Charles Stanley's
HANDBOOK FOR CHRISTIAN LIVING

Other Books by Charles Stanley from Thomas Nelson Publishers

Eternal Security
This best-seller has already comforted thousands of Christians. In it, Dr. Stanley offers the powerful, reassuring message that believers can be certain of eternal salvation and know peace and intimacy with Christ as a result.

The Gift of Forgiveness
Dr. Stanley shows readers how to give and receive forgiveness and experience the healing and freedom forgiveness brings.

How to Handle Adversity
Reassuring, Bible-based advice on how to understand and handle adversity in ways that glorify God and demonstrate His faithfulness.

How to Keep Your Kids on Your Team
Brimming with wisdom and practical advice, this book is a must for all Christian parents who want to ensure that their children grow to be loving and loyal—not only to their parents, but also to God and His Word.

How to Listen to God
This is Dr. Stanley's most popular book. It provides direction for Christians who are struggling to hear God's voice and to understand His will for their lives.

The Source of My Strength
Sharing his own journey through emotional pain, Dr. Stanley encourages readers to face the hurts of the past and receive God's healing and freedom.

Winning the War Within
A reasoned, scriptural approach to triumphing over temptation and coping with trials and inner struggles.

The Wonderful Spirit-Filled Life
Charles Stanley's best-seller on the power of the Holy Spirit for the journey of faith. In his conversational, illuminating style, Dr. Stanley gives believers the keys to living an abundant life, deepening their personal relationship with Christ, and applying biblical truths.

Charles Stanley's
HANDBOOK FOR CHRISTIAN LIVING

THOMAS NELSON PUBLISHERS

Nashville

Published in Nashville, Tennessee, by Thomas Nelson, Inc.

Unless otherwise noted, the Bible version used in this publication is THE NEW KING JAMES VERSION. Copyright © 1979, 1980, 1982 Thomas Nelson, Inc., Publishers. Scripture quotations marked NASB are taken from THE NEW AMERICAN STANDARD BIBLE. Copyright © 1960, 1962, 1963, 1968, 1971, 1972, 1973, 1975, 1977 by The Lockman Foundation and are used by permission. Scripture quotations marked NIV are taken from the HOLY BIBLE, NEW INTERNA-TIONAL VERSION®. Copyright © 1973, 1978, 1984 by International Bible Society. Used by permission of Zondervan Publishing House. All rights reserved. Scripture quotations marked PHIL-LIPS are taken from J. B. Phillips: THE NEW TESTAMENT IN MODERN ENGLISH, Revised Edition. Copyright © J. B. Phillips 1958, 1960, 1972. Used by permission of Macmillan Publishing Co., Inc. Verse on page 17 is from *The Living Bible,* copyright 1971 by Tyndale House Publishers, Wheaton, IL. Used by permission.

This book was previously published as *The Glorious Journey.* Published by Thomas Nelson Publishers © 1996.

Library of Congress Control Number: 00135742

Stanley, Charles F.
    Charles Stanley's handbook for Christian living / Charles Stanley.
        p.   cm.
    Includes bibliographical references and index.
    ISBN 0-7852-6702-6 (cloth)
    1. Christian life—Baptist authors.   I. Title.
BV4501.2.S71934   1996
248.4′861—dc20

Printed in the United States of America.

7 — 04 03

CONTENTS

CONTENTS

CONTENTS

RELATIONSHIPS

SERVICE AND OUTREACH

CONTENTS

INTRODUCTION

I love to take trips. When it is time to embark, I am prepared. For several weeks prior, I unfold and refold the appropriate road map several times; I mark and highlight my route; I calculate how many miles I must travel and get a good idea of the time involved.

Still, a map can only give the broad, generic view of travel. Five or six inches of interstate ribbon on the map can take me an entire day or more to navigate. I may encounter detours, inclement weather, mechanical malfunctions—any number of surprises. Similarly, my atlas can never convey the beauty of the pastures, valleys, mountains, and flowers I see along the way.

The Christian trek has several parallels. We have a map, the Bible, that tells us much about Christ. It is God's amazingly precise story, given to each believer as an infallible guide. The Bible tells how we may know Christ and follow Him. It imparts essential and accurate information.

Yet for all the wonderful truth we possess, the Christian life is a tremendous learning experience. We may know that we are to walk in the Spirit (Gal. 5:16), but doing it is something altogether different. We are certain that God wants us to pray and not to worry (Phil. 4:6), but keeping anxiety at bay in stressful times is a real feat.

The life of the Christian is a journey, and a glorious one at that. We have a supernatural, proficient guide and map in the Spirit-inspired Scriptures, but we face distinct temptations and trials. We know that we have been saved by faith in Christ and have heaven as our sure destination, but the intervening pilgrimage is unique. We need God's help.

This handbook is written from my perspective of more than forty years as a Christian and thirty years as a pastor. It is a compilation of the scriptural principles that I have learned and applied. Although it is not an exhaustive work, it is rich in content and counsel, if only because it reflects the instruction and encouragement that God in His grace has provided when I have failed or been in my need.

The book is divided into eight major categories: Church Concerns, Daily Living, Doctrine, End Times, Personal Growth, Relationships, Service and Outreach, and Spiritual Disciplines. Each major section has numerous topics that you will find interesting, stimulating, inspiring, and refreshing.

I suggest that you read the book according to your current need or interest. If you want a better grasp on the fundamentals of your faith, study and digest the section on doctrine. If you lack a real sense of accomplishment, the material on spiritual disciplines could propel you to spiritual progress.

I do not know where you are on your personal spiritual journey. Perhaps you are exhausted and spent. Maybe you have recently experienced signifi-

INTRODUCTION

cant growth, or you may have settled on a comfortable plateau because of an uncertain future.

But I do know this: God wants you to enjoy and complete the journey. He has pledged Himself to finish the good work He began at salvation (Phil. 1:6) and will keep you strong until the end (1 Cor. 1:8–9).

CHURCH CONCERNS

■ *An act of obedience whereby the believer publicly identifies through immersion with Jesus' death, burial, and resurrection.*

BAPTISM

MATTHEW 28:18–20

And Jesus came and spoke to them, saying, "All authority has been given to Me in heaven and on earth. Go therefore and make disciples of all the nations, baptizing them in the name of the Father and of the Son and of the Holy Spirit, teaching them to observe all things that I have commanded you; and lo, I am with you always, even to the end of the age."

A CLOSER LOOK

What people believe about baptism is usually determined by their heritage, specifically, their religious heritage. Debates continue while opinions are formed and lines drawn between different schools of thought that are grounded in denominational teaching rather than scriptural truth.

A look at some questions that arise out of the baptism issue lends insight into the sensitivity of the subject and the problems that continue to drive a wedge between what a person believes and what Scripture teaches. Each Sunday as our counselors talk with people who have come to join our church, these questions seem to come up regularly:

- "I believe Jesus died for my sins, and I have accepted Him as Savior. But I have not been baptized. Does that mean that I'm not a Christian?"
- "I was christened as a baby. Doesn't that mean I've been baptized?"
- "I was baptized by immersion when I was twelve, but I didn't really become a Christian until I was thirty-four. Does my baptism count?"
- "If baptism is not required for salvation, what is the big deal anyway?"

It's easy to see that the issue of baptism is shrouded in controversy and differences of opinion that people cling to with tenacity because "that's the way I was brought up." Things that are a part of our heritage are difficult, at best, to give up. Even when presented with what we can see is the truth, we resist. Thus, we are left with questions about baptism that separate denominations and divide churches, and the struggle to discern scriptural truth, as opposed to denominational dogma, is an ongoing effort.

Let's take an in-depth look at the root word *baptize,* discover its original meaning, and draw some pointed conclusions. I believe it can resolve many questions that continue to cause so many problems.

The term *baptize* is not a Baptist, Methodist, Presbyterian, or Catholic term; it is a Greek term. *Baptizo* in the Greek meant to "dunk," "dip,"

BAPTISM

■ *An act of obedience whereby the believer publicly identifies through immersion with Jesus' death, burial, and resurrection.*

Conrad Grebel (1498–1526) founder of the Anabaptists, defied the Zurich city council's ban on his activities, and performed the first adult baptism in modern history. He served two prison terms, totaling six months, before his early death.

During the Persian Gulf War, 51 men were saved on one of our warships. Thirty-seven asked to be baptized.

"plunge," "submerge," or "immerse." Originally, it had no religious connotation. Rather, the word *baptize* was used to describe a ship that had been sunk in battle or a piece of cloth that was dipped in dye. Other times it was used to refer to someone who had drowned or a cup that was dipped into a pitcher to drink from. Its use was general in nature.

The first time the word *baptize* was used in the context of religion occurred as a result of its incorporation into the Jewish culture. The Jewish faith was somewhat complicated with ceremonies, rituals, festivals, and laws. The term *baptize* was used to describe the ritual known as ceremonial washing. Now, we would not say, "Go baptize your hands before you eat." We would say, "Go wash your hands before you eat." Yet the term *baptize* was used to describe this function of washing.

There is a second way in which the term *baptize* was used in the Jewish faith. The Jews developed a way in which Gentiles could become Jewish. It involved a number of things, including circumcision, a covenant meal, the agreement to obey Jewish law, and a ritual bath. The term used to describe the bath was *bapto,* meaning "immerse." Persons desiring to become Jewish would baptize themselves. The "bath" was an outward sign that they were dying to the old life as a Gentile and were being resurrected to the new life as a Jew. As a pledge of allegiance to the new identity, those who desired to adopt the Jewish faith as their own participated by baptizing themselves as a sign of their commitment.

What happened next involved John the Baptist. John got his name because of what people saw him doing. His unique role of baptizing other people was something that had never been done before, so it was natural that people came to watch. He was literally John the Baptizer. John took an ordinary word that meant to "dip," "plunge," "submerge," or "immerse," and coined it for the specific task he was performing. Soon it became almost exclusively associated with Christianity, and thus the word *baptism* appears in the New Testament.

A Greek term that was used in a general sense took on a special meaning because of its close association with what was happening. That's how the term *baptism* took on its religious connotations. Those who saw what was happening associated the word *baptize* with it, and it wasn't long before *baptism* became the word to define the event or process. This understanding is extremely important because it allows us to isolate the form of baptism. In the case of *baptism* or *baptize,* the word is the form. *Baptize,* as we determined earlier, means to "dip," "plunge," "submerge," or "immerse."

Many who advocate another form of baptism admit that the original form of baptism was immersion. And there is evidence from Scripture. In Acts

Church Concerns

BAPTISM

8:38, we read, "He commanded the chariot to stand still. And both Philip and the eunuch went down into the water, and he baptized him." Matthew 3:16 describes this scene: "When He had been baptized, Jesus came up immediately from the water; and behold, the heavens were opened." Baptism was a public observance whereby a person was immersed for the sake of a religious decision. Again, because of its original meaning, the form of baptism is defined by the word itself.

The next question concerns the meaning or significance of baptism. Why should a person be baptized? From the very beginning, baptism represented the ideas of identification and allegiance. Remember how the Gentiles were changing their identity? Once they baptized themselves, they were no longer Gentiles; they were Jews. People who were baptized by John were identifying with John's teaching for repentance. That is why Jesus allowed Himself to be baptized by John. The identity factor is underscored in Acts where we find that those who were baptized to identify with John were rebaptized in the name of Jesus in order to identify with Him. Therefore, one reason for baptism is that we publicly identify with Jesus' teachings.

The great Southern Baptist pastor R. G. Lee baptized more than six thousand people during his ministry.

Second, baptism is a picture that carries the weight of cleansing and resurrection and allegiance. The visual picture of baptism represents (1) cleansing from the sin of the old life; (2) dying to the old life and being born to a new life; and (3) a sign of commitment or allegiance to a new Master or way of life. This visual picture of an inward decision is best summed up in the sentence "I am not ashamed." Baptism is the believer's declaration to the world that Christ is the standard by which he or she intends to live.

Another reason a believer should be baptized is that Jesus commanded us to be baptized, and following in obedience should be a part of every believer's life. In the Scripture reference at the beginning of this chapter, known as the Great Commission, Jesus instructed the remaining eleven disciples to "go therefore and make disciples . . . baptizing them." The disciples were instructed to lead people to know Jesus as Savior and then to baptize them as a sign of their allegiance and identification with Him. As obedient children, we must consider baptism as the next step after salvation, one that should be taken without delay.

Baptism and the Supper are for the saved alone, and only the saved can scripturally observe either ordinance.
—George W. Truett

Many people express one last concern about baptism and its connection to salvation. Baptism is an act of obedience whereby the believer identifies with Christ. Believing in Christ comes first, then baptizing. Think about the thief on the cross. He believed in the moments just prior to his death on the cross. There was no time for baptism; yet Jesus assured him that they would meet in paradise that day. Were baptism required for salvation, the thief

Baptism **5**

BAPTISM

■ *An act of obedience whereby the believer publicly identifies through immersion with Jesus' death, burial, and resurrection.*

would have missed out. It is clear from Jesus' words that the thief was saved the moment he believed. Paul says, "For Christ did not send me to baptize, but to preach the gospel" (1 Cor. 1:17).

Baptism should be a part of every believer's experience, but it is not a requirement for salvation. Since obedience is an integral part of becoming a mature follower of Christ, baptism is something that every believer should participate in. It is called "believer's baptism" to underscore the connection between believing and baptism.

APPLICATION

Baptism is not merely about being immersed, making a commitment, or joining a particular denomination or church. None of these things convey the real meaning of baptism. Baptism is about publicly identifying with Christ. It is an act of obedience. Baptism is an outward expression of an inward decision to align oneself with Christ and what He lived and died for.

If you were sprinkled as a child or christened, you have not been scripturally baptized. If you were immersed as an adult but had no intention of following Christ, you were not scripturally baptized. If you were sprinkled and have followed Christ since that time, you have not been scripturally baptized. If you were immersed and became a Christian later, you have not been scripturally baptized. Does that mean that Christ does not accept you or loves you less? Absolutely not. Does it mean that you are not saved if you haven't been baptized? No. It means that as a believer, you need to be obedient and be scripturally baptized.

GROWTH

If you struggle with the issue of baptism, find a church that teaches the scriptural truth about baptism, and seek the counsel of someone who can help you resolve your struggle.

If you have come to understand that you were not scripturally baptized, I encourage you to take the steps to follow in obedience to Christ's command.

Finally, if you are struggling with a part of your religious heritage that taught something different from what you now understand to be true concerning baptism, ask God to renew your mind through His Word and through prayer. Hanging on to the past just because it's a part of your upbringing is not a reason for resisting obedience to God. Ask for willingness to release the part of your heritage that prevents you from being obedient. Allow the Holy Spirit to guide you into the truth of Scripture. God will answer your prayers and enable you to move forward as you seek to be obedient to Him.

Church Concerns

■ Believers in Jesus Christ who join together in fulfilling their mission to make disciples.

CHURCH

SCRIPTURE

And I also say to you that you are Peter, and on this rock I will build My church, and the gates of Hades shall not prevail against it.

COMMENTARY

I can only imagine what Peter must have thought when Jesus made this sweeping statement as the disciples met and talked that evening. Peter's quick and confident response to Jesus' question concerning who the disciples believed He was prompted Jesus to designate Peter, as it were, to be the starting point from which Christ would build His church. Reference to the church is made throughout the New Testament as "the bride of Christ" and "the body of Christ," but I doubt that Peter understood it was his legacy to be known as the one Christ pointed to that day as the "charter member" of the church.

What did Jesus mean when He said that Peter was the rock upon which He would build His church? There were no architects with their sketches drawn of a new building on a new parcel of land. Jesus was not making reference to a building or a denomination. Peter had just confessed his belief in Jesus as the Son of the living God, and on that basis, Jesus established, or defined, the church. However, as the body of believers grew, the local church (i.e., First Church of Galatia or Ephesus Community Church) was a natural outflow. Thus, from the early days of the church down through today, we have come to associate the church with our particular fellowship of believers. Whatever name we apply to a particular fellowship, there is only one church, and it belongs to no particular denomination.

The church is made up of those who have placed their belief—their faith—in the person of Jesus Christ. Having established who the church is, Jesus commissioned those who believed in Him to "make disciples" (Matt. 28:19–20). It has always been the work of the church to bring others to belief in Christ and to experience a personal relationship with Him. Jesus came to save the lost. Those who believed in Him became His church and took on the responsibility that comes with belief—the commitment to continue the work Christ began.

> The Bible knows nothing of solitary religion.
> —John Wesley

A CLOSER LOOK

Jesus' reference to the church had a very different meaning from what we commonly think of today. Jesus was not referring to the First Baptist Church of Galatia when He spoke of the church. He was speaking of the body of

Church **7**

CHURCH

■ *Believers in Jesus Christ who join together in fulfilling their mission to make disciples.*

believers who had placed their faith in Him as the Son of the living God. When you and I speak of the church, we are apt to refer to a particular church or denomination that we are familiar with. To be clear, we must learn to understand the difference between who we are and the name we apply to our identity. *We are the church*. The place we worship and carry out our work is just that—a place.

I have been pastor of First Baptist Church of Atlanta, Georgia, for some twenty-five years. Many people come to Atlanta on vacation or business and visit First Baptist because they have seen me preach on television or have read one of my books. First Baptist is the church they have come to associate with our broadcast ministry. Perhaps during your youth you were a member of a church that you remember fondly, or maybe you are involved in the ministry of a church at this time. However, biblically speaking, the church is not a denomination or a building. The church is you and me. It's the woman who sings in the choir and the kid who leads a Bible study on Tuesday nights for his fellow high school students. The church is not a place. It is a people, the body of believers who share their faith in the person of Jesus Christ.

A denomination defines a particular group or belief system that focuses on a certain theological interpretation. Buildings house the body of believers in corporate worship and administration. When we fall into the trap of looking at the church as a place, we easily separate ourselves from its mission because we think of the church as a physical place to worship together instead of understanding the church as our identity with a specific purpose. The church leaves in the cars that exit the parking lot after Sunday worship and carries on its work throughout the week.

For our purposes here, let us agree that the church has one mission, although denominations may have different ways of accomplishing it. *The mission of the church is to make disciples—to lead people into a growing relationship with Jesus Christ*. It was true during the days of the disciples of the New Testament and it is true today; the church—those who believe in Christ—is to make disciples. In his book *A Church for the 21st Century*, Leith Anderson reaffirms where we get our marching orders and who set us on our path: "The church of Jesus Christ was founded by Jesus, is owned by Jesus, and is run by Jesus. It is a theocracy, and we are citizens under orders. We are stewards who have been entrusted with the care of that which belongs to Jesus." He continues, "The practical implications are significant. The church does not belong to any denomination, synod, presbytery, association, session, diaconate, pastor or membership. It is his to do with as he sees fit." So how do we accomplish this task?

Just as the passage of time necessarily brings change, the way we do things today may not necessarily be the way we did things last year or the way we will do them five years from now. Some things never change, as in our mission, but in a world that changes faster than textbooks can record the changes, the church must be accountable to its timeless mission. Nothing is more relevant to our day than the message of salvation through Christ Jesus. However, unless we are willing to make the changes that will equip the church to do its work, the relevancy of the gospel will likely never reach those who are lost.

An interesting book has taken a look at what it calls ten of today's most innovative churches. In the preface, Elmer L. Towns states, "Our culture is like a drag racer, rushing toward the future. But will the church be left behind? Too many congregations are hibernating churches, withdrawing from the world, refusing to meet the challenge of society. . . . Many churches are not keeping up, but falling behind."

Our world is far different from that of Jesus and His disciples. "It is risky to reach out to unbelievers. It changes a church when newcomers are unlike the old-timers. God's work is seldom neat, clean, or free of problems. Our world is changing around us. All healthy organisms adapt or die. The same goes for churches," writes Leith Anderson. He continues, "The church of the twenty-first century is dealing with a generation that is discouraged, depressed, tired, lonely, and feeling guilty. They are more interested in learning *what* to do about their sins and struggles than being *told they are sinners* and strugglers." That is not to say that people in Jesus' day did not experience some of these problems, but we live in a world of people overcome with despair. We must recognize the mind-set of those we would reach to be effective.

One change that appears to be taking place is that people no longer cling to denominational lines as tenaciously as before. Invitational counselors in our church routinely counsel people who come to join our fellowship from other denominations. It was considered true heresy in the fifties and sixties to cross denominational lines. Today most people feel it is more important to be in a church that teaches the Bible in a relevant way than to attend the church Mom and Dad always went to (although it may have served the parents' needs quite well). It is apparent from what I see in those who join our church and other churches that people are looking for Bible teaching that is practical and applicable; they are looking for churches that offer opportunities and ministries that meet their needs and the needs of their families.

In a Gallup study of the reasons why people who have dropped out of church decided to return, the top three reasons respondents gave were: (1) feeling an inner need to go back, (2) sensing an inner need to rediscover faith, and (3) desiring religious training for their children.
—*Clergy Journal*, March 1995

The Christian church is the largest institution that exists or has ever existed in the history of the world.
—D. James Kennedy

CHURCH

■ *Believers in Jesus Christ who join together in fulfilling their mission to make disciples.*

As we change, we must also stay the same. Contradictory? Not really when you consider that the church has one mission and many avenues by which to accomplish it. When we consider how to make the work that we are doing effective in today's world, it is wise to consider what made the church work in the days of Jesus. The key was recognition of the mission and willingness to change. The book of Acts is replete with illustrations of the church changing. The mission stayed the same, and as the church changed, it grew. What the church understood then, we must cling to now. As long as we keep our priorities straight and continue in the work Jesus commissioned us to do, we will seek better ways of reaching the lost for Christ without being threatened by the thought of change.

APPLICATION

As the church, we are going to change if we are to continue to lead people to Christ. With changing demographics, changing monetary needs, changing family structures, and other major considerations, the church must be equipped to minister to those within its reach and capabilities. Not every church has the same needs or abilities. Producing cookie-cutter churches would be a mistake. However, the church must keep abreast of some basic elements of a changing world and make an effort to incorporate them into its methods of reaching lost people for Christ.

Dr. George Hunter, dean of the school of world mission at Asbury Seminary, makes the following observations: "Effective churches recognize a number of things concerning reaching unsaved people. Among these are three that stand out in my mind: (1) know that people who aren't disciples are lost, (2) know that lost people matter to God, and (3) see the church as primarily a mission to lost people rather than a gathered colony of the faithful." That's a pretty good beginning for a church that wants to be effective in its mission. From there, ideas that equip the church to meet the growing needs of the lost are as numerous as there are minutes in a day. Having the wisdom to discern those that will work in a given situation is the benchmark of a church that effectively meets the challenges.

QUOTES

When the Lord asks a sick church, "Do you want to get well?" the answer is not always obvious. Getting well may require exercise of spiritual gifts, stepping forward on faith, incorporating newcomers who are unlike the old-timers. Comfort zones will be invaded. A new identity may have to be forged. While few churches will ever actually say no either to Jesus or to His question, their real answer is, "We would rather not!"

—Leith Anderson

The ministry is not called to fit the church's structure; the structure exists to further effective ministry.

—George Barna

CHURCH ATTENDANCE

■ *The habit of participating in a local church on a regular basis.*

HEBREWS 10:23–25 NASB

Let us hold fast the confession of our hope without wavering, for He who promised is faithful; and let us consider how to stimulate one another to love and good deeds, not forsaking our own assembling together, as is the habit of some, but encouraging one another; and all the more, as you see the day drawing near.

COMMENTARY

The book of Hebrews was written to Jewish Christians. The new believers were struggling with how to incorporate their Jewish heritage into their faith in Christ. The writer spent a great deal of time explaining that Jesus Christ prepared the way for uninterrupted fellowship with the Father. He was the new High Priest. His death provided the way for individuals to have personal access to God without a series of complicated steps.

That was difficult for the Jewish Christians to accept. They were accustomed to participating in a variety of ceremonial washings and offerings to be cleansed from their sins. Immediate access to God apart from those things was something new. But the writer of Hebrews insisted that they could go directly to the Father through Christ. Jesus Christ, the Chief Priest, provides unlimited access to the Father.

The author knew the challenge it would be for the recent converts to remain faithful to their newly formed faith. So he exhorted them to "hold fast." Then he took it one step farther. He instructed his readers to help one another "hold fast." He knew they would have a tendency to drift away from the truth. He anticipated their need for other believers to help them stay on track. So he said, "Stimulate one another to love and good deeds." The Greek term translated "stimulate" literally means "to irritate." In essence he was instructing them to spur one another along, watch out for one another, take responsibility for one another. With that backdrop he instructed them not to stop meeting together. They needed one another. To give up meeting together would spell disaster. In meeting together they found the mutual encouragement to keep going.

A CLOSER LOOK

God wants His children to meet with other believers on a regular basis. He wants His people in church! One reason so many believers don't take this admonition seriously is that they don't know the reason behind it. How often I have heard this refrain: "I can worship God at home. I don't need to go to church." Many believers are convinced that the primary reason we meet together is to worship. And understandably so. After all, we call it a worship service.

CHURCH ATTENDANCE

If worship was the primary reason we are commanded to meet, those who claim they can worship at home would have a strong argument. After all, in some instances it is much easier to worship at home. But worship is not the sole reason we are commanded to meet together.

Certainly then, it must be so that we can be taught the Word. Not entirely. We can turn on our radios and televisions and hear good Bible teaching and preaching. On the surface it would seem that anything we can do at church, we can do just as well at home alone.

So why are we commanded to meet? Why go to church? The writer of Hebrews says it is to safeguard against drifting.

We are surrounded by forces that work to blow us off course. Sheer individual commitment alone is not enough to keep us in line. There are times when we feel as if our faith makes no difference. We see no fruit in our lives, and we don't seem to be making any difference in anyone else's life, either. During those times, we are tempted to pull up anchor and drift. After all, everybody else is. At least that's the way it appears.

And then we drag ourselves to church and discover that we are not alone. We hear others share how God came through for them when they were in a tight spot. Someone else shares about the pain experienced when he left the faith. A new believer tells her story and rejoices in God's grace. And something begins to happen inside us. We are spurred on to faithfulness!

The accountability and encouragement found in church fellowship anchor us against the tides that work to sweep us away. We can develop a network of relationships with other believers that works to ensure we don't abandon our faith when the pressure is on to do so. To neglect the regular assembling with other Christians is to miss out on this essential element in the development of our faith.

In Hebrews 10:22, the writer said, "Let us draw near [to God] with a true heart in full assurance of faith." God desires a relationship with His children. By becoming active in a local church, you safeguard yourself against missing out on all that God has for you. Your participation in a local church protects your personal fellowship with God. When you drift away from the family of God, it is only a matter of time until you drift away from fellowship with God. Solomon said it this way: "He who walks with wise men will be wise, but the companion of fools will be destroyed" (Prov. 13:20).

There are an estimated 375,000 churches in the United States, and most of them are small. Half of these churches have seventy-five or less at worship on a typical Sunday morning.

GROWTH

If you attend a church where you are not encouraged and spurred to action and continued faithfulness, you may need to consider looking for a new

CHURCH ATTENDANCE

■ *The habit of participating in a local church on a regular basis.*

church. After all, if the church you attend does not accomplish the primary thing it was designed to do, what is the point in going? If you are like many believers, you feel guilty when you miss. But easing your conscience is not a good reason to go.

If attending your church or Sunday school class has the same effect on you as showing up at the garden club or the athletic club, you are fooling yourself. For all practical purposes, you have abandoned the spiritual stimulation of assembling yourselves together. Form without function is more dangerous than no form at all. You are lulled into thinking that everything is okay. After all, you're in church.

There must be a spiritual dynamic. If the teaching and fellowship do not challenge your character and behavior, it may have church in its title, but it is not functioning as a church. We are to be involved in order to be encouraged and held accountable. From God's perspective, to participate in a church that does not accomplish His purposes is not to have gone to church at all.

Attending a church that does not encourage you to remain faithful and hold you accountable in your walk with God is like joining and attending a health club but not exercising. What good does a health club do you if you attend three times a week to have coffee with a friend? Sure, you are in the building, but nothing is happening that will benefit you physically. No one could fault you on your attendance, but your health is not affected. You are in no better shape than when you joined.

"But wait," you say, "aren't you being a little hard on my church? We sing together, and our pastor always brings a well-reasoned sermon." Yes, but does being there, with that group of people, encourage you to cling to the hope that is in you? If not, I recommend you visit another church. Keep in mind, however, that there is no perfect church. Find one that accurately presents Scripture and practically demonstrates God's love. Remember, too, you have a responsibility to actively use your spiritual gifts for the benefit of other believers.

I also encourage you to carefully consider how God can use you in your present church. You may be so intent on having your needs met that you are overlooking how powerfully God can use you to help others. God may have you where you are, even if far less than ideal, for some significant ministry purpose. Try volunteering in an area in which you are comfortable, and your attitude may become the primary thing that changes.

> Churches usually hire one full-time pastor for every 175 people who attend Sunday morning worship.

LAWSUIT

1 CORINTHIANS 6:1, 5, 7

Dare any of you, having a matter against another, go to law before the unrigh-teous, and not before the saints? . . . I say this to your shame. Is it so, that there is not a wise man among you, not even one, who will be able to judge between his brethren? . . . Now therefore, it is already an utter failure for you that you go to law against one another. Why do you not rather accept wrong? Why do you not rather let yourselves be cheated?

COMMENTARY

The Corinthian church was made up of Greeks and Jews. The diverse backgrounds of the two groups made for interesting interaction within the church. One point of conflict was the handling of disputes. The Greeks loved to argue and debate. Consequently, taking one another to court was a common practice. They loved everything about litigation and court proceedings. It was sport.

The Jews, on the other hand, were taught to avoid public court. In their tradition, they were to settle their differences in the synagogue through the elders. To them, it was a family affair and needed to stay that way.

What would the courts—probably Roman courts—know about the Jewish lifestyle and traditions? And even in cases where a Roman magistrate might have been familiar with Jewish law and custom, he would not necessarily rule with that in mind.

The difference really became a problem when a dispute arose between a Jewish believer and a Greek believer. Where were they to go to settle their dispute? The Greek didn't want to go to the synagogue, and the Jew didn't want to go to court.

So Paul's congregation was made up of ready-to-sue-on-the-spot Greeks and reticent Jews. They were in the same church body. Paul had to deal with the issue of lawsuits, and one can only imagine what had brought the issue to a head. But in the church of Corinth, most anything was possible.

To sum up what Paul said in verses 1, 5, and 7: "How dare you!" and "I say this to your shame!" and "You are already defeated!" I would say his three-point outline got right to the point. It doesn't seem to be one of his more positive sermons, does it?

Let's take a closer look at the whole subject.

A CLOSER LOOK

We are living in an I've-got-my-rights society. People live with the motto, "I want my rights, and I'll get my rights, and if I don't, I'll take you to

LAWSUIT ■ *Legal actions between private parties in a law court; litigation.*

court." To make matters worse, nobody wants to assume responsibility for anything, especially personal behavior!

Some countries have 200 to 400 attorneys for every 100,000 people. In the United States, we have 5,000 lawyers for every 100,000 people. And we are increasing that number every day. There are many lawyers who work only for profit, but there are also great, godly people in law. In that way it's like any other profession.

The real tragedy is that the pursuit of justice seems to have been lost (or misplaced). The goal of our court system is no longer reconciliation or healing the breach so the two opposing parties can leave as friends. It is, rather, to see who has the best tactics to outshoot the other side, and it rarely matters how many are wounded.

When Christians come to court and want to know what their rights are, I believe underneath the legality are greed, bitterness, resentment, vengeance, retaliation, pride, and anger. The Christian's bottom line is the world's bottom line: I want it *all*.

Part of the problem is that church leaders have failed. Because we've failed to resolve things in the church house, we go to the courthouse. Paul offered a solution that should be going on in every church across the world.

For example, in a small church where there is one aisle, two families may sit on opposite sides of the aisle and never speak for years and years following a bitter lawsuit. Both sing the same songs, listen to the same sermon, and profess to love the same Father, and yet never speak. It happens in large churches, too, but it's easier to hide in a large one.

You may say to me, "You just don't know how I've been hurt." You are absolutely right. But we totally forget what Jesus said about forgiveness.

Whatever happened to what Jesus said to Peter about forgiving 70 times 7? He didn't specify that there were 490 different offenses. It could be the same thing over and over and over and more than 490 times. Whatever happened to forgiveness?

If God's people stayed out of the courts and healed their differences in a biblical manner, a big load would come off our overcrowded court system. And if we gave that money where it rightfully belonged, we would give more to the mission of the church than ever.

Is Paul saying that Christians aren't to go to court, period? When we look at 1 Corinthians 6:1–8, Paul makes it clear that Christians are not to take other Christians to court.

Sometimes an unbeliever takes a believer to court. You can't do much about that. But you need to participate with the right kind of spirit, willing to be wronged to keep your testimony.

Paul realized that unbelievers would not be coming to the church to settle a legal problem. First of all, it probably wouldn't occur to them to do such a thing. Second, they probably wouldn't be interested in a decision based on the Word of God.

For believers, however, it is different. The basis of his argument that godly counselors are to be consulted is that someday we will rule and reign with Jesus. In light of this future assignment, Paul was alluding to the fact that the things of this world aren't really too tough for Christians to handle (v. 2).

Verse 4 is somewhat confusing, but I believe it is saying one of two things. Paul is asking why the believers were going to outside judges who were not saved, or another possible interpretation is, "Even the least capable people in the church should be able to decide these things for you," as *The Living Bible* puts it. Either interpretation of this verse encourages Christians to seek arbitration within the church, not outside it.

Jesus had something to say about this as well: "Therefore if you bring your gift to the altar, and there remember that your brother has something against you, leave your gift there before the altar, and go your way. First be reconciled to your brother, and then come and offer your gift" (Matt. 5:23–24).

Before you go to court, remember the Cross. Jesus was willing to be wronged as an example to us. He didn't fight back.

You may say, "Yes, that's okay for Him, but He's God." Well, He lives in you. Jesus gave further instructions on how to make peace with your brother:

> If your brother sins against you, go and tell him his fault between you and him alone. If he hears you, you have gained your brother. But if he will not hear, take with you one or two more, that "by the mouth of two or three witnesses every word may be established." And if he refuses to hear them, tell it to the church. But if he refuses even to hear the church, let him be to you like a heathen and a tax collector (Matt. 18:15–17).

A process is described here. First, go alone and talk to the offender. If the person doesn't listen, take one or two other believers along. And if that doesn't work, take the issue to the church. It could be the whole body, or it could mean a representation of the local assembly.

This is where problem resolution should start and stop!

If you and I refuse to go to court even when we're wronged by another believer, God will assume responsibility to provide for us. I understand that is terribly hard to put into practice. But I am saying it is biblical.

Manufacturers offer a list of "tort taxes" that the public pays because of litigation: $20 of the $100 price of a ladder; $3,000 of the $18,000 cost of a pace maker.
—*U.S. News and World Report*, May 22, 1995

A million lawsuits a year are filed in New York and the city pays a staggering $230 million a year in personal-injury claims. Every pot hole is a lottery ticket.
—*U.S. News and World Report*, May 22, 1995

LAWSUIT

■ *Legal actions between private parties in a law court; litigation.*

Minnesota inmates have filed lawsuits demanding damages for being provided an improper variety of beans on the menu, a lack of salsa, a surfeit of bologna, and underwear that was too tight ("cruel and unusual punishment").

When you take another believer to court, you are taking things into your own hands. But when you don't take another believer to court, God assumes responsibility for putting pressure on the person who is wrong. It is amazing the ways God can get people's attention.

There are Christian organizations consisting of lawyers committed to reconciling people through the church. When a situation arises, they assemble a pastor, a Christian attorney, and someone who is a professional in the area in which there is a problem (for instance, real estate or finances). These people make the decision for the Christians who are having difficulty with an issue between them.

That is the spirit of the New Testament. I believe the church has been reluctant to get involved in the messy affairs of church members, and I feel we have been wrong. We have forced Christians to go outside the church. I believe Paul is teaching against that.

God's way is to confess, repent, and reconcile. Lose face if you have to. When a believer shouts with glee, "I won!" after having just defeated a fellow believer who is now hurt and wounded, that is utter hypocrisy.

When we win a court battle with a believer who may have been wrong and leave him in the muck of resentment and guilt and anger, what makes us think we've won anything in the eyes of God? Satan has won.

You have two alternatives when you've been wronged by a believer:

1. Let the church settle it.
2. Be willing to be wronged and defrauded and not go to court.

Christ said: "By this all will know that you are My disciples, if you have love for one another" (John 13:35). That verse strongly implies peaceable resolution of problems.

Paul is telling us not to settle our differences outside the church before a judge who has no clue how believers live. He encourages us to go to godly men or women in the church to help us settle our problems.

And he is going so far as to urge us that in the end, it is better to be wrong than go after rights.

You know how the world says, "Don't get mad; get even"?

If God treated us that way, where would we be?

He didn't get mad; He didn't get even. But He did satisfy His demands for justice.

The Cross says it all.

LAWSUIT

Two men went into business together. One supplied the "brains," and the other supplied the money. Over the course of time, they made a great deal of money.

One morning the man who had supplied the know-how went to the office. The doors were locked.

He got in contact with the other partner, who had supplied the capital, and explained, "I'm not sure what the problem is, but I can't get into my office."

The business partner replied, "Oh, I know you can't. You're out. You didn't put any money into this outfit, so you're out."

And the man was ousted.

Because their original agreement had been on a rather flimsy, meager document, there was a lot of verbal wrangling. Greed totally consumed the man who had put up the cash. The verbal battle was fierce.

The ousted business associate went to a counselor and asked, "Do you think I could win in court?"

After hearing all the story, the counselor agreed that he could win in court. But then he added, "Do you want to know what God's best is, or would you rather win in court? I don't believe God wants you to take your brother to court and sue him, even though you are right from a business standpoint."

The guy was livid. He lashed out, "I wish I had never met you! If I don't follow this through, I'll lose everything." But he kept his emotions in check and decided to put the matter into God's hands.

Two years passed. He received a telephone call from someone he did not know. "Sir, I'm interested in buying your former business. Do I understand that you were a partner and you were ousted?"

The Christian stammered and replied, "Why, yes, sir, that is correct."

The man on the phone asked again, "Do I understand that you no longer have a part?"

"Yes."

The caller explained his surprise offer: "Sir, I want to buy the business, but I am going to purchase it only if the present owner agrees to give you a percentage—which will amount to several million dollars."

I am sure the delighted Christian could only shake his head in amazement at God's goodness and gulp a "thank you."

Well, the gentleman made the offer to the owner. In essence he said, "I want to buy your business. But I want you to know that I am able to tie it

> **G**od says there is to be swift punishment: "Because the sentence against an evil work is not executed speedily, therefore the heart of the sons of men is fully set in them to do evil."
> —Ecclesiastes 8:11

LAWSUIT

■ *Legal actions between private parties in a law court; litigation.*

up so that you can't sell it to anyone else. You need to treat your brother right, whom you have wronged, and give him a percentage of the deal."

And they lived happily ever after. Well, at least two of the three did.

And if anyone sins, we have an Advocate [lawyer] with the Father, Jesus Christ the righteous.

—1 John 2:1

■ *The ability to help others move toward an agreed-upon vision.*

LEADERSHIP

SCRIPTURE

MATTHEW 4:19–20

He said to them, "Follow Me, and I will make you fishers of men." They immediately left their nets and followed Him.

COMMENTARY

Three general categories describe the leadership style of Christ. First, He was a leader with a clear mission. Jesus' primary motivation and purpose were glorification of His heavenly Father. Second, Jesus was a leader with consistent character. He lived what He taught and believed. Third, He was a leader with a capable team. He knew with committed, gifted individuals around Him, He would reach the world.

A clear mission serves as a compass to point you in the right direction. A mission is what you are to do as you fulfill God's purpose for your life. A mission focuses you on what's important. It's not uncommon for the driving force of families or ministries to be crises or instant gratification rather than their mission. Your mission keeps you on course.

A mission serves as a filter for new ideas. You reject an idea that does not line up with your purpose. It may very well fit in another arena, but for your purpose it is unnecessary.

A mission also serves as an evaluation tool. Ministries, families, or individuals have a tendency to drift from the original purpose. A mission statement properly placed within a system can sound the alarm once a ministry, family, or individual begins to change in an unhealthy manner. Conversely, the mission statement should stimulate change when an organization or individual becomes stagnant.

A mission should reflect priorities. When you look over your life, will you be able to say, "I poured my life into what really mattered"? Through the dynamic of a clear mission, you will use the talents God has given you to their maximum potential. Not only will you "spend" your life, but you will "invest" your life in what really matters.

A clear mission statement serves as a powerful tool to keep you focused on God's best. An unclear mission is just as powerful in allowing you to settle for good things but miss out on what really matters. Jesus had an uncanny ability of staying focused. He was mission driven and used interruptions as opportunities to apply His purpose.

Jesus understood why He was here. He knew where He was going and how He was to arrive at His destination. Jesus stated His purpose at twelve years of age. He explained to His parents, "Did you not know that I must

A true and safe leader is likely to be one who has not desire to lead, but is forced into a position of leadership by inward pressure of the Holy Spirit and the press of external situation.
—A. W. Tozer

LEADERSHIP

be about My Father's business?" (Luke 2:49). The business of His Father most concerned Jesus. In a phrase the mission of Jesus was to "glorify God."

Jesus described this mission in another fashion when He explained to His disciples, "My food is to do the will of Him who sent Me, and to finish His work" (John 4:34). Jesus' whole being was bent toward doing the will of God. With all of His heart and soul He wanted to please His heavenly Father. That is why when the temptation to quit was overwhelming and when Christ was at the point of physical exhaustion in the Garden of Gethsemane, He prayed to His heavenly Father, "My Father, if it is possible, let this cup pass from Me; nevertheless, not as I will, but as You will" (Matt. 26:39).

Out of Jesus' glorification of God flowed many other purposes, but those purposes were determined by His primary mission of glorifying the One who sent Him: His heavenly Father. This brings us to the next logical questions: What was His Father's business, and How did Christ carry out His Father's will?

Jesus made clear His mission when He prayed, "I have glorified You on the earth. I have finished the work which You have given Me to do" (John 17:4). Knowing He was about to die, Jesus evaluated His life and, with humility and quiet confidence, stated He had accomplished His purpose in life: the glorification of His heavenly Father.

Joseph H. Thayer defines *glorification* in this context, "To make renowned, render illustrious, i.e., to cause the dignity and worth of some person or thing to become manifest and acknowledged." Jesus revealed God in His life, and He was about to enter into the last stage of His glorification mission—the revelation of Christ in His death and resurrection. Jesus accomplished His life mission by glorifying His Father; however, His death and resurrection missions were accomplished by the Father glorifying His Son!

Jesus' personal rejection and suffering did not distract Him. Instead they drove Him to remain focused on His purpose. In the darkest hours He more fully revealed the nature of His heavenly Father. On another occasion He could have let the people make Him king, but He retreated to be with His heavenly Father to refocus on His mission (John 6:15).

Though His life was a portrait of God, He did not let the love of this life delay the culmination of His Father's plan. Jesus could have confined Himself to the synagogue to a lifetime of insightfully and accurately expounding the Scriptures, but He knew God's glorification was not limited to a building. He could have spent a lifetime in the humanitarian work of feeding and healing the people, but He knew God's revelation was not limited to the physical needs of people.

> We need to decide if we will be mere spectators in the struggle for humanity's mind and will, or whether we will exercise leadership in shaping the course of and outcome of today's battle of conflicting and competing values.
> —Carl F. H. Henry

LEADERSHIP

Jesus could have spent all His time with unbelievers, but He chose to use some of His time to build a team of believers. The point is that Christ experienced all of life and ultimately death. As He experienced life and death, He revealed His heavenly Father, so with our finite minds we can develop our understanding of who God is and what He has done for us. The leadership style of Jesus has at its heart an uncompromisingly clear mission. Not only did He have a clear mission, but He also lived what He taught with consistent character.

Mission is *what* we do; character is *how* and *why* we do it. Mission is action and getting things done; character is the motivation behind the work. Character validates our mission. Character gives credibility to our purpose. Without character, our mission becomes a catchy cliché that fails to affect our lives and the lives of others.

Character proves to others the seriousness of my commitment. Character expresses interest in the well-being of another's relationships as well as in getting the job done.

Character comes from within. Honesty, hard work, sensitivity, and courage flow from the life of Christ within the believer. The fruit of the Spirit is just that: the fruition of God's Holy Spirit working in the life of a believer. You can get things done. You can accomplish much, but without love, it is useless in this life and in the life to come.

There is a temptation to compromise character just to get the job done. But for the sake of God's kingdom and for the good of the individual and those around him, character and competence serve together. Flowing from character are trust and respect, two vital traits of an effective leader.

Character is what is within an individual. People see what's on the outside. God sees what's on the inside. A look into the life and teachings of Christ indicates that character seems to revolve around the heart. If your heart is right, your character is right. Your heart is your innermost being where motivation and desires reside. Jesus modeled a consistent character. Through His character, He proved Himself to be the Son of God. His character validated His mission and ministry. The key to Christ's character was purity of heart.

Walter Bauer defines *heart* in Matthew 15:8, 18 and Mark 7:6 as "the seat of the inner life in contrast to the mouth or lips, which either give expression to the inner life or deny it." Wesley Penschbachen's *Analytical Greek Lexicon* defines *heart* in Matthew 6:21; 22:37 as "the seat of feeling, impulse, affection and desire."

As followers of Jesus Christ, we must consider character essential. The Holy Spirit is in the character-building business. He will lead and teach us

Studies by the Alban Institute indicate that a pastor needs three to four years to build up credibility and trust. Constant turnover in pastoral leadership can be debilitating to a church.
—*Religion Watch*,
   Dec. 1995

True leaders are not afraid to surround themselves with people of ability and then give them opportunities for greatness.
—Warren W. Wiersbe

Leadership **23**

LEADERSHIP

to be more like Christ. In the long run, character will prove to be the great balancer. Character will help us give proper attention to the roles we are to fulfill. Consistent character earns the respect and trust of others. It's through their respect and trust that we can be effective leaders.

Christ wisely surrounded Himself with twelve men with great potential. His team certainly had not arrived. They were rough, though ready to meet the challenge with enthusiasm. They were not perfect, but they were open to growing and learning God's ways. They were from diverse backgrounds. The diversity was an asset rather than a liability. They built on the strengths of one another and valued the uniqueness of their perspectives. Let's examine this team, looking at Christ's method of recruiting, training, and relationship building.

Jesus sought His heavenly Father's wisdom before choosing His team. Jesus prayed all night, and at daybreak He called His disciples together and chose twelve as apostles (Luke 6:12–13). Seeking God's wisdom was Jesus' number one priority.

Jesus drafted men whom He had observed. He watched how they related to other people and saw the potential they could offer. Jesus also recruited people from various backgrounds. Included on the team of apostles were fishermen, a doctor, and a government official. None had formal theological training, though they would learn much from Jesus. They all seemed to exhibit an entrepreneurial spirit. They were adventurous and ready for change. They showed remarkable faith in leaving their jobs and following Him. They were trusting Christ for their needs to be met.

Jesus knew He needed apostles who represented all types of people. The majority of people were down-to-earth folks; thus, He had an equal representation from the apostles. They represented a diversity of backgrounds, expecting a life of faith as they abruptly left their occupations and, in some cases, families. Christ's followers were loyal and teachable. Recruitment was just the beginning. Training was also a vital part of Christ's teamwork philosophy.

Prior to commissioning the twelve apostles, Jesus was teaching, preaching, and healing. Jesus was a powerful teacher. He knew that what His followers could see and understand, they would retain. Jesus took everyday experiences and illustrated truth to the disciples. He taught about God's provision by pointing to the birds and the lilies. The birds were fed and the lilies grew not because of their efforts but because of God's faithfulness.

Consistently, the disciples heard this clear teaching. Over a span of three years, the words of Christ were recorded and discussed. His teaching helped

> **G**od may not call you to be a leader, but He may want you to help a leader do a better job.
> —Warren W. Wiersbe

them to begin a systematic way of belief. It all made sense. Loving God and loving people became the theme of the disciples' lives. The strongest teaching tool reached beyond Christ's words to His life.

The actions of Jesus were the greatest education for the disciples. Some of the most effective sermons Jesus preached occurred through His healing touch. His compassion for people who were sick was sincere and real. His disciples saw Him mingle among people with leprosy and other serious illnesses. He went to places that most people viewed with contempt. The disciples watched Christ. Many times they were astonished at His humility and servant spirit.

Jesus humbled Himself by washing the disciples' feet (John 13). He took on the role of a servant as an example to the disciples. He left for them a Technicolor example of what a disciple of Christ looked like. As Jesus washed their feet, there was misunderstanding, almost mutiny, but as they saw the sincerity and true servanthood of what Jesus was doing, they in turn were humbled and recognized their need for His cleansing. Jesus was an effective educator. He taught His followers by word and deed.

Jesus knew the value of relationships. He modeled a dynamic, loving relationship with His heavenly Father. Out of that relationship flowed a tender love with those around Him. Out of the twelve apostles, He developed an intimate relationship with Peter, James, and John.

During crucial and pivotal experiences, Jesus involved Peter, James, and John. He included them at His encounter with God on the mountain of His transfiguration (Matt. 17). His ministry was not isolated from sharing His feelings with friends. He confided in them in the Garden of Gethsemane: "My soul is exceedingly sorrowful, even to death. Stay here and watch with Me" (Matt. 26:38). Jesus needed the prayer and support of friends. Jesus showed His greatest love for His friends by dying for them (John 15:13).

> **L**eaders of the growing churches delegated responsibility without anxiety. They perceived delegation as a means to an end: it was a way to empower other people to do ministry.
> —George Barna

They saw Him grieving at the tomb of His friend Lazarus. They witnessed His anger toward the hypocrisy of those using the temple for financial gain. Jesus fulfilled His roles in an honorable manner. His family relationships were important as well. He looked at John while He was dying on the cross and asked him to take care of His mother.

Jesus knew strong, healthy relationships would weather persecutions and trials. Because of His three-year investment in relationships and the proof of His authenticity on the cross, His investment is still paying dividends. Recruitment, training, and relationship building were important to Jesus. I want to apply these principles more specifically to growing and building your team.

LEADERSHIP

■ *The ability to help others move toward an agreed-upon vision.*

A team is a group of uniquely gifted individuals committed to a common cause. Football is an example of a team sport where all commit to the good of the team.

A good coach will take skilled, capable people and lead them to work together. Though some positions attract more attention, each team member needs the others to reach the ultimate goal of victory.

Golf is a whole other sport. Golf revolves around individuals. You are on your own. Whether you win or lose, the game depends solely on you.

Leadership is like coaching a football team rather than hitting a golf ball. You can knock golf balls around, but not people. Wise coaches place people into positions according to their skills and giftedness. They coach these people to develop their skills and gifts. A good coach helps the average become above average and the above average become exceptional.

There are clear-cut benefits to building a team. I use the phrase "building a team" because it takes time. When you commit to building a team of leaders, expect the results to be cumulative. The results will come slowly, but they will build exponentially as time passes. Let's examine three benefits of team building.

The first benefit of a team is multiplication. Figuratively speaking, a leader can be in two places at the same time. By imparting his vision and cultivating friendships with other team members, he imparts purpose and meaning. People begin to live out the mission statement.

The second benefit is delegation. By surrounding yourself with gifted and capable individuals, you can trust them to carry out the task. They will take responsibility to carry out the mission in their area of expertise. The leader is able to "cast the vision" and make sure the team is making the right decision because competent men and women are implementing the mission.

The third benefit of a team is longevity and loyalty. People are highly motivated where there are contentment and fulfillment. They will endure longer or wait patiently for future reward, knowing what they are presently doing is making a difference. Team members commit for the long haul, and they develop a real loyalty to one another. Someone may struggle, but they all struggle together. If one is successful, they all feel a part of the success as well.

Good coaching begins with good recruiting. Great plans without great people lead to failure. A wise leader surrounds himself with capable and gifted associates. The impression they make on others represents that of the leader. How vital then for the leader to choose those who can represent him well.

> **D**o you wish to rise? Begin by descending. You plan a tower that will pierce the clouds? Lay first the foundation of humility.
> —Augustine

A wise leader chooses a variety of gifted individuals. He complements his strengths. In a church setting a pastor gifted in teaching could complement his ministry with an associate gifted in evangelism and follow-up. A strong evangelistic pastor may choose to serve with a gifted educator leading the Sunday school. A pastor may make the mistake of hiring people like him. This approach misses the synergy provided from the development and creativity of differently gifted individuals.

Compiling the team is the first step. You have all this diversity and potential, so what do you do next? It is like landscaping a new home. You have trees, shrubs, grass, flowers, and other types of vegetation. The layout and combinations are numerous. How will you coordinate and lay out a design that's best for the situation?

Part of the process involves getting to know and understand one another. This takes time. Different personalities come across in different ways. The goal is not to change people's personalities, but for everyone's personality to be under the control of the Holy Spirit. As we understand one another's gifts and perspectives, we work more effectively with one another.

> Sometimes the wisest tactic is to get out of the Holy Spirit's way.
> —Judith Couchman

Most team members have agendas and goals. A motivated individual will not sit back and wait for things to happen. That is why a clear mission statement is important; it keeps the team on the same track working together for the betterment of the team.

A good team leader will help team members work out differences and conflict. He will help team players stay mission driven and not spend all their time on hobby horses. Coaching also involves developing a game plan. We have already talked about mission, but that is only the beginning. Once purpose is determined, then comes the tedious task of hammering out objectives, goals, and strategies.

A leader/coach is also relational. He cares about the personal matters of his team members. If there is marital strife or family problems, the leader wants to be part of the solution. Offering some time off or providing a counseling resource may be just the remedy to get a fellow team member through a difficult time.

A leader/coach wants to be a friend, someone to listen and offer solicited advice. Having fun times together is just as important to a friendship as suffering through difficult times together. Though the working relationship is professional, there is still the feeling, "This person really cares about me."

A coach is also an educator. He knows how to teach, train, and motivate his team members. A leader/coach believes in practice, practice, and more practice.

LEADERSHIP

■ The ability to help others move toward an agreed-upon vision.

Educating takes on many forms. The most effective is modeling. People are more apt to do what they see. Personal involvement from the leader communicates importance. If prayer is taught to be a priority and the leader consistently participates in weekly prayer time, other team players will see it as a priority as well. Behavior preaches the loudest sermons. Modeling also helps people to better understand an expected role. Visual learning brings to life ideas and concepts that may still be trapped on paper.

 A CLOSER LOOK

Integrity and maturity are two character traits vital to the heart of a leader. Without them a leader has no credibility. No credibility means the leader forfeits the right to lead. The lifestyle of Jesus exemplifies these two areas.

Integrity is being honest with others and honest with myself. It is following through with my commitments. Integrity is not overextending myself so I can give quality time to key relationships like family and friends.

Integrity is recognizing my blind spots, sharing them with close friends, and asking for their prayers and accountability.

Integrity means being honest about the hurts and heartaches of my past by confessing them and receiving God's forgiveness and healing. This also involves my forgiving others and allowing God to heal my heart.

Integrity means making my yes my yes and my no my no. It is the act of candidly but with concern speaking the truth in difficult and potentially embarrassing situations. Integrity, in a word, means honesty. Honesty is the number one trait that's expected in a leader. James Konzes and Barry Posner in *The Leadership Challenge* discovered this in a survey of more than 2,600 top-level managers. Honesty is truly the best policy.

Jesus was a master at following through with commitments. His follow-through of His death on the cross affects us more than any other of His commitments.

In referring to His body, Jesus said, " 'Destroy this temple, and in three days I will raise it up.' . . . But He was speaking of the temple of His body. Therefore, when He had risen from the dead, His disciples remembered that He had said this to them; and they believed the Scripture and the word which Jesus had said" (John 2:19, 21–22).

The faith of the followers of Jesus grew rapidly as they saw Him do what He said He was going to do. Follow-through on our word builds trust and belief.

Integrity builds trust and credibility. People follow and trust someone or something they believe in. If their belief is strong enough, they will die for an individual or a cause. This is illustrated by Peter and James dying for their faith in Christ or soldiers giving their lives for the freedom of a country because of their strong belief in liberty.

Character involves integrity and maturity. Maturity balances courage with sensitivity. It takes the appropriate approach within different situations. Maturity understands that situations are not always black and white. Maturity gathers the facts, weighs the evidence, and makes a wise decision.

Maturity understands that some people respond better to a direct, candid approach while others need more understanding and explanation. Maturity understands what motivates an individual and then leads her by that motivation. If recognition is important, the mature leader delivers sincere compliments both privately and publicly. If status and position are important to others, the wise leader at the proper time will promote and place them in areas of their expertise.

Courage and sensitivity mean the leader is interested not just in the destination but in the quality of the journey as well. The mature leader balances sensitivity with accountability. He knows when to give a little and when to stand firm.

Jesus balanced courage and sensitivity. He could be candid, as He was with Peter before washing the disciples' feet (John 13). Peter refused to let Christ wash his feet. Jesus told him, "If I do not wash you, you have no part with Me" (v. 8). Later He showed consideration by offering an explanation for His unusual actions. He said, "For I have given you an example, that you should do as I have done to you. Most assuredly, I say to you, a servant is not greater than his master; nor is he who is sent greater than he who sent him. If you know these things, blessed are you if you do them" (vv. 15–17).

Jesus was wise to confront when He needed confrontation and to give a sensitive explanation when more compassion was required. Christ was consistent in His character; therefore, He earned the right to lead. People respected His ability to live what He believed. Integrity and maturity are important traits in character.

A clear mission, consistent character, and capable team are all essential for us to be the leaders of God's people. The example of Jesus gives us a pattern to follow. May all of us follow Him so we can lead others for His glory!

> **S**tudies have shown that few of today's pastors believe they have been gifted by God as leaders; that few say they were adequately prepared by their university and seminary educations to lead people; that only a handful have identified a vision for the future they feel called, by God, to pursue in tandem with their church; and that most of them find their mastery and their enjoyment of leadership lacking.
> —George Barna

GROWTH

Suggested reading for further study includes: *The Leadership Challenge* by James M. Konzes and Barry Z. Posner, *Spiritual Leadership* by Oswald J. Sanders, and *The Training of the Twelve* by A. B. Bruce.

LORD'S DAY

■ *The Christian Sabbath, observed on the first day of the week in celebration of Christ's resurrection from the dead.*

SCRIPTURE

HEBREWS 4:9–10 NASB

There remains therefore a Sabbath rest for the people of God. For the one who has entered His rest has himself also rested from his works, as God did from His.

COMMENTARY

As long as I can remember, church has always been on Sunday, the Lord's Day. At least that is true for the majority of those who worship, as I do, in a Christian church. Muslims worship on the sixth day of the week, and Jews adhere to the Mosaic Sabbath on Saturday, the seventh day of the week. So why did the early church of New Testament history change the day of worship from the seventh day to the first? What about God's moral law? Does our decision completely disregard the fourth commandment?

I believe three basic questions require in-depth study to understand why the Christian family has made this change.

1. Why was the Sabbath changed from the seventh day to the first day of the week?
2. Is this change consistent with the continuing validity of the moral law?
3. Does the change of day undermine the fourth commandment?

A CLOSER LOOK

Until the resurrection of Jesus Christ, the church observed its day of worship and rest on the seventh day (Saturday), or Sabbath. It is troublesome to some that we seem to have abandoned God's example and eliminated the fourth commandment altogether. I suppose the bottom line is whether or not the question of worshiping on Sunday has any real connection to the fourth commandment or is another issue that divides congregations and causes strife among believers.

The simplest path to take in this discussion is to point out that the New Testament church *immediately* began worshiping on the first day of the week after Christ's resurrection. With this ultimate act of love, Christ fulfilled His mission as God's chosen Sacrifice to restore sinful people to God's perfect redemption. Christ rose from the dead on the first day of the week, and His first appearance to the saints after His resurrection was on the first day of the week. Jesus appeared to the disciples on the evening of the first day of the week (John 20:19). Was this a coincidence, or was a pattern being set even then?

LORD'S DAY

I don't think it had anything to do with coincidence. One of the disciples, Thomas, was missing. Always the skeptic, Thomas couldn't hide his doubt when the other disciples reported Jesus' appearance. Yet, we learn that it wasn't until the *next first day* of the week that Jesus chose to return and disclose Himself to Thomas (John 20:26). It wasn't a coincidence. A pattern was being set.

I believe that we can accept the example of the early church. It is fitting for us to worship on the first day of the week in celebration of Christ's resurrection and our promise of eternal life through His shed blood and our willingness to accept what He did for us. But there is more to this new Sabbath than acknowledging Christ's resurrection. We know and believe that Christ's death, burial, and resurrection are assurance of eternal life to those who accept Him as Savior. What more can there be? Much more.

First, it is biblical suicide to suggest that the idea of Sabbath rest was presented for the first time in the fourth commandment. God spent six days in the process of creating the earth and its inhabitants, saving His finest creation for the sixth and final day. It was on the sixth day that God created human beings in His image. Having finished His work, He rested on the seventh day. There was nothing lacking. His work was complete. At that point of perfection God called human beings into His rest.

The perfection that existed when God placed Adam and Eve in the Garden is something that you and I cannot comprehend because we've never known anything but a fallen world. It sounds wonderful, but we have to pause only a brief moment to know what happened next. Perfection was sacrificed in the name of free choice, and sin entered the world. Once Adam and Eve made the choice to be disobedient and go their own way, the option to enter God's rest was impossible.

God's attitude toward the human sinful condition is evident:

> *For forty years I was grieved with that generation,*
> *And said, "It is a people who go astray in their hearts,*
> *And they do not know My ways."*
> *So I swore in My wrath,*
> *"They shall not enter My rest" (Ps. 95:10–11).*

This same declaration appears in Hebrews 3:11 when the writer of Hebrews recounted the plight of the Hebrews of Moses' day who failed to be obedient and urged the people of his day: "Today, if you will hear His voice, do not harden your hearts" (Heb. 4:7). The comparison is one that we can't miss.

Sunday honors God the Father by being the day of the dawn of creation; honors the Son by being the day the work of redemption was sealed by His resurrection; and honors the Holy Spirit by being the day the Spirit descended on the 120 in the Upper Room.
—*Vital Christianity,*
May 30, 1976

LORD'S DAY

■ *The Christian Sabbath, observed on the first day of the week in celebration of Christ's resurrection from the dead.*

Sunday replaces Saturday as the Sabbath because Jesus' resurrection occurred on a Sunday. It is sometimes called the Lord's Day.
—Mark D. Taylor

Just as the ancient Jews had the gospel preached to them in the desert, we have the gospel preached to us (Heb. 4:2). Unlike those who refused to accept the gospel, those who believe will enter God's rest (Heb. 4:3). We must be careful to recognize that the rest Scripture refers to is *God's rest*. The reference of Psalm 95 within Hebrews indicates that the rest is God's rest, not ours. Specific reference is made to God's rest on the seventh day: "Although the works were finished from the foundation of the world. . . . 'And God rested on the seventh day from all His works'" (Heb. 4:3–4).

It was never God's intention to enter the seventh day rest alone. He created us to be His intimate companions and enjoy the finished work of creation in all its glory. There was nothing lacking in God's creation and in His desire that we enter the rest possible only in relationship with Him. What was lacking was in us. Because of our sinful, rebellious, disobedient condition, Christ was the only hope for this to ever become anything more than a longing in God's heart. The key to understanding what this is all about is found in Hebrews 4:9–10: "There remains therefore a Sabbath rest for the people of God. For the one who has entered His rest has himself also rested from his works, as God did from His" (NASB). When Christ rose in victory from the grave, He made it possible for us to enter the rest that had been waiting for us since creation. From the cross, Jesus said, "It is finished," but I wonder if anyone really understood what He was saying to those present that day and to us today.

We miss the whole idea if we don't look carefully at the obvious comparison. God ceased His work of creation on the seventh day. It was complete. The first people sinned and separated themselves from God and the rest that God had called them to. Christ came as the perfect Sacrifice. He ceased His work of redemption on the first day of the week when He rose from the dead in triumphant victory over death itself. Once Christ had completed His work, He could rest, and humankind could enter the rest that God had intended from the beginning of time. Christ ceased His work on the first day of the week. When God finished His work, He rested. When Christ finished His work, He rested and opened the door for us to enter that rest by faith in Him.

Jesus Christ, the Lord of the Sabbath, is the Lord of the new covenant. His finished work has enabled us to enter God's rest. Sabbath keeping in the new covenant is on the first day of the week because that is when Christ rested from His labor. The thought is so simple, so absolutely perfect, that we almost miss it! The Father and the Son had their labor to perform. Nothing was lacking in God's creation, and nothing is lacking in the completion of Jesus' resurrection from the grave. Our path to the rest that God so lovingly calls us to is found in the cross of Christ. Our sinful condition no longer has to be a barrier between us and our Creator. The lesson of Hebrews 4:10 is that the moral law of the Sabbath has in no way been compromised by changing the day of worship. Rather, the law has been fulfilled in the finished work of Christ.

Scripture makes it abundantly clear that Jesus had no intention of destroying the law. It was His goal all along to fulfill it through His finished work. Matthew 5:17 gives us a close look at the mind-set of Jesus when He said, "Do not think that I came to destroy the Law or the Prophets. I did not come to destroy but to fulfill."

God wants your love. He wants a relationship with you. Your highest ambition should be to so love God that one day spent in worship of holy God would be the pinnacle of your week. How long has it been since you looked forward to Sunday worship? If you love God, you will keep this commandment willingly instead of moaning about all the other things you need to do. Your relationship with Him will influence all the other relationships that come into and go out of your life. Too many forces in the world want to capture your time and attention. You cannot afford to begin your week without having spent a day with the One who created you and still calls you today into His rest.

APPLICATION

Anytime we attempt to look at a subject such as this, there will obviously be more questions than there are time and space to address. However, there are some life-changing lessons to learn from even this brief study of what Scripture has to say about the Lord's Day.

We still have a moral obligation to observe the Sabbath.

The Christian Sabbath, through the new covenant, is the Lord's Day.

The Lord's Day is the first day of the week, Sunday, the day Christ finished His labor and rose from the dead.

The moral law was fulfilled through Christ, not abandoned.

GROWTH

It is exciting to look at a comparison of the truth that God gave us from the beginning of creation through the time of Christ's entrance into the world to redeem humankind. We are not slaves to the law, but we rejoice in our ability to observe this day of rest and worship our Lord, Jesus Christ.

The entire question about the Lord's Day and the Sabbath draws us to the central issue of who we allow to be in control of our lives, including our

LORD'S DAY

■ *The Christian Sabbath, observed on the first day of the week in celebration of Christ's resurrection from the dead.*

> **S**unday is nature's law as well as God's. No individual or nation habitually disregarding it has failed to fall upon disaster and grief.
> —Daniel Webster

time and activity. I pray that this study will lead you into a deeper relationship with the One who created you for Himself and longs for you to enjoy the rest that only He can appropriate to you through His loving grace. Only a perfect heavenly Father would have gone to such lengths to restore us to Himself. I cannot think of a better way to begin my week than to spend it with Him. Just as I would devote my full attention to someone I love dearly here on this earth, my full attention must be devoted to worshiping the God of creation. Celebrating the Lord's Day signals our allegiance to Christ and allows focused time for meaningful private and corporate worship.

LORD'S SUPPER

■ *A Christian ordinance in which bread and wine or juice are received as symbols of the body and blood of Jesus.*

1 CORINTHIANS 11:24–26

And when He had given thanks, He broke it and said, "Take, eat; this is My body which is broken for you; do this in remembrance of Me." In the same manner He also took the cup after supper, saying, "This cup is the new covenant in My blood. This do, as often as you drink it, in remembrance of Me." For as often as you eat this bread and drink this cup, you proclaim the Lord's death till He comes.

COMMENTARY

The two ordinances of the church are baptism and the Lord's Supper. Both are visual aids of our salvation. The first—baptism—is a one-time occurrence visually demonstrating our death and burial and resurrection with the Lord Jesus Christ. The second ordinance—the Lord's Supper—is observed on a continuing basis in response to Jesus' command, "This do, as often . . . ," and "For as often as you . . ." (1 Cor. 11:25–26). The exhortation is given that we are to observe this breaking of the bread and drinking of the cup until He comes (1 Cor. 11:26).

Churches differ on the frequency of the Lord's Supper. Some churches observe this ordinance every week, and some once a month or once a quarter. The book of Acts seems to indicate that the early church partook of the elements frequently and also that the event was tightly woven into the sermon ("apostles' doctrine"), fellowship together, and prayer time (Acts 2:42).

The early church usually held a love feast (called an agape feast) in connection with the Lord's Supper. During the time of fellowship, they corresponded with other churches and also collected money for orphans and widows.

A CLOSER LOOK

The Lord Jesus Christ instituted the Lord's Supper before His death. Three of the four Gospels record the event:

Then He said to them, "With fervent desire I have desired to eat this Passover with you before I suffer." . . . Then He took the cup, and gave thanks, and said, "Take this and divide it among yourselves." . . . And He took bread, gave thanks and broke it, and gave it to them, saying, "This is My body which is given for you; do this in remembrance of Me." Likewise He also took the cup after supper, saying, "This cup is the new covenant in My blood, which

Lord's Supper

is shed for you" (Luke 22:15, 17, 19–20; see Matt. 26:26–29; see Mark 14:22–25).

The apostle Paul refers to the new covenant, as well. *Webster's Dictionary* defines *new* as "other than the former or the old." That definition certainly fits here. Think about it.

The Messiah had come.

The law had been fulfilled.

The ultimate and final sacrifice for sin had been made.

No more animal sacrifices.

A new High Priest.

The veil in the temple was torn.

It was a *new* covenant all right. A *covenant* means an "arrangement made by one party which the other party involved can accept or reject but cannot alter." God, the "Arranger" of the new covenant, was offering through His Son a new and better way. We can accept or reject His offer. But we can't alter it.

So, we are to have a memorial service in honor of this One who came. It's kind of a celebration of a new covenant. It's not like a New Year's revelry, but it should be a glorious commemoration of "out with the old and in with the new."

I would be remiss if I did not comment briefly on a few things that are more controversial in the Lord's Supper. I will not go into great depth about these views but will touch on them. First, there is *transubstantiation*. This view is held by the Roman Catholic church and teaches that at consecration, the elements literally become the body and blood of Christ.

I do not personally believe the Bible teaches this. Henry Thiessen's *Lectures on Systematic Theology* mentions several reasons why this view is not held by Protestants. First, Jesus was present when He said that the elements were His body and blood. He had to be using figurative language. And second, the idea of eating human flesh and drinking human blood would be abhorrent to the Jewish mind. Drinking blood was strictly forbidden in Scripture (Gen. 9:4; Lev. 3:17; Acts 15:29). Just as the Passover was a symbolic feast of the deliverance of Israel from Egypt, so the symbolism of the elements in the Communion service would be in keeping with the symbolism in the Passover feast.

Another view is called *consubstantiation*. This is the position of the Lutheran church. Unlike the Roman Catholic view, the Lutheran view is that the elements themselves do not change but that the mere partaking of them

> This is the Lord's table. Human sentiment therefore is not to govern it. Long-established customs are not to govern it. Prejudices, tastes, or feelings are not to govern it.
> —George W. Truett

after the prayer of consecration communicates Christ to the participant along with the elements. I do not feel Scripture teaches this.

The Lord's Supper is like baptism in that both are symbols or reminders. Baptism is not our literally dying in the water and being literally resurrected. It is a picture of our salvation. In the same way, I believe the Lord's Supper is a picture of His sacrificial death to secure salvation for us.

In reading the book of Acts, I feel this is what the early church saw these ordinances to be as well.

Some hold firmly to closed Communion and some hold just as strongly to open Communion. Closed Communion is generally limited to believers who are members of that denomination, or in some cases that local church. Open Communion is received by those who have been saved and baptized, but not necessarily a member of the local assembly.

I see it as the Lord's Table. Not a denominational table. It is a joyful memorial for His children to remember Him. As a pastor, I would not feel comfortable at all saying, "This is the Lord's Table, but if you are a believer and have your membership somewhere else, please refrain from this." I have never said that, and I can't picture the apostle Paul telling the church of Corinth, "Oh, by the way, you fellows who dropped in for the love feast to bring us news from the church in Ephesus, please don't partake of the Memorial Service." I don't think that happened. After all, Communion is really between the person and the Lord anyway. No pastor can know the hearts of those sitting around him.

Christian speaker John DeBrine calls the Lord's Supper the most dangerous service in the church. I think that's true. Paul gave a stinging warning to those Corinthian believers to examine themselves before they partook. He was, in essence, saying, "Either you deal with your sin, or God will. Your choice" (1 Cor. 11:27–32).

> The Lord's Supper is the only thing Jesus ever asked His people to do whereby they might remember Him. Shall we deny Him this simple request?
> —George W. Truett

When we have our time of reflecting before the Lord's Supper, I like to imagine that I can turn 360 degrees and not think of a soul I have offended or a grudge I am harboring. Frankly, I think if we were really honest, during this time of reflection and examination, there would be rustling of people as one believer seeks out another to ask forgiveness.

A mother told me that she and her family were sitting on the fifth row at our church after they had moved to Atlanta and joined our fellowship. As the elements were slowly passed from person to person, her twelve-year-old daughter eyed them coming closer and closer to her. She squirmed. Finally, as she saw the tray only two people away from her, she knew she had to hurry and make things right. She leaned over to her mother and whispered

LORD'S SUPPER

as fast as she could, "Mom, you really hurt my feelings this week, and I've been really mad at you. Will you forgive me?"

The mother assured her of her forgiveness. And as the little girl partook—obviously with a clear conscience—the mother realized she needed to ask her daughter to forgive her for hurting her feelings. So the mom quickly cleared her conscience with her daughter as she was handed the tray.

A man was sitting up in the balcony one night when we received the Lord's Supper. During the time of reflection, he looked across the balcony and spotted someone he knew deeply disliked him. He got up and walked quietly to the other side of the balcony to get things cleared up. When the person refused to forgive him, they decided they needed to talk more about the problem, and they went to another room to talk it out.

Neither of them was in the sanctuary to partake of the Lord's Supper, but I am sure the Lord was pleased with two believers trying to get a complicated situation straight. Nothing worse than siblings fighting at a Memorial Service for their Father!

What a joyous celebration as we remember His sovereign will in choosing us, His substitutionary death in saving us, His Spirit sealing us, and His steadfast love sustaining us!

What a Savior! "For where a covenant is, there must of necessity be the death of the one who made it" (Heb. 9:16 NASB).

He died! He lives! He is coming back!

But remember, the Memorial Service is strictly limited by the Father to family members.

Many years ago, the former pastor at First Baptist Church of Dallas, Texas, Dr. George W. Truett, told this story before serving the Lord's Supper:

In the long ago a prince led an insurrection against his country and thereby legally forfeited his right to life. Though fleeing, he was finally captured and brought before the ruler whose authority he had despised. Looking upon him, the ruler asked him what he would give for his liberty. "The half of my estate," he answered. Again he asked him what he would give for the liberty of his children. "The other half of my estate," he quickly answered. And again, the ruler, looking upon the prisoner's wife, asked him: "And what would you give for her liberty?" Quick as the lightning's flash he answered: "Oh, sir, if you will spare her I will give you my life!" So deeply touched was the ruler's heart that he released them all. One day thereafter, when the pardoned prince spoke to his wife of the wonderful look of the ruler, on that momentous day when he set them free, she replied that she did not see him. "How could that be?" the husband asked. "Oh," said the wife, "I had eyes for nothing but the man who was offering to give his life to save me."

LORD'S SUPPER

At the Lord's Table—and throughout our lives—may we have eyes only for the One who offered His life to save us.

For most of us, Communion is a solemn time. We do not take lightly the body and blood of the Savior. And we are to examine ourselves closely. We hardly do that eagerly.

But it is not just a solemn time. It is also a celebration. He came! He lives! He is coming back!

The Lord's Supper is a memorial service. While we grieve over the price our salvation cost the Son of God, we also rejoice over the wonderful memories of what He has done in our lives.

Let me suggest four things to remember at the Lord's Table.

First, *remember by His sovereign will, He chose you*. Don't ever let the devil trick you into thinking that you decided one day to be saved. The Bible teaches you could not even choose Him had He not wooed you to Himself in the first place. According to Ephesians 1:4–5, we were chosen and predestined unto adoption. We can argue about predestination and free will all we want to, but He chose us before we chose Him. Period. All by His grace.

What a wonderful thing to remember: His sovereign will.

Second, *remember by His substitutionary death, He saved you*. You are no longer guilty. You're accepted. You're a joint heir with the Son. He stepped in and died in your place. Can you think of anyone you would die for? "For scarcely for a righteous man will one die; yet perhaps for a good man someone would even dare to die. But God demonstrates His own love toward us, in that while we were still sinners, Christ died for us" (Rom. 5:7–8).

God the Father looked through eternity and saw His Son, along with the spit and slaps of the jeering crowd and His ultimate death. And He still chose to instigate the new covenant through His sacrifice.

What a wonderful thing to remember: His substitutionary death.

Third, *remember by His Spirit, He has sealed you forever*. You are not His child for a season. He will not wake up in a bad mood and cast you out. He will not tear up the will where you're a joint heir. He will not shake His head in disgust that He adopted you. He will not say, "Now that you are My child, you must behave or you're not in this family anymore. Understand?"

No. "Having believed, you were sealed with the Holy Spirit of promise, who is the guarantee of our inheritance" (Eph. 1:13–14). You are sealed.

We know that church saints should periodically memorialize the death of Christ by breaking bread and drinking from the cup because the apostle Paul was told by special revelation that Christ's church should do this (1 Cor. 11:17–34).
—Dwight Pentecost

LORD'S SUPPER

The earnest or guarantee is like an engagement ring, securing you until the Beloved comes and takes you home. There are no broken engagements once He has made you part of His bride. You're eagerly awaiting the marriage supper of the Lamb.

And so you meet with others at His Table now as a foretaste of what will be.

What a wonderful thing to remember: His Spirit sealing you.

Fourth, *remember His steadfast love sustains you*. Paul wrote of numerous things that he was persuaded could not separate us from God's love. We can't think of one thing that doesn't fit into his list.

Read Romans 8:38–39. You'll be persuaded, too. Every single day and minute and second and megasecond—not to mention every heartbeat and brain wave—His love sustains you.

I understand some people have a difficult time feeling loved. A lot of it stems from their backgrounds. Some don't feel worth loving. Some have been hurt and will not soften their hearts again, lest they be broken. There are a thousand ways they stoically try to keep His love out. But you know what? He just keeps on loving them.

You may not feel loved. But you are loved. You are absolutely adored by the Father. He loves you to death.

What a wonderful thing to remember: His steadfast love sustains you.

Perhaps these four things can be a starting place in remembering Him.

■ *To return to a former state; to bring back to spiritual health.*

RESTORATION

GALATIANS 6:1

Brethren, if a man is overtaken in any trespass, you who are spiritual restore such a one in a spirit of gentleness, considering yourself lest you also be tempted.

What is our attitude to be when a fellow Christian stumbles? Galatians 6 gives us priceless insight and direction. Perhaps the most unsettling insight is that no one is exempt from the propensity to sin. No one has the right to stand in self-righteous judgment of another's actions because all are subject to stumbling.

It was from experience that Paul wrote, "For the good that I will to do, I do not do; but the evil I will not to do, that I practice. Now if I do what I will not to do, it is no longer I who do it, but sin that dwells in me" (Rom. 7:19–20). Some call this the sin principle, while others call it the old sin nature. Whatever name we place on it, our vulnerability to sin is obvious. Its influence is strong. Sin has no power over us, but we still have the capacity to sin within us. The choice is ours—and we make the choice all too often! That's why the principle of restoration is necessary. Otherwise, the one who has fallen could remain in unnecessary bondage to guilt or fail to come to terms with the sin and its effect on the relationship with God.

In Galatians 6:1, the word *overtaken* means when someone has been plotting to sin, and it can also mean that the person has been taken by surprise. Whether or not the person premeditated the sin, Scripture says we are to restore that person. Since that is the case, it is essential that we understand what the term means.

The term *restore* is an interesting one. In the Greek, it meant to set a broken bone back in place. If you have ever had this procedure, you know it isn't a pleasant process but is essential if the bone is to grow properly. There will always be an element of pain when a person is involved in the restoration process. When a person is broken by sin, our responsibility is to gently mend her so that she is whole again.

If restoration is something the church should be involved in, to whom should this responsibility be given? The phrase in our text, "you who are spiritual," gives us a hint but leaves us with questions. Does that mean only supersaints can restore a fallen brother or sister? Absolutely not. There are no supersaints anyway. We all have feet of clay. "You who are spiritual" refers to those who walk with the Lord Jesus and live through the enabling of His Spirit. These are not people who just appear to be pious. Scripture

Restoration **41**

RESTORATION

■ *To return to a former state; to bring back to spiritual health.*

speaks of the godly man or woman who recognizes his or her need for grace and is empowered by the Holy Spirit to reconcile a wandering brother or sister into a right relationship with God and the church.

A CLOSER LOOK

The steps to restoration are as follows:

1. The person needs to be led to *recognize* her failure. We need to help her see the nature of it, the consequences, and to call it by its right name: *sin*. As long as a person can rationalize her behavior as anything other than what it is, she will never be willing to take the next step of accepting responsibility.

2. The struggling soul needs to be led to acknowledge *responsibility* for his sin. Blaming others will do him no good whatsoever. That doesn't mean someone else was not involved, and it doesn't mean that another did not tempt him or put pressure on him. However, in the final analysis the person chose to sin and claiming proper responsibility is essential to restoration.

3. The fallen saint needs to be led to *repent*. We hope she will, through conviction of the Holy Spirit, feel remorse, regret, and grief. Repentance means a change of mind, and that, of course, will result in a change of conduct. Too often we get that backward and think we have to change behavior first. When Paul spoke to the church about being transformed by the "renewing of your mind" (Rom. 12:2), he was aware that our thinking must change first, then our actions will follow.

4. The person needs to be led to understand the necessity of making *restitution*. This is obvious in the case of stealing, but suppose the person criticized another in public? He needs to go to the one he offended and ask for forgiveness. There are some things he can't make restitution for, however, and he will need to be led carefully through the stages of grief. All of us are recipients of grace, and we must never cause a fallen saint to be defeated by staying in his guilt.

5. The one who has been caught in a trespass needs to be led to *receive* the message God wants to teach her through her failure. She may not want to hear this. Sometimes a person is stubborn and resistant and reluctant to learn. The one who is working with her in the restoration process needs to help her learn what God wants to teach her. I've come to understand that failure is only unprofitable when

we refuse to learn from the experience. If we learn and grow, we have not failed—we have taken the opportunity to learn more about ourselves and about our God.

6. The sinful believer needs to be led to *respond* to God's chastisement with gratitude. The one guiding can point out these verses that David wrote, "Before I was afflicted I went astray, but now I keep Your word," and "It is good for me that I have been afflicted, that I may learn Your statutes" (Ps. 119:67, 71). The person needs to be reminded—gently—that it is wonderful that God loves us enough to chastise us and to mend us. God is our most loving Father—the perfect Parent—who will discipline but will never crush the one He loves so dearly. A child rarely expresses gratitude to the parent during a time of disciplining but, years later, honors the wise parent for loving him enough to teach lessons the hard way.

> **O**ften the emptiness we feel when we stray in our fellowship from God is a warning that we are entering dangerous territory.
> —*In Touch*, March 1995

The spirit in which we restore a fallen brother or sister is vital. It must be done firmly but gently. There is to be a balance between firmness and gentleness. We are not putting bandages on people. We are setting broken emotional and spiritual bones. It is often a long and painful process.

Someone who is already hurting is as fragile as glass. She doesn't need our condemnation. We are to restore her "in a spirit of gentleness" (Gal. 6:1). We don't go to her in anger or to vent our hurt. We go gently, being very sensitive to her agony. The inability to express her grief should not be interpreted as a lack of remorse or repentance. She may suffer so greatly that she can't get close to the physical tears that her soul weeps for. We must be firm in our effort to restore a fallen sister, but we need to set the broken bones as tenderly as possible.

We are also to restore someone in the spirit of humility: "For if anyone thinks himself to be something, when he is nothing, he deceives himself" (Gal. 6:3). We can't go with a haughty attitude, as if that could *never* happen to us. That attitude is an affront to God. We have to remember that we are all vulnerable to sin. If we go to a hurting person with the attitude that we are way above him, he certainly won't respond to our help. In fact, it will build a wall that will prevent the restoration process. "Considering yourself lest you also be tempted" means to examine ourselves with a sharp eye.

> **G**od doesn't command us to feel a certain way; He commands us to forgive, that the relationship may be restored.
> —Mati Waymeyer

We are to go in love. Galatians 6:2 uses the word for burdens that means "heavy burdens." We need to get up under the heavy burden with the person and help him carry it. We need to vicariously feel what he is feeling. We must go with the right spirit, or we may as well not go at all. What an

RESTORATION

■ *To return to a former state; to bring back to spiritual health.*

incredible privilege we have, as believers, to help restore a brother who has fallen! What a marvelous thing to watch as his fellowship with the Father is restored, as well as the fellowship with other believers!

Not only is it a privilege; it is also our responsibility. Those who are walking with the Father are to get up under the load with the saint who has sinned. We need to lead gently, humbly, and lovingly into restoration. We must help her to recognize her failure, take responsibility for it, repent, make restitution, receive God's lessons, and respond to God's chastening with gratitude. It is an experience that we need to be involved in, being sure to check our attitude and motive. The restoration process is not for people playing church. It is for people who are serious about their walk with the Lord. It will be a difficult assignment for the one who has sinned and wants restoration and for the saint who is willing to be used in the process. It is a glorious calling for the Christian.

Those of us who belong to the Shepherd and have been in the valley and have had another believer lift us up know what it means. Although none of us would enjoy being a part of the process, because of the pain that is inevitable, all of us should gladly participate as the Spirit leads us to restore one who has fallen. What more thrilling experience can we have than to help restore a fallen saint into fellowship with the Father? We must never make the mistake of heaping unnecessary and inappropriate guilt.

When a child does something that causes a rift between himself and his parents, the child doesn't stop being a child. He stops enjoying the privilege of open fellowship with his parents until someone takes the first step in mending the gap that caused the problem. Our Father has already taken the first step by letting Jesus pay the ultimate price for our sin. He waits for us to follow His lead by restoring the fellowship of our brothers and sisters who have strayed from the path.

The apostle Paul was distressed about a man in the church at Corinth who had committed a sin and the church had failed to do anything about it. When they finally took action and disciplined him, Paul wanted to be sure that they went the next step to restore him: "This punishment which was inflicted by the majority is sufficient for such a man, so that, on the contrary, you ought rather to forgive and comfort him, lest perhaps such a one be swallowed up with too much sorrow. Therefore I urge you to reaffirm your love to him" (2 Cor. 2:6–8).

I believe the lesson is that if the man was not restored—gently, with love and in humility—he would be totally consumed with grief and unable to function in the body of Christ. Sin is never to be overlooked or ignored by

> **F**aithfully honoring the commitment of forgiveness . . . takes discipline and perseverance. . . . In the same way that an athlete trains his body to compete, we must train our minds to say no to thoughts of bitterness.
> —Mati Waymeyer

> **G**alatians 6:1 indicates that when someone sins against us our goal should be to restore them in a gentle manner that draws them back to God. . . . One of the ways to help restore someone is to confront them when they have sinned against us or offended us.
> —Wayne and
>   Miyako Meyer

the church, but it is also against God's Word to refuse to work toward restoration for the one who has strayed from God's way.

When Paul wrote in Galatians 6, he may have had this very man in mind.

APPLICATION

What can you learn from the restoration process? I think there is a lot for you to learn, and I think two key elements are involved.

First, you need to take it as a call to self-examination: What about me? How am I doing? Am I being extra cautious in this area?

Second, you need to see that Satan could use this to cause deception in believers and unbelievers. Let me explain. As a believer, you could smugly think, *Well, I've never been tempted in that area.* Our adversary takes full advantage of that attitude.

You might be the one to help restore a fallen brother or sister—or perhaps you are the one who needs to face the sin that has interrupted your fellowship with the Father and the church. You need to intercede and intervene under the Spirit's leadership. And you need to pray for purity in your life.

QUOTE

The granting of restorative grace is among the greatest and most unique gifts one Christian can give another.

—Gordon MacDonald

SUICIDE

■ *The act of intentionally killing oneself.*

2 SAMUEL 17:23

Now when Ahithophel saw that his advice was not followed, he saddled a donkey, and arose and went home to his house, to his city. Then he put his household in order, and hanged himself, and died; and he was buried in his father's tomb.

COMMENTARY

Is suicide the unpardonable sin, or does God forgive suicide? These questions have troubled the hearts of those who struggle with the temptation to end their lives and those who are left behind when a friend or family member chooses to take his or her life.

As we look at this most sensitive subject that exposes our most intimate thoughts and feelings, we realize that the subject of suicide affects those who do not profess to know Christ as Savior and many believers as well.

A CLOSER LOOK

Although the word *suicide* is never used in the Bible, there are several direct references to people killing themselves, and by definition, that is suicide. In 1 Kings 16:18, there is reference to Zimri, who reigned for a few days over Israel and then died in a fire that he started in his home. He was about to be overthrown and could not cope with defeat. Abimelech, the son of Jerubbaal, committed assisted suicide (Judg. 9:53–54) rather than have it said that he died at the hands of a woman. Saul fell on his sword after losing a battle against the Philistines. When his armorbearer saw that Saul had killed himself, he followed in like manner (1 Sam. 31:4–5; 1 Chron. 10:4–5). When he stopped allowing God to direct his life, Samson lost his unbelievable strength and suffered humiliation at the hands of the Philistines. Unable to tolerate the ridicule and the reality of his failure, in one final act of strength, Samson pulled the pillars down on himself and thousands of his captors (Judg. 16:25–30).

The inability to cope with failure. The inability to deal with relationships. The perceived loss of position or status. The unbearable pain of humiliation and a meaningless life. These were some of the reasons given for those who committed suicide during biblical times. A closer examination of the alarming number of suicides today reveals five motivating factors: (1) a cause that a person is committed to; (2) a pact between two or more people; (3) feelings of meaninglessness; (4) circumstances that overwhelm an individual; and (5) an extended illness involving intractable or unrelenting pain (note the growing debate regarding assisted suicide).

No matter what mode of suicide a person chooses, if we were to somehow explore the thoughts of those who have committed suicide (or are contemplating it), I believe that we would find one of these five motivating factors. The death certificate may list drug overdose or gunshot wound as the cause of death; yet the underlying cause often is never discovered because of the self-imposed isolation that most people experience prior to their suicide. We see the result on the coroner's report, but the true cause can usually be found within the list of these motivating factors.

Over the last ten to fifteen years, we have watched the results of suicides stemming from adherence to a cause. This has been portrayed in grim detail in the media in the suicides carried out in bombings in the Middle East when a soldier storms a building with a truck laden with explosives. The murder of hundreds of soldiers was an honorable deed for the one who killed himself in the truck that slammed into the army barracks. To die for such a cause is noble for one who considers the cause life's motivation.

The pictures of Guyana and the hundreds of bodies strewn across the ground were grim reminders that pacts between individuals can have tragic consequences. The followers of Jim Jones had a pact, and it resulted in their mass suicide.

A major cause of suicide is the despair of living without meaning or purpose. In a world overwhelmed with violence, divorce, homelessness, AIDS, and drug abuse, it is too often the norm to live life bouncing around without anything to hang on to that would give meaning and security to an otherwise lonely existence.

In his book *Fatal Choice,* John Q. Baucom states that of all the suicides committed by teenagers in 1984, 80 percent had alcohol in their systems: "Suicide is the second leading cause of death among teenagers. It is estimated that approximately 6,000 adolescents will take their lives annually. . . . During the past 25 years the teenage rate has tripled. One report indicates that nearly 12 percent of all school children will experience serious suicidal ideation at least once."

The fact that many children are finding suicide to be the logical choice underscores the impact that the pressures of life, even at such an early age, can have. They live in a world of isolation, rejection, and the perception that no one cares. Life becomes intolerable, and suicide becomes the "logical" answer. Depression is a key factor in most suicides.

Circumstances can often be the precipitating factor in suicide. What one person can deal with, another might find overwhelming. This can encompass any number of things, such as divorce, the loss of a job, or financial distress. In one sad incident, the inability to deal with the death of a friend resulted

Dr. Seymour Perlin, chairman of the board of the new Youth Suicide National Center in Washington, D.C., stated that two million adolescents between the ages of fifteen and nineteen attempt suicide each year.

The National Institute of Mental Health suggests that approximately 30,000 people successfully take their own lives annually. That is nearly one person every twenty minutes or more than seventy persons per day.

SUICIDE

in the suicide of a well-known professional football player. The young man lost control of his car while driving late one evening in Texas. A friend who was in the car died. Overcome with the reality of what had happened, the young man put a gun to his head and ended his life. His circumstance motivated his suicide.

The last of the motivating factors in suicide concerns the inability to cope with a debilitating illness and unrelenting pain. Assisted suicide has gained national and international attention in the media. Over the years, the idea of euthanasia has been discussed and debated, but never have so many sought to enlist the help of medical professionals in ending their lives. *Euthanasia* is defined in *Webster's II, New Riverside University Dictionary,* as "the intentional causing of a painless and easy death to a patient suffering from an incurable or painful disease." As people have become more aggressive in their "right" to end the suffering of terminal illnesses or the ravages of old age, the issue of assisted suicide has taken on monumental significance among many groups who wish to see euthanasia become one of the "rights" that all people possess. News reports are filled with stories of people seeking to end their lives with the help of a medical professional.

GROWTH

We need to consider the reasons why suicide is wrong and why it is not the way to avoid painful circumstances. As an act of rebellion, suicide is a sin against God. These are some of the reasons why suicide is wrong:

- It violates the Ten Commandments.
- Nowhere does the Bible condone a person ending life to escape circumstances.
- Life is a gift from God.
- Suicide is an expression of self-hatred, and the Bible says we are to "love our neighbors *as ourselves*."
- Suicide usurps the power that belongs only to God.
- A person who commits suicide short-circuits God's will for his or her life.
- It is an expression of lack of faith. Philippians 4:19 states, "My God shall supply all your need according to His riches in glory by Christ Jesus." This applies to financial needs and emotional and physical needs.
- Suicide is an act of selfishness.
- It hurts the cause of Christ.

SUICIDE

With this in mind, we can understand why there are so many questions concerning whether God forgives the person who commits suicide. After all, suicide is an act of rebellion against God. Fortunately for all of us, however, God's grace is without prejudice. Whoever believes will be saved. Nowhere in the Bible does God compartmentalize sin and reserve grace only for those who commit "acceptable" sins. There is no such thing. Does God forgive suicide? *Yes, He does.*

If the person who committed suicide at some time accepted Jesus' death on the cross as payment for his sin debt and asked Him into his life, he is forgiven. Absolute assurance of forgiveness is found in Romans 8:1: "There is therefore now no condemnation to those who are in Christ Jesus." If a person has ever taken that step and received Christ as Savior, nothing can alter the truth that, as children of God, we are forgiven. Even when we rebel against God, He is faithful to keep His Word. On the other hand, there is no such assurance for the one who commits suicide and has never taken that step of faith in Christ, except the assurance of eternal separation from God.

The fact that God's grace is sufficient and that forgiveness is available even in the case of suicide should *never* be taken as permission to follow through with the temptation to commit suicide. Suicide is never the right decision. No one enjoys suffering. All of us sympathize with those who hurt, both physically and emotionally. However, 2 Corinthians 12:9 is our assurance that in our weakness, God's grace is sufficient, and that is our hope when life becomes intolerable. When nothing we try works, God has promised that He is able to sustain us.

> **O**nly one thing will keep us from heaven and that is our refusal to turn to Christ in faith and trust.
> —Billy Graham

APPLICATION

If you have struggled with the meaning of life or are experiencing overwhelming pain (physical or mental) and are considering taking your life, I urge you to take these steps to get the help you need in your time of trouble.

Cry out to God. Read Psalm 34 and ask God to renew your mind with these verses:

> *The righteous cry out, and the LORD hears,*
> *And delivers them out of all their troubles.*
> *The LORD is near to those who have a broken heart,*
> *And saves such as have a contrite spirit.*
> *Many are the afflictions of the righteous,*
> *But the LORD delivers him out of them all.*
> *He guards all his bones;*
> *Not one of them is broken (vv. 17–20).*

SUICIDE

■ *The act of intentionally killing oneself.*

> The failure to control one's behavior and the depression evident during drinking are reasons why the suicide rate of alcoholics has been found to be six to twenty times higher than that of the general population in various studies.
> —Jay Strack

Call someone and ask for help. Don't let pride get in the way. Much of Satan's power to convince those who feel unloved and hopeless is found in his ability to keep them isolated and removed from those who can lift them up.

Ask Jesus Christ to give you new hope and to give your life meaning. His life indwells you, and His resources are constantly available in your most desperate moment.

If you are not the one struggling with the issue of suicide but have a friend or someone in your family who seems to have given up, there are some things you can do to help that person.

Be able to recognize clues the person may be giving, either consciously or subconsciously. Look for symptoms such as depression, signs of hopelessness, lethargy, and so on. Listen for threats and words of warning, such as, "I have nothing to live for." Be aware of whether the person becomes withdrawn and isolated from others.

Trust your judgment. If you believe there is an imminent threat of suicide, trust your instincts. Don't let others dissuade you from loving intervention.

Tell others. Don't worry about breaking a confidence if the person is obviously contemplating suicide or says he or she has a plan. As soon as possible, involve the help of others, such as parents, friends, spouse, teachers, ministers, physicians, anyone in a position to assist the distressed individual.

Stay with the person. If you believe the person is in danger of carrying out the plan, do not leave the person alone. Wait with the person until medical help arrives or the crisis has passed.

Listen. Encourage the person to talk to you. Refrain from giving pat answers that could further depress the person who is on the verge of giving up. Listen and empathize with the person.

Urge professional help. Stress the necessity of getting help for the individual.

Be supportive. Show the person that you care. Do what you can to help the person feel worthwhile and valuable to you.

Suicide is not the answer to life's pain, whether it be physical, mental, or emotional. Christ is the answer and in Him alone will we find healing from the problems that ultimately cause a person to end life before God has chosen to do so.

QUOTES

Most suicides occur in April or May. December has the lowest rate except around Christmas. There are a large number of suicides during the Thanks-

SUICIDE

giving, Christmas and New Year holiday periods. Suicides occur most frequently on Friday and Monday. Sunday runs a strong third. Three times more women attempt suicide than men. On the other hand, three times more men actually succeed. Men use more violent means to commit suicide, including the use of guns and explosives and by hanging. People with serious depressive reactions are 500 times more likely to commit suicide than others. Farm workers have the lowest incidence among occupational groups. Dentists and physicians take their own lives at the rate of 6½ to 1 over the general population. Lawyers commit suicide at a ratio of 5 to 1 over the general population.

—John Q. Baucom

Do you not know that your body is the temple of the Holy Spirit who is in you, whom you have from God, and you are not your own? For you were bought at a price; therefore glorify God in your body.

—1 Corinthians 6:19–20

> **I**n the past two decades there has been a dramatic change in the issue of teen suicides. The number of suicides has tripled. . . . The increase has been attributed to numerous causes, such as: family breakups, teenage pressure to compete, hopelessness, and substance abuse.

TONGUES

■ *Known dialects or unintelligible languages associated with the early church.*

1 CORINTHIANS 12:4, 7, 28, 30–31

There are diversities of gifts, but the same Spirit. . . . But the manifestation of the Spirit is given to each one for the profit of all. . . . And God has appointed these in the church: first apostles, second prophets, third teachers, after that miracles, then gifts of healing, helps, administrations, varieties of tongues. . . . Do all speak with tongues? Do all interpret? But earnestly desire the best gifts. And yet I show you a more excellent way.

The Lord Jesus Christ had come and gone. The church—newly birthed—was in a transition time. The new covenant was seen as a threat to the Jewish leaders; therefore, there was persecution for those who had chosen to follow Christ.

The new religion, in its infant stages, had no Bible, few leaders, and absolutely no support from the government.

Astounding that it survived, isn't it?

How in the world did it survive with so little going for it?

Power. Not just a force, but mighty, visible power.

This new church had speakers—apostles—but how were followers of Christ to know the speakers were authentic? How did the believers know that the men weren't making up things? If you were being persecuted for your belief, wouldn't you want to make sure the data you were risking your life for was accurate?

The Bible tells us, "After it was at the first spoken through the Lord, it was confirmed to us by those who heard, God also bearing witness with them, both by signs and wonders and by various miracles and by gifts of the Holy Spirit according to His own will" (Heb. 2:3–4 NASB).

God authenticated His message and the messenger through signs, wonders, and miracles. Anyone could have claimed to be a teacher or an apostle in the newly established church. The believers were rather naive and childlike and probably could have been easily misled. To validate His spokesperson, God sent power and accompanying miracles. God not only authenticated His message, but He also authenticated His messengers.

I personally believe there were sign gifts in this infant church as well as ministry gifts. They had different functions. The sign gifts, as previously stated, were to validate the message and messenger. The ministry gifts, listed in Romans 12:6–8, were for the members of the body to build one another up.

TONGUES

I believe that the gift of tongues was a legitimate sign gift and a genuine work of the Holy Spirit. I believe it validated the message and the messenger. But there is so much division today over this topic, I think we need to take a much closer look.

Because this subject is somewhat controversial and divisive, I want to be as sensitive and clear as I can possibly be. I was raised in a Pentecostal church. I have heard many people speaking in tongues. A lot of my family members did so.

In examining the whole scope of this subject, I think we need to look at the presence of tongues in the New Testament church as well as the position of tongues, the problem and purpose of tongues, the principles of regulation of tongues, and the permanence and practice of tongues in the New Testament church.

Let's look first at the presence of tongues in the New Testament church. Let me reiterate, I believe it was a genuine gift and work of the Holy Spirit. On the day of Pentecost the Holy Spirit enabled them to communicate in other tongues or languages. The Greek word for tongues is similar to our word *dialect*. It always means languages. The other Greek word for tongues—*glossa*—is never used outside the New Testament in any other writing to mean anything other than human language. There are thirty references to tongues in the Septuagint (which is the Greek translation of the Old Testament), and they all refer to a language.

The second chapter of Acts teaches that the apostles were speaking in other known languages to reach the people who had assembled from other parts of the world (Acts 2:4–12). This was a true miracle of God! Therefore, I believe in the presence of tongues in the New Testament church. Peter, Paul, Pentecost, and even Gentiles (Acts 10:45–46) attest to this fact.

But what was the position of tongues in the New Testament church? Jesus mentioned tongues only in Mark 16:17. And even though the work and person of the Holy Spirit are written about extensively throughout the Epistles, tongues are never mentioned. How could this be, especially if, as some hold, tongues are the main evidence of being filled with the Holy Spirit? I don't believe the Bible supports that belief.

In the listing of spiritual gifts in 1 Corinthians 12, the gift of tongues is mentioned last. What is the gift listed first? The first mentioned is the gift of being an apostle (1 Cor. 12:28). There are no apostles today because an apostle is someone who actually saw the Lord Jesus Christ in the flesh. Paul

TONGUES

was the last apostle, having seen Jesus according to his conversion account in Acts 9.

If we are not to desire the gift of apostleship, what gift should we desire? Right after the gift of apostle, the next gift mentioned is prophecy. You may be saying, "Sure, that's fine with me. If I can't be an apostle, I would love the gift of telling the future." But that's not the only meaning for the gift of prophecy. The word *prophecy* means to tell forth the truth. Telling forth the truth would have been essential in this early struggling church.

The purposes of prophecy were to (1) edify the church, (2) exhort the church, (3) console the church, and (4) evangelize unbelievers.

All gifts are not on the same level. The lesser gift seems to be tongues and the greater gift seems to be prophecy. Paul says that we are to "earnestly desire" the greater gifts (1 Cor. 12:31). He writes that we are to "desire spiritual gifts" and "pursue love" (1 Cor. 14:1).

I believe the position of tongues in the church was the position of the lesser sign gift. I believe the Bible teaches prophecy was the greatest sign gift. And I also believe it is amazing that we emphasize everything but to "pursue love," even though we love to read 1 Corinthians 13. We lose balance.

The early church got off balance easily, too. And this led to the problem of tongues in the New Testament church. Mystery religions were around during this time. Prostitutes spoke in a form of tongues in their religion. The church at Corinth was made up of people from all walks of life. Apparently, people stood up and appeared to be babbling. They didn't seem to care if there was an interpreter or not. Paul knew that a lot of this commotion was a counterfeit of a legitimate gift of the Holy Spirit.

He could see that their babbling was unprofitable to the church in that they were disrupting the service; it was unsettling to the church, and it was unintelligible to the world. It sounded like a madhouse during the church services. Paul admonished them, "For God is not the author of confusion but of peace" (1 Cor. 14:33).

We'll look together later at the regulations Paul put on them so that this problem could be handled.

Some feel that the purpose of tongues is to enable them to have a prayer language. I understand that some feel very strongly about this, and I have no desire to argue. However, *prayer language* is not a term used in the Word of God.

And gifts were given so that we could build one another up, not use them in private. Paul stresses that the church is to be edified. I believe this is a

> **E**ighty-five percent of males and eighty-five percent of females do not speak in tongues or a spiritual language when they pray.
> —George Barna

very important verse that we gloss over: "Even so you, since you are zealous for spiritual gifts, let it be for the edification of the church" (1 Cor. 14:12).

Some people claim to have a prayer language. I would urge only that we take any of our experiences—no matter what they are—and examine them in light of Scripture. If our experience does not line up with the Word of God, we have to negate the experience and go with the final authority, which is His Word.

I caution believers who speak in tongues to evaluate carefully their motivation. Is it for the glory of God, or is it because of pressure from a group? Do you feel that you would be a lesser saint than others if you did not speak in tongues? The Bible urges you to pursue love, not tongues.

Since confusion surrounded the practice of tongues, Paul set parameters to govern the use of tongues in the church. So, he gave the following regulations, according to 1 Corinthians 14:27–28:

1. Only two or at the very most three people were to speak in tongues.
2. Only one was to speak at a time.
3. Each was to have an interpreter. If no interpreter was present, the person was not to speak.

> In a 1980 Gallup Poll, 28.8 percent of all evangelical Christians identified themselves as "Charismatic Christians." Of those, 34.7 percent claim to have spoken in tongues.
> —Dr. Clyde Narramore

Those were the guidelines. We would do well to honor them today.

In Corinth, the immature Christians were trying to outdo one another spiritually. Some could have misused the gift of tongues as a spiritual show-and-tell. Paul was trying to grow them up. They were supposed to be helping one another grow up, and that is seldom done through babbling. Telling forth the truth, yes. Uninterpreted talk, no.

I have said several times that I firmly believe tongues was a gift of the Holy Spirit. I believe the gift was legitimate and for a purpose.

But what about the permanence of it? Is the gift still to be employed today?

I can almost hear some of my charismatic friends groaning, "Okay, here he goes."

Because I view the Bible as my Textbook, and I believe it to be the Word of God without error, I need to see what it says about faith and practice. And I would be remiss if I didn't see what it says about the gift of tongues.

We need to look again at the purpose of tongues as a sign gift—to validate and authenticate the message and the messenger. There is no need for that sign today because we have the complete revelation of God in the Bible. No new revelations are coming forth that need a sign to accompany them. The revelation is finished, and it does not need validation or authentication. The

TONGUES

■ *Known dialects or unintelligible languages associated with the early church.*

Holy Spirit gives illumination to His children so that we understand the truth in the Word, but the canon of Scripture is complete.

I believe maturity has been achieved in the church because of the completeness of the Word of God available to us so that sign gifts are no longer necessary. Nothing needs validation. The Word of God can stand on its own. And if the messenger is saying something that isn't in the Book, he is not a true messenger.

I want to be gentle and loving and yet tell you what I believe Scripture teaches. I know that many disagree with this, but I am telling you in love—which is what 1 Corinthians 13 is about.

I believe the practice of prophecy, words of knowledge, and tongues were associated with the infant stages of the new church. Paul knew that a day would come when the church would reach a level of maturity where it could put away the things of childhood (1 Cor. 13:11).

Please hear my heart. I am not saying that those who speak in tongues are immature in their faith. I believe that many who speak in tongues are in love with Jesus Christ and want everything God has for them.

I am saying, though, when one of the disciples asked for a sign after the Resurrection, Jesus told him, "Blessed are those who have not seen and yet have believed" (John 20:29). We are to live not by signs but by faith.

Evidently, the gift of tongues was given to one church, a carnal, immature one at that. They were out of balance, and all the indications point to the fact that tongues caused problems. Paul did not mention the gift in Galatia and Ephesus, where he spoke much about the Spirit.

If the gift of tongues was the only evidence that one is filled with the Spirit, I believe Paul would have made that clear. Not one verse supports that view. Not a verse. But we are admonished over and over again to be filled with the Spirit.

If I live for signs, I am a spiritual babe. Oh, I believe He heals and does miracles today, but they are not for a sign. He does them out of love for His children.

The emphasis in the New Testament church was evangelism and growth—not healing and tongues. Paul stated his focus, "For I determined not to know anything among you except Jesus Christ and Him crucified" (1 Cor. 2:2). He told the Galatian church, "But God forbid that I should boast except in the cross of our Lord Jesus Christ" (Gal. 6:14).

His emphasis is the Cross. It must be ours as well.

Who is magnified in tongues?

Who is magnified in the Cross?

> **I**t has been my observation that no one starts a "helps movement," or a "giving movement," or a "showing mercy movement." . . . Yet tongues are commonly linked with movements.
> —George E. Gardiner

Church Concerns

56

TONGUES

I fear that tongues is sometimes a strong and successful substitute for coming to the Cross. Galatians 2:20 tells of our being crucified with Christ. Romans 6—8 tells me how to have victory over sin. A person can speak in tongues and not have victory over sin and be crucified with Christ.

Tongues cannot be sought as a spiritual high. It is not the ultimate experience. The ultimate of the Christian life is "that I may know Him and the power of His resurrection, and the fellowship of His sufferings, being conformed to His death" (Phil. 3:10).

In India, there is a caste system. There are not just the "haves" and the "have-nots," but there are the "almost-haves" and the "mid-haves" and the definite "never-will-haves." The system determines every part of a person's life—economic, social, political, educational, and every other sphere.

In some churches, there is an invisible caste system. There are those who claim to have the sign gift of tongues and those who do not. That is totally unscriptural. When people say the "haves" have spoken in tongues and the "have-nots" have not spoken in tongues, they set up a harmful division between Spirit-filled believers.

How would an earthly father feel if the children in the family were constantly arguing about which child always got the best gifts from Dad? Suppose the children squabbled, and one pointed to a shiny new bike and stuck his chin up indignantly, boasting, "See, Dad loves me more than he loves you because I got the best gift."

Well, first of all that is a boastful, prideful attitude implying that gifts are earned by being the favorite. Second, it says little about the father's discernment in giving gifts to his children.

How do we think the heavenly Father feels when He loves all His children with perfect love, and then they squabble over who has the best gifts from Him? And even more divisive are some in the family of God who boast because they think they have earned some wonderful gift. Or that they have at least favored status.

You didn't earn your salvation. And you didn't earn your gift. God graced it to you.

And it's not anybody's prerogative to claim the Father has a caste system of "haves" and "have-nots." We might. He doesn't.

> It is estimated that less than one out of every seven Christians in America employs a charismatic gift in his or her times of worship, prayer, and personal ministry.
> —George Barna

 APPLICATION

More important than acquiring a specific gift is discovering the gifts God has given you. Do you know what your spiritual gifts are? Are you using

TONGUES

them in the body of Christ to benefit others? If not, you are robbing yourself of the joy of giving to others and robbing others of the benefit they would derive from your gifts. Ask your pastor for a spiritual gifts inventory. There are several kinds. Take a positive step toward discovering the gifts God has given you to serve the church and fulfill your special role in His body.

DAILY LIVING

COMPROMISE

■ *To make concessions in order to gain something.*

1 KINGS 11:4

SCRIPTURE

For it was so, when Solomon was old, that his wives turned his heart after other gods; and his heart was not loyal to the LORD his God, as was the heart of his father David.

COMMENTARY

The wise learn by watching others. Every person we come into contact with is a walking textbook on how to succeed or, as some would say, how not to fail. An invaluable lesson we learn from people who cross our paths concerns the ethic of give-and-take. If you've ever had to compromise on what restaurant you were going to eat at on Saturday night, or what you were willing to pay for the car you want to buy, you don't need me to explain how it works. *Healthy* compromise is demonstrated when we are able to give in without sacrificing our values and beliefs. Every relationship we enter into has an element of give-and-take if it is to remain healthy.

Our focus here is on a different kind of compromise. It leads us to abandon sound ideas or standards, and we are left morally and spiritually bankrupt. This compromise is always contradictory to God's laws and principles for living. It diverts us from the right attitude of obedience to the dangerous ground of independence apart from God. Those who have suffered as a result of compromise are examples that we would be wise to consider when faced with the temptation to make such dangerous choices.

One example of compromise that ended in tragedy is the story of Solomon. The Bible says, "So King Solomon surpassed all the kings of the earth in riches and wisdom. Now all the earth sought the presence of Solomon to hear his wisdom, which God had put in his heart" (1 Kings 10:23–24). He sounds like a man I would have wanted to know. Wise. Respected. The consummate ruler, who understood the value of obedience to God's laws. Yet he deliberately disobeyed God's warning in Deuteronomy 7:3 about intermarriage with people of other religions. There was not even the slightest hint or pretense about ignorance of the law. He compromised what he knew was true and took "seven hundred wives, princesses, and three hundred concubines; and his wives turned away his heart" (1 Kings 11:3). No man ever soared so high and fell so low.

If you are looking for a single event that brought Solomon to his ultimate end, you have to start with a thought. That's where compromise begins and spirals to its tragic conclusion. In Solomon's case, you can track the process. There were signs that he was headed in the wrong direction. Disobedience

This is a day of diplomats, not prophets. It is nicer to be an appeaser than an opposer. It is the day of Erasmus, not Luther; of Gamaliel, not Paul.
—Vance Havner

Compromise

COMPROMISE ■ *To make concessions in order to gain something.*

is the first clue. Ignoring God's warning, Solomon set the process in motion with a decision to do what felt good. The process went like this:

1. Admiration inevitably led to association.
2. Association was the prelude to involvement.
3. Involvement resulted in possession.
4. Possession concluded in collapse.

There wasn't anything terribly ominous or threatening in the beginning of the process—and that's the first point I need to make. Satan never comes on like a herd of wild horses to scare us away. Rather, he disguises his true intent. What started as a thought in Solomon's mind exploded into tragedy. Because of the enormity of the entire issue that surrounds this topic, a closer study is required of how a wise man, highly esteemed, could have taken the path he did. If one so wise could be swayed, what about us? It's something we tremble to think about, but we have no choice if we are to avoid the same fatal choices.

 A CLOSER LOOK

Why would one who had so much to lose be willing to risk everything? I do not believe Solomon understood he was risking everything when he first looked in the direction he had been warned to avoid. After all, he might say, all I *intended* to do was to admire the women from a distance. Strike one.

1. *Admiration* seemed harmless enough. Solomon was not plagued with the dilemma that some men face in their unsuccessful attempts to attract the opposite sex. He could have had any woman he wanted in Israel, but he looked elsewhere. As Scripture points out in 1 Kings 11:1, "King Solomon loved many foreign women." God's warning should have been sufficient to keep Solomon from taking the path he set out on that day. Obviously, something had changed. What had been important to Solomon took a backseat to other priorities. Obedience to God's law no longer held the place of importance in Solomon's life that it once had.

It is worth noting that his father, David, did the same thing with Bathsheba. An admiring gaze seemed harmless enough to them. The problem he faced comes as no surprise to anyone who has strayed away from the boundaries God established for relationships. Admiration, in and of itself, may be harmless, but it rarely (if ever) ends there. His problem was multiplied by the sheer number of women involved. The outcome of Solomon's admiration was totally predictable.

2. *Association* was the next step in the process: "Solomon clung to these in love" (1 Kings 11:2). What happens when you admire something over a period of time? You become intensely focused. Just looking doesn't give you the satisfaction it did in the beginning. Admiration inevitably leads to association. What looks like an innocent beginning assumes new and greater dimensions. Although wrongly focused admiration is extremely risky, association is downright dangerous because it can't help leading to the next step in the process.

3. *Involvement* was the natural outcome of association. The story of Solomon's involvement could have been written for a television movie, but Hollywood couldn't have come up with a more predictable ending: "For it was so, when Solomon was old, that his wives turned his heart after other gods" (1 Kings 11:4). How sad that this one who had been so totally devoted to God found himself with a divided mind and heart: "And his heart was not loyal to the LORD his God" (1 Kings 11:4). The pattern of ongoing compromise becomes unmistakably clear as we look at Solomon's struggle with truth and compromise. It felt good, tantalizing. Solomon's deeper involvement became a stronghold that Satan used to distract him from God's law. Solomon's dilemma cries out to us today about the cost of compromise—the risk of abandoning a standard.

4. *Possession* was the final step in the process. The conclusion was total abandonment to disobedience and idolatry that ended in collapse: "For Solomon went after Ashtoreth . . . and after Milcom. . . . And he did likewise for all his foreign wives, who burned incense and sacrificed to their gods" (1 Kings 11:5, 8). He was utterly possessed by wrongdoing, even to the point of worshiping other gods. It began with a look here, a gaze there—and before long, he was trapped. Along with possession, total abandonment to disobedience occurred. It didn't happen overnight. That's not the way it happens, not in Solomon's day or in ours. The compromise is usually subtle at first, and each step of the way the process becomes easier, not more difficult as we might assume. One day, too late, we forget where we began.

Like most tragedies, Solomon's began with something that looked perfectly harmless. When he crossed the line and began to relinquish what God never intended to be a bargaining point, he paid an enormous price. It all started with a thought. If we could go back and ask him what he was doing at that moment, he probably wouldn't remember. It was that insignificant to him.

> **A**s one of God's people, you need to establish a deliberate defense against the negative influence of unbelievers.
> —*In Touch*, March 1995

COMPROMISE ■ *To make concessions in order to gain something.*

It is impossible to compromise without giving up something. It works something like this. I make an adjustment in my thinking. I have to decide to give up something to receive something. But what I receive may not begin to equal what I have to give up. Those who say, "Well, everyone has to give in somewhere along the way," are really saying, "Everyone has to surrender something at some time in life." The question is, What do we need to compromise? Our purity? Honesty? Integrity? Our belief in the Word of God? Satan will whisper, as he did to Solomon, "Come on, no one's perfect. Everyone has to give up something to make it in this life." It sounds perfectly sensible in our world today.

We have to remember that Satan is the father of lies. Often distinguishing a lie from the truth is difficult because it is so cleverly veiled in perfectly sensible-sounding ideas. No one doubts that we are called upon to give up certain things in life. That is part of living. Satan conveniently forgets to make a distinction between what is okay to give up and what isn't. The implication is that there are no boundaries—that whatever he prods us to give up will ultimately lead us to greater happiness. That is a fallacy.

If it were possible for Solomon to give us his Monday-morning quarterback assessment of the process he went through, what do you think he would say? I think he would say that two things are certain. First, *compromise is costly.* When you compromise, it is an admission that you are willing to surrender, in different degrees, what is valuable to you. I have seen friends compromise what they once would have died to uphold. I have watched politicians promise their constituents one thing and, once the vote was a sure thing, compromise their values for the sake of another's cause. In each instance, a price was paid. For my friends who compromised their values to gain popularity, win influence, or obtain monetary favors, the loss of self-respect and the trust of their peers was a dear price to pay for what they received. There isn't enough money in the world to take the place of a loyal and devoted friend; yet every day people risk the respect of their friends for momentary gain. Politicians who sacrifice their principles to gain political power find success fickle when once-loyal friends become aware of their actions.

The high cost of compromise is apparent from the days of Solomon to the morning headlines of today's newspaper. Satan hasn't changed. Neither has the fact that there is a price to be paid for compromise. In some cases, the price has escalated dramatically. I think of young men and women who opt to go along with what they think the rest of the crowd is doing and compromise their purity. The price for such decisions has always been too high, with millions of babies being born out of wedlock. Today, there is an added cost of AIDS and other diseases. What used to result in a pregnancy, lost dreams, and broken lives today can kill. That's a pretty high price for compromise.

Second, not only is compromise costly, but *compromise also corrupts*. All we have to do is look at our Scripture passage. This king went from worshiping the one true God to worshiping idols. Totally corrupted! The goddess Ashtoreth had worshipers who practiced animal and human sacrifices. They threw little babies into the fire. They engaged in male and female prostitution. Solomon knew better. He became so corrupted that God began diminishing his wisdom. The very thing that was near and dear to Solomon—the thing he asked for—was being taken away because he kept compromising, he kept surrendering.

God's righteousness is forever. He doesn't wink at compromise. After the compromise and the corruption came *collapse*. These are potent words: "I will surely tear the kingdom away from you" (1 Kings 11:11). God didn't waste any words. He said He would rip the kingdom right out of Solomon's hands because of his compromising. God knew exactly how to get Solomon's attention.

Compromise is costly. It corrupts. It brings collapse.

Has God put His finger on something in your life? Did something come to mind as you read these pages that you've been flirting with? Perhaps you've crossed the line and are no longer flirting but have jumped headfirst into whatever you've been admiring. As long as you live in a fallen world, there will be temptations. Satan is cunning and powerful. If he can get you to give up what is important to you, he has begun a process that could cost you dearly. That is a guarantee. Is it really worth the cost? Your hope lies in the fact that you serve the God who created all that is good. His limitless power is your only defense against the schemes of Satan. You must never lose sight of the truth if you are to hold strong against the temptation to abandon the standards that God established.

> In making ethical decisions, 57 percent of Americans chose what would work best at the time, or situational ethics.
> —George Barna

APPLICATION

It would be nice if we could wipe our hands of this whole subject. After all, we haven't sold out to "seven hundred wives, princesses, and three hundred concubines." We haven't had our hearts turned away after other gods. We aren't pursuing detestable idols. We don't do evil in the sight of the Lord. We aren't building temples to an idol. We don't see any kingdom being torn from us.

COMPROMISE

■ *To make concessions in order to gain something.*

There doesn't seem much to apply. Are you sure? Before you answer, I urge you to consider carefully the idols you have built, the evil you have done. What idols? What evil? Anything that we value above the principles that God has given us is an idol. If I began naming the things that we "worship," the list would take up volumes. And what about evil? The pride of our hearts for what we have and the things we accomplish in life is evil in God's eyes because we have nothing outside the grace of God. Nothing.

Solomon compromised in the areas that we have discussed. We compromise in other areas. The point is, no one is blameless when it comes to this sensitive subject. Before we get too self-righteous, we better take a look at our lives. We do the same thing; we just dress it up with nice words and justify our actions, or so we think. What we allow in our lives that God forbids eventually conquers us. God warns us along the way. But, we often don't heed these warnings because we're so busy waving the white flag of surrender to the enemy.

None of us would admit that we are surrendering ground to Satan, but every time we give in and compromise standards that God has set for us, we are giving Satan a foothold in our lives to do with us as he pleases. He doesn't waste time or opportunity, and only the grace of God prevents us from suffering eternal consequences because of our stubborn insistence on doing things the way we choose.

What about the college student whom God has blessed abundantly? The time for term papers arrives, and he struggles to come up with an original idea. Nothing he thinks of is new. The thought crosses his mind that if he plagiarized a little on his term paper, it would speed things up. He is sure God wants him to get the paper in on time. After all, God knows how hard he has worked for the grades he has attained thus far. So, he cheats—just a little. No one finds out. No one guesses that he stole someone else's work. No hassles. Good grade. The next time it's not such a big deal. And the next.

Then there's the woman who is going to a dinner at church. It is important (she thinks) to present a good image, and she justifies her need for a new dress by telling herself that God put her in a position of leadership and expects her to look her best for His purpose. Financially stressed, she charges the dress; she wears it once and returns it the next day. No problem. No complications; in fact, a lot of compliments. She had no intention of keeping the dress. In her mind, she was leasing it anyway. The next time she needed a dress for a special occasion, she didn't struggle over what to do. Each time got easier until it didn't bother her at all.

COMPROMISE

Examples are endless. Each one has its own bottom line: when we choose to compromise, we pay a price, whether it becomes immediately apparent to anyone or not. The lie that Satan wants us to believe is that no one gets hurt in the process. That lie has cost men their jobs, it has cost children their innocence, and at times, it has cost people their very lives.

We start out compromising with no intention of being conquered by it. Ask people who have struggled with addictions if they started out with the intention of becoming alcoholics or drug addicts. I doubt many would step forward and say, "Yes, that was my goal the first time I drank a beer or smoked marijuana." We seldom start with big things. But compromise breeds corruption and ends in collapse.

The application for you and for me is demonstrated in the life of Solomon. He was a good man. Good men fall hard when they give up what they know is right. I'm sure if you had asked Solomon at the beginning of the process whether he would ever consider worshiping an idol, he would have passionately replied, "Never!" He began by admiring a pretty woman and ended up worshiping false gods. We are no more immune to the consequences when we compromise our principles than Solomon was.

> Twenty-three percent of Evangelicals said they were trying to live up to their moral and ethical standards but find it hard to do so.
> —James Davison Hunter

GROWTH

If I were to choose the best way to protect myself from the temptation to compromise my values, it would be through an accountability relationship with someone I respected and trusted. I make that same suggestion to you. As long as Satan can keep us isolated, he has a better chance at getting to our thoughts. Lonely, isolated people are prime targets for his schemes. Busy workaholics are equally vulnerable. There is one thing I am sure of, Satan doesn't want us talking to each other. The last thing he wants is for us to spend time together, revealing our weak points and praying for each other. That is why it is so important for me and for you to find someone (of the same gender) we can get real with, drop our pretenses with, and allow God to do His work through.

Since it is apparent that compromise has its birth in a thought that may seem insignificant at the time, we cannot take the directive to "renew our minds" lightly. If Satan works in our minds, that is where we must take special effort to protect ourselves from his attacks. Personal Bible study, corporate worship, or any opportunity you have to fill your mind with the truth is something you must be regularly engaged in. The mind will be either fertile ground for the truth or vulnerable territory for the lies of Satan. Don't be fooled by the notion that you can open God's Word once on Sunday

Compromise

COMPROMISE

■ *To make concessions in order to gain something.*

morning and be equipped to fight Satan's attack the rest of the week. That's what he wants you to believe. Don't fall for his lies. Study and equip yourself for the battle of a lifetime.

Finally, if you have ever attempted to journal your thoughts and decided it was leading nowhere, think again. I suggest that you write about the areas of your life that you are tempted to compromise. I have a friend who began writing things down on paper many years ago. He found great insight and comfort as he looked back over the years of written pages that chronicled his life's story. You don't have to worry about someone thinking you're weird or that you don't have the right answers. You can write from your heart, turn over your written thoughts to the One who loves you and gave Himself for you, and then profit by what He can teach you. Start today.

CONSCIENCE

1 TIMOTHY 1:18–20

This charge I commit to you, son Timothy, according to the prophecies previously made concerning you, that by them you may wage the good warfare, having faith and a good conscience, which some having rejected, concerning the faith have suffered shipwreck, of whom are Hymenaeus and Alexander, whom I delivered to Satan that they may learn not to blaspheme.

COMMENTARY

Webster's Dictionary defines the *conscience* as "the sense of what is right or wrong in one's conduct or motives, impelling one toward right action." I would narrow it down to eight simple words: the conscience is a person's internal alarm clock. It's the voice inside that yells when we're about to make a wrong move or do something that will hurt us or someone else. It's the unexplainable "something" that grabs our attention long enough to ask, "Is this right?" or "I'm not sure I ought to . . ." You know what I mean.

Paul's words to Timothy must have produced mixed emotions in the young man's heart. Paul stated that keeping the faith and protecting a good conscience were extremely important. On the one hand, Paul's words encouraged and lifted Timothy up for the days to come. On the other, they carried a grave warning of what would happen to anyone (himself included) who acted against the sense of what was right according to God's laws. Apparently, Timothy had been prophesied over earlier in life, probably during his ordination (1 Tim. 4:14). The prophecies pointed to his role as a leader in the church. In this letter, Paul reminded Timothy of his position and responsibility. As a footnote or a reminder, he included a chilling description of what happens when people ignore their calling. The lesson, if we went no further, is this: to ignore your internal alarm is dangerous!

It was not unusual that Paul's words were captured in nautical terms because the early church often used words associated with navigation to illustrate the process of Christian growth. Therefore, Timothy understood perfectly Paul's reference to Hymenaeus and Alexander being "shipwrecked" in their faith. What had they done to deserve such an indictment? It boiled down to Hymenaeus expressing his belief about the Resurrection (2 Tim. 2:17). Paul's graphic illustration indicates how unhappy he was with the idle talk that Hymenaeus had involved himself in. He used words like *cancer* to describe how such talk spreads. So, the words of Paul in this particular passage were double sided: (1) hold tight to your faith, and (2) don't ignore your conscience. Paul did not mince words about the devastating consequence of failing to keep a clear conscience.

Conscience

CONSCIENCE

■ *The moral faculty designed to distinguish right from wrong.*

God considers a pure conscience a very valuable thing—one that keeps our faith on a steady course. Likewise, He views a tainted conscience as detestable and worthy of severe judgment. So much so that He may allow rebellious people to shipwreck themselves. This is especially true if they persist in rebellion against what they know is right. Although it must break God's heart, He would rather do that than see the rebellion spread to others. Thus, Paul "delivered [them] to Satan that they may learn not to blaspheme" (1 Tim. 1:20). What a sobering thought!

A CLOSER LOOK

It is fair to say that God places enormous value on the state of the conscience. If you've ever asked yourself, Should I let my conscience be my guide? you've already considered the role your conscience should play in your daily decisions. Before I suggest an answer, a look at some questions about the conscience will clear up the confusion about its role in our lives. Perhaps the question will answer itself.

Where is the conscience located? We are made up of body, soul, and spirit (1 Thess. 5:23). I've heard it explained this way: "I own a body, I possess a soul, and I am a spirit." The body is the physiological component of our makeup. It's how we relate to our environment. The soul is the psychological element of what makes me Charles and you, Bill or Sarah. It's our thinker, feeler, and chooser, and it manifests itself through our personalities. The spirit is who we *really* are, and it provides us the means to relate to God since He is Spirit.

From the description above, I believe we would have to agree that the conscience operates from the soul. If that is the case and the soul has several compartments within it, what part of your soul do you think your conscience is housed in? Your mind, will, or emotions? I think probably all three play a role, but the conscience operates through your mind. I believe that is why Jesus made such a passionate case for continual renewing of the mind. He understood that the battle is fought there.

If everyone has a conscience, why do people react to situations differently? If everybody has a conscience, how can a child of sixteen kill his parents or rape a schoolmate and laugh at the camera as he is led into the courtroom for trial? The real scenes that come into our homes through television news make us wonder if some people are born without a conscience. The medical community has labeled those who seem to have no sense of right and wrong as sociopaths. Although some people test our capacity to believe that all people have a conscience, I believe it is a part of our nature that isn't left to chance.

The conscience is our God-given personal alarm system. Everybody has one. The key to our different behaviors is programming. Why else would two men act so differently about the same offense—one with great sorrow and one without any apparent remorse? Programming. Input. Those who program the thinker, feeler, and chooser with the truth of God will be much more disposed to respond with great remorse when they sin, as opposed to people who never put anything of eternal value into the conscience. No wonder we react and respond differently.

Computers begin with basic programs that allow users to perform the function of writer, analyst, or editor. Some programs add games and offer address books and places to keep appointments. You can buy groceries or order jewelry with a computer that has the right program and the necessary connection.

Like all good things, there is a dark side to the computer industry; it has brought pornography to the screens of home computers, exploiting and degrading moral values. Just as computers can be programmed positively or negatively, the conscience can be programmed with the truth of God or the depravity of the world. Depending on which source of information you choose to program into your conscience, you will react accordingly.

What does the Bible have to say about the conscience? The Old Testament term *leb* (translated "heart") is used frequently, often in reference to the work of the conscience. First Samuel 24:5 states, "David's conscience bothered him because he had cut off the edge of Saul's robe" (NASB). However, we need only look at the first husband-and-wife team to watch the workings of the conscience and the result of two people who ignored the truth.

Adam's and Eve's consciences were programmed with only one rule: obey God. Just that one very important directive. In Genesis 3:1, when the serpent first asked, "Has God indeed said . . . ?" Eve's internal alarm system went off. Her conscience was programmed by her Creator never to question what He said. When the devil tempted her, she knew what he was asking her to do did not fit in with how she had been programmed. Something wasn't right! It was Eve's chance to choose to follow God's instructions. Her conscience (thinker) told her not to listen to Satan's lies, yet her feeler won out. The rest of the story is chronicled throughout Scripture.

We are a totally shipwrecked people apart from Christ. Contrary to what some might think, God did not give us a conscience to spoil our fun. The exact opposite is true. God wants us to enjoy life to the fullest, and He

> **R**estful sleep: the reward of a clear conscience.
> —Bill Gothard

> **M**y conscience is captive to the Word of God. Here I stand, I can do no other.
> —Martin Luther

CONSCIENCE

■ *The moral faculty designed to distinguish right from wrong.*

knows that when we choose to ignore His truth, we can't enjoy it fully. You see, the conscience is a universal gift of God given to protect, not prohibit.

The New Testament also has numerous references to the conscience—thirty in all, nineteen of which are found in Paul's epistles. According to Romans 2:14–15, the conscience is programmed with certain truth: "For when Gentiles, who do not have the law, by nature do the things in the law, these, although not having the law, are a law to themselves, who show the work of the law written in their hearts, their conscience also bearing witness, and between themselves their thoughts accusing or else excusing them." These verses seem to point out what we've debated for years, that even the most primitive cultures possess a conscience.

Jesus told us to go to the uttermost parts of the earth. Most of us will never leave our homes for the mission field, but the testimony of missionaries supports the idea that all people, no matter how primitive, are born with some code of ethics. Ask a roomful of atheists what they think about murder and you will generally find a consensus of opinion that murder is wrong. Most criminals will rarely deny that their crimes were wrong. Some will, and they are the ones who have denied the truth for so long that their hearts have been hardened. Everyone is born with a sense of right and wrong—though people may argue about its source.

As believers, we know that our ethics and moral code are based on the Word of God. Counseling members of my church provides me the chance to see people make healthy choices to follow their consciences. However, there are times when I am counseling and say, "You know that is wrong." Nothing breaks my heart more than to hear that person say, "I know it's wrong, but I'm probably going to do it anyway." When a person knows that something is wrong and deliberately chooses to do it anyway, that person is approaching shipwreck.

God gave us the conscience to protect us. Without it, we would be left to the whims of the world without a safety net. Although we are wise to heed what we "hear" from the conscience, here are some things it is not intended to do. Clearing up the confusion is essential to our success or failure as to how we respond to the conscience God has gifted us with.

The purpose of the conscience is not to guide you. That pretty well answers the initial question, "Can you let your conscience be your guide?" You and I need an infallible guide, and your conscience and my conscience are not infallible. We have already established that the conscience is programmed. But with what? For example, children and teenagers are being falsely told that there are no absolutes and that everything is relative. Schools teach values that we would not have even considered twenty years ago. For

CONSCIENCE

those who do not have a godly father and mother to teach them the truth, a faulty monitoring system is a given that no amount of arguing will change.

The purpose of the conscience is not to make us feel bad. It is a warning system. Someone has said, "The conscience is the judge of the soul." I believe the Holy Spirit works in conjunction with the conscience. Where the conscience sends the signal, the Holy Spirit reveals the reason for heeding the alarm. The Spirit urges us and guides us. He reminds us, as the alarm system sounds, that we are accountable to God. Unsaved people have the alarm system, but they don't have the Spirit to explain or guide.

As something comes across the "radar screen" that is cause for alarm, the signal goes off, and the Holy Spirit whispers (well, sometimes He has to shout), "That doesn't fit who you are. Stay away!" Unbelievers struggle and say yes or no to their conscience. We have a Helper, One who has come alongside to woo us to do the right thing. As if that isn't enough, He empowers us to do what we know is right. There are several things we can agree on. The conscience is universal. It is given to protect. It is not given to guide or make us feel bad.

We must train the conscience. The conscience responds to programming. Input is output. The conscience is trainable. David refers to this aspect of the conscience in Psalm 119:11, "Your word I have hidden in my heart, that I might not sin against You." Note the cause and effect are present. I program my heart with God's standards—and when the alarm system goes off, I quickly know not only what standard is in jeopardy but also what to do in response to the alarm. That's a rather loose translation but what I believe this verse teaches. Everyone's conscience has some information, but we need to go beyond the basics and fill the conscience with truth that is not there when we are born. Content is essential.

So how does the conscience work? We began by agreeing that we are composed of body, soul, and spirit and that the soul is the conduit for the daily operation of the conscience. Why does the man who is in the store about to reach for a pornographic magazine almost hear the Voice say, "No, no. Don't touch!"? The conscience warns us when we are about to do wrong. If we had only a warning, we would be in a much more precarious position than we are with the Holy Spirit as our Helper and Enabler.

Even though the primary purpose of the conscience is to warn, not to accuse, it will let us know loud and clear when we've taken the wrong road! Still, before you decide the conscience is just an unpleasant watchdog in your soul, let me add that it also affirms when you do what is right. Someone has said, "That feeling of confirmation—the opposite of guilt—is God's pat

> Thirty-three percent of Americans would ask God how they can be a better person.
> —*100 Questions and Answers*

> In the mid-1990s there were 800,000 prisoners of conscience in the world.

Conscience

73

CONSCIENCE

■ *The moral faculty designed to distinguish right from wrong.*

on the back." I enjoy feeling His pat on the back more than His slap on my hand through my conscience, don't you?

To make an individual application about where you stand when it comes to your conscience, you need to look at the four kinds of conscience that the Bible speaks of and then ask the Holy Spirit to reveal the truth about you.

1. *The sacred conscience.* Paul spoke of a "good conscience" and a "sincere faith" (1 Tim. 1:5). This conscience is cleared of all guilt and is in harmony with the will and Word of God. Paul said he strived "to have a conscience without offense toward God and men" (Acts 24:16). Paul was doing his best to maintain a sacred conscience, which meant he was not treating it carelessly. He was maintaining it. Just as you put oil in your car for maintenance, you should check often to make sure your conscience is running smoothly. People with a sacred, or clear, conscience will be free and joyful. They relate well with others because they have nothing to hide. People love to be around transparent people. They are intimate people, free to share their hearts. There are no secrets or skeletons in the closet that jeopardize free expression of God's love and goodwill.

2. *The soiled conscience.* Titus 1:15 declares, "To the pure all things are pure, but to those who are defiled and unbelieving nothing is pure; but even their mind and conscience are defiled." People with a soiled conscience see everything soiled. It's as though they see through a murky filter that colors everything a dirty gray. There are several indicators that someone is living with a soiled conscience: a subtle desire to be punished, a sense of insecurity, a likely candidate for illness because of the stress derived from the guilt of disobedience, a compulsive worker to rid feelings of inadequacy, and a rebellion toward God. Whether singly or in combination, these indicators are clues to a dirty conscience.

3. *The struggling conscience.* In 1 Corinthians 8, Paul wrote to the believers who were really struggling. They had come out of idol worship, where they had sacrificed meat to idols. As Christians, they knew that was not right. When they would go to the meat market to buy food, they realized that some of the meat had already been offered to idols and that was wrong. Their question was: Do we eat the meat, or don't we? They struggled in their consciences. This is not necessarily wrong, especially when a believer isn't quite sure what is right or wrong and needs counsel. A wise person, even with a struggling conscience, seeks godly counsel on things that aren't clear-cut issues.

Tax cheating amounts to $180 billion a year. The IRS has a "Conscience Fund" for those who want to send in their money after having cheated the government.

A man's conscience re-echoes the condemnation—"all have sinned."
—Dr. Clyde Narramore

CONSCIENCE

4. *The seared conscience*. Paul spoke of some people "speaking lies in hypocrisy, having their own conscience seared with a hot iron" (1 Tim. 4:2). The Greek word for *seared* is our word for *cauterize*. This is a scary place to be. The conscience no longer functions because it's been so muffled, so ignored, so resisted, that it no longer works. It's the picture of putting a hot iron on a piece of tissue paper. It totally disintegrates it.

How does that happen? First, we can sear the conscience deliberately, not accidentally. We repeatedly do what we know to be wrong in spite of the alarm system going off. Second, we can sear the conscience by degrees, thinking that perhaps sin has no cumulative effect. Third, we can sear the conscience by being on the defensive. We say to others, and to ourselves, "Aw, c'mon. It's not that bad. Look what others do." Fourth, we can sear the conscience by being defiant. We dig our heels in the dirt and become like defiant children to God and to anyone else who mentions the sin.

Fifth, we can sear the conscience by being dead to the alarm system. It is like we have unplugged the life support alarm system in the conscience. We are no longer moved to do anything about the sin. I believe this is where the Bible makes reference to a "hard heart." Sixth, we can sear the conscience by becoming destructive and dangerous to ourselves and others. When we are so bent on having our own way, hurting ourselves or others is not a deterrent. The conscience becomes so seared, we are set on doing what we want and it matters not who is hurt in the process. Those are the people I've spoken of who are called sociopaths, the ones who can kill and laugh in the face of the camera, who *seem* to have no conscience at all.

The application is simple. You don't ever want to get to this place. So how do you avoid getting there? *Instant* obedience. The minute you hear the alarm, do what's right.

Do you have a sacred conscience? A soiled conscience? A struggling conscience? Or a seared conscience? If your conscience is soiled now, all you need to do is ask the Lord to show you the problem and then repent of it. That means turn around and go in a different direction. You may have to make things right with others if it is an offense that you've never resolved. If things have gotten so far out of hand that you can't even get close to the solution, you must find someone equipped to help in that situation and let that person lead you out of your dilemma.

Your conscience is your alarm system. It's your protection. Don't ignore it and find yourself reaping consequences for making wrong choices. Rather than view your conscience as your "soul police," praise God for His loving way of helping you through this fallen world in such a caring manner. If you believe, as I do, that we are creations of God, put here for the purpose of

> **C**huck Colson of Prison Fellowship warned that a loss of conscience in our young people threatens this country with anarchy.

> **W**e can teach our children that being honest protects from guilt and provides for a clear conscience.
> —Josh McDowell

> **A** bad conscience has a good memory.
> —Anonymous

Conscience **75**

CONSCIENCE

■ *The moral faculty designed to distinguish right from wrong.*

glorifying Him through our time on earth, how we listen to the conscience that lives inside our souls and how we allow the Holy Spirit to keep us accountable take on new and formidable dimensions. We are here not to do as we please but to please God. Put His truth in your conscience and then respond to its prompting and you will know Him intimately.

GROWTH

There are a number of ways to deal with a guilty conscience. Confession is one. Find a trustworthy friend and talk about the things you need help with. If you need more, ask your pastor to refer you to a godly counselor who can guide you through the struggles you face, factoring in the truth of Scripture, separating truth from lies. However, your best defense is to study and renew your mind with God's Word. As many times as I repeat that admonition, it remains true. Satan does not want us in God's Word. He wants to confuse us and cause us to doubt. Stay in the truth. Arm yourself with the Word of God, and your conscience will sound off loud and clear when you're headed in the wrong direction.

■ *The price we pay or the benefit we derive from our decisions.*

CONSEQUENCES

GALATIANS 6:7

SCRIPTURE

Do not be deceived, God is not mocked; for whatever a man sows, that he will also reap.

COMMENTARY

For the believer who lives with the consequence of poor decisions in the past, Paul's words may seem rather harsh. For the young Christian who has yet to feel the sting of sin in a significant way, Paul's words may not seem all that important. But for people on both sides of the aisle, the apostle's words hold great significance.

After all, it affects our lives every day. But as familiar as we are with this cause-and-effect relationship, there is still confusion about how it fits in with the forgiveness of God. At the moment of trusting Christ as Savior, many who struggle with the idea of grace and forgiveness hit a brick wall regarding the continuing consequences of their sins. It seems strange to speak of forgiveness and consequences in the same breath. Contrary to what many believe, forgiveness and consequences are not opposite ends of a spectrum. Rather, they run parallel. Together they accomplish an essential part of God's plan for believers.

The questions most commonly voiced among those who struggle with this seeming contradiction are understandable considering what the world has to say to us about our actions. The prevailing ethic implies there are no consequences for our choices and that we are not responsible for our choices. Watch any morning television talk show and you will find ample assurance that someone else is responsible for the things you've done. In other words, we can't be expected to pay the price for something that wasn't our fault to begin with. If we believe what the world teaches us, it's easy to understand why so many struggle with God's forgiveness and the consequences of sin.

Observation, however, leads us to a different conclusion. We all know about consequences. We all know that we pay a high price, at times, for our actions. It's a principle that no modern-day philosopher can adequately rebut. Paul's words to the church at Galatia ring true in our ears and our lives today: "He who sows to his flesh will of the flesh reap corruption" (Gal. 6:8). It wasn't a debatable issue. Paul did not modify or soft-pedal his statement. He laid down a principle that has served as a reminder throughout history to those of us who trust God's Word: whatever we do, there is a consequence.

Consequences **77**

CONSEQUENCES

■ *The price we pay or the benefit we derive from our decisions.*

While we all know the verse about sowing and reaping, we fail many times to grasp the big picture, and we focus only on our negative consequences. This is true for several reasons, but primarily because all too often we dwell on the negative rather than celebrate the positive side of this valuable principle. Yes, there is a positive side—depending on the choices we make. Just as Paul made it clear that sowing to our sinful nature will result in destruction, he added the promise of what will happen if we choose to do what will please God. "He who sows to the Spirit will of the Spirit reap everlasting life" (Gal. 6:8). When we choose to do what is pleasing to God, we will enjoy the benefits of our actions.

Because we spend much of our time focusing only on the negative side of this two-part equation, many are left with the continuing dilemma of the apparent problem that exists between God's forgiveness and the truth about consequences. It's not "one or the other" as we would like to believe; both stand true throughout Scripture as principles of God's grace. After all, the negative consequences of sin may lead us in quiet desperation to the throne of God's forgiveness.

A CLOSER LOOK

Very few things motivate us to give God our undivided attention like being faced with the negative consequences of our decisions. Regardless of our guilt and our shame, we find the courage or the nerve to turn to Him for help and oftentimes for a miracle. We make promises. Suddenly, we are concerned for the welfare of others. We look for whatever leverage we can find to get God to do something on our behalf. But the truth is, God is under no obligation to remove all the consequences of sin. In many cases, He chooses to allow us to live with some of the consequences.

So many believers experience tension because they live daily with the consequences of past sins *after* accepting Christ as Savior. Mistakenly, they thought or hoped or were told that once they accepted Christ as Savior, God would miraculously erase the consequences. With the daily evidence that God has not taken away the consequences, many believers conclude that God has not forgiven them. If God's Word was true, they surmise, if He *really* loved me and *truly* forgave me, surely He wouldn't allow me to continue to suffer as I am. It's understandable that so many people feel this way because we think these two principles stand at opposite ends of the spectrum. It seems to us that to move in the direction of one (forgiveness) is to move away from the other (consequences).

CONSEQUENCES

We expect the financial problems that threaten our very existence to disappear once we accept God's forgiveness. We count on God to miraculously heal our marriages or return a runaway child to the home once we accept Jesus as Savior. The new Christian who has lived a promiscuous life and is at high risk for AIDS is convinced that this new relationship with God will eliminate this most horrific nightmare.

Seldom is that the reality. More often, God allows the consequences to continue as He faithfully loves and teaches us the lessons that we otherwise would never learn. It is one of the harder lessons to accept, but very often we learn our most valuable lessons as a result of the continuing consequences for something that happened long before we became Christians.

The response I hear most often is, "It's just not fair! I quit drinking five years ago, and I'm still not able to get a decent job, and the bank manager laughs when I suggest that she can trust me to repay a loan that I need. It's just not fair!" My heart goes out to these people. However, I have to remind them that their thinking is off course. I don't think fair is really what we want. We want the easy way out. God knows that, and sometimes He chooses to answer our prayers and eliminate the consequences. When He does, He is showing us another side of His incredible grace. It is not something He is obligated to do. Just because we've joined the family, so to speak, doesn't mean the Father is obligated to give us what we want.

If you struggle to understand why God allows you to continue to suffer the consequences of your sin, perhaps it would help to understand the difference in these two principles. Forgiveness is relational. Our relationship with Jesus is the totality of the reason behind God's forgiveness of our sins. He allowed His Son to pay the greatest price for our sin. He has already eliminated the greatest debt we owe. He allowed Jesus to die instead of us, as we deserve to. Understanding that forgiveness is relational is the first part of the equation that leads to understanding why God allows the consequences to continue many times.

Consequences are circumstantial, not relational. The man who drank for so many years and develops cirrhosis of the liver knows that his disease has a direct link to his drinking. He knows, even though he may deny the truth, that as a result of drinking, he is experiencing the negative effect. The woman who gave in to the temptation to have an affair with a coworker knows in her heart that her ruined marriage is a consequence of her choice to sow to her sinful nature. It is a result of the circumstances that occurred within the choice made that ruined the marriage. Therefore, it makes it easier to factor in the second part of the equation regarding forgiveness and consequences.

Alcoholism is America's third largest health problem, following heart disease and cancer. It afflicts ten million people, costs sixty billion dollars, and is implicated in two hundred thousand deaths annually.
—Jay Strack

Consequences

CONSEQUENCES

■ *The price we pay or the benefit we derive from our decisions.*

Forgiveness is relational. Consequences are circumstantial. If we can begin to understand the importance of both, we can begin to get past our problems with the reality that oftentimes God does not remove the consequences from our lives upon our acceptance of Christ as Savior. As much as we argue about fairness and grace, we know as we allow God to renew our minds that each is a principle in line with His grace. Thank God that He understands and doesn't make things too easy for us. If there were no consequences, as the world tries to convince us daily, where would we be? Headed for trouble, most likely.

There are many illustrations, as I've already presented. But, perhaps the most compelling illustration comes from the Cross itself. Jesus gave us an example that can't be argued or debated. As He hung there, dying for you and me, He was in the process of teaching us priceless truths for our lives today.

Remember the criminal on the cross? Jesus made it clear to him and to us that the man was completely forgiven. Yet, moments later, he died a painful death. Forgiveness and consequences stood side by side. He was as forgiven as anyone could be; yet he suffered the full extent of the consequences of his sin.

Down through the ages, this act of forgiveness stands as a testimony of God's grace, while the stark reality of sowing and reaping is portrayed for all of us to behold. Unlike many of us who rededicate our lives at some point as Christians and vow to live as we should, that man didn't have time to rededicate or live in service to God. He died within minutes of his miraculous experience with Jesus. Forgiven, yes. Free of consequences, no.

APPLICATION

The thief died, even though he acknowledged his need for a Savior and accepted Christ just before his death. Was he forgiven? Absolutely. And the lesson that we can learn is that even though God often chooses to eliminate certain consequences from our lives, there are many times God chooses not to take the consequences away. We must trust Him, whether He does or not.

In spite of what the world might try to tell us, we are accountable for our choices, and consequences are a guarantee. The key is whether they will be good or bad, and that is up to each of us as we decide daily to sow to the sinful nature or to the Spirit. There are times when it seems that everyone we know is getting away with sin: the man who promiscuously has affairs with many women and never gets caught by his wife, the woman who steals money from her job and no one finds out, or the kid who drinks and flirts

CONSEQUENCES

with recreational drugs and never becomes a dropout but instead graduates at the top of his class and goes on to college with a scholarship. It can be confusing if we focus on the circumstances and not on the truth of God's Word.

Rest assured, consequences are a guarantee. They are not a maybe but an absolute, whether you and I witness the ultimate consequences. We are blessed, though, in that we can determine the consequences we are required to experience by our choices. And there are times when we sow good seeds that we can actually turn negative consequences around. I've seen couples who made bad financial decisions and paid dire consequences for many years begin to make wise decisions. Over time they experienced the benefit of their right choices.

It is never easy to face the negative consequences when we struggle daily to live as God wants us to. However, nothing is so bad that we can't rejoice in the grace of God and the forgiveness that is our eternal assurance. Many people who have become most effective in leading the lost to know Jesus as their Savior bear the scars of consequences that God has chosen not to eliminate from their lives. We all have scars. They, too, have a purpose, not to cause us grief as a daily reminder of sin but as a tribute to God's mercy and grace. Once again, the way we look at the scars makes the difference in how we face the consequences God has chosen not to eliminate. Whatever the consequences, whatever the scars, the attitude will determine how we relate to our heavenly Father. Either we will reach a point of understanding and thank Him for the daily reminders of His grace, or we will become bitter.

> **S**tudies show that 10 percent of drivers involved in accidents resulting in minor property damage and 15 percent of drivers involved in extensive property damage have a raised blood alcohol concentration of 0.5 percent.
> —Jay Strack

If we asked God each day to give us the ability to view our scarred lives as monuments to His grace, instead of looking at the scars we bear as ongoing punishment, we would enter into a new realm of trust. I encourage you to look at your scars as proof of healing for a certain length of time (say, six weeks), and then step back and look at the changes that have taken place in your life. I can guarantee that you will change. Instead of your circumstances (or consequences) changing, your ability to trust God in situations that before have tested your faith will take on new and exciting dimensions.

The choice is yours to make. You can end your workday at five o'clock, like your coworkers do, and spend time at home with your spouse and children and reap the benefits of their love. You can choose to fix up the old car rather than go into debt for a new car and make the wise decision that will ultimately return to you a sound financial standing. You can walk away from the friends who tempt you to do things that you know are not what

CONSEQUENCES

■ The price we pay or the benefit we derive from our decisions.

God would have you do and become an example to your friends of one who chooses character over popularity. You have choices. The consequences you reap will be determined by the choices you make.

GROWTH

Just as God has promised that you will reap what you sow with respect to negative consequences, He has equally promised that it works the other way. The consequence doesn't have to be negative. It can be positive, depending on whether you sow to your sinful nature or to the Holy Spirit.

It is absolutely essential to have Christian friends that you can be accountable to. There is power in the community of believers who stand against the lies that Satan puts in your path each day. There are any number of ways to involve yourself with your local church, through Sunday school, a small home group Bible study that focuses on the promises of God, or a one-on-one mentoring relationship where those who have already traveled the road and come face-to-face with consequences share their experiences with younger believers just beginning their walk.

Guard your heart and mind from things that would come between you and the truth. Don't underestimate the impact of television, books, movies, and newspapers on how you think and what you do. I don't mean you have to sit at home and talk to the four walls and never watch television or read the newspaper. I am, however, reminding you to be cautious about what you put into your mind. Just as God speaks to you through your mind, Satan can use your thought processes for his devastating work, also.

Remember that you are instructed to renew your mind with the truth, and this must be a daily habit. It is something that you can't do when you feel like it because you are probably too busy and too tired to do anything other than what you absolutely deem necessary. That is why it must be a priority in your daily schedule. Renewing your mind with God's Word is the best practice to help you avoid the unpleasant consequences of unwise decisions.

Instead of spending the bulk of your time trying to figure out some way to get God to remove the consequences from your life, try praising Him for the wisdom He demonstrates in allowing these reminders to keep you away from further sin and the consequences. As you humble yourself before Him, ask God to give you the strength and courage that you need to walk away from sin and walk toward His almighty arms. He may never change your circumstances, but He will renew your strength and He will change your life.

EMPLOYMENT

SCRIPTURE

COLOSSIANS 3:22–24 NASB

Slaves, in all things obey those who are your masters on earth, not with external service, as those who merely please men, but with sincerity of heart, fearing the Lord. Whatever you do, do your work heartily, as for the Lord rather than for men; knowing that from the Lord you will receive the reward of the inheritance. It is the Lord Christ whom you serve.

COMMENTARY

With so much emphasis placed on picking the right career, it is amazing that so few people are satisfied with their jobs. Most people work day after day in jobs that offer little fulfillment, jobs that often cause them to develop ulcers, chronic headaches, and extended periods of depression. Many folks fantasize about being one's own boss, only to discover that being one's own boss doesn't ensure a joy-filled workplace if you are a perfectionist who can't allow anyone—including yourself—the privilege of making mistakes.

Since the bulk of adult life is spent in some type of work environment, the wise individual devotes considerable time and energy to the choice of career. Only those who follow God's direction will enjoy the peace of mind and joy of being in the center of His will. Even then, unless we are quick to take inventory of our dedication to the work we are given to do, we will fall short of our best.

The apostle Paul placed enormous importance on giving our best to our employers. It was at the top of his priority list, along with the role husbands, wives, parents, and children should assume in the relationship with each other. Immediately following his discourse about relationships, Paul addressed the workplace. Paul was writing to slaves. Although the specific situation no longer applies to our free society, the principles are similar. If Jesus were standing here with us today, I believe He would say, "Listen, learn, and be wise."

The comparison between those days and the day in which we live, however, is inescapable. In biblical days, some slaves were treated well and some were not. In our society, some employees are treated well and some are not. In Paul's day, some masters were fair and some were not. In our day, some employers are fair and some are not. The fact remains that we have more in common with the master-slave relationship than we would care to admit. Some masters treated their slaves with respect uncommon to the relationship. There are good employers with bad employees, just as there are bad employers with dedicated employees. If we are willing to look at what God wants

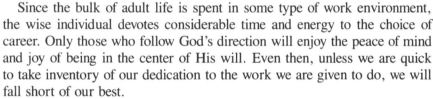

In the 1990s, Americans older than fifty-five became the most likely to be displaced from their jobs.

Employment

EMPLOYMENT

■ *A person's work or occupation.*

In 1973, 15.9 percent of nonagricultural workers worked 49 hours or more. In 1994, the figure rose to 20.9 percent.

us to experience through our workday, there is plenty within the pages of God's Word to tell us what our attitude should be.

Paul admonished slaves to be the best at what they did. We fuss about work our employers give us to do, but a brief look at the job description of a slave leaves us with no room to complain! One of the more demeaning tasks of a slave was to remove the dusty sandals of guests in the home of the master and wash the smelly feet. Yet Scripture says the slave was to do this job with enthusiasm, "as for the Lord." Taking into consideration the landscape of the day, the sandals probably bore the stench of the roads the people traveled. Paul told the feet washers to do the best job possible. If slaves were required to give their best, even to such contemptible labor, how much more should we give our best to jobs that encompass considerably more prestige.

What is your attitude toward your work? Do you feel like you're accomplishing something or just spinning your wheels? Do you fuss and complain? Would the people you work with be surprised that you are a Christian, given your prevailing attitude? Do you give it your all, or do you get by with as little as you can?

In an age when much is said and done to assure that those just entering the workforce are placed in jobs that will fulfill their dreams and aspirations, it is worth our time to look at what Scripture has to say to them—and us— about how we spend the normal forty-hour period of time we call our workweek. A closer look might give you new and life-changing ideas about the way you treat the responsibility you've been given through your career.

A CLOSER LOOK

The Bible says a lot about work. It goes so far as to say that those who won't work shouldn't eat (2 Thess. 3:10). None of us would argue that all people are capable of working; likewise, we are acutely aware of the impact of having millions of people on the welfare rolls. It has become far too easy to let someone else pay the bills rather than take responsibility and follow God's teaching with respect to work.

Some people are enthusiastic about their jobs, while others treat their jobs like diseases they want to stay away from. Whatever your attitude concerning your job, the Bible tells you how to get the most out of it. God said, "Six days you shall labor and do all your work" (Ex. 20:9). He did not say, "Six days you shall take the path of least resistance and then worship Me with all your heart on the Sabbath."

EMPLOYMENT

Working is a scriptural imperative, with a number of practical results attached to what you do.

First, of course, is a paycheck. From a purely practical standpoint, you are given a responsibility that requires you to pay your bills and take care of your family. A paycheck is God's method of providing for your financial responsibilities. If, however, a paycheck is all a person wants from the job, the viewpoint is shortsighted. There is a danger of getting caught up in the "got to have more" syndrome that keeps the acquisition of money at the top of the priority list. That is a dangerous place to be. If your only objective is to make more money, you will always have a sense of insecurity because there is never a guarantee of that happening. It is illogical to invest all of your time, energy, and skills just for money.

Second, an inevitable outworking of a job is the development of skills. Everyone has some skill, be it technical or artistic. I strongly believe that God is the source of our talents and that He expects each of us to make good use of them. Having your skills refined day in and day out in a job is not a waste of time. It is a valuable use of time because of the potential for you to excel. It is wonderful to behold a skilled craftsperson, no matter what the field. If you've ever watched a glassblower practice his art and you've seen the piece take shape, you have been caught up in the mystery of how it all happens and the wonder of his giftedness. Not all of us can be glassblowers or rocket scientists, but all of us can take our talents and use them to glorify our Father by using them responsibly.

Third, work develops character. In the trials and challenges that come with any job, you can learn patience, faithfulness, and submission to authority. One of the truths of life is that these wonderful qualities are usually learned *only* in times of trial and tribulation. I can hear you saying, "Boy, where I work, I am being stretched beyond character development!" Perhaps it won't change your environment or make your boss a more understanding individual, but I guarantee that what you learn about yourself, God, and others will be worth all the pain you might encounter along the way.

Fourth, your job can build your sense of self-worth. Knowing you've given your best is a source of fulfillment. You feel good about yourself when you know that you gave it your all. Even when no one else knows or everyone knows but says nothing, you have the satisfaction of knowing you did a good job—even a great job! You are the epitome of Colossians 3 in serving the Lord Christ, and your self-esteem can reflect that. I don't mean to act haughty. Rather, you react from a biblical sense of knowing you did what you were asked. All of us desire the respect and appreciation of our peers and our superiors at work, but it is possible to enjoy your work without

> **F**orty-three percent of men have changed employers at least once within the last five years.

> **S**ixty-one percent of Americans confess to having regularly lied to their boss.
> —*The Day America Told the Truth*

EMPLOYMENT

Over a life span, the average American worker will spend 76,900 hours on the job.

their attention or appreciation. That happens when you work to glorify God first and the boss second.

Fifth, you can develop meaningful relationships with people you come into contact with every day at work. With the right attitude and motivation, long-lasting friendships will develop. I have seen large corporations where Bible studies are held and wonderful Christian friendships are formed. What an encouragement to believers to realize they are not lone Christians in the corporation! Even if you are in a small business and there are no other believers, your attitude in the workplace is a testimony in itself. Many times, you will be the only light in an otherwise dark and dismal situation. Your only hope of survival in this atmosphere is to keep your focus on the One who makes the sun rise every morning and causes all things to work together for good to those who are called according to His purpose. Keep focused on the One who gave us His very best and you'll shine so bright, others will want to know where the light comes from.

Sixth, another practical outcome in your employment is the sense of accomplishment and achievement. When you see your project completed—no matter how menial—that signals to you that you are making progress in your life.

A woman told me that her father used to build ships. It often took years to build aircraft carriers and other huge ships. She said she remembers as a little girl going with her dad to the launching of the ships. It was a celebrated event with many dignitaries on hand, including the president's wife or some other woman striking the bow of the ship with a bottle of champagne. She recalled how proud she was of her dad and the look on his face when the whistles and horns would blow as the ship eased into the water, flags waving in the breeze.

Not everyone who finishes a project has dignitaries present or whistles blowing and flags waving. But the sense of accomplishment is just as real. Very little you do on earth rivals the wonderful feeling of a job well done.

A man's business is not chiefly his way of making a living but his altar where he serves the King.
—Henry P. Crowell

Seventh, your job gives you a sense of joy that you have made a contribution. Sometimes that's hard to grasp, particularly if your job elicits little praise or attention. Nonetheless, if you are working to glorify God, the sense of accomplishment will prevail over the sense of being a nobody. If you work on an assembly line and you think your job counts for little, let me assure you that you are doing something that is making life easier for someone else. That is one of life's highest callings, I think, to serve others. Jesus was a servant and set the example for us all.

Suppose, for instance, that someone works on an assembly line and puts a certain bolt or screw in a dishwasher minute after minute and hour after hour. He may think this counts for nothing, but ask any woman with a dishwasher if she thinks that person's work is of value and you will hear a resounding "YES!" People who work on an automobile assembly line contribute to those who drive their automobiles. The millions of people who depend on their cars count heavily on the fact that a faithful worker somewhere on an assembly line did her part well. No matter how menial the task, a worker contributes to the lives of others.

So, you are the benefactor of a number of positive benefits as a result of the work you do. A paycheck, honing of skills, character development, a sense of self-worth, rewarding relationships, a sense of accomplishment, and contribution to the lives of others are some of the more practical outworkings of employment.

I am sure that every employed person really wants to get the most out of work. I seriously doubt that anyone longs to be miserable on the job. No one really likes to live and die by the sordid motto, "Another day, another dollar." There has to be more to your attitude about your occupation than that. I guess the next question would be, How do you get the most out of your work?

Let me give you some suggestions.

You get the most out of your work when you view yourself as a servant. Your employer is over you in authority, but Jesus Christ is your Lord. You work for Him. And you do it as His servant. The means whereby you demonstrate your servanthood may be in a company or corporation, but you will get much more out of your work if you see that you are a servant of Jesus Christ.

When the Lord Jesus Christ became your Savior, you became His follower. He said that if someone wants your shirt, give your coat, too. Or if someone wants you to go one mile, go two. Or if someone slaps you on the right cheek, turn the left one to him, also (Matt. 5:39–41). This does not sound like someone who is fighting for rights. This is the lifestyle of someone who has given up rights—like a servant.

The Lord Jesus Christ took upon Himself the form of a bond-servant. We do well to heed these verses: "Have this attitude in yourselves which was also in Christ Jesus, who, although He existed in the form of God, did not regard equality with God a thing to be grasped, but emptied Himself, taking the form of a bond-servant" (Phil. 2:5–7 NASB).

Jesus washed feet (John 13:5). Who do we think we are when we regard ourselves so highly that we can't see ourselves as servants? We scream, "I want my rights!" How wonderful to know that on the road to Calvary there was One who did not demand His rights.

> **F**ifty percent of Americans will procrastinate at work and do absolutely nothing about one full day in every five.
> —*The Day America Told the Truth*

> **G**od owns my business and God owns me. I have every confidence He will take care of His property.
> —*Stanley Tam*

EMPLOYMENT

■ *A person's work or occupation.*

> **T**here is no work better than another to please God; to pour water, to wash dishes, to be a cobbler, or an apostle: all is one.
> —William Tyndale

Some may say, "Well, I'll never get a promotion. I may as well reconcile my life to a series of mediocre slave jobs." But look at this verse: "Whoever desires to become great among you, let him be your servant" (Matt. 20:26). The pathway to promotion is servanthood. Whoever wants to be a leader must adopt an attitude of a servant. A prideful employee is seldom seen as a "promotional person." It is the humble worker who diligently labors with a godly attitude that management sees as leadership material. Never doubt the impact of your attitude on everyone around you—the boss included!

If you feel you have plodded long enough and hard enough, realize God has you where you are for a purpose and He could change your position at any moment. I have a friend who went through a period when she was troubled emotionally, eventually finding herself placed on Social Security disability because of her overwhelming addiction to drugs. After many years of seemingly hopeless addiction, this woman discovered the grace of God and the truth set her free. Several years after God delivered her, she was working for the very agency that once declared her hopeless and said she would never work again! Thankful for the opportunity to work, she knew God had placed her in the specific job for a purpose, but her daily confrontation with the dysfunctional government system brought her to a point of despair. "How can I continue working where so much is wrong? I just want out," she cried. It took a while, but God worked in her heart and reminded her of the time when no one thought she'd ever work again and how she was given a second chance to use the skills and gifts He had given her. Humbly, she asked God to renew her heart to His truth and to give her a new vision for her job.

> **W**e may see unemployment as a disaster, but the same God who has given us a season of unemployment will take us safely through it. If God can create light and darkness, He can create a job at the proper time.
> —Doug Erlandson

Nothing changed at work. She was confronted on a daily basis with things that she knew must grieve God's heart. What changed was her ability to look at the people she worked with through new eyes. God thought better of changing her circumstances. He thought it more profitable to change her! When God is in control of a person's life, there is always an opportunity to change for the better.

It takes persistence to do things that are boring or tedious. Many times we wish we could quote a Scripture that would relieve us of the responsibility to do things we are required to do at work. Scripture hasn't given us that option. The only limitation set on us about obeying those in authority is that we cannot violate Scripture. If you are asked to do something that violates your conscience and/or the clear teaching of Scripture, you need to confront the issue. Don't be slothful or exhibit a bad attitude to prove your point. By all means, don't march into the manager's office with a family Bible tucked under your arm and expect everyone to understand your plight.

EMPLOYMENT

You might respectfully request a meeting with the person over you in authority and say, "I really appreciate the privilege of working here. But I need to ask you a question concerning the thing you have asked me to do. Would you really want me to violate God's Word and be disobedient to God? Would you honestly want me to go against my Christian conviction?" In handling it in this manner, you are putting the responsibility back to the one in authority. You are approaching it with the attitude of being able to win the other person. Give God time to change the person's mind, but if she insists that you do what God has clearly said not to do, you need to continue to obey the Higher Authority over you. (And over her!)

I know of a person who was told to do something dishonest. Because, as a believer, he could not do it, he was fired. He told his boss, "I don't mind being fired if I can walk away from this with a clear conscience." As he finished out his day, his boss came back and said, "If you would like your job back, I want you to have it. I really want you to work for me."

If you are an employer and someone tells you he can't violate his conscience, you need to respect him because that's the kind of employee you want. Character and integrity are in short supply in the workplace, and the employer blessed with a godly employee who chooses integrity over the love of money or status should hang on to that employee.

Next, you get the most out of your work not only by being a servant, but also by realizing you are working for the Lord Himself: "Slaves, in all things obey those who are your masters on earth, not with external service, as those who merely please men, but with sincerity of heart, fearing the Lord" (Col. 3:22 NASB).

You make a terrible mistake by segmenting life. You may think that Monday through Friday you work, Saturday you play, and Sunday you worship. The truth is that God has never seen life that way. If Jesus Christ is your Savior, you can't exclude Him from any part of life. It isn't right to teach a Sunday school class with everything you've got but meander into work the rest of the week.

Paul reminds you not to do your work to be seen of men. You should do your work whether anyone is watching or not because you know God is watching. You should do your very best because the Holy Spirit is equipping and energizing you.

Do I mean that your mundane Monday job is the Lord's work? Yes! *Ministry is not just what you do at church.* You worship Him Sunday through the next Sunday. On Sunday, it is in a church; on Monday through Friday, you worship Him by doing a good job. You see, as a child of God, you

> **W**hen the prop of a job is knocked away, men often feel worthless.
> —Doug Erlandson

> **A**bsenteeism at work accounts for $10 billion a year.

Employment

EMPLOYMENT

■ *A person's work or occupation.*

dignify your work. Your office or place of employment should never be the same because *you* work there.

There is another way to get the most out of your job. That is by viewing Christ as your ultimate authority: "Whatever you do, do it heartily, as to the Lord and not to men" (Col. 3:23). If you are a Christian, Jesus Christ is the Boss at your place of work. He allows others to be over you, but He is ultimately the Boss. You and I need to give a full day's labor whether or not we think management is fair because He is ultimately the Boss. If Paul tells slaves to do their work heartily (and they received no paycheck), what about the rest of us who get paid for what we do? I understand that you may not get paid adequately. But taking longer lunch hours, clocking out early, or coming in late is not the way to even that out. If you are paid for eight hours, you need to give eight full hours. You serve the Lord Christ.

You may say, "In the business world this is the way we do it. I work harder than anyone in my office, but they don't pay me more than they pay anyone else. I see nothing wrong in leaving early." That may be the way "they" do it in the business world, but because you serve Jesus Christ, I trust it is not the way you do it in the business world.

A sixteen-year-old had her first job. She was hired by the insurance agency because of her sweet attitude when she went in to sign up for car insurance after getting her driver's license. But during her summer job, she noticed that no one came at 9:00 A.M. She couldn't start on time because she had no key. Finally, she persuaded some to get there on time to let her in. They did and drank coffee until 9:30 or so until management arrived. But she plugged away as a servant of Jesus Christ. When she went back to school, she left behind a strong testimony.

Is your testimony in the marketplace a good one for Jesus Christ? Are you one of the most faithful employees because you serve Him? Does your attitude reflect the joy you have in seeing His name on the door as the real CEO?

You get the most out of your work when you view your fellow workers as persons of worth. You must never judge people by your position or by their positions. If you are in management, don't look down on others. Watch yourself and seek an accountability partner (yes, at work) so that when you start to fall into the wrong kind of attitude, that person can steer you back to where you should be, according to God's work in your life. You need to treat others justly and fairly. Never put such pressure on a person that she is forced to neglect the family. That is unfair and unjust.

For instance, a salesman has a certain territory and faithfully works it. He begins making a lot of money. Before long, corporate officers decide there is too much of the pie going to one person, so they cut the territory in half. Perhaps they bring in a novice they don't have to pay as much. This is inequitable. A woman has been at the same business forty-two years. Upper management does everything possible to make her life miserable so that she will quit and they can hire a few part-timers to work more cheaply. Greed is the culprit. Setting unfair quotas, taking advantage of someone, and requiring more than someone can physically do are wrong.

When managers see themselves as servants, they are creating a faithful, productive workforce. How can managers be so unwise as to mistreat their employees? Don't they see they are stifling their workers?

You get the most out of your work when you realize your pay comes both now and hereafter. Paul wrote, "Knowing that from the Lord you will receive the reward of the inheritance" (Col. 3:24).

Of course, you must get paid. But if you have done your very best and given all you have, you will never really get paid all you are worth. The wonderful thing to remember is that you may get paid down here, but you get rewarded up there! God is going to equalize it all in the Judgment. There is a payday someday, and the Boss who has watched you all these years will reward you justly.

When you feel trapped in your job, ponder Hebrews 6:10: "God is not unjust to forget your work and labor of love which you have shown toward His name." God knows how many extra hours you've put in. He knows all the times you've gone in when you didn't feel like it. He will not forget your work—or lack of it.

Do you see yourself as a servant? Have you reached the point where you can see Him as the One you're working for? Do you see others as having great self-worth? Have you realized that the reward may come later, that you may not get what you deserve here on earth? Last, but most important, have you come to a point where you can do your work "unto the Lord," no matter how menial or boring it might be? If so, you are getting the most out of your work.

APPLICATION

When you get off from work, you are tired. In a big city, you may go at a snail's pace through traffic home. There is supper to fix or eat. Children to care for. A spouse to be with. Mail to read.

Why not leave work and, as you start the long, slow, frustrating drive home, begin praising Him? Thank Him for the privilege of being employed. Thank Him for your skills. Thank Him for all that He is teaching you.

EMPLOYMENT

■ *A person's work or occupation.*

Thank Him that the true reward of your labor comes from Him. Tell Him you are giving your day's labor as an offering to Him.

Be as specific as you care to be. You might say, "Lord, today when I answered the phone and the person was rude, I thank You for the patience You gave me. I give that back to You as my labor of love." The Lord will help you with creative ways of praising Him as you leave work.

Traffic won't seem nearly as bad.

It surely beats "another day, another dollar."

Remember, your Father is President of the company.

QUOTE

My work is my worship.
—Anonymous

GOVERNMENT

ROMANS 13:1–2

Let every soul be subject to the governing authorities. For there is no authority except from God, and the authorities that exist are appointed by God. Therefore whoever resists the authority resists the ordinance of God, and those who resist will bring judgment on themselves.

COMMENTARY

At best, government is second best. At worst, government is stifling, stripping away human worth. What do I mean by these statements?

Let me explain. I love history. I majored in history in school. I am from Virginia, which is steeped in American history. I am fascinated by the history of other countries whcre I travel. The reason I say that government at its best is only second best is due to its historical beginnings.

Human government was not God's first plan for His people, the Israelites. His initial plan worked very well. He was the King, the Ruler, and He, in love, told His people what was best for them. It was not a complicated system. He had laws for them so they could get along with each other. He had nutritional laws so they would be healthy. He had laws so they could honor Him as their Ruler. Theologians call these the moral, civil, and ceremonial laws of God.

The Creator, who knew what His people needed, ruled and loved His people. But the people rebelled. They looked around at other nations and liked what they saw. So they whined. They were sick of judges, whom God had raised up to give them guidance. They wanted a king just like the nations around them.

The elders of Israel got together and visited the prophet Samuel. Samuel had just appointed his sons—who were dishonest and took bribes—to be judges in his place. The elders appealed to the paternal sadness in Samuel: "You are old, and your sons do not walk in your ways. Now make us a king to judge us like all the nations" (1 Sam. 8:5).

The Bible tells us that displeased Samuel. It also displeased their King: "And the LORD said to Samuel, 'Heed the voice of the people in all that they say to you; for they have not rejected you, but they have rejected Me, that I should not reign over them'" (1 Sam. 8:7). Samuel was sad. God was very, very sad.

God instructed Samuel to tell the people that they could have their wish but not without warning. God could have just lowered the boom. "You want a king? I'll give you a king. But you will be sorry." Because God loved His people—even when they demanded something that was contrary to His will—

> **T**he government of a country never gets ahead of the religion of a country. There is no way by which we can substitute the authority of the law for the virtues of men.
> —Calvin Coolidge

GOVERNMENT

■ *The system of authority that rules over a nation, state, city, or other organization.*

He did His best to ensure that they went into the new venture with their eyes open.

Samuel warned this whining group of government lobbyists that the new king would take thousands of their men to do his gardening, he would take their sons to ride before his chariots, and he would use thousands of other men to make his weapons of war. The king would use their daughters to make perfume and bake luscious food. He would demand their best fields and vineyards and olive groves. He would take one-tenth of their food for his officers and servants. He would take their servants and their donkeys for his work. He would take one-tenth of their flocks.

It hardly sounds like a winning platform for a king to campaign on. God told Samuel the people would regret their decision, and He would not listen to their complaints. He was giving them fair warning.

Some of the saddest words in Scripture follow:

> Nevertheless the people refused to obey the voice of Samuel; and they said, "No, but we will have a king over us, that we also may be like all the nations, and that our king may judge us and go out before us and fight our battles." And Samuel heard all the words of the people, and he repeated them in the hearing of the LORD. So the LORD said to Samuel, "Heed their voice, and make them a king" (1 Sam. 8:19–22).

And they got their tall, handsome king. Saul was literally head and shoulders above everyone. They had every right to be proud. They had a king everyone could see. They didn't just have a King who boomed from the heavens, who was in a fiery pillar or swirling cloud, or who somehow opened seas for them to go through. No. Here was a real king with skin.

That's the history of human government. From the time of Adam and Eve right on through today, we have not been content to have God as our Ruler. We have always opted for a second-rate system.

That being the case, why, in our opening passage, are we told to obey the government? And are there exceptions when we are not to obey?

Let's take a closer look.

A CLOSER LOOK

We need boundaries. Because of our sin nature, we don't do well coloring outside the lines. Because of our sin nature, we often color all the way off the page if left to ourselves.

So God instructs us to stay under the authority of government. The speed limit applies to believers and unbelievers. It makes no difference if we name

---

the name of Christ or not, we pay taxes. A judge will not be impressed by the title Christian if we have just shoplifted.

The Bible teaches that we are to be in submission. Color inside the lines. They are there for a purpose. Paul tells us in Romans 13 that those who fear the law to a healthy degree have very little to worry about. We drive without looking in the rearview mirror for police officers because we drive correctly. No problem.

But what do we do when we know our tax money is going to fund abortions? What do we do when we know our tax money is going toward public school sex education with a totally humanistic approach? What do we do when we know our tax money is funding paintings euphemistically called art?

The Bible does not specifically answer each of these difficult questions. The closest we can get, I think, is the Lord Jesus' admonition to "render therefore to Caesar the things that are Caesar's, and to God the things that are God's" (Luke 20:25). He was responding to a tax question. The motive of the people asking—the Bible calls them spies—was to get Jesus to denounce the Roman government, thereby giving them some reason to arrest Him. Humanly speaking, we can see a thousand reasons why He could have denounced the pagan government of Rome. But He did not. He, as a man, had placed Himself under the authority of the earthly government. Should we do less?

Another time, the IRS called on Peter. Peter didn't answer the question correctly, and Jesus spoke to him about it. The tax collectors had asked Peter if Jesus was going to pay the temple tax. We can see how Peter was not sure if the One who had cleansed the temple wanted to contribute to it. So he told the collectors that he didn't think Jesus would pay. Jesus explained to Peter that His followers were to pay taxes. And to put a huge exclamation point to His words, He provided enough temple taxes for Himself and Peter through a coin in a fish (Matt. 17:24–27).

We can almost picture talkative Peter giving the coin to the tax people, wanting desperately to give an I-don't-agree-with-all-the-goings-on-of-the-Roman-government speech. Not to mention where the coin came from!

Soon after Christ's ascension, we see the same Peter defying the local government. Hadn't Jesus made His point about authority clear? Why did Peter do such an about-face? Can we? When?

Peter had preached at Pentecost. Many were saved. There were healings. God got the new church's attention through the deaths of Ananias and Sapphira. A lot was going on! Peter and the rest of the apostles were preaching and teaching, preaching and teaching. It was not only the government

> The Supreme Court commands the allegiance of only one in four Americans.
> —The Day America Told the Truth

> Thirty percent of adults said the U.S. Supreme Court has gained influence compared to its standing five years ago. Forty-four percent said its influence remained unchanged.
> —George Barna

GOVERNMENT

■ *The system of authority that rules over a nation, state, city, or other organization.*

that was unnerved by their actions; the religious section wasn't too happy, either. Peter and his friends were "commanded" to be quiet (Acts 4:18).

Peter and John prayed differently from the way some of us would have. They said, "Now, Lord, look on their threats, and grant to Your servants that with all boldness they may speak Your word" (Acts 4:29). They were carrying out the Great Commission. They had an unction from on high and had set about to proclaim it.

The government said one thing.

God said another.

That's when we have to make the choice.

They finally ended up in jail, were released by an angel, and went back to preaching. The religious leaders were irate. Furious. Red-faced from anger and embarrassment. After all, they probably had never been released from anything by an angel. They shouted, "Did we not strictly command you not to teach in this name?" (Acts 5:28).

Here is the key: "But Peter and the other apostles answered and said: 'We ought to obey God rather than men'" (Acts 5:29). They knew whose strict orders to obey when man's edict plainly violated God's instructions.

A learned teacher used illustrations of some other troublemakers who had come and gone and told the council to leave Peter and John alone, thinking the novelty would wear off. Little did he know: "And daily in the temple, and in every house, they did not cease teaching and preaching Jesus as the Christ" (Acts 5:42).

Would Peter and John have obeyed the speed limits in their chariots? Yes. Would they have paid inflated property taxes on their little homes? Yes. Would they have stopped talking about the Cross because someone told them to? No.

If Peter were a teenager and had the opportunity to speak at graduation, would he delete the mention of the Lord's name because the Supreme Court said to? If Peter worked in an office and the office manager said not to bring his scrolls—or Bible—and lay them on his desk, would he still do it?

The Bible does not say. Each situation differs and God's wisdom must be sought. Consequences must be seriously considered.

I want us to look primarily at the government of the United States of America because we are leaders in the world. We were leaders in military might, leaders in strong moral fiber, leaders in affluence, leaders in sending the most missionaries out. We are still leaders. Leaders in crime. Leaders in drugs. Leaders in teen pregnancies. Leaders in illiteracy. Leaders in pornography. Leaders in debt. And fast losing in our preeminence of sending forth missionaries. What on earth happened?

GOVERNMENT

Many government buildings in Washington, D.C., have Scripture etched throughout. On a Christian-oriented tour of the city, the guide points out the Word of God in each setting.

Not only do our buildings proclaim our nation was founded on the Word of God, but our coins proclaim "In God We Trust." The Ten Commandments hang above the Supreme Court justices. In the Senate and House chambers are inscriptions of "In God We Trust." The president and government officials are sworn into office with a hand on the Bible that children cannot read in school.

Noah Webster said in 1832, "The principles of all genuine liberty and of wise laws and administrations are to be drawn from the Bible and sustained by its authority. *The man or woman who weakens or destroys the divine authority may be accessory to all the public disorder which society is doomed to suffer.*"

George Washington said, "It is impossible to rightly govern the world without the Bible and God."

Andrew Jackson proclaimed about the Bible, "That Book, sir, is the rock on which our Republic rests."

Such Christian notions are scarce now. Religion is viewed cynically by government and legislation seeks to isolate Christian influence. The result is moral chaos.

According to 2 Chronicles 7:14, uprighting our national ship begins with prayer. God has placed the solution into the laps of those who acknowledge Him. God's strategy for change goes something like this.

First, we must humble ourselves. We agree that we are not worthy to be fixed. Although we are the greatest nation on earth, we're not that great. We must take personal responsibility: "Father, *my* country is in the shape it's in because *I* have not done my part to change it."

Second, we must pray. We plead for this land. We pray for every Supreme Court justice by name. We pray for our president, those who counsel him, the Senate, and the House. Get the names of local authorities and pray specifically.

Third, we must seek His face. We seek or desperately want what He wants: "Lord, what can *I* do? Where do *I* fit to make the most impression for righteousness?" One man said that as he prayed specifically like this, God impressed him not to buy gas where lottery tickets were sold. He thought that was fine until God impressed him further to explain to the gas station owner close to his home why he no longer bought gas there. He said that was harder. It was even more difficult when fellow believers told him that the small amount of gas money he withheld made absolutely no difference in whether or not the gas station sold lottery tickets. But he said he had sought God's face and believed he needed to be obedient in this small area.

Eighty-four percent of the people in the United States believe in the Ten Commandments.

GOVERNMENT

■ *The system of authority that rules over a nation, state, city, or other organization.*

From its earliest biblical beginnings of a theocracy all the way through history to the present-day democracy, government boundaries are interesting to study.

But the boundaries are changing.

It is indeed wonderful to know that the highest court in our land is not really the highest court. The term *supreme* might be used to describe it, but it is a poor term. By definition that word means "highest in rank, power, final, ultimate." It probably should be called the Subsupreme Court. Or the Not-Quite-Supreme Court.

Because we belong to the Judge of all the earth. He's supreme.

This supreme Judge has told us through His Word to be subject to the government. Pay taxes. Drive the speed limit. Wear seat belts. Serve on jury duty. Vote. Don't pollute. Don't chop down trees in national parks. Don't hunt out of season. Put tags on your car. Get emission stickers.

It is not complicated. So far.

But then the government goes way outside the lines: "Don't talk about Jesus."

The righteous Judge of all the earth—the true Supreme Court—says, "Go and make disciples of all the nations." In other words, talk about Jesus.

That's when Peter would have stopped fishing for a coin and gone to jail. We may have to do the same thing one day. But if we pray and take our stand now, it may not come to that.

We need to appeal to the true Supreme Court.

Rev. Tony Evans is very well known in Dallas, where he serves his church, and all over the world as a bold leader. The civic leaders in Dallas asked Dr. Evans to give the invocation at a city affair. He was glad for the opportunity, since his church has a tremendous outreach to the young people there. After asking Dr. Evans to come to their function and pray, they added, "Oh, by the way, don't pray in the name of Jesus. That could be offensive to some. Just pray." Dr. Evans quickly responded, "If you don't want me to pray in the name of Jesus, don't ask me to pray. Get someone else."

This pastor saw through the supposed opportunity to be involved in a civic affair. The opportunity was there. As a citizen of Dallas, he would have been delighted to have been included. As a citizen of heaven, he drew the line.

APPLICATION

Because the problems are so big that they are overwhelming, getting a grip on any of them is a challenge. Let me isolate one area that shows decline because our government took a stand against the Word of God under the guise of separation of church and state.

Forty years ago, while Bible and prayer were still in the school system (and seminaries), these were the major problems in school: (1) talking in class, (2) chewing gum, (3) making noise, (4) running in the halls, (5) getting out of line, (6) wearing improper clothing, and (7) missing the wastebasket.

Today these are our problems: (1) drug abuse, (2) suicide, (3) alcohol, (4) pregnancy, (5) rape, (6) murder, and (7) assault. Sounds like the description of a penitentiary instead of a school.

Based on this example, we can see that talking in class versus drug abuse is not even comparable; that chewing gum versus suicide screams to the world, "SOMETHING WENT WRONG!"

It sure did. We decided prayer and the Word of God should have no part in the school system. And the foundation crumbled. Administrators have put in security systems in many school systems to make sure weapons stay out.

Paul declared, "For the weapons of our warfare are not of the flesh, but divinely powerful for the destruction of fortresses" (2 Cor. 10:4 NASB). There is no security system in the world strong enough to keep out our invisible weapon of prayer. We've got to pray. Not just for the school system. Our entire system of government needs to get back to the Word of God. And the answer rests with believers petitioning the true Supreme Court.

What are you doing?

 QUOTES

Within the covers of this Bible are all the answers for all the problems that men face. The Bible can touch hearts, order minds and refresh souls.

—President Ronald Reagan

It was the Lord who put it [the discovery of America] in my mind. I could feel His hand upon me. There's no question that the inspiration was from the Holy Spirit because He comforted me with rays of marvelous inspiration through the Holy Scripture.

—Christopher Columbus

All men must be controlled either by a power from within or a power from without. Either by the Word of God or by the strong arm of man. Either by the Bible or the bayonet. But men will be controlled by one way or another.

—Robert C. Winthrop

GREED

■ *An inordinate desire for something, particularly wealth.*

SCRIPTURE

LUKE 12:13–21 NASB

Someone in the crowd said to Him, "Teacher, tell my brother to divide the family inheritance with me." But He said to him, "Man, who appointed Me a judge or arbiter over you?" And He said to them, "Beware, and be on your guard against every form of greed; for not even when one has an abundance does his life consist of his possessions." And He told them a parable, saying, "The land of a certain rich man was very productive. And he began reasoning to himself, saying, 'What shall I do, since I have no place to store my crops?' And he said, 'This is what I will do: I will tear down my barns and build larger ones, and there I will store all my grain and my goods. And I will say to my soul, "Soul, you have many goods laid up for many years to come; take your ease, eat, drink and be merry."' But God said to him, 'You fool! This very night your soul is required of you; and now who will own what you have prepared?' So is the man who lays up treasure for himself, and is not rich toward God."

COMMENTARY

Jesus used the parable of the rich man to remind His audience that there are several types of greed. In the parable, the rich man died before he could use all that he had stored in his barns. He mistakenly believed that the wealth he had amassed was his alone. Jesus viewed his attitude as a form of greed.

When we concentrate our efforts on amassing wealth and material things and ignore God's plan for our resources, we violate one of His key principles. If we plan only for this life, we are heading for eternity empty-handed.

Notice the warning, "Beware, and be on your guard against every form of greed; for not even when one has an abundance does his life consist of his possessions" (Luke 12:15 NASB). Jesus was striking out against one of the most common misconceptions, that life equals possessions. The more possessions a man or woman has, the better life will be.

But it's a lie. Our lives are not defined by what we have. We brought nothing into this world, and we take nothing with us when we leave. Furthermore, how much of what we own would we be willing to give up to save our lives if the need arose? In most cases, everything. Why? Because at the core of our being we know that life does not consist of the abundance of our possessions; there is much more to it than that. But we forget God. And when we forget, we become greedy.

A CLOSER LOOK

Greed is a trap that ensnares many believers. Greed is like a prison that locks us in and others out. What begins as an exercise of our freedom (how we choose to spend our money, time, or talents) can grow into selfishness to the point that we lose freedom, no longer able to help others. This selfish waste of God's precious resources goes against God's will for our lives.

The sin of greed may begin innocently enough. We may think that because God has blessed us, we are entitled to use our financial and spiritual gifts as we choose. Slowly, we fall victim to Satan's snare of desire for more, leaving us unfulfilled.

Our view of giving, whether through money, time, or talents, may have been negatively influenced by a family member, friends, or even a bad experience in church. Our upbringing, theology and, most especially, our commitment to Christ or lack of commitment, affect our attitude. A sense of guilt may wash over us when the offering plate passes or a request is made to assist someone in need. Why? Because we have made greed a priority over giving to God and to others.

In Proverbs 1:19, the writer admonishes us that being "greedy for gain" is a trap. When we fall for Satan's suggestion that we can't live without more money or possessions, our desire grows until it becomes an obsession.

The most graphic illustration of greed in the Bible is that of Judas. One of Jesus' twelve disciples, Judas held an important position—keeper of the money bag. Yet Judas allowed greed to enter his life and so consume him that he was willing to sell the life of his Master, Lord, and Savior for thirty pieces of silver!

Mary took a pound of spikenard and poured it on Jesus' feet. Judas was furious that Mary would take an expensive perfume, pour it on Jesus' feet, then wipe His feet with her hair. He loudly objected to what he thought was a waste of money.

Although Jesus never said anything about it, He probably knew that Judas had taken money from the disciples' money bag for his own use. Jesus knew Judas's heart and explained that Mary's act was not meant to ignore the poor and spend lavishly. Mary was publicly acknowledging her faith in Jesus as her Messiah. The pouring of the perfume was the anointing that anticipated the burial of Jesus.

> **P**erhaps the most significant economic change of the second half of the 20th century was the discovery of instant prosperity (called credit) by millions of American families.
> —Larry Burkett

> **I**n 99.9 percent of the cases we see, the problem is not too little money; it's too little stewardship.
> —Jerry and Ramona Tuma

APPLICATION

The Scriptures also reveal warnings that if we are consumed with greed, not only do we disobey God, but we will miss the opportunity to allow Him to use us as instruments for others.

God wants to do more than convict us of our sin. He wants us to make proper use of our resources the priority. Jesus lived and died so that we might

GREED

> **G**reed is evil because it substitutes material things for the place of honor that the Creator ought to have in an individual's life and is therefore idolatry.

have abundant life. He knows that greed is a major barrier to experiencing the quality of life God desires for us.

Genesis 14 details Lot's greedy desire for the best of everything. A desire for more success and more possessions led him into sinful surroundings and cost him his freedom. He was captured and tortured: "They also took Lot, Abram's brother's son who dwelt in Sodom, and his goods, and departed" (Gen. 14:12).

Like Lot, we can fall prey to becoming involved with people or activities we shouldn't. We crave prosperity and popularity. Failure to make God's motives our motives causes us to behave in a manner unworthy of God's children.

Desires may not be wrong, but the sin enters when we allow the desire to become greed. Numbers 11:34 describes this situation: "He called the name of that place Kibroth Hattaavah, because there they buried the people who had yielded to craving." The Israelites craved fine food and believed it was their right to have it; the desire for food was not wrong, just a wrong perspective. The Israelites dwelled on fine food to the degree it was all they could think of; it affected their perspective on God's provision of manna. In the same way, we may become so preoccupied that we allow what could be a harmless desire to grow into lust and covetousness.

Even if we concentrate on God's motives, we must be wary of those who do not share our perspective. The main ambition of Moses was to serve God, but Numbers 16 relates the story of Korah and a group of 250 Israelites, including some Reubenites who rose up against Moses. They falsely believed that Moses, Aaron, and his sons were trying to make the Israelite priesthood into something political. Korah and his group were greedy for power.

GROWTH

To be the person God wants you to be, you must seek first His kingdom and make Jesus the Lord of your life. Only when you acknowledge Him as the Creator of all that you have and ever hope to have can you have victory over greed. Acknowledging His lordship means allowing Jesus Christ control of your finances, talents, time, and relationships.

You don't have to fret over the future or become anxious about your financial status. Jesus knows your needs and supplies your needs, and occasionally your desires. A scriptural principle is the wise investment of resources for today and tomorrow. Jesus said, "For where your treasure is, there your heart will be also" (Luke 12:34).

Furthermore, in Hebrews 13:5, you are told to keep your life free from the love of money and to be content with what you have because God said He would never leave you or forsake you.

You can live with less and be content if you make giving a life principle. Instead of becoming bitter over what you don't have, you can express appreciation and gratitude to the Lord for what you do have. God reflects His love in what He has provided. His love will endure for all eternity; your money and possessions will not.

QUOTE

The sense of ownership in general is always to be encouraged. The humans are always putting up claims to ownership which sound equally funny in heaven and in Hell, and we must keep them doing so. . . . And all the time the joke is that the word "mine" in its fully possessive sense cannot be uttered by a human being about anything. In the long run either Our Father or the Enemy will say "mine" of each thing that exists, and specially of each man. They will find out in the end, never fear, to whom their time, their souls, and their bodies really belong—certainly not to them, whatever happens.

—C. S. Lewis

GRIEF

■ *Intense emotional suffering caused by loss; acute sorrow.*

JOHN 11:32–37

Then, when Mary came where Jesus was, and saw Him, she fell down at His feet, saying to Him, "Lord, if You had been here, my brother would not have died." Therefore, when Jesus saw her weeping, and the Jews who came with her weeping, He groaned in the spirit and was troubled. . . . Jesus wept. Then the Jews said, "See how He loved him!" And some of them said, "Could not this Man . . . also have kept this man from dying?"

The Bible records at least three occasions when Jesus grieved: at the tomb of Lazarus, over the city of Jerusalem, and in the Garden of Gethsemane before His death. He is the "Man of sorrows and acquainted with grief" (Isa. 53:3).

Referring to the Scripture reference in John 11, people often wonder why Jesus would weep over the death of His friend Lazarus when He knew he would come forth within minutes.

His knowledge of the future did not keep Him from identifying with the sorrow of people around Him. "Jesus wept." He was moved with emotion at the sight of Mary and Martha's sorrow. He was touched by their love for their brother. He was not emotionally isolated from the pain suffered by those whose perspective was different from His own.

Jesus weeps over our sorrow as well. He is sensitive to what we are feeling: "For we do not have a High Priest who cannot sympathize with our weaknesses" (Heb. 4:15).

A scientific study has revealed that the chemical content in tears of grief differs from the content in tears of joy. Toxins are released from the body through tears of anguish. What a loving Creator who has given us a physical release of emotional pain!

Christians are told not to stifle their grief or to behave unscripturally stoic. I use the word *unscripturally* because the Lord Jesus gave us an example of how to grieve—not how to feel neutral. The Bible tells us concerning grief, "That you may not grieve, as do the rest who have no hope" (1 Thess. 4:13 NASB).

One of the most painful times in my life occurred when I lost my mother. She and I were very close. After her stroke, I watched her die a little each day. It was as if a Band-Aid was being pulled off an open wound a bit at a time. It stung beyond anything I had ever known. I had dreaded losing her, and the thought of doing so made me feel physically ill.

Although I was sixty years old when she died, I felt orphaned. I learned that is a common feeling when any child—younger or older—loses a parent.

The emotional wound was deep and oozed many months. When well-meaning friends remarked, "We're so happy your mom is in heaven!" I became very angry. Without their realizing it, they were trying to short-circuit my grief.

It was then that I realized grief was a necessary part of emotional healing. I recognized that it was hard work and that no one could circumvent it.

No two people grieve alike. A couple who cared for a disabled child for many years noticed the strain the care put on their marriage. The couple finally realized they were grieving differently. Each needed to give the other room to work through personal pain the way each needed to. The wife thought it was insensitive for her husband to go hunting, and the husband couldn't fathom how walking through a mall and eating a hot dog could soothe his wife.

We cannot be critical of how someone hurts. The intensity of pain is different for everyone, as are the variety of coping skills.

A loss need not be a death. Some losses seem to be far worse than death. There are job losses; a move to a different city, which means loss of relationships and familiarity; an empty nest; loss of promotion at work; loss of a dream as your child becomes rebellious; loss of a child in miscarriage; loss of youth or good health; loss of a pet; and loss of a spouse in separation or divorce.

The process of working through the loss is the *process* of grief. It is hard work but a necessary part of healing. And no one can do it for another, although we can be there to listen to someone who needs to talk. The process can be a lengthy one with the time varying from individual to individual.

The first stage is shock or numbness. This is almost a heavenly Novocain so that the person is not totally overwhelmed. This is one reason the hurting person cannot assimilate advice or even a lot of Scripture at first. Her mind is dulled. Her emotions are overloaded.

Second, as the numbness wears off, she says to herself—and sometimes to others—"This can't really be happening." This is denial. It seems significant that the most often used response to bad news is, "Oh, no." That is a verbal response to a soul saying, "No, this just can't happen. It happens only to others." Sometimes the denial gives way to bargaining, such as, "Lord, if You will ease the pain, I will . . ."

You cannot live without experiencing grief in a thousand different ways!
—Granger E. Westberg

I shall look at the world through tears. Perhaps I shall see things that dry-eyed I could not see.
—Nicholas Wolterstorff

GRIEF

> he tears . . . streamed down . . . making . . . a pillow for my heart.
> —Augustine

When the bargaining doesn't seem to work, anger becomes predominant. Comments, some of which seem uncharacteristic, such as, "How dare management select him over me! I hope the company fails," take some off guard. Frequently, widows or widowers will be angry with the one who died and made them such. Or some are angry with the doctor for not having saved a friend. And many get very angry with God since He could have prevented the hurt in the first place. Although a lot of the grief is irrational, it needs to be verbalized and not trivialized by those who hear it. There will be time for explanations.

The fourth stage of grief is guilt. "If only" or "I should've" hits the wounded heart. This is common for someone who lost a loved one in death and was not with the person when she died. The grieving person feels he "should have" somehow known. There is no limit to the guilt. Loss of health: "I should've eaten better, exercised more." Loss of a child to rebellion: "It's all my fault. I should've been a better parent." Divorce: "I should've been a better partner." Loss of job or promotion: "I should've worked harder." Even though some of these might have an element of truth, in grief the guilt is totally out of proportion to reality.

Then, finally, the grieving person works through to resolution or acceptance. She is able to acknowledge the loss did occur. It was dreadfully painful. It still hurts to think about it. It made her angry and guilt ridden. But she will go on. She will get out of bed in the morning. She will resume some activities, perhaps a bit at a time.

The unhealthy part of the grieving process is getting stuck in one stage for a long time. Although it is normal to fluctuate in emotions and hit different stages randomly, it is not healthy to get bogged down in one. For instance, staying numb for six months and denying your son is on drugs are not working through a process. Total denial is no help to you or your son.

One of the things I have discovered since my mom died is that grief hits at the most unexpected—and inconvenient—times. Last year I lost two of my dear friends in death on the same day. I preached their funerals within hours of each other. I was overcome as I walked into the pulpit on Sunday and saw the pews where each man had sat. Thousands of others were sitting there, but that could not compensate for the two I had lost. My sad reaction took me off guard.

A mother who lost her child said her most difficult part of grieving was done in the grocery store. Food was about all she could buy for her sick child for many years. She commented to a friend she met at the checkout counter, "I've come a long way. I just made it through the cereal aisle without crying!" But that was months after the child's death. She said she

> hirty countries with 11 percent of the world's population (or 519 million people) registered 75 or greater on the Human Suffering Index.

still has a twinge of hurt when she sees moms with little boys playing with Matchbox cars. She feels, in time, the pain of that will lessen but may never be totally eradicated.

I thought one thing she said about the loss of her child was revealing. She said, "People would say to us, 'Well, you know that's only a shell in that grave.' But what they'd forgotten, in their desire to be helpful, was that 'shell' was precious to me. I had carried that 'shell' in my body. I was there when that 'shell' breathed his first breath. I taught that 'shell' to walk and talk and ride a bike. His daddy baptized that 'shell.' I bathed that 'shell.' I loved the way his hair curled and his feet were shaped like his dad's and his long eyelashes gave the 'shell' an impish look. I stood over that 'shell' in an intensive care unit for months. And then I kissed a cold 'shell' forehead before his daddy pulled the sheet over a 'shell' he and I helped to create. So saying it was *just* a 'shell' was no comfort. Theologically, I know what they were saying, but maternally and emotionally, I wanted to scream, 'I did everything for that precious "shell" I knew to do and it stopped breathing and it's now in a grave. That hurts.'"

Just looking over the grieving process, we can see it is necessary, complicated, and hard work. But recognizing the stages and giving ourselves, or others, permission to grieve are parts of healing. If we understand that no two people grieve exactly alike, on the same time schedule, much less in the same stage at the same time, we are on our way to healthier relationships in a hurting situation. And we will be more prone not to be discouraged when we understand we may bounce from one stage to the other before acceptance finally finds a home in our hearts.

A non-Christian psychiatrist told a grieving woman that he was amazed at her coping skills. She had explained to him that she was a Christian, and while she grieved, she did so "with hope." He explained that "talking out loud to anyone—even God—is helpful when you are hurting." The Christian woman smiled and explained that praying out loud was not her last resort but her first option. The doctor was not sure what to do with the information, but he could not deny the results were wonderful.

Discussing each *why* in your heart and each feeling of dismay with the One who loves you and understands is the most healing thing you can do. This Friend will never say, "Snap out of it!" This Wonderful Counselor will listen to every feeling. He is not shocked by anger, even if it is directed toward Him. He understands every human emotion and is never tired of repetitive laments. He is unchanged through every changing emotion you experience. He understands your need to grieve better than you do, but He

Because we know so little about grief, we become panicky when it strikes us.
—Granger E. Westberg

To say a person is deeply religious and therefore does not have to face grief situations is ridiculous. Not only is it totally unrealistic, but it is also incompatible with the whole Christian message.
—Granger E. Westberg

GRIEF

■ *Intense emotional suffering caused by loss; acute sorrow.*

longs "that you may not grieve, as do the rest who have no hope" (1 Thess. 4:13 NASB).

QUOTE

If God would make manifest the fact that "He giveth songs in the night," He must first make it night.

—William Taylor

■ *A feeling of responsibility or remorse for some real or imagined offense.*

GUILT

SCRIPTURE

This righteousness from God comes through faith in Jesus Christ to all who believe. There is no difference, for all have sinned and fall short of the glory of God, and are justified freely by his grace through the redemption that came by Christ Jesus.

COMMENTARY

In the third chapter of his letter to the church at Rome, Paul explained in no uncertain terms that apart from God's intervention, people are hopelessly, helplessly lost. He went to great lengths to dispel any notion that righteousness existed in anyone, no matter the heritage. He wrote,

> What then? Are we better than they? Not at all. For we have previously charged both Jews and Greeks that they are all under sin. As it is written:
>
>> *"There is none righteous, no, not one;*
>> *There is none who understands;*
>> *There is none who seeks after God"* (vv. 9–11).

Certainly, if Paul had ended his description of guilt there, it would put people in a hopeless state of guilt that drives many to despair. However, he assured us of a way out when he added, "And are justified freely by his [God's] grace through the redemption that came by Christ Jesus" (v. 24 NIV). That's it. If resolving guilt any other way was possible, what Jesus did at Calvary would have been worthless. That is why Paul made such a point to remind the church at Rome (and us today) that we can't work out our guilt; freedom from guilt is a gift.

Our response to God's offer of freedom from guilt determines whether we walk free of guilt or live in bondage to it. Too often the struggling believer gets stuck in the "for all have sinned" part of Romans 3:23 and fails to grasp the glory of the "and are justified freely" part of verse 24. Later, Paul wrote, "Therefore, having been justified by faith, we have peace with God through our Lord Jesus Christ, through whom also we have access by faith into this grace in which we stand" (Rom. 5:1–2). A few chapters later Paul assured believers, "There is therefore now no condemnation to those who are in Christ Jesus" (Rom. 8:1). There is no reason to live in bondage to guilt. It doesn't make anyone holier. In fact, it keeps believers from experiencing the fullness of our identity and holiness in Christ.

GUILT

■ *A feeling of responsibility or remorse for some real or imagined offense.*

A difficulty we face in resolving guilt is that we don't understand what it is. That may seem strange. Guilt means you've done something wrong. That's true. A rose is a rose. Right? Yet, stop and think about it for a minute. Just as there are many variations of roses, there are different kinds of guilt as well. Here is where we must begin to understand why we have such problems handling guilt. Until we are able to differentiate between the various types and sources of guilt, it is impossible to find freedom.

In his book *Healing for Damaged Emotions,* David A. Seamands writes, "Immature and sensitive believers can become neurotic perfectionists who are guilt-ridden, tight-haloed, unhappy, and uncomfortable." Do you recognize that description? We all know people like that—or perhaps that description fits the person in the mirror! Immature believers have never caught hold of the grace that is extended to them through Jesus' sacrificial death, and they continue to strive for forgiveness and acceptance through guilt-based service or, in many cases, give up completely and live in dreadful pain that is a direct result of unresolved guilt.

There are basically four types of guilt: civil, theological, psychological, and true. Let's look at each one.

1. *Civil guilt* is the outcome of violating human law. When we exceed the speed limit or fail to report a certain amount of income on our taxes, we are guilty of breaking the laws of the land. We may not feel guilty, but that doesn't change a thing. Civil guilt is an objective fact. It is not based on feelings. When you break the law, you are guilty whether you know it or not, whether you admit it or not.

2. *Theological guilt* is the violation of divine law and is an objective fact, just like civil guilt. The Bible teaches that we are all born in sin. As a result of our sinful condition, we break God's moral laws through our thoughts, words, and actions. The Bible is clear about our guilt (Rom. 3:23).

3. *Psychological guilt* is the guilt we feel. Generally, it results from our upbringing. This type of guilt is not necessarily linked to the other two. Oftentimes it isn't linked to anything real. It is perceived guilt. It is possible to assume guilt because of something that happened to us as children and carry it into adulthood, never realizing that we are carrying a burden that doesn't belong on our shoulders (i.e., "Mother and Daddy got a divorce because I did . . . ," or "Uncle Bob wouldn't have abused me if I hadn't . . ."). Psychological guilt is usually destructive because it often isn't attached to anything genuine and therefore is impossible to deal with.

4. *True guilt* is real guilt that leads to constructive sorrow. Constructive sorrow is the only response to wrongdoing that produces lasting change for

What the devil loves is that vague cloud of unspecified guilt feeling or unspecified virtue by which he lures us into despair or presumption.
—C. S. Lewis

the right reasons. It doesn't incorporate the feeling of self-condemnation or psychological guilt. This guilt is healthy because it is our cue that we have done something wrong and need to confess it to resolve the effects (broken intimacy with God, broken relationships with others). Constructive sorrow leads to remorse, confession, repentance and, ultimately, freedom.

With these four types of guilt in mind, we can see why we live in a world that depends on tranquilizers, alcohol, sex, and work to divert attention from what seemingly is an impossible load to bear. The effects of guilt are numerous. The guilty party gives up completely or resorts to methods of escape. Most people handle guilt through saying the following:

- "I give up."
- "I'll show you."
- "I'm not that bad."

"I give up" is one of the easiest ways to deal with guilt and one of the most dangerous. It can lead to depression, feelings of worthlessness and hopelessness. If not dealt with, it can result in suicide. For some, suicide seems the only way out.

"I'll show you" is grounded in anger about being caught. You've seen this type of response, for example, when a child is reprimanded for doing something he knows is wrong. Or the employee is chided for cheating on her time card and secretly vows to "show them" by sabotaging the morale of the office through rumors and false accusations. The "I'll show you" response is usually triggered when a person knows he is guilty, but he doesn't want to face the consequences.

The "I'm not that bad" response is deadly because of the denial involved. I've seen this many times when a person tries to make herself look good by comparing what she has done to what someone else has done. For example, the person cheats on income tax returns and then rationalizes by saying, "Well, what I did didn't hurt anyone. Look at that guy on trial for killing his wife. At least what I did didn't hurt anybody!"

The effects of guilt are endless: feelings of rejection, projection of feelings onto other people, the inability to say no, depression, anxiety, obsessive-compulsive behaviors, blame shifting, spiritual loss of intimacy with God, addictions, and continuing indulgence as a result of the "blackmail" that Satan brings against the believer once a sin is committed.

The good news is that God's program of reconciliation and forgiveness works! Obviously, until we come to an understanding of the real problem and the solution that was set into motion two thousand years ago, we will

> "Large" and "small" are not words for the vocabulary of conscience. It knows only two words— right and wrong.
> —Alexander Maclaren

GUILT

continue to run in circles and collectively sigh at the apparent hopelessness of our state of being. We are not the first. The Psalms are full of despair: "My guilt has overwhelmed me like a burden too heavy to bear" (Ps. 38:4 NIV). God understands that heavy burden, and He provided a way to resolve it. He declared us not guilty through Christ's death on the cross, yet we continue to hang on to the guilt as though we know more about it than He does.

Several years ago a woman showed up in one of our worship services seeking financial aid. One of our pastors talked to her after the service and discovered that her problems went beyond the realm of finances. Her past included years of addiction to drugs and a history of childhood sexual abuse. After several months, one of our counselors suggested she get treatment for her addiction as a first step to healing. During treatment, she realized that something deeper needed to be addressed. One night, very late, she called the pastor she had originally talked to and said she needed to know how to become a child of God. She had grown up in the church, but she was so overcome with guilt (real and imagined) that she couldn't get close to healing.

He told her, "When you went into the hospital, you couldn't pay for your treatment, so your insurance paid for it. *Jesus was your insurance. You couldn't pay for your sins, so He did.*" That might not seem like a very spiritual version of the gospel, but it was just what she needed to hear! He put her "sin debt" and the "payment plan" in terms that she could relate to. That night the woman accepted Christ as Savior.

But this is not where "and she lived happily ever after" comes in. That happens only in fairy tales. Unable to rid herself of the guilt of a wasted life, she eventually returned to drugs and almost died of an overdose. Unable to trust anyone with her pain, she began to write to the person who had saved her life.

The pain of her past—the realization that she had sinned against God, others, and herself—was more than she could bear. After she relapsed into her addiction, the guilt was so overpowering that it looked hopeless to everyone. For several years she existed in torment, unable to face the day without the drugs to assuage her guilt. In sheer desperation one night she prayed a prayer that many have prayed, "God, either let me die or release me from the pain of my life." The process took time, and it wasn't easy. Contrary to what she (and the rest of us) would prefer, quick fixes rarely occur.

First, she had to come to an understanding of what she was told that night in the hospital—that Jesus had paid the price for her sin (guilt) and that she

In the New Testament, Jesus stressed the importance of right heart attitudes as over against outwardly correct acts, and taught that there are degrees of guilt, depending upon a person's knowledge and motive (Luke 11:29–32; 12:47, 48; 23:34).

no longer had to live under its condemnation. Then she had to reckon with the guilt she had carried around for things that were not her fault.

Finally, she had to deal with the guilt of things she knew she had done to others and to herself. That is what we called true guilt earlier. Dr. David Augsburger addresses this guilt in his book *The Freedom of Forgiveness:* "Guilt is a much maligned emotion. This comes as no surprise to anyone, since the pain that guilt causes is one of the earliest sources of intense inner discomfort. Yet guilt is not only necessary for healthful living, it is a gift to be used wisely as well as a burden to be lifted." We must be able to recognize our wrongs to resolve them, and guilt is the avenue through which we can achieve this.

The path to freedom wasn't easy or painless. However, this woman would tell you that the process was worth it because of the freedom she experiences today. Once she accepted God's forgiveness and the grace that He extended to her, she was able to move to the next step of resolving the guilt she felt for the past that had held her captive. Every part of the process was necessary to reach her final destination—freedom from guilt.

APPLICATION

Every believer needs to understand the grace of God's forgiveness and be able to incorporate it into the daily walk. If you are dealing with guilt that won't allow you to enjoy the peace that God has promised to those who believe in Him, you need to begin the process to discover what is holding you back.

Ask God to renew your mind about who you are in Him and to release you from the guilt, whether it is real or imagined. Perhaps you need the support of a small group in which you can work with others to fully understand God's grace and His acceptance of you. Prayer is essential when a believer is stuck in the pits of unresolved guilt. He wants to give you freedom, and your forgiveness is already in place. Spending time with the One who holds you blameless will lead to the freedom that you search for daily.

GROWTH

In researching what other people have determined about guilt and ways to resolve it, I came across a plan of action in David Augsburger's book *The Freedom of Forgiveness.* He wrote, "Guilt is a goad to prod us toward repentance and forgiveness. Guilt should move us toward regret and perhaps remorse. And remorse is only a step away from repentance." Do you see

GUILT

■ *A feeling of responsibility or remorse for some real or imagined offense.*

> The feeling of being, or not being, forgiven and loved, is not what matters. One must come down to brass tacks. If there is a particular sin on our conscience, repent and confess it. If there isn't, tell the despondent devil not to be silly.
> —C. S. Lewis

the progression of events? The steps to resolving guilt, according to Dr. Augsburger, are these:

1. Face it.
2. Confess it.
3. Forsake it.
4. Live it.

The first step is difficult because of the pain of admission. However, once you can face the guilt, denial can no longer hinder the process, and so you can move to the next step of confession. The old saying, "Confession is good for the soul," is true. First John 1:9 is a standard by which you should abide. There is another side to confession that you might not think of readily—and that is confession of allegiance to Christ and dependence on Him. To confess your total dependence on the grace of God is to free you to take the next step. Forsaking your guilt has to do with constructive sorrow or repentance. It means being willing to turn from the source of your guilt. Finally, it is necessary to live your forgiveness, to live as a forgiven child of God. To do otherwise will result only in continuing false guilt that will destroy any opportunity for intimacy with God and others because of the shame that drives a wedge between you and them. Accept your freedom, and live in the knowledge of the grace that God has extended to you. Live your forgiveness!

QUOTES

To condemn is to blame, to pronounce guilty, to declare unfit for use. No condemnation means that God does not condemn or blame me. He does not reject me. In Christ I have forgiveness.

—Tim Sledge

He touched my mouth with it, and said:
"Behold, this has touched your lips;
Your iniquity is taken away,
And your sin purged."

—Isaiah 6:7

Who shall bring a charge against God's elect? It is God who justifies. Who is he who condemns?

—Romans 8:33–34

Emotionally, we may live so long under guilt and self-condemnation that the very idea of being free is threatening.

—Charles Stanley

Surrender is the positive side. To find release from guilt, you must also confess your faith. A faith in Jesus Christ who removes guilt of all shapes and sizes.

—David A. Augsburger

HARD HEART

■ *The ability to say no to God in spite of overwhelming evidence and pressure to say yes.*

SCRIPTURE

EXODUS 7:3–4

I will harden Pharaoh's heart, and multiply My signs and My wonders in the land of Egypt. But Pharaoh will not heed you.

COMMENTARY

Have you ever met someone who was just plain stubborn? Probably you know people within your circle of friends who insist on having their way. They are hardheaded and obstinate about what they want. Well, God put it another way. God called it a heart problem. A moment of reflection causes us to laugh uncomfortably at the suggestion that we might know something about this self-centeredness—you know, personally. Yet the problem has existed from the beginning of time, documented in the lives of people we read about in Scripture as well as people we live and work with today.

Pharaoh is probably the best illustration in the Bible of a person with a hard heart. He was exposed to the truth over and over again, yet refused to respond accordingly. Notice God said, "*I* will harden Pharaoh's heart." God engineered the situation we read about in Exodus. In doing so God provides us with a blueprint for what happens when a person refuses to accept and bend the will to the truth.

Pharaoh was presented with overwhelming evidence. Plague after plague, sign after sign, miracle after miracle, and still he refused to let the Israelites go. Pharaoh refused to accept God's warnings. Even when faced with undeniable evidence that he was wrong, Pharaoh wouldn't give in. God gave him the ability to act on what was in his heart. Unfortunately, Pharaoh's overexposure and underresponse to truth proved to be extremely costly.

God repeatedly presented Pharaoh with the truth of who He was. Yet Pharaoh wouldn't bow. He refused to acknowledge that another was greater than he. His pride and hard-heartedness almost cost him his kingdom.

In Exodus 7:8–10, we read the account of Aaron's encounter with Pharaoh when he threw his staff on the floor and it turned into a snake. Unimpressed, Pharaoh called in his magicians who repeated the same feat without a blink of the eye. That "anything you can do, I can do better" attitude was obvious in Pharaoh's reaction to Aaron. However, the story didn't end there. In Exodus 7:12, we read, "Every man threw down his rod, and they became serpents. But Aaron's rod swallowed up their rods." The evidence was clear and convincing, or was it? Even in the face of undeniable evidence that there was One mightier than himself, Pharaoh refused to acknowledge God. "And

> **G**od has promised to replace our calloused, stony heart with a new heart of flesh. . . . You will always know when you have a new heart by the attitude change that comes to you.
> —Dick Mills

HARD HEART

Pharaoh's heart grew hard, and he did not heed them, as the LORD had said" (Ex. 7:13).

All of us have experienced the stubborn desire to have things the way we want them, even when "our way" wasn't God's way. That's what Pharaoh was doing. If we are wise, we will learn from his experience. Are the extremes that Pharaoh went to so far-fetched to us as believers today? Every time we say no to God, we skirt the edges of a "once too often" rebellion, stubbornly asserting our selfish will over God's will for our lives. Just as Pharaoh stubbornly clenched his fist and said no over and over to God, we cannot do that for long without developing a hard heart that will lead to destruction.

God has given us example after example to clear up any confusion on our part. Nevertheless, we stand in danger of following in the footsteps of Pharaoh if we refuse to submit to God's standard. The more we can be duped into believing that we're right and God is wrong, the more we are in danger of developing a hard heart.

Although we must be careful, we need not despair. We can rejoice in the graciousness of God as we study the blueprint (or lesson) He gave us. The very reason I believe God initiated this entire sequence of events was to provide us with a lesson plan for *not* following in the way of Pharaoh. God wouldn't leave us without a way to experience victory over our tendencies to assert our rights over God's truth. It's our responsibility to study the lesson and apply its truth to our lives.

> **N**obody talks so constantly about God as those who insist that there is no God.
> —Heywood Broun

A CLOSER LOOK

Let's be honest. We all want things the way *we* want them. We all want what we want when we want it. I'm more comfortable when things are the way I like them. Most people are. The tension comes into play when what we want is not what God wants, when the two conflict. Refusal to act on the truth time and time again will corrode the heart of the believer until nothing can melt the hardness.

Paul wrote, "Although they knew God, they did not glorify Him as God, nor were thankful, but became futile in their thoughts, and their foolish hearts were darkened" (Rom. 1:21). It's dangerous to say no to the truth because there will come a time when God allows us to have our own way: "Even as they did not like to retain God in their knowledge, God gave them over to a debased mind, to do those things which are not fitting" (Rom. 1:28). You can count on this: frequently saying no to God will eventually result in God's letting you have your way. Sounds pretty good? Don't bet on

Hard Heart

HARD HEART

■ *The ability to say no to God in spite of overwhelming evidence and pressure to say yes.*

> **I**n whatever man does without God, he must either fail miserably, or succeed more miserably.
> —George MacDonald

> **G**od cannot give us happiness and peace apart from Himself, because it is not there. There is no such thing.
> —C. S. Lewis

it. How many children have cheered their independence from Mom and Dad only to weep in the dark of the night because they discovered that having their own way was not always as appealing as it seemed?

To avoid the pitfalls that are sure to occur in our paths, we must understand the danger signs of a hard heart. Otherwise, we can and will rationalize ourselves right into disaster! The saga of Pharaoh supplies us with signs to use as a checklist for a hard heart.

The first sign (and one that we all struggle with) is *stubbornness*. Pharaoh was eaten up with a stubborn spirit when confronted with God's truth. We can't point a finger at him, however, without pointing it at ourselves. It's the way we react when we know we shouldn't do something, and we respond, "I know I shouldn't, but I'm going to anyway." When we have been confronted with truth over and over again, our lack of response to God demonstrates a hard heart that no doctor can fix.

A lack of concern for spiritual things is the second sign of a hard heart and is evidence that God's work is second to our own. An insensitivity to God's work is a sure sign that we are developing a hard heart. A lack of concern for spiritual things means that you are more concerned about your business than God's business. The selfishness of that attitude is evidence that when God's business gets in the way of your plans, you choose to do things the way things work best for you.

Ignoring the testimony of other people demonstrates the making of a hard heart. Similarly, when a person repeatedly *ignores undeniable evidence,* there is no doubt that he is developing a hard heart. Together these two tendencies combine to make up the fourth sign of a hard heart. Whether the evidence comes via a person or an event, ignoring it can result in tragic consequences.

The fourth sign of a hard heart is *recognizing need (sin) and refusing to deal with it.* Many Christians sort of feel good about feeling bad. They know cheating on income tax is wrong, but they do it anyway. They understand that there is a speed limit for a reason, but speeding is just something they do. They shake the pastor's hand on Sunday and with great sincerity say, "That sermon sure did step on my toes, pastor!" I know, as do most pastors, that they are victims of the "feeling convicted" syndrome. They have no intention of doing anything about their sin. They just feel bad for a time. And feeling bad relieves some of the guilt. But that's as far as it goes.

The fifth sign of a hard heart is *pride*. It could be summed up as the "I know better than anyone else" disease. Men suffer from this disease quite often. We pretend to be experts about everything. No matter what anyone else says, our way is the right way. Often it is hard for us to take instruction from anyone. When we know we are wrong, we argue instead of facing up to it. And the tragedy is, everybody knows our problem is pride. Pride is a sign of a hard heart. The root of Pharaoh's hard-heartedness was pride. He considered himself a god. He wasn't about to let some other God get the best of him.

The sixth sign of a hard heart is *acknowledging sin but making a deal with God*. Instead of turning from sin, we rationalize it and try to make deals with God so that we can continue sinning and not be plagued by our consciences. Think about the young man who is scared he has gotten his date pregnant. It would be interesting, at best, to listen in and hear him try to make a deal with God: "God, if You will just fix it where she's not pregnant, I will go to church on Sunday, and I'll even volunteer to help out with the three-year-olds! After all, it takes two, and it just happened!" Do you think God is impressed one bit? A woman who plays the same game, blaming her plight on the man she chose to be with, is just as guilty of the attempt to bargain with God. While we may attempt to make deals with God, our efforts lead to more problems, and the gap between His truth and our desires gets wider as our hearts harden.

> When man forsakes the fountain of living water, he cannot get rid of the thirst . . . and there is still within him the same absolute necessity for a revelation of God.
> —Joseph S. Exell

We should have thankful hearts that the signs of a developing hard heart are made unmistakably clear to us. We don't have to wonder or assume things, for God has given us a description of the problem and what we must do. We can promise and bargain and rationalize, but unless we come to an accurate understanding of our purpose on earth, we will miserably fail in our efforts to succeed. It's not our behavior that needs to change so much (although it certainly needs to change) as it is our hearts that need restoring. Once that happens, behavior will change, and we will know what is right or wrong. We sometimes focus too much on changing behaviors when we should be focused on doing what will result in changed hearts.

We must be sure of two things when we contemplate the problems of a hard heart: (1) the warning signs or red flags that God has given us through Scripture, and (2) how to avoid taking the same road Pharaoh did. Applying the truth that we've obtained through study is the key to victory in this (or any) situation!

APPLICATION

The confusion that comes with saying a continual no to God is evidenced every day in the things that we don't give a second thought to. Some people think that because they tolerate soap operas on television or don't protest the smut that is flashed on the movie screens of our nation, they have become

HARD HEART

more mature or sophisticated. *As we grow as Christians, sin should bother us more, not less.* Yet every day we spend hours being entertained by the very sin Christ died for! We rent it at the video store, view it at the theater, watch it on television, or read it in books. "But I never thought of it that way, pastor." Why? Over time, we have changed the rules, and our hearts have come to accept things that we wouldn't have dreamed we'd accept a few years ago. Do you remember when bad language really bothered you? Perhaps now it hardly affects you. That's a sign of a hard heart.

Our response to truth determines whether our hearts will be hardened or remain pliable and ready to have God make them after His own. Unless we allow God to apply the truth that we know, we acknowledge what we know and continue to go our own way. Again, it's a sure sign of a hard heart.

GROWTH

There is only one absolute answer to the problem of a hard heart. Nothing short of honest repentance will bring about the change needed. I don't mean rededicating your life. I'm talking about allowing God to change your heart to the point where your no becomes a yes to His truth. True repentance manifests itself in a changed life.

Results happen when you understand the big picture. God's priority for you is that you take Him seriously when He says, "Go into the world and change it!" When you lead people to know Christ as Savior, you change the world. Recognizing that puts your response to truth in a totally different perspective. You're not in this world just for your pleasure or well-being. God put you here for a purpose, and it was not to spend your days fulfilling selfish needs at the expense of those He would have you bring to know Him personally.

Putting all things into perspective, if you continue to insist on your way, there will come a time when God's truth no longer matters to you at all. When Paul wrote in Romans that "God gave them over to a debased mind" (Rom. 1:28), he made sure that we understood what would happen to us if we continued to insist on our way long enough. God will back off and let you have what you think you want! Sounds great until the reality of your depravity destroys your life and the lives of others.

Perhaps you would benefit by returning to the signs of a hard heart. Does one (or more) jump out of the page at you? You have to understand the big picture to understand why developing a hard heart can bring about disaster—not just in your life but in the lives of those whom Christ wants you to bring to Him.

HARD HEART

God's tender mercy and grace are proven cures for the hard heart. Humble yourself before God, and receive His unconditional forgiveness. Select specific Scriptures that apply to your circumstances. Focus on the goodness and love for Christ who can transform a hard heart into one that responds obediently and cheerfully.

RESTITUTION

■ *The act of making good or compensating for loss, damage, or injury.*

MATTHEW 5:23–24

Therefore if you bring your gift to the altar, and there remember that your brother has something against you, leave your gift there before the altar, and go your way. First be reconciled to your brother, and then come and offer your gift.

Has it ever happened to you? You're right in the middle of time with God when you remember something that happened months ago. You just can't turn the thought off. Needless to say, these times are at the very least uncomfortable and, if unresolved, can affect your relationships with your family, your coworkers, and God.

The principle of restitution is a key concept in the New Testament. Making right a wrong isn't just good morality; it's thoroughly biblical. Our relationships with others are of vital concern to the Father. As we find in Matthew 5, commonly known as the Sermon on the Mount, there is specific reference to this dilemma with instruction on what to do. Jesus lays out the perfect plan for those who are devoted to God. The pure in heart. The peacemakers. The description of a godly man or woman is beautifully portrayed within the more familiar verses of this sermon. Yet many times we fail to continue our study and, thus, fail to recognize the importance of what Jesus was saying to those present in His admonition regarding their personal relationships and unresolved issues.

Jesus did not admonish the crowd on the mountain to get their hearts right with God. Instead, He urged them to put God on hold for a time! "First be reconciled" (Matt. 5:24). The term translated "reconciled" is used only here in the New Testament. It literally means "change." In other words, "Change things." Do whatever you have to do to right a wrong.

This directive leaves no doubt that getting things right with God isn't enough. There are other people to consider. Our relationship with the Father doesn't let us off the hook for things we did that hurt other people, things for which we never attempted to make restitution. He said, "First be reconciled . . . and [second] then come and offer your gift." As much as we would like to forget the past and reap the benefits of being new creatures in Christ, Jesus observed that our relationship with God is affected by the way we deal with our past.

When you consider this passage in light of personal experience, you may note that you're doing a great job at being faithful in your relationship with

RESTITUTION

God. You have your quiet time every day. You tithe. Then when you least expect it, you remember! It could be any number of things. A financial obligation that you haven't taken care of—and worse, you've avoided the calls from the one you owed. It could be that you injured someone in an accident and left the scene. Perhaps you lied on a job application. The possibilities are endless. The bottom line is, there are people you've hurt, people you've offended, and you've never resolved the situation.

"But that was a long time ago" is a familiar excuse. Or, "God has forgiven me" sounds pretty good. "I wasn't a Christian then" and "They have probably forgotten" are excuses I hear all too often. And though all of these statements may be true, a person of character must take responsibility for actions now, tomorrow, and yesterday!

You can't be right with God while something is wrong between you and another person and you are to blame for the conflict. The reason for the connection is that the main thing that distinguishes a believer from the rest of the world is *love for others*. When God leads you to deal with the past wrongs and you don't, progress stops. There is an obstacle in your relationship with God that cannot be solved until you deal with the problem.

Why? God will not be used. Jesus paid a high price to reconcile us to Himself. We are responsible for working restitution. Zacchaeus understood the connection between what he did in regard to others and his relationship with God. He paid back those he owed four times as much as he stole from them! No matter what we try to tell ourselves, the consequences of unresolved hurts will affect us despite our best efforts to deny the truth.

One of the first consequences is the sincerity of our prayers, our services, and our counsel. There will always be the nagging thought: *Yeah, but what about that time when . . . ?* As long as someone is back there that you know you need to call or write or repay, you will never be able to put your whole heart into your service or your pursuit of God. It is like carrying around extra weight; it taxes you mentally, emotionally, and oftentimes physically. Many people struggle with attitudes and habits that they can't shake, and the reason is they have never taken responsibility for their past actions.

The second consequence is that Christianity becomes ritual instead of relational. People who refuse to deal with the past often do and say all of the "right" religious things. Yet as time goes on, they put less and less heart into it, and God seems a bit distant. A quick survey of people seated around you on Sunday morning might pose quite a picture. The women are dressed just right. The men have on their best suits. Children are groomed better than they'd like to be! The smiles are polished and the handshakes are firm.

The command is clear: Go. Both parties are obligated to seek reconciliation, no matter who is at fault (and often both are, to some extent). As Jay Adams points out in *The Christian Counselor's Manual*, ". . . ideally they ought to meet one another on the way to each other's house seeking reconciliation."
—Matt Waymeyer

Restitution is different from reparation in that the latter normally involves the repairing or replacement of damaged goods or property, whereas restitution has a much wider legal and ethical scope.

RESTITUTION

■ *The act of making good or compensating for loss, damage, or injury.*

Yet inside there is a terrible feeling, and the thought comes through, *I wonder if they know about . . . ?* The guilt of unresolved relationships is a primary reason why some Christians live defeated lives. They try to live as new creatures while strangling on the guilt of past sin that has never been resolved.

The third consequence is limited intimacy. This is a direct result of the fear that someone will find out about the past, which automatically creates a sense of isolation and aloneness. I think about men who fathered children and walked away. The fear of someone discovering the dark part of the past that they've tried to escape will always result in a lack of intimacy in any new relationships that such men will encounter. It is something that cannot be avoided when there are unresolved relationships.

APPLICATION

If you want to know how important this whole idea of restitution is, turn the idea around for a moment. What difference would it make to you if someone who really hurt you came back and made things right? For example, what if the parent who rejected you a long time ago showed up at your doorstep and apologized? What would happen if the boss who treated you so badly apologized? What if that old friend who stabbed you in the back came back to say, "I'm sorry"? What would happen if that ex-spouse called to apologize?

For many, it would be the beginning of healing. That is why God insists that we take time out to deal with the past so that we can then be ministered to in our relationship with Him.

It might be a bitter pill for us to swallow as Christians, but there are times when it seems that secular methodology has a better grip on matters of the heart than we do. Members of Alcoholics Anonymous have long understood the importance of making restitution.

A friend who once belonged to this organization gave me the solution that AA has found to handling problems of the past—which are many for those who become members. As a part of the twelve steps, restitution is found in steps eight and nine where members pledge, "We became willing to make amends to those we had harmed," and then "Made amends to such people, except when to do so would injure them or others." My friend advises me that those who find sobriety have discovered the importance of not carrying around the extra weight of conflicts that remain unresolved. These two steps present a picture of one becoming willing to take responsibility for the past and then doing something about it.

Forgiveness and reconciliation through Christ bridge the gap between God and man and between man and man to overcome the distance and alienation due to race, culture, and religion (Eph. 2:11–22).

RESTITUTION

The problem with making restitution is that it means you have to deal with some unpleasant situations from the past that you'd rather ignore or forget. However, as a believer, you must face up to the past to fully experience the intimacy that God withholds for those who are willing to abide by His principles. He said to love one another, and it's impossible to do that with past offenses hanging over your head.

Consider these two things as you think about the past and what you need to make restitution for: (1) what you are giving up by holding on to the past, and (2) what you could gain by writing the letter, making the phone call, or dropping by the place of business that you've avoided for so long. You are giving up peace of mind and peace with God. If you become willing to take responsibility, you will gain the opportunity to express love and experience it.

If you are ready to take responsibility for your past actions as well as for what you do today, I urge you to ask God's guidance and, then with His strength, to begin changing the past. Some things you can't change. Others you can. Start from the point where you know you can begin to make restitution, and God will open doors for you to achieve what He demands you do—be reconciled to others.

God, grant me the serenity to accept the things I cannot change, the courage to change the things I can, and the wisdom to know the difference.

—Serenity Prayer

WORLDLINESS

■ *Having the same purpose, perspective, and priority as those who live in this world but who do not know God; being of the world.*

JOHN 17:14–18

I have given them Your word; and the world has hated them because they are not of the world, just as I am not of the world. I do not pray that You should take them out of the world, but that You should keep them from the evil one. They are not of the world, just as I am not of the world. Sanctify them by Your truth. Your word is truth. As You sent Me into the world, I also have sent them into the world.

COMMENTARY

It is a marvelous thing that our Intercessor prays for us. This particular prayer was in light of the following chapters that would record His trial, His death, His resurrection, and His ascension. The Lord Jesus, knowing that He would be leaving soon, prayed for those of us who would be staying.

Why would He pray that? He knew the Holy Spirit would come to equip those He left behind, so why would He be so focused on praying for those left in the world? He had spent three years primarily with twelve men. As God, He knew all about them. As man, He had walked and talked with them. He knew how easily they could fall prey to the world's charm.

We need to take a closer look at how vulnerable we are and at the One who left us here *in* the world but continues to intercede for us that we may not be *of* the world.

A CLOSER LOOK

I believe we would agree that as those who belong to Jesus Christ, we are called to be *in* the world but not *of* it (v. 16). But on a practical level, what does that mean? We use the freeway system of this world; we shop at the world's grocery stores; we use the world's school systems; we buy at the world's malls; we go to the hospitals of this world.

So what are we to do?

But there is more to it than that. When Jesus was praying in John 17, His very first prayer request was, "Holy Father, keep [them] through Your name . . . that they may be one as We are" (v. 11). He was not talking about essence. He was talking about function.

Jesus' number one prayer request was extremely practical. He knew that He faced the Cross. He knew that the disciples would be without Him. He knew that they needed to function as He and the Father had functioned.

WORLDLINESS

He knew the potential to defect lay in all the disciples. And in us. Thus He prayed, "I do not pray that You should take them out of the world, but that You should keep them from the evil one" (John 17:15). In other words, He didn't want them to go on any tangents or to get sidetracked. He wanted them to be stable, dependable. The enemy wanted them unstable, easily distracted.

The same battle is raging. I feel it just as you do.

After Jesus prayed for them to be one—to function as one in His new system of life—He prayed for them to be sanctified: "Sanctify them by Your truth. Your word is truth" (John 17:17). Jesus was not talking about a second work of grace. The word *sanctify* means to "set apart for a special purpose."

Those called-out ones had a special purpose. They were set apart. Not set aside. Set apart. Different. Upstream kind of guys. Not only were they otherworldly, in a proper sense, they were also other purposed from those around them. They probably were not the most popular people around. Upstream people aren't.

They had known since He called them that *He* had a special purpose, but now He was talking to the Father about *their* special purpose. Jesus prayed, "And for their sakes I sanctify Myself, that they also may be sanctified by the truth" (John 17:19). It's like a steady stream from the Father to the Son to the disciples to the world with glory back to the Father. Jesus was setting Himself apart all the way to the Cross. The disciples needed to set themselves apart to proclaim what He did. The stream dare not be clogged by a filthy world system or disciples who wanted to be their "own man."

Disciples today have the same criteria. The same privilege. We need to function as one in His system and purpose. We need to be set apart and get in on what He started two thousand years ago. Can you imagine any greater privilege than being linked in purpose with the God of the universe?

You live "in order that _____." What? Fill in the blank. If you define your purpose in living, you can pretty well tell whether your purpose is the same as others. Is your goal to take the message of eternal life from the Father through the Son to you to the world? Does that drive you? Is that your greatest passion? Is that why you get up in the morning?

Or is your greatest passion to own a house, car, or boat or have CEO as your job description? The world operates like this: every man for himself; get all you can.

Not only is our *purpose* to be opposite from the world's purpose, but our *perspective* is to be different from the world's.

John seemed to refer to this order and system in relationship to thinking, ideas, and motivation. He wrote later, "Do not love the world or the things

> The socially prescribed affluent, middle-class lifestyle has become so normative in our churches that we discern little conflict between it and the Christian lifestyle prescribed in the New Testament.
> —Tony Campolo

> Surveys suggest that American Christians may be far more worldly than we realize.
> —Paul Benware

> A society that pursues pleasure runs the risk of raising expectations ever higher, so that true contentment always lies tantalizingly out of reach.
> —Paul Brand and Philip Yancey

WORLDLINESS

in the world. If anyone loves the world, the love of the Father is not in him. For all that is in the world—the lust of the flesh, the lust of the eyes, and the pride of life—is not of the Father but is of the world. And the world is passing away" (1 John 2:15–17).

Worldliness is a permeating perspective. So what exactly is the world's perspective? "Me, myself, and I." That is, what makes me happy and what makes my family comfortable.

If our purpose is to be a vital link in the eternal purpose of giving the Word of the Father to the world, how should our perspective be different from the world's? If it's not "me, myself, and I," what is it?

If our perspective is today centered, it is exactly like the world's. We need to sing more often, "This world is not my home, I'm just a passin' through." We act a lot like settlers instead of "sojourners and pilgrims," as Peter talked about (1 Peter 2:11). It was the same Peter who earlier asked Jesus, "See, we have left all and followed You. Therefore what shall we have?" (Matt. 19:27).

We can't be too hard on Peter as if the question has never occurred to us. Peter was talking about the here and now. Jesus responded with a "then and there" answer: "When the Son of Man sits on the throne of His glory . . ." (Matt. 19:28).

This present world isn't all there is. We've heard the expression, "They live like there's no tomorrow." How descriptive of the world's perspective! But is it descriptive of ours as well?

Moses' perspective is a profound example of otherworldly thinking. The writer of Hebrews tells about Moses' life, but one verse sums it all up: "Esteeming the reproach of Christ greater riches than the treasures in Egypt; for he looked to the reward" (Heb. 11:26). He knew a better day was coming. He knew this world isn't the stopping point. Moses considered, counted the cost (and it was a pretty hefty price for him), and contemplated eternity. Eternity won out over Egypt.

If eternity doesn't permeate our here and now, we are living exactly like the world. Our perspective is wrong. But if we live with eternity's values in view, our perspective is Christlike.

Not only are our purpose and perspective to be unlike this world's, but priorities are to be different as well.

When considering our priorities, let's look at Luke 12:34: "For where your treasure is, there your heart will be also."

Jesus spoke more on our "treasure" than on any subject other than the kingdom of God. He went right to the heart of the matter. Right to the core of our priorities. He was kind of saying, "Look at your checkbook. Where's your priority?"

In one sense, this is an easier test than the rest because it's more black and white. We can get a bit off target trying to figure our purpose and perspective, but a checkbook ledger is concrete. Jesus was saying that how you spend your money is a primary indicator of where your heart is.

We have in common with the world the need for food, clothing, and shelter. The world spends most waking hours figuring out how to have the best food, the best clothing, and the best shelter. That's high on the priority list.

Christians also need to have food, clothes, and shelter. In the Sermon on the Mount when Jesus was discussing the three categories, He said, "For after all these things the Gentiles seek. For your heavenly Father knows that you need all these things. But seek first the kingdom of God and His righteousness, and all these things shall be added to you" (Matt. 6:32–33).

If we take care of His priority—reaching the world—He takes care of our needs. We seek to tell about His kingdom, and He makes sure we have the things we need to live.

We understand our possessions are only tools to reach the lost, but we have somewhere learned that if we polish and hoard our things, we are wonderful stewards of what God has given us. He says, "Nope, that's not even close. Use them to reach the lost!"

Everything we have belongs to the One who gave it to us in the first place, and we are managers of His things. You're right, the world would think we are ludicrous in this. But that's okay. We aren't out to win any popularity contests; we are out to win people.

Possessions are not just tools; they really are a test. When we buy something, we don't hear a voice out of heaven saying, "This is a test. This is only a test. In the event of a real . . ." But the way we use our money and our things is really a test of where the heart is and who is Lord in our lives: "Do not lay up for yourselves treasures on earth . . . but lay up for yourselves treasures in heaven. . . . For where your treasure is, there your heart will be also" (Matt. 6:19–21).

We need to change our thinking and ask, "How much can I get into the kingdom?" Ask God to help you make this a thought process. Ask Him how you can turn the temporal into the eternal. And remember, good stewardship is using things to reach others until you can't use them anymore. Hoarding is not a scriptural principle, even if it has leather seats.

Possessions are also a trademark of the ultimate lordship of Jesus Christ in our lives. To think otherwise is worldly.

> Ten years ago, Americans spent $300 billion on leisure and recreation. Today it has probably doubled.
> —Tim Hansel

> Two out of three adults (63 percent) concur that the purpose of life is enjoyment and personal fulfillment.

> Fifty-two percent of adults assert that in the end, their first responsibility is to themselves.

WORLDLINESS

We have looked at how our purpose is different from that of the world; our perspective is different from that of the world; and our priority is different from that of the world.

Up to this point, we have looked at the internal focus of our lives. Let's look for a while at the external. Almost everyone is familiar with Romans 12:1–2. Paul urges us to present our bodies to God because that's a reasonable act of service. In verse 2, he tells us not to be conformed to this world.

Basically, Paul is writing for us to change our way of thinking. In the same verse when he tells us to prove what the will of God is, the word *prove* means to "discern, sort out, and weed through external issues." He wants us to saturate our minds with truth. The world does a marvelous job saturating us with error. All we have to do is watch television commercials to see that. Reading the newspaper or watching the news will surely convince us that we need to renew our minds with truth and to discern all day long.

GROWTH

Since the antidote for worldliness is a renewed mind, let's look at some specific truths from God's Word that fly in the face of the world's philosophy.

First, "For as we have many members in one body, but all the members do not have the same function . . ." (Rom. 12:4). *God's truth:* the world does not revolve around you. You can exercise your spiritual gift because others exercise theirs. It's body life. *The world's lie:* you are number one, and if you don't look out for number one, no one else will.

Second, "'Vengeance is Mine, I will repay,' says the Lord" (Rom. 12:19). *God's truth:* you back off from trying to repay those who have offended you and leave it to God. (I agree, it's harder than it sounds.) *The world's lie:* "You get me, I'll get you back."

Third, "Owe no one anything except to love one another" (Rom. 13:8). *God's truth:* you need to love—and dote on—others just like you do yourself. *The world's lie:* love is totally conditional on the other person and how you happen to feel at the time.

Fourth, "Receive one who is weak in the faith, but not to disputes over doubtful things" (Rom. 14:1; note verses throughout the rest of the chapter). *God's truth:* learn to accept someone with different opinions without passing judgment. *The world's lie:* "There's one view of this situation, and it's mine. Don't bother me with the facts. I have a perfect right to my opinion, so don't mess with me or it."

We are indeed free in Christ, but if we retain this freedom and our rights to do anything we want, not caring whether or not it hinders others' growth,

Fifty-six percent of adults strongly agreed that each of us has the power to determine our own destiny.

we are worldly. The world holds tightly to rights, and if we, under the spiritual guise of freedom grip ours as tightly, we are pressed into the world's way of thinking and acting.

Fifth, "We then who are strong ought to bear with the scruples of the weak, and not to please ourselves" (Rom. 15:1; vv. 2–6). *God's truth:* get involved. There are hundreds of places where we could get involved and "not to please ourselves." The emphasis in the rest of the verses is encouragement to the weak, that is, those who are without emotional strength. That takes effort. That takes time. And that takes selflessness. *The world's lie:* don't get involved. Life goes so fast—you have a job to work, bills to be paid, places to go, things to do, children to raise. Why let someone emotionally weak sap your precious strength? It doesn't make sense. I mean, after all, what's the payoff for you?

Sixth, "Wherefore, accept one another, just as Christ also accepted us" (Rom. 15:7; vv. 8–13 NASB). *God's truth:* remember how Christ accepted you. Jesus Christ stepped out of the ultimate comfort zone—heaven—to mingle with you. Can you do any less with others who are so different from you? *The world's lie:* hang around with those who are like you. You'll be more comfortable. They'll be more comfortable. You'll mesh.

Each of those truths deals with externals: how you view yourself, revenge, government, love, differing opinions, emotionally weak people, and acceptance of others who are different from you. But God's truth is so diametrically opposed to the world's way of thinking, is it any wonder we are to be transformed in the way we think?

The Lord Jesus Christ is still praying for us. He wants us to be in the world but not of it.

> **L**ess than half of born-again Christians who attend evangelical churches strongly agreed that they have the responsibility to share their convictions with people who hold different beliefs.

He who dies with the most toys . . . still dies.
—Anonymous

 QUOTE

DOCTRINE

The scriptural process by which God establishes a relationship with the person who trusts in Christ as Savior.

ADOPTION

ROMANS 8:15–16

SCRIPTURE

For you did not receive the spirit of bondage again to fear, but you received the Spirit of adoption by whom we cry out, "Abba, Father." The Spirit Himself bears witness with our spirit that we are children of God.

COMMENTARY

Paul encouraged us to think of our heavenly Father in the most intimate way, as a Daddy. This relationship is in contrast to one of fear, which commonly existed between a slave and a master. God desires an intimate relationship with us. He has taken it upon Himself to remove every possible barrier.

Paul echoes the same idea in his letter to the Galatians: "But when the fullness of the time had come, God sent forth His Son, born of a woman, born under the law, to redeem those who were under the law, that we might receive the adoption as sons" (Gal. 4:4–5).

Paul makes the connection between adoption and justification. The grammar of these verses indicates that our justification was merely a means to an end. God's ultimate goal in salvation is the relationship made available through our adoption. A necessary step in that direction is being declared not guilty.

Whereas Jesus speaks of our being born into the family of God (John 3:3), Paul uses the term *adoption*. Both are pictures of the same spiritual reality—those who were outside the family being brought into the family. Again, the emphasis is relationship—Father and child.

A CLOSER LOOK

God does not intend for us to consider Him a stern Judge peering over the bench at the accused. Yet many believers have this perception of Him. For some reason they never get out of the courtroom and into the family room. To them, God is always a Judge and never a Father.

This view is so unfortunate. But even worse, it is a precursor to doubting other basic doctrines of the faith. I've talked with Christians who fear that the gavel may strike again—this time with a guilty verdict. The good news is that after the Judge pronounced us not guilty, He welcomed us into His family. That is apparent from Jesus' words in John's gospel: "Most assuredly, I say to you, he who hears My word and believes in Him who sent Me has everlasting life, and shall not come into judgment, but has passed from death into life" (John 5:24).

Adoption

ADOPTION

■ *The scriptural process by which God establishes a relationship with the person who trusts in Christ as Savior.*

As a believer, you will never be judged for your sins. That is a settled issue. It is so settled in the mind of God that at the moment of your salvation, knowing all the sins you were yet to commit, God adopted you into His family.

Let me say again, adopting us into His family was not a courtesy God extended to poor, wretched sinners. It was His goal from the very beginning. And not just from our very beginning but from the beginning of time: "Just as He chose us in Him before the foundation of the world . . . in love, having predestined us to adoption as sons by Jesus Christ to Himself" (Eph. 1:4–5). God chose to adopt you as His child before the foundation of the world. Why? For one reason and one reason only: He wanted to. That is what Paul means by the phrase, "according to the good pleasure of His will" (Eph. 1:5). No one forced Him. God wanted you as His child. God did not send Christ to die because He felt sorry for you. He sacrificed His only begotten Son so that He could make you His adopted child.

I have heard of many unwanted pregnancies; I have never heard of an unwanted adoption. Couples adopt children because they want children. God adopted you into His family for the same reason. He knew your shortcomings. He knew your inconsistencies. He knew all about you. But He wanted you just the same.

APPLICATION

Paul's reliance on the concept of adoption is a strong argument for eternal security. To lose your salvation, you would have to be unadopted. Within that errant system there must also be provision for readoption. The very idea sounds ludicrous. If the logistics of such a belief system are not enough to make you wonder, consider the relational problems. Could you really put your total trust in a heavenly Father who may unadopt you?

Let me put it another way. Can we pledge unconditional loyalty to a God who promises only conditional loyalty in return? Isn't it unrealistic to think that we could ever grow comfortable thinking of God as our Dad when we know that if we drift away and fall into sin, the relationship will be severed?

Persons holding to a view that allows for someone to be unadopted must confront another major theological hurdle. Why would God choose before the foundation of the world to adopt someone He knew He would eventually dismiss from His family? To believe we can be unadopted is to believe that we are able to thwart the predestined will of God!

The permanency of our adoption is best illustrated by Jesus Himself: "A certain man had two sons. And the younger of them said to his father,

ADOPTION

'Father, give me the portion of goods that falls to me'" (Luke 15:11–12). With those words Jesus had His audience's undivided attention. From what we understand of first-century Jewish culture, no son with any respect for his father would dare demand his share of the inheritance. To make things worse, the younger son was making the request. What he did was unthinkable!

Jesus continued, "So he divided to them his livelihood. And not many days after, the younger son gathered all together, journeyed to a far country, and there wasted his possessions with prodigal living" (Luke 15:12–13). Not only did he demand his share of the inheritance, but the younger son left town with it. Apparently, he had no concern for his father's welfare. He was concerned only about himself. So he took the money, went to a distant country, and squandered his gift.

No doubt Jesus' listeners were rehearsing in their minds what they thought the disrespectful brat deserved. How dare he take such a large portion of his father's hard-earned estate and throw it away!

But then the story took a surprising turn: "But when he had spent all, there arose a severe famine in that land, and he began to be in want. Then he went and joined himself to a citizen of that country, and he sent him into his fields to feed swine. And he would gladly have filled his stomach with the pods that the swine ate, and no one gave him anything" (Luke 15:14–16). The crowd must have become almost nauseous as Jesus described the condition in which the boy found himself. The Pharisees would not go near swine, much less feed them. By definition, the young man was ceremonially unclean.

They listened carefully as Jesus continued:

> When he came to himself, he said, "How many of my father's hired servants have bread enough and to spare, and I perish with hunger! I will arise and go to my father, and will say to him, 'Father, I have sinned against heaven and before you, and I am no longer worthy to be called your son. Make me like one of your hired servants.'" And he arose and came to his father (Luke 15:17–20).

I imagine everyone who heard Jesus that day had an opinion about what the father should say or do when the boy began the speech. I doubt any of them would have ended the parable the way Jesus did: "But when he was still a great way off, his father saw him and had compassion, and ran and fell on his neck and kissed him" (Luke 15:20).

> **G**od's adopted son has the right of access to the Father and a share in the divine inheritance.

ADOPTION

■ *The scriptural process by which God establishes a relationship with the person who trusts in Christ as Savior.*

The Pharisees must have cringed at the thought of embracing someone who had spent time feeding swine. Jesus then added,

> The son said to him, "Father, I have sinned against heaven and in your sight, and am no longer worthy to be called your son." But the father said to his servants, "Bring out the best robe and put it on him, and put a ring on his hand and sandals on his feet. And bring the fatted calf here and kill it, and let us eat and be merry; for this my son was dead and is alive again; he was lost and is found." And they began to be merry (Luke 15:21–24).

Culturally speaking, what Jesus described in the parable was a worst-case scenario. The son could not have been more disrespectful. He could not have been more insensitive. And he certainly could not have been a greater embarrassment to the family.

No one would have blamed the father if he had refused to allow the son to work for him as a menial servant. The son didn't deserve a second chance, and he knew it. He recognized how foolish it would be to return as a member of the family. That was not a consideration. In his mind, he had forfeited all the rights to sonship. He was of the conviction that by abandoning his father and wasting his inheritance, he had relinquished his position in the family.

His father, however, had a different perspective. In his mind, once a son, always a son. The father's first emotion as he saw his son returning wasn't anger. It wasn't disappointment. He felt compassion for him. Why? Because the young man was his son!

The father said, "This my son was dead and is alive again" (Luke 15:24). He did not say, "This was my son, and now he is my son again." On the contrary, there is no hint that the relationship was ever broken, only the fellowship.

The imagery of adoption is a powerful one. It is powerful because it is volitional on the part of God; He chose to adopt us. Also, it is a powerful picture because it is permanent. Once a child, always a child.

It is by the Spirit that we have an inner assurance of our identity as children of the Father, and it is by the Spirit that we can know our Father intimately and maintain a relationship of love with him.
—Gordon T. Smith

■ *Confidence that one is a child of God forever.*

ASSURANCE

1 JOHN 5:13

SCRIPTURE

These things I have written to you who believe in the name of the Son of God, that you may know that you have eternal life.

COMMENTARY

John's first epistle was written to Christians to assure them that they were in the faith and that God is true to His Word. This is the same John who wrote the familiar words, "For God so loved the world that He gave His only begotten Son, that whoever believes in Him should not perish but have everlasting life" (John 3:16).

John was reminding believers in his epistle what he had written in his gospel. God loved. God gave. We believe. We have. Period.

I love the phrase "that you may know that you have eternal life" (1 John 5:13). He did not say "hope so" or "wish so" or "maybe have." What comfort would that be? He said "know." Assured of; confident of; insured for eternity.

A CLOSER LOOK

It would be a terrible thing for children—or adults—to wonder how they fit in their families. When I was growing up, I never really knew if my stepfather would be in a good mood or a bad mood. The uneasiness in my young soul often was troublesome.

And while that is terrible in an earthly family, it is even more unsettling in the spiritual family. Many Christians live with the thought that they are just not sure how God sees them. Is He in a good mood or a judgmental mood? Are they in the family, or has their Father decided He has had enough?

What a horrible way to live! How incredibly sad for children of the King to live as beggars! I surely am not being critical. I find it heartbreaking for people whose sin debt has been paid in full to squirm under the uncertainty of whether they belong in the family of God.

Let's look at some basic reasons people tend to doubt their salvation:

First, *sin in their lives*. Sin brings a feeling of estrangement from God, a feeling of isolation. In John's first epistle, he warns Christians to take close inventory of their salvation if they continue in sin and do so merrily and often and long: "No one who is born of God practices sin, because His seed abides in him" (1 John 3:9 NASB). In other words, if sin is the constant bent of your life, you should wonder about your salvation.

ASSURANCE

> **K**ept by His power—
> that is the only safety.
> —Oswald Chambers

On the other hand, if you sin and feel perfectly miserable, this is really an indication that you belong to Him. The non-Christian can sin all day long and not sense any isolation from God; only His children experience a lack of harmony with their Father.

But sin in the life damages faith and could make someone doubt his salvation.

Second, *false teaching*. This false teaching is primarily in two camps. The first camp includes liberal pastors who do not hold to the view that all the Bible is the Word of God. They discount certain parts, verses, and authors. How is a person to know 1 John 5:13 is even in the Book to stand on it? Or John 3:16 for that matter?

False teaching that deletes portions of the Word of God leads to doubts of salvation; the other camp includes teachers who believe the Word of God from cover to cover but overemphasize performance.

I have been criticized for emphasizing grace so strongly. But I was raised in a legalistic church where performance was stressed. I was also taught that my salvation depended on my works. I was saved at twelve, but many times I was afraid that I hadn't worked hard enough or long enough to keep my salvation. How does someone know when she has worked enough? What is the standard?

Third, *an overemphasis on emotions*. There are those who place a lot of importance on "feel good" religion. I am all for joy in the Christian life. But when the entire Christian life is based on emotions rather than doctrine, assurance is rare. Heartaches will come. Financial setbacks come. Sorrow comes. Disappointments come. Doubt multiplies.

We can't live on feelings. We don't live on feelings in the world—for instance, when the alarm clock rings. When we sit in the dentist chair and hear the whir of the drill, we are not thrilled. We do not send a check to the IRS because it makes us deliriously happy. Why do we think the Christian life is always going to feel euphoric?

> **T**hirty-six percent of the adult population might be described as born again because they have made a "personal commitment to Jesus Christ . . . and they believe that when they die they will go to heaven."
> —George Barna

Fourth, *failure to take God at His Word*. Follow this logic. Pastor asks, "Do you believe Acts 16:31 that whoever believes in the Lord Jesus shall be saved?" Parishioner: "Well, yes. But I don't know if I am." Pastor: "Did you believe on His name?" Parishioner: "Yes, but I don't know if it worked." Pastor: "Why do you insist on calling God a liar?" Red-faced parishioner: "I would never call God a liar." Pastor: "Did He or did He not say, 'Believe in the Lord Jesus and you shall be saved'?" Parishioner: "He said it. I know He said it. I just don't know if I'm saved."

You see, there is very little logic.

ASSURANCE

If I came up to you and said, "I am very happy you're reading this book," and you responded, "Oh, I don't really believe you mean that!" you are doubting my sincerity.

That is exactly what we are doing when we doubt what God has said. We are doubting His trustworthiness.

Sometimes I meet people and they say, "Well, I used to be saved." I will ask, "How'd you get lost?" They name something they've done or thought. But John wrote, "If we confess our sins, He is faithful and just to forgive us our sins and to cleanse us from all unrighteousness" (1 John 1:9).

I have written a whole book on the subject of eternal security and so I will not deal with that issue here. But if we take Him at His Word—and if He is indeed trustworthy—we won't wonder if we were bad enough to lose it. Or good enough to keep it, for that matter.

Fifth, *satanic attacks*. Satan will be happy to whisper, "Look at you. Look how you're acting. A Christian doesn't act like that." Not only will Satan whisper that, but he often uses others as his unsuspecting agents. A mother scolds her child, "A Christian girl wouldn't behave like that." What conclusion is the little girl supposed to reach? And the mother can't understand why her daughter doesn't have assurance of her salvation.

Satan is the accuser of the brethren. We need the Word of God to answer him.

There are, however, some truths God wants us to understand, to counter the enemies of assurance.

First, we understand God's will for our salvation. In referring to God, 1 Timothy 2:4 states, "[God] desires all men to be saved and to come to the knowledge of the truth." God's desire is for us to be saved, not for us to be condemned. Peter tells us that He is "not willing that any should perish but that all should come to repentance" (2 Peter 3:9). He is standing with open arms, just like the father of the prodigal son, to welcome us into His family.

Second, we understand the provision God has made for our salvation. He has done everything possible to get us saved. He gave "His life a ransom for many" (Matt. 20:28). He "Himself bore our sins in His own body on the tree, that we, having died to sins, might live for righteousness" (1 Peter 2:24). He paid the price for salvation, and it would be totally illogical to think, after He paid such a high price—the shedding of blood—that salvation is capricious. He died in our place so we could know we belong to Him.

What earthly father would provide everything his child needs, only for the child to wonder, "Are you sure you wanted me to have it, Daddy?" Of course, that is what the daddy wants. He is grieved that his child is so

ASSURANCE

■ *Confidence that one is a child of God forever.*

insecure in his love. Our heavenly Father is the same way. He has provided everything we need for salvation.

We have a responsibility. Jesus did not die, rise again, ascend, and thus automatically save us. The Bible doesn't teach universal salvation—that is, that all people by virtue of the fact they're created are Christians. John says, "But as many as received Him, to them He gave the right to become children of God, to those who believe in His name" (1:12). And John further says, "He who believes in the Son has everlasting life" (3:36).

A verse in John 5 summarizes the issue: "Most assuredly, I say to you, he who hears My word and believes in Him who sent Me has everlasting life" (v. 24).

We need to believe in Christ and receive Him as our very own. There must be a definite decision. You may not remember the definite time—such as the very date and minute—but you know that you received Christ and have passed from death to life.

GROWTH

If you are still struggling with assurance, apply these three tests:

1. *Do I believe the Word of God?* God said it; I believe it; that settles it.
2. *Do I have the witness of the Holy Spirit?* Read 1 John 5:6, "And it is the Spirit who bears witness, because the Spirit is truth." It is conviction, not feeling. "The Spirit Himself bears witness with our spirit that we are children of God" (Rom. 8:16).
3. *Do I have the walk of the believer?* Are you different? Do you have a deep desire to please the Lord Jesus? "Therefore, if anyone is in Christ, he is a new creation" (2 Cor. 5:17). You will sin from time to time, but the Holy Spirit convicts you. The unsaved person feels guilt when he sins, but he can harden his heart so that eventually his conscience doesn't speak anymore.

Those who were saved very young often need to reaffirm or make sure of their salvation when they are in their teens. This does not insult God. Teens go through a long process of making sure they are making their own choices and not resting on their parents' decisions for them. They may need to resettle the issue. Don't be alarmed. Many who were saved at a young age have never doubted their salvation. People are different, and God deals with us where we are.

ASSURANCE

As I have said, I was saved at the age of twelve. I remember where I was sitting in the church. A woman was preaching, and I went forward and accepted Christ. So much emphasis was subsequently placed on performance, I wondered if I was still saved. But as I would get down beside my bed to pray, I would say, "God, I know I'm not doing everything right. But something inside me says I'm not lost."

I didn't know that was the witness of the Holy Spirit in my young heart. But He was there, assuring me that I belonged to the Lord Jesus Christ. There was no ethereal feeling. I had a blessed assurance.

Based on His wonderful Word—all of it—we can *know* that we have eternal life. It has nothing to do with feeling. But it has everything to do with the trustworthiness of God. He wants us saved. He has done everything possible through Christ to make that happen. Once we receive Him as our own, we can rest on the Word of God and in the witness of the Spirit.

Once you're in the family of God, by faith in His Son, your name is written in the Book of Life.

Several times a year, we conduct cruises through In Touch Ministries. It's a wonderful time of Bible study, special music, and fellowship. I look forward to each one.

On one cruise, a worker on the ship sat in the back during a Bible study session. He came to me later and asked if we could talk. I was delighted. We sat down and I explained the way of salvation to the young man.

He wasn't quite sure about the whole thing. He asked more questions, and I tried, as best I knew how, to answer them from the Word of God. He left to go back to work on the ship, still uncertain.

The next afternoon at lunch, the same fellow came up to me, smiling, and said, "Dr. Stanley, I got it!"

He knew he'd been born again. The smile and enthusiasm were not from a hope-so or maybe-this-will-work experience. He knew, according to 1 John 5:13, that his name was written in heaven and that he was a child of God. He just took Him at His Word. Literally.

When the seas of his life get rocky, he has an anchor.

Blessed assurance.

APPLICATION

The most frequently asked question I hear is, "How can I *know* I'm saved?" That is the dilemma of many people.

Not long ago during the invitation at our church, an older woman came forward. She took my hand and said she'd wondered about her salvation for years, and she needed to know.

ASSURANCE

■ *Confidence that one is a child of God forever.*

The longing look in her aged eyes broke my heart. She'd needlessly wrestled for many years. With great delight she was able to meet with one of our counselors and settle it once and for all.

Maybe you are like that woman. You have prayed, you have read the Scripture, you have done everything you know to do, but you still don't have any assurance of your salvation. John wrote his epistle so that his audience could indubitably know they were part of God's family. You can know as well. Tell God you are ready to settle this issue once and for all. Tell Him that you are taking Him at His Word. Salvation is not a feeling; it is a fact based on the finished work of Christ at Calvary. The truth is, once saved, always saved. Once a family member, always a family member.

QUOTE

I've lived under the "obey God or else" and it's awful. Now I rest on His Word.

—Anonymous

BAPTISM OF THE HOLY SPIRIT

■ *The initial coming of the Holy Spirit into the hearts of believers.*

MATTHEW 3:11

I indeed baptize you with water unto repentance, but He who is coming after me is mightier than I, whose sandals I am not worthy to carry. He will baptize you with the Holy Spirit and fire.

As the forerunner to Christ, John the Baptist's responsibility was to prepare the people for His arrival. Four hundred years had passed since the last legitimate prophet had spoken to the Jewish nation. People were suspicious. John had a challenging mission.

John often spoke about the baptism of the Spirit. He continually emphasized that once the Messiah arrived, He would baptize His followers with the Holy Spirit.

In all probability, the people of that day had no idea what it meant to be baptized by the Holy Spirit. They may have had ideas, but nobody knew exactly what John meant.

Jesus did not speak about the baptism of the Holy Spirit until He prepared to ascend into heaven: "And being assembled together with them, He commanded them not to depart from Jerusalem, but to wait for the Promise of the Father, 'which,' He said, 'you have heard from Me; for John truly baptized with water, but you shall be baptized with the Holy Spirit not many days from now'" (Acts 1:4–5).

In these verses, Jesus equates the baptism of the Holy Spirit with "the Promise of the Father" and, more important, with "[that] which . . . you have heard from Me." Think for a moment. What is He referring to? What had the Father promised? What had they heard from Jesus about the Holy Spirit?

Jesus is referring to a series of conversations with His disciples just before His arrest. He promised to send the Holy Spirit after He departed: "And I will pray the Father, and He will give you another Helper, that He may abide with you forever—the Spirit of truth, whom the world cannot receive, because it neither sees Him nor knows Him; but you know Him, for He dwells with you and will be in you" (John 14:16–17).

Notice that He said He would ask the Father to send the Spirit and the Father would do it. Jesus made a promise on behalf of His Father. That is the same as the Father promising the Holy Spirit.

Jesus was describing the baptism of the Spirit. He didn't use the exact phrase. But His comments in Acts 1:5 link these two discussions. He was

BAPTISM OF THE HOLY SPIRIT

not talking about two different events—the coming of the Holy Spirit (John 14) and the baptism of the Spirit (Acts 1:5). They are identical.

At Pentecost, the Holy Spirit was given to the church. There is no mention of the baptism of the Spirit! The Bible says they were all filled with the Spirit: "And they were all filled with the Holy Spirit and began to speak with other tongues, as the Spirit gave them utterance" (Acts 2:4). What's going on here?

Why doesn't it say, "And they were all baptized with the Holy Spirit"? Isn't that what Jesus promised would happen? Isn't that what John the Baptist predicted? Isn't that what the Father promised?

Absolutely. And that is exactly what happened. They were baptized, filled, indwelt, filled with rivers of living water (John 7:38–39) and empowered. There is no distinction. It's all the same. Jesus, Matthew, John, Mark, Luke—they all used these terms interchangeably to describe the initial coming of the Holy Spirit into the hearts of believers.

Long after the actual day of Pentecost, Luke and Peter added two more figures of speech to the list. Peter was in the middle of preaching to a group of Gentiles when all of a sudden, in Luke's words, "the *Holy Spirit fell* upon all those who heard the word. And those of the circumcision who believed were astonished, as many as came with Peter, because the gift of the Holy Spirit had been poured out" (Acts 10:44–45, emphasis added). Now we have the Holy Spirit "falling" and "being poured out." Is this a new ministry of the Spirit? Of course not. It's just another way of describing the initial entry of the Holy Spirit into the heart of a believer.

We know this from Peter's interpretation of what happened. Notice what he compared the incident to:

> And as I [Peter] began to speak, the Holy Spirit fell upon them, as upon us at the beginning. Then I remembered the word of the Lord, how He said, "John indeed baptized with water, but you shall be baptized with the Holy Spirit." If therefore God gave them the same gift as He gave us when we believed on the Lord Jesus Christ, who was I that I could withstand God? (Acts 11:15–17; see Acts 15:8).

A group came to faith, and immediately—with no begging, praying, pleading, or prompting—the Holy Spirit came. According to Peter, it was the same event that occurred in the Upper Room. And it was the same experience John the Baptist predicted in the beginning.

Now, to really tie it all together, take a look at how the leaders in Jerusalem interpreted what happened to those Gentiles: "When they heard these things

BAPTISM OF THE HOLY SPIRIT

they became silent; and they glorified God, saying, 'Then God has also granted to the Gentiles repentance to life'" (Acts 11:18).

The baptism of the Spirit signifies that men and women have put their faith in Christ. That is why years later the apostle Paul could write, "For by one Spirit we were all baptized into one body—whether Jews or Greeks, whether slaves or free—and have all been made to drink into one Spirit" (1 Cor. 12:13). Every believer has been baptized by the Holy Spirit. Baptism symbolizes our identification with the body of Christ. To be baptized into the body of Christ is to be placed in Christ. This happens at the moment of salvation.

 APPLICATION

No ministry of the Holy Spirit has been more misunderstood than the baptism of the Spirit. As an adolescent, I always heard the baptism of the Holy Spirit described as an experience that took place sometime after salvation. I would meet people from time to time who spoke of "getting the baptism" or "receiving the gift." I discovered that those phrases described the experience of being baptized by the Holy Spirit. Such phrases are still used today.

It was some years before I dug into the Scriptures to discover what God's Word had to say about the baptism of the Holy Spirit. When I did, I reached two conclusions:

1. The Bible is clear and consistent in its explanation of the baptism of the Spirit; the confusion is unnecessary.

2. There is very little similarity between what the Bible teaches concerning the baptism of the Spirit and the experiences of many who claim to have been baptized by the Spirit.

I decided early in my ministry to allow the Bible to determine my conduct and to interpret my experience. By "determine my conduct," I mean the Bible is my standard for living; it is my code of conduct. When I say "interpret my experience," I mean I will always give priority to what the Scriptures say over my experience. I will not interpret the Scripture through my experience. To do so is dangerous. It elevates me to the place of judge and jury over the Bible. I want God to conform my experience to the truth of His Word.

I know many believers who have had a significant experience following their salvation. Some have attributed this experience to the baptism of the Spirit. It is not my place to judge whether or not something has happened to these people. I feel it is my place, however, to warn them against justifying

Baptism of the Holy Spirit

BAPTISM OF THE HOLY SPIRIT

> **O**ur Lord does not mean that life will be free from external perplexities, but that just as He knew the Father's heart and mind, so by the baptism of the Holy Ghost He can lift us into the heavenly places where He can reveal the counsels of God to us.
> —Oswald Chambers

or explaining their experience at the expense of the integrity of God's Word.

Occasionally, someone will walk up to me and ask me if I have the baptism. I always answer, "Yes." Sometimes I elaborate, "But not in the way you may think." What disturbs me most about that question is that it sets up a false dichotomy in the body of Christ. Remember, one of the roles of the Holy Spirit is to enable believers to work together, to build unity in the body. The "do you or don't you" mentality works against the unity of the body. Therefore, it cannot be of the Spirit.

The Bible does not support the notion that there are two levels of believers—gifted and nongifted, baptized in the Spirit and not baptized in the Spirit. This way of thinking opposes everything the Bible teaches about spiritual gifts and the body of Christ.

I have talked to dozens of sincere believers who claim that the baptism of the Spirit dramatically improved their Christian experience. Their prayer lives are better; they have more boldness; their hunger for the Word has increased. To which I say, "Fantastic!" I am all for an enhanced Christian experience. "But why," I ask them, "do you have to call whatever happened to you the baptism of the Spirit? Call it something else. You are just confusing the issue." Some respond by saying it is "the second baptism of the Spirit." That's even worse. The Bible never speaks of a second baptism of the Spirit.

First Corinthians 12:13 teaches that every believer has been baptized by the Holy Spirit. Baptism symbolizes our identification with the body of Christ. To be baptized into the body is to be placed into the body. This happens at the moment of salvation. To avoid confusion, I must allow the Bible to interpret my experience, no matter how I may feel.

It is easy to misinterpret our experiences. We have to be careful. It's dangerous to jump to conclusions. As long as we align the interpretations of our experiences with the teaching of Scripture, we will be fine. When we use the Bible to sanction the validity of our interpretations, we get into trouble. If you have trusted Christ as your Savior, you have the baptism. Not only that, you have been indwelt, filled, and therefore have everything you need to experience the wonderful Spirit-filled life.

A CLOSER LOOK

Some people think you can receive the Holy Spirit through the laying on of hands. They point to a delay between salvation and the baptism of the Spirit found in Acts 8. There we find Philip preaching to the Samaritans and performing signs to validate his message. A large number of Samaritans expressed interest, and many came to faith.

BAPTISM OF THE HOLY SPIRIT

When the apostles in Jerusalem heard about that, they decided to send Peter and John to Samaria to help with the work and to check on Philip. When they arrived, they discovered that the new believers had not received the Holy Spirit. Luke writes, "For as yet He had fallen upon none of them. They had only been baptized in the name of the Lord Jesus. Then they laid hands on them, and they received the Holy Spirit" (Acts 8:16–17).

Some use this incident to support the idea that the baptism of the Holy Spirit comes by way of laying on hands. But that is not the point here at all. If that was all there was to it, Philip could have laid his hands on the new believers. After all, God was performing miracles through the hands of Philip (Acts 8:6). Why didn't he lay his hands on this group? Why did they have to wait for Peter and John?

As you may know, the Jews despised the Samaritans. They considered them inferior. It wasn't unusual for Jews to travel miles out of their way to avoid going through Samaritan-held territory. If the Samaritan believers had automatically received the Holy Spirit the day Philip preached to them, what do you think would have happened? There would have been a First Church of the Samaritans and a First Church of Jerusalem. The delay forced the Jews to acknowledge that their God accepted the Samaritans just as He accepted them. The delay united the early church.

The significance of this incident is not the delay. Neither is it the relationship between the laying on of hands and the baptism of the Spirit. The significance is that the apostles had to lay their hands on the Samaritan believers. In doing so, they put their stamp of approval on the whole Samaritan missionary movement.

> **C**hrist baptizes believers in the Spirit into the body of Christ. This baptism takes place at the moment of salvation. The rite of water baptism symbolizes Spirit baptism.
> —Henry Thieseen

 QUOTES

I am delighted to hear of increased faith, zeal, earnestness in prayer, and the rest. My concern is not with the meaningfulness of the experience but with the understanding of the meaning of the experience. It is the interpretation of the experience that tends to go against Scripture. Our authority is not our experience but the Word of God.

—R. C. Sproul

In my own study of the Scriptures through the years I have become convinced that there is only one baptism with the Holy Spirit in the life of every believer, and that takes place at the moment of conversion.

—Billy Graham

CANON

■ *In regard to Scripture, an officially accepted list of books.*

SCRIPTURE

LUKE 24:27, 32, 44–45

And beginning at Moses and all the Prophets, He expounded to them in all the Scriptures the things concerning Himself. . . . And they said to one another, "Did not our heart burn within us while He talked with us on the road, and while He opened the Scriptures to us?" . . . "These are the words which I spoke to you while I was still with you, that all things must be fulfilled which were written in the Law of Moses and the Prophets and the Psalms concerning Me." And He opened their understanding, that they might comprehend the Scriptures.

COMMENTARY

If we had no other verses than these to give authenticity to the three sections of the Old Testament, these verses are enough. The Lord Jesus Christ was referring to the writings of Moses, the writings of the prophets, and the writings of the psalmists.

How do we know the *same* writings of Moses, the *same* writings of the prophets, and the *same* writings of the psalmists are the ones we have? I believe these are fair questions.

If our entire faith hangs, balances, and is supported by one Book, we need to ask some serious questions about the Book. And if our eternity rests on that Book, we need to do some investigation. God is not intimidated by our questions. The Bible encourages us to handle "accurately the word of truth" (2 Tim. 2:15 NASB).

In our passage, we read about the Lord Jesus Christ, risen from the dead, showing up on a road to talk with two men. Evidently, He quoted freely from sections of the Old Testament. Those portions were all about Him! And the effect on the men was supernatural. They claimed that their hearts burned within them while He explained the Scriptures. We can hardly imagine this happening if someone was discussing the *Reader's Digest*.

Does He still want to explain the Scriptures? And if He does, how do we know what Scriptures He wants to explain?

These are not irrelevant questions. These are wonderful questions. The church in Berea was complimented on being "more fair-minded than those in Thessalonica, in that they received the word with all readiness, and searched the Scriptures daily to find out whether these things were so" (Acts 17:11). We can't help wondering what the people at Thessalonica did in regard to the Word. Did they not care? Did they gloss over it? Did they not ask Paul any awkward questions concerning the Scriptures that indicated they really meant business? I think we would rather be counted in the ranks

> **C**ould I accept the New Testament canon alongside that of the Old Testament? I had no other choice . . . when confronted by the internal evidence of Jesus and the other writers.
> —Dr. Louis Goldberg

of the Berean fellowship! Digging. Comparing texts. Researching. Learning about translations.

And as we do these things, our hearts will burn within us as He explains to us what we need to know.

Let's do some digging together now.

A CLOSER LOOK

I love this Book above all my earthly possessions. I have given my life so that others may love it, too. I do not take this subject lightly. I literally base everything I am now and all my future on this Book. I firmly believe that "All Scripture is given by inspiration of God, and is profitable for doctrine, for reproof, for correction, for instruction in righteousness, that the man of God may be complete, thoroughly equipped for every good work" (2 Tim. 3:16–17).

I must admit to writing as one who loves not only the Book but also the Author. In that sense, I am not objective. But I believe as we look at historical facts together, we can objectively study how the Bible came to us.

One of the most exciting discoveries of Scripture portions actually happened in my lifetime. In 1947, a young Bedouin shepherd made an incredible discovery. In a cave close to Jericho, the shepherd boy found many leather scrolls rolled and hidden in pottery jars. Two scrolls contained the entire book of Isaiah and the first two chapters of Habakkuk. In 1952, further excavations found fragments of all Old Testament books except Esther. There are some fragments of Psalms, Jeremiah, and Daniel.

A study of the finds from the cave indicated that the pottery was from the Hellenistic age. And in comparing the writing with others of that period, experts discovered that the manuscript was a thousand years older than any previously studied.

In 1951, an expedition from the Jordan Department of Antiquities guided and assisted by Bedouin excavated four caves close to the Dead Sea. Another expedition in 1952 investigated the area and found two rolls of thin copper into which a Hebrew inscription had been impressed. The biblical materials far exceeded the other treasures of the first cave. Almost every book of the Old Testament is now represented.

In comparing those manuscripts with what we already had in our Bibles, experts discovered the variation was minuscule. Absolutely minuscule.

It would have been easier, indeed, had the Holy Spirit prefaced each of the sixty-six books that make up our Bible with "thus entereth into the canon

The rabbis who compiled the Talmud, completed by about A.D. 500, affirmed that the Old Testament canon of books is fixed as we know it.
—Dr. Louis Goldberg

CANON

■ *In regard to Scripture, an officially accepted list of books.*

of Scripture." But He chose not to do it that way. It's more complicated than that, but that does not mean the Holy Spirit was not in charge.

Since God loves me and gave His Son for me, it is perfectly logical to conclude that He communicates through His chosen agency, the Bible, and that it is accurate. If we fail to grasp that, we have a very small concept of God. He is greater than papyrus; He is greater than scribes; He is greater than those seeking to destroy the Book, and He is going to make sure the people He loves get the right Love Letter.

The Old Testament was written in Hebrew, the New Testament in Greek. The original manuscripts were painstakingly copied. The copiers were called scribes, and the sacred calling was confined later almost exclusively to monasteries. From the ninth century through the fifteenth century, cursive manuscripts were produced in great numbers. The scribes' chief business in life was copying the sacred Scriptures. The profession of the scribe was so revered that a writer of the sacred Book was exempted from working in the gardens of the monastery, so the skill of his pen wouldn't be marred by injury to his hands.

There were guidelines for the scribes. It was not a profession that someone chose because he had a good hand with calligraphy. The men saw it as a high and holy calling. How would you feel if you were copying the Word of God for others?

The first guideline was wearing full ceremonial dress when copying the Scriptures. They were about very important business for the King, and they dressed accordingly. Everyone in the monastery knew they were called to regal service.

Second, scribes were so concerned about accuracy that they counted all of the verses and even the letters in the various books. They made notes of the middle verse, the middle word, and the middle letter of each book. After they had finished their copying, they counted the words and verses in what they had copied, and if the count did not tally with the notations that had been made, the scribes had to either meticulously correct the manuscript or start again.

Third, each scroll had to have a certain number of lines per inch with a certain margin on each side. (All this without computers!)

Fourth, the distance between each letter had to be the same on every scroll, and even the scroll had to be a perfect width, length, color, and skin from a perfect animal.

Fifth, the scroll was copied letter for letter and not word for word. I depend so much on the spelling checker on my computer, I can see why the men would copy letter for letter. It is so easy to leave out a letter here and there when we think in words.

Sixth, they wrote from right to left, and the writing had to end perfectly on the scroll or the entire scroll was discarded. I can see the temptation to want to crowd some letters at the end. But they couldn't do that because the distance between each letter had to be the same. It was very precise work.

As we think about these ancient manuscripts coming to us in Hebrew and Greek and copied so carefully, how do we know that what's in our Bible is really what God wanted us to have? We could suppose that other caves are there with other pottery and other manuscripts. Or we could suppose that there had to be a slipshod scribe someplace.

Because the manuscripts of the Old Testament are not as plenteous as those of the New Testament, we have to rely on Jewish history and Jewish historians to help us understand.

Early in history, God began the forming of His Book. The Ten Commandments were written on stone (Deut. 10:4–5); Moses' laws were written in a book (Deut. 31:24–26); copies of this book were made (Deut. 17:18); Joshua added to this book (Josh. 24:26); Samuel wrote in a book and laid it up before God (1 Sam. 10:25). This book was known four hundred years later (2 Kings 22:8–20); prophets wrote in a book (Jer. 36:32; Zech. 1:4; 7:7–12); Ezra read this book of God publicly (Ezra 7:6; Neh. 8:5).

The Jewish people revered the Scriptures. It is a wondrous thing to watch orthodox Jews today handling the Old Testament. They do so with reverence and awe.

In Jesus' day the book was called the Scriptures and was taught regularly and read publicly in the synagogues. Jesus repeatedly called it the Word of God. Just looking back at our verses in Luke 24, we see how He opened to them the Scriptures and quoted things about Himself from all three major divisions. The Jews readily accepted these Scriptures. Jewish history asserts that as the books were written, beginning with Moses, they were recognized as the inspired Word of God and placed in the tabernacle or temple. Copies were made as needed. But in the Babylonian captivity they were scattered, and many copies were destroyed. Ezra, after the return from the Captivity, reassembled scattered copies and restored them as a complete group to their place in the temple.

Josephus, a Jewish historian, believed the Old Testament canon was fixed from the days of King Artaxerxes, during the time of Ezra. Josephus was born in A.D. 37. He received an extensive education in Jewish and Greek culture. He was governor of Galilee and military commander in the wars

Sixteen percent believed the Bible is an ancient book of legends, history, and moral precepts, recorded by people.
—*U.S. News and World Report*, April 4, 1994

The New is in the Old contained. The Old is in the New explained.
—Augustine

CANON

with Rome, and he was also present at the destruction of Jerusalem. You can go to any library and read the works of Josephus.

This is what he said about the Old Testament books that we possess:

> We have but 22 books, containing the history of all time, books that are believed to be divine. Of these, 5 belong to Moses, containing his laws and the traditions of the origin of mankind down to the time of his death. From the death of Moses to the reign of Artaxerxes the prophets who succeeded Moses wrote the history of the events that occurred in their own time, in 13 books. The remaining 4 books comprise hymns to God and precepts for the conduct of human life. From the days of Artaxerxes to our own times every event has indeed been recorded; but these recent records have not been deemed worthy of equal credit with those which preceded them, on account of the exact succession of prophets. There is practical proof of the spirit in which we treat our Scriptures; for, although so great an interval of time has now passed, not a soul has ventured to add or to remove or to alter a syllable; and it is the instinct of every Jew, from the day of his birth to consider these Scriptures as the teaching of God, and to abide by them, and, if need be, cheerfully to lay down his life in their behalf.

Josephus is accepted in secular history. Yet he is commenting on the books of the Old Testament. The difference in numbers—he mentions twenty-two books—can be accounted for in the way the books were divided up. Before the division as we now know it, the Hebrew Old Testament contained twenty-four books because Samuel, Kings, and Chronicles were each one book, instead of the two books of each that we now have. Also, Ezra and Nehemiah were one, as were the twelve Minor Prophets. Josephus further combined Ruth and Judges and Lamentations with Jeremiah, making twenty-two and corresponding with the Hebrew alphabet.

Although the number differs, the Hebrew Old Testament contains *exactly* the same books as our English Old Testament.

Another historical preparation for us to receive the Old Testament was between A.D. 600 and 950. The Hebrew manuscripts had no system of vowel indication, just consonants. There were certain consonants to indicate long vowels. But between A.D. 600 and 950, Jewish scholars, called the Masoretes, invented a full system of vowels and accents to punctuate the text. This work providentially prepared it for the advent of the printing press five centuries later.

Looking at the Lord Jesus Christ quoting from the three sections of Hebrew Scripture in Luke 24 (and many other places in the New Testament),

The canonical books were also called "books of the testament," and Jerome styled the whole collection by the striking name of "the holy library," which happily expressed the unity and variety of the Bible.

the labor of scribes and the testimony of history, we can accept the Old Testament as inspired of God.

The Old Testament is primarily the history of a nation, but it is much more than that. The Old Testament combines with the New Testament to tell of One who died for us. The Old Testament set the stage. God preserved His Word through the ages so that we could know One to come.

There are more than five thousand Greek manuscripts of the New Testament. God made sure we have what He wants us to have.

The third Council of Carthage (A.D. 397) rendered one of the earliest decisions on the Canon. The Council stipulated that only "canonical books" be read in the churches. Then it listed the present-day twenty-seven books in our New Testament.

To be canonical, the books had to (1) be considered *the* revelation of God; (2) be considered "God-breathed" and inspired in a different sense from all other literature (1 Tim. 3:16); (3) be considered to disclose God's plans and purposes for the ages of time and eternity; and (4) be centered in God incarnate, the Lord Jesus Christ (Heb. 1:1–2).

The Holy Spirit gave guidance:

> And so we have the prophetic word confirmed, which you do well to heed as a light that shines in a dark place . . . knowing this first, that no prophecy of Scripture is of any private interpretation, for prophecy never came by the will of man, but holy men of God spoke as they were moved by the Holy Spirit (2 Peter 1:19–21).

We can study ancient history, we can study evidence, we can study all we can study, but the bottom line is: God is big enough to watch over His Word.

We are not left to chance on which to rest our lives and eternity. "God, who at various times and in various ways spoke in time past to the fathers by the prophets, has in these last days spoken to us by His Son, whom He has appointed heir of all things, through whom also He made the worlds" (Heb. 1:1–2). These are incredibly powerful verses.

If He spoke to us through His Son, and if He set the stage to do that in the Old Testament, why do we have so many translations and paraphrases?

We know the Old and New Testaments were not suddenly bound together in burgundy calfskin, complete with ribbon markers and thumb indexing. God used people and a process to get the Hebrew and Greek translated for us.

There were many translators over the years, and many versions, but several are more significant than others in the large scheme of things. Because we are not dealing with all of church history, we need to look at several to get a clearer picture.

It is not possible to be certain when the Pentateuch reached its final form, but part of it at least was laid beside the ark of the covenant in Moses' lifetime (Deut. 31:24ff.), an action parallel to the ancient practice of keeping treaties in sacred places.

CANON

Wycliffe's version is the first complete translation of the Bible into the English language. It is a manuscript Bible, made before the invention of printing around 1450. Wycliffe's New Testament was completed in 1380 and the Old Testament in 1382. John Wycliffe was born in England, and he went to Oxford University. Later, he taught at Oxford.

Wycliffe believed in the right and duty of everyone to read the Scriptures. The people were so thrilled with the Word of God in their language that they paid large sums for it. One writer tells that a whole load of hay was paid for the use of a complete New Testament *for one day.*

In 1384, this great and brave man was suddenly stricken with paralysis. On December 31, Wycliffe died.

John Wycliffe, no doubt, had many enemies because not everyone agreed that the Word of God should be available for all. Some considered him a heretic. One such enemy wrote,

> John Wycliffe, the organ of the devil, the enemy of the church, confusion of the common people, the idol of heretics, the looking glass of hypocrites, the encourager of schism, the sower of hatred, the storehouse of lies, the sink of flattery, was suddenly struck by the judgment of God, and had all his limbs seized with the palsy. That mouth which was to speak huge things against God and against His saints . . . was miserably drawn aside, and afforded a frightful spectacle to the beholders; his tongue was speechless and his head shook, showing plainly that the curse which God had thundered forth against Cain was also inflicted on him.

Another enemy, Archbishop Arundel, complained of "that pestilent wretch, John Wycliffe, the son of the old Serpent, the forerunner of Antichrist, who had completed his iniquity by inventing a new translation of the Scriptures."

Wycliffe's was the only English Bible for 145 years, and some of our familiar Bible expressions, such as "the strait gate," "the narrow way," the "mote," and the "beam," have come from his translation.

One of the largest mission boards in the United States is named after Wycliffe. The mission? To translate the Word of God into the languages of the peoples of the earth. What would Wycliffe's enemies say to that? What do some of the tribal groups who are being reached say to that? What does Wycliffe's Lord say to that? "Well done" comes to mind, doesn't it?

Johannes Gutenberg, of Mainz, Germany, invented the printing press around 1450, and four years later, he invented printing from movable type. The very first book off the press was the Latin Vulgate Bible. Printing

The Bible, particularly the King James Version, has had more impact on the literature of the English language than has any other single source.
—Mark D. Taylor

presses soon found their way into Italy, France, and then England. It revolutionized how quickly the Word of God could get to the people. In Wycliffe's day, it had taken a scribe ten months to produce one copy of his Bible, and the price was very high. After the invention of the printing press, thousands of copies could be produced swiftly and distributed widely. The price was much lower so that more people could have a copy of the Bible. The printing press produced a "spiritual earthquake." People were hungry for the Word of God, and it became accessible to them.

> *But the word of the LORD was to them,*
> *"Precept upon precept, precept upon precept,*
> *Line upon line, line upon line,*
> *Here a little, there a little" (Isa. 28:13).*

William Tyndale was born in England about 1494. He was educated at Oxford. He later went to Cambridge and studied Greek and theology. He felt strongly that the Bible should be translated into the language of the people. Tyndale became proficient in seven languages, so much so that one said he was "so skilled in . . . Hebrew, Greek, Latin, Italian, Spanish, English, and Dutch, that whichever he might be speaking, you would think it to be his native tongue."

He had to leave England because of the prevailing policy against Bible translation and ownership. Since he was committed to circulating Scripture, he needed a safer place to translate. He had been working on his translation in England and realized that no printer would dare to print it. He left for Germany, lamenting, "I understood that not only was there no room in my lord of London's palace to translate the New Testament, but also there was no place in all England."

In Wittenberg, Germany, he met Luther (we can only imagine what conversation occurred there!). He also saw the Reformation in full swing and saw the people reading the Bible in their own language. There he evidently translated some of the New Testament.

Tyndale's New Testaments were soon smuggled into England in cases of merchandise, barrels, bales of cloth, sacks of flour and corn, and in every secret way that could be found. Although there was diligent watch at every port, the Bibles were scattered throughout the country. When some of the opposition realized what had happened, they bought as many as they could and burned them.

Tyndale remained in hiding, yet continued to study. He was diligent in the study of Hebrew, and in 1529, his translation of the Pentateuch was

> The books of the Bible were written by many different authors over a long period—possibly as long as 1,500 years (1400 B.C. to A.D. 95).
> —Mark D. Taylor

CANON

ready for the presses. He lost several of his friends to burnings during persecutions. He, too, was a hunted man.

During that time, he translated Jonah, 1 John, and the Sermon on the Mount. In the next two years, he revised many of his earlier works of the New Testament, and some of the Old Testament books, Proverbs and the Prophets, for use in church services. In 1535, another revised and improved edition of the New Testament appeared, with chapter headings in the Gospels and Acts. But before it came from the press, Tyndale was imprisoned in Belgium.

Deceived by a so-called friend, he was persuaded to go to England where he was imprisoned. During his imprisonment, he translated other portions of the Old Testament.

I find this so interesting because it reminds me of another, jailed for his faith. A single letter written in Latin by Tyndale has been found. In it, he asked for a cloak. Above all he wanted permission to have his Hebrew Bible, Hebrew grammar, and Hebrew dictionary so that he could study. Does that not sound similar to the apostle Paul: "Bring the cloak that I left with Carpus at Troas when you come—and the books, especially the parchments" (2 Tim. 4:13)? I want to weep when I read that.

On Friday, October 6, 1536, Tyndale was led out and allowed a few minutes for prayer. With typical zeal he cried in a loud voice, "Lord, open the King of England's eyes." Then his feet were bound to a stake and an iron chain placed around his neck and a rope loosely tied in a noose. That saint of God was strangled to death and then the body burned.

Our King James Version is practically a fifth revision of Tyndale's Bible. We have much to thank him for.

I have belabored Wycliffe's and Tyndale's roles because they are so significant. What a price the men paid for us to have the Scriptures in our own language. I personally hold in high esteem those today who are still laboring so that the Word is available in various tongues. Many modern-day saints, serving in remote fields, start with an alphabet, teach the people to read it, and then put the Scriptures in their language.

Just a brief word about the Apocrypha. This name is given to some books between the Old and New Testaments. They are not accepted in the Protestant church as part of the canonical books. They were written after Old Testament prophecy, oracles, and direct revelation had ceased. The historian Josephus rejected them as a whole. They were never recognized by the early church as of canonical authority or of divine inspiration. Jesus never quoted from them, and only one is referred to in the New Testament—Enoch in the book of Jude.

The New Testament canon in its present form was largely in place by about A.D. 200, and the first exact listing of the twenty-seven books we now know as the New Testament was included in a letter of Athanasius in A.D. 367.
—Mark D. Taylor

CANON

When we look at all the historical evidence, when we look at the men who labored and gave their lives for the God of this Book, when we see how methodically God worked to give us His Word, and when we see that the One who loves us chose to communicate through the Bible, we can do nothing but praise Him for His faithfulness.

"I testify to everyone who hears the words of the prophecy of this book: If anyone adds to these things, God will add to him the plagues that are written in this book; and if anyone takes away from the words of the book of this prophecy, God shall take away his part from the Book of Life, from the holy city, and from the things which are written in this book" (Rev. 22:18–19). With an admonition like that, we need to be very careful not to tamper with the canon of Scripture.

We may be very good at adding and subtracting, but neither has a place in the Word of God. The only mathematical term we need is multiplication—that is, multiplying the translation of this wonderful Book into more languages: "Behold, a great multitude which no one could number, of all nations, tribes, peoples, and tongues, standing before the throne and before the Lamb" (Rev. 7:9).

Hallelujah! What a Savior! "Did not our heart burn within us while He talked with us . . . ?" (Luke 24:32). When we read this Book and then we pick up a magazine, we know there is a difference, a Divine difference.

 QUOTES

I believe the Bible is the best gift God has ever given to man. All the good from the Savior of the world is communicated to us through this Book.
—Abraham Lincoln

It is impossible to rightly govern the world without God and the Bible.
—George Washington

If there is anything in my thoughts or style to commend, the credit is due to my parents for instilling in me an early love of the Scriptures.
—Daniel Webster

It seemed fitting for me as well, having investigated everything carefully from the beginning, to write it out for you in consecutive order . . . so that you might know the exact truth about the things you have been taught.
—Luke 1:3–4 NASB

CREATION

■ *Bringing into being; the fact or state of being created.*

SCRIPTURE

GENESIS 1:1

In the beginning God created the heavens and the earth.

COMMENTARY

In his book *The Life of Samuel Johnson,* James Boswell quotes Mr. Johnson, an English author, with these words: "There are innumerable questions to which the inquisitive mind can in this state receive no answer. Why do you and I exist? Why was this world created? Since it was to be created, why was it not created sooner?"

Without question, creation is a mystery. There was nothing. Then there were heaven and earth—and they were just starts! Reason says such an event couldn't happen. Yet our faith in God takes us beyond reason to the wonderful truth of God's creation. Just because we can't explain or understand how the earth came from nothing doesn't give credence to the theories suggesting otherwise.

If we were completely honest, we'd have to admit that creation is impossible to understand intellectually. Our minds—our ability to comprehend and reason—are finite and restricted by our humanity. Something from nothing is incomprehensible. There had to be a first before there could be a second. That is true only in our finite minds. God is not bound by our limitations.

As believers, we are not without sufficient evidence from which to draw conclusions. God knew it would be difficult for us to understand, so He left us a written record of what took place.

We must understand the words as they were used in the original Hebrew. Just as there are many words in our modern language that have similar meanings, the same was true in the original language. Yet it is fascinating—and even exciting—to discover the exclusive use of the words in the creation story because it leaves no doubt that God created this universe! A close look at the word *created* as it appeared in Genesis 1:1 leads to only one conclusion: that before God spoke the words that brought the heavens and earth into being, *nothing* else (but God Himself) existed.

Bara is the Hebrew word used in the original account of creation. Other words used in Scripture have been translated "create" or "make." However, none of the other words hold the exclusive meaning that *bara* does. *Vine's Complete Expository Dictionary of Old and New Testament Words* explains the true meaning of this word: "This verb is of profound theological significance, since it has only God as its subject. Only God can 'create' in the sense implied by 'bara.' The verb expresses creation out of nothing, an idea seen clearly in passages having to do with creation on a cosmic scale." Although *bara* is a technical term, *Vine's* points out that "'bara' is a rich theological vehicle for communicating the sovereign power of God, who originates and regulates all things in His glory."

Think about what occurred that first day. It's overwhelming. God set the universe into motion. Heaven and earth were His focus, adding day (light) and night (darkness) before He finished His work for that day. Quite enough for one day. I am sure that God could have completed His creation in a single day—even in a single breath. It was His creation, and He gave it to us in His time.

A CLOSER LOOK

Three concepts have shaped the way we view creation today.

The first is *materialism,* the second is *pantheism,* and the third is *theism.* Because creation is so widely debated and even taught to our children, I believe it is important for us to understand each of these concepts.

Basically, materialism contends that matter is eternal—has always been and will always be. "The physicist claims 'energy can neither be created nor destroyed,'" writes Norman L. Geisler in *Knowing the Truth About Creation.* Geisler continues to explain that within materialism are two divisions—those who involve God and those who don't: "Many ancients, including the Greeks, believed in creation by God out of some previously existing, eternal lump of clay." Plato was one of those people. One drawback to this view puts God in the role of a builder or architect, not a Creator.

The second division of materialism (generally called atheism) holds to the position that matter is simply there and does not need God to explain it or give it meaning. Again, Geisler offers insight into this view: "If questioned on where the universe came from, the strict materialist may ask in reply: where did God come from? For it makes no more sense to them to inquire who made the universe than to ask who made God." One of the foremost proponents of this theory is the astronomer Carl Sagan. Sagan writes in his book *Cosmos* that "the Cosmos is all that was, is, or ever will be."

The next view of creation is known as pantheism. Unlike those who believe in materialism (creation out of matter, *ex materia*), those who profess a belief in pantheism believe in creation out of God *(ex deo).* What does that mean? There are two basic divisions within this view—those who deny the existence of matter absolutely and those who hold that matter is a manifestation of God.

CREATION

■ *Bringing into being; the fact or state of being created.*

It goes something like this. Absolute pantheists claim that everything we call matter is an illusion; only the mind truly exists. It would take more than the space we have here to go deeper into this philosophy, but there are two classical representatives of this view: Parmenides (a Greek) and Shankara (a Hindu). There is help for understanding what absolute pantheists believe. Sagan writes, "To think we are not God is part of the illusion or dream from which we must awake. Sooner or later we must all discover all comes from God, and all is God." For the more moderate pantheists, there is some flexibility; yet they still believe there is no absolute distinction between the Creator and creation: "Ultimately Creator and creation are one. They may differ in perspective, as two sides of a saucer. . . . Even for those who believe the world is real, Creator and creation are simply two sides of the same coin. There is no real difference between them," Sagan states. One of the most vocal proponents of pantheism is the actress Shirley MacLaine. In her television movie *Out on a Limb,* she waved to the ocean and proclaimed, "I am God, I am God!" For those who believe in pantheism, as Ms. MacLaine, there is no difference in the Creator and the creation. They are one.

Theism is in stark contrast to both materialism and pantheism. It is Judeo-Christian in nature. Theism is based on the belief that God created the universe (including mind and matter) out of nothing. There is absolute difference between the Creator and His creation.

Theism is the belief in God as the Creator of the universe that we hold to as Christians. We can't explain it. We can't reason it out. Yet we know that God is absolute and that He existed before time. Only He created what we know. Creation is the first doctrine to be stated in the Bible (Gen. 1:1) and one of the last (Rev. 4:11). God created the very ability to think and to reason. Yet He knew it would bring questions. That is why He gave us His inspired Word so that we could know and believe.

Concerning the foundational truths that we find in Genesis, Theodore Epp writes in *The God of Creation,* "It presents Him as the Creator, as the King, and as the determined Redeemer. Genesis does not tell us where God came from but reveals beyond question that God exists. Genesis does not make a defense of God—it does not reveal His nature nor declare His methods nor state His ultimate purposes."

As we consider the views discussed here, neither materialism nor pantheism is worthy of the intelligence that God Himself gave us. To discount God but allow for some kind of Mind that helps us along defies the evidence of creation's rational order.

Because I trust the inerrancy of Scripture, I believe that Genesis 1 is the only accurate account of the creation of the universe. It's not my interpreta-

CREATION

tion. It's what happened. From the first verse of the creation story through the book of Genesis, the history of firsts is set out for us to recall and learn from. A widely read commentary presents a study of Genesis 1:1 that encourages the hearts of believers as we gather a clear understanding of God's power and His desire to create something of great beauty and also extreme mystery. In *The Matthew Henry Commentary,* the editor refers to the first verse of Genesis as "the work of creation in its epitome and in its embryo."

Continuing, the editor observes that we can gather four things from these few short words: "In the beginning God created the heavens and the earth." The first observation is "the effect produced—the whole frame and furniture of the universe." The second observation is "the author and cause of this great work," God is the Author and Cause. The third is the manner in which this work was effected: "God created it, that is, made it out of nothing." Again, we have confirmation of how the word *bara* is the exclusive word for "created out of nothing." And the fourth observation concerns when the work was produced—in the beginning. This is the reference of not only the beginning of the universe but also of all that we understand about time. From that point on, all of life would be measured in days and by light and darkness. Before that time, nothing existed except God.

Can so much be gathered from ten short words? I believe so. Creation is the end result of the Creator.

GROWTH

You must be equipped with the truth of God in order to stand against the culturally appealing philosophies that challenge your trust in God. To prevent that from happening, you should study Scripture and ask God to posture it in your heart and mind. I encourage you to undertake a study of the creation story. I believe it will solidify your belief in your Creator and will equip you to share the truth with those who get tangled up in culturally reasoned theories.

A number of excellent books have been written on this topic. It would be good if you (perhaps with a few friends) picked one of them and began a small group study in your home. The more you know about God, the more you want to know.

QUOTE

Father, I want those you have given me to be with me where I am, and to see my glory, the glory you have given me because you loved me before the creation of the world.

—John 17:24 NIV

DOCTRINE

■ *A specific set of beliefs; tenet.*

1 TIMOTHY 1:3-7

As I urged you when I went into Macedonia—remain in Ephesus that you may charge some that they teach no other doctrine, nor give heed to fables and endless genealogies, which cause disputes rather than godly edification which is in faith. Now the purpose of the commandment is love from a pure heart, from a good conscience, and from sincere faith, from which some, having strayed, have turned aside to idle talk, desiring to be teachers of the law, understanding neither what they say nor the things which they affirm.

The aged apostle Paul asked Timothy to stay in Ephesus while he ventured to another city. Apparently, Paul felt the need to move on, but he felt a burden for the people in Ephesus, also. After reading in Acts 19 how the people at Ephesus reacted to the gospel, we can imagine Timothy wanting to say to Paul, "Thanks for the offer and the opportunity. But I think I'll pass on this one."

Not only was Timothy to emphasize sound doctrine to those folks who obviously enjoyed a good tangent, but he was to be firm. The mystics were no longer to pay attention to fables and genealogies, which were endless. Timothy was to stop the talk dead in its tracks.

Ephesus was a proud city, boasting of commerce and the goddess Diana, among many gods and goddesses. To silence Paul, on one occasion, the people shouted for a solid two hours, "Great is our goddess Diana." Can you imagine Paul trying to preach while hordes of intellectual pagan people tried to drown him out for two long hours? I am sure Paul was one weary open-air preacher when he went back to his home that night.

Timothy was admonished to instruct those people. It is entirely possible, though no one knows for sure, that Timothy had the letter from his mentor Paul to the church at Ephesus. What a gold mine to refer to! If he did not have the letter, he surely had been schooled in the wonderful truths about the Lord Jesus Christ by Paul.

The Ephesian people—early Gnostics—were steeped in "wisdom" and culture and false gods. And traditions. And genealogies—linking them to Old Testament patriarchs in some instances.

Youthful Timothy—who was not to be despised because of his youth—needed to step in with pure doctrine. Solid stuff. He had to look beyond the "wisdom" and the loud boasting and proclaim Jesus Christ. That's not an easy calling for an aspiring preacher.

DOCTRINE

Do we know enough about sound doctrine that we could defend it, much less proclaim it? Even when the crowd tries to drown us out?

We need not only to know "whom we have believed," as Paul wrote to young Timothy, but we need to be steeped in what we believe, or sound doctrine.

Let's take a closer look at what that involves.

A CLOSER LOOK

Stop the man on the street and ask, "Could you define psychology for me?" Chances are, he will probably be able to give you a workable definition. Stop the same man on the street and ask him to define theology. He may have a harder time. Ask another man coming out of a church the same question and he may be equally perplexed.

I am not being critical because most theological terms are not used by the mainstream of society. It is far more important that we understand the basic doctrines of Scripture than that we understand the long titles.

But allow me to use the theological terms briefly, and then we'll look together at the basic doctrine under each term.

Theology is the study of God and His relation to the universe. Theology is a broad stroke of the brush that colors various categories. When we are studying God, we know the study has to be multifaceted.

Bibliology looks at the inspiration of Scripture.

Angelology is the study of angels.

Anthropology is the study of humankind.

Christology is the study of the person and work of Christ.

Soteriology is the doctrine of salvation.

Ecclesiology is the study of the church.

Eschatology is the study of things to come.

These subjects take on a whole new meaning when we look at them as children discovering wonderful things about our Father. Timothy was not to stay in Ephesus and throw out big words. He was to teach sound doctrine.

First, theology, the study of God, is a vast subject. Basically, the *sound doctrine about God* is that He is the living, eternal One who is self-existent (Ex. 3:14). He is omnipresent (everywhere at once); omniscient (all-knowing); omnipotent (all-powerful); and immutable (unchanging). He is sovereign (He's in charge!). God is righteous, holy, just, good, loving, and full of grace and mercy.

He exists in three separate, equal persons: Father, Son, and Holy Spirit. The word *Trinity* is not used in the Bible, but the teaching of this doctrine is there (Gen. 1:26; Matt. 28:19).

There are thirty thousand religions in the world.

DOCTRINE

About 74 percent of Americans strongly agree that "there is only one true God, who is holy and perfect and who created the world and rules it today."

Some *unsound doctrines* about God include atheism, which denies the existence of God, or agnosticism, which holds that all knowledge is relative and we can't really know anything for sure—God included. Then there is pantheism, which teaches God is all and all is God. Pantheism emphasizes nature and God's oneness with all that is. Polytheism holds that there are many gods.

To sum up the *sound doctrine about God:* there is only one eternal God, existing in three equal persons, with characteristics only deity can have.

Second, the *basic sound doctrine concerning the Bible,* according to 2 Timothy 3:16, is that the Scripture is fully and verbally inspired by God, inerrant and infallible. Totally. The Father wanted His children to know Him, and He sent His Word to tell us the story of redemption without error.

The *unsound doctrine* concerning the Bible is that it is partially inspired. The problem is knowing what parts to accept if one holds this view. There is also the theory that the thoughts, not the words, are inspired. Paul specifically said that he spoke "not in words which man's wisdom teaches but which the Holy Spirit teaches, comparing spiritual things with spiritual" (1 Cor. 2:13).

To sum up the *sound doctrine of the Bible:* all the words of the Old and New Testament autographs are inspired of God and are free from any error of any kind. God has preserved His Word, and the Bible is absolutely reliable for belief and lifestyle.

Third, the *sound doctrine about angels* is that they were created by God for His glorification through worship and service. Nehemiah 9:6 states,

> You alone are the LORD;
> You have made heaven,
> The heaven of heavens, with all their host. . . .
> The host of heaven worships You.

A Gallup Poll indicates 78 percent of Americans polled believe they are going to heaven. Although 60 percent of Americans polled believe in hell, only 4 percent think they are going there.

Angels are ministering spirits for the saints, as Hebrews 1:14 explains. They possess knowledge but are not omniscient (1 Peter 1:12); they possess great strength but are not omnipotent (2 Peter 2:11).

The Bible teaches there are fallen angels, as Satan is. He sought to be like the most high God and was cast out of heaven (Isa. 14:12–15). Because Satan has a host of fallen angels at his command, there is constant warfare in the heavenlies between the angels of Jehovah and the angels of Satan.

The *unsound doctrine* concerning angels is more apparent today than ever before. In our mysticism, we have elevated them far above what the Bible teaches. We have talked about angels, written multitudes of books about them, and have gotten to the place of nearly revering our "guardian angel." At one time we never considered them at all, and now we seem to be going to the opposite extreme. I trust that we will strike a balance in this wonderful doctrine of angelology.

To sum up the *sound doctrine about angels:* angels were created by God to worship Him and to serve the saints.

Fourth, the *sound doctrine of humankind* is that we are the highest form of creation. We are unique. Genesis 1:27 declares, "God created man in His own image; in the image of God He created him; male and female He created them."

We were created perfect and by a free act of will chose to disobey God. The penalty for sin is physical death and eternal death with a life of bondage to sin and no fellowship with God. We are totally depraved (Rom. 3:10, 23). (That's the bad news; the good news is, He provided a way to be redeemed.)

The *unsound doctrine* of humankind is that we evolved into being, and that we are still evolving—getting better every day. (It's hard to believe that the people who hold to this view read crime statistics.) Another unsound view is that we are little gods. That is humanism at its best—or worst—and does not have a shred of biblical support.

To sum up the *sound doctrine of humankind:* God created us in His image, but we chose to separate ourselves from Him by sinning. We are depraved and in need of redemption.

Fifth, the *sound doctrine of the study of the person and work of Christ* is summed up in this: "Jesus said to him, 'I am the way, the truth, and the life. No one comes to the Father except through Me'" (John 14:6). The Lord Jesus Christ existed in the heavenlies with the Father before He was born of a virgin (John 1:1; Luke 1:31–35). He is in His divinity everything that God is and in His humanity everything that we are. He was subject to temptation but never once sinned (2 Cor. 5:21). As the sinless God-man, He was the Lamb of God who could take away our sins through His blood sacrifice: "[He] bore our sins in His own body on the tree . . . by whose stripes you were healed" (1 Peter 2:24).

His bodily resurrection attested to the fact that sin and death were forever defeated: "For if when we were enemies we were reconciled to God through the death of His Son, much more, having been reconciled, we shall be saved by His life" (Rom. 5:10).

He is now seated at the right hand of the Father, and He intercedes for us (Heb. 7:25). His next act will be to come again for His children.

Among adults who describe themselves as born-again Christians, fewer than expected could correctly explain these four terms: the Great Commission (25 percent), John 3:16 (50 percent), evangelical (43 percent), and the gospel (84 percent).

Forty-three percent of Christians concur "all religious faiths teach the same lessons about life." —George Barna

DOCTRINE

■ *A specific set of beliefs; tenet.*

The *unsound doctrine* about the Lord Jesus Christ is that He was merely a nice man, a good teacher, just a Jewish rabbi, and certainly not virgin born.

To sum up the *sound doctrine of Christ:* He is 100 percent God and 100 percent man. The shedding of His blood thoroughly atoned for the sin of humankind. He is alive and interceding and will return for us.

Sixth, the *sound doctrine of salvation* is summed up in this: "For God so loved the world that He gave His only begotten Son, that whoever believes in Him should not perish but have everlasting life" (John 3:16).

Because sinful humankind is separated from a holy God, God Himself breached the gap to bring His creation to Himself. He sent His Son, the Lord Jesus Christ, who was perfect, without sin, to take our punishment: "He [God] made Him [Jesus] who knew no sin to be sin for us, that we might become the righteousness of God in Him" (2 Cor. 5:21).

When the blood of Jesus Christ was shed, God's demand for justice for sin was satisfied. He did what we could not do for ourselves. With Jesus' resurrection from the dead, sin and death were defeated once and for all.

Salvation was accomplished by the God-man.

The *unsound doctrine* of salvation is called works. Those who hold to this theory believe that if a sinful man is somehow good enough, he will meet the standards of God and thus enter heaven someday. The Bible teaches the very opposite: "For by grace you have been saved through faith, and that not of yourselves; it is the gift of God, not of works, lest anyone should boast" (Eph. 2:8–9).

Another means for salvation that is unscriptural is trusting in one's heritage or denomination. If belonging to a certain family or denomination or being baptized would guarantee salvation, Jesus Christ would never have died in our stead. Martyrdom for a religious cause, which seems to be on the increase, does not guarantee salvation and is not taught in the Word of God, though it is in other religious literature.

A summary of the *sound doctrine of salvation* is that Jesus Christ willingly paid the sin penalty in full with His precious blood (death) and His resurrection. There is no other way (Rom. 10:9–10).

Seventh, the *sound doctrine of the church* emphasizes that Christ loved the church and gave Himself for her (Eph. 5:25). The universal church is a group of called-out saints, a spiritual organism made up of born-again believers across the globe. The wonderful promise is that one day some from "every tribe and tongue and people and nation" (Rev. 5:9) who make up the universal church will be with the Lord Jesus in heaven.

DOCTRINE

There is not only the church universal but the local church as well. It is made not of brick and mortar but of flesh and blood. One friend who lives in the parsonage next to the church he pastors tells his small children, "It's time to walk over to the church building." He said he wants to instill in them at an early age that there is a difference between the actual building and the church made up of people for whom Christ died.

The local body of believers assemble for worship, edification, evangelization, and participation in the ordinances of baptism and the Lord's Supper.

The *unsound doctrines* concerning the church vary from the belief that "our church is the one and only" to "we'll all blend in to one mystical church and it doesn't matter what we believe."

To sum up the *sound doctrine of the church:* the church is a spiritual organism made up of born-again believers who are in fellowship with a local assembly for worship, teaching, mission outreach, and partaking of the ordinances.

What is the *sound doctrine concerning end things*? Because the Bible mentions this doctrine more than three hundred times, and whole chapters are given over to this subject, as well as several biblical books, it is difficult to be brief. After Jesus' ascension, an angel spoke to those nearby and asked, "Why do you stand gazing up into heaven? This same Jesus, who was taken up from you into heaven, will so come in like manner" (Acts 1:11).

Paul wrote to Titus about our "looking for the blessed hope and glorious appearing" (Titus 2:13). Elsewhere he wrote that we can be comforted by this wonderful hope (1 Thess. 4:13–18).

The Bible is clear that He is coming again. I personally believe that according to Revelation 20:4–6, He is coming before the Millennium. And I hold to the pretribulational view, based on Revelation 3:10–11: "Because you have kept My command to persevere, I also will keep you from the hour of trial which shall come upon the whole world, to test those who dwell on the earth. Behold, I am coming quickly!" These are my personal persuasions.

Some *unsound doctrines* referring to future things are the setting of dates for the end of the world. The Bible states that no one knows when Jesus will return (Matt. 24:42). Others teach an interim known as purgatory, a place for cleansing. This teaching dismisses the full atonement of the death of Jesus Christ. Purgatory and soul sleep, which also teaches an intermediary holding pattern for the soul, are dealt with in this verse: "Absent from the body and to be present with the Lord" (2 Cor. 5:8).

Some liberal scholars declare that despite minor differences in detail, all religious myths converge.
—Donald S. Whitney

Two out of three people reject the notion of absolute truth.
—George Barna

DOCTRINE

■ *A specific set of beliefs; tenet.*

Annihilationism is an unsound doctrine that believes the unsaved are extinguished at death. Revelation 14:11 teaches that the "smoke of their torment ascends forever and ever; and they have no rest day or night."

To sum up the *sound doctrine of eschatology:* Jesus is coming personally, unexpectedly, suddenly, in the glory of His Father with angels, and triumphantly. The Bible is very clear on that. If you want to study further about the Millennium or the Tribulation, I recommend the book *Things to Come* by Dwight Pentecost. Dr. Pentecost deals thoroughly with all of these issues.

As we review our study of theology, bibliology, angelology, anthropology, christology, soteriology, ecclesiology, and eschatology, I think we agree it's not as difficult as it sounds!

In the New Testament, Jesus is called a teacher numerous times. Paul and the other apostles were teachers.

Christianity doesn't consist of mere sentiment. It is based on facts. Becoming a Christian is not just a plunge in the dark. We must have an intelligent grasp of the meaning of what we believe. But doctrine does not exist just for its own sake. Doctrine points to the One who loves us and wants us to know Him and live for Him. It makes sense.

We think back to young Timothy. Where do you think he started with the people at Ephesus? What sound doctrine do you suppose he started with? When they chanted louder, which doctrine did he move on to?

Whatever doctrine he taught wasn't mere data. I imagine it was cloaked in love, as Paul had taught him.

Shouldn't that be our approach?

GROWTH

Get a book on theology and do a personal study on the doctrines in Scripture.

Purpose not to argue over minor differences within the body of Christ.

Purpose, according to 1 Peter 3:15, to be able to defend the major doctrines of the Bible. But do it in love.

QUOTE

The teaching of biblical doctrine is as rare as it is valuable! . . . Those who hope to survive with any measure of emotional sanity and mental stability must have a solid diet of sound biblical theology, clearly understood, consistently digested, regularly put into action.

—Chuck Swindoll

■ *The belief that once you become a*
Christian, you are always a Christian.

ETERNAL SECURITY

1 JOHN 5:13

These things I have written to you who believe in the name of the Son of God, that you may know that you have eternal life.

God assures believers of eternal life. This assurance is based on belief in Christ. Why is belief in Christ conditional for eternal life? Belief is conditional because God's purpose for Christ's death was the payment for a debt we could not pay. That debt was sin. My experience has been that those who have problems with the doctrine of eternal security have a distorted understanding of what took place at the Cross. That may sound as if I am being critical. But in reality I am more puzzled than anything else. When I think of Calvary, and the price that was paid to provide me with eternal life, the thought of my having the power to undo all that seems preposterous. What people believe took place on the cross determines what they believe about eternal security.

On the cross, Jesus Christ literally became your Sin Bearer. Not only did He bear your sin, but He gave you His righteousness in return (2 Cor. 5:21). When you believe in Christ, you receive His life, and He forgives you of your sin debt. Christ's death was a permanent transaction. Because the transaction was permanent, so were the results: forgiveness and eternal life (John 6:40). Your belief in Christ's death on the cross as the payment for your sin assures you of eternal life.

Faith is the means by which the saving work of Christ is applied to the individual. Specifically, you are saved when you trust in Christ's death on the cross as the complete payment for sin.

The biblical support for this idea comes from a grammatical construction that occurs repeatedly when faith is mentioned in connection with forgiveness and salvation. This construct consists of the Greek word that means "believe" followed by a little word translated "in" or "on," depending on the context of the passage. The combination of the term for "believe" and this little preposition is unique in the New Testament. The writers of the New Testament were forced to coin a new phrase to accurately communicate their unique message (John 6:40; see also 1:12; 2:23).

The Gospel writers understood that Jesus was calling people to do more than believe in His existence. They knew from their experience that Christ was calling on sinners to put their trust in Him, in His life, in His words, and ultimately in His death as payment for their sin. "Wait!" the skeptic

It is the rightful heritage of every believer, even the newest in the family of faith, to be absolutely certain that eternal life is his present possession. To look to self is to tremble. To look to Calvary's finished work is to triumph.
—Larry McGuill

Eternal Security

171

ETERNAL SECURITY

■ *The belief that once you become a Christian, you are always a Christian.*

> The Christian's relationship to God as a child to his Father is not only intimate, but sure. So many people seem to do no more than hope for the best; it is possible to know for certain.
> —John Stott

counters. "What about the sins you commit after He declares you not guilty?"

Good question. But think about it. Which of your sins did Christ take to the cross two thousand years ago? Which of your sins was He punished for? If He died for only part of your sins—for instance, the ones you had committed up to the point of salvation—how can you ever get forgiveness for the sins you commit after that? Would Christ not have to come and die again? And for that matter, again and again?

If all your sins were not dealt with on the cross two thousand years ago, there is no hope for you. God declared you not guilty based on the once-and-for-all provision of His Son. Christ, unlike sheep and goats, needed to be offered up only once. And God accepted that as the once-and-for-all sacrifice for all of human sin (Heb. 9:24–28).

From the historical vantage point of the Cross, all of your sins were yet to be committed. If Christ died for one of them, He died for all of them. What is the difference? He will not come again to pay for sin (Heb. 9:28). On the cross He took upon Himself all the sin of humankind—past, present, and future.

How can anyone possibly undo all of that? If Christ took upon Himself all your sin, what can cause God to reverse His verdict of not guilty?

Not a thing!

APPLICATION

If we reject eternal security, several things are at stake. First of all, our assurance. If our salvation hinges on anything but the finished work of Christ on the cross, it will be difficult to live with much assurance. Hope, yes; assurance, no.

Where there is no assurance of God's acceptance, there is no peace. Where there is no peace, there is no joy. Where there is no joy, there is a limitation on the ability to love unconditionally. A person with no assurance is by definition partially motivated by fear. Fear and love do not mingle well. One will always dilute the other. Furthermore, fear spills over into worry. Let's be realistic for a moment. If my salvation is not a settled issue, how can I be anxious for nothing (Phil. 4:6)? No security contributes to no assurance.

Forgiveness is at stake as well. When Christ died, which of your sins did He die for? Which sins were you forgiven of when you trusted Him as Savior? If the sins you commit after becoming a Christian can annul your relationship with the Savior, those sins were not covered at Calvary. Forgiven is forgiven. To differentiate between forgiven and unforgiven sins is to make a distinction foreign to Scripture. The timing of your sins is irrelevant since they were all in the future from the perspective of the Cross. On the cross, Christ paid for all your sins, even those yet to be committed.

A third area of doctrine that is affected by the notion of losing one's salvation is that of salvation by faith alone. Once good works are introduced into the salvation process, salvation is no longer by faith alone; it is by faith and works. To imply that salvation is maintained by good works (or not sinning) is to take the daily burden of our salvation upon ourselves. In that case, there will be room for boasting in heaven. Our salvation is based on faith alone and not a combination of faith and works. Because of the permanency of our salvation, we are assured of eternal security.

Christians who are insecure in their relationship with God have a difficult time sharing the love of God with others. They often find it impossible to get beyond their own struggle. Not everyone who rejects the notion of "once saved, always saved" has this problem. But I have met many for whom this barrier is real.

These are just a few of the things affected by the stance on the question of eternal security. This subject is not just for theologians to debate. This issue has a great deal to do with your life right now. The view you adopt will have a great impact on your perception of yourself, God, and others. For these reasons I pray you will study and restudy until this issue is settled in your mind once and for all.

> **C**an we be born into God's family one moment and repudiated from it the next? The Bible indicates that it is a permanent relationship.
> —John Stott

A CLOSER LOOK

Let's examine two questions related to eternal security. The first question is, What happens if someone stops believing? In other words, Does my unbelief undo my promise of eternal life? The second question is, What does it mean to fall from grace? Or stated another way, Can my disobedience cause me to lose my salvation?

First, let's take a closer look at the question of unbelief. Those who believe salvation can be lost often ask an insightful question about the relationship between salvation and faith. The question goes something like this: If our salvation is gained through believing in Christ, doesn't it make sense that salvation can be lost if we quit believing? To answer this question, we must see what saves us. Paul tells us that we are saved by grace (Eph. 2:8–9). The instrument of salvation is grace. God came up with a plan and carried it out through Christ. We didn't take part in it; we didn't deserve any part of it. It was grace from start to finish. We are saved by grace through

ETERNAL SECURITY

■ *The belief that once you become a Christian, you are always a Christian.*

faith. "Through faith" is important, but often misunderstood. "Through" is translated from the Greek word *dia,* which carries the idea of "means" or "agency." Faith was the agent whereby God was able to apply His grace to the life of the sinner.

Faith is *simply* the way we say yes to God's free gift of eternal life. Faith and salvation are not one and the same any more than a gift and the hand that receives it are the same. Salvation stands independently of faith. Consequently, God does not require a constant *attitude* of faith in order to be saved—only an *act* of faith in Christ.

You and I are not saved because we have enduring faith. We are saved because at a moment in time we expressed faith in our Lord. Notice how Paul ends Ephesians 2:8–9: "It is the gift of God, not of works, lest anyone should boast." "Salvation," Paul says, "is a gift." I don't know about you, but I have learned a gift that can be taken back is no gift. True gifts have no strings attached.

You can say, "What if I give it back?" You can give it back only if the giver accepts the return. In the case of salvation God has a strict no-return policy. Christ came to seek and to save the lost. Why would He take back what He came to give?

And faith? Faith is our way of accepting God's gift. Faith serves as our spiritual hands by which the gift is received at a particular moment in time. Again, saving faith is not necessarily a sustained attitude of gratefulness for God's gift. It is a singular moment in time when we take what God has offered. Eternal life is received by grace through faith. It is a once-and-for-all transaction that can never be undone. Because of the nature of God's grace, once you become a Christian, you are always a Christian. Before we move to the question of falling from grace, let's look at your relationship with Christ.

We have learned that faith is the means by which we accept God's gift of eternal life. With this in mind, let me ask you this: Has there been a time in your life when you accepted God's free gift of salvation?

When I was twelve, I prayed a prayer similar to the one I've included here. If you are not sure you are saved, why not make sure now? If you recognize your need for forgiveness and you believe Christ's death made your forgiveness possible, you are ready. Pray, "God, I know I am a sinner. I know my sin has earned for me eternal separation from You. I believe Christ died in my place when He died at Calvary. I accept His death as the full payment for my sin. I accept Him as my Savior. Thank You for saving me. In Jesus' name I pray. Amen."

> Nothing can ever change God or the reality of redemption. Base your faith on that, and you are as eternally secure as God Himself.
> —Oswald Chambers

ETERNAL SECURITY

For many people falling from grace is synonymous with losing salvation. This perception is unfortunate. Equally unfortunate is that the majority of people I talk to about "falling from grace" have no idea where the phrase came from or to what it originally referred.

To compound the problem, these three words have become a common expression for losing favor with someone. All of this has resulted in confusion over this phrase, which appears only once in the New Testament and was never intended to be lifted from the text as a theological maxim.

The book of Galatians finds Paul refuting a group of "teachers" who arrived in Galatia after he left. The group, commonly referred to as the Judaizers, proclaimed a gospel different from Paul's. Yet it was similar to the apostle's teaching in enough ways to confuse the Christians in Galatia.

The group believed and taught that salvation was found through having faith in Christ along with keeping portions of the law. Their distorted view centered on the importance of circumcision. Paul's letter indicates that the Judaizers were successful in persuading some Gentile believers to be circumcised to ensure their salvation (Gal. 5:2).

So, what has all of that to do with falling from grace? Paul's primary concern was not that the Galatian believers were drifting into gross immorality or consciously abandoning God. In one sense, the opposite was true. They were about to adopt a form of religion that further restricted their freedom. They were in danger of committing themselves to a way of life that would demand more in the way of works (Gal. 5:1).

Listen to how he says it in Galatians 5:4: "You have become estranged from Christ, you who attempt to be justified by law; you have fallen from grace." In this context, falling from grace has nothing to do with being lost or unsaved. The opposite of grace here is not becoming unsaved or lost; it is attempting to be saved by the works of the law. To fall from grace, then, is to abandon the salvation-by-grace model for justification and to adopt the salvation-by-works model. Paul was not threatening them with the loss of salvation, just a loss of freedom (Gal. 5:1). He didn't say they were falling from salvation. His concern was that they were falling away from God's system of grace, which would lead them right back into the frustration of living under the law. You may fall from grace, but you will never fall from salvation. Nothing can separate you from the love of God (Rom. 8:37–39).

> **E**ternal life is not a gift from God, eternal life is the gift of God.
> —Oswald Chambers

 QUOTE

That soul, though all hell should endeavor to shake, I'll never, no, never, no, never forsake!

—"How Firm a Foundation"

FAITH

■ *Confidence that God will do what He has promised.*

HEBREWS 11:1–2 NIV

Now faith is being sure of what we hope for and certain of what we do not see. This is what the ancients were commended for.

There is no clearer explanation of faith in all the Scriptures than the one found in Hebrews 11:1 (NIV): "Faith is being sure of what we hope for and certain of what we do not see." The two key words here are *sure* and *certain*. Faith is about being sure and certain of something. This raises the question at the heart of the confusion often surrounding the topic of faith: Sure and certain about what? When can we be sure and certain God is going to act? When can we know for sure He is going to do what we ask?

Fortunately, the author (whose identity is a mystery) answers that question in no uncertain terms. Interestingly enough, he introduces his explanation in this way: "This is what the ancients were commended for." *This* refers to faith. The people whose stories he is about to recount were all men and women who had faith; they were sure and certain about something. They were sure and certain about the right things.

As he recites the experiences of some of our favorite Bible characters, along with some of the most spectacular events recorded in Scripture, it becomes evident why the ancient men and women were so sure and certain. Furthermore, the author gives us some unmistakable clues about the things we can be sure and certain about.

He begins with the creation story and moves right on through the story of Abraham. He takes us on a historical journey through the life of Moses including the parting of the Red Sea. He speaks about Joshua, Gideon, David, and Samuel. Each man's life is associated with "by faith."

But something else is associated with each of these characters. In some cases it is stated outright. In others it is merely implied. That something else is *a promise*. The men and women were so certain and sure because each had received a promise from God. They were confident that God would do exactly what He promised. And that is the essence of faith.

The term *promise*, or some derivative, appears eighteen times in Hebrews. It appears seven times in this one chapter alone. What is the significance of that? Faith and the promises of God go hand in hand.

Where there is no promise, there can be no faith—only hope. Notice the connection in the following verse: "By faith Abraham, even though he was past age—and Sarah herself was barren—was enabled to become a father

> It may be true that I have much less to live on than I did a year ago, but it is certainly true that I have just as much to live for. The real values of life are unshaken and solid; a financial crisis can rob us of all that we have, but it cannot affect what we are.
> —Claiborne Johnson

because he considered him faithful who had made the promise" (v. 11 NIV). The basis of Abraham's faith was the promise of God. He believed he and Sarah would have a child in their old age because God promised they would. Their faith followed a promise. Every person mentioned in this chapter was given a promise of some kind. Faith was grounded in the promise of God.

Faith, then, is confidence in the promises of God or, as stated earlier, confidence that God will do what He has promised.

APPLICATION

To apply our faith is to live as if God will keep His promises. A question I often ask myself is, How would I conduct my life if I really believed God is who He says He is and if I really believed the Bible is His Word? That is what living by faith is all about—taking God at His Word.

So, what about you? How would you conduct your life if you really believed God is who He says He is and if you really believed the Bible is His Word? How would that affect the way you do business? How would that affect your giving? How would that affect the way you treat your neighbors?

Living by faith requires that we become familiar with God's promises to us. The Bible is filled with promises for believers. Nothing is more encouraging or nurturing to our faith than reviewing God's promises. Every morning when I awake I review a list of promises that I have assembled. I rehearse in my mind His promises regarding my forgiveness, my protection, my relationship with Him, and the future inheritance He is preparing for all His children. I have also made it a habit to claim certain promises for my children.

A CLOSER LOOK

I have met many Christians who are disappointed with God. They feel as if God has let them down, as if He didn't answer their requests as they had desired. It is not unusual for people in this situation to stop reading their Bibles, stop attending church, and stop praying. In some cases their disappointment turns to anger and even bitterness.

Disappointment with God usually stems from confusion over the meaning of faith. Most people who are disappointed with God misunderstand what faith is. To them, faith is some sort of power or force. They think if they have enough faith, God will do whatever they ask Him. So when a crisis comes along, they try to move God into action through their faith. When God doesn't respond, they become disappointed. Their misunderstandings lead to unrealistic expectations. And their expectations eventually lead to disappointment.

FAITH

■ *Confidence that God will do what He has promised.*

Faith is not a power we tap into. Faith is not a lasso we slip around God's neck to force our will on His. Faith is not a button we push to prod God into action. Faith is confidence that God will do what He has promised. That is what all those men and women in Hebrews 11 were commended for.

Part of the problem is that the concepts of faith and hope have been confused. If you wrote me a letter inviting me to your home for dinner, you wouldn't include statements such as, "We have perfect faith that you are coming; we know you will be here; we are claiming your arrival; by faith we are announcing to all our friends that you will be here."

On the contrary, you would say things like, "We hope you can join us; we would love to have you; please check your schedule." You would be foolish to believe I was coming until I told you. Once I called you and confirmed the date, you could have faith. Why? Because I told you I would be there; I made a commitment to come; you have a promise to hang your faith on. You can start cooking at some point. And if I don't show up, your disappointment is justified—I broke my promise. But until you heard from me, you could only hope I was coming.

As children of God, we are free to ask God anything we please. And once we ask, we can *hope* He will give us exactly what we've asked for. But to *believe* He will do something He has not promised to do is not faith; it is presumption! I fear that much of what is passed off as faith these days is really presumption.

Part of the reason for the confusion in this area is poor teaching. But another reason is that we want to be in control. We want God to do our bidding. We don't want to submit to His will; we want Him subjected to ours. We don't really want God to function as the Lord of our lives; we would rather have Him operate like a vending machine. We put in a little faith, and He sends out whatever we think we need. But He doesn't operate that way. And to approach the Christian life as if He does is to set yourself up for disappointment. Faith is not an escape hatch from all the trials and tribulations in this life. It is confidence that God will keep His promises.

Another area of confusion has to do with the foundation of faith. Believers tend to judge God's interest and involvement in their lives according to what happens around them. When things go well—their health is good, their finances are solid, their family members get along—they are quick to praise God for His faithfulness. But when things take a turn for the worse, they doubt. "Where is God?" they ask. "Has He forgotten me? I thought He loved me!" They make the mistake of drawing conclusions regarding God's faithfulness based on what is happening then.

FAITH

The writer of Hebrews warns us against this. His original audience made the same mistake two thousand years ago. Their situation, however, was a bit more severe than anything most of us will face. He was writing to a group of Jewish Christians who were being persecuted for converting from the Jewish faith. The persecution was so intense that they began to doubt whether they had made the right decision. God wasn't honoring their faithfulness in any tangible sort of way. On the surface it looked as if He had abandoned them. They were judging His love and concern for them on the basis of what was happening around them. Consequently, some believers abandoned the faith.

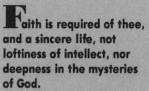

Faith is required of thee, and a sincere life, not loftiness of intellect, nor deepness in the mysteries of God.
—Thomas à Kempis

To combat this defection, the writer of Hebrews reminded them of the foundation of their faith. He took the entire first three chapters of his letter to demonstrate for them the superiority of Christ over Abraham, Moses, and even the angels. He summarized his argument with these words: "Seeing then that we have a great High Priest who has passed through the heavens, Jesus the Son of God, let us hold fast our confession" (Heb. 4:14). In other words, "Since our Savior, Jesus, died and rose from the dead and went to be with the Father, we have every reason to hang on to our faith. What He has done is enough to merit our faithfulness regardless of what happens in the meantime."

His point is that the primary support for our faith is not what is happening now but what happened two thousand years ago at Calvary and later at the tomb. Jesus has demonstrated His faithfulness to us in a way that far surpasses bailing us out of unpleasant circumstances, that far surpasses answering a prayer or two. The fact that He would die on the cross for our sin settles the question of His love and concern. The fact that He could rise from the dead settles the question of His reliability and His right to call Himself Lord. The fact that He passed through the heavens and is seated at the right hand of the Father is overwhelming support for the reliability of His promise to return.

The question of whether or not God loves you and is concerned about you has nothing to do with the circumstances surrounding you right now. That question was settled a long time ago. We never, regardless of our circumstances, ever have reason to doubt God's love, care, and concern. It is an open-and-shut case, never to be reopened.

 GROWTH

Begin a journal of God's promises. As you see promises in God's Word, write them in a notebook. Eventually, you may want to categorize them.

Faith

FAITH

■ *Confidence that God will do what He has promised.*

> **F**aith is a voluntary anticipation.
> —St. Clement of Alexandria

Use categories such as "Personal," "Family," "Financial," "Friends," "Business," "Temptation," and "Rewards."

Memorize one promise for every category.

Every parent knows that what is best for the child is also sometimes painful for the child. Every trip to the doctor or dentist is an act of love on the part of the parent and yet a time of fear and potential pain for the child. Discipline is the same way.

From a child's perspective this can be confusing: "Why would someone who says he loves me hurt me or allow someone else to hurt me?" Yet from our vantage point, it all makes sense.

Imagine that you are sitting in the waiting room at your dentist's office. You look over and see a four-year-old child crying and begging his daddy not to make him have his cavity filled. You walk over to the child and ask this question, "Do you think your daddy loves you?" Under these circumstances you wouldn't be shocked to hear, "No, my daddy doesn't love me. He made me come to the dentist." The child's faith in the goodness of his father would be at a low point. These circumstances don't communicate love to a four-year-old. And he doesn't have the maturity to think through all the other good and sacrificial things his dad has done for him in the past. The child's attention is riveted to the present.

You realize that this is a timing problem. The child doesn't have all of the information. He doesn't realize the importance of having the cavity filled. However, ask him the same question a few hours later when his dad is rewarding him with a chocolate shake!

We are the same way. When things aren't going our way, it is hard to look beyond the here and now; it is hard to remember the goodness of the Lord; we forget the significance of the sacrifice made for us at Calvary. Consequently, our faith runs low; we begin to doubt.

But as we learn to refocus on what happened at Calvary two thousand years ago, our faith will grow strong. We will be able to join in with the psalmist who wrote,

> *But I have trusted in Your mercy;*
> *My heart shall rejoice in Your salvation.*
> *I will sing to the LORD,*
> *Because He has dealt bountifully with me (Ps. 13:5–6).*

■ *God's kindness toward humanity, without regard to the worth or merit of those who receive it, and without their deserving it.*

GRACE

EPHESIANS 2:8–9

SCRIPTURE

For by grace you have been saved through faith, and that not of yourselves; it is the gift of God, not of works, lest anyone should boast.

COMMENTARY

It is no small wonder that these two verses are frequently memorized. They sum up the gospel of grace. Every heart's desire is grace.

We surely don't want justice. If we got what we deserved for our sin, we would all be condemned. We want what we don't deserve, and that is grace.

Ephesians 2:8–9 teaches that our salvation has nothing to do with our works. Salvation is a gift which we receive by faith.

Even the faith to believe comes from God, so it is grace from start to finish. This is not something that we work up or even something we work on. Works have nothing to do with it. If that were not the case, we could boast, "I did this," or "I did that." Only God can say, "I did this: I provided all that these sinners need through My Son."

Paul knew about boasting. In Philippians 3, he referred to his past. And it was quite an impressive past! If anyone could boast, Paul could have. Talk about religious credentials! He wrote that he was "circumcised the eighth day, of the stock of Israel, of the tribe of Benjamin, a Hebrew of the Hebrews; concerning the law, a Pharisee; concerning zeal, persecuting the church; concerning the righteousness which is in the law, blameless" (Phil. 3:5–6). He said that if anyone could boast or "have confidence in the flesh . . . I more so" (Phil. 3:4).

He was impeccably religious. But he confessed in the next verse, "Yet indeed I also count all things loss for the excellence of the knowledge of Christ Jesus" (Phil. 3:8). He looked at his impressive past and counted it all rubbish. "Be found in Him, not having my own righteousness, which is from the law, but that which is through faith in Christ, the righteousness which is from God by faith" (Phil. 3:9).

According to Romans 3:23, none of us deserves salvation. We have all sinned. But grace greater than our sin was offered. All we need to do is receive Christ. If we think that any of our works add anything to the Cross, that insults God.

May we never lose the wonder of amazing grace.

> **G**race is but glory begun, and glory is but grace perfected.
> —Jonathan Edwards

Grace

GRACE

A CLOSER LOOK

Have you ever looked at your circumstances and thought, *My, how I would love to have a chance to do that again?* Or *If I could just change that, I would. I need another chance.* That is what grace is all about. I don't mean after we die, we get another chance to receive the Lord Jesus as Savior. The Bible does not teach that. I mean in this lifetime, He lavishes His forgiving love on us after we have thoroughly blown it. We are never outside God's grace.

Most people hear the gospel many times before they receive the Lord. That is grace. He does not give up on wooing us to Himself. You see, He is the God of the second chance—and oftentimes a thousand chances. He sends someone our way to tell us of the Savior. We reject the truth. Because He is a God of grace, He sends another. We reject the truth again. Because He is a God of grace, He sends yet another. Sometimes this process goes on for years until finally one day—because of pursuant grace—we become children of God.

This should encourage us to pray for unsaved people. This should encourage a Christian wife who has prayed for years for an unsaved husband. God's grace is pursuing him. This should encourage parents who have prayed for an unsaved child. God's grace is pursuing that son or daughter. We may give up. God does not.

Some of us were saved early in life, and some were saved late in life. But the wonderful fact is, it takes the same amount of grace to save a twelve-year-old boy as it does a sixty-year-old man. Grace is abundant, no matter the age.

God is beyond time. It's like being in a helicopter and seeing all of a parade at one time. That's the way God sees time. When God forgave Adam and Eve for their sin, He did so based on what in His mind was already accomplished—the crucifixion of the Lord Jesus Christ. His substitutionary death makes it possible for God to say to us, "I'm going to give you another chance."

Paul starts most of his epistles referring to this God of grace in the salutation. Paul's message is one of grace. He knew if it were not of grace, it would be of works; if it were not of grace, it would be of the law. You can't have both at the same time. It can't be grace and law or grace and works.

Many struggling Christians understand they have been saved by grace, but they still want to pay Him back with good works. Some even think this is necessary to remain saved. The Bible teaches neither.

I heard a pastor explain it this way: "God's love for us flows from His character, not ours; it is not dependent on anything we have done or will

The grace of God is outrageous. By normal human reason, it doesn't make any sense.
—Leith Anderson

GRACE

do." He continued, "In fact, if you do nothing to serve Him the rest of your life, He will not love you any less."

One listener reacted somewhat negatively. She could not comprehend that kind of grace. Later she confessed that she felt she had to earn God's love and acceptance. In time she was able to accept God's unconditional grace.

After accepting this truth, she found that she still wanted to serve Him, but her motivation was different. She served Him because she loved Him, not to earn His approval.

This is certainly a liberating truth. God isn't keeping score. We can't pay Him back for His grace. No amount of good works can pay the debt of love we owe.

There is no ritual involved. He loves us and draws us to Himself. We love Him and serve Him. Balancing the scales of indebtedness has nothing to do with it, either before or after we are saved.

You can't do anything to make Him love you any more. And you can't do anything to make Him love you any less.

The book of Galatians was written to those who were adding law to grace. Paul wrote to them, "Therefore the law was our tutor to bring us to Christ, that we might be justified by faith. But after faith has come, we are no longer under a tutor" (Gal. 3:24–25). There is no way we could keep God's moral code perfectly. We need a Savior.

Even after we become Christians, God does not want us to add law to His grace. He wants obedience, of course. But the obedience is an overflow of a heart full of love, not legalism.

When Jesus tells us to keep His commandments, He emphasizes that obedience shows others that we love Him. The moral law shows us our need of a Savior. The corresponding imperatives in the New Testament help us see that we cannot obey the Lord Jesus, even after we are saved, without His help. It is not *ought to, should, must* to gain His favor. It is children wanting to please the Father because we love Him.

This delivers us from legalism and keeps us on the ground of grace, not only for salvation, but for living the Christian life.

What about those who abuse grace? Paul anticipates this when he asks, "What shall we say then? Shall we continue in sin that grace may abound?" (Rom. 6:1).

The answer is no. Paul answered the question in the very next verse, "Certainly not! How shall we who died to sin live any longer in it?" (Rom. 6:2). The implication is that it is unthinkable that a Christian would be comfortable continuing in sin. Sin does not stay dormant. It grows. It enslaves.

> Thank God, He does not measure grace out in teaspoons.
> —Amy Carmichael

> God makes us pure by His sovereign grace.
> —Oswald Chambers

Grace

GRACE

■ *God's kindness toward humanity, without regard to the worth or merit of those who receive it, and without their deserving it.*

If people are saved, sin cannot destroy the relationship with God, but it surely can damage their testimony and their fellowship.

In the Greek, the prefix on the word *abound* means "super." So the verse is really saying, "As sin comes in, grace comes in a greater way." Or "Where sin abounds, grace superabounds." Sin may overflow a bit, but grace is like a flood. Sin reached the top of Mount Sinai, but grace goes all the way to heaven. No matter how great the sin, there is always more grace. If your sin weighs two pounds, grace weighs one hundred. Sin cannot reign over the Cross!

But we do not have license to sin. Abundant grace spurs us to obedience.

Remember when Jesus answered Peter's question about how often he needed to forgive his brother? Peter thought seven times sounded extravagant. Jesus answered, "Peter, seventy times seven." Jesus was telling Peter to forgive countless times. Jesus did *not* say, "Well, Peter, I see how someone would really want to take advantage of you." Peter may have wondered that, but Jesus emphasized forgiveness, not keeping score and not worrying about being taken advantage of.

If Jesus told Peter that, how much more does He, the Son of God, exercise forgiveness toward us? Surely, we have sinned more than 490 times. And it is the sheer grace of God that He is not counting!

The extravagant grace of God does not encourage sin. Grace comes into our lives when we receive Jesus Christ as our personal Savior. He delivers us from the penalty of sin and also the power of sin in our lives. Romans 6 emphasizes that we do not *have* to sin. What wonderful liberty is given to us to do what is pleasing to Him!

Let's look at the riches of His grace, according to Ephesians 1. First, the riches of the grace of God are bestowed by God the Father (v. 3). Second, these riches are freely given to us (v. 6). That means we don't merit these riches; they are extensions of His character of grace. Third, this grace is given to us in abundance (v. 7). Nowhere is stinginess hinted at. He has given immeasurable grace. Fourth, His grace is given to us instantly (v. 3). The verb tense in verse 3 indicates once-and-for-all completed action. Everything we need, He gave us the moment we were saved. My capacity to enjoy these riches and to experience them grows as I know more about this God of all grace, but I have His riches from the moment I was born into God's family. Fifth, the riches come simultaneously. God does not justify me here and redeem me later and forgive me over there and reconcile me down the line and glorify me here and sanctify me later. Simultaneously, all these things, and more, became mine when I was saved. Sixth, these riches are totally on the merit of what Jesus did, not on any of our merit (v. 7). His death bought the riches for us. He paid the debt in full.

The riches are eternal. Money can't buy them, and death can't take them away. We are redeemed, reconciled, and freed from the law. We have a relationship in the family of God. We are children of the King who lavishly gives us everything we need to live. As children of His kingdom, we are sealed and set apart for Him (Eph. 4:30). Why on this earth do we often live like paupers?

Someone might say, "Well, that sounds pretty good, but I don't feel rich." We are talking about our wonderful, abundant spiritual assets, not material wealth. And whether or not we feel rich has nothing to do with our wealth. Our riches are in the One we belong to, and He will never change.

The Bible says, "For you know the grace of our Lord Jesus Christ, that though He was rich, yet for your sakes He became poor, that you through His poverty might become rich" (2 Cor. 8:9). This is how we are partakers of His riches. This is the great exchange.

The obvious question comes to mind: If we are so rich and He is so great, why do Christians suffer? Second Corinthians 12:9 gives the promise in the midst of suffering, "My grace is sufficient for you, for My strength is made perfect in weakness." Paul learned there was something far more important to him than reengineered circumstances. He was discovering the sufficiency of God's grace.

I was speaking to a group of ministers, and I asked them how many of them wanted to know God like the apostle Paul did. Each pastor raised his hand. I then asked how many were willing to go through stonings, beatings, shipwreck, prison, being left for dead, and many other persecutions that the apostle experienced. No one raised his hand.

I understand the hesitancy. No one enjoys pain and hurt. But we prove His immeasurable grace in the middle of terrific heartache.

Paul was consumed with the gospel of grace. He was willing to die for it. He was willing to live for it. (Sometimes that's harder, you know.) Think how we would feel if he called it the gospel of the law of God. Sounds scary. Or suppose he wrote about the gospel of the holiness of God? Sounds intimidating. But he reveled, as can we, in the gospel according to the grace of God.

When men and women have the conviction that they are doing the work that God has given them to do, in their souls are zeal and courage that all the forces of this world cannot destroy.

> **G**od's grace is sufficient.
> —Gordon T. Smith

> **G**race is pardon; grace is power; grace is promise.
> —Lewis B. Smedes

GRACE

■ *God's kindness toward humanity, without regard to the worth or merit of those who receive it, and without their deserving it.*

We could spend most of our lives doing a word study on the word *grace*. There are so many facets to it. It affects the core of our being and spills over into our finances, our relationships with others, and our prayer life.

In Hebrews 4, the writer tells us to "come boldly to the throne of grace" (v. 16). I was wondering how we would feel if he had written about our coming boldly to the throne of judgment. That term doesn't engender an attitude of wanting to come at all, much less with boldness. Or suppose he invited us to come to the throne of condemnation? Who on earth would want to come?

Entering the throne room of God and coming before the very throne of grace require no security measures. Nobody checks you out. You don't have to stand in line. You don't even have to make an appointment. You just come. You rightfully belong there because of grace.

When John F. Kennedy was president of the United States, security was frequently tight. But one picture captivated the hearts of America as his tiny little son, affectionately called John-John, sneaked by all the security personnel and curled up close to his daddy. He had instant access. It didn't matter what any of the Secret Service agents said, John-John could come anytime he wanted to because he was the son.

Grace brought us to the Savior, often after we spurned Him on many occasions. Grace brings us back to Him when we fail. Grace lavishes us with all the things we need to live for Him. Grace implores us to do good works, out of sheer gratitude. Grace displaces us when we test the limits. Grace tells us we're accepted on Another's merits. Grace is more than what we need when we suffer. Grace superabounds where sin abounds. Grace invites us to a throne where we find One to help in time of need.

QUOTES

When you experience grace and are loved when you do not deserve it, you spend the rest of your life standing on tiptoes trying to reach His plan for your life out of gratitude.

—Charles Stanley

And if by grace, then it is no longer of works; otherwise grace is no longer grace.

—Romans 11:6

INSPIRATION OF SCRIPTURE

■ *God-breathed; supernatural divine influence on the prophets, apostles, or sacred writers by which they were qualified to communicate truth without error.*

 SCRIPTURE

2 TIMOTHY 3:16–17

All Scripture is given by inspiration of God, and is profitable for doctrine, for reproof, for correction, for instruction in righteousness, that the man of God may be complete, thoroughly equipped for every good work.

COMMENTARY

The Bible claims that *all* Scripture is God-breathed. The part about Adam and Eve? Balaam's donkey talking? Jonah and the fish? A real flood in Noah's day? The Red Sea parting?

All Scripture? A raven feeding a man? Battles fought—and won—with trumpets?

All Scripture? A virgin birth? Miracles of disabled people walking, blind people seeing? A little boy's lunch feeding more than five thousand people? A little child actually raised from the dead? A disciple walking on the water? A Savior rising from the dead?

All Scripture. God-breathed. For us.

It claims to be the very Word of God? All of it? How do we know?

A CLOSER LOOK

Is the Bible the Word of God? If we want to be intellectually honest, we will study the evidence. It is not a simple question, and I don't want to give simplistic answers. We can see how people would ask, "You really mean that the Bible came from God, through the Holy Spirit, through human writers, through original manuscripts, through copies of manuscripts, through ancient versions, through quotations from the church fathers, then through printed editions of the text, through more modern versions to us?"

That's a legitimate, thoughtful question.

First of all, we need to realize that we cannot prove history. The only thing we can prove is what is repeatable and observable. History is based on evidence, not proof. Our whole court system is based on this. In a courtroom, evidence is introduced. The jury looks at evidence. Jurors have to decide, using probable cause, whether or not the eyewitnesses or others involved are telling the truth.

In looking at the evidence that the Bible is the Word of God, we also can make decisions on what is probable, not what is possible. And we must be

Inspiration of Scripture

INSPIRATION OF SCRIPTURE

intellectually honest when we look. As apologist (and former lawyer) Josh McDowell put it, it is "evidence that demands a verdict." That is, once we weigh all the evidence, we need to do something with that information. We cannot be neutral with our verdict. No hung jury or mistrial.

In a study of historical manuscripts of any type, three tests are used to determine the reliability: (1) the date they were written, the origin, and the condition of the manuscripts; (2) the character of the writers; and (3) the content of the documents (do they appear mythical or read like someone is hallucinating?).

This is true in studying any historical documents, whether biblical or not. For instance, two Oxford students began in 1895 a systematic search for papyri. Over a period of ten years they found more than ten thousand manuscripts and parts of manuscripts in Egypt. They were dug out of sand-covered rubbish heaps, stuffings in mummy cases, and embalmed crocodile bodies. They consisted mostly of letters, bills, receipts, diaries, certificates, and almanacs. Some of them were valuable historical documents dating as far back as 2000 B.C. Most of them were dated, however, from 300 B.C. to A.D. 300. Among them were some early Christian writings.

> **T**he most influential book cited by 223 corporate CEOs and college presidents is the Bible.

Along with those finds, there was a fragment of John's gospel. It is a tiny scrap of papyrus, 3½ inches by 2½ inches, containing on one side John 18:31–33, and on the other side John 18:37, 38. It is a part of one leaf of a manuscript that had been originally 130 pages, 8¼ inches by 8 inches. Because of the shape of the letters and style of writing with certain dated manuscripts, scholars assign it to the first part of the second century. It is the oldest known Bible manuscript, and it is evidence that the gospel of John was in existence and was in circulation in Egypt in the years immediately following John's death.

If we apply the very same tests to this gospel of John that we applied to the almanac and diary, we produce evidence of its reliability. Because an ancient almanac and ancient diary demand very little in our belief system, and have virtually nothing to do with our behavior, it is easier to be objective when looking at them than when looking at biblical documents.

But since we have determined we want to be intellectually honest, let's continue to look closer at the reliability of the Bible.

During the first century, two important Romans wrote history. Almost no one else wrote about the subjects they covered, so everything we know about the events like the Gallic Wars is from these two men. Although Caesar wrote during the first century, the writings were not discovered until nine hundred years after they were written. We have only ten copies of this book. There are a few scattered fragments, but there are only ten copies.

INSPIRATION OF SCRIPTURE

Caesar's book is quoted in other history books. No one doubts its authenticity, even though there are few copies and many years between the writings and their discovery.

The other writer of Roman history, Tacitus, was hired by his father-in-law, who was a general going into battle. He wrote *The Annals* about the battles in which his father-in-law fought. Virtually nothing is known about these battles other than what Tacitus wrote. He fills many gaps in the chronological history during that time.

We don't even have all of his letters or manuscripts. We have only twenty copies, about 60 percent, and those copies, too, are dated about 900 or 950. Even though we do not have a lot of copies and even though there is a significant time lapse between the writing and the finding of the writings, this man's work is accepted as ancient history. No one doubts the authenticity of his work.

> **F**ifty-seven percent of young people said no objective standard of truth exists.
> —Josh McDowell

In light of the writings of these two men, how does the Bible stand in comparison?

A copy of Matthew, Mark, Luke, and John was found together in one volume—not separate—in A.D. 250. A copy of the gospel of Luke, just as it appears in our Bible, is dated A.D. 175. The fragment mentioned earlier from John's gospel was dated A.D. 150. It is believed that the Lord Jesus Christ died in A.D. 30, so there is a very small time span between His death and the writings. When I stated that the fragment was found in Egypt, it is even more noteworthy that so soon after the gospel events, people started distributing copies not just nearby in Jerusalem but in Egypt.

By A.D. 350, there were five thousand Greek manuscripts of the New Testament. This is incredible evidence that the news needed to get out to the whole world.

In light of the test of the date, origin, and condition of the manuscripts, the New Testament evidence is more reliable than ancient history.

Although we don't have the originals of any ancient manuscripts, we do have copies. The earliest manuscripts were written on papyrus. Papyrus was made of slices of a water plant that grew in Egypt. Two slices, one vertical and the other horizontal, were pressed together and polished. Ink was made of charcoal, plant gum, and water.

Papyrus was not very durable. It became brittle with age or rotted with dampness and soon wore out. Paper does not last very long today, so we can only imagine the lack of durability in the paper used in ancient writings.

We can see why copies were necessary. But this is true of all ancient documents. It was true of the writings of Homer—of which, by the way,

INSPIRATION OF SCRIPTURE

there is not a complete known copy available from earlier than A.D. 1300— as well as other documents.

Our faith can only be strengthened to see how the New Testament manuscripts so closely followed the actual event, and there were so many of them. The people who copied the documents were known as scribes, and they took their profession very, very seriously. Scribes who copied ancient history did so with care, and those who handled what they considered to be the Word of God did so with utmost reverence and awe.

Our first test in the evidence for the reliability of the Bible is the date, origin, and condition of the manuscripts. The Bible is better documented than ancient history!

The New Testament writers, often poor and relatively unknown, had their writings better cared for than writers in the powerful, influential Roman Empire. Could it have been the Story itself that was so powerful? Surely, the Romans had their own historical stories, but nothing to compare with the Story written by some lowly fishermen and seemingly insignificant followers. Although the Romans were very interested in getting their history spread throughout the world, the followers had Someone orchestrating the distribution of their manuscripts.

Because there were so many manuscripts—which increases the chances of accuracy—those working on the canon of Scripture took the similar manuscripts and compared them. There were some differences, but the differences were minimal. There were primarily grammatical differences such as an *s* on a noun in some and only the singular noun in other manuscripts. In studying variant texts, we can see that not one thing in the manuscripts affects truth. The only substantial variations are in $^1/_{1000}$ of the New Testament. This amounts to about ¼ of one page of the Greek text.

The comparisons were not lightly done. There is a scientific, technical process in comparing variant texts. But there is not one shred of evidence in any of them that the Word of God is not trustworthy.

Let me give an example in English of how the texts differed. If you should get a telegram one day that reads, "You inherited a million," you probably would take that seriously. You probably would not say, "A million what? I don't like this telegram. It doesn't give enough information." The next day, you receive another telegram that reads, "You have inherited a million dollar." You probably would not complain that the *s* is missing on the word *dollar*. You compare it with the first telegram, and you like what you read. The next day, you get another telegram: "You've inherited a million dollars." You probably would not say, "Okay, which is it: You or you've? Dollar or

INSPIRATION OF SCRIPTURE

dollars?" And on the fourth day, you get the final telegram, "You have inherited a million dollars."

These are "variant texts" telegrams. But comparing one with another only sheds more light on your good news; it doesn't make you doubt because a letter was left off or the verb changes. And you have only four telegrams to compare. Suppose you got five thousand telegrams with only that little variation. You would probably believe that you had inherited a million dollars! Those are exactly the types of minute variations in the biblical manuscripts.

All those manuscripts, spread throughout the world, copied over and over, still bore no discrepancies that would affect the truth. That, in itself, is strong evidence that the Bible is the Word of God.

The New Testament gets an A+ when we apply the test of the date, origin, and condition of the manuscripts. If we do not accept the biblical manuscripts, we need to throw out all of ancient history because the historical manuscripts so widely accepted just do not pass the tests with flying colors like the biblical texts.

The second test that should be applied to see if a manuscript is authentic is the character of the writers. For example, it would be hard to take seriously the writings of a group of known liars.

Let's look at the four Gospels first. Matthew claimed to be an eyewitness of what he wrote. Mark probably interviewed people, and some think he may have questioned Peter at length. Luke interviewed a group of people. John was an eyewitness.

The four men could have gotten together and come up with a collective fabrication. Or they could have had individual fabrication. Or they could have written the truth.

What does one story that is told from four perspectives sound like? There is a certain pattern when four individuals or groups of people tell the same story: different emphasis, different details, general agreement about focus, and apparent contradictions.

I put this question to a test. I heard four people, who had not collaborated, tell about an exciting play in an Atlanta Braves baseball game. It was amazing. After I listened, I knew I was hearing about the same play, but the details each gave were totally different.

One girl told about her father jumping up and down in excitement and breaking his sunglasses in the excitement. The other three did not mention that because it was not important to them. They told about other things. One had given up on watching the game on television and had gone to bed,

By all those inconceivable means at the disposal of the sovereign God, the Holy Spirit used the writers of Scripture to produce through them the message that He wished to communicate to man.

Inspired Scripture is . . . written revelation, just as the prophet's sermons were spoken revelation.

Inspiration of Scripture

INSPIRATION OF SCRIPTURE

listening to it on the radio. One mentioned a player standing behind home plate, and another mentioned someone else standing behind home plate.

There were enough apparent contradictions in their stories that I knew they had not collaborated, but there were enough similarities that I knew they were telling about the same play. They just told it from their vantage point.

The writers of the Gospels gave the Story with enough distinctions that it is obvious they did not collaborate. The differences in their writings only persuade us that it is not a collaborated lie because the details vary enough to let us know they were writing from different vantage points.

But the similarities, the threads, running through their letters let us know that they are telling the same wonderful Story. There are many striking parallels. So the seeming contradictions give credence to the truth of the Gospels, as do the parallels.

When Matthew wrote to the Jews, he wrote about Jesus as King of the Jews. Mark wrote with a different thought; he presented Him as the Servant. Luke, the physician, wrote about Him as the Son of man. John wrote about Him as the Son of God. That is four men, writing from four different vantage points, with four different emphases. But the Story didn't change.

We need to look at the men themselves. They didn't become wealthy or well known. If they were in it for the money or fame, they were dismal failures. Why would four men spend their whole lives writing without reward? What did they expect in return? They preached Christ until their death.

People don't die for something they know is a lie. A person will lie in order to keep living, but no one dies for a lie.

So, as eyewitnesses or interviewers of eyewitnesses, they knew they were writing—and dying for—the truth. They didn't die for a religious ideology or philosophy. They died because they knew what they had seen and heard was the truth: there was One named Jesus, virgin born, worker of miracles, crucified and risen, and seen of many after He arose. They were willing to die rather than deny what they had beheld.

Dying for something doesn't make it a true belief. There are those willing to die for false theology. The difference in these men is that it was not some theory they had come up with and chose to believe. The men were dying for what they saw and heard. There is a big difference in ideology and firsthand reporting.

The biblical narratives fare better—much better—than ancient history when we hold them up to the three objective tests for reliability: origin,

> **A**ll which comes within the category of Scripture is God-breathed and thus profitable for guiding both faith and life.

INSPIRATION OF SCRIPTURE

date, and condition of the manuscripts; character of the writers; and the content.

But how do we know that it is the Word of God? Remember the question, "You really mean that the Bible came from God, through the Holy Spirit, through human writers, through original manuscripts, through copies of manuscripts, through ancient versions, through quotations from the church fathers, then through printed editions of the text, through modern versions to us?"

The Bible is not a book. It is a library. There were sixty-six books written by many generations of many men over hundreds and hundreds of years. Our faith does not rest on a discount store paperback. Our faith is based on an entire library.

These sixty-six books, written by about forty men, all converge to tell the same Story. It's almost as if there was one main Author, using writers to tell the Story that He wanted told. Of course, we believe that is exactly what happened.

Jesus said it was the Word of God. He confirmed the Old Testament, and He predicted the New Testament.

A religious group called the Sadducees tried to confuse—and discredit—Jesus. They did a rather poor job by asking a totally ridiculous question, based on the Old Testament (Matt. 22:23–46). Jesus admonished them by saying, "You are mistaken, not knowing the Scriptures" (Matt. 22:29). (He referred to the Mosaic writings as the Scriptures.) He quoted a verse to them from the Old Testament and asked, "Have you not read what was spoken to you by God?" (Matt. 22:31). Jesus was equating the Old Testament as God's Word.

Jesus was born into a Jewish community where the Old Testament was accepted as the Word of God. Most Jews today believe it, also. So when He went into the temple and read from Isaiah, or during His temptation by Satan when He refuted each temptation with a quote from the Old Testament, He was referring to the Word of God.

He referred to David's writings in the book of Psalms and said that David spoke "in the Spirit" (Matt. 22:43–46).

Also in Matthew 22, we read that as Jesus was having the discourse with the Sadducees, the Pharisees were lurking around. They prided themselves on knowing (and supposedly keeping) every jot and tittle of the law. But when Jesus was quoting the Old Testament, the Bible says the Pharisees and Sadducees gave up trying to outsmart Jesus. He knew the Old Testament! He regarded it as the Word of God!

> The overriding reason for accepting the divine inspiration and authority of Scripture is plain loyalty to Jesus Christ.
> —John R. W. Stott

Inspiration of Scripture

INSPIRATION OF SCRIPTURE

Jesus talked about Noah and the Flood. He referred to the Second Coming and compared the evil days with the ones in Noah's time. He did not refer to the Flood as an allegory. He referred to it as a historical happening (Matt. 24:37–39). Since Jesus believes the Scripture is true, it seems rather foolhardy for the rest of us to question it.

He even referred to Jonah! He was talking about His death and being dead three days and three nights before His resurrection. It would have been ludicrous to have used a myth to illustrate the Crucifixion. But He said, "For as Jonah was three days and three nights in the belly of the great fish, so will the Son of Man be three days and three nights in the heart of the earth" (Matt. 12:40).

He mentioned the ancient city of Sodom (Matt. 11:23–24). He used it as an illustration of judgment, and it would be unthinkable for Jesus to use mythical stories to illustrate judgment. He would use something His followers were familiar with and would take very seriously. Every one of the followers knew about Sodom, and they knew it was historical fact because they had heard about the city from the Old Testament.

Jesus not only freely quoted the Old Testament and gave His stamp of approval that it was the Word of God, but He also intimated the origins of the New Testament when He said the Helper, the Holy Spirit, would teach them the new truth and remind them of what He had told them (John 14:26).

In 1 Timothy 5:18, Paul quoted Luke as an inspired writer. In 2 Peter 3:15–16, Peter referred to Paul and even said that some things Paul wrote are hard to understand. (That should encourage a lot of us!) Peter referred to the prophets and apostles as inspired writers (2 Peter 3:2). Paul claimed that his writing was inspired (1 Cor. 2:7–13; 14:37). John, writing the book of the Revelation, claimed inspiration (Rev. 1:2).

The church fathers quoted almost all of the New Testament.

Although it was not a world of railroads, airplanes, televisions, and radios, there was communication. But it was slow. Printing was unknown then, and making copies by hand was hard work. It was also a time of persecution, and some Christian writings had to be hidden.

There were no councils or conferences where the early believers got together and compared notes on what writings they had. That didn't happen until the day of Constantine.

But when we look at the Old Testament and the New Testament and apply the tests of reliability, we can be intellectually honest and accept them together as the Word of God.

Some use the word *inerrant* to describe the Bible. That means it is without error. It is a reliable document when it refers to faith, and it is a reliable

> **N**ever has a skeptic been able to overturn or overthrow the evidences for the inspiration of the Scriptures.
> —D. James Kennedy

Doctrine

INSPIRATION OF SCRIPTURE

document when it speaks about history and science. It is a reliable document. Period.

What an encouragement to us! When we started out, we looked at the importance of evidence and probable cause. We decided we could use our minds, not just our hearts, to see whether the Scriptures are reliable.

After looking at the many manuscripts, the writers themselves, the dates of the earliest manuscripts, the way the four Gospel writers told their stories, and the way the Lord Jesus Christ quoted from the Old Testament, I think we can be intellectually honest and say the evidence is there, and there is more than enough probable cause that the Bible we hold is the Word of God.

God loved His creation enough that He wanted us to know of His plan of redemption. He would not give us an inaccurate account of such an important plan. He would make sure we got the full picture, especially since our eternity rests on it.

It only stands to reason that He loves us enough, and loves His Word enough, that He watched over every writer and every scribe so that we have the greatest Love Story ever told. I believe if we have a weak view of Scripture, we have a weak view of God. He is the Great Communicator. We just need to read what He communicated about Himself to us in His Word.

It really is evidence that demands a verdict. Remember, no hung jury.

APPLICATION

So we have a Love Letter. What do we do with it?

A young woman told of getting a lengthy love letter from her fiancé before he went to the mission field for a short term. Everyone teased her because of her utmost care—and frequent reading—of the one letter. She read it over and over. She even had it memorized after a while.

What made this letter different from her other mail?

She was in love with the author.

And the author was in love with her.

That makes all the difference in the world.

JUSTIFICATION

■ *Process by which sinful human beings are made acceptable to a holy God.*

SCRIPTURE

ROMANS 5:1

Therefore, having been justified by faith, we have peace with God through our Lord Jesus Christ.

COMMENTARY

The Greek verb tense used in this verse means a once-and-for-all transaction. We have been justified—that is, declared not guilty once and for all.

The word *justify* is not only a theological term, but it is a judicial or legal term as well. As far back as the book of Genesis, the question was asked, "Shall not the Judge of all the earth deal justly?" (Gen. 18:25 NASB). If we accept the Lord Jesus Christ who died in our place, we are justified, at peace, spared from the penalty.

How can God be righteous when He acquits a man and declares him righteous? How can He do this and maintain His integrity?

The apostle Paul makes the problem even more acute by showing that all people are sinners (Rom. 3:23). So if God declares someone righteous, He is declaring one to be righteous who is unrighteous. How can He possibly do that?

In the most wonderful way imaginable.

The process of declaring us not guilty starts and ends with the Godhead. Romans 3:26 states that He is "just and the justifier" of those who believe.

Because He is just—acknowledging the gravity of our sin—and the *Justifier*—paying the penalty for our sin—He does not violate His attributes.

The book of Romans refers to Abraham's justification: "For if Abraham was justified by works, he has something to boast about; but not before God. For what does the Scripture say? 'And Abraham believed God, and it was reckoned to him as righteousness'" (4:2–3 NASB).

The word *reckoned* here is not used in the vernacular sense. It does not mean "I guess so; I hope so." The Greek word used means "credited"; it was *credited* to him as righteousness. There is no guesswork in any aspect of justification.

A young woman was stopped by a policeman for speeding. She was newly married and had just obtained a driver's license in the state where many speed limit restrictions had been removed. The policeman peered into her car window and asked if she realized how fast she was going.

Having just studied the driver's manual, she boldly answered, "Oh, yes, sir. But the manual states that a resident of this state can drive as fast as she wants as long as she thinks it is safe. I felt I was safe."

> **W**e . . . being called by His will in Christ Jesus are not justified by ourselves . . . but by that faith which . . . has justified all men.
> —Clement of Rome

> **A** real Christian expects to go to Heaven on the virtue of another.
> —A. W. Tozer

JUSTIFICATION

The policeman smiled and responded, "That law is only applicable where there are no speed limit signs posted. And mainly on rural roads. You are within city limits with signs posted everywhere. You should've read the manual more carefully."

Should the young woman have not been let off with just a warning by an amused policeman, she would have wanted a merciful judge. The duty of the judge, however, would be to uphold the limits set.

Our manual, the Bible, tells us the limits are posted. Therefore, violation is possible. The Bible also makes clear every one of us is a violator.

He satisfied the demands of the law to remain as the righteous Judge and enforce laws, but also to be the merciful Judge.

The Judge Himself took the place of the condemned. Penalty for sin was paid so that the laws of justice were satisfied. But the penalty was paid with a great price.

Once we are justified, we are free to change— and change is exciting.
—Tim Hansel

APPLICATION

In 1829 in the state of Pennsylvania, George Wilson and others were arrested for robbing a train. They were tried and found guilty. The penalty for their crime was death by hanging. George Wilson's brother, a politician, tried to get him a pardon. The governor of Pennsylvania could not help because it was a federal crime. The governor suggested he see the president of the United States. The president was convinced that a pardon was in order, and he signed a presidential pardon.

George Wilson, however, refused the pardon, saying, "I did it. I will pay for the crime." The warden didn't know what to do. The case was sent through various courts, all the way to the Supreme Court. The highest court ruled that if a pardon was refused, the penalty must be paid. In April 1830, George Wilson was hanged by the neck until he was dead.

He would not receive the pardon.

The president can pardon crimes without payment of the penalty. But God can pardon crimes only with the payment of the penalty by a qualified substitute.

The Substitute was the Lord Jesus Christ. The pardon, however, must be received to be effective.

A CLOSER LOOK

The Word of God deals with the marvelous dichotomy that although we previously were "without excuse" (Rom. 1:20), we are now seen "free from sin" (Rom. 6:18).

JUSTIFICATION

■ *Process by which sinful human beings are made acceptable to a holy God.*

One can almost picture a courtroom drama. Satan, our accuser, seeks to prosecute. He gleefully points out to the Judge why we are condemned.

But our Advocate, or Lawyer for our defense, pleads our case. The Bible calls Him our *paracletos* or the "One who is called alongside." I can visualize in our modern judicial system the Lawyer sitting alongside us. He says, "My client is not guilty. Exhibit A is My pierced hands; Exhibit B is My pierced feet; Exhibit C is the wound in My side." Even as Satan shouts, "I object!" the righteous Judge will respond, "Objection overruled."

Why? Because He is the perfect Substitute. The penalty was paid. The one who receives the pardon by faith is fully justified.

The verdict? NOT GUILTY.

QUOTE

It is not "just as if I've never sinned." That is too shallow. It is "*although* I am a dirty sinner, He died for me and sees me as clean."

—Charles Swindoll

■ *To purchase; to buy back.*

REDEMPTION

1 PETER 1:18–19

SCRIPTURE

Knowing that you were not redeemed with corruptible things, like silver or gold, from your aimless conduct received by tradition from your fathers, but with the precious blood of Christ, as of a lamb without blemish and without spot.

COMMENTARY

In our natural way of thinking, it seems logical to repay debt with money. But Peter states that sin debt is never paid for that way. One can give large offerings. One can leave everything to the church or a philanthropic cause, but the sin debt is still there.

To understand redemption, we need to see an overview of the sacrificial system in the Old Testament. To cover sin, the sacrificial lamb needed to be without blemish, and its blood had to be shed. Practically every sacrifice included the sprinkling or smearing of blood, teaching that redemption involves life for life.

The high priest not only had to offer an animal for the people's sins, but he also had to offer one for his own sin first. The Lord Jesus Christ, our High Priest, was sinless and offered Himself as the One who would die for our sins, not His own, for He had none. The whole book of Hebrews describes His once-and-for-all offering as the final blood sacrifice (Heb. 7:27).

In the Old Testament, the animal sacrifices were a foreshadowing of the Lamb of God. The sacrifices were in seed form what the Lord Jesus did in a fully developed form later on. The blood of goats and sheep covered sin; the blood of Jesus removed it completely!

He could give His life in our place because He was sinless. We were purchased at great price. But silver and gold had nothing to do with it. Our sacrifice—dying once and for all—was the spotless Lamb of God. Blood had to be shed. If the blood of animals would have done the job, God would never have sent His Son.

Someone has called it "the terrible price of the priceless blood."

But He came. Sinless. Willing. One for all. Once and for all. Redemption!

A CLOSER LOOK

Each of us had a sin debt, and it needed to be paid. We were all born as slaves to sin who needed to be purchased for freedom. The word *redemption* indicates how the debt was paid and the freedom purchased, how the account was settled.

REDEMPTION

The whole Bible is a story of redemption. A scarlet thread runs from the first book to the last book.

After Adam and Eve disobeyed God, they tried to cover themselves—and their disobedience—with fig leaves (Gen. 3:7). But God, wanting them to know they could not cover sin with their works, provided for them. He did not take vegetation, which must have been plentiful in the lush garden. He clothed them with "tunics of skin" (Gen. 3:21). The word *tunics* is plural—one for each of them—but the word *skin* is singular. One sacrifice.

In the very first book of the Bible, with the very first people, a blood sacrifice was offered. God did for them what they could not do for themselves.

As the thread of redemption continues to weave throughout the Word of God, we see the Israelites being led out of bondage. What a glorious picture as the blood of the Passover lamb was put on the doorpost and lintel of the house! The death angel would spare those covered by the blood (Ex. 12:7, 13), a vivid reminder that the blood must be applied to the doorpost of our hearts!

After the deliverance through the Red Sea, Moses spent forty days and forty nights with God. There God gave him the rituals of worship that are recorded in the book of Leviticus. Perhaps no other book in the Bible portrays and prophesies the sacrifice of the Lamb of God as the book we read infrequently because we don't understand the significance behind the blood sacrifices.

As the Old Testament foretold and illustrated redemption in a figurative way, the New Testament boldly tells of the One who purchased our redemption. He was the Lamb of God whom John spoke of (John 1:29).

The perfect Sacrifice.

The meaning of *redemption* is two Hebrew roots that designate a process by which something alienated may be recovered for its original owner by paying a sum of money. This alluded more to slaves being redeemed by money. We have already seen in 1 Peter 1:18 how "silver or gold" could not redeem us. We were alienated from God, although He was our original owner. So, He paid the ransom.

Why was a ransom necessary? Throughout church history, several views have been held. One is that Christ was the ransom paid to the devil to redeem people who had become slaves to Satan. This view has always been met with strong opposition and has never been accepted as doctrine.

To counteract this teaching—that God owed Satan a ransom—an opponent of this view came up with a contrasting belief. Abelard in A.D. 1141 taught that there could be nothing in the "divine essence that required satisfaction."

> **Y**ou are a new creation, not a "recycled" one or one wearing a disguise.
> —*In Touch*, March 1995

He wrote that the Cross was only an exhibition of divine love and its effect was only a moral one—that the Cross would merely serve to woo sinners.

Neither view is right.

God owes Satan nothing. The ransom for sin was not paid to Satan. Redemption was a necessary act, but the necessity was not imposed from without. If that were so, God would not be God. The necessity for redemption was imposed from within, by virtue of His just nature. Holy God not only required a ransom; He paid it.

The other view—that the Cross is some sentimental expression—totally misses the horror of the Crucifixion. If God wanted to impress us, He would surely have devised a way that would not have required the death of His only begotten Son.

The Bible nowhere teaches that the Cross was merely a moral victory. What cheap theology! When we see the awfulness of sin, we see why the ransom was such a costly one. We have a spiritual debt, and it is sheer pride to think it as simple as a moral deficit.

What more could God do? "He made Him who knew no sin to be sin for us" (2 Cor. 5:21). God foretold His coming and foreshadowed it in blood sacrifices throughout Scripture. The sinless Lord Jesus shed His blood to ransom sinners back to a holy God. He was the perfect Substitute.

He didn't die for His sin; He died for ours. God accepted the payment. When Jesus cried on the cross, "It is finished," He used the word that means "paid in full." It is the same word that was stamped across bills when they were paid. The debt was canceled. The ransom paid.

Not only were the children of Israel told to celebrate their redemption (Ex. 12:47) and not only did the psalmist sing, "Let the redeemed of the LORD say so" (Ps. 107:2), but an unparalleled celebration is yet to be. The book of Revelation tells us of a huge celebration where those who have "washed their robes and made them white in the blood of the Lamb" (Rev. 7:14) will forever sing redemption's story. The Lamb, who shed His blood to purchase us, will be at the center. Redeemed ones from all nations, tribes, peoples, and tongues will cry joyfully with a "loud voice" (Rev. 7:9–10).

Redeemed, how I love to proclaim it. Redeemed by the blood of the Lamb. The old account was settled long ago!

A little boy worked side by side with his father in the workshop. The loving dad taught his young son how to build a tiny boat. The small fellow worked hard at his task. He listened carefully how to cut pieces of wood and how to use the right nails. His father put his large hand over his son's hand as they gently hammered together. The boy thought the blue paint was

> **I**t became clear that the narrowness of God's redemptive plan was rooted in his perfect standard of justice and in the grievousness of sin.
> —*Decision,* Feb. 1995

REDEMPTION

■ *To purchase; to buy back.*

just the finishing touch and could hardly wait for it to dry so he could sail his masterpiece.

Several days later the young master builder sat next to the tiny lake on their farm. He clapped with glee as the boat floated. As the blue treasure bobbed back to him time and again, he pushed it out in the water just a little farther. One big push, however, sent the boat way out of the boy's reach, and he sadly watched it sail out of sight.

Dejected, the lad went into the house. The parents prodded the story out of a silent, sad little son. The father, trying to ease the brokenhearted boy's pain, promised to take him to a nearby town to buy an even better boat. As the two walked the street the next day, the little boy spotted something in the window of the small pawn shop. He quickly took his father by the hand and went in. In excited childish fashion he exclaimed to the owner of the shop, "That's my boat in the window! The blue one in the window is my boat! I made it!"

The gruff proprietor was not moved. "Listen, that boat was found on the lake and brought in this morning. If you want it, you gotta pay for it."

Wide-eyed, the boy queried, "Pay for my boat? The one I made? But it's mine!"

Irritated, the owner answered, "As far as I know, it was a lost boat that someone found and brought in. If you want it, you gotta pay for it."

The little boy reluctantly gave a few coins to the man. And the man gave the small blue boat to the little boy.

As he and his father left the pawn shop, the lad clutched his boat and said, "You belong to me twice. Once 'cause I made you. And twice 'cause I bought you back."

When God made His creation, He was prepared to pay whatever price to buy us back. And He did. Paid in full.

APPLICATION

Following an exhilarating ball game, a fan remarked: "Well, our team redeemed themselves with that good showing, didn't they?"

What did he mean? He meant that the team had vindicated themselves. They had done poorly, but they had balanced things by doing well. That's wonderful for a sport, but in a spiritual sense it doesn't work that way. First, no matter how much good we do, it does not vindicate us—we still fall short. We are debtors. Second, "redeem ourselves" is a foreign idea when applied to spiritual life. The Bible teaches it is "not of yourselves; it is the gift of God" (Eph. 2:8).

The team members congratulated one another on their skills and good showing, but we cannot boast of such. Anticipating we just might, Paul addresses the fact, "lest anyone should boast" (Eph. 2:9).

When looking at redemption as a gift of God, we can only be humbled at the price of such a gift. Free to all? Yes, free for the taking. But the cost is immeasurable. Free to all? Yes, but the gift is not a cheap one. The payment was the death of God's Son.

Thank God we don't have to do extra good on Tuesday to redeem ourselves from a poor showing on Monday. The price of redemption was paid at Calvary, and our works have nothing to do with it.

 QUOTES

Every tiny bit of my life that has value I owe to the redemption of Jesus Christ. Am I doing anything to enable Him to bring His redemption into evident reality in the lives of others?

—Oswald Chambers

Those of us who know the wonderful grace of redemption look forward to an eternity with God, when all things will be made new, when all our longings will at last find ultimate and final satisfaction.

—Joseph M. Stowell

REPENTANCE

■ *A change of mind resulting in a change of behavior.*

PSALM 51:1–4

Have mercy upon me, O God,
According to Your lovingkindness;
According to the multitude of Your tender mercies,
Blot out my transgressions.
Wash me thoroughly from my iniquity,
And cleanse me from my sin.
For I acknowledge my transgressions,
And my sin is always before me.
Against You, You only, have I sinned,
And done this evil in Your sight—
That You may be found just when You speak,
And blameless when You judge.

COMMENTARY

Two counterfeit forms of repentance are often passed off as the real thing. One of them goes something like this: "Lord, I'm really sorry I got caught." The other sounds like this: "Lord, I'm really sorry I sinned. I certainly hope I can do better next time." Both of these are prompted out of guilt or embarrassment, not a heartfelt sense of remorse over the fact that God has been grieved. Usually, these people have no intention of changing. They are attempting to get God off their backs.

Genuine repentance involves several things. First of all, confession. Not just, "Lord, I'm sorry for my mistake," but, "Lord, I have sinned against You." Confession acknowledges guilt. Second, repentance involves the recognition that the sin was against God. Notice what David said in verse 4, "Against You, You only, have I sinned." That doesn't mean he failed to recognize that he had sinned against Bathsheba and her husband. He realized that his sin was primarily against God.

All of us need to recognize that our sin is primarily against God. Other people may be hurt as well, but when we hold our sin up to the unconditional love and grace of God as expressed through the giving of His Son, we see that is where sin is darkest. Repentance begins with confession of our guilt and recognition that our sin is against God. But genuine repentance goes farther.

Repentance includes taking full responsibility for our sin. David accepted full responsibility for his actions with Bathsheba. He said, "I acknowledge my transgressions, and my sin is always before me." He doesn't rationalize, "Now, Lord, You know it takes two. I wasn't the only one involved. She

> **R**epentance is not a thing of days and weeks . . . to be got over as fast as possible. No, it is the grace of a lifetime, like faith itself. . . . that is not true repentance which does not come to faith in Jesus and that is not true faith in Jesus which is not tinctured with repentance.
> —Charles H. Spurgeon

should have been more careful. You know I am only human." David never accused Bathsheba. He never mentioned her name.

Whenever we catch ourselves blaming someone else for our sin, our repentance is incomplete. If we are truly repentant, we take full responsibility for sin, no matter what happened or who was involved. Regardless of the nature of the temptation, we are ultimately the ones who make the decision to sin.

Last, repentance requires total honesty with God. Repentance is not complete without honesty. I believe God is looking for us to be honest about our sin—honest about our weaknesses, our failures, and our frustrations. Honesty promotes fellowship. As long as we continue to be open and honest with God, He can continue to work with us, even after we have committed our most grievous sin.

We get into trouble when we start to cover things up: "Now, Lord, I know I have made a mistake. But after all, everybody makes mistakes. Nobody's perfect." Responding like this is avoiding the real issue and is therefore dishonest. As long as we approach God in that fashion, there is not much He can do with us.

> **T**rue repentance hates the sin, and not merely the penalty; and it hates the sin most of all because it has discovered and felt God's love.
> —William Mackergo Taylor

APPLICATION

What happens when we delay our repentance? Are there consequences? God's discipline is connected to repentance. The Bible teaches that God disciplines those who are disobedient. It is full of illustrations of God's discipline. The story of David and Bathsheba is one of the best examples.

When David committed adultery with Bathsheba, he didn't repent immediately. It was some time later before David faced up to what he had done. And even then, he didn't do it on his own accord. God had to send a prophet to confront him (2 Sam. 12). Only after Nathan told him the story of the man who had many sheep stealing from the man who had only one sheep did David realize the great evil he had done. That was when David repented of his sin. The discipline that followed, however, was severe in nature, and part of the reason for the severity was David's failure to repent sooner.

It is my conviction that if you and I deal with our sin genuinely, openly, and immediately, God can lessen the severity of our discipline. This makes sense in light of the nature of discipline. Discipline is for the purpose of getting us to change, to obey. If God sees that we want to cooperate and that we have purposed in our hearts to obey the next time, stern discipline is not usually needed.

> **R**epentance always brings a man to this point: I have sinned. The surest sign that God is at work is when a man says that and means it.
> —Oswald Chambers

Repentance

REPENTANCE

■ *A change of mind resulting in a change of behavior.*

When we perpetuate our sin with no intention of stopping, we won't escape the disciplining hand of God. For our own sake, and for the testimony of His kingdom's sake, He cannot let us continue in our sin. The longer we put off repentance in our lives, the greater God's discipline. Those who are wise will repent quickly.

A CLOSER LOOK

What does repentance mean for the unbeliever? Repentance for those outside Christ means a change of mind. The unbeliever is to change his mind about what he believes concerning Jesus Christ. He moves from unbelief to belief that Jesus Christ paid the penalty for his sin. An unsaved person admits that she cannot save herself. She trusts Christ instead of her goodness for eternal life. She changes her mind about God and His payment for our sin. It is important to understand repentance for the unbeliever is not referring to cleaning up his life. If he can earn forgiveness of sin and a home in heaven by changing his life through self-effort, there is no need for the Cross.

Peter proclaimed the need for repentance: "Repent, and let every one of you be baptized in the name of Jesus Christ for the remission of sins; and you shall receive the gift of the Holy Spirit" (Acts 2:38). Peter was compelling them to believe that Jesus was more than a man from Nazareth. He was the resurrected Lord and Christ. He was the Messiah they had longed for. They needed to change their minds from believing that Jesus was just a man to accepting His deity. Peter said the evidence pointing to His deity was miracles, wonders, and signs, but most of all, God raised Him from the dead. He challenged them to think of Jesus as more than a local person who was a good teacher. Peter was instructing the Jewish people to change their beliefs about Jesus (Acts 2:22–36).

Repentance and belief are so intertwined that they are almost synonymous. You cannot have one without the other. They are two sides of the same coin. Jesus used *repentance* as synonymous with *belief* when He said, "Thus it is written, and thus it was necessary for the Christ to suffer and to rise from the dead the third day, and that repentance and remission of sins should be preached in His name to all nations, beginning at Jerusalem" (Luke 24:46–47). Someone may say, "But doesn't Acts 20:21 teach that repentance and belief are not the same?" The verse states, "I have declared to both Jews and Greeks that they must turn to God in repentance and have faith in our Lord Jesus" (NIV).

I like the way Charles Ryrie explains this passage:

> **W**hatever is foolish, ridiculous, vain or earthly, or sensual, in the life of a Christian is something that ought not to be there. It is a spot and a defilement that must be washed away with tears of repentance.
> —William Law

Summarizing his ministry in Ephesus, Paul said he testified to both Jews and Greeks of repentance toward God and faith in Jesus Christ. Does this not show that faith and repentance are not synonymous? Or at least that repentance is a precondition to faith? No, because the two words, repentance and faith, are joined by one article which indicates that the two are inseparable, though each focuses on a facet of the single requirement for salvation. Repentance focuses on changing one's mind about his former conception of God and disbelief in God and Christ; while faith in Christ, of course, focuses on receiving Him as personal Savior.

After you receive Christ, you will continue to repent as you grow in Christian faith and character. This repentance is a change of mind that leads to change of behavior.

RESURRECTION

■ *A rising from the dead.*

SCRIPTURE

1 CORINTHIANS 15:13–14, 17

But if there is no resurrection of the dead, then Christ is not risen. And if Christ is not risen, then our preaching is empty and your faith is also empty. . . . And if Christ is not risen, your faith futile; you are still in your sins!

COMMENTARY

According to these verses—in fact, according to the entire chapter of 1 Corinthians 15—our faith rests on the fact of the resurrection of Jesus Christ. According to the apostle Paul, if the resurrection of Jesus Christ is not fact, we have no sermons to preach, we have nothing to base our faith on, and we are still in our sins.

The Resurrection is a fact. Those who are not quite sure, and who do not trust the Bible's account, can go to the library and investigate Josephus's historical accounts.

And for those of us who do believe the Bible is an accurate account of the life, death, and resurrection of Jesus Christ, we have much to rejoice about.

A man from the former Soviet Union spoke to our church. He related how Easter is the favorite day of the year in his part of the world. He compared our country's emphasis on Christmas with his country's emphasis on Easter.

We can see that people whose world has been so dismal for so long, and whose faith has been challenged on every hand, would take great joy in celebrating Easter. Life! Resurrection! Those in the early church greeted one another with the salutation, "The Lord is risen," to which the other would add, "He is risen, indeed."

A CLOSER LOOK

Resurrection is not just New Testament theology. Job believed in the resurrection from the grave. (The book bearing his name is considered to be one of the oldest books in the Bible.) In his deep pain and sorrow, he asked,

> *If a man dies, shall he live again?*
> *All the days of my hard service I will wait,*
> *Till my change comes (Job 14:14).*

It was not an unusual thing for Job to cry out in his anguish. Nor is it unusual for us to cry out in ours, "Is this it?" But Job shouted out through

RESURRECTION

it all, "I know that my Redeemer lives, and He shall stand at last on the earth" (Job 19:25).

We can picture suffering saints through the ages crying out those words with Job, "I *know* that my Redeemer lives." And we can almost hear those anguished, yet rejoicing, believers add in song, "And because He lives, I can face tomorrow." Only because of the Resurrection do we have such hope.

David spoke of the Resurrection in the book of Psalms, and Isaiah proclaimed, "He will swallow up death forever, and the Lord GOD will wipe away tears from all faces" (Isa. 25:8).

Daniel wrote,

> And many of those who sleep in the dust of the earth shall awake,
> Some to everlasting life,
> Some to shame and everlasting contempt (Dan. 12:2).

Hosea added these words of the Lord: "I will ransom them from the power of the grave; I will redeem them from death" (Hos. 13:14).

The Sadducees were a New Testament religious sect that did not believe in a resurrection. In an effort to trick Jesus, they asked Him about a woman whose husband had died and who then married a series of family members as each one died. Their question was, When this woman is resurrected, which man will she be married to? Jesus, knowing the religious men were schooled in the Old Testament, cut through all their questions, not to mention through their motives, and answered, "But concerning the resurrection of the dead, have you not read what was spoken to you by God, saying, 'I am the God of Abraham, the God of Isaac, and the God of Jacob'? God is not the God of the dead, but of the living" (Matt. 22:31–32). Jesus believed in a resurrection.

In the Old Testament, we read about the widow's son being raised from the dead (1 Kings 17:17–22). The resurrection of her son gave greater credence to Elijah's words to this mother. She already knew he was a prophet sent from God, for she treated him with honor in providing a room for him and gathering up a few remaining morsels of food. She exclaimed with great joy, "Now by this I know that you are a man of God, and that the word of the LORD in your mouth is the truth" (1 Kings 17:24).

J. Vernon McGee said he could just picture the apostle Paul going to the major cities on his missionary journeys with his Old Testament parchment to expound from. After Paul finished preaching about the resurrection of the Lord Jesus Christ, Dr. McGee said he could visualize the Jews arguing

In the fourth century, Jerome wrote, "From India to Britain, all nations resound with the death and resurrection of Christ."

Jesus tasted death. But hell's party was canceled after only three days. —Joseph Stowell

RESURRECTION

■ *A rising from the dead.*

with Paul, "That's not in our Scriptures!" And he could imagine Paul fingering his parchments and saying, "I'd like to remind you about Isaac and Abraham. Abraham received that boy back from the 'dead' in essence. Now remember, God spared not His own Son but freely gave Him up for us also."

Dr. McGee went on:

> Then, he probably turned to the Mosaic system of sacrifice and the book of Leviticus and showed Jesus as the Sacrifice; and then he'd talk about the Day of Atonement and the two goats which pictured Christ's death and resurrection. Then he'd tell them about Aaron's rod that budded, and the book of Jonah, which is a picture of resurrection. Then Paul would read the Messianic Psalms of chapter 22 and 16 and then Isaiah 25 and 53.

> This is the most important issue you will ever have to decide. Did Jesus rise from the dead or not?
> —Michael Green

Often, we think of one resurrection—and of course, Christ's resurrection was by far the most important—but other people were raised from the dead in Scripture. In the New Testament, Jairus's daughter was raised (Matt. 9:23–25). In Luke 7:11–15, the widow's only son was raised; in John 11:43–44, we read about Lazarus's "coming forth"; Dorcas was raised (Acts 9:36–40). One significant event that is seldom preached about was at the tearing of the veil of the temple when Jesus was crucified. The Bible records, "Behold, the veil of the temple was torn in two from top to bottom; and the earth quaked, and the rocks were split, and the graves were opened; and many bodies of the saints who had fallen asleep were raised; and coming out of the graves after His resurrection, they went into the holy city and appeared to many" (Matt. 27:51–53).

Every one of these people who died and was raised, whether in the Old Testament or the New Testament, had one thing in common: they all died again. Christ's resurrection was unique. The Lord Jesus Christ died. He was resurrected. He ascended. He never went back into any grave.

But we have more than internal evidence. Before we look at the external evidence, we need to address several theories that have surfaced from time to time that are intended to discount the resurrection of the Lord Jesus Christ.

The swoon theory maintains that Jesus was not really dead but only swooned on the cross. After He was laid in the tomb, the cool damp environment of the cave revived Him.

There are numerous problems with this from a biblical, as well as a practical, viewpoint. The Bible said He was dead. He "yielded up His spirit" (Matt. 27:50). The angels said He was dead. Even the Pharisees wanted the tomb sealed, "lest His disciples come by night and steal Him away, and say to the people, 'He has risen from the dead'" (Matt. 27:64).

From a practical point of view, those who hold to the swoon theory do not realize the horrors of crucifixion. Even the soldiers who started to break His legs realized they did not have to because He was dead. They were not His friends; they were His enemies, men whose job was to ensure that Jesus was dead. Furthermore, no one who had just awakened from a swoon could push away the huge stone that sealed the door to the tomb, much less subdue the guards stationed there.

Some hold to the theory that the body was stolen. Two groups of people could have stolen it: His friends or His enemies. Many of His friends died as martyrs. They went to their graves still claiming that Jesus was the Christ and that He rose from the dead. People don't die for what they know to be a lie. Think about it. If you had stolen His body to convince everyone that He had really risen—and then your life was on the line for this false message you had been proclaiming—wouldn't you recant? Wouldn't you admit to the lie? Sure you would. So would I. So would they.

His enemies had a better opportunity to steal the body because they could have struck a deal with the soldiers standing guard. After all, they were allies. However, what purpose would stealing the body have served for them? They had no reason to have it. But if they had stolen His body for some sordid reason, when news of His resurrection started surfacing, wouldn't they have produced it to disprove the resurrection rumors? Of course they would. The only reasonable explanation is that He died, He was buried, and He arose. And after rising from the dead, He walked the earth for forty days.

> The evidence for the resurrection of Jesus Christ has been examined more carefully than the evidence for any other fact in history!
> —D. James Kennedy

After He arose, He appeared to Mary Magdalene (John 20:11–18); the other woman (Matt. 28:1–10); Peter (1 Cor. 15:5); the two on the Emmaus Road (Luke 24:13–27); ten of the disciples (Judas was dead and Thomas wasn't there, in John 20:19–24); and eleven disciples eight days later (Thomas was there, in John 20:26–29). According to John 21:1–23, He met with seven disciples, and 1 Corinthians 15:6 tells of five hundred followers seeing Him at once. He appeared to James (1 Cor. 15:7); all the disciples at the Ascension (Acts 1:3–11); Paul (1 Cor. 15:8); and finally the apostle John (Rev. 1:9–18).

When skeptics question that perhaps a disciple here or a woman there in grief only imagined seeing the Lord Jesus, they have a hard time refuting His appearance to five hundred people. It is impossible to think that all five hundred would imagine the same thing, no matter how grief-stricken they were.

RESURRECTION

The grave was empty. No one stole His body. He was seen and touched. He ate with them. He talked with them. Their lives were transformed. Many became bold to the point of martyrdom. He had said He would rise, and He did. Even the day on which we worship was changed from Saturday to Sunday to celebrate His resurrection.

There was a time that I would almost become physically ill when I thought about having to bury my mother someday. She and I were very close. We were a team as I grew up. My father died when I was nine months old, and my mother worked very hard to put food on the table and wisdom in my soul. She loved me with all of her being, and I loved her. The thought of her dying was overwhelming to me.

On Easter Sunday, she was preparing to come to our early church service, and she fell down some basement steps. It was not long after that she suffered a stroke and was hospitalized. In November of that same year, God took her to Himself.

Although deeply saddened, I knew it was not a final parting. I knew I would see her again. And it is because of the resurrection of Jesus Christ that I can say that. If I served a Savior who was still in the grave, I would have no hope whatsoever that my mom is also alive. I think if there were no Resurrection, I would despair beyond anything I can imagine. But I know He arose! And I know that "because He lives, all fear is gone." The thing I dreaded for so long was cloaked in His victory. There is no way to explain it.

But it is so very, very real.

A woman told of how she went to the cemetery to put Easter lilies on her son's grave. She stood there and read the inscription on her son's headstone. She wept. She looked at the pink dogwood tree just above the grave. The buds were about to break open into new life once again. She said she talks to God a lot when she's out there, and after she saw the almost budding dogwood tree that had looked so dead all winter, she couldn't contain her joy.

She said she could almost hear the Lord Jesus say, "Why do you seek the living among the dead?" as an angel had asked after Christ's resurrection (Luke 24:5). She knelt down and adjusted the Easter lilies and said, "Father, I know it's because of the Resurrection that someday this grave is going to burst open."

Today, in our society, a doctor is helping people end their lives. He is sometimes referred to as Dr. Death. Basically, those two terms are not thought of as being compatible—*doctor* and *death*. If you go to a doctor, you want him to be a doctor of life.

> **I**n the early church, as in many churches today, believers greeted one another on Easter by saying, "Christ is risen," to which the others would respond, "He is risen indeed."
> —Mark D. Taylor

RESURRECTION

The term *risen Savior* is compatible. When you come to a Savior, you want Him to be alive.

He is. So's my mom.

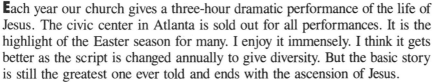

Each year our church gives a three-hour dramatic performance of the life of Jesus. The civic center in Atlanta is sold out for all performances. It is the highlight of the Easter season for many. I enjoy it immensely. I think it gets better as the script is changed annually to give diversity. But the basic story is still the greatest one ever told and ends with the ascension of Jesus.

Each year as I sit there and anticipate the Resurrection scene, I feel as if I am going to explode with excitement. I am extremely tense during the trial and the beating of Jesus. I get incredibly angry at the Roman soldiers (who are my church members!) as they yell at and hit the Savior. I am weary and sad during Gethsemane and the Crucifixion scenes. I am sometimes exhausted after those scenes because they seem so real to me.

Then the music changes. The mood changes. Disciples and women are running across the stage looking for Jesus, wondering where His missing body could be. Women weep. Disciples shake their heads. Jesus' mother is pondering. I want to stand up in the civic center and shout, "He's risen, just as He said!" I never have done that and I'm sure those around me are grateful, but I've wanted to.

The strangest feeling overtook me one year. As the disciples peered into the tomb and as angels hovered nearby and they cradled His folded graveclothes in their hands, I wanted to get up out of my seat and walk up on the stage to look in the tomb, too. I knew it was empty, but I wanted to experience the thrill that those first disciples must have felt when they walked into the empty tomb.

We can't imagine their despair and then their feeling of utter amazement and victory!

His resurrection assures our resurrection. There would still be the sting in death if He had remained dead. But He was the firstfruits of resurrection (1 Cor. 15:20). He paved the way for us.

Of course, we grieve when someone we love is taken in death. But we grieve differently from the way the world does. We do not grieve as those who have no hope. We can look forward to a wonderful reunion someday with them and with the One who died—and lives—for us!

If He had remained dead, we would have nothing.

Nothing.

> **C**hristianity is in its very essence a resurrection religion. The concept of the resurrection lies at its heart. If you remove it, Christianity is destroyed.
> —John Stott

RESURRECTION

No hope. No faith. No comfort.

But we have a living Savior, who transcended the laws of death and smashed them forever.

A little girl took a caterpillar and put it in a metal box that once held Band-Aids. She shut the lid tight to keep the caterpillar in and then went on her way, virtually forgetting about her wonderful catch. The caterpillar spun a tight cocoon inside the box.

One day while the girl was at school, her mother was cleaning her room. The mom opened the box to see what treasure the little girl had hidden. Out crawled a beautiful butterfly.

The mother closed the bedroom door tightly, so she could show this creation to the little girl when she came home. She could hardly wait. She met her daughter at the door and said, "Guess what! You've kind of become a mother!"

The child couldn't imagine what on earth her mother was talking about. But then the mother slowly opened her door and showed her the butterfly basking in the sunshine on the window sill.

Butterflies, although a beautiful illustration of new life emerging out of something seemingly dead, do not adequately portray the Resurrection. Jesus was not in some flimsy metal box. He was in a sealed tomb with guards standing nearby. He was wrapped in a cocoon of death, yet He broke forth.

The stone was rolled away from the tomb not so Jesus could get out but so the world could look in. His resurrection assures yours. Because He lives, you will live forever.

SPIRITUAL GIFTS

■ *Special abilities given to believers at conversion by the Holy Spirit for building up the body of Christ.*

1 CORINTHIANS 12:4–11

SCRIPTURE

There are diversities of gifts, but the same Spirit. . . . But the manifestation of the Spirit is given to each one for the profit of all: for to one is given the word of wisdom through the Spirit, to another the word of knowledge through the same Spirit. . . . But one and the same Spirit works all these things, distributing to each one individually as He wills.

COMMENTARY

Of all the sermon series I have preached, none have captured our people's attention like my series on spiritual gifts. People are interested in the gifts of the Spirit. Much has been published on the topic. You can take all kinds of tests to determine your gift or gifts. And yet in spite of all the information available, there is still confusion, even controversy.

I believe much of the confusion over the gifts stems from an attempt to understand them apart from the Spirit-filled life and our roles in the body of Christ.

Each person's role in the body of Christ is determined by the spiritual gift. A spiritual gift is a special ability from God. William McRae, who wrote *Dynamics of Spiritual Gifts,* defined it as "an ability to function effectively and significantly in a particular service as a member of Christ's body, the church." In *The Holy Spirit,* Billy Graham compares spiritual gifts to tools. Each member of the body of Christ has been given one of these tools to use in building the body.

There is much discussion about the differences between a spiritual gift and natural talent and ability. The Bible, however, is silent on this subject, so I will be, too. I do know that both spiritual gifts and talents are from the Lord.

Through the distribution and networking of spiritual gifts, God has created a system ensuring that (1) every believer has a significant role in the body of Christ, and (2) believers work together to accomplish His overall purpose.

The Holy Spirit distributes gifts according to His will. And His will is in accordance with the Father's plan for the church. Three truths need to be emphasized.

1. Spiritual gifts are manifestations of the Spirit (1 Cor. 12:7). When a believer exercises her gift, it is an exhibition of the Spirit's power through her. It is not simply a matter of doing something she is good at. Spiritual gifts are a manifestation of the Holy Spirit. This is readily acknowledged

Spiritual Gifts

SPIRITUAL GIFTS

when the more spectacular gifts are exercised. For example, we are quick to give the credit to God when someone is miraculously healed. But when someone with the gift of mercy exercises his gift, we say things like, "Isn't he sweet?" or "He is such a good listener." The gift of mercy or giving or administration is no less a manifestation of the Holy Spirit than the gift of healing or the effecting of miracles (1 Cor. 12:10).

Now, I want you to think about something. If walking in the Spirit involves sensitivity to the promptings of the Holy Spirit, and if the Spirit manifests Himself through the gifts, is it possible for someone to walk in the Spirit without exercising her gift? Absolutely not. The Holy Spirit will reveal Himself in a special way through you, through the exercise of your gift. To refuse to use your gift is to say no to the Holy Spirit.

2. Spiritual gifts are for the common good of the body (1 Cor. 12:7). The primary purpose of spiritual gifts is building up the body, not the personal gratification of the individual member. Your nose is worthless apart from its service to the body. And the same holds true of any particular spiritual gift. Its worth is determined by its usefulness and availability to the body.

The more spiritual men or women are, the more involved they will be with the body of Christ. Why? Because as they give free rein to the Holy Spirit, He will continually lead them to exercise their spiritual gifts for the common good of the body. And that necessitates involvement.

I know many believers have been hurt by organized religion. But despite their protestations, they are part of an organized body. A body in which each member has a significant part. A body that cannot function as well without them as it can with them. To experience the power of the Holy Spirit in their lives to His fullest extent, they must put themselves in a position where the Spirit is free to express Himself through them for the common good of other believers.

Men and women who are being led by the Spirit will exercise their spiritual gifts within the body of Christ.

When we speak of building up the body, we are not talking necessarily about building a bigger body. The gifts were given to aid in developing a healthy body as well. Spiritual gifts are God's way of administering His grace to others. When we exercise our gifts, we function as the hands and feet of Christ. For example, when a man loses his wife, it's comforting for him to know that he will see her again someday. But that is not nearly as comforting as having friends around to succor him. Believers with the gift of mercy gather around him to listen. Another with the gift of administration takes care of all the funeral arrangements. A neighbor with the gift of

Do you tend to be a spiritual lone ranger? If so, begin today praying that God will give you a desire to be interdependent with the body of Christ.

Have you identified the areas in which the Holy Spirit has especially gifted you?

hospitality invites him to spend several nights with his family. When these things happen, it is as if Christ Himself reaches down to take care of one of His own. Through the exercise of these gifts, this wounded soul is dispensed a healthy portion of God's grace.

When a man or woman with the gift of giving pays another believer's electric bill, it is God's grace. When a pastor gifted as an exhorter stands to deliver a message, it is God's grace to the people. When a believer with the gift of service gives time to meet a need, it is God's grace in action. In these instances, Christ is at work through His body. It is more than a matter of people being *nice*. It is Christ manifest on earth.

Many believers miss what God is doing. What they see as purely human can be a divine act. When we serve others through the use of our gifts, we are channels through which the grace and power of God are manifested. When you hear about believers in need, don't stop at praying, become part of the answer. Exercise your gift. After all, isn't it a bit strange to pray for a friend who has a financial need when you have the resources to meet it? Do you think God is going to create money and drop it out of the sky? Of course not. His plan to meet the needs of His people is *His people*. That is why He has gifted us. When one hand gets a splinter, what does the other hand do? It goes to work to remedy the problem. And when you use your gift to remedy the problem of another believer, you become the hand of Christ.

3. Spiritual gifts are distributed as the Holy Spirit wills (1 Cor. 12:11). The last point I want to make in regard to Paul's comments on spiritual gifts is that the Holy Spirit decides gift assignments. There is emphasis these days on getting certain gifts. But we must leave the administering of the gifts to the Holy Spirit. Notice what the apostle Paul says: "But one and the same Spirit works all these things, distributing to each one individually as He wills" (1 Cor. 12:11). And a few verses later, "But now God has set the members, each one of them, in the body just as He pleased" (1 Cor. 12:18). God has the big picture. He knows exactly how much of what is needed in the church. From His perspective, things can be kept in perfect order and balance.

Paul instructs the believers in Corinth to place a high value on spiritual gifts. "Hold them in high regard," he says, "especially the greater gifts." He implies that believers should hold the gift of prophecy in such high esteem as to envy (not covet) those with that particular gift, for that is the greatest gift next to apostleship. When it comes to pursuing something, however, "pursue love," he says (1 Cor. 14:1). We can't get enough of that. And suddenly, we have gone full circle! For Paul defines love as a life

> **H**ow can you plug in and get your gifts functioning in a way that maximizes your contribution to the body of Christ?

> **F**our prerequisites needed to find your gift are being a Christian, believing in spiritual gifts, being willing to work, and praying.
> —C. Peter Wagner

SPIRITUAL GIFTS

characterized by the fruit of the Spirit (1 Cor. 13). To sum up Paul's entire argument, "You can have all the gifts in the world, but if your life isn't characterized by the fruit of the Spirit, they don't mean a thing!" Gifts are important. But apart from the fruit of the Spirit, they are worthless.

The presence of fruit, not gifts, demonstrates a believer's dependency on the Holy Spirit. Everybody has a gift. Possessing a gift says nothing about a believer's compliance with the promptings of the Spirit. As the apostle Paul says, the focus of the pursuit should be love.

APPLICATION

The Spirit-filled life is a life of interdependency. We are to depend on the Holy Spirit. But we are to live interdependently with other believers. Just as the members of a physical body work interdependently with one another to accomplish the will of the brain, so the members of Christ's body are to work together to accomplish His will. The apostle Paul described it this way in 1 Corinthians 12:12–27. Let's take a fresh look at this familiar analogy of the body.

You are a part of a living organism called the body of Christ—or the church. If any member of your physical body began functioning independently of the others, or stopped functioning at all, you would take immediate action to correct the problem. You wouldn't say, "Well, it's just my lung. After all, I have two." Or "I've got nine other good fingers, I'll just work around this broken one." The members of your physical body are so interdependent that they make it a priority to care for one another. Back to Paul's illustration: "And the eye cannot say to the hand, 'I have no need of you'; nor again the head to the feet, 'I have no need of you'" (1 Cor. 12:21).

What is true for our physical bodies is true for the body of Christ. I cannot say of any member, "I don't need you. I don't need to restore my relationship with you. I can do fine without you. I can go my way, and it will have no impact on me whatsoever." To do so is to deceive myself.

Referring to the actual body of Christ, Paul says, "There should be no schism in the body, but that the members should have the same care for one another" (1 Cor. 12:25). Did you get that? There should be *no* schism, or division, in the body. On the contrary, we should make a priority of caring for one another because when one member suffers, we all suffer—just like a physical body.

What would happen to a physical body if ailing members were untended? First of all, the functioning members would be forced to carry the load of the dysfunctional members. Eventually, the disproportional workload would

SPIRITUAL GIFTS

cause undue wear and tear on the good members, and they would begin to break down as well. An early grave would be unavoidable. Sound familiar? It ought to.

Take a close look at the condition of the church in America. I see scores of dysfunctional members of the body either going unattended or refusing attention. I see healthy members doing their best to pick up the slack left by the dysfunctional members and working themselves to death in the process.

The Head of the body is Christ (Eph. 5:23). He functions as mission control for the church. We are to take our cues from Him corporately as well as individually. He has a plan and purpose for His church, just as He has a personal will for your life. In fact, the two overlap. *As a member of His body, what you do or refuse to do as an individual affects the whole body.* Your participation counts. God's will for your life includes discovering your niche in the body and fulfilling your corresponding responsibility.

We resist this kind of accountability. Most of us would rather freelance the Christian life. Regardless of how far you advance in your personal holiness, you will always need other believers. Not because you are weak. Not because God isn't sufficient for you. On the contrary, God planned it that way. It is by His design. Walking in the Spirit is not a solo mission. It is not an excuse for you to become isolated from other Christians. A believer who pulls away from the body to do his or her own "spiritual" thing is not walking in the Spirit.

You can't walk in the Spirit apart from functioning in the body of Christ. It won't work. It has never worked. It wasn't designed to work that way.

Spirit-controlled Christians don't function as lone rangers. They don't buy into the "me and God are a majority" bit. Instead, they actively pursue relationships with other believers. They look for ways to be involved. They don't sit back and let others do the work. Spirit-filled men and women jump at the opportunity to carry their fair share of the load. I was reminded of this principle on a recent vacation.

I was taking pictures in a beautiful canyon. Later, I was walking along the creek bed looking for a place to sit when I slipped and fell hard into the rocky bed. Like any conscientious photographer, the first thing I looked for was my camera. Amazingly enough, it was still in my right hand. Not a scratch on it. I rolled over to check the damage to my arm. My arm and shoulder were fine. But my wrist was broken in two places.

I laid my camera down and got up slowly. I looked for a place to regroup. My eyes spotted a big flat rock a few yards away. I made my way over and sat down. Before long my friends caught up with me.

"How did you keep from dropping your camera?" they asked.

> Not everybody has spiritual gifts. Unbelievers do not. But every Christian person who is committed to Jesus and truly a member of his Body has at least one gift, or quite possibly more.
> —C. Peter Wagner

SPIRITUAL GIFTS

"I'm not sure," I replied. "When I went down, I probably instinctively held it up and stuck out my left arm to break my fall."

My doctor confirmed my suspicions after a couple of X rays. I had used my left arm to break the fall. If I hadn't, I could have really been hurt.

The whole situation reminded me of how dependent each member of the physical body is on the other members. My wrist took the shock of the fall. My legs picked me back up. My eyes located a place to sit down. My feet took my wounded wrist (and ego) to safety. And my other hand and arm nursed my wound as we made our way out of the canyon.

Now let's use our imagination for a moment. Imagine that my arms, legs, hands, and wrists all had personalities of their own. What if, as I started falling, my left arm shouted to my right arm, "Hey, you better get ready to absorb some extra weight"?

To which the right arm responded, "Are you kidding? He's falling toward you, not me! Besides, it's foot's fault. If he had been watching where he was going, none of this would have happened."

About that time the nose joined in the conversation, "Somebody do something! This is going to be serious."

"Don't yell at me," replied left arm. "I didn't do anything. And I'm not . . ." By that time I'm face down on the rocks with a lot more to worry about than a broken wrist. If the members of our physical bodies began acting independently of one another, we would be in a terrible mess!

 A CLOSER LOOK

I'm afraid the modern church has lost sight of the members of the body serving one another. Instead of organizing to meet the needs of the body, we expect pastors and staff to do it. When the pastor's performance demonstrates a deficiency in one or more gifts, he gets traded in on a new model. The new model usually has the gifts the old one didn't have but lacks the strengths of the first. Once the weaknesses surface, the search continues.

God didn't give pastors to the church to meet the needs of the body. Pastors were given to train the other body members to meet one another's needs: "He Himself gave some to be apostles, some prophets, some evangelists, and some pastors and teachers, for the equipping of the saints for the work of ministry, for the edifying of the body of Christ" (Eph. 4:11–12).

The gifts listed above are what I call the equipping gifts. Their purpose in the body is to equip the other members to carry on the ministry—not do the ministry themselves.

Think about this. If spiritual gifts are God's primary means of administering grace to His people, what does that say about believers who refuse to exercise their gifts for the good of the body? Four things come to mind.

1. They are robbing the body of Christ.
2. They are forcing other members of the body to carry their load.
3. They are dead weight on the body, dysfunctional limbs.
4. They are out of step with the Spirit of God.

Not a very encouraging report. Once again we are reminded that no one is a spiritual island. Our spiritual progress, as well as the progress of the whole church, hinges on our willingness to work together.

What about you? Are you plugged in? Are you using your gift for the common good of the body? Are you encouraging other members of your family to use their gifts? Or do you get in the way?

I know you are busy. Busyness has become the rule rather than the exception. Sunday may be the only time you can do things as a family. If you travel during the week, you may need Sunday afternoon to prepare for the following week. PTA, Rotary Club, and Little League may make it impossible for you to attend the midweek service at your church or serve on any committees. But these don't excuse you from your responsibility to the body of Christ. You have an important role, a role only you can fill. Your God-given gift may serve you well in your secular pursuits. But those must be secondary to your involvement in God's work. It is God's will for you and your family to be exercising your gifts for the common good of His people. If the church you attend does not provide you with flexible enough opportunities to do so, find another one. But whatever you do, exercise that gift! Peter exhorted the believers of his day in a similar fashion when he wrote, "As each one has received a gift, minister it to one another, as good stewards of the manifold grace of God" (1 Peter 4:10).

Again, we see an emphasis on the importance of using our gifts to serve others, not ourselves. Peter was so convinced that God ministers directly through our gifts that he went so far as to say that the person who has a speaking gift should speak as if he was actually speaking for God. The one with a serving gift, he said, will serve with the strength of God.

This latter illustration explains a phenomenon I have seen in churches all over the country. When people serve within the context of their spiritual gifts, they seem to do so effortlessly. There is little stress. And they don't tire easily. They emerge from their service with such excitement that they are generally ready for more. On the other hand, assign that same job

> **H**ow do we know what our gifts are and how do we use them? We need to ask four questions: 1. What do I naturally do well? . . . 2. What do others say I do well? . . . 3. What can I do better? . . . 4. What can I do to use my gifts?
> —Jim Watkins

SPIRITUAL GIFTS

description to someone who isn't gifted for it and it becomes dreadfully stressful.

Mary Gellerstadt is a perfect example of what I'm talking about. Mary served on our church staff for many years. Her gifts are in the areas of administration and organization. No matter how much responsibility I gave her, she handled it. Actually, she seemed to thrive on it. Thinking about her responsibility stressed *me* out! I never saw her get in a hurry. To my knowledge, she never missed a deadline. As long as she was administrating and organizing, she was in her element. She looked forward to tackling new responsibilities that called upon her to exercise her gifts.

On the other hand, I love to get up in front of a large group and speak. What an opportunity! I can't wait for Sunday mornings to roll around. Sometimes I am so excited on Saturday nights, I can't sleep. Nothing motivates me like preaching the Word. I feel almost no stress when I'm preaching. And I'm just as motivated at the end of our services as I was at the beginning.

When we minister to others through our gifts, we are tapping into the inexhaustible energy and motivation of God. When we exercise our gifts, the Holy Spirit works through us. We are doing what we have been called and equipped to do. We experience an extra measure of energy and joy.

Serving outside our gifts is a different story altogether. I believe this is the primary reason so many Christians get burned out on church work. Instead of finding a position where they can use their gifts, they sign up for whatever task is available. They do their best as long as they can take it, then they quit.

I know a man who attends a Sunday school class where they take turns teaching the lesson. He loves the Lord and loves his class, but teaching is not his gift. He dreads the Sunday he is assigned to teach. In his words, "I would rather cut a truckload of wood."

Some misinformed soul may hear a comment like that and be tempted to say, "Well, I guess he isn't very committed!" But nothing could be farther from the truth. It's not a question of commitment. It's a question of giftedness. This same man serves on the long-range planning committee for his church. When his church decided to build a new building, it was suggested that the pastor and several members of their committee visit other churches and look at their buildings. This fellow immediately volunteered to fly the group in his private plane at his expense. From what I know of this man I would welcome his participation on all our committees. But I wouldn't ask him to teach.

SPIRITUAL GIFTS

Probably the most common question asked in connection with gifts is, "How do I find out which ones I have?" When people ask me that question, I always respond with, "What do you enjoy most about serving the Lord?" Notice, I don't ask, "*How* are you serving the Lord?" I am interested in what they *enjoy* doing.

You will enjoy exercising your gift. You will look forward to the responsibilities you are given that call on you to use your gift. On the other hand, you will not be as motivated for tasks that are outside your giftedness.

There are several good gift tests available today. (For an excellent description of all the gifts as well as some helpful hints for discovering your gift, see *Dynamics of Spiritual Gifts* by William McRae.) But probably the best way to discover your gift is to serve in a variety of ministry situations. When you find the area that suits your gift, you will know it.

A delightful woman volunteers at a church in Mississippi. She organizes a large youth conference every spring involving several churches from around her area. She is a master organizer. She secures the facility, the speakers, and the musician. She organizes a committee to handle registration. And she puts together all the promotional material. Hundreds of teenagers have been blessed as a result of her hard work and dedication.

Someone asked her how she got started working with teenagers. She said she knew God wanted her to get busy serving Him, but she didn't think she had anything to offer.

"I tried working in the nursery, but I found myself dreading that," she said. "Then I thought about teaching, but the thought of it scared me. Then I heard they needed some help putting together meals for our summer youth camp. I thought, hey, I can do that. Before I knew it, I was in charge—and loving it."

The youth minister in the woman's church recognized that she had skills in organization and administration. His gifts were more in counseling and discipleship. So he turned much of the administrative aspects of the ministry over to her. She had found her niche. She didn't know much at the time about spiritual gifts. She just knew she had found something she couldn't get enough of.

While serving as a volunteer assistant to the youth minister, she began thinking about putting together a youth conference. Fortunately, her church recognized her gifts and encouraged her in her pursuit. The following spring they had their first conference. This past spring they celebrated their eighth anniversary.

> **O**ur challenge as Christians is to continually seek the best way to serve God with the gifts He has given us, rather than using them solely for our own gratification.
> —Elsa Houtz

SPIRITUAL GIFTS

Most people discover their gifts like this woman. They just do it. If you decide to approach it this way, remember that it may take a while. Don't be afraid of change. Remember, you are not quitting. You are searching for a place to settle in for the long haul.

The second piece of advice I would give those in search of their gift is this: concentrate on bearing fruit, and eventually, you will discover your gift. The Holy Spirit wants you to know your gift. Follow His lead, and you won't miss it.

Don't forget. You are a unique blend of talents, skills, and gifts, which makes you an indispensable member of the body of Christ. You can do what only you can do. So don't cheat the rest of us. Get out there and get busy! For this, too, is a part of the wonderful Spirit-filled life.

UNPARDONABLE SIN

■ *To attribute the work of the Holy Spirit to the power of Satan in the face of undeniable evidence to the contrary.*

MATTHEW 12:31–32

Every sin and blasphemy will be forgiven men, but the blasphemy against the Spirit will not be forgiven men. Anyone who speaks a word against the Son of Man, it will be forgiven him; but whoever speaks against the Holy Spirit, it will not be forgiven him, either in this age or in the age to come.

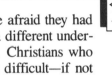

I have talked with Christians and non-Christians who were afraid they had committed the unpardonable sin. Just about everyone had a different understanding of exactly what it was, but they all felt hopeless. Christians who believe they have committed the unpardonable sin have a difficult—if not impossible—time accepting the doctrine of eternal security. This is the main reason we need to deal with the issue.

Hundreds of verses in the Bible promise the forgiveness of our sins, but only one passage refers to an unforgivable sin. Let's examine it to gain insight.

Jesus had healed a demon-possessed man who was blind and could not speak, "so that the blind and mute man both spoke and saw" (Matt. 12:22). The multitudes following Jesus began to say, "This man cannot be the Son of David, can He?" They wondered if He was the Messiah.

On the other hand, the Pharisees accused Jesus of casting out demons by Beelzebub, the ruler of the demons. Jesus' response to their accusation led Him to conclude what He said in Matthew 12:31–32. In this passage He refers to blasphemy.

The term *blasphemy* may be defined "defiant irreverence." We would apply the term to such sins as cursing God or willfully degrading things considered holy. In this passage the term refers to the declaration of the Pharisees who had witnessed undeniable evidence that Christ was performing miracles in the power of the Holy Spirit. Yet they attributed the miracles to Satan. In the face of irrefutable evidence they ascribed the work of the Holy Spirit to that of Satan.

I agree with a host of biblical scholars that this unique circumstance cannot be duplicated today. The Pharisees had seen proof of Christ's deity. But instead of acknowledging Jehovah God, they attributed the supernatural power to Satan instead of the work of the Holy Spirit.

Christ is not in the world as He was then. Although the Holy Spirit still accomplishes supernatural things through His servants, they are merely

> Christians who fear they have committed the unpardonable sin demonstrate by their repentance that they have not done so, and the forgiveness of God is freely offered to them.
> —Mark D. Taylor

UNPARDONABLE SIN

representatives of the King. The circumstances of Matthew 12 make it impossible for this sin to take place today. This incident, I might add, is the only one in which a sin is declared unforgivable. The Bible states, "Whoever calls on the name of the LORD shall be saved" (Rom. 10:13). No invitation to salvation carries with it an exception clause, "unless you have committed the unpardonable sin."

No matter how evil our sins, there is pardon for them. God forgave David for his adultery, dishonesty, and murder (2 Sam. 12:13; Ps. 51). Simon Peter's denial of our Lord accompanied by profanity was forgiven (Matt. 26:74–75). The apostle Paul was forgiven of his preconversion merciless persecution of Christians (Acts 9:1). Just about every possible sin is listed somewhere in the New Testament. And every one of them falls into the category of forgivable.

APPLICATION

Unpardonable sin is not a singular event for which a person later feels remorse. It is an ongoing, willful, and active rejection of the testimony of the Holy Spirit concerning the person and truth of Christ, and it can only be committed by an unbeliever.
—Mark D. Taylor

Although there is no unpardonable sin today, there is an unpardonable state—the state of continued unbelief. There is no pardon for a person who dies in unbelief. The Bible refers to this in terms of having a hard heart. The hardening of the heart is not a one-time act. It is the result of a gradual progression in which sin and the conviction of the Holy Spirit are ignored. The hardened heart has no desire for the things of God. But if you have a desire in your heart for God, as expressed through concern that you have committed some sort of unpardonable sin, you do not have a hardened heart. Your concern confirms your innocence. God always welcomes those whose hearts are sensitive toward Him.

On the other hand, if you are unsaved, that can be remedied this very moment. Salvation is by faith alone—faith in the death of Christ for your sin. You can place your faith in Christ by praying a simple prayer expressing trust in Christ alone for the payment of your sin. Acknowledge your sin, accept Christ's payment, receive His forgiveness, and thank Him for the gift of eternal life.

■ *God's personal, moral, and providential plan for His creation.*

WILL OF GOD

EPHESIANS 1:3–5

Blessed be the God and Father of our Lord Jesus Christ, who has blessed us with every spiritual blessing in the heavenly places in Christ, just as He chose us in Him before the foundation of the world, that we should be holy and without blame before Him in love, having predestined us to adoption as sons by Jesus Christ to Himself, according to the good pleasure of His will.

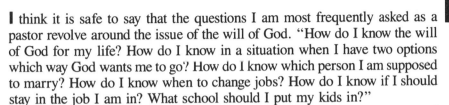

I think it is safe to say that the questions I am most frequently asked as a pastor revolve around the issue of the will of God. "How do I know the will of God for my life? How do I know in a situation when I have two options which way God wants me to go? How do I know which person I am supposed to marry? How do I know when to change jobs? How do I know if I should stay in the job I am in? What school should I put my kids in?"

As Christians, we believe that God is interested in these decisions and that, in fact, He has a plan for our life. We believe that God has a preference as to which direction we should take. But discovering His will can be a frustrating process.

God definitely has a will for you. If you were to take a concordance and look up the phrases "the will of God" and "God's will," you would find that, in the New Testament, the phrases fall into two categories. One category is "God's moral will." The other category is "God's personal will."

God's moral will in Scripture is the "dos" and "don'ts." "Thou shalt do this." "Thou shalt not do this."

For instance, Peter says that it is God's will that we obey human government. In 1 Thessalonians 4:3–4, Paul writes that it is the will of God that we be sanctified, that we abstain from moral impurity. There are almost a dozen other instances in the New Testament where God says, "This is My will."

The other category that we are usually interested in is God's personal will, which is His personal agenda for your life—the things that He has specifically designed for you.

Paul says in 1 Corinthians 1:1 that he has been "called to be an apostle of Jesus Christ through the will of God." God didn't call everybody to be an apostle. That was God's specific will for Paul.

Let's look at how to discover God's will. First, why do we even have to discover God's will? If I am His child and He is my heavenly Father, why

WILL OF GOD ■ *God's personal, moral, and providential plan for His creation.*

doesn't He just make it plain? Why all the seeming mystery? Why all the tension? Why all the pressure? Why all the tears and the fasting and the praying?

The answer to that question lies behind this whole issue of knowing God's will. As you read the New Testament and the Old Testament, you find that God is always more interested in revealing Himself than simply revealing details about His will for us. God does not want to function simply as an information center in our lives; He wants to be involved in our lives in the most intimate of ways through a relationship that revolves around faith and trust. In times of pressure and questioning when we seek His will, God has the intention of drawing us into a more intimate relationship with Him.

Think about a time when you had to make a big decision; you prayed diligently and finally came to a conclusion about God's plan. Not only did you arrive at an action plan, but you also emerged from the situation amazed at the goodness and grace of God. You had not only more information about what He wanted you to do, but also an awareness of who He is and how much He loves you.

God is involved in this process. And while we might want simply information, He wants us to trust Him. The principle of discovering God's will is couched in the context of a relationship. He is working to reveal Himself to you because He wants you to walk away from the process with your faith greater and your relationship more intimate.

There is an island in the Bahamas called Inagua. And from that island they export salt. There is a harbor that has been dredged out and is large enough for big ships to dock and get the salt. The water is not very deep, so the ship captains have to be careful once they come inside the reef to stay inside the channels.

I was photographing in the area and noticed a very interesting phenomenon. On the mainland behind the harbor on this particular island was a large pole. About forty yards behind that one, farther inland, was another one. Another was positioned in alignment in the distance. I figured this had something to do with the ships' navigation but wasn't sure how it worked. I asked a man standing nearby to explain their function. He said, "Well, those are channel markers."

I responded, "Channel markers are usually in the channel. These are on the island. So how does this work?"

He responded, "What happens is, as a ship approaches the island, the captain of the ship can see these three poles. He has to keep maneuvering his ship so that all three poles line up. And once they are aligned he knows he is in the channel and can approach the island safely."

> To know the will of God is the greatest knowledge! To do the will of God is the greatest achievement.
> —George W. Truett

WILL OF GOD

What God has done for us through His Word is give us channel markers that assure us that when these things line up, we can know we are following His will. I want you to be impressed with the incredible, practical approach God gives us to discern His will. It is not some kind of mysterious journey. He has given us objective channel markers to help us know whether or not our decisions agree with God's will for our life.

The first channel marker is God's moral will. God will never lead you to do anything that is in conflict with His moral will. Any decision you make or any option you are looking at that is in conflict with God's moral will is not of God.

He will never lead a husband to leave his wife for a more spiritual woman. It won't happen. That is not God. God will never lead a teenager to rebel against his or her parents. That is not God's way. God will never lead you to cheat on your income tax in order to give more money to the church.

God's moral will plays another important role. Obeying His moral will, the things that are clear, is the foundation for decision making in the more challenging arena of discerning His personal will. In John 14:21, Jesus puts it this way: "He who has My commandments and keeps them, it is he who loves Me. And he who loves Me will be loved by My Father, and I will love him and manifest Myself to him."

The man or woman who develops a lifestyle in harmony with God's moral commands will experience God's guidance in a special way. When you and I live lives of obedience, we are consistently in step with God's thoughts and God's ways. It makes sense that we are able to discern His voice more easily.

You are going to have a difficult time discerning God's personal will if you ignore His moral will. Why? Because as I said earlier, God is not interested in simply being an information center. He is interested in an intimate relationship with you.

There is a second marker—the principles of God's Word. The difference between God's moral will and His principles is this: God's moral will is clear commands. "This is what you do. This is what you don't do." Principles, however, are more like equations—an equation where God says, "If a man does this he can expect this to happen. If a woman does this, she can expect this to happen."

A principle is the law of sowing and reaping. We always reap what we sow. Another principle is this: things that you hold tightly to diminish; things that you scatter and give are multiplied and returned. "There is one who scatters, yet increases more; and there is one who withholds more than is right, but it leads to poverty" (Prov. 11:24).

> **H**as it ever struck you that the vast majority of the will of God for your life has already been revealed in the Bible? That is a crucial thing to grasp.
> —Paul Little

Will of God **229**

WILL OF GOD ■ *God's personal, moral, and providential plan for His creation.*

The Bible is full of principles. And here is the key: at some point in your decision making, your options will intersect with the principles of God's Word. The Bible is so incredibly packed with principles, there is no way for you to face any decision and not intersect with the principles of God's Word. God has given us His principles as a check and balance in the decision-making process.

Discovering the will of God is not the result of spending hours in a spiritual darkroom. That is not the picture. God has made it far simpler than that. He has given us principles that intersect with all the choices we must make. God wants to renew your mind with His principles. It is not a mystical thing. It is very practical.

Principles take precedent over a sense of inner peace. God does not want us to be slaves to vacillating feelings. He is far more practical than that. If you will keep God's moral will and constantly renew your mind to what is true, then, as the decisions come along, you will be able to sort out the options and discern what the will of God is for you. How practical. How wonderful.

Do you spend time in God's Word every day? If you don't and if you are not in some sort of systematic discipline to fill your mind with God's principles, you are going to have a difficult time making the right decisions, because the key to decision making is the principles of His Word. Promises have a role, but they are girded by the principles.

There is a third marker—wisdom. Ephesians 5:15 says, "See then that you walk circumspectly, not as fools but as wise." God has called us to ask of every invitation, every opportunity, every business transaction, every family decision, this important question: Is this the wise thing to do? In light of my present state of mind, in light of the present state of my relationship with my wife or my husband, in light of what's going on at work, in light of what's going on in my life right now, is this the wise thing for me to do? In light of where I want to be in the future, in light of the kind of marriage and the kind of family I want to have, in light of where I want to be financially, in light of where I want to be in terms of my career, in light of where I want to be in terms of my ability to serve God, is this the wise thing to do?

This question will quickly reveal your motive. It will reveal the selfishness in your relationships. It will reveal the greed in your financial decisions.

So in decision making, the place to start is measuring the decision against God's moral will. You have to measure it against the principles of His Word, and you have to measure it against this penetrating question: Is this the wise

> **I** find that doing the will of God leaves me no time for disputing about His plans.
> —George MacDonald

thing to do? If you do these things and still don't know God's mind, an example from Paul's missionary journeys is helpful.

Do you know how Paul decided which cities to visit? Paul apparently went where he wanted. He wasn't trapped by thinking, *Oh, what if I do the wrong thing? What if I step out of God's will?* He understood the incredible principle that God's will is not a tightwire that we fall off of. Acts 16:7 gives insight: "After they had come to Mysia, they tried to go into Bithynia, but the Spirit did not permit them."

A key word is *tried*. They tried to go to Bithynia. It is where they wanted to go. We don't know how, but somehow Jesus said, "Paul, this isn't the right route."

Paul, in his own way, said, "Okay, no problem." He did not get depressed or discouraged; he just started out in a new direction.

God, through His Word, has demonstrated that if children of God are willing to be honest and, to the best of their ability, do what God wants them to do, He will intervene if they make faulty decisions.

APPLICATION

Do you realize that God has made a commitment to tell us what we need to know when we are trying to make wise decisions? God doesn't want you making foolish decisions. Read the book of Proverbs. It is full of wisdom because He wants us to make wise decisions.

It is evident that God is interested in directing and guiding our lives, providing helpful wisdom for effective decision making. Let's ignore the ridiculous. Don't worry about what color socks you are going to wear. That is not the issue. We are talking about decisions in your life that matter— who you are going to marry, where you are going in your vocation, how you are going to spend or invest your time, what you are going to do with your money or your relationships with your family.

Remember, we belong to God. We do not have the right to make up our mind about what we are going to do and how we are going to do it independently of the will, the purpose, the plan, and the desire of God. You forsook that right when you said, "I receive the Lord Jesus Christ as my Savior." In that moment, He became the Lord of your life, whether you acknowledge it or not, whether you understood it or not.

We are to meditate on the Word of God. Scripture gives an understanding of the ways, the will, and the purpose of God. "Your word is a lamp to my feet and a light to my path" (Ps. 119:105). As we search and think deeply on the Word of God, asking God to speak to our hearts, He will work in such a way to help us understand His will.

The only way to know the mind of God is to know the Scriptures. The Scriptures sift, purify, and clear up our thinking process so we are able to think after God.

Sometimes God will give us wise counsel through others. However, you want to be sure that you are getting wise, godly counsel. Before you seek somebody's counsel, first examine his life. Is that person living in obedience to God? Is his lifestyle one of submission to the will of God?

A godly counselor is going to tell you the truth whether you like it or not. If somebody is committed to God's principles, he is going to be honest with you. So counselors are often God's way of giving us direction.

The Holy Spirit has an essential role in helping us know God's will. "Now we have received, not the spirit of the world, but the Spirit who is from God, that we might know the things that have been freely given to us by God" (1 Cor. 2:12).

One of the purposes of the Holy Spirit is to show you the truth. Remember what Jesus said in the Upper Room? He said, "When He, the Spirit of truth, has come, He will guide you into all truth" (John 16:13).

There will be times when we are suddenly faced with a decision. In that moment, we may not be certain what to do, which way to turn. As one of His prescribed, designated, divine responsibilities, the Holy Spirit unfolds and unveils God's will for you by interceding in your behalf with God the Father to reveal the mind of Christ in that given issue.

You cannot trust your feelings when it comes to discovering God's will. "Oh, I just feel wonderful about this. I think this is what we are going to do."

"Well, is that what God wants?"

"I feel good about it."

"Is that what God wants?"

"Well, it looks like everything is working out."

"Well, have you asked God about it?"

"No."

If you have sin in your life—willful, deliberate sin—trying to discover God's will is frustrating. You are saying, "God, I really want to know Your will in my life in this area. Whatever You say to do, I am willing to do. But God, don't worry about this area of sin right now. I'll take care of that later. I have got to know Your will now. I'll deal with that later." God is not going to let you ignore sin. I am not saying you will never know the will of God if there is sin in your life. Sometimes God may show you exactly what to

M**an proposes, but God disposes.**
—Thomas à Kempis

do, but then He will say it will never work until you deal with the sin problem. There is danger in praying and asking for God to show you His plan in a major decision when there is willful sin in your life.

Something is already wrong in your thinking process if you are tolerating sin. You have rationalized a given area that God says has to be dealt with. Here is the problem: our evaluation of sin is not the same as God's! He hates it. He wants it out of our lives, and He sees it as a stumbling block to His best for us.

Sometimes God delays revealing His will because He is getting us ready. He knows we are not prepared to fulfill His plan. You may lose your job and say, "Lord, what am I going to do?" God knows that in three months He has the most fantastic job ready for you, but He is working on some character traits such as perseverance and faith in your life in the interim.

GROWTH

Suggested reading for further study includes: *Knowing and Doing the Will of God* by J. I. Packer, *Affirming the Will of God* by Paul Little, and *God's Guidance* by Elisabeth Elliot.

END
TIMES

ANTICHRIST

■ *One who is to come; a political leader who will falsely set up a covenant with Israel and lead the world during the Tribulation.*

1 JOHN 2:18

Little children, it is the last hour; and as you have heard that the Antichrist is coming, even now many antichrists have come, by which we know that it is the last hour.

One visit to your local Christian bookstore should be enough to convince you of the immense interest in end time events. An issue that continues to intrigue much of the Christian community is the identity of the Antichrist.

Is he alive today? Is he in power somewhere in the world? Which nation will usher this seemingly dauntless leader onto the stage of world affairs? These are just a few of the questions many have sought to answer about this person. Several writers have developed intricate numeric schemes in an effort to identify either his name or his identity. Others have approached the subject from the standpoint of current world events.

The Bible, however, teaches that when the Antichrist comes onto the scene, there will ultimately be no doubt about his identity. His deeds and doctrine will eventually expose him to the world.

In his epistles and the book of Revelation, the apostle John made it clear that many people would come along in the spirit of antichrist. But there will come a day when one world leader will rise to power who will be the embodiment of evil, one who is empowered and directed by the devil himself. This will be *the* Antichrist. The benchmark by which these false prophets were to be tested concerned their attitude toward the incarnate person of Jesus Christ. Their refusal or failure to acknowledge that Jesus had come in the flesh would expose the spirit of antichrist, according to John. Therefore, if we take our cue from John, we can assume (accurately) that antichrists have come and gone since the day John penned his letters.

In the book of Revelation, John refers to the final and ultimate Antichrist as the Beast. The Beast will be the embodiment of the entire spirit of antichrist. He will have supernatural power and global influence.

The Beast first appears as a political leader, who will make a covenant with Israel and assume world leadership. Later he takes on the role of a religious leader who is worshiped. Supported by his sidekick—the False Prophet—the Beast will deceive the world. He, his prophet, and Satan will form an unholy trinity to rule all of creation.

> **A**ntichrist's power will extend to every area of life in every part of the world. His dictatorship will be religious, political, and economic. He will have supernatural abilities, including the power to counterfeit miracles.
> —George Sweeting

Antichrist

ANTICHRIST

Although we derive much of our thinking about the Antichrist from the descriptions of the beasts found in Revelation 13, the word *Antichrist* appears only in the epistles of John. As discussed earlier, John's reference was more pointed to a false doctrine than to a particular person. However, because of the interest in the "person" or "persons" described in Revelation, a brief look at the connection between John's idea concerning antichrist and the beasts described in Revelation is essential.

Two meanings go along with the prefix *anti*. The first carries the thought of "instead of" or "a substitute." A better way of putting this would be "false Christ." The second meaning is probably the one most often thought of—"against," or "against Christ." If you are antisomething, then you are against it. This, I believe, is the more accurate meaning of the term used in John's epistles.

The latter definition lends itself to the description of the first beast in Revelation 13:1, "I stood on the sand of the sea. And I saw a beast rising up out of the sea, having seven heads and ten horns, and on his horns ten crowns, and on his heads a blasphemous name." Scripture says this first beast will set himself up in direct opposition to Christ, falsely pledging to give Israel the land, bringing about peace for the first three and one-half years of the tribulation period. For this reason, many evangelicals believe this first beast to be the Antichrist.

The description of the first beast—especially the ten horns and seven heads—has led many to conclude that the first beast will be a political leader. He will achieve worldwide control through his plan for peace. This ruler will be in this position for the entire seven-year tribulation period.

Who will he be? Will he be resurrected from the dead, as many believe because of the reference to a fatal wound that has been healed? No one knows, and our most educated guesses are just that.

In direct cooperation with the first beast is a second beast known as the False Prophet, who will assume a place of leadership in the religious community that rightly belongs to Christ. Reference to this second beast is found in Revelation 13:11: "I saw another beast coming up out of the earth, and he had two horns like a lamb and spoke like a dragon."

There is much to be learned about the False Prophet from the description in Revelation 13:11–17. The description that he had two horns like a lamb but spoke like a dragon signifies his religious role. The word *dragon* has been used as a name for Satan; thus, the False Prophet is described in terms such that he will look like a lamb (Christ) but speak like a dragon (Satan). The role of this second beast is to support the first beast—the political leader.

Christians have identified various evil rulers through the centuries as the Antichrist, but none of them has fulfilled the role described for the Antichrist in Revelation.
—Mark D. Taylor

ANTICHRIST

The authority that this False Prophet claims is derived from Satan and the political leader. His role is to cause the inhabitants of the earth to worship the first beast, thus fulfilling the third part of the false trinity.

Many terms have been used to describe or define antichrist(s) or the Antichrist. One that comes to mind most often is *the deceiver*. Based on further study of Scripture, we can see that there will be an onslaught of false teaching that will cause many to form a new world religion. Those drawn to this new theology will be deceived into believing Satan's lies, as taught by antichrists (those who teach against Christ) and the False Prophet who deceives those who listen to his lies.

As the religious leader of this time, the False Prophet will gather credibility among the earth's peoples by performing great and miraculous feats. Although all who believe in the only true and living God recognize His ability to perform miracles, many forget that (within limitations) Satan can also perform miracles. With power derived from Satan, the False Prophet is able to induce the inhabitants of the earth to worship the Beast, thus deceiving them with false teaching.

In addition to the use of miracles, the False Prophet will require everyone to wear the mark of the Beast on the hand or forehead as a sign that he or she has worshiped the Beast. Many have speculated on what the mark will be, with the most common thought being some use of the number 666. Again, this is speculation at best, and I will leave those studies to others. Suffice it to say that Scripture says there will be a mark, and whatever that mark is, it will be placed on everyone who worships the Beast. Without it, Scripture says the right to buy and sell would be prohibited.

The false religious system that will eventually come into being will be a clever, but nonetheless false, imitation of the divine Trinity. In his unholy schemes, Satan desires to be worshiped as God the Father, with the first beast (the Antichrist) assuming the place of Jesus Christ and the second beast (the False Prophet) taking the place of the Holy Spirit.

> **P**aul used the term "man of lawlessness" in 2 Thess. 2:3ff. to refer to the [Antichrist]; he opposes religion, claims to be God, owes his power to Satan, but will be defeated by Jesus.

APPLICATION

What application can be made concerning things that are yet to come? Perhaps that question overwhelms you and causes you to fear what is to come. If that is where you are, I urge you to consider solemnly your position in Christ and rest in His absolute control of future events.

Although the descriptions found in Revelation and in other places through the Bible that deal with the end times can be frightening, our trust in Christ is our ultimate weapon against fear. If you have a personal relationship with Jesus Christ, your future is secure.

ARMAGEDDON

■ *The name of the valley where the final war between God and the kings of this world—led by the Beast—will take place.*

REVELATION 19:19–21

And I saw the beast, the kings of the earth, and their armies, gathered together to make war against Him who sat on the horse and against His army. Then the beast was captured, and with him the false prophet who worked signs in his presence, by which he deceived those who received the mark of the beast and those who worshiped his image. These two were cast alive into the lake of fire burning with brimstone. And the rest were killed with the sword which proceeded from the mouth of Him who sat on the horse. And all the birds were filled with their flesh.

COMMENTARY

While exiled to the isle of Patmos, the apostle John was the recipient of wondrous revelation from God concerning future events. Thus, the name *Revelation* is given to his prophetic writings. One out of every twenty-five verses in the entire New Testament refers either to the Rapture or to Christ's second coming.

God, however, uses vivid language to portray not only the beauties of heaven but also the heinousness of the last battle, the Battle of Armageddon.

For instance, an angel summons all the birds to clean up the carnage left behind. The buzzards are to be ready to eat the flesh of the rotting bodies (Rev. 19:17–18). Blood will flow "up to the horses' bridles, for a distance of two hundred miles" (Rev. 14:20 NASB). This battle will signal the end of this world as we know it. It is the final battle between good and evil.

A CLOSER LOOK

The whole subject of eschatology—or the study of things to come—is vast and complex. It is difficult to single out one aspect or event because all are interrelated; each builds upon the other. For this reason, I encourage you to read all of the chapters in this book related to end times. Together they present the overview concerning the future. Our primary concern in this chapter, however, is the Battle of Armageddon.

The word *battle* is a modest description. This is not a little skirmish; this is a war. *The war.* The big one. The last one.

Lest some saints wonder if they will be forced to hold out during all of this, let me hasten to add that I believe the Bible teaches we won't be here. I believe the Bible teaches that we will have been raptured. Paul writes,

For the Lord Himself will descend from heaven with a shout, with the voice of an archangel, and with the trumpet of God. And the dead in Christ will rise first. Then we who are alive and remain shall be caught up together with them in the clouds to meet the Lord in the air. And thus we shall always be with the Lord. Therefore comfort one another with these words (1 Thess. 4:16–18).

Although the actual word *rapture* is not in the Bible (the word is from the Latin, which means to be "caught up"), Paul is telling us that we are going to be caught up—raptured—before this final war breaks out. That is why we can "comfort one another with these words." Besides, the very fact that when He comes back to set up His kingdom, He is bringing us back *with Him* leads to one conclusion—we are *with Him,* not down here in the carnage. More on that later.

So, we need not fear that we might have to hold out. I am not saying we will not be persecuted for our faith because as the end of the age draws near, that is surely more and more a distinct possibility. But I am saying we will not be here when the Antichrist rules, breaks his peace covenant with Israel, and the war breaks loose. Praise God for the blood of Jesus Christ, which provides the way of escape for those who trust Him!

As the stage for this last war is being set, it is interesting to see that the Middle East has risen to world power in an unusual way. That spot on the globe finds its way into the headlines just about every day. From the standpoint of prophecy, that is electrifying evidence that the scene is getting set for Armageddon.

John F. Walvoord writes that a unified Europe will need more than 2.8 billion barrels of imported oil. He further emphasizes that a staggering amount of oil will be needed to guarantee Europe's prosperity as it moves into the twenty-first century. What part of the world has the oil and the bargaining power that it affords? The Middle East.

The oil crisis of 1973 was a drop in the bucket compared to what may be coming. In our country, fights broke out because people were irritated that they had to stand in a line to pump gas into their cars. If tempers flare that quickly over such a small thing, imagine when oil is tightly controlled throughout the whole world. The Antichrist will use this bargaining tool to the hilt.

Remember several years ago during the Persian Gulf crisis how Saddam Hussein, the Iraqi president, literally burned the precious oil in the fields. He knew the black billows of smoke would get the attention of the world. And he was right.

Not only will the Antichrist have economic power and political power, he will have religious savvy. Because of the Antichrist's ecclesiastical influence,

> **W**hether we Christians live or die, we have nothing to fear because Jesus will come either with us or for us!
> —Warren W. Wiersbe

> **T**he Church historically has taken this belief that Christ is coming again to judge the world literally.
> —John F. Walvoord

> **S**ince His return is imminent, refuse to set any goals without relying on His input.
> —In Touch, March 1995

ARMAGEDDON

the apostate church, so blind and so deceived, will follow along. This leader will break his peace covenant, not only with Israel but with his religious following as well.

During this explosive reign of the Antichrist, as demonic forces motivate kings and generals, the whole world will go to war. Because the saints of God had been raptured before all this, the restraining power of the Holy Spirit is gone (2 Thess. 2:6–8). It is hard to imagine what the world will be like when the salt and light of the saints are no longer here and the Holy Spirit is no longer at work to restrain. Utter evil will reign. Human depravity will go unbridled.

Plagues. Mourning. Famine. Torment. Blood flowing two hundred miles four and one-half feet deep. Chaos. Earthquakes. Screams. Fire.

The pot will be boiling over. Spewing.

And the good news is this:

> *Then the LORD will go forth*
> *And fight against those nations,*
> *As He fights in the day of battle.*
> *And in that day His feet will stand on the Mount of Olives,*
> *Which faces Jerusalem on the east.*
> *And the Mount of Olives shall be split in two,*
> *From east to west,*
> *Making a very large valley;*
> *Half of the mountain shall move toward the north*
> *And half of it toward the south (Zech. 14:3–4).*

There is a fault running east to west right through the Mount of Olives. It would take only one small earthquake for it to be split.

When the Lord Jesus ascended to heaven from the Mount of Olives, two angels asked those gazing into the clouds, "Men of Galilee, why do you stand gazing up into heaven? This same Jesus, who was taken up from you into heaven, will so come in like manner as you saw Him go into heaven" (Acts 1:11).

I think it is extremely significant that He was sitting on the Mount of Olives when the disciples asked, "When will these things be? And what will be the sign of Your coming, and of the end of the age?" (Matt. 24:3).

Zechariah tells us that not only will the Lord Jesus come back, but all the holy ones will come with Him (14:5). One angel smote 185,000 men dead (Isa. 37:36). We can only imagine what all the accompanying heavenly hosts can do when they come back with Him.

ARMAGEDDON

The language of Scripture is vivid as Christ descends from heaven to launch the final assault against the Antichrist.

Now I saw heaven opened, and behold, a white horse. And He who sat on him was called Faithful and True, and in righteousness He judges and makes war. His eyes were like a flame of fire, and on His head were many crowns. He had a name written that no one knew except Himself. He was clothed with a robe dipped in blood, and His name is called The Word of God. And the armies in heaven, clothed in fine linen, white and clean, followed Him on white horses. Now out of His mouth goes a sharp sword, that with it He should strike the nations. And He Himself will rule them with a rod of iron. He Himself treads the winepress of the fierceness and wrath of Almighty God. And He has on His robe and on His thigh a name written: KING OF KINGS AND LORD OF LORDS (Rev. 19:11–16).

What an ending! What a beginning!

Satan will be bound for one thousand years, and we will reign with the Lord Jesus Christ during the Millennium. Righteousness will flourish, peace will be universal, and productivity will be greatly increased.

After this one-thousand-year reign, Satan will be loosed and given one last opportunity to regain his power (Rev. 20:7–9). But in the end he will be defeated: "The devil, who deceived them, was cast into the lake of fire and brimstone where the beast and the false prophet are. And they will be tormented day and night forever and ever" (Rev. 20:10).

Politically, the stage is being set today. Economically, the stage is being set today. Religiously, the stage is being set today.

After we are raptured, the Antichrist will wield his power, break his treaties, and the war will begin.

We know who will win.

Actually, He already has.

APPLICATION

Since eternity past, God has been planning the progress of redemption. The first prophecy in the Bible concerning Jesus is in Genesis 3:15:

> And I will put enmity
> Between you and the woman,
> And between your seed and her Seed;
> He shall bruise your head,
> And you shall bruise His heel.

ARMAGEDDON

Satan's head was bruised fatally at the Cross. We are no longer prisoners of war. We can stop cowering.

And at the final battle, Satan will be cast aside forever.

As someone said, "When Satan reminds me of my past, I remind him of his future."

Praise the Victor!

QUOTES

I've read the back of the Book—and we win!

—Anonymous

These will make war with the Lamb, and the Lamb will overcome them, for He is Lord of lords and King of kings; and those who are with Him are called, chosen, and faithful.

—The Apostle John

■ *The final abode of Satan, his angels, and anyone who dies without trusting Jesus Christ as Savior.*

HELL

SCRIPTURE

Do not fear those who kill the body but cannot kill the soul. But rather fear Him who is able to destroy both soul and body in hell.

COMMENTARY

The term *hell* comes from the Greek word *Gehenna*. Gehenna was a valley south of Jerusalem where locals dumped their garbage. If you have ever been to a city dump, you know the kinds of things that one would find in Gehenna. There were fires burning around the clock. The smell was sickening. Vultures and other animals of prey made the valley their home.

The valley of Gehenna was the most undesirable place known to the inhabitants of Jerusalem. In time it came to represent the place of future punishment for the wicked.

Another Greek word is translated "hell" in some translations. This term is *hades*. Unlike hell, hades is not the final resting place for anyone. It is best described as a loathsome holding tank. Hades consistently refers to the place where unbelievers go to wait for the Judgment (Luke 16:19–31). Hades is a place of torment and agony. At the Judgment unbelievers will receive their sentences. Only then will they enter into hell.

Now, this brings us to an interesting point. Since the Judgment is still in the future, and hell is reserved for those who have been judged and sentenced, we must assume that no one is in hell at this present moment. Everyone who has died in unbelief is waiting in hades for the coming judgment. Their wait is torturous.

Further evidence for this is found in Revelation 20:14–15. There the apostle John makes a distinction between hades and the ultimate place of punishment. In doing so, he introduces us to a new term, *the lake of fire*. John informs us that death and hades will be thrown into the lake of fire. The lake of fire and hell are the same place. Both refer to the ultimate place of punishment for those who die without trusting Christ. The lake of fire is the place reserved for people who have been judged and found guilty of unbelief.

The most accurate terminology to use in referring to the ultimate destination of the lost is the lake of fire. Unfortunately, Bible translators are not consistent in their translations of the terms *Gehenna* and *hades*. This makes things a little confusing for the English Bible reader. The good news, however, is that most study Bibles will inform you when "hell" is used to translate the term *hades*.

> **I** hate thinking about it, teaching about it, and writing about it. But the plain truth is that hell *is* real and real people go there for eternity.
> —Bill Hybels

HELL

■ *The final abode of Satan, his angels, and anyone who dies without trusting Jesus Christ as Savior.*

APPLICATION

The existence of hell seems to fly in the face of what the Bible says about God's love, forgiveness, and grace. How could a God of love send people to hell forever? Furthermore, it doesn't seem reasonable. How is it that seventy or eighty years of sin merit an eternity of punishment?

These questions reveal an error in our overall understanding of sin and the nature of God. If a man's eternal destiny was a matter of counterbalancing his bad deeds with good, these questions may have some credence. If hell was a system wherein a person paid God back for her sin, seventy years versus eternity would be an issue. If God arbitrarily came up with the rules that governed who goes to heaven and hell, we would have good cause to call His fairness into question. But none of these things has any bearing on the question of why there is a hell and why the people who go there go there forever.

Hell is a reality because of an incompatibility problem. Holy God and unholy humankind are incompatible. And no amount of time apart can change that.

The rules that govern who goes to heaven and hell are established by God's nature. Things are the way they are because God is the way He is. That makes them unchangeable because God cannot change.

Take fire, for example. Fire is hot by nature. Fire doesn't make itself hot; it *is* hot. That is the nature of fire. If you stuck your hand in a campfire to retrieve a hot dog that fell off your stick, you would be burned. You wouldn't get mad at the fire. You wouldn't say, "I can't believe that fire burned me. I never did anything to the fire! Why would it treat me like that?"

Fire and your hand are incompatible. They don't do well together. You can protect your hand with a fireproof glove, but that doesn't make your hand and fire more compatible; that doesn't change the nature of fire.

God is holy by nature. And He can't change. Unholy things don't do well around holy God. It is hard for us to grasp the power and awesomeness of God's glory and holiness. John—who knew Jesus well—saw Jesus in all His glory and fell down as a dead man (Rev. 1:16–17). Why? He was overwhelmed by the glory of God.

The only solution to this dilemma was for God to change us. That is why Christ came and died—to pave the way for a change in our very nature. Those who accept Christ's death as the payment for their sin are made holy (2 Cor. 5:21). That is why we are referred to as saints. That is why the Holy Spirit is able to dwell in us. At salvation there was a fundamental change in our nature. We were taken out of darkness and placed into the kingdom of God. We became heavenly citizens.

Percentage of adults who believe in heaven, hell, and the devil:

	Heaven	Hell	Devil
Total	90%	73%	65%
Men	86%	71%	63%
Women	93%	75%	68%

HELL

Unbelievers go to hell because they are incompatible with heaven. They don't go to hell to pay God back. The severity of their sin doesn't send them there. The quantity of their sin doesn't send them there. The problem is that they aren't suited for heaven. They have not been cleansed of the sin that makes them unholy.

A CLOSER LOOK

Although hell is not the most pleasant topic discussed in the Bible there is some good news. Like heaven, hell will not be the same for everybody. I heard a teenager say, "I don't care if I go to hell when I die. All of my friends will be there!" The young man was confused, to say the least. He saw hell as one big dark room where he and his buddies could be together forever. This is a common misconception.

On one occasion as Jesus was sending His disciples out to preach in the surrounding villages, He made a notable comment about the Final Judgment:

Whatever city you enter, and they do not receive you, go out into its streets and say, "The very dust of your city which clings to us we wipe off against you. Nevertheless know this, that the kingdom of God has come near you." But I say to you that it will be more tolerable in that Day for Sodom than for that city (Luke 10:10–12).

Jesus said, "more tolerable," indicating that there will be different degrees of punishment. The Judgment—and hell—will be more tolerable for some than for others. People in the towns that His disciples would be visiting would be more responsible than the people in Sodom because they had been exposed to more teaching and miracles; they had more light. They had less excuse for not believing.

In John's description of the Final Judgment, we find further evidence for hell not being the same for everybody: "The sea gave up the dead who were in it, and Death and Hades delivered up the dead who were in them. And they were judged, each one according to his works" (Rev. 20:13). What a person does in this life does not determine *where* he will go when he dies; but it does determine *what it will be like* when he gets there.

The Bible does not elaborate on exactly how punishment in hell will differ from one person to the next. Neither does it outline which sins will incur a greater punishment. All we know is that Christ will take into account the type of life each person lived before He hands down the sentence.

> **I** believe in hell. I believe in it rationally. I believe in it emotionally. I'm not neurotic about it, but I have to admit that it impacts me every day. It bothers me. It jars me out of complacency. It sparks my energies.
> —Bill Hybels

Hell **247**

HELL

■ *The final abode of Satan, his angels, and anyone who dies without trusting Jesus Christ as Savior.*

GROWTH

The fact that hell will not be the same for everybody in no way implies that it will be a good place for anybody. People in hell will be separated from God and all that is good forever.

As much as I dislike the idea, I do believe that the lake of fire (hell) is a real, literal place. And as hard as it is to grasp, I do believe people will eventually be sent there to live for eternity.

I believe it because Jesus believed it. I know Jesus believed it because of the price He paid to provide a way to escape. If He hadn't believed in hell, He would not have gone to such extreme measures to save us from it. His belief was so deep and His picture was so clear that it drove Him to leave His throne and His glory to die an excruciating death.

So how should you respond? Christ's desire to rescue you from hell motivated Him to die for you. It certainly ought to motivate you to reach out to and pray for lost people.

QUOTE

In righteousness God reveals chiefly His love of holiness; in justice, chiefly His hatred of sin. . . . Neither justice nor righteousness . . . is a matter of arbitrary will. They are revelations of the inmost nature of God.

—Augustus H. Strong

■ *One thousand years; in Scripture, the thousand-year earthly reign of Jesus Christ.*

MILLENNIUM

REVELATION 20:4

SCRIPTURE

I saw thrones, and they sat on them, and judgment was committed to them. Then I saw the souls of those who had been beheaded for their witness to Jesus and for the word of God, who had not worshiped the beast or his image, and had not received his mark on their foreheads or on their hands. *And they lived and reigned with Christ for a thousand years* (emphasis added).

COMMENTARY

As the apostle John gazes into the future, he is privileged to see the glorious day we all long for—the day when Christ returns and establishes His kingdom on this earth. It is impossible for us to comprehend what it will be like to see Jesus face-to-face. Yet the Scripture declares that Jesus will come again and take up residency on earth. The next time He appears, however, He will come not as a babe in a manger but as the Ruler and King of all creation! The peace that has escaped the world thus far will be the benchmark of the thousand-year reign of Christ known as the Millennium. Satan will be bound, and Christ will be in charge.

Yet, just as is true with all prophecy, until the time is fulfilled, there will be questions and debate over particular meanings and whether these prophecies can be taken as literal or as a figurative expression of what is to come. With increasing interest and growing debate over future events, many have taken sides on the issue of the Millennium. Some doubt that there will be a literal millennium. Others are divided over questions concerning when and where it will transpire.

Among those who debate these questions, there have evolved three positions regarding the Millennium. The three positions are (1) amillennialism; (2) premillennialism; and (3) postmillennialism. As you will discover, these positions are hotly debated by their proponents and are vastly different in their conclusions. However, there is almost universal agreement that this period of time is the fulfillment of promises made in both Old and New Testaments. Jews and Christians alike believe that this is the promised time when Jesus (or another Messiah) will reign for a thousand years. As to when this will take place, these three positions have garnered their own debate teams with Scripture in hand and knowledgeable scholars to validate their positions.

A CLOSER LOOK

Where do you stand on the millennial question? Perhaps you believe, as I do, in the premillennial position. However, unless you have done considerable

Millennium

MILLENNIUM

■ *One thousand years; in Scripture, the thousand-year earthly reign of Jesus Christ.*

study on the subject, you probably don't know where you stand. Therefore, a quick look at each of these positions will equip you to make an informed decision.

One position is *amillennialism*. The roots of amillennialism can be traced as far back as the third and fourth centuries, to Augustine and others. The general point of agreement among those who hold to this belief is the denial of a literal reign of Christ on the earth. Holding to the belief that Satan was bound at the first coming of Christ, amillennialists believe that this present age (between the first and second coming of Christ) is the fulfillment of the millennial kingdom. One area of tension among amillennialists is the question of whether or not the Millennium is being fulfilled at this moment here on earth or whether it is being presently fulfilled by the saints in heaven.

There are obvious divisions among those who hold to this belief that affect the relevancy of major portions of Scripture and its impact on this present age. If the Millennium is presently being fulfilled on earth, the conclusions drawn from Scripture would take on an entirely different meaning than if it was being fulfilled spiritually by the saints in heaven. With so much debate even among those who hold to this position, their points of agreement are few: (1) a millennial age after the second coming of Christ is denied, and (2) prophecy regarding this subject should not be taken literally.

The second position—*premillennialism*—is the oldest of the three positions. Premillennialists support their view by a more literal interpretation of Scripture. For example, when the apostle writes, "They lived and reigned with Christ for a thousand years," those holding to a premillennial understanding believe that verse refers to a literal one-thousand-year period of time on earth. Premillennialists take the Scripture's description of the chronology of events literally as well.

Specifically, premillennialism derives its meaning from the belief that the second coming of Christ will occur before (pre) the Millennium—the thousand-year reign of Christ. Therefore, it is called premillennial.

Premillennialists believe that the present age will end suddenly when Christ appears. At that time, the wicked will be judged, the righteous will be rescued, and Satan will be bound. Furthermore, God will pick up where He left off in His dealings with Israel. In the premillennial scheme of things, Israel and the church are two distinct entities. Premillennialists hold to the belief that the Jewish nation will be restored—including the repossession of their ancient land when Christ returns to earth. Furthermore, they believe that Satan will be bound, that a theocratic kingdom will be established, and that those who have died "in Christ" will be raised to share in the blessings of this time.

MILLENNIUM

The premillennial position concerning the thousand-year reign of Christ on earth holds to a plain interpretation of the prophecies that speak of a righteous kingdom of God on earth.

The third of the three primary positions regarding the Millennium is *postmillennialism*. Daniel Whitby, a Unitarian, is often given credit for originating this view. Those holding a postmillennial view believe this present age will end with a worldwide spiritual revival resulting from the gospel being preached to all nations. Essentially, the postmillennial position adheres to the belief that the whole world will be Christianized and brought to submission to the gospel *before* the return of Christ. Those who adhere to the postmillennial position believe that the Millennium will occur prior to the second coming of Christ. Postmillennialism is based on a more figurative interpretation of scriptural prophecy.

Those holding the postmillennial position do not believe in a literal reign of Christ on the earth. They are confident, however, that the world will be Christianized by the successful preaching of the gospel, that the kingdom of God will triumph in this world in this age.

The postmillennial and amillennial positions hold in common a belief that the Final Judgment of people and angels is one single event that will occur after a general resurrection of all people and before the eternal state begins.

One thing is clear: there is considerable difference in opinions and theology concerning the millennial kingdom. The most literal viewpoint concerning this subject is found within the position of premillennialism. As I concluded earlier, all the questions surrounding this subject (and other subjects that concern prophecy) will be answered only when the actual prophecy is fulfilled. However, one constant throughout Scripture gives us all rest in the middle of the debate. Our sovereign God knows the future and is in control of it. Whatever happens in that day and time will be in His time and under His control. That should give us all peace when we seem to have so many questions that elicit so many different answers.

> Amillennialism is the view that does not believe in a future literal reign of Christ on earth for a thousand years in fulfillment of the Old Testament promises of God.
> —Robert P. Lightner

GROWTH

As with all the Scriptures that concern prophecy, study can be exciting and can lead to a much greater dependence on God for what we know and understand—and what we leave in His hands. If you find the subject of prophecy interesting and want to know more, I encourage you to find a study group that makes use of the many excellent studies written on biblical prophecy.

MILLENNIUM

■ *One thousand years; in Scripture, the thousand-year earthly reign of Jesus Christ.*

Premillennialism describes the belief that Christ will return before the millennium and in fact will establish it when He returns to the earth.
—Robert P. Lightner

As with any study or study group, it is essential to accurate understanding and teaching that two elements be held to without fail. The first is to be sure that the material being used is reliable and comes from a source that is committed to belief in the inerrant Word of God. Second, be sure that the one who teaches is a godly person who has studied Scripture thoroughly and has drawn conclusions from what the text says rather than from opinions.

If you feel somewhat overwhelmed and out of your league when it comes to Bible prophecy, don't give up. Keep reading. Keep learning. Seek God's guidance in finding a good Bible study or Sunday school class that can lead you through your fear and insecurities concerning the Scriptures.

■ *The sudden removal of the church (believers in Christ) from earth to be with the Lord.*

RAPTURE

SCRIPTURE

Then we who are alive and remain shall be caught up together with them in the clouds to meet the Lord in the air. And thus we shall always be with the Lord.

COMMENTARY

Have you ever had the experience of closing your eyes as you listened to some brilliant piece of music and later remarked that you were carried away by its beauty? Well, that's what it means to be raptured—to be carried away. Whereas in the realm of music we talk of being carried away in figurative terms, Paul talked literally of the church being carried away in the air. Paul's words to the Thessalonians give us just a glimpse of what that day will be like for those living when Christ returns for the church.

There is considerable discussion today among believers and unbelievers concerning this topic. When will it happen? Who will go? Is this the second coming of Christ that Scripture speaks of? Paul takes great effort to educate the Thessalonians concerning these matters. Earlier in this same chapter Paul speaks of the resurrection of those who have died "in Christ," indicating that immediately prior to the rapture of the living believers, believers who had died during the New Testament period and afterward would be resurrected.

Tom Constable explains these verses well in *The Bible Knowledge Commentary.* He writes,

> Then *the dead in Christ* will be resurrected, that is, believers of this dispensation will be raised. Old Testament saints, it seems, will be raised at the end of the Great Tribulation (Dan. 12:2), for the phrase "in Christ" usually refers exclusively to Church-Age saints. The bodies of the dead in Christ will *rise* before the living Christians are caught up to meet the Lord in the air.

The basic idea of the Rapture is drawn from the Latin term for "caught up"—*rapturo*. It means that the church of Jesus Christ, those who have trusted in Christ as their Savior, will literally be transported from earth to heaven in an instant. There will be no death for those who are raptured. They will be taken—caught up—in the air to be with Jesus! Paul believed that Jesus' return was imminent, and that brought great comfort to him in his daily struggles. It is not difficult to understand Paul's longing for this to occur when faced with the trials we are confronted with daily. However, no one knows when this will happen. We do know that we are given His Word as the assurance that it will happen.

> **W**e're not to predict; we're to watch and wait. But that does not mean we are to be idle. There are still marriages to grow and children to tend. There are churches to build and souls to win.
> —Jerry Jenkins

Rapture **253**

RAPTURE

■ *The sudden removal of the church (believers in Christ) from earth to be with the Lord.*

If you have made any attempt to study scriptural references to what the future holds, you know that the major discussion among believers today concerns the point of time that the Rapture will take place in relation to the Tribulation. There are several theories, but two dominate. The first is the pretribulation view. This is the belief that the church will be raptured prior to the Tribulation. I believe this is the view Scripture supports. The second is the posttribulation view, which is the belief that the church will not be raptured until the very end of Tribulation; that the Rapture and the second coming of Christ are a single event rather than two separate events as held to by those who adhere to the pretribulation Rapture.

In his book *What You Should Know About the Rapture,* Dr. Charles Ryrie compares these two theories concerning the Rapture. But he also asks a very important question for anyone who is about to study the end times. He asks, "Does it really make any difference when the Lord will come? Is it not His coming that is important? If His coming should be pretribulational, then we will praise Him for the fact that we missed that terrible time. If it is posttribulational, then we will gladly suffer for His sake. Either way, we still have the blessed hope of His coming."

The fact that God has chosen to reveal some things regarding the timing of the Rapture is significant. Additionally, the time factor is important as it relates to the power and motivation of an impending event or events that are soon to come.

If the Rapture is to occur prior to the Tribulation, it could happen at any time, and that adds anticipation to the thought of being raptured into the heavens with Jesus. On the other hand, if the Rapture is not to occur until the very end of the Tribulation—after all the prophecy concerning the events of the Tribulation has transpired—we certainly won't find ourselves living as if He could appear at any moment. The two views have different effects. Clearly, the question of *when* is important in light of what we can expect and the revelation of God to the church.

The fact that Revelation 3:10 promises to keep us from the *hour* of temptation is the basis for my belief that the church will be raptured prior to the Tribulation: "Because you have kept My command to persevere, I also will keep you from the hour of trial which shall come upon the whole world, to test those who dwell on the earth."

The only way to keep us from the hour of the temptation is to eliminate our presence, and the means of doing that is the rapture of the church into the air to meet Jesus! Others argue the point. There is nothing wrong with

Regardless of secondary issues such as the timing of the Rapture, Christians of all persuasions have always agreed on the essential issues of the end times. . . . They agree that Christ is physically coming again, that there will be a judgment, and that there will be an eternal state.
—Ron Rhodes

debate, and questions have never changed the truth. Whatever you believe about when it will happen, rest assured, the time will come.

In addition to what you believe about *when* the Rapture will happen, there is much to be gleaned concerning exactly what the Rapture is. From the definition, we have determined that it means the church will be caught up or carried away into the air to be with the Lord, but exactly what does that mean? Well, I believe it covers a number of things.

First, Christ will return. That this event will be one of great drama is vividly portrayed in Scripture. His coming will be accompanied with a loud command from what will sound like the voice of an archangel. This will be accompanied by the trumpet call of God. The implication is that these sounds will be heard all around the world.

The second thing we can know about the Rapture is that there will be a resurrection of those who have died "in Christ." The dead will be raised even before those who are living will be changed. And yet both groups will experience their respective changes "in the twinkling of an eye" (1 Cor. 15:52). Neither will be a process occurring over a period of time. It will be as Scripture describes it—instantaneous.

Third, there will be a rapture of living believers who will be caught up to be with Jesus without experiencing death. Although we have used the word *rapture* to encompass the entire experience, the Rapture specifically refers to the transformation of living believers into immortal bodies without the event of physical death. Paul calls it a mystery, and I can add nothing beyond that description. Whatever happens in that instant is a mystery, but what a glorious one to consider!

The fourth aspect of the Rapture relates to the reunion with loved ones who have died and our union with Christ. Can you imagine what that will be like? Perhaps you never met your father or grandmother because each died before you were born. Many children born during times of war lost their fathers without knowing them. Just think about what kind of reunion that day will entail! And yet, it holds no comparison at all to what it will be like when we see Jesus. The very thought makes my heart long for the day.

There is one more truth regarding the Rapture we need to take a look at. This is the most practical of the five. The doctrine of the Rapture is to be a source of comfort and encouragement. Paul writes, "Comfort one another with these words" (1 Thess. 4:18).

It is not difficult for me to find comfort in Paul's words. I never knew my father. The knowledge that we will be united in heaven is comforting to

Live as though Jesus is coming any moment, but *plan* as though you have 100 years!
—Dick Mills

While Scripture presents many signs of Christ's Second Coming and the establishment of His Kingdom, there are no predicted events preceding the Rapture. It could happen at any time.
—John F. Walvoord

RAPTURE

■ *The sudden removal of the church (believers in Christ) from earth to be with the Lord.*

me. Several years ago my mom died. To know that one day we will be reunited is comforting.

GROWTH

There will be questions about future events. However, the fact that Jesus is coming back is the bottom line and the source of comfort for me as a believer, as I hope it is for you. Whether you believe that the Rapture will happen prior to the Tribulation or at the very end, the fact that it's going to happen should encourage your heart as you look to the future with great hope.

QUOTE

The resurrected or translated bodies of all Christians will be united with Christ and with each other at the Rapture. From that time on and forever, thereafter they will be with the Lord. The Lord will take living believers to the place He is presently preparing for them (John 14:2–3).

—Tom Constable

TRIBULATION

■ *The seven-year period immediately preceding the second coming of Jesus Christ; a time of unparalleled suffering.*

MATTHEW 24:21–22

For then there will be great tribulation, such as has not been since the beginning of the world until this time, no, nor ever shall be. And unless those days were shortened, no flesh would be saved; but for the elect's sake those days will be shortened.

Christians and non-Christians are interested in the future. Everyone has questions. Some are motivated by curiosity, others by fear and anxiety. For the most part the future is a mystery. I say "for the most part" because certain future events have been revealed by God.

Many of the questions that Christians ask surround the period of time known as the Great Tribulation.

What will happen to Christians when the Tribulation happens? Who will be spared? We are certainly not the first to question the future. Jesus was prompted by His disciples to describe the events to come that signaled the end of the age.

The first reference to a seven-year period of time when the earth would be besieged with great suffering is found in the ninth chapter of Daniel. Though there is considerable debate among theologians concerning many details surrounding this period of time, it is commonly called the seventieth week of Daniel, indicating the seven-year period that we know as the Tribulation. A further study of chapter 9 describes the beginning of the Tribulation, marked by the signing of a pact or treaty with the leader of the revived Roman Empire (the Antichrist).

The Great Tribulation is divided into two distinct periods. Jesus says that in Matthew 24:14 when He says, "And this gospel of the kingdom will be preached in all the world as a witness to all the nations, and *then* the end will come" (emphasis added).

The halfway point (three and one-half years) in the Tribulation defines the end of a lesser degree of suffering and the beginning of unequaled woe. Jesus describes this first half of the Tribulation: "For nation will rise against nation, and kingdom against kingdom, and in various places there will be famines and earthquakes. But all these things are merely the beginning of birth pangs" (Matt. 24:7–8 NASB). Just like an expectant mother feels the pains of birth in various stages, so will the earth feel the pains of the Tribulation in differing degrees. He continues, "Then they will deliver you

TRIBULATION

to tribulation, and will kill you, and you will be hated by all nations on account of My name" (Matt. 24:9 NASB). His words indicate that this period of seven years will be divided. To put it in terms we are more familiar with, things get bad and then they get worse!

With the beginning of the Tribulation marked with the signing of the treaty, the second half begins with the breaking of the same treaty. In *The Bible Knowledge Commentary,* Louis Barbieri writes,

> At the middle point of the seven year period preceding Christ's second coming, great distress will begin to be experienced by Israel. The Antichrist, who will have risen to power in the world and will have made a protective treaty with Israel, will break his agreement at that time (Dan. 9:27). He will bring great persecution on Israel (Dan. 7:25) and even establish a center of worship in the temple in Jerusalem (2 Thess. 2:3–4).

A CLOSER LOOK

What those who are living during this period can expect is summed up in *One World* by John Ankerberg and John Weldon:

> The Tribulation period is composed of seven years, the first three and one-half years constitute a period of apparent relative peace when the Antichrist signs a peace treaty with Israel. The last three and one-half years involve massive destruction that is described as the Great Tribulation. This leads to the final world conflict of Armageddon.

Several characteristics define the first half of Tribulation: (1) false christs, (2) wars and rumors of war, and (3) occurrences in nature such as famines and earthquakes. It is easy to understand why many people believe we are in the midst of the Tribulation now when you think about these signs and then turn on the television news and listen to the day's events. However, because I believe that Scripture supports the conclusion that the church will be raptured *before* the Tribulation, it is apparent that the Tribulation has not begun, or I would not be writing this book!

After the first half of the Tribulation ends, then begins the time when there will be inconceivable anguish on the earth. Dwight Pentecost describes it this way: "The tribulation period will witness the wrath of Satan in his animosity against Israel (Rev. 12:12–17) and of Satan's puppet, the Beast, in his animosity against the saints (Rev. 13:7). Yet even this manifestation of wrath does not begin to exhaust the outpouring of wrath of that day." What could be worse than Satan's wrath? God's, of course.

The Greek word *thlipsis,* translated *tribulation* or *affliction* in many English Bibles, occurs twenty times in the New Testament.
—Marvin Rosenthal

TRIBULATION

Dr. Pentecost writes, "Scripture abounds in assertions that this period is not the wrath of men, nor even the wrath of Satan, but the time of the wrath of God." Many verses support this suggestion. Zephaniah 1:18 states,

> *Neither their silver nor their gold*
> *Shall be able to deliver them*
> *In the day of the LORD's wrath.*

Isaiah 26:21 states, "The LORD comes out of His place to punish the inhabitants of the earth for their iniquity." Because this time of tribulation comes from God Himself, it will be earmarked by the kind of suffering and also by the intensity of the suffering.

I am sure of two things: (1) the Tribulation will happen, and (2) the church will not be present during this time. Why? What reason is there for the Tribulation? Primarily, there are two reasons: (1) to prepare Israel for her Messiah, and (2) to pour out judgment on unbelieving people and nations. This brings us to the question concerning what we, as believers, will experience at this point in history. With the second purpose being to judge *unbelieving* people and nations, I believe this gives credence to the belief that the church (believers) will not be present.

Among the verses that support this idea is Revelation 3:10: "Because you have kept My command to persevere, I also will keep you from the hour of trial which shall come upon the whole world, to test those who dwell on the earth." Suffice it to say, I believe that Scripture indicates the church's absence on earth prior to this period of time.

APPLICATION

We can conclude a number of things about the Great Tribulation, but these conclusions are tempered by where we stand—with Christ or without Him.

If you are among those who have taken that crucial stand and have confessed Christ as your Savior, I believe Scripture affirms that you and I will not be present during the Tribulation. Yet the church is not exempt from normal suffering. On the contrary, Scripture asserts that believers will suffer for faith. There are two considerations here: (1) what we believe, and (2) what we will experience in the way of trials and tribulation. No one is exempt from suffering, but there is a difference in the trials that we experience and the tribulation of those left after the Rapture.

The application of this study is far different for the unbeliever. Because I believe that the church (those who believe in Christ as Savior) will be raptured before the Tribulation, your status is rather tenuous. Knowing Christ as your Savior is your security for now and eternity.

GROWTH

I would add a word of caution to anyone who attempts to study this topic. Only God and His Word are infallible. In your attempt to discern what Scripture says about the future, be careful that it comes from the truth of Scripture and not your own interpretation. I believe we can know certain things about the future, but not everything.

Know this for sure: if you are a believer, God will provide for you today and tomorrow. Whatever the future holds, He is in control. With that in mind, what have you to fear?

PERSONAL
GROWTH

ARMOR OF GOD

EPHESIANS 6:10–11

Finally, my brethren, be strong in the Lord and in the power of His might. Put on the whole armor of God, that you may be able to stand against the wiles of the devil.

COMMENTARY

If you asked most believers whether they would like to know how to stand firm against temptation, they would be very interested. Most of our problems stem from our inability to say no to certain temptations.

In the verses quoted above—as well as those that follow—the apostle Paul gives us a formula for success when facing temptation. In essence, Paul gives us a promise. We could paraphrase it this way: "If you put on the full armor of God, you will be able to stand." And the reverse is true as well: "If you don't put it on, you will fall."

The devil is very good at what he does. He does not go about his work haphazardly. He has a plan. The apostle refers to the enemy's strategy as "wiles." Satan designs a plan of attack against each of us. His attacks are specific, direct, and relentless. They are always perfectly timed. They are tailor-made for us. And more often than we would like to admit, his attacks are successful.

On the other hand, our defenses are generally sloppy—a little prayer here, some Bible reading there. Usually, just enough to feel good about ourselves.

Although we spend time preparing for work, meals, vacation, school, and other activities, when it comes to preparing for the wiles of the devil we are lazy. Consequently, we are often defeated repeatedly in the same areas.

But it doesn't have to be that way. There is an effective defense. Paul refers to it as the armor of God. And those who take the time to put it on will stand against temptation.

A CLOSER LOOK

The pieces of armor Paul refers to in Ephesians mirror those worn by Roman soldiers in that day. By associating the believer's spiritual defenses with the armor of a Roman soldier, Paul provides his audience with an illustration of how spiritual defenses work.

The first piece of armor is the thick leather apron the Roman soldier wore around his waist. This apron served as a belt as well as protection for the abdominal area. It was the first piece of armor the soldier put on.

Paul says to "Stand therefore, having girded your waist with truth" (6:14). The truth is as the foundation for all the other pieces of armor. It is truth

■ *The central truths of Scripture that make up the spiritual defenses of the believer.*

that provides the perspective to successfully face the trials and temptations of the day. The truth allows us to see and interpret all of life from God's perspective. The truth raises us above our human understanding of things and allows us to see things from an eternal perspective.

Next, Paul mentions the breastplate. The breastplate of a Roman soldier was usually made of leather and metal. It protected the chest area and thus many of the vital organs. Often, the breastplate was marked in such a way as to designate which army or battalion a soldier belonged to.

Paul refers to it as the "breastplate of righteousness" (6:14). We are to be known for our commitment to righteousness. Along with that commitment, we must guard our hearts from unrighteousness. By putting on the breastplate of righteousness, we renew our commitment to do what is right. And we take a stand against things that have the potential of leading us into unrighteousness.

In ancient days, men believed the emotions resided in the chest. This belief probably arose from the fact that so much of what we feel emotionally is felt in that part of the body. With this in mind, it could be that Paul uses the picture of the breastplate of righteousness as an admonition to guard our affections, to keep our emotions under control. The battle between righteousness and unrighteousness is often a battle between what we know and what we feel. By guarding our emotions, we ensure that they do not control the will and thus move us in the direction of unrighteousness.

Next, Paul moves to foot coverings: "And having shod your feet with the preparation of the gospel of peace" (6:15). The foot covering of the Roman soldier was a thick leather sandal. It wrapped around both the foot and the ankle. Sometimes the bottom was covered with spikes or nails to allow him to keep his footing in hand-to-hand combat.

The shoe is associated with the readiness to share the good news of the gospel wherever we go. Part of our defense against the enemy is verbalizing our faith and how that affects where we stand on particular issues. By making our position and faith clear, we draw a line of demarcation between us and those who may otherwise be tempted to draw us into sin.

Notice that Paul refers to our message as the "gospel of peace." *Peace* certainly describes the nature and message of the gospel. After all, the theme of the gospel is that we can have peace with God. But *peace* should also be our goal as we move in and out of people's lives. There should be something special about us and our behavior that draws men and women to our message.

Next, we are instructed to take up the shield of faith, "with which [we] will be able to quench all the fiery darts of the wicked one" (6:16). The

We don't have to fight or wrestle *with* God, but we must wrestle before God *with things.* Beware of lazily giving up. Instead, put up a glorious fight and you will find yourself empowered with His strength.
—Oswald Chambers

ARMOR OF GOD

focus shifts here from clothing to a defensive weapon. The shield in view here is not a little round shield like we see portrayed in movies about this era. The word translated "shield" comes from a Greek word that is also translated "door." Some of these shields were as large as doors.

They consisted of an iron frame with thick leather stretched over it. Some of them had metal on the front as well. A soldier could kneel down behind his shield and be completely protected in the front. On occasion, Roman soldiers would soak their shields in water so that the enemies' flaming arrows would be extinguished on impact.

Faith is taking God at His Word. The arrows that come against us are the lies the enemy constantly tells us. He lies about God's faithfulness, love, and concern for us.

Without the promises of God we would not know what to believe about— or expect from—God. We wouldn't know what He thought about us. We would be lost in a sea of doubt. The promises of God give us something to anchor our faith to; they give us something to hold on to.

Using the shield of faith is a matter of claiming the promises God has made to us. It becomes God's Word against the lies of the enemy. Without His Word, we have only our speculations and emotions to rely on.

From the shield, the apostle turns his attention to the helmet: "And take the helmet of salvation" (6:17). The helmet was the most costly and most ornate piece of a soldier's armor. It was designed to protect the head.

Here we are reminded of our eternally secure position in Christ. Our salvation is a source of confidence in the midst of temptation. No matter how severe the temptation, our relationship with God is unaffected.

The helmet is also a reminder of the presence of the Holy Spirit. The Spirit of Christ dwells in each of us. Just as Christ—through the Spirit—was able to overcome temptation, we, too, have the potential to say no. His presence in us has empowered us to overcome the devil.

The last piece of armor is the only offensive piece Paul mentions—the sword: "And the sword of the Spirit, which is the word of God" (6:17). The Roman sword was designed for close combat. It resembled a dagger more than a sword.

The Word of God is pictured here as a sword because of its ability to overcome the onslaught of our enemy. By renewing our minds with the truth of God's Word, we are able to recognize the lies that set us up for sin, the lies we would otherwise use to rationalize our sin. By memorizing and quoting the truths of God's Word, we can resist even the strongest temptations.

> We Christians are not told that we will never have to face demonic opposition. We are told to "get tough," to put on our spiritual armor, to fight the good fight of faith, and to win battles in the name of the Lord!
> —Dick Mills

Armor of God

ARMOR OF GOD

■ *The central truths of Scripture that make up the spiritual defenses of the believer.*

APPLICATION

One of the best habits you can develop is putting on the armor of God every morning. This is spiritual armor, so you put it on by faith. The best way to explain this is to walk you through a routine I follow every morning. I'm sure there are other ways of putting on the armor of God. Paul didn't leave directions. The main thing is that you put it on!

Each morning I say something like this:

Good morning, Lord. Thank You for assuring me of victory today. By faith I choose to follow Your battle plan and to prepare myself according to Your instructions.

To prepare myself for the battle ahead, by faith I put on the belt of truth. Renew my mind to what is true. Fill me with truth. Expose in my heart the lies that I am tempted to believe. The truth is that You are a sovereign God who loves me and cares for me. The truth about me is that I am Your child—bought and paid for. Nothing can separate me from Your love.

By faith I put on the breastplate of righteousness. Today I am committed to doing what is right. I pray that I would be known as one who does what is right regardless of what it costs me. Allow the righteousness of Christ to shine through me today.

By faith I put on the sandals of the gospel. I am available to You. Use me in the lives of others. I pray that in my conduct and speech I would accurately represent You. Make me a calming presence everywhere I go.

I now take up the shield of faith. My faith is in You and You alone. Apart from You I can do nothing. In You, I can do all things. Everything that comes against me must come through You for I am in You. As You walked without sin on this earth, live without sin through me today. By faith I claim victory over _____ [then I list some of the temptations I know I will face that day]. When I face these temptations, remind me that the victory has already been won.

By faith I put on the helmet of salvation. Thank You for saving me. Thank You for forgiving me. Thank You for sending the Holy Spirit to live inside me. Holy Spirit, I surrender my will to You today. I surrender my thoughts to You. I choose to take every thought captive to the obedience of Christ.

And last, I take up the sword of the Spirit, which is the Word of God. [Then I claim several specific promises from Scripture.]

So, Lord, I go now rejoicing that You have chosen me to represent You to this lost world. May others see Jesus in me. May Satan and his hosts shudder as Your power is manifest through me. In Jesus' name I pray, Amen.

> **B**y putting on the whole armor of God, it is possible to have the entire Christian personality and character completely covered. We can stand our ground in the battle between light and darkness, good and evil.
> —Dick Mills

Can you think of any better way to start the day? You may be thinking, *But aren't you just psyching yourself up?* Exactly! But unlike most positive mental attitude programs, I am not telling myself things that I hope will one day become true, I am reminding myself of what God has said is true. There is a big difference. And our goal in all of this is not self-confidence. It is Christ confidence. It is not my armor I'm putting on. It is the armor of God. Once again, apart from Him we can do nothing.

 GROWTH

A Roman soldier would not dream of going into battle without every piece of his armor secured and ready for battle. To have done so would have meant certain death. In the same way, you have no business venturing out into this evil world without putting on the whole armor of God.

CHARACTER

■ *Doing what is right because it is right.*

SCRIPTURE

ROMANS 5:3–4

And not only that, but we also glory in tribulations, knowing that tribulation produces perseverance; and perseverance, character; and character, hope.

COMMENTARY

The word *character* appears in the Bible only a few times. Yet the references indicate that character is something to be sought after. In the passage cited above, the apostle Paul points out the unique relationship between tribulations, perseverance, and character.

The tribulations he is referring to were the trials and difficulties experienced by believers who were being persecuted for their faith. He says these tribulations would produce perseverance. He was assuming, of course, that those who were being persecuted would faithfully and courageously endure their persecutions; that they would not break under the pressure and deny their faith in Christ.

Then he gets to our word, "And perseverance, character" (Rom. 5:4). Notice the difference. Perseverance is something we do. We persevere under pressure. But character is not something we do—it is something we have or don't have. Character is about what we are or, as some would say, what we are made of. Paul's conclusion is that those who persevere through trials regarding their beliefs are men and women of character. Their character was made evident by their response to what was happening around them.

A CLOSER LOOK

We defined *character* as "doing what is right because it is right." In biblical terms we are talking about righteous men and women, men and women who do what is right for the right reason.

Our definition presupposes two things. First is an absolute standard by which to define right and wrong. People of character don't make up the rules as they go along. They have agreed upon the rules beforehand. They don't ask, "What's right for me?" They ask, "What's right?" They believe there is a standard of right and wrong that overshadows the entire human race, one to which all people are accountable.

Those who know the Lord recognize that we are accountable to God's standard. According to His nature, He has set limits on human behavior. He has determined what is and is not permissible; what is and is not fair; what is and is not moral. And His code of conduct does not shift with a particular culture. It never changes.

CHARACTER

A second thing that our definition presupposes is the ability and willingness to obey. Agreeing with the rules of a game is one thing. Playing by the rules is something else entirely. Men and women of character have not only agreed to God's code of ethics and morality. They live it. They do what is right.

Whereas achievement and fulfillment are the chief pursuits of many in this age, it is different for men and women of character. They are not opposed to achieving certain goals. They are not against personal fulfillment. The difference is their priorities. For them, personal obedience takes priority over personal achievement. Self-control takes precedent over self-fulfillment. It is all a matter of priorities. I have never met anyone who is against character. It's just that few people make it their priority. They are quick to compromise their character if that is what it takes to reach the next rung on whatever ladder they choose to climb. Today, what a person *is* on the inside is not nearly as important as what he or she can *do*.

So, to be persons of character, we must first submit ourselves to God's code of conduct. We must agree with Him that His ways are right when we understand, don't understand, and misunderstand. We must in effect say, "Lord, before You even tell me what the right thing to do is in my particular situation, I want You to know that I believe You are right."

And second, we must follow through. We must do what is right. Why? Because we will always come out looking good? No. Because it's what we want to do? No. Because it will keep us out of trouble? No. People of character do what is right because it is right.

> **W**atch your thoughts; they become words.
> Watch your words; they become actions.
> Watch your actions; they become habits.
> Watch your habits; they become your character.
> Watch your character; it becomes your destiny.
> —Dr. William Mitchell

APPLICATION

Think for a moment about all the places in your community where you could go to improve your outer appearance. Most shops in most shopping centers and malls are geared toward making us look or feel better. We are bombarded from every direction by products designed to improve our looks and our health. Just pick up a magazine and flip through the ads.

Now, think for a moment about the places in your community that are geared toward developing your character. Your second list is likely much shorter. Other than church, you don't have much to choose from. There was a time when you would have put school on that list, but that is not necessarily true anymore.

I think you agree we live in a society that is totally committed to the outer person and neglects the inner person. Yet the social problems in this nation—the ones commentators and politicians constantly complain about—are not

> **L**ife is built on character, but character is built on decisions.
> —Warren W. Wiersbe

Character

269

CHARACTER

> **C**haracter is built into the spiritual fabric of personality hour by hour, day by day, year by year in much the same deliberate way that physical health is built into the body.
> —E. Lamar Kincaid

> **I**f you want to know what people are really like, find out what makes them angry, what makes them weep, and what makes them laugh.
> —Warren W. Wiersbe

> **G**od has to hide from us what He does until by personal character we get to the place where He can reveal it.
> —Oswald Chambers

rooted in our appearance. On the other hand, most of our problems as a nation stem from a lack of character among our leaders and citizens. Our biggest deficit in this nation is not a budget deficit; it is a character deficit.

It's an old story. We would much rather complain about the way things are than make the sacrifices to change them. And character certainly takes sacrifice. But those of us who know the Lord have been called to make that sacrifice; we have been called to live on a higher plane. Christians, above any other group, should be known for character. That means we need a plan.

If you don't have a personal plan for developing character, you won't. You will fall in line with everybody else. The only difference is that you will go to heaven when you die. My point is, we don't drift into character. It takes effort; it takes a plan. Even as Christians, we are prone to allow the cares of this world (which are external by nature) to choke out any time for working on the part of us that is most crucial to our genuine happiness and success—our character.

Part of my plan is a list of seven things I want to be known for. I have written them on a card and placed it inside my desk drawer. Several times a day I rehearse my list mentally. I meditate on Scriptures that deal with these seven things. I pray every day that God would work on my character to the point that these seven characteristics would shape my public reputation. I want to be known as a man in which these seven things are true.

Begin by thinking through the kind of person you want to be. Not what you want to accomplish, but what others perceive you as being in your heart. Start a list. Don't let it get too long. And don't try to come up with all of them at one time. Praying that God will help you develop character is one thing. But when you start to get specific, you will begin to see change.

After you have made your list, look for practical ways to work the qualities into your life. You will be amazed at how your personal plan unfolds. You may change your list from time to time. That's fine. But keep it going. This way you will see your progress, and you will stay involved in the process.

Character is to relationships what oil is to a motor. If you took apart the engine of a new car, you would find that each part was made to work perfectly with all the other parts of that engine. They were made for each other. Yet if you run that engine without oil, certain parts of that engine will eventually destroy the parts around them. Why? Friction and heat. The fact that the parts were perfectly suited for each other isn't enough.

The same is true in relationships. When there is a deficit in character, you pay for it in your relationships. It doesn't matter how perfectly suited you are to your spouse, your job, or your club. If you don't have character, there is going to be friction.

Character is what a man is in the dark.
—D. L. Moody

The God-given capacity to lead has two parts: giftedness and character. Integrity is the heart of character.
—Dr. J. Robert Clinton

CHILDISH THINGS

■ *Immature and foolish behavior stemming from background that people cling to in adult years.*

1 CORINTHIANS 13:11

When I was a child, I spoke as a child, I understood as a child, I thought as a child; but when I became a man, I put away childish things.

COMMENTARY

Have you ever walked into the living room Christmas morning and found your husband or father sitting in the middle of the floor playing with a new train set? Well, my children could tell you stories about my love for trains and the Christmas mornings they had to wait while I got to play first! That's part of the benefits of being the dad—I got to try the train out first. Now that my children have children of their own, I may find myself watching on the sidelines as they exercise their parental "rights." That is fine. It's even refreshing. There is nothing basically wrong with a grown man or woman taking a few minutes out of an otherwise physically and emotionally taxing day to have fun. It is another matter altogether when an adult copes with important matters of life from the emotional standpoint of a child.

While memories of those Christmas mornings bring a smile (and a tear) to my face, the old saying that a man is just a grown-up boy is all too true for many men. I've heard it said that the only difference between a man and a boy is the cost of his toys! Likewise, women are often referred to as grown-up little girls, who still live out of the emotional vacuum they grew up in.

If you are married to a fifty-year-old kid, who doesn't know when it's time to be the father or husband, after a while the cuteness of your husband's antics is replaced by a growing resentment that he has abdicated his role as husband and father to relive his childhood. If your wife still acts like she's a college girl, when she is approaching her fifties or sixties, the fun of having a wife who enjoys being "young" is quickly replaced with a need for a companion who recognizes the need for maturity and intimacy in the latter years of marriage.

I am not suggesting that we walk around with frowns on our faces, never letting the child inside all of us out to play. I am suggesting the need for balance. You've all known or lived with a proverbial child who is going on forty, fifty, or sixty. Unable to make decisions from the healthy stance of adult maturity, this person either jokes his or her way through life or pitches a temper tantrum to get his or her way. Either response is inappropriate and

> **Y**ou ought not to practice childish ways, since you are no longer that age.
> —Homer

leaves many relationships fractured or broken because a spouse is unable to assume the role of adult. Why do some men and women react to life from the emotional vantage point of a child?

What we fail to remember is crucial to our understanding. All of us have a history that is hidden by years of conditioning and grooming. It is still there, no matter how "good" we look on the outside. It's the same as when we look at a tree. We only see part of it. The part we don't see is the foundation that holds it upright during storms and wind. Deep beneath the surface are the roots. Most of the time we never see beneath the surface of those we come into contact with. To the one observing, the man who throws a temper tantrum is a spoiled brat, but the roots of bitterness are at the core of every bit of acting out he subjects his family to. God understands what lies beneath the surface and He knows that we have to go deeper—to the very roots—to develop into mature sons and daughters of the living God. That is where our foundations were laid and where we will discover (if we persist) what makes us act childishly instead of prudently.

Many weddings include some reading of or reference to 1 Corinthians 13, commonly called the love chapter. Yet I rarely hear the part about "childish things" repeated in the marriage ceremony. Rather, couples entering marriage are quick to include "love never fails" in their vows to each other. Could it be that we don't want to be reminded of what childish behavior can do to a marriage? When Paul spoke of putting away childish things in 1 Corinthians 13, he recognized the importance of allowing God to invade our lives and mature us as His children.

I believe Paul mentioned the childish (or immature) ways we cope because he knew that kind of acting out is the hidden enemy of love. When a husband or wife holds on to a grudge, lets resentment brood until it blossoms into full-grown anger or hatred, the consequence is obvious. When a man or woman has to be first all the time, ahead of the other family members, feelings of abandonment and rejection can quickly get out of hand.

We are often emotionally disabled in adulthood because of the baggage we bring with us from the past. It would be the worst form of denial to conclude that our past has no effect on our present. Paul asks us to render our past dead to what we know as reality today. He encourages us to grow up physically, spiritually, and emotionally. When he says to put away this childish mind-set, the verb he uses means to render it *totally inoperable* and to put it out of commission.

All of us would agree that we love to see a man or woman who can get down on the floor and play with the kids—enjoying life as a family. However, it's a different story when the man or woman has to be the center of attention

> **A** psychologist a few years ago conducted a study on how people think, and he concluded that those who had more positive thoughts had a much greater likelihood of enjoying the following:
>
> - Better eyesight
> - Healthier bodies
> - Better bodily function
> - Better memory
>
> —Dr. William Mitchell

> **I**t's in devoting ourselves to things outside of the self—particularly to other people and, I would also argue, primarily to God—that we gain our self. Those who narcissistically hold on to looking out for number one will lose their life.
> —Paul Vitz

CHILDISH THINGS

and get his or her way every time. Certainly, when the little boy or little girl takes over the adult, there are major problems. And love's hidden enemy springs up all around in relationships.

Let's take a closer look at how childishness affects love life.

A CLOSER LOOK **B**ecause what we learned as children continues to influence the way that we look at things in our adult years, we need to get a handle on what needs to be discarded and what should be kept. Much of our mental and emotional programming was faulty, yet we cling to it.

If you questioned counselors concerning the basic problem behind a person's way of coping with life, I believe that you would hear the same answer repeated time and time again: *performance based behavior.* Psychiatrists, psychologists, social workers, and counselors are extremely familiar with the terminology. Whether or not you know what to call the behavior, you know the consequence of its impact on the lives of men and women who still think they have to *do* something to be of value. It's not a new idea, but one that has come into its own in recent days. A look at some of the thought patterns that have grown out of this learned behavior might surface some rather uncomfortable ideas in your way of dealing with life.

"I have to be perfect." This develops perfectionism to an extreme because we want perfect behavior so that we will be accepted. I've seen children who are afraid to bring home a B on a report card because Mom or Dad won't be satisfied. Who is the child in that picture? Those who believe worth is based on doing it perfectly set themselves up for a lifetime of disappointment that filters into their children and grandchildren. A perfectionist can't allow anyone to fail, especially anyone within the family. It wouldn't look right.

People who believe that love is based on their ability to measure up never feel safe or secure. People trying to be lovable become self-centered, thinking of how to be more lovable. They suspect others of having ulterior motives if they exhibit any love toward them, so they end up pushing people away. Not only do they feel the impact in their relationships with spouse and children, but they translate the same idea into their relationship with God. It's a tragic way to live.

"You'll never amount to anything." The person who has grown up hearing that repeated develops an inferiority complex. It puts pressure on a relationship that is often deadly. The one who believes the lie that says, "You'll

never amount to anything," is set up for a life of failure, draining anyone who dares to get close in an effort to help or befriend.

"I'm a failure and inadequate." This is the natural outgrowth of the programming discussed in the previous paragraph. As an adult, this translates into feeling, "I've never pleased anyone, and I'll probably never please you." A person who believes she is a failure will either try to overcompensate by being "too good" or will give up completely and avoid any relationship that requires intimacy. In a marriage, this attitude creates tension and defensiveness that will destroy the relationship before it can grow unless both partners are committed to seeking God's answer to this faulty belief system.

"If you can't have your way, throw a fit." Adults teach this attitude to their children because of the way fathers and mothers get their way. This attitude says, "If you act ugly enough, you'll get what you want." That translates into adults perfecting their tantrums into silence or pouting or yelling. Each adult who was taught this has his own way of getting what he wants, and he knows which way is the most effective. Children are quick to pick up on their parents' way of coping. Many parents have had to deal with a child who pouts until they give in, and they wondered how the child learned such obnoxious behavior.

"You must have things to be secure." This way of thinking is also based on performance because of the need to have material possessions. Ones who don't perform well won't ever have the financial means to get what they mistakenly think will make them secure. That translates into a no-win situation where materialism and financial stress can quickly destroy a relationship. Greed always demands more.

Other faulty belief patterns that need to be addressed aren't specifically based on performance but are linked indirectly to how we perceive the value of those we interact with on a daily basis.

Women were taught, *"You can't trust men."* God knew what He was doing when He established the man as the head of the household. If a woman grows up thinking men can't be trusted, the outcome is inescapable. As an adult woman, she becomes overly jealous and suspicious. No wonder the word *submission* has been deleted from most marriage vows. What we teach our little girls affects their marriages. Whether you believe that or not, the truth is inescapable.

"Sex is dirty." To an adult, that translates into devastation in the marriage. There can be untold problems stemming from this idea, including physical symptoms in both partners. God created sex to be enjoyed within the boundary of marriage. Some men and women decide to have an affair because the spouse is unable to function as a sexual partner in addition to being a

> **I**f we could expel all pride, vanity, self-righteousness, self-seeking, desire for applause, honor and promotion—if by some divine power we should be utterly emptied of all that, the Spirit would come as a rushing mighty wind to fill us.
> —A. J. Gordon

> **W**e Americans no longer are willing to accept responsibility for our actions. Not only have we redefined the things that matter most to us, but we have also moved away from accepting responsibility for the consequences of our actions.
> —George Barna

CHILDISH THINGS

Christian maturity may be tested in how one answers the following questions. How do I react to trials? How do I resist temptation? How do I respond to truth? How do I restrain my tongue?
—Lehman Strauss

Nine-tenths of our unhappiness is selfishness and is an insult cast in the face of God.
—G. H. Morrison

companion, friend, and parent. There is no excuse for extramarital affairs, but Satan has used this lie to tempt many to ignore marriage vows for the fulfillment of sexual needs. A child who grows up believing sex is dirty has quite a problem on the honeymoon night when all that was dirty is supposed to be expected, much less beautiful.

"God and the church are not important." That translates into a marriage with a lot of friction, especially on Sunday if this person is married to someone who was taught differently. It not only causes enormous strain in the marriage, but it can also totally confuse the children about what is important. When a man and a woman get married and one believes God is relevant to everything in life and the other uses "god" only in the context of profanity, there will always be confusion and disagreement. The Bible's instruction not to be unequally yoked is for our well-being.

Although these faulty belief systems have significant impact on our lives, there are countless more we haven't discussed. The hidden enemies of love are everywhere Satan can get a foothold. What is the simplest and quickest way to deal with the lies you grew up believing? If you are like most people, you blame the other person, keeping a running record of the other person's faults, and refuse to examine yourself. That is the quickest way to deal with false belief systems, but is that the way to health and maturity in relationships? Absolutely not. While it might get the heat off personal inventory, it's like taking a water pistol into mortal combat. The effect is nil.

If blaming is the wrong way to deal with these problems, what is the proper method of dealing with these hidden enemies of love? There are five steps, which are not simple and quick. However, they work. I can only tell you what they are. The Holy Spirit will have to convict you of your need to apply them to your experience.

First, *take responsibility* for your part in the problem. You need to acknowledge the part that is your fault. This is contrary to everything that you want to do, but it is the first step in putting away childish things. You know what it's like to keep arguing about who is to blame. Nothing positive gets accomplished, and feelings of anger and resentment keep the battle at a fever pitch.

Second, *get to the root of the problem,* however difficult that might be. You need to peel the layers off your life. What you find may make your eyes water. The potential for pain keeps too many people from enjoying the benefit that results from doing the difficult work necessary for a marriage, a parent-child, or Creator-created relationship to be healthy.

Third, *seek godly counsel*. Notice, I said godly counsel. If the counselor doesn't refer to the Word of God as the source, you need to find one who does. I've heard the men and women who work in our counseling center talk about the wounded souls who come to see them after years in therapy. Often, after months or years a man or woman will finally reach the point of despair and come to see one of our counselors. Inevitably, these words come out: "What my counselor told me made things worse." Many times it takes months and months to undo the damage of unsound counseling.

Fourth, *surrender fully to the Lord*. Say, "Father, whatever You want me to do, I'll do." As long as you cling to your "rights," you prevent God from doing what needs to be done to break you and bring you to your knees in absolute surrender. I believe people can't fully experience healing until they have been broken of the pride and stubbornness that keep them from admitting their sinfulness. As long as you keep saying, "But . . . but I . . . but . . . ," you haven't reached the point of surrender. I know from experience that until you give up your rights, you won't get it right.

Fifth, *trust God to bring about healing*. Don't get it in your mind that you can manipulate God. That's not what I mean. However, before God can heal you, you must have a pure heart that says, "I trust You whatever You choose to do with my life." That's when you are primed for God's healing—whether it is spiritual, emotional, or physical.

Only God can wean an adult from her childish behavior. But the adult must be willing. God, as the heavenly Parent, may gently pry loose the false ragged blanket. Or He may jerk at it. When that happens, the person needs to look at why she resists giving up what she thinks makes her secure. She needs to identify her "security blanket" and just hand it to Him. He'll gladly take it.

 APPLICATION

Enemies are hard to deal with when you can see them. But when they are hidden, they are really difficult. It's like getting up at night, wandering through the dark house, trying to identify the strange noises you thought you heard. Once the lights are turned on, the hidden enemy is no longer hidden.

Paul admonishes us to turn on the lights in our lives and spotlight hidden enemies of love. It's a painful and long process. It's even more painful when you must take part of the blame and say, "I have met the enemy: me."

In the end, it's worth it.

I am *not* talking about any pop psychology. I am talking about honesty. I am talking about discovering through hard work what makes you tick. I am talking about realizing that what makes you tick may be ticking off someone

CHILDISH THINGS

else. I am talking about finding the hidden enemies of love in your life and putting them away, *once and for all*.

Jesus Christ will help you. He won't usurp your free will. If you want to continue to throw temper tantrums or pout until everyone gets tired of your childish behavior and walks away, He'll let you go right ahead. But remember, Jesus understands how wounded you are. He knows about pain and sorrow. He has already fought the greatest enemy of all and won.

He just wants to help you in your battle.

Let Him.

GROWTH

Look through the list of enemies and see if what you learned as a child is among the things mentioned. Are you acting in that childish manner now? When do you plan on putting away childish things?

It would be beneficial to find a trusted friend, counselor, or pastor to help you work through your personal belief systems, searching out the faulty programming and committing yourself to renewal. Ask a trusted Christian friend to point out areas that you need to confront. The truth is, few of us would address our problems without a little push (or a big one) from a person who really loves us enough to say, "This is something you need to work on."

The only way to bring about real change in your behavior is to renew your mind to God's truth. If there was one truth I could give you that has changed my life, it would be the truth contained in Romans 12, that we are "transformed" by the renewing of our minds. Paul did not say by the renewing of our behavior. He understood that change begins in the mind and blossoms into the behavior. The childish things that keep you from experiencing the fullness of mature relationships with family, friends, and God will soon become evident. Then you can begin to put them away and allow God to grow you into the man or woman who can still play with trains on Christmas morning.

QUOTE

If I am soft to myself and slide comfortably into the vice of self-pity and self-sympathy; if I do not by the grace of God practice fortitude, then I know nothing of Calvary love.

—Amy Carmichael

■ *Accepting God's sovereign control over all of life's circumstances.*

CONTENTMENT

SCRIPTURE

PHILIPPIANS 4:10–13 NASB

But I rejoiced in the Lord greatly, that now at last you have revived your concern for me; indeed, you were concerned before, but you lacked opportunity. Not that I speak from want; for I have learned to be content in whatever circumstances I am. I know how to get along with humble means, and I also know how to live in prosperity; in any and every circumstance I have learned the secret of being filled and going hungry, both of having abundance and suffering need. I can do all things through Him who strengthens me.

COMMENTARY

The apostle Paul knew something that most of us have missed. He knew how to be content in *any* circumstance. That is a bold claim. But when you think about the life of Paul, such a claim moves from the realm of bold to amazing! He was personally commissioned by Christ to take the gospel to the Gentiles. And after only a few years of work, he was sidelined in a Roman prison. There he sat, under house arrest, waiting for his trial; well aware that the various churches he planted needed his immediate attention and leadership, driven by a desire to get the gospel to unreached cities, and yet content.

Notice he said, "I have learned the secret." The word *learned* implies a process. As Paul grew in his spiritual life, he discovered the truth about contentment. He referred to it as a secret because the truth he discovered is a truth that eludes so many believers. It is a truth that we search for in our own way and yet miss.

He learned the secret of being content in and through circumstances. It wasn't the secret of changing—or getting God to change—his circumstances. Real contentment does not hinge on circumstances. It goes beyond that.

Paul's discussion regarding contentment closes with a verse that many of us learned as children. "I can do all things through Him who strengthens me" (4:13 NASB). Unfortunately, for a lot of us, no one explained the context of this popular verse. Paul was referring to his ability to be content in every circumstance. To paraphrase, "I can endure any circumstance without losing my peace and my joy because of the strength I gain through my relationship with Christ."

> **I**f we have not quiet in our minds, outward comfort will do no more for us than a golden slipper on a gouty foot.
> —John Bunyan

APPLICATION

Let's take a closer look at Paul's secret. What is the secret of contentment? From what he says, I believe it has to do with our willingness to accept three powerful truths.

CONTENTMENT

■ *Accepting God's sovereign control over all of life's circumstances.*

First, real contentment hinges on what's happening inside us, not around us. We are all tempted to believe the lie that our contentment—or our happiness for that matter—hinges on our ability to control what is going on around us. We spend a great deal of energy and time trying to control our environment and the people in it. But real contentment has to do with what's going on inside us, not around us.

Think about it this way. When we become discontented, the first two things we lose are our peace and joy. But the Bible teaches that peace and joy are to be fruits of the Spirit. Their source is the Holy Spirit; He is producing them in us. If we can lose our peace and joy when our circumstances turn bad, the peace and joy we were experiencing were not fruits of the Spirit; they were fruits of good circumstance.

As long as our contentment can be destroyed by a change in our environment, we can never be content in any circumstance. Such is the fragile nature of externally oriented contentment. That is certainly not the contentment Paul knew. Circumstances didn't steal his peace and joy; what happened around him didn't overwhelm what was happening in him. His contentment was internal from start to finish.

To experience contentment, we must begin by refusing to blame our circumstances (or the people who make up our circumstances) for our lack of contentment. As long as we blame what's going on around us, we will never understand what's happening in us. When circumstances rob us of our peace and joy, we must take responsibility. We must acknowledge that we are looking to what we cannot control to provide us with our contentment. Only then can we begin to look in the right direction for our contentment.

Second, contentment is need, not want, oriented. God will meet all our needs; He is going to take good care of us. Much of our discontentment stems from not getting what we *want*. God has not promised to meet all of your wants according to His riches in glory. As long as our peace and joy hinge on getting what we want, we are on an emotional roller coaster.

God is a perfect heavenly Father. He knows what you need. He knows what you don't need. He knows what you want. He knows what you can handle. And He is committed to doing what's best for you.

Ask yourself this question: Is God meeting my needs? If the answer is yes, stop and thank Him. Don't allow your emotions to attach themselves to your wants. That is a no-win proposition. The secret of contentment, then, includes distinguishing between what you need and what you want. It means rejoicing over the promise of God to meet your needs.

CONTENTMENT

This brings us to the third truth we must accept if we are to learn Paul's secret: contentment is a matter of trust. If we really trust God—if we really believe He loves us and has our best interests in mind—when things fall apart around us, things don't have to fall apart inside us. Contentment is trusting God even when things seem out of control.

Discontentment, on the other hand, is really a lack of faith in God's love and concern for us. To express discontent is to suggest that God has lost control, or that He doesn't care.

Paul's resolute faith in God allowed him to say, "I can do all things through Him who strengthens me" (Phil. 4:13 NASB). And later in the same chapter, "And my God shall supply all your need according to His riches in glory in Christ Jesus" (Phil. 4:19 NASB). He trusted God completely. When things around him fell apart, he kept trusting. And consequently, he was content.

Overcoming discontentment requires mental discipline. The following five suggestions will help you begin internalizing some of the things discussed above:

1. Memorize and meditate on Philippians 4:10–13.
2. When feelings of discontentment creep in, refuse to blame your circumstances; take responsibility for your feelings.
3. Admit to the Lord that you have allowed your contentment to become too attached to your circumstances.
4. Distinguish between what you need and what you want.
5. Thank Him for meeting your needs.

Let's take a closer look at the flip side of contentment—discontentment. Discontentment always causes three things to happen.

First, discontentment erodes relationships. Discontentment usually translates into a burning desire to change the people around us. If others would act the way we think they should act, we would be fine, right? But as soon as we try to change others to suit our particular taste, mood, or style, we are no longer able to love them. Love is replaced by manipulation. And manipulation is to a relationship what fire is to paper.

The only person you are responsible for changing is yourself. But a discontented person usually expresses discontentment by attempting to change others.

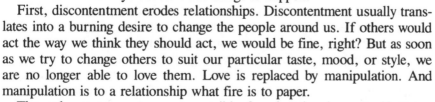

Contentment

CONTENTMENT

> **I**t is right to be contented with what we have, but never with what we are.
> —Sir James Mackintosh

Second, discontentment clouds the decision-making process. Discontentment makes it almost impossible to wait. Discontented people want change—and they want it now. Consequently, their decision-making abilities are skewed. The emotions that accompany discontentment are so strong that they often override reason.

People in marketing understand this all too well. Part of any effective advertising campaign is to make potential customers discontented with their existing product. The feelings that accompany discontentment are enough to make people buy things they don't need or can't afford. Discontentment clouds the ability to make wise decisions.

Have you ever noticed how bad your car looks when you drive it onto a new car lot? Have you ever become self-conscious about what you have on when shopping for new clothes? Have you noticed how small your house feels after visiting in a larger and newer home? These feelings get you in trouble if you don't keep them in proper perspective.

Discontentment causes people to make foolish marital decisions. It causes people from all walks of life to make foolish financial decisions. I have seen men make unwise career changes because of discontentment. Discontented people tend to make foolish decisions.

Third, discontentment distorts our view of God. Discontented people attempt to control God. Worship, prayer, Bible study, and church attendance become a means to an end—getting God to change whatever they think needs changing. Even faith is reduced to another tool to use to move God in their direction. Discontented people reduce the heavenly Father to the status of a heavenly automatic teller machine. And Christianity becomes a lifelong attempt to find the right code to get from Him what they want. Discontented believers will never know God for who He is. Their discontentment distorts the picture.

GROWTH

Like many, I struggle with contentment. How much is enough? Should I be satisfied with what I have or seek more? Is ambition bad? What kind of goals should I make? The answers are not simple, but I believe Scripture provides the balance we need to cultivate godly contentment.

We must live on a daily basis. Jesus said to pray for our "daily bread"—sufficient provision for daily needs. Contentment flees when we worry about the future. God controls that, and we must leave tomorrow's problems with Him. Today I can bring my needs to Christ. Today His grace is sufficient. Jesus "daily bears our burden" (Ps. 68:19 NASB).

CONTENTMENT

The key to contentment is learning that I can do everything God wants me to do through His strength. I can establish objectives that are in God's plan. Ambition is all right so long as my primary aim is to glorify Christ. We cannot do everything, but He will help us do what He has planned for our lives. We can be content knowing that He enables us to deal with all the vacillations of life as we depend on Him.

Contentment is a daily struggle. It is something we learn by adhering to the basics—cultivating a growing relationship with Jesus Christ, living daily, and knowing that Christ strengthens us for every challenge.

 QUOTE

True contentment is the power of getting out of any situation all that is in it.
—G. K. Chesterton

Contentment

ENDURANCE

■ *To stand; to tolerate; to continue.*

SCRIPTURE

2 TIMOTHY 2:5–6, 8, 10, 12

And also if anyone competes in athletics, he is not crowned unless he competes according to the rules. The hardworking farmer must be first to partake of the crops. . . . Remember . . . Jesus Christ. . . . I endure all things for the sake of the elect. . . . If we endure, we shall also reign with Him.

COMMENTARY

Paul uses several word pictures in this chapter to illustrate and encourage endurance. He refers to a soldier (v. 3) who doesn't yell, "I surrender!" in the foxhole. He withstands the hardship, the rain, the cold, and the dreadful fear of the enemy because of his commitment to the people he is fighting for.

He is single-minded. The Bible says he doesn't get entangled in everyday life because a good soldier can't bother himself with trivial things. In other words, he travels light. Small rations. Few letters from home. Filthy clothing. Unshaven. Matted hair. Seeing the bigger picture, the soldier endures.

From there Paul directs his audience's attention to the field of athletics. As I write this, Atlanta is counting the days—literally—until the 1996 Olympics come to our city. There are gigantic preparations going on in every sphere of our city life.

But our preparation as a city is nothing compared to the preparation of the athletes. Some have been in training since they were very young. Their families have spent vast sums of money for their training. Parents have arisen early to get their children to the ice rink before daybreak. Some athletes have left home for better training. Their eating is regimented. Their sleeping is regimented. Their socializing is regimented. And their bodies are whipped into shape on a daily basis so that they can perform to their highest capacity.

They live, eat, and sleep their chosen sport. What we see at the Olympics is just a fraction of the endurance they demonstrate. I believe that is one reason the Olympics hold such charm for the world—the competition is the ultimate in discipline and endurance.

Then Paul changes the nature of his illustrations when he refers to farmers. Farmers endure in a different way from that of soldiers and athletes. Farmers are forced oftentimes to endure disappointment.

> Endurance is not just the ability to bear a hard thing, but turn it into glory.
> —William Barclay

Every so often, during floods or drought, we'll see a farmer survey his ruined crops. But very few will say, "This land has been in my family for one hundred years, but I can't go on." The majority *endure*. They scrimp and save and figure out a way to feed the family until the next harvest.

Spring comes, and they till the soil that they love so much.

ENDURANCE

They do it with no guarantee that there will be no more floods or parched land again. They do it out of determination because they are farmers and this is their job. *And they endure.*

Like the soldier, are we single-minded and unentangled so we can fight to the end? Like the athlete, do we know anything about daily discipline so that we can compete and not give up before the finish line? Like the farmer, do we not give up after a huge setback because we know what we're called to do and we press on till harvest?

How's our endurance?

Let's take a closer look.

A CLOSER LOOK

You may say, "My life is more complicated than that of a soldier or athlete or farmer. It's not all as simple as you make it sound."

You're right. Life is not simple. There are many bumps and turns in the way. The rat race is real, the battle continuous, and the painful experiences piercing.

But our environment doesn't determine our endurance.

In Hebrews 12:1, the writer begins, "Therefore we also, since we are surrounded by so great a cloud of witnesses." What does that verse have to do with endurance? When we look at why the *therefore* is there, the writer directs us back to chapter 11.

Chapter 11 of Hebrews is populated with people who endured. You may say, "Well, sure they endured. I mean, look how their story turned out!" Well, *they* didn't know how their story was going to turn out. And you don't know how yours is going to end, either.

A young man who is now a pastor had to memorize the entire chapter of Hebrews 11 in the fifth grade. Of course, when children learn large portions of Scripture, so do their parents who are helping. His mother says that exercise was probably one of the most important parts of his entire education, although he went all the way through seminary.

He committed to memory this repertoire of godly people who endured. They seemed like his friends. When he was going through a rough time in his ministry, the Lord reminded him of these great people of faith who endured.

What is involved in endurance?

Endurance involves encouragement from others. That is why the writer of Hebrews encourages us to look at others in Hebrews 11. He refers to the

William Carey, when asked the reason for his success as a missionary, replied, "I can plod."

ENDURANCE

"cloud of witnesses" (Heb. 12:1). The children of Israel had a literal cloud to guide them.

Our cloud of witnesses from the Word of God includes people we cannot see, but we can read about them and glean from their endurance.

I really hope that you have a visible group of encouragers in your life. I believe everyone needs someone to say, "You're doing fantastic," or "I'm praying for you." We all need someone who will cheer us on.

I know some people will gloat over your failures. May God, in His grace, raise up those who will rejoice with you in your victories and weep with you when you weep. That's encouragement.

When I look back at the unseen cloud of witnesses, I think of Joseph, who endured though life was so unfair. I think of David, who endured though he was so lonely, and Moses, who took no shortcuts through the land with the grumbling people. I think of Peter, stumbling and falling, stumbling and falling, and getting up again and again.

We can say, "God, if they endured, so can I because You love me just as much as You loved them."

One encourager in my young life was my grandfather, although I spent little time with him. Once he said to me, "Charles, obey God and leave the consequences to Him." I have never forgotten that. That statement from an encourager has sustained me through many battles.

We are fellow runners in this race. The Bible says this cloud of witnesses *surrounds* us. I hope you are surrounded by encouragers, those who cheer you from the grandstands or run beside you.

Endurance involves laying aside anything and everything that hinders us: "Let us lay aside every weight, and the sin which so easily ensnares us" (Heb. 12:1).

How do we lay aside things that slow us down in the race so that we can endure?

First, we need to identify the hindrances. But what is a hindrance for one person might not be to another. The same weights that keep the scuba diver under the water are the same weights that wreak havoc for a runner.

You need to identify *your* weights, the things that slow *you* in your race. You need to identify the things that make *you* want to quit, or at least not run as fast.

Second, we need to lay aside "the sin which so easily ensnares us." What is the difference between a sin and a weight? Sin is a very specific disobedience. A weight, or an encumbrance, is more subtle and not as easy to see.

> **W**hile women weep . . . I'll fight. While little children go hungry . . . I'll fight. While men go to prison . . . I'll fight. While there is a drunkard left . . . where there remains one lost dark soul . . . I'll fight! I'll fight to the very end!
> —William Booth

ENDURANCE

Notice the word *sin* is singular. Satan knows which sin will throw each of us off course. We generally hear that referred to as a besetting sin. It's the sin you deal with habitually. It's the sin that you thought you had conquered and then it raised its ugly head in an unexpected place.

The writer is telling us if we want to endure, we need to lay aside subtle weights and the sin that constantly nags at us.

Endurance involves running the race. Note the last part of verse 1: "Let us run with endurance the race that is set before us."

God knows the Christian life is not easy. It will never get easy no matter how long you live. There is never a gliding time. It's always a battle. You will deal with the world, flesh, and the devil until you die. Satan is not going to say, "Well, he is sixty-two now and retired, so I'll give him a break, too." Satan never operates that way. The enemy has an incredible endurance record.

I am not trying to be discouraging. I am trying to be realistic. Endurance requires something that doesn't come easily. We have to stand *for* something and *against* something. But running the race involves laying aside—purposely—weights that bog us down and sin that defeats us, and then running with endurance.

Let's look at the race together.

The stadiums in Rome were built a lot like our stadiums. Sporting events had a significant role in Roman life. Racing in the arenas was one of their favorite sports. The people we read about in the book of Hebrews understood the race analogy. They understood that sometimes we run in adverse conditions.

But when the going gets rough—and it will—we don't run away. We can't be quitters. The longer we push the limits, the stronger our faith becomes. We become ready for greater service and expanded ministry. We become strong, stalwart, and steadfast.

It's the same principle that applies to exercise equipment. The more we work out, the stronger our muscles become. The more we run, the greater our endurance level.

A woman noticed a friend was hobbling along. She asked what the problem was, and her friend sheepishly answered, "I am trying to lose weight through exercise, and my personal trainer is killing me."

We have a Personal Trainer who wants us fit for the race but will not "kill" us in the meantime. He knows our individual racetrack. He knows which pace we need to take. He knows what goal He has set for us. And He knows what weights or sin gets us off track. He knows what tires us out.

When John Wesley died, one secular magazine hailed him as "one of the few characters who outlived enmity and prejudice."

ENDURANCE

■ *To stand; to tolerate; to continue.*

It's your unique race. But not so personal that you aren't surrounded by a great cloud of witnesses.

Verse 2 tells us the entire motivation for the endurance: "Looking unto Jesus, the author and finisher of our faith, who for the joy that was set before Him endured the cross, despising the shame."

The One who endured the Cross lives in you so that you can endure yours. If you stumble, He is there to pick you up, just as He lifted Peter when he took his eyes off Jesus and sank into the water.

Peter's key is your key: fix your eyes on Jesus.

If your trail gets real narrow or the bridge is out, don't turn around. Keep your eyes on Jesus.

Do you want to endure? Listen to the throngs encouraging you. Make sure you're in a church where there are present-day clouds of witnesses to cheer you on. Do you want to endure? Lay aside everything that slows you down in your race. Put aside the debilitating sin that gets you off course.

Do you want to endure? Then run your particular race inside your particular track. Don't look back. Keep your eyes on Jesus.

Have as your goal to write in your journal what the apostle Paul wrote, "I have fought the good fight, I have finished the race, I have kept the faith. Finally, there is laid up for me the crown of righteousness, which the Lord, the righteous Judge, will give to me on that Day" (2 Tim. 4:7–8).

Don't quit. Endure.

I know a woman who goes to the Special Olympics each year. She goes for no other reason than to cheer. She sits in the stands and watches the youngsters with disabilities run in the races. They get distracted easily. They often get confused as to which way to run. They have to concentrate hard on limbs that won't cooperate.

But running alongside them are encouragers. That's all they are there for. They run and keep calling out the children's names. They praise the children. They discourage them from looking at the other runners. In fact, they encourage them to keep their eyes fixed on the hugger at the finish line. Someone is there for no other reason than to hug the winner.

They don't win because they beat the other contestants. They win because they finish the race. That's the criterion.

But they need to listen to the encouragement from the stands. They need to listen to personal encouragers running with them. And they need to keep their eyes on the hugger at the finish line.

In a sense, we are in a very Special Olympics. And in a very real sense, we have disabilities.

> **T**he way in which you endure that which you must endure is more important than the crisis itself.
> —Sam Rutigliano

There are encouragers along the way.
But we have to focus on the Hugger at the end of the line.

When you received the Lord Jesus as your Savior and He set you on your course, He had it all mapped out—bumps, quick turns, detours, up hills, down valleys.

He didn't just fire the starting pistol and you took off, hoping to find your way. He brought the Holy Spirit, who is called alongside you, to indwell you.

You aren't running alone. And you don't have to clench your fists so you can endure.

Remember the verse we read about Jesus' enduring the Cross?

Suppose—just suppose—in Gethsemane He said, "I can't do this. I just can't"? That's hard to conceive, isn't it?

Okay, suppose He lasted through Gethsemane and the trial but when the nails appeared, He cried, "That's it. I quit. There's got to be another way."

We know He didn't quit. He *endured*.

The writer in Hebrews declares, "You have not yet resisted to bloodshed" (Heb. 12:4).

He endured the Cross. Our race pales in comparison to that. We've not shed blood.

But the One who did runs with us.

GROWTH

Memorize Hebrews 11.

QUOTES

Jesus is our running companion. He runs in front of me to show the way, by my side to pick me up, and behind me to encourage me.

—Charles Stanley

When you fall and skin your knees and skin your heart, He'll pick you up.

—Charles Stanley

FREEDOM

■ *The capacity to exercise choice.*

GENESIS 2:16–17

And the LORD God commanded the man, saying, "Of every tree of the garden you may freely eat; but of the tree of the knowledge of good and evil you shall not eat, for in the day that you eat of it you shall surely die."

COMMENTARY

Unlike us, Adam and Eve didn't have to worry about very many rules and regulations. In fact, Adam and Eve had only one rule to abide by. Just one. But they still blew it.

What can we learn from their experience? First of all, it tells us a whole lot about God. Contrary to what some people have surmised, God is not hung up on rules. Rather, He is a God of freedom. In a world that was exactly like He wanted it, He had only one rule. There was only one "thou shalt not," and it was put there to establish His authority over human beings. God knew that under His authority, people would find maximum freedom. God doesn't impose rules just for the sake of having rules. It was His desire that His creation experience the joy of freedom, and He knew that could happen only under His care.

Second, freedom in the Garden of Eden meant the ability and authority to do anything they wanted to within the parameters God established. Even in a perfect world, freedom was not the power to do *whatever* they wanted to with no consequences. That freedom does not exist. It *never* has, and it never will. Freedom, from God's perspective, has not changed since the Garden. The purest example for freedom was established in the Garden, as the ability and authority to exercise our will within the parameters God establishes.

The third thing we can learn from the experience of Adam and Eve is that sin, not God, robbed people of freedom. Satan lied to Eve and Eve (and Adam!) fell for it! What ensued is history. If this was a "happily ever after" story, I would joyously relate how people learned from the grave error Adam and Eve made in the Garden when they chose to disobey God. That's not what happened. The lie continues and people keep falling for it. Have you ever heard someone say something like the following?

- "God is trying to limit your freedom."
- "You cannot trust Him."
- "You can be absolutely free from all rules."

Satan has been using the same lines since Adam and Eve's experience in the Garden. Looking back at their experience, we wish we could step into

> **F**reedom can be uncomfortable. Given choice, it is always possible to make the wrong decision.
> —*Observer*

history and stop them from making such a devastating choice; yet we fall for the same rationale. When Adam and Eve opted to exercise their free will, instead of gaining freedom, they lost most of the freedom they already had.

They lost their freedom to live in the Garden.

They lost their freedom from shame, guilt, fear, pain, and suffering.

They lost their freedom to walk with God.

They lost their freedom from conflict with each other.

They became slaves to sickness and death.

Sin always results in the loss of freedom. Can you imagine living in a world where words like *blame* and *it's your fault that I'm so unhappy* were never spoken? Adam and Eve had that opportunity and lost it in the pursuit of freedom. Whenever you step outside the boundaries that God established, you take a step away from freedom. Obedience is the path to maximum freedom. With so many voices telling you how to be free, you are at risk of relinquishing your freedom unless you remain vigilant and equipped for Satan's attack. Instead of setting yourself free of the rules and regulations that seem to weigh you down, you will find yourself in bondage.

You cannot be free outside a relationship with God. Anyone who tells you otherwise does not have your best interest at heart. While some would argue that there is no such thing as freedom if it has strings attached to it, a closer look will help you redefine freedom from God's perspective—the only outlook worth your time and attention.

> **T**wenty-five percent of men surveyed strongly agreed that "freedom means being able to do anything you want to do." Thirty-three percent strongly disagreed.
> —George Barna

A CLOSER LOOK

Freedom with parameters and boundaries doesn't seem like freedom to us. Every day we are offered the same lie offered to Adam and Eve: "Maximum freedom is found outside the boundaries," or "Try it just once," or "You're missing out." We are tempted to reach for something that doesn't exist—freedom to do whatever we want to, whenever we want to, with whomever we please, with zero consequences. We often have to learn the hard way that real freedom lies in obedience to God's truth.

Whenever we cross God's moral guidelines in an effort to express or gain freedom, we are the losers. We are tempted to seek freedom outside the boundaries of obedience concerns in our finances. This is such a problem in a world that seeks to find significance through things. The person who spends what he doesn't have sets himself up for bondage that no one wants to experience. Anyone who seeks freedom by spending money loses the freedom of being free from the stress of financial debt, bill collectors,

FREEDOM

collection agencies, and court-enforced garnishments. More couples divorce over financial problems than for almost any other reason. The love of things has cost persons their freedom.

We seek freedom in entertainment—what we read, watch, and listen to. The television and movie industries are multibillion-dollar industries, with more money being spent in an effort to attract consumers, with less and less concern for the moral values.

We seek freedom in speech. Verbal abuse leaves "bruises" that aren't readily apparent to the naked eye. Yet its tragic effect is evident as years of verbal abuse tear down the spirit of a child, who grows up believing she is unworthy of love and sells herself to anyone who will spend time with her. As children, we learned, "Sticks and stones may break my bones, but words will never hurt me." Even as a child, I knew that was a lie. It really doesn't matter if the one who continually tells a child that he is stupid means to be abusive; the words become a life script that often leads to a tragic end. Words are a powerful tool that can either uplift or tear down.

There are unbelievable pressures on teenagers to exercise their "right" to be free of parental control. Some have even gone so far as to sue their parents so that they can make their own choices without parental interference. Husbands and wives are constantly bombarded with the propaganda of the world's standard that says, "You don't have to abide by the boundaries of marriage the same way your parents did. That was then. This is now. Things have changed." Truer words were never spoken. Things have changed. People used to go to bed at night without locking the doors to their houses. Today we have dead bolts and multiple locks on doors and windows to keep out criminals. We are living in a world that values protecting the rights of the criminal over the welfare of the victim. It should not surprise anyone that we have come to this place. Every time people choose to abuse a freedom, they lose a freedom.

God wants us to be as free as we can possibly be, but He understands the big picture and knows that maximum freedom can be found only under His authority. Because God desires for us to enjoy as much freedom as we possibly can without being hurt, He has established limits to provide for and protect our freedom. That's why He made up that one rule in the Garden—to provide for an order of authority, setting into motion the framework for an optimal relationship between Creator and created. It was God's intention to protect Adam and Eve from evil by establishing certain parameters that they were to adhere to for their well-being.

The same principle applies to us. There are reasons for the rules God gives us. Granted, we have a lot more than Adam and Eve had to contend

> **T**here are two freedoms: the false where one is free to do what he likes and the true where he is free to do what he ought.
> —Charles Kingsley

> **R**eal freedom means to welcome the responsibility it brings, to welcome the God-control it requires, to welcome the discipline that results, to welcome the maturity it creates.
> —Eugenia Price

with. But there are so many rules because of sin, not because of God. We live in a dangerous world, and the more dangerous our environment, the more precautions we have to take. Twenty years ago, no one had heard about AIDS. While there have always been consequences of engaging in sexual relationships outside the boundary of marriage, the cost has never been so high. Now it can cost you your life.

God's rules have always been given to provide the framework for the best possible relationships, both vertically (with Him) and horizontally (with one another).

The most liberated marriages function under the canopy of honesty, trust, faithfulness, and respect. In the marriages that are falling apart, one person starts breaking the rules. Almost immediately, trust is gone and so is freedom in the relationship. Contrary to what the world might tell you, a liberated marriage is not a marriage without rules. Without rules, it's just another encounter with no lasting commitment involved.

God created us, and He knows how we function best. Freedom is found within the confines of His laws, boundaries, and commandments. Just as God places boundaries in our relationships to provide the best arena for them to grow, He gives us rules to protect us from sin and its consequences. You'd think we would remember this from childhood, but we forget so easily. Our parents gave us rules we didn't understand or agree with, but later on, we look back and understand. Soon we pass along the same rules to our kids— and they don't understand, either.

Instead of learning from the experience with childhood rules, we continue to make excuses. Instead of learning, we repeat, "I don't see anything wrong with . . . ," or "I can handle this; nothing is going to happen." Sin always enslaves, always robs us of our freedom. The scriptural warning that we reap what we sow has never changed.

What causes the problem with the principle of obedience versus freedom? We don't know why He established certain rules. When we don't know the *why,* we aren't aware of the consequences. Without the *why,* we aren't motivated to take the rule seriously.

Josh McDowell, one of today's most prolific writers and speakers, relates how he went into churches and asked teenagers whether or not they would lie to avoid painful circumstances. He said that he couldn't remember a student who said, "No." Now we're talking about church kids; yet right in church, they admitted they would lie to avoid painful consequences. Then Josh asked, "Have your parents taught you that lying is wrong?" They all responded, "Yes." They added that they were taught that the Bible says lying is wrong. Then Josh asked the question that stumped them all, "Why does

> We must exercise our freedom of choice by seeking and following God's direction. Wise decision making comes from seeking God's wisdom. Wise choices come from seeking God's will. They result in following His ways.

> When you do your task in life as best you can, when you know you are in touch with your own conscience, when you have prayed about, thought about a tough decision, and you have finally made up your mind, and you go ahead with a free spirit no matter what anyone else says or thinks, then you finally have found a precious freedom.
> —Lewis B. Smedes

FREEDOM

the Bible say you shouldn't lie?" He never got an answer. The overwhelming truth that we can't avoid is that we all know *what* we should or shouldn't do, but we do it anyway because we don't understand *why* the rule is enforced.

For every what to do, there is a why to do it! Knowing the why usually informs us as to how the rule provides for us and protects us. God doesn't make up arbitrary rules any more than a caring parent does. His rules flow from His perfect character and from His concern for us. You can be sure of one thing. For every precept, there is a principle, and the principles flow from the character and nature of God. If we ended this discussion here, that should be enough motivation for us to cheerfully adhere to the rules that God establishes for His children. He is a loving Father, the perfect definition of love, and He will not ask us to do something (or *not* do something) just for the sake of putting another rule on the books. His motivation is always our well-being. Love cannot do otherwise.

I have the considerable joy of watching my two children, Andy and Becky, as they are beginning their role as parents. As a grandfather, I get to enjoy the benefits of spoiling my grandchildren while leaving the disciplining and teaching to my children as they parent their children. Often as I observe my children in their new role as parents, I am reminded of things that happened to them as children. One such experience that Andy went through when he was eleven years old is a perfect illustration for our discussion of freedom.

One of the families in our church had invited my family to their farm after church along with some other friends. As the adults sat inside talking, Andy and another boy his age ventured outside and explored the woods just beyond a fenced-in pasture. After they had walked around the pasture for a few minutes, the boys came up with a brilliant idea. Why not climb under the barbwire fence and cut across the pasture to the pond? Sounded like a good idea since it would eliminate quite a distance they would otherwise have to walk. Glancing from one side of the pasture to the other, all they saw was a herd of cattle quietly grazing at the other end. Confident that they were safe, they lifted up the wire, crawled under, and began walking toward their destination.

For some reason, Andy looked back, only to see a charging Brahma bull. They could have won the Olympics with the speed they began running, gasping for breath as they reached the fence and crawled underneath it! Once safely on the other side of the fence, lying breathless on the ground, they peered up to see the cattle standing just across the fence staring at them.

You're probably way ahead of me, but I can't resist making the application to the "moral of the story" for those who might miss it. What had appeared

> **Y**ou are free to make decisions in the light of a perfect and delightful friendship with God, knowing that if your decisions are wrong, He will lovingly produce that sense of restraint.
> —Oswald Chambers

to be a hindrance, something that stood in Andy's way, was there for his protection and safety. What had been a nuisance a few minutes earlier was a welcome barrier between him and the bull headed straight for him. He learned a lesson that he's never forgotten. The hindrance became his safety. There is always a why connected to the what. Why was the fence put there? Was it to get in his way and make him have to walk farther? No, it was put there to protect him from the animals. Taking the time to find out why God has given us certain rules and boundaries will eliminate a lot of the problem we have being obedient.

APPLICATION

All of us enjoy the benefits of living in the United States. It's a great country, even with all its problems. Yet none of us would have the freedom we enjoy without some rules. There will never be *absolute* freedom. It doesn't exist. However, we can enjoy *maximum* freedom by letting God have His way in our lives, by being obedient to the rules we often fuss about.

To do what you want, when you want, with whom, without consequences is a fairy tale that has no place in the real world. Our Creator understands us because He made us, and He knows that we will enjoy maximum freedom only under His authority. There, we will find the most nourishing relationships, the best plan for our protection, and the greatest provision for our well-being. What more could we ask for? Those of us who have asserted our "right" to free choice understand the high price we pay when we choose freedom over obedience to God. That's the choice we make every time we go outside God's will and act out of selfish motive for our own satisfaction.

Next time you are faced with the choice between doing what feels good or doing what God requires of His children, remember there is a why behind every rule. Rules were created not to spoil your fun but to protect and provide for you.

GOALS

■ *The things we aspire to achieve.*

SCRIPTURE

PROVERBS 21:5

The plans of the diligent lead surely to plenty,
But those of everyone who is hasty, surely to poverty.

COMMENTARY

The writer of Proverbs knew the importance of goals. Without them, our lives are at best a toss-up, with priorities being determined by the boss, the pediatrician, the loan officer at the bank, and/or the child's schoolteacher. If we don't give serious thought to our goals and how we can reach them, our time, money, and emotions will be dictated by others.

A wise person said, "If you aim for nothing, you are bound to hit it every time." The truth within these words is evident in people who wander through life with no specific ambition. It's common sense to set goals you want to attain and then map out a plan of action.

God felt that setting goals was vitally important. Although Jesus said, "Don't worry about tomorrow," He didn't say, "Don't *think* about tomorrow." God's Word is clear. He wants us to make plans and that means setting goals. Think about it for a minute. We set goals all the time. Try having a wedding without a goal (a plan). Try starting a new business without a business plan. Try building a house without a blueprint. The outcome would be a disaster. Most people who work understand the importance of goals and plans in the business world, yet too many fail to see the importance of goals and plans in personal life.

It is obvious from the way we plan our careers that we understand, in a limited sense, the value of setting goals. We know that goal setting is effective in reaching our career objectives. The top salesperson in the company has a sales strategy, a plan that will ensure her rank among the other salespeople. She wouldn't dare enter the competitive field of sales without a plan detailing the way she intends to reach the established goal. This person often collects the largest bonus at the end of the year. The application seems obvious. Yet, very often, we act as though it is unspiritual to set goals in personal life and for spiritual growth. If we believe what Scripture says, just the opposite is true.

A CLOSER LOOK

There are many seeming contradictions between living by faith and setting goals. I say "seeming" because there is no contradiction at all. Following are four observations about goals that illustrate that the walk of faith and plans for the future are not mutually exclusive.

First, *setting goals establishes priorities*. If you don't establish your priorities, someone else will. It is true, also, that spiritual growth can be monitored and measured by your priorities. When you become a Christian, your priorities change. You grow and mature in your relationship with God; the things you value (your priorities) will change. Likewise, if you fall away from the Lord through unwise counsel or fleshly desires, your priorities again will change. An honest look at the way you spend your time and how you spend your money will give you a good look at your spiritual growth— or lack of it.

Setting goals is one way you can be sure that you will focus your efforts on the main things so that trivial matters will not become your focus. There is so much to distract you. Your goals will ensure that you keep first things first. They will keep you from allowing this world to establish your life's agenda. It's a way of saying, "If I don't do anything else, I want to make sure I . . ." It's your safety belt in a world that too often makes the things that have no eternal significance seem so essential.

Second, *setting goals enables you to move from remorse to real change*. As you read this page, you have probably already thought about something you intended to change but let slip through last year without ever making the effort to alter what was wrong. You are not alone. We all regret things we did or didn't do last year, but regret and remorse are no guarantees that anything will change. On the contrary, you can spend your life regretting things and never make it across the line that separates regret from rejoicing in an accomplished goal. That's because you had no goal in place.

If you don't have a plan, if you don't set goals, you are left with good intentions, remorse, and regret, and year after year the cycle repeats itself. It is amazing to me how many people admit they have a problem in a particular area but are unwilling to come up with a concrete plan to change. Let's suppose you invited friends over for dinner next Saturday night. You would look pretty silly if you didn't plan what you were going to have to eat. Your intentions may be as pure as gold, but they never accomplish a thing without a plan of action.

Third, *goals are a tool for character building*. Setting goals is one of the most effective character-building tools that God has gifted you with. It teaches you discipline through delayed gratification. As you mature and understand the positive side of setting goals and working for them, you reap the rewards of delayed gratification and learn invaluable lessons. One of the most valuable character traits that many have put aside today is that of self-

Perseverance is more than endurance. It is endurance combined with absolute assurance and certainty that what we are looking for is going to happen.
—Oswald Chambers

Paths of righteousness have a goal to which they unerringly lead.
—J. R. Miller

GOALS

■ *The things we aspire to achieve.*

> **E**very person in the church needs to feel important, and indeed they all are. Give people a purpose and they will thrive.
> —Brian Jones

control. Having goals is a sure way of learning self-control. If your goal is to pay off your debts by next year, you will learn to exercise control in your spending habits.

The same is true when you think about living for tomorrow rather than for the thrill of today. Sin never makes sense in the long run, but if your focus is shortsighted, you are prone to look at the immediate situation and not consider the long-term implications. The pie that your next-door neighbor brought by to thank you for your kindness looks tempting, but if you have a goal to lose weight so you can become healthier, it makes sense to look at the long-term benefit of not eating the pie. Living for the future puts things in perspective. It puts choices you make, as well as the sins you are tempted to commit, in their proper perspective. One way to make sure you stay focused on what you desire to achieve is to have a plan of action in place.

Fourth, *goals are evidence that you are serious about your God-given responsibilities*. This is perhaps the most important reason to set goals. Too many people have bought into the popular belief that it's okay to live only for the day and refuse to accept responsibility for their lives. The news is full of stories about people who spend their entire lives seeking out new and better ways to avoid accepting responsibility for their choices.

God never meant for us to shirk the responsibilities that He has given us during our time on earth. As a father, I am acutely aware that fathers must accept responsibility for setting the agenda for their families, the direction and pace that their families will go. Parents either accept the responsibility to parent their children or face the reality that others will assume that responsibility. Yet for many parents, the job of parenting is too threatening, so they leave it to whoever happens to be around. That choice can be deadly for kids.

With so many things working against you, these four reasons are powerful motivation to push you from your complacency when it comes to setting goals to beginning today to establish goals that will bring about deeper relationships with your family and with God. If you went no farther, you would benefit from this life-changing principle of setting goals that line up with God's will for your life. It's not so hard to determine the goals that God would have you strive to attain. It just requires taking some time out of your busy life to seek God's will.

APPLICATION

The application for this subject is not to write down your New Year's resolutions (whether it's January or July) and then put the list away in a drawer to be forgotten. Instead, there are some practical ways to accomplish what you need to in setting goals that will lead you into a deeper relationship with God, a healthier relationship with your family and friends, and the peace of mind that results from a well-planned strategy.

Write down each of your goals. Then write beside each one *why* it is important to accomplish the goal. The *why* will be your motivation.

For instance, your goal may be to pay off your mortgage this year. Why? Perhaps you want to live without debt or have the assurance that you would have a safe place to live should something unfortunate happen to your health or your job. The *why* will motivate you to continue in your efforts when other things come up that tempt you to use the money you've budgeted for this goal.

Marriage goals are crucial. Why? Because you want to demonstrate to your spouse that he or she is a priority in your life and, in doing so, enhance your life together. Perhaps you want to become a better parent to your children.

A third goal is that of character—what you want to become. Thousands of self-help books describe how to be healthier physically and have a better and longer life, but little is said about character. You might ask yourself, What do I want to become as a person and why? That would certainly be a question worth spending some of your quiet time thinking and praying about.

You must have a better understanding of what your goals are and why they are worth attaining if you are to be successful and achieve your ambitions. I could offer many illustrations, but this one is very personal to me.

I have long understood the value of setting goals in my life, but as I have watched my son, Andy, and daughter, Becky, grow into mature adults, I have seen each of them determine the importance of this principle and take the steps to set goals and determine priorities.

Andy shared a goal that has to do with who he wants to become. It has three parts:

1. A husband worth respecting
2. A father worth imitating
3. A leader worth following

> A goal is different from a dream. A dream is a picture of the world the way we want it to be or as it should be. A goal is a picture of the world the way we are willing to work to make it become.
> —Dr. William Mitchell

Here is how he answered the question of why it is important to become the three things listed above: "That is what God has called me to be. To move in this direction will lead to a deep sense of accomplishment and satisfaction. To become these things will make my time on this earth worth having been here for. . . . It will set a pace and direction for my children that if followed will ensure for them the best quality of life they can experience as well."

The *why* is a guarantee that Andy will work to attain this character goal. It will help him in the choices he makes and will guard him when temptation comes. Without the *why,* the goals are just nice words that bring tears to your eyes and mine. I have every reason to believe that Andy will achieve this goal. It is evident in the way he lives his life that this goal has established what is important to him.

Another facet of following through with your goals is accountability. Find someone to hold you accountable. Knowing that someone else knows and is going to check up on you to see if you are on track will keep you focused.

GROWTH

Just as there are always areas in my life that I need to focus on and make goals for in order to grow, I'm sure there are some in your life. I'd like to suggest some areas that you might consider in your goal-setting adventure.

Your *spiritual life goals* are of utmost importance. Perhaps you need to look at your quiet time—or start one if you don't already have one. Determine for yourself when you're going to have a quiet time and how many times a week. Don't leave it to chance. If you don't have a plan, you will come to the end of your week and realize that other things occupied your time. If you don't have a plan, you have in reality planned not to have a quiet time.

Another spiritual life goal would be to join a small group within your church—Sunday school, a prayer group, or a support group that seeks to find God's answers to difficult questions. If you don't see a small group within your church, you might offer your time and energy to facilitate one.

Service is another spiritual life goal to consider. Perhaps this year you need to find a place to serve the Lord, get involved, and stop enjoying the benefits of the fellowship without putting something into it. You may need to join the fellowship of believers that you have become associated with but have never committed your membership to. Whatever your spiritual life goals, you will not achieve them if you don't have a plan to go by.

Character goals are vital to your growth as a parent, child, friend, pastor, boss, or passing acquaintance. You can ask some questions to determine what your goals should be:

- What would I like to become?
- What one thing would I like to see God change in my character?
- What character quality—if developed—would make me a better parent, sibling, friend, and so on?

GOALS

Once you've thought about it, determine the areas that need specific goals, and go to work. They may be marriage or financial goals. They may be social or fitness goals. Whatever they are, don't spend another year wasting your time being sorry you didn't do something. Instead, begin today to establish where you want to be six months or a year from now, and ask God to give you the strength to stay on track.

Let me remind you that as you set your goals and make your plans, keep your mind and heart open to God's desires for your life. Proverbs 16:9 reminds us, "A man's heart plans his way, but the LORD directs his steps." It doesn't mean you aren't supposed to make your plans and set your goals; it means that you will, from time to time, need to adjust the goals as God reveals His plan for your life. Your responsibility is to maximize your time and potential to lift the Lord's name up and to glorify Him in all you do. Your time is perhaps your most valuable asset. It equals your life. It is your God-given responsibility to use it for His glory and not waste it with things that don't matter in the long run.

> **I** will go anywhere, provided it be forward.
> —David Livingstone

To ensure that you don't waste it, sit down and plan the best way to use your time in the coming days. When the year ends, you will be among the minority—those who have ended the year with more accomplished and less left undone. I guarantee you, that's a much better place to be than to finish the year knowing you let the time go by again without doing the things that you knew were important. It's not too late, but you must make your plan and set your goals.

GODLY MAN

■ *Devout person, whose heart is bent toward God.*

SCRIPTURE

DANIEL 6:4–5

So the governors and satraps sought to find some charge against Daniel concerning the kingdom; but they could find no charge or fault, because he was faithful; nor was there any error or fault found in him. Then these men said, "We shall not find any charge against this Daniel unless we find it against him concerning the law of his God."

COMMENTARY

I love this verse about Daniel: "Then this Daniel distinguished himself above the governors and satraps, because an excellent spirit was in him; and the king gave thought to setting him over the whole realm" (6:3). That wonderful verse describing Daniel is followed by our text.

Apparently, some fellow "governors and satraps" were jealous of Daniel because of God's favor. They looked for a way to discredit him before the king and could find "no charge or fault, because he was faithful" (6:4).

This is even more amazing when we realize that Daniel was a statesman! He was in politics!

In the Word of God, nothing negative is written about Joseph or Daniel. Joseph, too, was promoted in the king's court. Joseph, too, stood alone for what was right. Daniel was thrown into the lions' den; Joseph was thrown into a pit by jealous brothers and later into prison. Daniel interpreted dreams; Joseph interpreted dreams. Neither changed the interpretations to save himself.

Daniel refused to pray to an idol, knowing he could be cast into the lions' den. He boldly prayed three times a day to his God, realizing the king would be furious.

They were men of God. They exhibited godly character qualities. They never once backed down or compromised.

As readers of the book of Daniel, and also of Joseph's life in Genesis, we have an advantage that neither one of these godly men had—we know how the stories turned out. They may have been interpreters of dreams, but they were not clairvoyant. They could not see that Daniel would be delivered from the lions' den and Joseph would be sold into slavery and end up as the administrative leader in Egypt.

They did the right thing without knowing the end of the story.

Let's take a closer look at what a godly man is.

> A man's man is a godly man. He's humble. He's vulnerable. He's transparent. That's a real man.
> —Bill McCartney

GODLY MAN

In a day when we have a desperate need for godly people in our homes, at work, among friends, and as leaders in our land, perhaps it would do us well to determine the characteristics of a godly man.

We could look at many passages of Scripture, but I think the very first psalm gives us a wonderful characterization of what a godly man looks like, acts like, and thinks like.

First, the person orders his life around godly counsel: "Blessed is the man who walks not in the counsel of the ungodly" (v. 1). A man who follows the Lord with his whole being does not want to seek advice from others just because they are successful. A godly person is not too proud to seek advice or too self-centered to ask. He understands that he can still learn and that there is much he doesn't know. He wants to dip into the well of godly advisement.

Second, a godly person seeks friends with fellow believers, not with the lost: "Nor stands in the path of sinners" (v. 1). That does not mean he does not have friendships with unsaved people because he knows being a friend is part of bringing them to Christ. But I believe the Bible means that a godly man's closest friends are believers.

He realizes that no matter how successful, sophisticated, or influential unsaved men are, he longs to have as his closest friends those who have godly character and a tender conscience.

Third, the godly person gets enjoyment, encouragement, and refreshment from the Word of God: "But his delight is in the law of the LORD" (v. 2). He loves the Bible more than television, his hobby, or magazines. He delights in the Word of God. The godly person meditates on the Word: "And in His law he meditates day and night" (v. 2). Meditation is gnawing on what was just read. It is different from memorizing. Meditation asks questions such as, What did this just tell me about God? What did this just tell me about Jesus? What did this just tell me about myself? What do I need to change? How does it apply to my work and my friends and my home?

Meditation is absorbing the truth into our very being. It is totally different from a cursory reading of the Scripture.

When Joshua was overwhelmed with his new responsibilities of leading the children of Israel, God encouraged him: "This Book of the Law shall not depart from your mouth, but you shall meditate in it day and night, that you may observe to do according to all that is written in it. For then you will make your way prosperous, and then you will have good success" (Josh. 1:8).

Everyone wants to be successful. I have never met one person who said he wanted to be a failure. We need to teach this principle to our children.

> Although it's great to be called a PGA Tour player, and it's probably greater to be called a PGA Champion, I don't think there's any greater gift than is mine, to be called a child of God.
> —Paul Azinger

Godly Man

GODLY MAN

■ *Devout person, whose heart is bent toward God.*

If they want to succeed, they need to meditate on the Word of God. Teach your children how to be saved, how to pray, and how to succeed by loving and meditating on His Word.

Fourth, the godly person will successfully stand the storms of life: "He shall be like a tree planted by the rivers of water" (v. 3). The roots go down deep. The godly man has a taproot all the way to Jesus Christ. He is continually being refreshed by the rivers of water. Water is not just for nourishment and refreshment but also for cleansing.

A godly person can stand all the winds of life because he is firmly rooted.

The wife of one of our deacons had been very sick for ten years. After she died, the deacon shared with me that during those ten years, someone sat with his wife on Sundays so that he could teach his Sunday school class. He did not complain. He said, "God has been so faithful." He was not blown away by the winds of adversity.

Fifth, a godly person is a fruitful person: "That brings forth its fruit in its season, whose leaf also shall not wither" (v. 3). He is more interested in investing in a life than merely spending his. He is interested not only in how much fruit but also in its quality.

He is a patient man, knowing that fruit will come in season. He understands that all the fruit doesn't come at once. When Charles Haddon Spurgeon got saved as a little boy, he had gone to the church in a snowstorm. The preacher probably thought it was a dismal morning with only one little lad receiving Christ. But fruit came forth in God's timing.

Evangelist Mordecai Ham preached faithfully all over the country. The tent meetings were probably very hot, and I'm sure attendance wasn't impressive in each city. But one night, a teenage boy named Billy went forward and got saved. He'd wanted to be a baseball player, but his plans radically were changed that night. Fruit was born in Billy Graham's life. And think of the fruit that has come since that time!

A godly person is fruitful. He plods away at investing his life in the lives of others. He doesn't live for a paycheck. He understands that winning others to Christ is more important than reaching the top in his profession. He is a faithful employee, but he loves bearing spiritual fruit.

And his "leaf also shall not wither." He sticks with it. You can count on him. He doesn't wither under pressure. He is consistent.

Sixth, a godly person prospers in all he does: "And whatever he does shall prosper" (v. 3). He prospers in his home, in his work, in his finances, and in his relationships. This does not necessarily mean that he will be wealthy, which is the way the world defines prosperity. There is so much more to life than money. I believe this verse means he flourishes in all that he does.

Seventh, a godly person is contented. He is not anxious or fretting. He is not harassed. A sweet quietness marks him. It is wonderful to be around someone like that. He is "blessed." He is at rest.

And why shouldn't he be? If Jesus Christ is in charge of all of his life, there is no reason for him to be agitated. He knows His grace is sufficient. He knows he is equipped, no matter the task.

The beginning of being a godly man is receiving Jesus Christ as Savior. That's the foundation to build on.

That's the beginning of a godly person.

Homes need him. Churches need him. The world needs him.

Psalm 1 defines him.

I hope you know one.

I hope you are one.

APPLICATION

When we look again at the life of Daniel, we see an incident that is astounding. After a lengthy time of intense prayer, he was very tired. Guess who showed up? The angel Gabriel! Daniel said he came in "my extreme weariness" (Dan. 9:21 NASB). Gabriel addressed Daniel as one who was "highly esteemed" (Dan. 9:23 NASB).

Imagine being exhausted and an angel showing up by your easy chair to announce that you are highly esteemed. One better than Gabriel has called you not only highly esteemed and of great value, but He gave His life to make you a godly man.

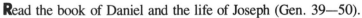

GROWTH

Read the book of Daniel and the life of Joseph (Gen. 39—50).

List the times they could have taken the easy way out but didn't. Now list the times you could have taken the easy way out but didn't.

Read some biographies of godly men. Read *Spiritual Disciplines for the Christian Life* by Donald S. Whitney and *Discipline of a Godly Man* by R. Kent Hughes.

QUOTE

God does not require a perfect, sinless life to have fellowship with Him, but He does require that we be serious about holiness, that we grieve over sin in our lives instead of justifying it, and that we earnestly pursue holiness as a way of life.

—Jerry Bridges

Godly Man

HUMILITY

■ *An attitude of dependence as we recognize that all we have is a gift of God.*

SCRIPTURE

LUKE 18:9, 14

He spoke this parable to some who trusted in themselves that they were righteous, and despised others . . . "For everyone who exalts himself will be humbled, and he who humbles himself will be exalted."

COMMENTARY

Humility expresses a genuine dependency on God and others. Humility recognizes that we live the Christian life in the same manner we become a Christian—by the grace of God. God extends His grace to the humble person, but He resists the proud (James 4:6).

The parable referred to in the Scripture above speaks about two men who went to the temple to worship. This would be our modern-day equivalent of a Sunday morning worship service. Both men appeared and sounded religious. As the story unfolds, we quickly understand the focus of each man. The Pharisee trusted in himself and looked down on others. He was proud he was not like the robbers, adulterers, and tax collectors. He looked on the outward appearance. He was consumed with his behavior to a fault. He spent little time evaluating the motivation behind his actions. He overlooked the fact that God is concerned about not only what we do but also why we do it; God looks at the heart.

The man was so rigidly self-righteous that he missed the opportunity for God to change him from the inside out. The Pharisee overlooked the humility required to apply God's grace to his life. But then, that is the very nature of pride. It shuts out the need for God and people.

The tax collector, on the other hand, was keenly aware of his sinfulness, and he looked to God for mercy and forgiveness. His attitude was, "God, be merciful to me a sinner!" (Luke 18:13). He recognized that humility puts us in position to hear from God. We more clearly understand the heart of God when we approach Him with dependence rather than smug self-sufficiency.

Humility is an attitude of the heart. When God sees humility, He sees someone with whom He can entrust His grace. God responds to the humble prayer while the proud prayer is like talking to yourself. It goes no farther than your lips. The humble prayer is powerful. Humility arrests the attention of God! He says in His timing, the humble man will receive the proper recognition he deserves while the proud man will be brought low.

APPLICATION

Let's look at three truths concerning humility.

First, humility is quick to confess sin and slow to point out sin in others. The tax collector asked God to be merciful to him, a sinner. Humility asks

God to surface sin so he can repent. Pride, on the other hand, is slow to confess sin and quick to point out sin in others. We can almost hear the pride in the man's voice as he told God, "I thank You that I am not like other men" (Luke 18:11). Outwardly, his actions looked right, but inwardly, his heart was ravaged by pride and selfishness. He was not teachable; he was not humble; he knew no compassion or mercy. To him, it was his way or no way. Pride says if you don't look, talk, and act just like I do, you are wrong.

Second, humility asks for and receives God's forgiveness and in turn is quick to forgive others. Once someone has received God's forgiveness, she recognizes the need to forgive others. She realizes she cannot expect perfection from others until she gets to heaven. On the other hand, a proud person sees no need to ask for God's forgiveness; he doesn't forgive or seek the forgiveness of others. Pride says, "I will never forgive you for that." This is where a lot of people are today. Because the offended holds on to the wrong and does not forgive, anger, bitterness, and pride are free to reside in the heart. There is nothing the offending person can do to compensate for the wrong. Only through humility and forgiveness can the relationship ever heal.

Third, humility is content to be behind the scenes. The tax collector stood at a distance (Luke 18:13). A humble person is secure, knowing her service is just as important to God as the service of the one who is in the spotlight. Pride insists on being in the spotlight; it wants everyone to know that time and energy are being sacrificed for God's "work." Pharisees loved the best seats in the synagogues so they could be seen. Pride is always causing conflict because it insists on being the center of attention. Jesus said the proud love to hear the praises of people. Jesus also said that the praises of people were their reward—nothing more. But to the humble, Jesus has promised that though they may never hear the praises of people, they receive their reward in heaven.

God hates pride. Pride made sin a reality in God's creation. And pride brought sin into the world:

> *The fear of the LORD is to hate evil;*
> *Pride and arrogance and the evil way*
> *And the perverse mouth I hate (Prov. 8:13).*

God hates pride so much that He is willing to allow adversity into the lives of His children to root it out. As we will see, God has such a disdain

> The call to humility is a call to serve God with sober minds—with full awareness of our gifts and our limitations.
> —Gordon T. Smith

> Humility is simply living in the truth—recognizing the reality and character of God, and living in personal dependence on God as Creator and Savior.
> —Gordon T. Smith

HUMILITY

■ *An attitude of dependence as we recognize that all we have is a gift of God.*

for pride that He is willing to go so far as to send adversity to keep pride from becoming a problem.

In his second letter to the Corinthian church, Paul spoke of his "thorn in the flesh." Apparently, it was some form of adversity—probably physical—that caused him much discomfort and anxiety. The adversity drove him to his knees and caused him to do serious self-examination. After begging the Lord three times to remove his thorn, he discovered something about himself. During Paul's time of intense soul-searching, God revealed to him the reason for the "thorn."

Paul described it this way: "And lest I should be exalted above measure by the abundance of the revelations, a thorn in the flesh was given to me, a messenger of Satan to buffet me, lest I be exalted above measure" (2 Cor. 12:7). The thorn in the flesh was God's way of doing some preventive maintenance. It was His way of assuring that Paul's popularity and special spiritual privilege would not cause him to think more highly of himself than he ought. God knew Paul's potential for His kingdom. And He was going to do everything He could to ensure that Paul's ego did not get in the way of his ministry.

In light of our potential for the kingdom and the devastating effect of pride on our relationship with our heavenly Father, it is understandable that God would go to great lengths to keep us humble. Imagine how much God must have loved the apostle Paul. He allowed him to pen half the New Testament! Yet He also allowed Paul's thorn in the flesh. The only way to reconcile such privilege with such pain is to realize how much God hates pride.

Is not our potential for God's kingdom as important to our Lord as Paul's? Is He any less interested in having an intimate relationship with us than He was with the apostle? Of course not. Therefore, God uses some adversity to inject healthy doses of humility.

The tragedy is that some people are clever enough to weasel their way through or around the adversity God intends to use. Through ingenuity and determination, they manipulate things in such a way as to temporarily bypass God's plan for keeping them humble. This may work in the short run, but nobody outsmarts or outmaneuvers God. For a while these people continue functioning or ministering as if nothing has changed. But slowly, what is true privately surfaces publicly.

But the humble man can count on productivity and peace. He entrusts the results of his labors to God and credits God for his success. His future is ever bright.

> Nothing sets a person so much out of the devil's reach as humility.
> —Jonathan Edwards

> To say Thank God, I know I am saved and sanctified is in the sight of God the acme of humility, it means you have so completely abandoned yourself to God that you know He is true.
> —Oswald Chambers

HUMILITY

The meek man is not a human mouse afflicted with a sense of his own inferiority. Rather he may be in his moral life as bold as a lion and as strong as Samson; but he has stopped being fooled about himself. He has accepted God's estimate of his own life. He knows he is as weak and helpless as God declared him to be, but paradoxically, he knows at the same time that he is in the sight of God of more importance than angels. In himself, nothing; in God, everything. That is his motto.

—A. W. Tozer

 QUOTES

They that know God will be humble, and they that know themselves cannot be proud.

—John Flavel

SIFTING

■ *The process of separating or filtering the good from the bad, the desirable from the undesirable.*

LUKE 22:31–32

Simon, Simon! Indeed, Satan has asked for you, that he may sift you as wheat. But I have prayed for you, that your faith should not fail.

When I think of sifting, I picture my mom making biscuits. She had a handheld sifter that she would squeeze and shake at the same time to get lumps out of the flour. What seemed like an endless, tiresome process to me was a gift of love from Mother.

The Bible refers to a different kind of sifting. It is the same principle we are familiar with but on a larger scale. When Satan asked to sift Peter, his purpose was not to get rid of what was undesirable in order to keep the best. His purpose was to shake Peter's faith so that nothing was left. God allowed the sifting, but He had a different purpose in mind. And that made all the difference between defeat and victory.

If you are like most people, the last place you would expect to read about sifting would be the Bible. You would expect to find the word *sift* or *sifting* in a cookbook or women's magazine, full of wonderful recipes and ideas for new and better ways to cook. The idea, as we consider it here, might be better understood with the use of words such as *filter* and *purify*. When Jesus advised Peter that Satan had asked (implied, *demanded permission*) to sift Peter, He made specific reference to the way wheat was sifted to separate grain from stubble, the good from the bad. Jesus understood Satan's attempt to interfere in Peter's life as villainous.

Immediately prior to this startling announcement, the disciples had been thrust into a chaotic debate over loyalty and significance. It was an unforgettable scene that illustrated both their love for Jesus and their insecurities. Jesus had broken the bread, and He had disclosed the news about His impending betrayal and death. With a collective gasp, the disciples began looking around in utter disbelief. What happened was inevitable. They began to argue and grew suspicious—quickly asserting their loyalty and love for the Master.

With all the tension that Jesus' revelation to the disciples stirred up, I suppose it was natural that the debate evolved into a discussion of which one of them was the greatest or most loyal. It was a biblical version of "anything you can do, I can do better." Jesus, however, made His thoughts clear about such childish behavior: "He who is greatest among you, let him be as the younger, and he who governs as he who serves" (Luke 22:26).

Lord, let me not live to be useless.
—John Wesley

SIFTING

There was probably a moment of awkward silence, before someone dared to speak.

Peter—the outspoken, natural-born leader—may have been the one to speak first. Perhaps he said something like this: "The greatest? I walked on water. Did any of the rest of you? Did Jesus change your name to the Rock, like He did mine?" Although that is purely conjecture, we don't have to guess about what Jesus had to say. To understand why Jesus' words were so unsettling to everyone present that evening, we need to take another look at the Scripture itself. It appears at first glance that Jesus was talking directly to Simon Peter when He said, "That he may sift you as wheat" (Luke 22:31). However, the word *you* is plural in the Greek. Jesus may have been looking at Peter, but His message was all-inclusive.

I don't know how you feel, but it makes me shudder to think Satan might specifically request permission to sift me *by name*! That's a little too personal for my comfort zone, but it clears up any doubt I might have that Satan knows my name. If I were not aware that God alone has the final word in my life, it would be unsettling. Even though He allows Satan to have limited influence over the lives of His children, Jesus left no doubt that He would supervise the process.

We need to recognize the devil had to get permission from Christ. Satan doesn't have a free hand with saints. The "accuser of our brethren" (Rev. 12:10) had to get God's approval before any grinding or sifting took place. Apparently, God said, "Okay." If God allowed Satan that kind of hands-on experience with His disciples, we must be acutely aware of his continued influence on believers today. A closer look at the biblical process of sifting is worth our time and attention.

> **H**e screens the suffering, filtering it through fingers of love.
> —Joni Eareckson (Tada) and Steve Estes

 **A CLOSER LOOK**

Questions about sifting can lead us to a deeper understanding of the way God conforms us into the persons He created us to be. Jesus was not fooled by Satan's plan to sift the disciples. He knew that Satan's mission was to defeat and destroy. Yet He had His own mission and chose to allow Satan's influence in their lives to accomplish His purposes.

The only way we can successfully struggle through these times is to focus on the Author of truth and not on our circumstances. While He may allow us to be severely tested, God has faithfully promised to never leave or forsake us.

Biblical references to sifting wheat are often accompanied by pictures that depict something unfamiliar to us today. Those assigned to the task would

SIFTING

■ *The process of separating or filtering the good from the bad, the desirable from the undesirable.*

winnow the wheat on large six-pronged forks. The people who held the forks waved them in the wind until the chaff blew off. There were times that the process required more, when the undesirable chaff tenaciously clung to the fork and wouldn't let go. When that happened, the women took the wheat and put it on a large sifter and wrapped their arms around it. They shook the sifter back and forth so that all the chaff was discarded and all that remained was the best wheat. Their purpose was not to destroy the wheat but to get rid of what was not desirable and keep the very best.

God has a purpose in sifting saints or in allowing us to be sifted. What is most obvious is this: God uses sifted people. There is nothing random about it. With the goal ever in sight, God sifts us for His service. Paul says we are "His workmanship, created in Christ Jesus for good works" (Eph. 2:10). Have you ever wondered why God leaves us here on earth if not to serve Him? Why didn't He save us and immediately take us to be with Him so that we could avoid the suffering that is inevitable as long as we are here on earth?

In Titus 2:14, we discover why this process is centered in God's plan for our lives: "Who gave Himself for us, that He might redeem us from every lawless deed and purify for Himself His own special people, zealous for good works." It was a part of the plan. Because this principle is so vital to our relationship with the Father, a closer look at why God allows the process of sifting saints is useful.

He allows us to be sifted in order to *bring honor and glory to Himself.* He uses weak, imperfect people. The strong—those who are self-assured, confident in their abilities—have little (obvious) need for salvation, for God. They think they can make it on their own and would be insulted at the suggestion that they need a Savior. Those of us who have faced our weaknesses head-on and watched as God took control of our inadequacies, using them for His glory, understand that siftable souls are precious in God's eyes. They are refined gold.

God allows us to be sifted to *grow us up.* About all a baby can do is drink her bottle, sleep, and cry in order to alert those who care for her that she is hungry or in need of a clean diaper. It would be silly to expect a baby to take care of her parents, to meet their needs. Likewise, a spiritual baby is not equipped to serve. In the process of sifting us, God pushes us beyond our capabilities so that we have to trust Him. He lets us fail at times so that we do not lose sight of our frailty and His perfection. There are times when a mother or father has to let a child fall down and scrape his knee in order to learn that skateboarding without the proper protection is not the wise thing to do. No parent, who loves the child, will allow a three-year-old to drive a car. A skinned knee is one thing. Loving parents would never put a child in the driver's seat of the car. That would be suicide. However, within certain boundaries—certain limits—wise parents allow their children to fail at times to teach them lessons they would never learn otherwise.

Jesus didn't leave Peter stranded, on his own, without hope. He said, "Satan has asked for you, that he may sift you as wheat. But I have prayed for you, that your faith should not fail; and when you have returned to Me, strengthen your brethren" (Luke 22:31–32). Jesus was praying that Peter's faith would not utterly and ultimately fail. He gave us a hint in His prayer that it was a temporary setback when He said, "And when you have returned to Me" (v. 32). Jesus was in essence saying, "Peter, you and your friends are going to be sifted. I mean *really* sifted, as you've never been sifted before. You will be shaken, perhaps until you think you will die. But it's not going to be fatal. You may wonder and doubt, but you'll come around. When you stand on the other side, don't forget what you've learned. That's when you need to encourage the others."

And what was Peter's answer? Can't you just hear him? "Oh, listen. Don't worry. You can count on the Rock! Nothing could shake me to the very core." In the very next verse (v. 34), Jesus tenderly but firmly told Peter again that he would deny Him. The Rock was going to crack.

So what's that got to do with us and our sifting? All we need to do is look at Peter. On the night we've read about so often in the story leading up to Jesus' death on the cross, he denied that he ever knew Jesus. Yet God used Peter at Pentecost in ways Peter never could have imagined. How do you think Peter felt when things turned around, when God fulfilled His plan and used him so mightily? Do you think he waved his hand in victory, turning to the crowds to receive their adoration? I think, rather, that he quietly closed his eyes and thanked God for loving him enough to allow him to go through the entire process.

Sifted saints understand the value of the process that takes them from the heights of their self-sufficiency to the awareness of God's firm hand in conforming them to His image. Peter was sifted by Satan, but God had a different agenda for allowing the process. Talk about sifted to serve! God is still sifting His people today. Our responsibility is to stay focused on God's truth and not be swayed or distracted by temporary circumstances.

In north Georgia, there is an area where tourists pan for gold. They are equipped with a tiny tin pan with miniature holes in it. As they dip the pan into the cold, shallow water and scoop up sand, they shake the container gently. They watch carefully to see the sand fall through the holes. Some of the coarser sand needs harder shaking, but the people watch closely to make

> To wrestle continuously with "unanswerable questions" about the economy of God is to falsely assume that God intended for us to know all things or is obligated to tell us.

> God whispers to us in our pleasures, speaks in our conscience, but shouts in our pains; it is His megaphone to rouse a deaf world.
> —C. S. Lewis

SIFTING

■ *The process of separating or filtering the good from the bad, the desirable from the undesirable.*

sure only the sand and pebbles are sifted and not the precious gold they are after.

Some find tiny bits of gold and some find fool's gold and others find nothing. But they have to sift a long time to reveal whether they have anything worthwhile to take home.

God sifts us gently at first. Then He sometimes has to shake a little harder. He'll stay with us as long as necessary until the tiny bits of gold character sparkle in our lives.

There is always a purpose for the sifting God allows in our lives. If we are faithful to the process and refuse to turn and run, we will see God take our times of sifting and turn them into glorious monuments to His grace and mercy.

APPLICATION

Although you might want to be the supersaint who never lets God down, reality sets your course in a different direction. However, contrary to what someone who means well might tell you, God will use your faith failures to bless others. Once you get through a sifting process, you have an obligation to strengthen your brethren who are presently being shaken and feel as if they are on the prong of a winnowing fork.

My mom used a small handheld sifter. The Jewish workers used large sifters. What kind of sifter does God use?

His sifter is tailor-made for the person being sifted. What may shake me may not shake you. What may make the impurities in your life fall through the holes in the sifting process may not work for me. So, He has God-sized "designer sifters." They're not too small or too big; the shaking doesn't go on more than necessary.

Some sifters God may use include these:

- Physical suffering. During physical suffering, He brings to the surface your priorities. You may have great plans, but if the doctor's report isn't a good one, your plans totally change and your priorities take on a whole new meaning.
- Financial sifting. During financial sifting, what you trust in as your security surfaces.
- Temptation sifting. During temptation, your dependence on Him—or the lack thereof—rises to the top.
- Vocational sifting. During this sifting, your identity is on the line. Is it anchored to a job or Christ? Also, do you want God's will or yours?

SIFTING

You've been in the sifter from time to time, haven't you? It is comforting to know that God governs all sifting. He says to Satan about your sifting, "This far and no farther." God limits the sifting. He knows which method works best in your life. He knows the intensity of the shaking in the sifting process. And He has parentheses around the length of the sifting.

You are not at the mercy of Satan! Your life is Father filtered, and Satan cannot sift you without His knowledge and limitations. Okay, so you're in the sifting process. It's not a once-and-for-all deal. You are sifted throughout life as He brings other things to your attention for the wind of the Spirit to blow away.

What is your response to His sifting?

You can rebel. You can blame God. Or you can blame someone else. You can run. Or you can try to jump out of the sifter.

I guess we've all tried those responses to a degree.

But God's response to such rebellion is to eventually bring us to repentance. In bringing us to repentance, He will not violate our free will. He'll bring a lot of pressure, but He won't force repentance without his cooperation.

There are saints along the way who choose to submit in the sifting process and not stubbornly resist. When we submit, do you know what God does? He expands our ministry and makes us more useful. Sifting is for a purpose. And that purpose is to make us better servants.

STRESS

■ *Our emotional and physical response to the pressures of life.*

SCRIPTURE

1 PETER 5:6–7

Humble yourselves under the mighty hand of God, that He may exalt you in due time, casting all your care upon Him, for He cares for you.

COMMENTARY

Peter gives us a valuable insight regarding stress. He cites obedience as a stress reducer. He knew that there is no rest living outside God's moral and ethical boundaries. The farther we go outside God's protective guidelines, the closer we edge toward a life of frustration, anxiety, fear, and unrest. Obedience is the key component in two aspects of reducing stress.

Obedience removes a layer of actual potential stress. Some stress in our lives is the direct result of sin, sometimes ours, sometimes others, most of the time both. For instance, when husbands don't love their wives as Christ loved the church or wives don't treat their husbands with respect, stress fills the home. An air of tension permeates when kids don't obey their parents and the parents ignore scriptural principles of discipline. When a man or woman breaks the law and is worried about being audited, a great deal of energy is expended unnecessarily in not getting caught.

Peter targets this disobedience that compounds our stress. In the passage, he notes that the disobedience originates in our desire to become or to appear to be something we aren't, or to exalt ourselves. Our pursuit of this step creates stress.

How does this happen? In an attempt to become more popular, a teenager compromises. In an effort to build a reputation, you take unnecessary risks. In the desire to speed up the wheels of success, we make quick decisions, ignoring the counsel of others. The solution is to humble ourselves under God's mighty hand and recognize His right to rule.

When you do, God will exalt you because He is for maximizing your potential. God promises to work things out if you submit to His plan. In verse 6, Peter says God will work things out in due time. How often do you precipitate stress because you try to do it your way and in your time?

To humble yourself positions you to trust God with life's unavoidable pressures. Peter reveals the concept of stress management in verse 7 when he says to cast your cares on Him. The Greek word for cast means "to throw." To cast your cares is to give God the responsibility for things you have no control over. Why does God give this privilege? Because God cares. You are important to Him, and He cares about you.

Every hope or dream of the human mind will be fulfilled if it is noble and of God. But one of the greatest stresses in life is the stress of waiting for God.
—Oswald Chambers

STRESS

The Old Testament prophet Elijah illustrates the importance of viewing circumstances from God's perspective as the means to prevent stress. First Kings 17—19 is Elijah's story. God sent him to rescue Israel from its moral and spiritual decline at the hands of wicked kings. Elijah confronted and defeated the prophets of Baal and prayed for rain. God protected Elijah and sent rain.

Jezebel promised to kill Elijah because of the dead Baal prophets. Instead of holding fast to God's faithfulness, Elijah panicked and ran. God asked Elijah why he was hiding in a cave. Stressful situations often drive us to inappropriate responses to life's pressures.

Elijah's lesson is applicable to believers. Once Elijah was reminded of God's past faithfulness, he realized it was sufficient for his present circumstances. He recognized that God had protected and provided for seven thousand others in Israel. Elijah rested and returned to his mission for God. God was involved in Elijah's life, although Elijah thought He had become silent. Elijah is a model for us to follow—rest in God, recall His faithfulness, and trust Him for the future.

> **I**n a world where there is so much to ruffle the spirit's plumes, how needful that entering into the secret of God's pavilion, which will alone bring it back to composure and peace!
> —Archbishop Trench

A CLOSER LOOK

Stress is the intangible partner of progress. Defined as "the normal, internal, physiological mechanism that adapts us to change," stress is something we all feel at one time or another. The more demanding life becomes, the more stressed we become in our attempt to keep up the pace.

Sources of stress are everywhere. The unique problems of our age seem designed to create and almost force us to live in a state of stress and tension. Many personal relationships are fraught with stress. Although affirming relationships are probably the single best protector against stress-induced damage, we live in an impersonal world.

Certain personalities, especially in the corporate world, contribute to the stress of everyone they encounter. Type A personalities are considered driven by a need to control others. Aggressive and competitive by nature, they exhibit a need to win in everything they do and show a tendency toward self-destruction. These time-pressured individuals who do not enjoy vacations are carburetors set on high, ready to surge into overdrive at the slightest provocation. This lifestyle often causes varied health problems including heart attacks.

Our progressive modern age overstimulates us, and we pay a price physically. The major systems of the body—the heart, brain, nervous system, liver, and immune system—are on a constant standby to adapt to change.

STRESS

■ *Our emotional and physical response to the pressures of life.*

The effects of stress result in alarming rates of executive burnout and absenteeism. Add the continued corporate downsizing and we have a workforce on edge.

Stress is not just a circumstance; it is the response to circumstances. Stress can be particularly harmful in three vital relationships:

1. Relationships with family members. Nobody gets your undivided attention. Relationships get squeezed, and your capacity for giving and receiving diminishes.

2. Relationship with God. You can't concentrate when you pray or when you are in church. You can't worship or hear God because your attention is riveted elsewhere.

3. Relationship with the body of Christ. You have no time to disciple or be discipled. You have no time to care for others.

APPLICATION

God doesn't intend for you to lead a stress-filled life. Jesus knew incredible pressure. Luke notes that His response was to go away and pray (Luke 5:15–16). You would do well to follow the Savior's lead in this matter. If He found relief from the pressures of life by pulling away to be with the Father, I imagine you can, too.

Stress can be managed as you realize God's intimate care for the details of your life. He is willing to bear your burdens, and He assumes complete responsibility for the person committed to Him.

Make a list of each area of concern that adds significant stress. Take time to thoughtfully pray about each one. Take confidence in God's promised help and provision. He has equipped you to handle life's loads with a standing offer to bear their emotional weight.

Things can be very difficult for us, but nothing is too hard for Him. Believing and resting in that truth will protect your mind, heart, and spirit from the overload of stress.

■ *Mental pictures and ideas passing intentionally and unintentionally through the consciousness.*

THOUGHTS

SCRIPTURE

PHILIPPIANS 4:8

Finally, brethren, whatever things are true, whatever things are noble, whatever things are just, whatever things are pure, whatever things are lovely, whatever things are of good report, if there is any virtue and if there is anything praiseworthy—meditate on these things.

COMMENTARY

The significance of these words can be appreciated only when we picture the environment from which they were penned—a filthy first-century prison. How could Paul write about such positive things in such a negative place? Why didn't he mention the stench, the cold, the bugs, the mistreatment, the loneliness, and the poor nourishment suffered in the prison from which he was writing?

The answer to this question is found in the verse itself. Because he wasn't focused on those things. And he didn't want the church at Philippi—or us—to focus on the negatives. In this joyous book, Paul tells us to center our thinking on what is true, noble, just, pure, lovely, of good report (or admirable), virtuous, and praiseworthy. Then, and only then, will we have peace.

If we are constantly thinking about our circumstances, we never will have peace. Our thought patterns are extremely important to our mental, physical, and spiritual health. We can literally think ourselves into mental and physical distress. Doctors attest to the fact that a large percentage of physical illness has a psychological basis.

Solomon wrote, "A joyful heart is good medicine, but a broken spirit dries up the bones" (Prov. 17:22 NASB). That being the case, how does one get a joyful heart? Through joyful circumstances? No. Paul's circumstances were not joyful. There was nothing joyful about being in prison.

Yet he could write, "The things which you learned and received and heard and saw in me, these do, and the God of peace will be with you" (v. 9). Paul is saying, in essence, "I am constantly thinking about what is true, noble, just . . ." He was their visual aid.

In his commentary, Matthew Henry wrote, "He [Paul] could propose *himself* as well as his doctrine to their imitation. It gives a great force to what we say to others when we can appeal to what they have seen in us."

I can picture Paul sitting in his cell, perhaps on a cold stone floor. He may have thought about the Damascus Road and how he had met the One he had hated. He may have rehearsed his conversations with Ananias. Thought about the scales falling from his eyes. Being lowered in a basket. Missionary journeys. New churches. Disabled people healed at Lystra.

> Whenever you allow something into your inner life through reading, listening, or seeing, make sure that it passes the test of pleasing God.
> —Sammy Tippit

Thoughts

THOUGHTS

■ *Mental pictures and ideas passing intentionally and unintentionally through the consciousness.*

Demonic slave girl delivered. Singing with Silas. The experience with the Philippian jailer. Lydia. The viper shaken off. No doubt he reflected on those happenings during the long days and cold nights.

Some would call this Paul's power of positive thinking. But there is so much more to this than just positive thinking. The apostle is talking about meditating on these things.

For this to be a part of our lives—because this is not a natural process—there has to be a *renewal* of the mind. I am talking about an actual renewal that can take place in our thinking patterns.

Think for a moment. Are you constantly thinking about your personal "prisons," or have you been freed through breaking down those walls by disciplining yourself to think on what is true, noble, just, pure, lovely, of good report, virtuous, and praiseworthy? "Impossible!" you say. Not at all. Let's take a closer look at thought life.

A CLOSER LOOK

The power of the mind is awesome. It is evident when we realize the mind is the control tower of character, conduct, and conversation. We can think profitably or unprofitably, rightly or wrongly, and the rest of life will be influenced by this thinking. Our thinking now will affect our behavior years down the road. That's the power of the mind. We can't *think* evil and *live* righteously. It just doesn't work that way. Godly living is the result of godly thinking.

If our thoughts are really that powerful—and they are—and if they really influence us that much—and they do—the logical question is, How do we deal with problems in our thinking? We know we think erroneously at times. Where does that thinking originate? And how do we cope with it?

We all have unique thought patterns. These patterns were carefully put into our thinking by our parents, our teachers, our peers. Families have unique thought patterns, and these are etched in our minds. Right or wrong, they're still there.

The problem is, when the Lord Jesus saved us, He didn't erase all the faulty thought patterns. Our peculiar mind-set is still intact. Satan likes to capitalize on this past erroneous programming. The devil doesn't want us to think like the apostle Paul told us to think. He doesn't care if we don't think at all, but he really doesn't want us to think about positive things.

No one is forcing us to watch rubbish, listen to rubbish, and read rubbish. Satan is delighted to bring it to our attention, but he doesn't force it on us. *We make the choice.* And we pay the price in thought life.

God's cure for evil thinking is to fill our minds with that which is good.
—George Sweeting

THOUGHTS

The problem with poisoning our thinking through the world's system is that we eventually become hostile toward God. The underlying message of the world's thinking is, "Be independent." The message of the Word of God is, "Be dependent on Him." Slowly but surely, our dependence on Him and His Word is eroded because we are unconsciously adopting the world's thinking.

We leave the Word and become more thirsty for the world's thinking. We sometimes don't even want to read the Bible because it makes us feel guilty. It is almost like we are magnetized to the world's culture.

Haven't you ever been in prayer, and suddenly, you are overwhelmed with a horrible thought? Or at night before you fall asleep, your mind is going one hundred miles an hour on things you know aren't of God? When that happens, Satan is having a field day with your thinking.

Satan's mental strongholds are often what we call addictions. These addictions could be centered on sex, drugs, pornography, gossip, or anything. In each case, it all starts in the mind.

The battle is won or lost in the mind.

Someone has said, "You are what you eat." I believe the Bible teaches you are what you think.

Now that we've looked at the power of the mind and the problems associated with our thinking, what are we supposed to do? The picture may look bleak to you. Perhaps you're always thinking negatively—not anything like Paul suggested. Or perhaps your mind wants to feed at the world's trough.

Is there hope? Are you trapped in your mind until heaven?

Yes, there is hope, and no, you aren't trapped.

Freedom, however, is not instantaneous. Freedom is found through reprogramming or renewing your mind. You need to reprogram your thinking.

In reprogramming, you need to do four things.

First, you need to recognize you have the mind of Christ (1 Cor. 2:16). He is abiding in you. When He saved you, He gave you the capacity to think like He thinks. What a wonderful privilege! Notice I said the *capacity* to think like He thinks. The potential is there even when performance is lacking.

Second, you need to choose to think rightly. This is not easy. Paul said, however, "If then you have been raised up with Christ, keep seeking the things above, where Christ is, seated at the right hand of God. Set your mind on the things above, not on the things that are on earth" (Col. 3:1–2 NASB).

The "keep seeking" implies it's not a once-and-for-all deal. You will fight this battle of the mind until you get to heaven. But you are to keep battling. It's basically spiritual warfare for control of your mind.

> **L**earn to turn thoughts into discussions with God.
> —Bill Gothard

Thoughts

321

THOUGHTS

■ *Mental pictures and ideas passing intentionally and unintentionally through the consciousness.*

You have a choice. As one saint said, "I can't keep the birds from flying overhead, but I can keep them from making a nest in my hair." A fleeting wrong thought might hit your mind, but you make the choice whether or not to consider it. You need to let it pass right on by—quickly—and replace it with thinking in keeping with your new identity as God's disciple.

Third, you need to sift your thoughts through the Word of God to the will of God. You need to ask, What does the Word of God say? A wonderful, familiar verse tells how powerful the Word of God is in helping you to decipher what to think about: "For the word of God is living and powerful, and sharper than any two-edged sword, piercing even to the division of soul and spirit, and of joints and marrow, and is a discerner of the thoughts and intents of the heart" (Heb. 4:12).

If you want to know whether you're thinking correctly, check it out in the Word. Paul says you are to take "every thought into captivity to the obedience of Christ" (2 Cor. 10:5). You can do that. You can lasso every thought and control it if you want to.

You can even redirect your thinking. For instance, suppose you are angry. I mean, everything has gone wrong at work. Your coworkers have been insensitive. Your boss is cranky. You are steaming. You catch yourself thinking every unkind thing you can think. Then the phone rings with unsuspected good news from a family member. Almost immediately a change takes place. You are overjoyed.

You hang up the phone and realize you have totally refocused your thinking. The anger has been replaced by joy. Your mind has been redirected. Redirecting your thinking is a powerful tool in learning to control your thinking. You cannot *not* think about something. If I say, "Don't think about a red car," your thoughts turn to the very thing I have told you not to think about. It would be impossible to follow that command without redirecting your thoughts. You can think about good and right things if you choose.

Fourth, you need to refuse to think about some things. You don't have to think about the things Satan throws at you. Remember, the battle is in the mind. Suppose you are watching television and you know immediately the program is something you should not be watching. *Turn it off.*

Suppose you go to a movie in which the plot is not what you thought. You realize the language, the innuendos, and the value system are not what the Word of God honors. *Get up and walk out.* The people at work or school are telling jokes that are "only a little off-color." *Walk away.* The only magazine at the barbershop is a gossip tabloid. *Don't pick it up.* The billboard flashes an image you don't want in your mental computer. *Turn your eyes away.*

Refuse the input.

I know it is difficult. But it isn't impossible.

Remember, you have the capacity to think like Christ.

You need to reprogram and renew your mind.

Paul wrote, "And do not be conformed to this world, but be transformed by the renewing of your mind" (Rom. 12:2). There is absolutely no way to live godly without the Word of God saturating your mind and renewing it.

To neglect the Word is to open yourself up to deadly doses of the world's philosophy. No reprogramming goes on without the Word of God filling over your mind. God's Word is to be the focus of your thinking. Redirect your thoughts toward it.

We *must* meditate on His Word, or we don't have a chance of thinking correctly. Meditating on His Word isn't an option if we want to renew our thinking patterns. It is a matter of survival.

The mind is indeed powerful. It influences everything you do. It is no wonder then that your thoughts are a trophy highly sought after by the enemy. To counter his intense pursuit of your thought life, you have been given the mind of Christ; it is indwelling you. Therefore, you have a choice about what to think about. You are to be intentional with your thoughts. That is, you are not to let your mind wander. You are to direct your thoughts in a specific, predetermined direction.

My mom used to make Jell-O. She took the powder, mixed it with water, poured it into the mold, and chilled it. When it was all congealed, she turned the mold upside down on a plate. The Jell-O had conformed beautifully to its mold.

The world has a mold. The mold has various ridges and craters. The devil wants us to be conformed to the world's mold, especially in our thoughts. He spends a lot of time stirring things around and adding ingredients to ensure that his purposes are accomplished.

God said, "And do not be *conformed* to this world." Or as one translation states, "Don't let the world around you squeeze you into its own mould" (PHILLIPS). You are to be poured into the mold of the Lord Jesus Christ, conformed to His image.

Your thoughts are the determining factor as to whose mold you are conformed to. Control your thoughts and you control the direction of your life.

Whenever a thought comes to my mind that I know is not of God, I immediately pray, "Father, thank You for the blood of Jesus Christ. That precious blood is cleansing my thinking right now."

 APPLICATION

THOUGHTS

■ *Mental pictures and ideas passing intentionally and unintentionally through the consciousness.*

I am not sure how it works, but I know it does.

You can pray this when bombarded with one thought or many thoughts that you know are not of God. Then you can purposely think on things that are true, noble, just, pure, lovely, of good report, virtuous, and praiseworthy.

And if you can't think of any of those, think back to your experience when you met the Lord. That will set you free from your prison of wrong thinking.

QUOTES

Every major spiritual battle is in the mind.

—Charles Stanley

Meditate on His Word and your mind will be in the heavenlies even though your feet are on the ground.

—Charles Stanley

■ *Measurable period in which something takes place.*

TIME

EPHESIANS 5:15–17 NASB

SCRIPTURE

Therefore be careful how you walk, not as unwise men, but as wise, making the most of your time, because the days are evil. So then do not be foolish, but understand what the will of the Lord is.

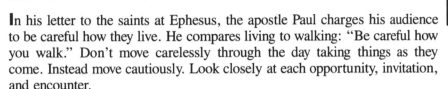

COMMENTARY

In his letter to the saints at Ephesus, the apostle Paul charges his audience to be careful how they live. He compares living to walking: "Be careful how you walk." Don't move carelessly through the day taking things as they come. Instead move cautiously. Look closely at each opportunity, invitation, and encounter.

As followers of the Lord Jesus Christ, we need to walk carefully. Cautiously. Wisely! Keep in mind that this world is a hostile place for those who seek to do what is right. Walking wisely involves using our time carefully. Not spending it, but investing it. As we surrender the use of our time to the lordship of Christ, He will lead us to use it in the most productive way imaginable.

In another letter Paul encourages believers to "conduct yourselves with wisdom toward outsiders, making the most of the opportunity" (Col. 4:5 NASB). The term translated "opportunity" is the same Greek word used in our text of "making the most of your time." (The New King James Version translates it "redeeming the time.") From God's standpoint, time equals opportunity. To waste your time is to miss opportunities.

A CLOSER LOOK

The two most commonly asked questions in any given day are, "How are you?" and "What time is it?" Time is something that can irritate or impel us. We wonder how long the red light will stay red. We wonder why the line at the bank or post office moves so slowly. We wonder why the express lane at the grocery store isn't "express" at all. We get irritated when the cleaners don't have our shirts ready when they promised.

We have microwaves for quick meals. We have instant tea, coffee, and most everything else. We travel on fast jets. We fax. We E-mail. We have pagers and cell phones for instant access.

We live in the *now* generation. Time is important to us. When things are done has become as important as how well things are done.

But with all of these timesaving devices, we don't have any more time than we did before. Where did the time go? If, indeed, we still have twenty-four hours per day, how do we spend it? Do we spend it, save it, or invest it?

TIME

■ *Measurable period in which something takes place.*

Isn't it strange that we use these same three verbs when speaking of our money? Money is more tangible than time, and in one sense we can see it slip through our fingers. But our time slips away as well.

This is the reason we are admonished to be wise, to walk carefully, and to watch how we invest our time. We need to make it count. To make the most of our time, we need to understand some things about it.

First, God created time. Time began at creation, with evening and morning being the first day. We still live in that framework.

In eternity past, there was no time, and there will be no time in eternity future. Time is peculiar to our sphere now. As someone has said, "Man's time sequence has bookends."

When the Lord Jesus said, "Before Abraham was born, I am," He was telling the scribes and Pharisees that He was eternal—a claim they did not take lightly. For in saying so, He professed His deity.

A second thing we need to know about time is that God rules over time. Not only did He create it, He is in charge of it. He is the One who caused time to stand still during a crucial Old Testament battle. "The sun stood still in the midst of heaven, and did not hasten to go down for about a whole day. And there has been no day like that, before it or after it" (Josh. 10:13–14).

The Bible doesn't tell us if the tides or creation was affected; it just lets us know God is in charge of time. He created it, and He can do anything He wants with it. He is not bound by it, as are we.

God used a span of time to let His servant Noah know how long he had before the rains started: "For after seven more days I will cause it to rain on the earth forty days and forty nights" (Gen. 7:4).

God has used time in the lives of His children, and He had a time—an exact time—for the birth of His Son. The eternal God entered time. God had been preparing the world for the coming of His Son.

Jesus was not premature. He was not late. He came at the exact moment in time that His Father had planned: "When the fullness of the time had come, God sent forth His Son, born of a woman, born under the law" (Gal. 4:4).

God has also appointed a time for judgment: "Because He has appointed a day on which He will judge the world in righteousness" (Acts 17:31). Just as surely as He had a time for morning and evening, for Noah, for Joshua, and for His Son's arrival, He has a time for judgment.

We cannot delay the time; we cannot speed it up. It is fixed. And no one knows the time but God Himself. We can ask God all we want to in reference to the Judgment, "What time is it?" and He will not tell us. He points to signs, but He has reserved the exact time for Himself.

> **P**eople's free time was rated as more important than most other aspects of life, including their religious lives, money, and community.
> —George Barna

Because God is in charge of time, nothing will keep us alive one second longer than God has appointed. For example, haven't we all known some people who have survived a very serious illness when the doctor gave them no hope? And have we not known some who have experienced an "untimely" death, as we call it? God is in charge of our time.

A third important insight regarding time is that God has given us responsibility to manage it. The way we use our time reveals our values and priorities. The Bible talks of some who have wasted their time and have nothing to show for it: "If anyone's work is burned, he will suffer loss" (1 Cor. 3:15). And the Bible tells us that someone who has invested time in good works, "he will receive a reward" (1 Cor. 3:14).

It saddens my heart when I ask someone, "Hey, what are you up to?" and she responds, "Oh, I'm just killing time." That is the same as saying, "I'm just wasting time."

Don't we realize that we can't add to or subtract from our time? You can't loan your time out for someone else to use. You can't say to a friend, "You're running short on time today? Here, take an hour from me. I'll just use the twenty-three hours left." No, each of us has twenty-four hours in a day, and how we use our time reflects our priorities.

If, for example, you put your mind in neutral for four hours daily in front of a television set, that reflects your value system. If you spend time in the Word of God, that reveals what you value as well.

In regard to managing time, not one verse of Scripture says, "Just do what comes naturally." The very opposite is true. Not only does Paul tell you in our text to make the most of your time, but Peter tells you to employ your spiritual gift (1 Peter 4:10). That means you are to use your time to serve others and get your eyes off yourself.

God brought you to birth at a certain time. He knows the exact time you will die. And He has a will for your time now. It is a sin to waste it.

In regard to the responsibility to manage time, there are some cautions.

Caution #1. In Ecclesiastes 3:1–11, where the familiar "there is a time . . ." passage appears, no verse says, "And there is a time to do nothing." The opposite is also true. No verse says, "There is a time to run and hurry." The caution is to be balanced in time. And for some of us, this is extremely difficult.

There are those who are workaholics, and there are those who are slothful. Neither is biblical.

The Ten Commandments emphasize balance in time: "Six days you shall labor and do all your work, but the seventh day is the Sabbath of the LORD your God. In it you shall do no work" (Ex. 20:9–10).

> **S**ixty-two percent of adults claim they spend time reading books for pleasure in a given week. (This has dropped from 75 percent in '91.)
> —George Barna

TIME

■ *Measurable period in which something takes place.*

Nothing in this passage talks about a four-day workweek. God didn't give us too much free time. Neither are we commanded to work seven days a week.

We are given a specific amount of time to work. And the days that we work should be productive. Of course, that does not necessarily mean that all six days are at a place of employment. Yard work, house work, and other types of labor are necessary.

Caution #2. Rest is important. The One who told us how long to work also told us to rest. And when we abuse His plan, we pay for it both physically and emotionally. Rest is a wonderful investment of time, as is work.

Caution #3. We are cautioned not to think, *I can get saved any time I want*. Remember when Paul was before Felix and the apostle shared the Lord Jesus Christ with him? The Bible records, "Felix was afraid and answered, 'Go away for now; when I have a convenient time I will call for you'" (Acts 24:25). That's all the Bible tells us about Felix's response to the gospel.

Caution #4. Don't overlook the timesaving power of prayer. Prayer is like a compass. It gives direction. God already knows every second of your day. He already knows every interruption. He already knows every crisis. Through prayer, He is giving you directions through your own personal minefield. None of it is hidden from Him.

I cannot prepare a sermon without prayer. I work and try, but it just doesn't mesh. However, if I first come to the Father and ask for direction, it's amazing how it all fits together. There is no way I can justify prayerlessness by preaching the gospel. The best investment of my time when it comes to sermon preparation is the time spent on my knees.

Before I go to bed on Saturday night, the last thing I do is read over my sermon. Sometimes the Lord will wake me up with fresh insights that I'd never thought of. His sweet intervention in response to my prayer is a wonderful time-saver.

One afternoon I was in my darkroom trying to develop some film. I was disappointed because there were some streaks on the side of the picture that I had taken of my granddaughter. I had worked hard to get rid of those streaks. Finally, I knelt down and said, "Father, I know what is important to me is important to You. This is important. I've done all I can do. Would You please tell me how to get rid of those streaks?"

I stood up and noticed a book lying on a table. On page two there were explicit instructions for getting rid of those streaks.

> **O**ur greatest danger in life is in permitting the urgent things to crowd out the important.
> —Charles E. Hummel

TIME

I had spent two hours trying to figure it out myself. I wish I had prayed earlier!

We need to live in such a way that we get the most for our time. We are to live as if every minute counts—because it does. We can always make more money, but we cannot make more time. Once it is gone, it is gone forever. And when our time on this earth is over, we will give an account to the One who gave us our allotment of this precious commodity.

The Lord Jesus was sensitive about time. He began His ministry at age thirty and ended it a mere three years later.

His life was jammed with people with immediate needs. Sick. Dead. Scared. People pushed through crowds to touch Him.

In Mark 1:35–37, before sunrise, Christ spent time with the Father. Peter and his friends "searched for Him. When they found Him, they said to Him, 'Everyone is looking for You.'"

In Matthew 14:23, He spent time with the Father in the evening. In Luke 6:12–13, He spent the night in prayer. And in Luke 5:15–16, we see that He slipped away into the wilderness to spend time with the Father.

He had three short years to teach, preach, heal, and lead. But the most important thing in His life was the time He spent with the Father.

If it was that important for Him, as the God-man, what about you?

APPLICATION

Since we are to walk wisely and make the most of our time, we need to know what we are aiming at.

Are we filling up time, or are we investing it? Do we have anything to show for our time, other than a paycheck?

Ask God what His purpose is for you and write out your personal mission statement. You could start, "Father, under Your divine guidance, I choose to invest my time by _____."

GROWTH

Figure up how many days you've lived. Subtract that number from 25,500 days (which is the average seventy-year span). What do you plan to do with the days you have remaining?

WAITING

■ *Remaining in our present circumstance for further instruction.*

PSALM 27:14

Wait on the LORD;
Be of good courage,
And He shall strengthen your heart;
Wait, I say, on the LORD!

In this hurry-up world, waiting for anything can cause us to lose our temper, our good sense, and our tongues more frequently than we care to admit. I don't know anyone who enjoys waiting in a line. We don't like waiting at stoplights. We don't like waiting in an airport. We don't like waiting for dinner. We don't even like waiting for good things—like for fish to bite. We want what we want *now.*

This frenetic propensity brings up a whole list of questions concerning waiting on God. Is God ever late or early? Does Omnipotence not have the power to change our circumstances? God has *never* been late (or early), and He certainly has the power to change our circumstances. That's not the problem. The problem is waiting when we want to move forward.

Why is it so hard to wait?

Perhaps we misunderstand what waiting is all about. Have you ever asked any of the following questions? Is waiting on the Lord the same thing as twiddling my thumbs? Should I clear my mind of everything? If you've ever asked even one of these questions, you can rest in the knowledge that you are not the first or the last.

The answer to all these questions is *NO!* Waiting has nothing to do with twiddling our thumbs in boredom. Waiting is not passive. It is an activity. It is a quiet, active stillness. Waiting is a directed, purposeful expectancy. It is a definite directing of our attention toward God, waiting for His intervention in our circumstances. It is like standing on tiptoe waiting for His further instructions.

One way we will know His instruction is through His Word. You've had the experience, as I have, of reading a Scripture and knowing that it has your name on it. You just know that verse or promise is for you. Although I am aware that there is a tendency of some to take Scripture out of context to make it fit their particular need, those who earnestly seek God's leading will be tuned to the prompting of the Holy Spirit. Scripture was not made for us to prove our point but to speak God's truth to our spirits.

Another way we will know God's instructions is through the changing of our circumstances. The Holy Spirit will give discernment to know this

> Two signposts of faith:
> Slow Down and Wait Here.
> —Charles Stanley

because not all change in circumstances is instruction from the Lord. Sometimes we are so close to the experience that we want to believe God has ordered the change that has occurred in our lives—particularly if the change is for the better. We are to listen to what the Spirit says to us through God's Word and the counsel of godly friends.

God is rich in mercy. He always has a specific reason for telling us to wait. Our responsibility is to trust Him, and that is perhaps the root cause behind our decisions to jump ahead in disobedience. What arrogance, to think we can work out things better than God can.

The writer of the scriptural passage said to wait—and he said it twice in one verse. He probably repeated himself because he knew no one likes to do it. If you've ever wondered whether it is always wise to wait, a closer look at this subject will answer your questions.

A CLOSER LOOK

It is *always* wise to wait on God.

First, it is wise to wait because God gives clear direction only when we are willing to wait. Remember, we don't operate like the world operates. We live in the now generation. Instant gratification of need defines society. But we, as believers, live differently. We belong to a different family. We live in light, not darkness. We don't take our cues from the world. We take them from God.

God will give clear direction, whether it is guidance for making a move or changing a career or choosing a mate. However, much to the distress of many, He seldom does it quickly. We must wait until He is ready to give direction. The world will think we are very foolish. "Take the bull by the horns," they'll say. Or "What are you waiting for? Looks to me like you're wasting time and just sitting around!" That kind of shame has prompted many a well-meaning believer to make rash decisions. Satan uses that tactic to take our eyes off God's direction and cause us to jump ahead of Him.

God says, "I will instruct you and teach you in the way you should go; I will guide you with My eye" (Ps. 32:8). We must wait until He is ready to give counsel to us. I know it's hard. No one ever said it would be easy. I just said it would be worth it.

I have struggled at times in my life with waiting. I have learned that the longer He takes to give direction, the more He has to teach me. When things aren't going smoothly, I have to trust His love for me and not complain. Once in the thick of the battle, no matter how dark the clouds, how heavy the fog, how hot the fire, and how fierce the fight, wait on God's instruction.

You can't step in front of God and not get in trouble. When He says, "Go 3 steps," don't go 4.
—Charles Stanley

WAITING

> **W**hat then is the chief end of man? Man's chief end is to glorify God and to enjoy Him forever.
> —The Westminster Larger Catechism (1861)

Once you've made it through and His direction has become evident, you can usually look back on those struggles as times He was able to teach you the most effectively.

Second, it is wise to wait because God uses that waiting time to *get us in step with His timing*. I have come to recognize the importance of being in step with God's timing. I will have a sense of peace. When I run ahead of Him, I have no sense of calm. Instead of peace, I will constantly be trying to figure out how to make my decision work. If you are in His timing, you won't have to worry about making it work. God wouldn't have you do something if He hadn't already figured out how to see you through.

Delayed timing, from our perspective, is perfect timing from God's point of view. Most of the time, our decisions affect others' lives. In His timing, He perfectly meshes it all together. When the poet said, "No man is an island," he was affirming the truth of how one life affects another. When what we decide to do affects another person, being in God's will is doubly important because we have more than our lives at stake.

Third, it is always wise to wait because God uses the time of waiting to *prepare us for the answer*. For instance, God may say to a young man, "Yes, you may marry her—but you need to wait." Wait? Why? Sometimes God does the same thing in business deals or purchases: "Yes, this is My plan for you—but you need to wait." It is so unnatural to wait. But the wise person does what is best, not what feels good at the moment.

As earthly parents, we don't give our children everything they ask for. Sometimes we know that the timing isn't right. How much more our heavenly Father knows this for His children. One night at supper, my son, Andy, said, "I want to thank you for not giving us everything we wanted because most of my friends got everything they wanted and it messed them up."

Fourth, it is always wise to wait because waiting *strengthens our faith*. We might want to say, "Okay, God. I've learned as much faith as I care to. You can act now." But when we realize that God is more interested in our character than in our comfort, waiting is a lot more palatable.

> **A**voiding the present moment has almost become a habit in our society.
> —Tim Hansel

Fifth, it is always wise to wait because God *gets our attention and sifts our motives*. While waiting and praying for the promotion at work, we have time to think through our motives. Why do we really want that promotion? Do we want it to get more money or so others will think we are powerful? Could it be we want the promotion so we have a greater platform to serve the Lord? If we allow God to sift through our motives, the truth will surface—good or bad. It is amazing what we learn about ourselves through this waiting period.

So it is wise to wait because

WAITING

1. He gives clear direction.
2. He gets us in step with Himself.
3. He prepares us for what He has in store for us.
4. He strengthens our faith.
5. He gets our attention and sifts our motives.

If it is wise to wait, how do we do it? We do it *actively*. We wait where we are, doing what God says to do, until God intervenes or tells us to do something different. It is probably not a good idea to quit your job until God has led you to another one. Most of the time He is not going to say, "Do nothing and shut down your life until further notice."

Not only do we wait actively, but we wait *patiently:* "Rest in the LORD, and wait patiently for Him" (Ps. 37:7). We must be willing to endure until He works. We all know this is much easier said than done. But waiting patiently will be easier when we're resting in Him.

We wait actively, patiently, and *silently.* One of my favorite verses is, "My soul silently waits for God" (Ps. 62:1). Remember Saul's amazing conversion on the Damascus Road? Wouldn't the natural tendency be for him to want to get to Jerusalem and the city square as fast as he could and give his dynamic testimony? After all, he had quite a reputation for having earlier persecuted the churches. Instead of going to Jerusalem, Paul went to the Arabian desert. He was alone with God.

We wait actively, patiently, silently, and *expectantly.* This is a period of time in which we sharpen our discernment and learn to look for evidences of God's working. We live in anticipation of what God is going to do.

We wait *courageously* because we are *standing on the Word of God:* "I wait for the LORD, my soul waits, and in His word I do hope" (Ps. 130:5). When I say we wait courageously, I don't mean the absence of fear. We have a calmness and stability in the midst of fear, an inner sense of leaning on the arms of a perfect heavenly Father. We wait courageously, claiming the promises from His Word that He loves us and will do what's best for us. Just because He doesn't work as quickly as we think He should is no proof of His indifference to our needs. Romans 8:28–29 contains promises to be believed.

What are the consequences of *not* waiting?

When we fail to wait, we get out of God's will. Even if we do the right thing at the wrong time, it is disobedience. Running ahead of God is not obedience. When we fail to wait, we not only get out of God's will but also delay God's planned blessing in our lives. If God is waiting so that He can

In a survey, 77 percent of people said that God had assisted them in making a decision in their lives.
—*Discipleship Journal,* March–April 1994

Forty-six percent of praying adults claimed they take the time to await God's answer.
—George Barna

Waiting **333**

WAITING

■ *Remaining in our present circumstance for further instruction.*

stretch our faith and we run ahead, He may have to wait *longer* to make sure we've learned the lesson. We only lengthen the training time!

Failing to wait also brings confusion in our lives. We feel no sense of direction because we are going so hurriedly, we don't take time to reflect on where we are headed. We speed through important intersections in our lives and refuse any four-way stops. This is especially disastrous because some decisions—such as the choice of a mate—are lifetime decisions.

Some of life's greatest lessons are learned while we wait. Some of life's hardest classrooms are waiting rooms. But there are vast rewards in waiting. God graciously uses the long pauses in our lives if we let Him.

Let's look at six rewards of waiting.

First, when we wait, *we discover God's will and purpose* in whatever we're concerned about: "The LORD is good to those who wait for Him, to the soul who seeks Him" (Lam. 3:25). God is not stringing us out to tantalize us. He is not saying, as do earthly parents, "Well, we'll see." No. He is working all things together for our good and His glory as Romans 8:28 assures us constantly.

Second, when we wait, *we receive supernatural physical energy and strength*. The promise in Isaiah 40:29–31 can be claimed.

> *He gives power to the weak,*
> *And to those who have no might He increases strength.*
> *Even the youths shall faint and be weary,*
> *And the young men shall utterly fall,*
> *But those who wait on the LORD*
> *Shall renew their strength;*
> *They shall mount up with wings like eagles,*
> *They shall run and not be weary,*
> *They shall walk and not faint.*

The promise is that during our waiting on Him, He supplies us with supernatural physical energy for the short term and the long term. Our impatience makes us weary and worn. Actively waiting on Him energizes us.

One time I had to preach seven times in one day with only ten minutes between preaching assignments. After the first three times, I decided that I couldn't make it physically. I put my overcoat on the concrete and lay on it, putting my Bible under my head for a pillow. I prayed, "God, I've got about ten minutes for You to energize me and put wind beneath my wings. I need to run and not be weary." Then I quoted Isaiah 40:31 to Him and to me. I discovered that five or ten minutes of waiting on Him is like a two-hour nap. Waiting on Him is not wasted time!

Third, when we wait, *we win battles:* "The LORD favors those who fear Him, those who wait for His lovingkindness" (Ps. 147:11 NASB). How wonderful to have the Lord favor us and to be on our side! Most of the time we're defeated because we do it our way, in our hurried time. Contrary to what it might look like on the surface, waiting will ensure our victory if God has led us to wait rather than precipitously act.

Fourth, when we wait, *we receive answers to our prayers:* "I waited patiently for the LORD; and He inclined to me, and heard my cry" (Ps. 40:1). One reason we don't see more answers to prayer is that we want the answers on our schedule and not His. We have become such an indulgent society that thinks it's unfair to put off personal gratification: God knows just the right timing.

Fifth, when we wait, *we see the fulfillment of our faith:* "They shall not be ashamed who wait for Me" (Isa. 49:23). We won't be embarrassed. When others encourage us to forge ahead instead of waiting on the Lord, we need to remember that we will not be put to shame in the end. I know that during the long wait, it is easy to say, "But, Lord, suppose it doesn't work out?" He will not let us down.

Sixth, when we wait, *we see God working in our behalf.* Isaiah spoke of the God "who acts for the one who waits for Him" (Isa. 64:4). Isn't that a wonderful promise? While we actively wait, He actively works. Think of this: every single day we have the greatest Mediator working on our behalf when things go wrong or when they go right.

Waiting. We need to transform our way of thinking about waiting, and the only way we can do that is to understand why God asks us to wait and learn to trust Him even when it doesn't make sense.

Waiting is one of the more difficult things in the Christian life. It is not wasted time. God gives instructions through times of actively watching. He may change our circumstances while we wait. He keeps us in step with Himself and prepares us for His answers. He uses the time to sift our motives and strengthen our faith. He wants us to wait patiently, silently, expectantly, and courageously trusting His Word.

When we choose to wait, He rewards us by allowing us to discover His will and renews us with physical energy. He enables us to win battles and receive answers to prayer. He fulfills our faith while working on our behalf.

The question comes: With all the advantages of waiting, why do we rush ahead as if we don't have a trustworthy Father? We need to hit the pause

> The growth of the soul is usually so slow that it is hardly measurable or visible. This is the perfect reason why many Western Christians are not marked with, as Celliet called it, the Presence. They do not have the patience that spiritual development requires.
> —Gordon MacDonald

> Patiently waiting is valuable because the Lord has instruction for us. While we are waiting, He has our attention. We are ready for correction . . . reproof . . . personality adjustment . . . lessons in obedience.
> —Dick Mills

WAITING

■ *Remaining in our present circumstance for further instruction.*

> **Q**uiet waiting before God would save from many a mistake and from many a sorrow.
>
> —J. Hudson Taylor

button in our lives and take our lives out of the fast-forward mode. God will amaze us at what He is doing while we expect His surprises.

Several years ago we were searching for a new building for our In Touch Ministries. We found a building that seemed to be adequate, but God kept speaking to my spirit to wait. I mentioned to the Lord that we didn't have a lot of time—as if He didn't know. Finally, I felt that it wasn't the right place.

I felt led by God to suggest our leadership go somewhere for several days to pray. We usually go to a location that takes a long time to get reservations, but after calling, we were told we could go on the following Monday.

We had discussed another building that seemed perfect because of its location and size. There was one enormous drawback. The building cost more than $2 million. We did not have the funds. We prayed earnestly for God's guidance and provision.

When we returned, there was a note on my desk saying that a man I had never met had called. I returned his call, and he explained that he was wondering if we had any needs since we didn't mention them on the broadcasts. I assured him that we always have needs. He persisted in asking. I explained that one pressing need was a building for In Touch but that the one we had selected was more than $2 million, and we did not want to violate our policy of no indebtedness. The man responded that he would underwrite the cost.

And he did. While we were in the mountains praying, God was burdening the heart of someone in another part of the country.

How sad if we had not waited!

We would have missed His very best for us.

 APPLICATION

When we plant a garden, we put seed under the soil.

Then we water. Then we wait.

And wait. After sun and rain pelt the earth, the seeds begin to grow. And we finally see evidence of what we planted. Suppose we had gotten impatient and dug up our seeds because nothing was happening? We would have ruined the garden. But that is exactly the way we live our lives.

God sends sunshine and rain, and yet we don't want to wait to see what He is growing in our lives. We get impatient and want to dig up what the Vinedresser is bringing forth (John 15:1).

In the process, we ruin the fruit that He is working on in our lives.

Some fruit takes a long time to mature. The One who wants to bring it forth in our lives knows exactly how long we need to wait.

Waiting is not wasted time. It brings forth the most luscious fruit of all.

WAITING

My case is urgent, and I do not see how I am to be delivered; but this is no business of mine. He who makes the promise will find ways and means of keeping it. It is mine to obey His command; it is not mine to direct His counsels. I am His servant, not His solicitor. I call upon Him, and He will deliver.

 QUOTE

—Charles Haddon Spurgeon

WISDOM

SCRIPTURE

EPHESIANS 5:15–16 NASB

Be careful how you walk, not as unwise men, but as wise, making the most of your time, because the days are evil.

COMMENTARY

In these verses, the apostle Paul commanded the believers in Ephesus to live wisely. The phrase "be very careful" means to scope things out, to think things through, to look at things from every angle. It is all-encompassing. Believers are to demonstrate caution in relationships, finances, decision making, business transactions, family matters, everything. Notice it says, "How you walk," that is, in every facet of life.

This is contrasted with how unwise people live. The implication is that they go blindly into situations without giving much thought to the outcome; they don't consider the consequences. Unwise men and women go with the flow. They tend to make unsound decisions.

The text also describes a common characteristic of those who live wisely; they make the most of time. Wise men and women waste no time. They take advantage of every opportunity to do what is right. They look for opportunities to move forward in their faith and service.

Paul gave his readers a reason for his instruction: "Because the days are evil." This is a reference to the moral climate of his culture as well as the culture of his audience. They were surrounded by people whose values were diametrically opposed to everything Christianity stood for. It seemed as if everything was working against them. For that reason, they needed to walk wisely.

> **T**he greatest good is wisdom.
> —Augustine

APPLICATION

It is easy to get swept along by the current of our society. There is something in all of us that wants to take the path of least resistance. But to do so is to disobey Paul's command to "be careful." The essence of wisdom, from a practical standpoint, is pausing long enough to look at our lives—invitations, opportunities, relationships—from God's perspective. And then, acting on it.

Many issues we are forced to deal with on a daily basis are not mentioned specifically in Scripture. Complicated situations arise, and there seems to be no biblical parallel to use as a guide. In these situations we are to turn to wisdom. We are to ask, "What is the wise thing to do?"

Wisdom takes us beyond the realm of mere right and wrong. Wisdom takes into account our personalities, our strengths, our weaknesses, and even

WISDOM

our present state of mind. As we have seen, wisdom also takes into account our environment. In this way, wisdom is often the tool God uses to personalize His will for our lives. What is wise for you may not be wise for me—and vice versa.

All of us are tempted to excuse things because they are not overtly wrong. No specific verse of Scripture prohibits them. But wise men or women don't ask, "Is there a verse that prohibits this?" We ask, "What is the wise thing for me to do?" It is not enough to merely stay on the right side of the line that divides right from wrong. In many cases, God would have us stay a safe distance away from the line itself.

Proverbs tells us that the fear of God is the beginning of wisdom (Prov. 9:10; see also Ps. 111:10). In this context fear refers to reverence and respect. Wisdom begins when we acknowledge God for who He is, when we recognize that His ways are best. Wisdom begins when we submit ourselves to His will, trusting that if we could see our lives from His perspective, things would make perfect sense.

We have a large number of single adults in our church. One of the recurring questions that surfaces in my discussions with them has to do with dating non-Christians. Usually, they ask this way: "What does the Bible say about dating non-Christians?"

"That's easy," I say. "Nothing. It doesn't say anything about dating at all, so maybe you shouldn't!"

After a brief look of panic, they realize I'm kidding. I answer this question by asking a series of questions. First, "Do you think that you will eventually marry someone you fall in love with?"

"Of course," they say.

I continue, "Do you think you will fall in love with someone you date for some length of time?"

"Probably."

"Do you want to marry a Christian?"

"Absolutely!"

"Well, if you are going to marry someone you fall in love with, and if you think it's likely that you will fall in love with someone you are going to date over a period of time, and you are committed to only marrying a Christian, is it really wise to date a non-Christian?"

Reactions are usually mixed. Someone will almost always refer to the original question: "But where does it say that in the Bible?"

"The Bible," I say, "instructs us to walk wisely. In that context, the Bible does have something to say about dating non-Christians. It is unwise."

> "And what is this valley called?"
> "We call it now simply Wisdom's valley; but the oldest maps mark it as the Valley of Humiliation."
> —C. S. Lewis, *The Pilgrim's Regress*

> Wisdom is seeing things from God's perspective.
> —Bill Gothard

> Wisdom is the right use of knowledge. To know is not to be wise. Many men know a great deal, and are all the greater fools for it. . . . But to know how to use knowledge is to have wisdom.
> —Charles Haddon Spurgeon

Wisdom

339

WISDOM

■ *Looking at life from God's perspective.*

A CLOSER LOOK

The moral state of Ephesus was much like what we face today. Everything was permissible. Ephesus was a port city on the Mediterranean Sea. It served as a hub for commercial trade in that region of the world. Consequently, it was an affluent city. But it was also a city filled with pagan religions. The temple to Diana served as a centerpiece for the pagan rituals of the day. Commerce made it necessary for the citizens of Ephesus to keep an open mind about all religions and religious practices. Many of the religious rituals included various forms of immorality. What was off limits to the Ephesian believers was part of the religious ceremonies of many of their neighbors.

As you can imagine, it was difficult for the believers in Ephesus to maintain high standards. Their hostile environment made it that much more important for them to begin asking, "What is the wise thing to do?"

IDEALS & GOALS

Before you accept an invitation.
Before you implement a plan.
Before you sign your name to anything.
Before you agree to participate in a venture of any kind.
Ask yourself these three questions.

- What is the wise thing to do in light of my past experience?
- What is the wise thing to do in light of my present state of mind?
- What is the wise thing to do in light of my future goals and dreams?

Parents, teach your kids to ask these questions as well.

QUOTE

The theme of Proverbs is wisdom, the right use of knowledge. This wisdom is more than an intellectual pursuit; it also involves devotion to the Lord. The wise person fears the Lord, trusts Him, and seeks to obey His will. The wisdom described in Proverbs is like a spiritual sixth sense. It enables you to evaluate circumstances and people and make the right decisions in life.

—Warren Wiersbe

■ *To be anxious or troubled.*

WORRY

SCRIPTURE

Be anxious for nothing, but in everything by prayer and supplication, with thanksgiving, let your requests be made known to God; and the peace of God, which surpasses all understanding, will guard your hearts and minds through Christ Jesus.

COMMENTARY

Praying is often the last thing we want to do when the worries of life overwhelm us. Our natural reaction is either to hastily solve our own problems or to sit around and worry about them. And yet, from a Roman prison, the apostle Paul instructs us to face our anxieties with prayer. Let's take a look at what he says.

Notice his first point of instruction. "Be anxious for nothing." If you are like me, you may be tempted to respond, "That is easy for you to say. You don't know my circumstances!" Paul, in his wisdom, knew that every believer would face situations that are worrisome. We should, therefore, heed his advice.

There are many times when I've felt the pressure and needs of life in the ministry to be overwhelming. If I gave in to worry, what would happen? Circumstances would worsen, and I would not allow God in His sovereign will and time to work things out. Especially at those times I do just what Paul says—I pray.

Prayer results in an indescribable and immediate sense of peace. That peace allows me to continue with what I need to do, in the confidence and assurance that God will work everything out.

> **P**eople wrestle with two primary fears:
>
> 1. Fear of failure
> 2. Fear of the future
>
> —Ron Blue

APPLICATION

The most effective way any believer can prepare for the stress of the day is to begin with God. Begin your day with time alone in which you can make your requests known to Him. Tell God the issues and concerns weighing you down. The heavier the burdens, the longer it will take, but when you walk away, you'll feel relieved and at peace.

Anticipate the stressors in your schedule, and ask God to give you peace in the midst of them. Remember God's faithfulness in the past. How did He help you yesterday, last month, last year? Rehearse His faithfulness for today, and thank Him for it.

Maintain a journal of requests. Record when and how they were answered. Use this journal as your visible proof of God's presence each and every day. When stress comes, as it will, you may claim His promises.

WORRY

A CLOSER LOOK

Luke records the constant pressures Jesus lived with. "I have come to bring fire on the earth, and how I wish it were already kindled! But I have a baptism to undergo, and how distressed I am until it is completed!" (Luke 12:49–50 NIV).

Jesus felt crowded and hemmed in by the crowds eager to hear Him. In three years, He had a lot to accomplish—disciples to teach, people to heal, and a world to save. Yet He never allowed His schedule to interfere with His relationship with God or people. Jesus didn't become distracted and ignore others; He didn't become self-centered. He was distressed. Why didn't He take matters into His own hands? He was God, wasn't He?

Worry is an attempt to control the future.
—Ron Blue

Luke relays Jesus' response: "[Jesus] often withdrew into the wilderness and prayed" (Luke 5:16). Jesus left to pray so many times that the disciples realized there was more to prayer than they knew. The disciples asked Jesus to teach them to pray.

The busier we are, the easier it is to worry. The greater the temptation to worry, the greater the need to be alone with God. Jesus had reason to worry, but He had a greater reason to spend time with the Father.

GROWTH

To break the habit of worry, you must develop the habit of prayer. It is there in the lonely place that you will gain the perspective and peace you need to handle the stress of life without sacrificing your relationships and health along the way.

RELATIONSHIPS

ACCOUNTABILITY

■ *A relationship between believers wherein one has invited the other to monitor the development of character in one or more areas.*

LUKE 17:3

 SCRIPTURE

Take heed to yourselves. If your brother sins against you, rebuke him; and if he repents, forgive him.

COMMENTARY

Some things taught in the Scriptures make us so uncomfortable, we tend to ignore them. The notion of being personally accountable to someone else for our actions is certainly one of them. Yet the passage quoted above could not be any clearer about our responsibility to our brothers and sisters in Christ. When fellow believers drift off into sin, it is our responsibility to confront them.

When Jesus said to "rebuke" a sinning brother, He took His disciples by surprise. It is a strong term. It is the same term used to describe Jesus' interaction with demons in several instances (Matt. 17:18; Mark 1:25). On another occasion Jesus "rebuked" a storm (Mark 4:39). To ask them to rebuke a brother was a stringent thing to do. Yet Jesus didn't hesitate. He operated from the basis that believers were accountable to one another for their behavior.

This same idea is echoed in what Paul told the believers in Galatia (Gal. 6:1–3). Paul said that if a believer is caught in sin, the strong members of the church are to help shoulder the responsibility of that person's sin. They are to work with the offending party and help him get back on track. As believers, we have a responsibility to bear the burdens of other believers. Their burdens are our burdens—and vice versa.

In both passages, accountability is assumed. The fact that the offending and confronting parties were believers was enough to justify the one holding the other accountable. Whether we know it or not, whether we agree with it or not, whether we practice it or not, whether we like it or not, we are accountable to one another.

 A CLOSER LOOK

Generally speaking, accountability is a willingness to share our activities, conduct, and fulfillment of assigned responsibilities with others.

Accountability

ACCOUNTABILITY

Accountability is not a new concept. Each of us is accountable in many ways to different organizations and people. If you have a job, you are accountable to your employer, who expects certain things of you. If you don't fulfill your responsibility, the employer has every right to ask you why. If you are married, you are accountable. Your spouse and family expect certain things. If you are not faithful to your responsibilities, more than likely they will voice their disappointment or concern.

But when it comes to our character and spiritual development, we are prone to resist accountability. "After all," we reason, "that's between me and God. It's nobody else's business."

Many believers mistakenly believe that the personal nature of our relationship with God excludes our need for mutual accountability. Although it is true that our relationship with God is *personal* in nature, it is not true that it is *private*. The Bible teaches that we are accountable to one another for our conduct and character.

Specifically, what we are talking about is inviting a person or small group of people to monitor you in one or more areas of your life. For instance, it could be as simple as asking your spouse to check with you from time to time about the consistency of your quiet time. You may want to ask a friend to check with you periodically on how much time you are devoting to your family. I know several men who have accountability partners to keep a check on their choice of entertainment when they are traveling alone.

GROWTH

An area where accountability can really make a difference is that of recurring temptations. Temptations carry with them emotional stress. This results from the internal struggle and then the guilt once we give in. An accountability relationship provides an outlet for the feelings and frustrations that otherwise have no outlet. Part of the deceptiveness of sin is that we feel the only way we can deal with the internal pressures is to go ahead and sin. Sin, however, only compounds the problem.

Having someone to whom we can be totally honest provides us with a temporary substitute for the frustration we feel as well as the sin we are tempted to commit. I say "temporary" because until we allow God to deal with the root issues, the pressure will eventually return.

Many times when I have been frustrated, I have turned not only to the Lord but to my friends as well. I tell them everything I am feeling; what I would like to do; what bothers me. Usually, by the time I am finished, I am all right. I don't need for them to say anything. Just knowing that they will

ACCOUNTABILITY

listen with open minds and hearts is enough. Most of the time there are some things that need to be dealt with in the areas that cause me frustration. But after I pour out my heart, they seem much more manageable.

We all need someone who will listen, pray, and offer wise counsel when appropriate. Individuals who have someone like that in their lives will find it much easier to deal with temptation. This is just one other benefit of establishing an accountability relationship.

APPLICATION

The Bible doesn't outline a program for accountability groups. There are no rules that govern when and how often you should meet with your accountability partner or partners. I have seen it work in a variety of ways. My daughter, Becky, gets together with her accountability partner once a month. Andy meets with a group every week. I know of groups that meet for breakfast. Some people keep up with one another by phone.

Accountability partners don't necessarily need to have a formal meeting. Some people choose to work their accountability around a hobby they do together. Others keep up with one another as they carpool to work. I know of several groups that exercise together. The point is, accountability can be an informal exchange.

An accountability partner should be someone of the same sex, someone you have things in common with, someone you enjoy spending time with. An accountability partner should be someone you respect spiritually, someone whose walk with God challenges you to pursue a deeper walk.

If you feel you need accountability in several areas, you may want to choose several people and ask each of them to hold you accountable in one specific area. For instance, if you need accountability in your finances, you will probably want someone who is capable in that area to hold you accountable. If you need someone to help you monitor the time you spend with your kids, you would probably want someone who has dealt with that issue.

Accountability does not have to be a two-way relationship. That is, an occasion may arise when you want someone to hold you accountable in a particular area, but circumstances make it awkward for you to hold that person accountable. For instance, there may be a situation when you need someone older and wiser to hold you accountable. The accountability would go only one way.

Accountability is about mutual encouragement, not criticism. The last thing you want is a relationship with someone who rakes you over the coals every time you get together. At the same time you don't want someone who

> The effective mentor strives to help a man or woman discover what they can be in Christ and then holds them accountable to become that person.
> —Howard Hendricks

Accountability **347**

ACCOUNTABILITY

hesitates to provide godly correction when necessary. The key is to strike a balance between encouragement and exhortation. The relationship should be about 75 percent encouragement and 25 percent exhortation or instruction.

Most accountability partners I know did not begin their relationship with that in mind. They were good friends who eventually felt comfortable sharing their personal struggles with each other. The more natural it is, the better: "A man of many friends comes to ruin, but there is a friend who sticks closer than a brother" (Prov. 18:24 NASB).

IDEALS & GOALS

If you are not in a formal accountability relationship with anyone, it is time to begin. Here are some tips on getting started.

List the areas in which you think you need accountability.

Beside each area, write the name of a person you know who seems to have that particular area under control, someone you respect in that arena of life.

Beside each area, write the name of a friend who would benefit from some accountability in that particular area in his or her life.

Ask God to open the doors for you to approach these people about beginning an accountability relationship.

■ *Boys or girls before puberty; sons or daughters.*

CHILDREN

SCRIPTURE

MARK 10:13–16

They brought little children to Him, that He might touch them; but the disciples rebuked those who brought them. But when Jesus saw it, He was greatly displeased and said to them, "Let the little children come to Me, and do not forbid them; for of such is the kingdom of God. Assuredly, I say to you, whoever does not receive the kingdom of God as a little child will by no means enter it." And He took them up in His arms, laid His hands on them, and blessed them.

COMMENTARY

It would be easy to wonder about the disciples in some situations. When we see how ordinary they were, the rest of us can have hope! In the book of Mark, we are not told how much time elapses between some events, but apparently, it is only a brief time span between what's recorded in Mark 9 and Mark 10. Even if the time was extensive, it's hard to figure how the disciples could have forgotten what Jesus said about children.

Their fuzzy memory seems to underscore how unimportant they thought the subject was. In Mark 9, after the glorious time on the Mount of Transfiguration and Jesus' talking about His coming death and resurrection, the disciples went with Jesus into a house.

It was an intimate setting—more so than the crushing crowds on open hillsides. Jesus took the opportunity to ask His disciples an awkward question—a question to which He already knew the answer: "What was it you disputed among yourselves on the road?" (v. 33).

The feeling that pervaded was probably somewhat like that of being caught with your hand in the cookie jar. The house probably felt smaller. There was no open sky to gaze into or grass to pull at. No room for maneuvering.

The Bible says, "But they kept silent, for on the road they had disputed among themselves who would be the greatest" (v. 34).

Can you imagine Wisdom Himself looking at you, knowing that you and your friends had been talking about who was most deserving of a promotion? Can you imagine Perfection gazing at you, knowing you and your friends had been discussing which one was the closest to being perfect? Can you imagine the King of kings inquiring, knowing all along that you and your cronies had been toying with who was the greatest?

"He took a little child and set him in the midst of them. And when He had taken him in His arms, He said to them, 'Whoever receives one of these little children in My name receives Me'" (Mark 9:36–37). This was Jesus' visual aid to His disciples. A child. We cannot help wondering how the child felt being used as a positive illustration. He probably never forgot this

Children

incident the rest of his life. We can wonder that if the child's father was not in the house at the time, how the proud Jewish mother must have greeted her husband that night, "You'll never guess what happened to our Benjamin today!" That's only conjecture on our part, of course, but what parent wouldn't want that to happen?

After Jesus used this child as an object lesson of humility, in Mark 10 we see another interaction.

"They brought little children to Him." The word *they* in the Greek dialect is indefinite. But the word *them* in the latter part of the verse is a masculine pronoun. So it could be assumed that along with mothers, fathers and perhaps even brothers or sisters were bringing the children to Jesus. Among the Jews, it was a custom to bring children to great men to have them blessed.

It is not clear how old the children were. The Greek word used in Mark indicates a twelve-year-old, but Luke used another Greek word that means babies. We can assume that there was a great range of ages, but none were too old for Him to touch and take in His arms—or too young.

Mark is the only Gospel writer who records that Jesus was indignant when He saw the disciples try to turn the little ones away. Didn't they remember the incident in the house not too long ago?

Even though their motives could have been noble, trying to protect the privacy of Jesus, or thinking He should spend His time with more important people, Jesus overruled them: "'Let the little children come to Me, and do not forbid them.' . . . And He took them up in His arms, laid His hands on them, and blessed them" (Mark 10:14, 16).

The Greek word implies He blessed them fervently. We wonder if He prayed to His Father out loud for each child. Perhaps He used an Old Testament benediction. We can be sure the parents never, ever forgot what they saw and heard.

Perhaps the disciples didn't, either.

A CLOSER LOOK

Not too long ago I gained an impressive title. I cherish it above most of my other titles. I had little to do with when the title was bestowed. I didn't do a whole lot to achieve it. And although I have received it five times up to this point, it hasn't become old hat. The title is "grandfather."

I enjoy saying it. I bask in being one!

I'm not sure if my aging makes youth look all the more wondrous. I don't mean to imply I would ever want to be young again. Never. What I mean is, I find the childish questions, the unsure tiny steps, and the stumbling words of my grandchildren incredibly precious.

I remember the awe I felt when Andy and Becky were born. But the years have deepened that awe as I watch my grandchildren. I can hardly be with them enough. I want to savor every moment.

When I was a young boy, I spent only a very short time with my grandfather, George Washington Stanley. I learned about obeying God in that short time. I wonder if he sensed that I was a dry sponge who soaked up everything he said?

I think that because my grandfather made such a profound impression on me, I understand to a degree how important being a grandparent is. I want to do it right. I want to have eternal input into the hearts of my grandchildren. I read an article about a retiree that blessed my heart. He looked forward to the day when he would become a grandfather, but that didn't seem imminent. He became a volunteer cuddler for premature babies at a hospital. After filling out the application, he had to wait eighteen months. He explained, "There were many grandmothers who were cuddlers, and none of them wanted to quit." Because touching affects the growth of the body and mind in a child, he never wants to quit his newfound job.

"They brought little children to Him, that He might touch them" (Mark 10:13). When I think of the gentle touch of the Lord Jesus on the children, I find child abuse incomprehensible. When we see that Jesus was indignant because the disciples turned the children away, we can only imagine what Jesus would say and do had He seen any parent—or anyone, for that matter—physically, sexually, or emotionally abuse a little one.

God's heart must be broken to see helpless little children hurt. He has given a stern warning that "whoever causes one of these little ones who believe in Me to stumble, it is better for him that a heavy millstone be hung around his neck, and that he be drowned in the depth of the sea" (Matt. 18:6 NASB). People who hurt little children will not go unnoticed or unpunished by the One who carefully knit them in the mother's womb.

More is mentioned here in Matthew 18 than just the physical hurting of boys and girls. Many well-meaning Christians hurt children spiritually. I don't mean just by being inconsistent in their walk, although that is surely detrimental. I'm talking about those who take lightly the salvation of children. This is the primary context of Matthew 18. Jesus uses children in the first part of the chapter as an illustration to the disciples of the simplicity of being converted. He later speaks of the little ones "who believe in Me." And He severely warns those who cause them to stumble. You know the

Eighty-five percent of those who came to Christ did so before the age of fifteen.

CHILDREN

main way we cause them to stumble? By telling them they are too young to receive the Lord.

We need to be very careful about dissuading a child who wants to become a Christian. It would be better to assume the Spirit of God is wooing that sweet tender heart than it would be to get close to causing that child to stumble by denying him the privilege. If you're going to err, err on the side of being too early, not too late.

Each of my children was saved at the age of five. As a pastor, I am thrilled to watch parents bring little ones up the aisle to tell me they have received Jesus and want to be baptized. They come wide-eyed and trusting. We don't have to wade through years of garbage that has accumulated in their lives. We don't have to untangle twisted relationships that have infiltrated their world. We don't have to try to help with a long-term drug or alcohol or sex addiction. We don't have to try to figure out how to make them financially solvent so they can serve the Lord unencumbered.

All we do is lead them to Jesus. And they are trusting enough that to them, it is the most natural thing in the world. Think of the years of heartache missed because they met Him as little children.

The daughter of Billy and Ruth Graham, Gigi Graham Tchividjian, received the Lord when she was three years old. She wrote about her children coming to Christ,

> When our oldest son was three, he was sitting beside his daddy on the balcony of our home in Switzerland enjoying the view. Suddenly he asked, "Daddy, how can I ask Jesus into my heart?" That day our eldest became a child of God and has never wavered. Years later, as a teenager, he was putting his youngest sister to bed. As he tucked her in, he quoted the verse, "Behold, I stand at the door and knock; if anyone hears My voice and opens the door, I will come in to him, and will dine with him, and he with Me." (Rev. 3:20) He explained that this was Jesus knocking at the door of her life. Would she like Him to come in and live with her? She said "yes" and prayed to receive Christ.

Gigi went on to say, "The great theologian Karl Barth was once asked what he thought was the greatest theological truth. He answered, 'Jesus loves me this I know, for the Bible tells me so.'"

I love what that great preacher Charles Haddon Spurgeon said, "A child of five, if properly instructed, can as truly believe and be regenerated as an adult."

After seeing Jesus use a child as an illustration of how to come to Him, we could reverse Spurgeon's statement and say, "An adult, if properly in-

> **C**hildren are not casual guests in our home. They have been loaned to us temporarily for the purpose of loving them and instilling a foundation of values on which their future lives will be built.
> —James Dobson

structed, can as truly believe and be regenerated as a child." The adults, not the children, have the hang-ups.

The best people in all the world to lead children to Christ are the parents. I encourage dads to baptize their children. I have found nothing in Scripture that indicates only a pastor can baptize. I believe children will never forget that day when Daddy, who has loved them and brought them to Jesus, baptizes them.

A parent who is never home or who never has time to be with the children possibly will not be available when the Holy Spirit pricks a tiny heart.

Anne Graham Lotz, another daughter of Billy and Ruth Graham, was telling about her mother,

> What my mother has taught me and that which I seek to pass on to her grandchildren, is that God is enough—period. Growing up, I had a bedroom directly over hers. No matter what time I went to bed at night, I could see the light from her room reflected on the trees outside. Were I to slip downstairs, I would find her on her knees beside her bed. There was no use waiting for her to rise—she would be there, in prayer, for hours at a time. No matter what time I arose in the morning, I would see the light from her room. When I arrived downstairs, she'd be at her desk reading one of 14 different Bible translations. *She knows God well.*

What a tribute! She knows God well. How many people can you say that about? Could your children say that about you?

I firmly believe that if at all possible, Mom should be home when the children are there. I explained how I was raised by a single mom who had to work. I know the financial issues. But it does not lessen the trauma or the loneliness because both parents work out of necessity.

In a recent minimagazine in our local newspaper, twenty pages were given to the subject of what to do with the children during the summer months. I don't mean "with" like companionship. I mean "with" like "to accommodate." One article was "Learn to Be Latchkey." I was a latchkey kid, long before the term was thought of. I remember exactly what the key looked like. I remember what it sounded like. I remember the sickening feeling in my stomach when I inserted it into a keyhole and knew no other human being was on the other side of the door. I felt totally alone.

Another article for parents offered tips on making sure the latchkey child has all the bases covered: "Your child should carry an emergency packet . . . and money for a pay phone or taxi, pinned inside a pocket"; "your child should be able to keep up with keys and know how to lock and unlock

CHILDREN

doors"; and "your child must know what appliances you have approved for his use." It mentioned first aid kits and fire and then ended with, "Work out a schedule of self-care activities together; include interesting things the child can do to alleviate loneliness and boredom."

One article told the parents that if they use the pool as a childcare facility, they need to make sure their kids have the things they need to spend the day in the sun. The schedule would be for the child to spend every day there throughout the summer. If the pool closes due to rain, where does the child go?

There are now twenty-four-hour day care services. One advertises that it tries to make bedtime "cozy like home." That is commendable. But it just isn't possible.

A woman I know was the director of a day care facility. She decided since people use day care, they might as well have Christians caring for their children. She said that when she arrived in the dark at 6:00 A.M. each morning, the tiny babies would begin coming. Some were six weeks old. Their parents would sometimes come back for them as late as 6:30 P.M. Again, it was dark.

She said that she saw so many two-year-olds with their noses pressed against the glass wailing as their parents drove away, she couldn't take it any longer. She finally had to quit. The owner sold it eventually because he couldn't take it, either.

I don't say this to inflict guilt on anyone. God knows your circumstances. You may be saying, "Well, Dr. Stanley was a latchkey kid raised by a single working mother for many years, and he turned out okay." But you have not seen all the years of working through the feelings of isolation and loneliness that accompanied my early childhood. It is the sheer grace of God—and I give Him all the praise and glory for what He has done in my life.

If you must work and your children must be cared for by others, bathe them, and the caregivers, in prayer. Pray. Pray. Pray. God knows your circumstances. He loves your children more than you do.

Children are treasures. We live in a time when many see them as totally expendable before birth. Some see them as expendable after birth. We want them to hurry and grow up.

Erma Bombeck tells of how she was always saying to her children, "Why don't you grow up?" It's a common statement among parents, especially if the behavior is grossly immature. But then she laments the empty nest:

> It's not time yet. It can't be. I'm not finished. I had all the teaching and the
> discipline and the socks to pick up and the buttons to sew on, and those lousy

meal worms to feed the lizard every day. . . . There was no time for loving. That's what it's all about, isn't it? Did they ever know I smiled? Did they ever understand my tears? Did I talk too much? Did I say too little? Did I ever look at them and really see them? Do I know them at all? Or was it all a lifetime of "Why don't you grow ups?"

I walk through the house and mechanically shut a refrigerator door that is already shut. I stoop to retrieve a towel that has not fallen to the floor but hangs neatly on the towel rack. From habit, I smooth out a spread that is already free of wrinkles. I answer a phone that has not rung and with a subtlety that fools no one, I hide the cake in the oven.

And I shout, "WHY DON'T YOU GROW UP?"

And the silence where once had abounded frustration, fear, disappointment, resentment, compassion, joy and love echoes, *"I did."*

Children are treasures in our world. They are treasures in the home. God gave thorough instructions to the children of Israel on how to instruct their little ones. That was important to God. It is no less important today.

We need to instill in our children, as well as children around us, that they are important. I smile at the story about a little fellow who went out to eat with his parents. As the waitress took their food orders, she looked at the little boy and asked what he wanted to eat. He stammered out his order. After the waitress walked away, the lad looked at his parents and said, grinning, "Gee, she thinks I'm real."

I like that story because I think it illustrates a subtle message that we give to children. We underestimate their thinking, their desires, and their abilities. We give underlying messages to them that they are inferior.

I understand that balance is needed. Children's rights are getting way out of hand in our country. Solomon wrote, "Foolishness is bound up in the heart of a child; the rod of correction will drive it far from him" (Prov. 22:15). The verses "A child left to himself brings shame to his mother" (Prov. 29:15) and "Correct your son, and he will give you rest; yes, he will give delight to your soul" (Prov. 29:17) remind us of the need to bring consistent discipline.

But balance includes heaping huge amounts of love, also. That's what our heavenly Father does. He disciplines. The Bible says if He did not discipline us, we wouldn't be treated like His children (Heb. 12:8). On the other hand, He heaps love. He constantly affirms us through Scripture. We are precious in His sight. He tells us that over and over. But He is not into His children's rights, although in a wonderfully unique way, He preserves our self-esteem by assuring us we are chosen by Him and so valuable His Son died for us.

Child abuse is the second leading cause of death among those between birth and twelve years old.

CHILDREN

■ *Boys or girls before puberty; sons or daughters.*

One young father wrote about working diligently to make sure his daughter developed proper self-esteem. He related,

My goal is to raise secure children with a good imagination. I realized I might be too successful one Saturday morning when I lost my four year old daughter at a roller skating rink. I was scanning the crowd when an announcement came over the loud speaker: "ATTENTION SKATERS! We have a lost little girl named Sleeping Beauty." Dozens of skaters were smiling as I skated over to claim my daughter.

Can't you imagine how many times that daddy tucked that little girl in and said, "Good night, Sleeping Beauty," or woke her up in the morning with the greeting, "Good morning, Sleeping Beauty!" She had gleefully internalized the message.

Our culture needs more children with positive messages oozing out of them. What we as believers pour into their hearts about their importance is not the same thing as what the world system pours into them. We don't want to produce a bunch of cocky kids demanding their rights. That's not biblical. It's not biblical for a bunch of cocky adults to demand their rights. We are servants. We've given up our rights to the One we serve.

God, in His marvelous wisdom, has the divine fine line of seeing us as servants and as children. Of demanding obedience. Of heaping love. He doesn't call us anywhere in Scripture adults of God. He calls us children of God. There is no verse that says, "Why don't you just grow up?" Plenty of verses encourage us to grow, some verses push us toward maturity, but we'll never fully grow up spiritually. Our loving Father hangs in there with us, assuring us of our value and bringing in the necessary discipline—never too harsh or too easy—to help us to grow to take on the family attributes.

"We are precious in His sight." Every child should have the privilege of singing that. Somebody needs to be around to make sure children know it.

We can learn a lot from children. I had gone to visit my daughter and her family during the winter. My oldest grandson and I got bundled up against the strong cold winds and walked through the snow carrying the circular sled. Many people had the same idea, and Jonathan enjoyed watching them going down the huge mountain on their sleds. I could only imagine how far down the bottom of the slope looked to him because it looked pretty far to this grandfather.

Jonathan and I surveyed the situation a while. He looked up at me and looked down the slope. He looked up at me again and down the slope again. I wondered what he was thinking, although I had a pretty good idea.

One million children, most from middle-class families, run away each year.

Finally, Jonathan placed a little mittened hand in mine and said, "Let's go, Gramps!"

That is one of the greatest compliments I have ever had. He trusted me. He knew I'd be on the circular sled with him, holding him tight as we went round and round, up and down, this way and that.

He had faith in me.

That was not only one of the greatest compliments I've ever had; that was one of the greatest lessons in faith I've ever had.

"And a little child shall lead them" (Isa. 11:6).

QUOTE

In 1962, 40 different categories of statistics relating to national morality broke. . . . The only thing that happened in 1962 to explain this is that we took prayer out of our public school system.

—Carman

FAMILY

■ *One man and one woman united in marriage for life and, if God chooses, children either biological or adopted.*

SCRIPTURE

GENESIS 2:18–24

The LORD God said, "It is not good that man should be alone; I will make him a helper comparable to him." . . . And the LORD God caused a deep sleep to fall on Adam, and he slept; and He took one of his ribs, and closed up the flesh in its place. Then the rib which the LORD God had taken from man He made into a woman, and He brought her to the man. And Adam said:

> "This is now bone of my bones
> And flesh of my flesh;
> She shall be called Woman,
> Because she was taken out of Man."

Therefore a man shall leave his father and mother and be joined to his wife, and they shall become one flesh.

COMMENTARY

This is probably one of the most familiar passages in the entire Bible. Children learn about Adam and Eve in Sunday school. Unfortunately, our tendency is to gloss over it because we've heard it all before.

But the Word of God is so wonderful, so powerful, and so full of truth that despite its familiarity, there is much gold to be mined from its depths. The same is true of the story of creation, specifically the first family.

The first family did not live in the White House. The first family lived in a luscious home prepared for them by their Creator. What an ideal setting! Nightly, their Creator would visit them. I would think they anticipated these evening interludes with Omniscience.

I often wonder what Omnipotence sounded like walking in the Garden. One can almost imagine Eve hurrying up with supper—if they had supper—and saying, "Adam, it's almost time for Him to come." Can you imagine welcoming Omnipresence into *your* family after supper?

God is relational. He made man "after His own image" so that they could fellowship together. God saw that even though Adam was surrounded by every sort of animal—in pairs, no less—he needed someone to correspond to him. God gently put Adam (Ish, in the Hebrew) to sleep and fashioned Eve (Isha, in the Hebrew) from his rib.

When Adam awoke, he was ecstatic with God's handiwork and exclaimed in our vernacular, "Wow, this is it!" Whatever Eve's response, that was the beginning of the first family. The man and the woman were incredibly alike and mysteriously different.

> As the first community to which a person is attached and the first authority under which a person learns to live, the family established society's most basic values.
> —Charles Colson

But they didn't live happily ever after. They became the first dysfunctional family.

The '92 presidential election did us a favor. It brought family values to everyone's attention. Very few people saw it as a pastel issue; most vehemently saw it as black or white. Nightly news blasted it into our homes.

Pulpits alluded to it. And mothers and fathers with 2.7 children scratched their heads. And a lone woman in the house with 4 children scratched her head. And a single man and a single woman who shared an apartment scratched their heads.

So, what was right? Who was right? Is there a right?

Before we look more in depth at the subject, let's define some terms.

A *value* is something that's important to you. That's not a complicated concept. Values—or what's important to people—determine what they ought and ought not to do. We call that our value system. For instance, if a person values his car, he knows he ought not park too close to another car in a parking lot, especially if he values a car door that is free of dents. That's his "parking lot ought." Or his "driving ought not" is not to drive excessively fast and dart in and out of traffic. His value system—valuing his car—has determined his oughts and ought nots.

But there's a hitch. Even though a fellow may really like his car, sometimes he wants to park where he wants and drive any way he wants. So he has a problem. His "ought to" and his "want to" don't always match.

Sound familiar? Christians, as well as non-Christians, share in the struggle that what we want to do doesn't always match what we should do. The common solution? Change the rules. Change the oughts. It certainly eases guilt.

Oftentimes, our values are determined by our behavior. And the creed today in society is this: self-control is out; self-expression is in. For example, suppose there was a country where there was no food and everyone was starving. Imagine this scenario. The government in that country comes out with a report: "We have good news for our nation. We have *redefined* the minimum daily nutritional standards. So you really aren't starving!"

Everything looks wonderful on paper. The leaders look great. The leaders wouldn't have to do anything because suddenly, there is no problem. They changed the rules.

You know what we've done? We've changed the rules, too. We used to say to teenagers, "Don't have sex before you're married." But now we say,

> Apart from religious influence, the family is the most important unit of society.
> —Billy Graham

FAMILY

■ *One man and one woman united in marriage for life and, if God chooses, children either biological or adopted.*

Grandparents or other relatives are now raising some 1.5 million American children.

In a recent survey by *Career and Colleges* magazine, teens were asked, "Whom do you most admire?" Mom and Dad were the top choices. For girls, 79 percent picked their mothers; for boys, 73 percent picked their fathers.

"Be sure to practice safe sex." We changed the oughts and ought nots. Sure must make a lot of teens feel better. Sure looks better on paper. Sure alleviates a lot of pressure on leaders.

We've tried to do the very same thing with the definition of family. We've gone from the "form" to a "feeling" definition.

In fact, 22 percent of those polled in a *Life* magazine survey thought that a family consisted of people who were related by blood, marriage, or adoption. Twenty-two percent? The magazine went on to explain that the definition preferred by 74 percent was much broader. They thought a family consisted of people who loved and cared for one another. (Actually, people didn't come up with these definitions off the top of their heads. They were given a choice of answers and could choose a definition shown to them.)

Sounds pretty cozy. And it almost sounds right.

But *feeling* doesn't define family. Cozy doesn't cut it.

If we defined a family as a group of people who feel good about one another, some could say, "My goodness, we're not a family. I don't feel good about my wife or anyone else in this house!" If commitment defined family, some men are more "family" with their workplaces than their homes. If caring and commitment defined family, two men who have strong feelings for each other could be a family. Or if children didn't feel caring and committed to their parents, they could divorce them. Or if the parents had strong words with a rebellious child, they could disown her and fracture the family.

Early in life, we were taught not to base a relationship on feelings. Ask any pregnant teenage girl. She'll agree. Cozy didn't cut it.

Even in the business world, we don't work this way. We don't look at someone and say, "So, do you feel good about this contract? Well, gee, so do I. I feel really good about it. Naw, let's not sign anything. I feel too good about it to mess it up with legal jargon." What will the judge say to that when you come to him with your messed-up noncontract? Cozy doesn't cut it.

Taking this line of reasoning one step farther, suppose one day, God got really put out with you. "Well, sorry, but you just can't stay in My family anymore. I don't feel good about you." How horrible! And how contrary to the doctrine that nothing shall snatch you out of His hand (John 10:28). Spiritually, we are children in a forever family.

We could look at it another way. Suppose you woke up feeling lousy. You didn't want to read your Bible. You didn't want to pray. You were depressed. You had a headache. You didn't feel good about your walk with the Lord at all. You didn't even feel saved. What a blessed assurance that you don't have to feel saved to be saved! By faith you received Him, according to Ephesians 2:8–9, and feelings have nothing to do with it. It's faith, not warm fuzzies, in the family of God.

Let's see what God says about earthly families. The word *family* is mentioned throughout the Bible. There is a common thread throughout the passages where it is mentioned. There is no exception to this common thread in the Word of God. *In the Bible, the word* family *always refers to people who are attached biologically or legally.*

Think of Joseph. What a story! You can read about Joseph in Genesis 37—50. This is not a "Seven Brides for Seven Brothers" kind of story. This is more like "Sibling Rivalry Revisited." His brothers hated him and did terrible things to him. But at the end of the story, Joseph, having been greatly honored of God in spite of his siblings, identified himself to them as their brother. Although it is a long story in the book of Genesis and there are plenty of plots and subplots, warm and cozy doesn't describe any of them. But he still called those scoundrels his brothers.

Something was fundamentally deeper there than feelings.

God calls Himself Father. There are more than 275 references to God as Father in the New Testament, with more than 100 of them in John's gospel. God uses legal terminology to describe how we belong to Him, "to *redeem* those who were under the law, that we might receive the *adoption* as sons. And because you are *sons,* God has sent forth the Spirit of His Son into your hearts, crying out, 'Abba, Father!' Therefore you are *no longer a slave* but a *son,* and if a *son,* then an *heir* of God" (Gal. 4:5–7, emphasis added).

Looking at how the word *family* is used in Scripture, we can come up with this definition: *Family*—"one man and one woman united in marriage for life and, if God chooses, children either biological or adopted."

If you look in a modern dictionary, you will find different definitions for the term *family.* We would do well, however, to stick with the Creator's definition. And His definition is grounded in form, not feeling.

In Genesis 2, God is describing what happens when one is married: "Therefore a man shall leave his father and mother and be joined to his wife, and they shall become one flesh" (v. 24). God is presupposing—which seems like a strange word referring to God—that a family has both a father and a mother. He does not say, "Leave his father *or* mother." He uses *and.* God sees a father *and* a mother in a home as His norm.

But that doesn't work in our society. His norm isn't our norm. Instead of our adjusting to His norm, we change the definition. In our world, when a kid gets married, the bride or groom may not leave a father and a mother

The Census Bureau estimates that the percentage of cohabiting unmarried couples has doubled since 1980 and older couples are keeping pace.

In 1960, one in twenty children was born to an unmarried mother. Today the rate approaches one in three.

FAMILY

■ *One man and one woman united in marriage for life and, if God chooses, children either biological or adopted.*

because the father has already taken off. Or the mother may have already left. Or the young groom or sweet bride isn't sure who is being left because of spending alternate weekends at Mother's or Father's house for years.

See, we say, God's definition just doesn't work.

But changing the definition doesn't work for the same reason telling the starving people in that drought-stricken country that they aren't starving doesn't work. First, a principle of life is being violated. Second, the wrong can't be righted if everyone agrees that it really isn't wrong; it only appears that way.

And do you know who ends up holding the short end of the stick?

Single parents.

Precious, struggling, lonely, tired, frustrated single parents are told it isn't so bad. God didn't mean His definition for everybody, and besides, He is used to our breaking His laws. Since this law is broken so often, He is probably used to this one getting broken. No big deal.

Oh, yes, it is. Ask a single mom or dad.

Ask a kid who misses his daddy.

Ask a girl who doesn't have a mother.

As politically incorrect as it is, the term *broken home* is still the most accurate description of a home where Mom or Dad is absent. I honestly don't say this to be discouraging. I was raised by a single mom, for the most part. I understand the pain. I am writing—and God knows my heart—out of a deep desire to help families, and that certainly includes single-parent homes.

So let's follow this to a biblical conclusion. Don't be discouraged and give up reading because you don't fit the definition. Hang in there with me.

In trying to see God's ideal, we need to wade through some telling statistics. The National Commission on Children noted that in a single-parent home, children had more problems with mental health; there were more problems with juvenile delinquency, more alcohol and drug problems, more teen pregnancies, and more dropping out of school.

You know what our culture says? "No problem. We can fix this. We need more money for education. Let's create a lottery or somehow come up with the money. If these kids knew better, they'd make wiser choices."

You don't have to know a lot of Scripture to know education isn't going to solve such massive problems. You don't need to know Scripture. Period. All you have to do is look around.

We are self-destructing. We have changed the rules. We've lost hope for anything better. We're stuck in the mire of our muddy substandards.

> **W**hat kids want to be when they grow up: 39 percent happily married, 24 percent rich.

FAMILY

God hates divorce but loves divorced people. He hates divorce because He knows the statistics; He sees the broken lives; He feels their pain. He has already looked into the prisons and the juvenile homes. He has already seen the hospitals. While we've been busy compiling our statistics, God has been acutely aware of the sorrow and has seen the hearts behind the statistics before we ever got started.

Newsweek magazine tracked kids from dysfunctional homes over a period of years to see what made the difference in the ones who "made it," that is, the ones who grew up to be responsible adults. The researchers thought that the adults would have a great inner resilience.

But they found that the adults who had come from a broken or dysfunctional background had one thing in common, and it was not inner resilience. The tremendous thing they shared, *in every single case,* was that they had a responsible adult who came alongside them during their lives.

That was true in my life. My father died when I was an infant. As a lonely adolescent, I delivered newspapers. A Sunday school teacher at our little church was discerning that this fellow needed a man in his life. Craig would wait on the street where I delivered papers so that he could buy one from me. Then he would talk to me. Craig didn't know I was aware of the fact that he had the paper delivered to his home. He used buying a paper from me, which he did not need, as an excuse to talk to me, which I desperately needed.

I believe with all my heart that I could have been one of those statistics had it not been for the grace of God using my mom and a man named Craig. He came alongside me. He showed me what a man talked like and acted like. He listened to me. I had no inner resilience. But I had a friend.

I was a better father to Andy and Becky because of this man, who went out of his way to befriend a lonely boy. My grandchildren will profit from a sensitive man talking to this paperboy.

What a tremendous opportunity we have in the body of Christ to reach out to children in our churches or neighborhoods in single-parent homes! We could be a "Craig" to someone.

But denying the problem exists, or changing the rules, accomplishes nothing in anyone's life. We have come so far from God's ideal in the family that people think it's abnormal to be married for a long time. A couple took a little trip to celebrate the twenty-fifth wedding anniversary. They didn't expect employees in the little shops to act as if it were some quirk of nature when the proud husband told them of his "bride" of twenty-five years. They called to others to gaze on this odd couple. The wife said, "I couldn't figure out what we'd done. I thought maybe we were the millionth customer or

Five out of six adult criminals are from broken homes.

A family is a place where principles are hammered and honed on the anvil of everyday living.
—Charles Swindoll

Family **363**

FAMILY

■ *One man and one woman united in marriage for life and, if God chooses, children either biological or adopted.*

something. Then they kept asking how we did it. I wanted to say, 'Well, we just walked in the door. Where's the prize money?' But they explained what they meant. Apparently, they don't know a lot of people married for twenty-five years. I didn't think that was unusual. I wondered when being married over ten years became somewhat of an oddity."

Turn back to look at our definition again. God apparently doesn't see a couple married for a long period of time as anything but the norm.

Name a dozen couples you know where neither spouse has been divorced. God's norm isn't the norm in society. A healthy family takes a lot of work. A lot. And a few miracles sprinkled along the way.

Let me mention something about mothers. Some mothers have to work outside the home. My mom did. She worked to feed us and clothe us and put shelter over our heads. She left early in the morning and came home late.

I understand there are those who *have* to work outside the home. My mom did. But that didn't lessen my loneliness.

A recent poll showed that 67 percent of the women who work do so by choice and not by necessity. What values do children pick up? The values of parents who are never there?

The father needs to be in the home. Not dropping in for visits. Not coming home from work after the children are in bed. He needs to be in the home, loving the mother and loving the children. The mother may set the emotional tone for the home, but the father sets the value system. If work is more important than his wife and children, the children will pick up on this value system in a minute. They internalize, "Work is more important than I am. Therefore, I must not be very important at all." They'll spend the rest of their lives trying to get someone's attention with good behavior or bad behavior—it doesn't matter to them as long as someone pays attention.

This chapter is not a how-to chapter. There are many excellent books on the market on how to have a successful family. What I have wanted us to see together is the basic definition of a family. This is a what-is chapter.

Perhaps you are saying, "It would be wonderful if we had this home with the picket fence, the hardworking yet committed husband, and the wife who stays home and cares for perfectly behaved children, with the dog nestled nearby the open hearth. Wake up and smell the coffee. It just isn't like that."

I know. God knows.

His ideal, however, remains.

He is in the business of binding up broken hearts.

Do you want to break the chain? Or do you want your children and grandchildren to reproduce a messed-up home? Of course, you want to break the chain. Let me give you some practical ways to deal with the negative traditions that you may have picked up along the way from your background.

Your parenting skills and your "spousing" skills were greatly influenced by what you saw around you as you were growing up. The negative, as well as the positive, things in your home seeped into your soul. You probably were not aware of it, but they were seeping in all the time. Day in. Day out. Year in. Year out. They are deeply ingrained into your personality. They overflow in the way you teach your children and respond to your spouse.

If you are single, they are ingrained. You just may not have seen them manifested yet. Take heart! You may be well ahead of your married friends in breaking negative traditions because you have the luxury of time to become aware of them and to deal with them.

By traditions, I don't mean what night you put the Christmas tree up and what kind of dressing you had with the turkey at Thanksgiving. I am talking about what unique things made your family into your family. I am even talking about deeper level things than who always got to use the remote control to the television in your home or who would have controlled it had there been one in your home when you were raised.

Forty-two percent of children of divorced parents hadn't seen their father for a year or longer.

The traditions were unconsciously passed down. The way Dad talked to Mom. The way Mom looked at Dad. The way they talked to you. Meals. Holidays. Tuesdays. Birthdays. Saturday mornings. Graduations. Death. Sicknesses. Bedtimes. Report cards. Shouting. Whispering. Slamming doors. Retreating into silence. Drinking. Pouting.

A million things that made up your life. Daily things. Sometimes inconsistency was the only consistent thing. But you know what? Your emotional computer picked it all up. And try as you might, hitting the delete button hasn't worked.

Let's look at some ways to break negative traditions that you don't want to bring into your home. I am working on this in my life, and it isn't easy. But it's worth the effort.

First, *identify* the negative family traditions. Sometimes this is more apparent than others. A hint would be when your spouse says, "You sound just like your father [or mother]!" Among Christians especially, trying to see negative things that were passed down may seem dishonoring to parents. If we understand our parents reacted the way they did because of what they learned from their parents, it is easier to understand where the negative traditions came from. If we don't identify them in our parents, we'll never see them in ourselves. Pray that God will help you to scale sacred walls and remember the negative as well as the positive things.

FAMILY

■ *One man and one woman united in marriage for life and, if God chooses, children either biological or adopted.*

Be specific when you identify things. I know this is really hard, but if the past is unresolved, it becomes the present. It also demands your emotional focus. What happens to you when you are emotionally focused on anything—conscious or unconscious? That's right, you take on the characteristics of the thing you are focusing on. (That gives a whole new meaning to the song, "Turn Your Eyes Upon Jesus," doesn't it?)

Second, *refocus*. Make a list of how you would like your spouse and children to remember you. What specific behaviors do you want to model?

One pastor said he wanted to be remembered by his children as one who laughed. Of course, he listed more than that, but he is working daily on keeping a light heart with his spouse and children. Pray through the list specifically. The things on your list become like electrical fence posts that shock you when you overstep your goals and boundaries.

Third, *take responsibility* for your choices without blaming. You see, when you let others in your past dictate your choices, you are admitting they have a great deal of control over you. They are pretty much mastering your life. That isn't what any of us want. We want one Lord and one Master whom we obey. How can anyone serve two masters? No one can. It's either your parents or Jesus Christ. No more excuses.

Fourth, *seek* a positive role model. Find a person who shows you what a healthy, Christian family looks like. If you are a man, find a Christian man whom you have observed honoring his wife and children. Spend time with him. Lots of time. If you're a woman, find a godly woman who respects her husband and loves her children. Spend time with her. Lots of time. You know what you're doing? You're being remodeled.

The original modeling took years and years, and the remodeling won't happen over a quick lunch with someone. To use a computer analogy, it's more like slow reprogramming.

God, in His grace, has given us a way to reverse negative things. Suppose you were raised in a home where Dad ran when the pressure got hot and heavy. Or Mom withdrew. Or the refrigerator held the bottled answer. Or lying seemed to work. Some of these coping mechanisms could be the operational style in your home now.

Jesus Christ is greater than tradition. That sounds trite, but it is the truth. If we were left to the mercy of how we were programmed in our homes, we would all be in bad shape.

Nonetheless, the One who created the first family is the One who is interested in yours and in mine. The God who adopted you into His forever family knows how to make earthly families work.

The USA has the highest divorce rate of any industrialized nation. Italy has the lowest divorce rate of any industrialized nation.

FAMILY

The family was instituted before the church. Although it is the smallest unit in society, it is the most vital one. Once these little foundational units start crumbling, the entire superstructure—commonly called a nation—falls apart, one family at a time.

Family—one man and one woman united in marriage for life and, if God chooses, children either biological or adopted.

We can't change God's ideal. Well, I guess we can. Adam and Eve did. And humankind has been paying the price ever since.

God provided the Cross to break their negative family traditions.

You could call the Cross God's family tree.

The former president of Columbia Bible College, Dr. J. Robertson McQuilken, resigned to care for his wife, Muriel. She has Alzheimer's disease, and her personality and behavior are quite different from those of the girl Dr. McQuilken married. In a moving tribute to his wife, he summed up how she had so faithfully cared for him and the children over the years. He said, "I don't *have* to take care of Muriel. I *get* to take care of Muriel."

What a visual aid for the family! Sticking with it. Priorities. We can only guess what their children are learning from watching Dad take care of Mom. One man and one woman for life.

Positive traditions.

 APPLICATION

Researching family trees can be humbling. Some branches we are more proud to claim than others. Some families would love to lop the whole tree down right at the base of the trunk.

God is different. He takes care of the branches on His tree. No matter the background. In fact, in John 15, He speaks of caring tenderly for the branches.

We're back in a garden setting again, but this time, not the Garden of Eden. The garden is not as important as the Gardener. The One tending the branches is significant.

The Lord Jesus calls Himself the Vine. Life flows from the Vine to the family branches. And the Father oversees it all as the Vinedresser. You and I are the branches on this tree.

Most branches really want to produce fruit. They want to produce fruit most of all in their families. So they work and work. They squint their little branch eyes and try all the harder. These weary branches don't just do this in their families, they do it in every part of their lives. Sweat. Worry. Work. Sweat. Worry. Work. Branches become tired and droop.

FAMILY

■ *One man and one woman united in marriage for life and, if God chooses, children either biological or adopted.*

But the good news is that branches don't have to work that hard to produce fruit. The job description of a branch is to *bear* fruit, not *produce* it.

Listen to the Vine speak, "Abide in Me, and I in you. As the branch cannot bear fruit of itself, unless it abides in the vine, neither can you, unless you abide in Me. I am the vine, you are the branches. He who abides in Me, and I in him, bears much fruit; for without Me you can do nothing" (John 15:4–5).

In our lives as well as our families, the life of the Vine flowing through our branches enables us to do what we need to do.

He is very clear that apart from that principle, we can't do it. We can try and work and sweat.

The principle for having a healthy family is the same principle for having a healthy Christian life: the life of Jesus Christ flows through you. *You don't have to do it alone.*

The discourse in John 15 about the Vine and the branches follows the wonderful passage in John 14 that is a favorite of many people. The Vine is talking about His family and the Father of the family. He says, "In My Father's house are many mansions; if it were not so, I would have told you. I go to prepare a place for you" (John 14:2).

Isn't that a lovely way to describe a family? The Father and the Son fixing up a home for the family.

Whereas the first family became dysfunctional, the last family will be complete.

I can hardly wait.

> **M**ore wives (24 percent) than husbands (18 percent) said they thought at one time or another their marriage might not last.
> —*Modern Maturity*

■ *People who accept you just as you are and love you too much to leave you that way.*

FRIENDS

PROVERBS 13:20 NASB

SCRIPTURE

He who walks with wise men will be wise, but the companion of fools will suffer harm.

COMMENTARY

Who influences your life the most? It is a question I've heard asked of presidential candidates, actors, teachers, and just plain folks like you and me.

Proverbs 13:20 promises that you will be affected significantly by people you choose to relate to. You will become wise by associating with those who are wise, or you will suffer the painful consequences of imprudent relationships.

What exactly does the Bible mean when it refers to someone being wise? A wise man or woman is someone who asks of every opportunity and invitation, What is the wisest thing for me to do (1) in light of my past, present, and future and (2) in light of what God says? On the other hand, a fool is someone who knows the difference between right and wrong and chooses to do wrong anyway. A fool is the person who buys the pack of cigarettes, reads the warning on the side, and engages in this harmful behavior anyway!

Proverbs 13:20 promises that change will occur if you associate with wise people. By spending time with wise people, your life will change for the better. Likewise, if you associate with fools, you will change. Scripture does not say you will become a fool; instead it says you "will suffer harm." It's a choice that seems simple.

Still, my appointment calendar is filled with folks who have chosen to be companions of fools and now suffer the harm Proverbs mentions. This kind of negative behavior is good reason for us to take a closer look at this principle.

A CLOSER LOOK

Friends have such an amazing impact on us because we are driven by a desire to be accepted. Everyone wants to fit in somewhere. I have noticed two things about the need to fit in. First, the kind of home life you grew up in will determine the intensity of your need to fit in. If your home life was insecure, you will feel the need to fit in far more than the person who grew up in a secure environment. Second, your relationship with your dad will

FRIENDS

■ *People who accept you just as you are and love you too much to leave you that way.*

greatly affect your need to fit in. The more insecure that relationship, the greater lengths you will go to in order to be accepted.

Acceptance plays a significant role in friendships. However, acceptance is not a sufficient reason for choosing friends. God's criteria for friends go beyond acceptance. God knows that you need friends who will love you, not merely accept you. *A real friend will accept you the way you are but will love you too much to leave you that way.* That's hard for some people to swallow. The argument I hear repeatedly goes something like this: "A friend who loves me will not try to change me." That sounds good, but it's the kind of "warm fuzzy" the world would have you focus on instead of looking at the truth of the situation. Have you ever had a friend who was sinking deeper into destructive behavior? Did you sit by and tell yourself it was none of your business, or did you step in and intervene in his best interest? I hope you were the kind of friend who cared enough to do what was best for your friend. A mistake the church makes is to listen to what the world says about acceptance and love. God accepts you just as you are, yet He is continually at work to conform you to His image. That is love, and He is the standard you must pattern your behavior by.

A loving friend will tell you the truth. I've seen many people make bad decisions while their "friends" stood around and said nothing. "It's none of my business" is our way of justifying not taking a stand with friends we know are making unwise decisions. I've seen people make terrible decisions that range from whether to get married, stay married, have children, or buy a larger home. Often friends can clearly see a couple about to make a disastrous decision, but they never say a word because interfering would be presumptuous. Seek friends who will warn you when you are about to do something that will cause you great harm down the road! Some call that interference. A better term would be *tough love*.

A friend who loves will be more concerned about what is best for you than being accepted by you. Although all of us want our friends to accept us, real friends will sacrifice acceptance to do what is right. A real friend's number one concern is not the relationship—it's *you*! How many of us are willing to go that far to be a true friend?

What kind of friends do you have? Are they wise or are they fools? If your friends are dragging you down, you have two choices:

1. Step back. The first thing you have to do is conduct the relationship on your terms, not theirs. You set the agenda; you lead the relationship. You decide how often you spend time with these friends. You decide what you do, where you go. It is essential to your well-being to know your boundaries and make them clear to your friends—churched or unchurched.

2. Step away. Some relationships will require you to do more than step back. No matter what you try to do, the relationship keeps pulling you down and pulling you away from the values that belong first in your life. When that happens, nothing will fix things. The toughest thing you have to do in these circumstances is to step away completely. I can hear the objection: "But what's going to happen to them if I just walk away? I'm the only Christian they know." Or "I can't do that. They will think I consider myself too good for them!" I understand how you feel, and I don't mean to be insensitive to these questions. However, there is another question: What's going to happen if you don't walk away?

That is a very difficult question to consider, but a necessary one. You must never sacrifice your relationship with God for the sake of a relationship with another person. You must always remember that your relationship with God positions you to affect the lives of others. If your relationship with God is not primary, you will not be the friend you need to be. If God loves them (as He loves us all), don't you think He is capable of putting someone in their lives to take your place?

God has a plan for your friendships because He knows your friends determine the quality and direction of your life. The real issue that must be answered is this: Is God the Lord of your friendships? I have never seen anyone make a life-altering decision for Christ who did not have to make some adjustments to friendships. Was it painful? Often it was. Was it worth it? Absolutely. In the long run, the decision to walk wisely determined future success. Before you can have the kind of friends who will positively influence your life, you have to become that kind of friend.

When my son, Andy, was a college student, he associated with a friend who was not on the same wavelength Andy was on. To say he was wild would be an understatement. They both loved music and enjoyed playing together. Still, even in Andy's youth, he recognized that it was a relationship he needed to look at wisely. He tried stepping back, but it didn't work. He had to tell his friend that they could no longer be friends. It came down to this: don't call; don't come by the house; we can't be friends any longer. I know it wasn't an easy decision for Andy to make, but in light of his purpose for living (to glorify God), he knew it was something he had to do.

A few years ago, Andy was preaching. When it was time for the invitation, he saw a young man coming down the aisle who looked familiar, but he couldn't remember who he was. When the man reached the front and shook Andy's hand, he said, "Andy, do you remember me?" Instantly, it came back to him. He was the guy he'd had to step away from years ago. With a gulp, Andy said, "Yes, I remember you. Are you still speaking to me?"

> **S**piritual friendship includes a willingness to confront, to challenge motives, actions, and priorities.
> —Gordon T. Smith

> **S**ome friendships are made by nature, some by contract, some by interest, and some by souls.
> —Jeremy Taylor

The fellow laughed and said, "Yes, Andy. Do you remember when you told me you couldn't be my friend anymore?" Andy nodded. Then he said, "Andy, I know why you had to do that. Now that I've asked Christ into my life, I can see why it was necessary."

The bottom line was this: God loved Andy too much to let him stay in the relationship, and He loved this fellow enough to bring someone else into the picture who could bring him to Christ! God knows our needs so much better than we do. Although Andy probably felt badly when he walked away that day, God knew the big picture. He understood what Andy needed and what his friend needed. The world would have called Andy insensitive and uncaring. Looking back, he was the best friend anyone could want because he did what was wise, not what felt good. They both grew from the experience and today share a relationship that God has blessed.

APPLICATION

You must make God the Lord of your friendships, or you will end up suffering harm because you have chosen inappropriate relationships. Are you spending time with wise friends, who accept you but are willing to risk the friendship you share to tell you the truth? If so, thank God for their commitment to you! If you are walking with friends who are fools, friends who know the difference between right and wrong and do wrong anyway, consider where the relationships are headed and change direction. A wise friend never stays in a relationship just for acceptance. A wise friend is willing to risk the relationship in the best interest of a friend.

■ *The feeling of being alone or isolated.*

LONELINESS

2 TIMOTHY 4:16–17

SCRIPTURE

At my first defense no one stood with me, but all forsook me. May it not be charged against them. But the Lord stood with me and strengthened me.

COMMENTARY

Paul was imprisoned in Rome when he wrote this letter to his son in the faith, Timothy. More than likely, he knew that his own death was imminent. It is sobering to read how he admonished Timothy to keep the faith and to finish well. Paul wanted to finish well: "I have fought the good fight, I have finished the race, I have kept the faith" (2 Tim. 4:7).

What an incredible statement! Every believer should long for those words to describe him or her. Not everyone finishes well. And Paul knew it. He referred to some who were troublemakers. He mentioned Jannes and Jambres, who had opposed Moses (2 Tim. 3:8). And then he got closer to home by mentioning Demas's forsaking him, and Crescens and Titus and Alexander the coppersmith for not standing with him (2 Tim. 4:10, 14).

We would think out of all the people Paul had led to Christ, some would support him during his time of imprisonment. Paul, however, was considered as an enemy of Judaism. He specifically tried to reach the Jews and used texts from the Law and the Prophets, including a lengthy quote from Isaiah (Acts 28:17–31). The Bible tells us that some believed and some didn't (v. 24), although he preached to them "from morning till evening" (v. 23). After so many of the Jews rejected what he was preaching, Paul let them know he would preach to Gentiles (v. 28). That caused no small stir, and Paul was not winning friends with his statement!

We do a disservice to the biblical characters and ourselves when we think the biblical characters did not have feelings like we do.

Paul faced prison alone. He, as a man, must have felt isolated. Joseph was lonely after his brothers threw him into the pit. Moses was lonely when he led the squabbling children of Israel out of Egypt. (One can be very lonely though surrounded by lots of people.) David was lonely as he evaded Saul's pursuit, providing the backdrop for some of the great psalms. Jeremiah and so many of the prophets were lonely men. In the New Testament, Mary, no doubt, was lonely when she was expecting—out of wedlock—her Son. Surely, few of the village women believed her incredible story and wanted to associate with her.

Loneliness

373

LONELINESS

■ *The feeling of being alone or isolated.*

The biblical characters were often isolated, estranged, and desolate. In the last months of Paul's life, he gives us the wonderful secret of what to do in times of intense loneliness and pain.

Let's take a closer look.

A CLOSER LOOK

What was Paul's secret in dealing with loneliness?

First of all, he was aware of the presence of God. He said, "But the Lord stood with me and strengthened me" (2 Tim. 4:17). Paul couldn't change or fix his situation, but in that lonely damp prison cell he was aware that One was with him.

God had strengthened him at other times during his ministry. After some had resisted his preaching, Paul literally shook his garments out and exclaimed, "Your blood be upon your own heads; I am clean" (Acts 18:6). "The Lord spoke to Paul in the night by a vision, 'Do not be afraid, but speak, and do not keep silent; for I am with you'" (Acts 18:9–10). The implication is that Paul had been afraid. He had feelings just like we do.

On another occasion, Paul was brought before the Sanhedrin, and the Sadducees and Pharisees got into a heated argument about him. It got so raucous that the commander was afraid Paul would be torn to pieces. The Bible says, "But the following night the Lord stood by him" (Acts 23:11).

Paul was a mighty warrior for the faith, but he was still a man and he still experienced a range of strong emotions. But Paul was aware of the presence of God in each predicament.

Another secret Paul had in dealing with loneliness was his awareness of God's strengthening him (2 Tim. 4:17). We often quote Philippians 4:13: "I can do all things through Christ who strengthens me." Paul was in jail when he wrote that verse, also.

The Lord strengthened Paul. Paul was infused with strength. He knew no one could take his life without God's permission. He had God's strength coursing through his spirit.

When the Lord Jesus Christ was in the Garden of Gethsemane, "an angel appeared to Him from heaven, strengthening Him" (Luke 22:43). We should never be too proud to ask for strength. Jesus Himself needed to be strengthened in His hour of trial.

Paul was aware of His strengthening in his hour of trial.

The last secret Paul had in dealing with loneliness was his awareness that he had an awesome privilege of fulfilling God's purpose for his life. What

> **J**esus frequently sought out "lonely places" for prayer and meditation. Loneliness may be turned to solitude when it is dedicated to a cause, a project, or God. When loneliness turns to solitude, its promise is fully experienced.
> —Steven S. Ivy

incredible encouragement that is—to know we are part of God's providential plan.

Paul was aware of the presence of God; he was aware that the Lord stood by him, when others didn't, and strengthened him; and he was aware that he was supernaturally enabled until God had fulfilled through him all that He wanted to.

But in his aloneness, he treasured his friends. After mentioning those who did not stand with him, he wrote that Luke was with him. And he wanted Mark to come. He mentioned four people by name who were with him: Eubulus, Pudens, Linus, and Claudia (2 Tim. 4:21). Isn't it amazing to realize that we know absolutely nothing else about those four people other than they stuck with the apostle Paul? That has to be one of the greatest compliments they could be paid!

I hope and pray that I am a faithful friend to some lonely pastor out there. I hope and pray that I am that kind of friend to my grandchildren—that when they feel terribly lonely, they know Gramps will be there for them. I have friends like that in my life, and I praise God for them.

Paul asked Timothy to bring a cloak with him, obviously to ward off the chill in the damp prison, and some books, "especially the parchments" (2 Tim. 4:13). The books may have been the Gospels, and the parchments may have been the Hebrew Scriptures. We are not told. But knowing the apostle Paul, who wrote about the precious Word of God to Timothy (2 Tim. 3:15–17), we may assume that he hungered for his copies of the Scriptures.

William Tyndale, who was imprisoned fifteen hundred years after Paul for putting the Word of God into the language of the common people, wrote a friend to bring him a "warmer cap, something to patch my leggings, a wool shirt, and most of all my Hebrew Bible." Tyndale knew what the apostle Paul knew—in the hour of great loneliness, the Word of God is of great comfort.

Feeling isolated and alone is a feeling that seeps into the bones. We all experience it from time to time. Some experience it for only a short while; others for a lifetime.

We can take comfort from the biblical characters, and specifically from the apostle Paul, that God's presence is with us; He is strengthening us (whether or not we feel that He is); and we are being used in a greater way than we imagine fulfilling His plan in our lives.

We can take comfort from the Word of God.

And we need to make sure that we are faithful friends to others who may be hurting and lonely.

> **M**ost loneliness results from insulation rather than isolation.
> —Dr. James Dobson

> **N**early half the population honestly feel that nobody knows them.
> —*The Day America Told the Truth*

LONELINESS

■ *The feeling of being alone or isolated.*

The Lord Jesus Christ was totally alone as He faced and endured the Cross. As man, He was alone because the Bible says that "all the disciples forsook Him and fled" (Matt. 26:56). And as the God-man, He was totally alone when He cried, "My God, My God, why have You forsaken Me?" (Matt. 27:46). He knows what loneliness feels like. He knows as well the joy of being carried through the loneliest of times on the wings of faith—faith that His Father and your God will never abandon one He loves. In this way Jesus stands as the ultimate example of One who faced the perils of loneliness without losing heart.

APPLICATION

We may never be thrown into the pit by our families, lead a group of squabbling people, tend sheep on hills, be forsaken by the whole city because of a virgin birth, or sit alone in prison for our faith. But we still have pits, lonely hills, and prisons.

We belong to One who knows exactly what we feel.

But unlike Him, we will never, ever have to ask, "My God, why have You forsaken me?"

He is standing with us and strengthening us. He will never leave us or forsake us (Heb. 13:5). Our feelings may betray us, but the truth is, He is with us.

Just read the parchments.

QUOTES

We have Sovereignty standing with us.
—Charles Stanley

Do not hide Your face from me;
Do not turn Your servant away in anger;
You have been my help;
Do not leave me nor forsake me,
O God of my salvation.
When my father and my mother forsake me,
Then the LORD will take care of me.
—Psalm 27:9–10

It is not until Jesus is all you have that you know He is all you need.
—Anonymous

■ Agape *love—sacrificial commitment, dedicated to the well-being of another.* Phileo *love—brotherly affection.* Eros *love—sexual affection.*

LOVE

1 JOHN 4:19 NASB

SCRIPTURE

W̲e love, because He first loved us.

COMMENTARY

In the 105 verses in 1 John, love is mentioned more than forty times. That's a lot of verses in such a short epistle about love. With seven words, however, the apostle John summarizes his teaching on this important topic, "We love, because He first loved us." We love Him because He first loved us, and we love others because He first loved us.

Love starts and stops with God. He is the Author. He created it out of His very nature, and He desires that we share and experience this wonderful gift to humankind.

When you think about it, our similarities to God are few. We are not omniscient, omnipresent, or omnipotent. But God *is* love, and He wants us to share that attribute with Him and with others. What a marvelous privilege! We are most like God when we love.

I think it is interesting to compare the most familiar verse in the Bible with another verse that John wrote. Most people can quote John 3:16, but look at 1 John 3:16: "By this we know love, because He laid down His life for us. And we also ought to lay down our lives for the brethren."

I understand that the numbers or references on the verses are not in the original, but the two 3:16 verses have a complementary message: love gives sacrificially. The world knows little about sacrificial love.

In defining love, I needed to provide three different definitions to give the full scope. That, in itself, shows how complex the subject is.

Agape is the highest form of love. Of the many times love is referred to in the New Testament, most of the references are to agape love. This is what John 3:16 speaks about. This love is totally sacrificial and committed to the well-being of another. This is God's kind of love. It is a fruit of the Spirit who indwells us (Gal. 5:22). When we look at the fruit of the Spirit in Galatians 5:22, we can look at it like this:

- Joy is love enjoying.
- Peace is love resting.
- Patience (or longsuffering) is love waiting.
- Kindness is love reacting.

S̲uppose that I understand the Bible and . . . am the greatest preacher who ever lived! The Apostle Paul wrote that unless I have love, "I am nothing."
—Billy Graham

Love **377**

LOVE

■ Agape *love—sacrificial commitment, dedicated to the well-being of another.* Phileo *love—brotherly affection.* Eros *love—sexual affection.*

- Goodness is love choosing.
- Faithfulness is love keeping its word.
- Gentleness is love being able to empathize.
- Self-control is love being in charge.

This kind of love is not something we can work up on our own; it is an outflow of the Holy Spirit.

The second kind of love mentioned is *phileo*. This is a brotherly kind of love. The Bible says to "be kindly affectionate to one another with brotherly love, in honor giving preference to one another" (Rom. 12:10). Furthermore, we are admonished to "let brotherly love continue" (Heb. 13:1), implying that it can diminish if not watched over and cultivated. This healthy form of love should saturate the body of Christ.

The third type of love is *eros*. This is sensual or sexual love. Though this word is not used specifically in Scripture, it is certainly implied through the admonitions concerning marriage. Although the world has tried its best to distort this—and this seems to be the type of love that is written about, sung about, and acted out the most—God invented eros love for the most intimate part of marriage.

I think that sums up the definitions and also gives us the background that John was setting for us. It is amazing that love is so complex we cannot define it easily, and yet John, "that apostle whom Jesus loved," summarizes it so beautifully by saying, "We love, because He first loved us."

> **K**indness is a language which the deaf can hear and the blind can see.
> —Mark Twain

A CLOSER LOOK

If I asked you why God created you, what would your answer be? Why were you born?

You and I were created so that God could express His love to us and we could respond with love. Because He is love, and because that is His very nature, He wanted an object for His love. So He created man and woman. You and me.

How does God express His love? In many ways, but let's look at a few.

First, God expresses His love through creation. The trees, the lovely flowers, the gorgeous mountains, the bright stars, the moon in all of its stages—these are tangible expressions of His love. I enjoy the outdoors immensely. I love hiking and photographing all the beauty God has given us to enjoy. There is no way to travel and see the beauties of the world and not feel very loved by the Creator. I look at the ocean and think, *The One who makes the tides ebb and flow cares for me.* I climb the mountains in all of their majesty and think, *The One who created these is omnipotent in my life*. God expresses His love for us through creation.

Second, God expresses His love in giving us the freedom to choose. That sounds strange, doesn't it? It almost seems that He would love us more if He had made the parameters a bit tighter. His love is so great, however, He has given us the freedom to say no. No one wants to be married to a robot. The wonder of love is when a person chooses to love you. He delights when we choose to love Him out of our free will, which in love He gave us. In giving Adam and Eve the free will to choose to sin, He showed a new dimension of His love—He loves willful sinners.

Third, God expresses His love by putting us in a family. I love this truth. I grew up without my natural father, and to think I have a supernatural Father who cares for me is beyond my comprehension. You and I are part of a large family—God is Father, Jesus Christ is our elder Brother, the Holy Spirit is our indwelling Comforter. Beyond that, the body of Christ comprises our brothers and sisters! A woman who is an only child said she loved knowing that she really has siblings, and in reality they are blood relatives. Think of the security, the protection, and the fellowship the family of God affords.

Taking church lightly, and attending sporadically, is ingratitude toward the One who put us in a family. It's akin to refusing to show up for family reunions because we have other things that are more important.

Fourth, God expressed His love in sending the Holy Spirit to live within us. He said He was going to send One just like Himself to reside in us. He did not just love us; He empowered us to love Him and others!

Fifth, God expresses His love by engineering our circumstances for our good and His glory. Almost everyone can quote Romans 8:28, but few of us really grab hold of the truth that He loves us enough to make *all things* work together for good. He is vitally interested and involved in everything that interests or involves us. God expresses His love toward us in being intensely involved in our lives.

Sixth, God expresses His love toward us by providing heaven. We had absolutely nothing to do with it. His Son is still busy preparing a place for us, and we get there only by the grace of God.

Seventh, God expresses His love toward us by His uninterrupted presence in our lives. One writer put it this way: "For He Himself has said, 'I will never leave you nor forsake you'" (Heb. 13:5). This Presence is there during the death of loved ones; during sleepless nights over a wayward child; during bad results from medical tests; during financial woes. Often the numbness of pain keeps us from sensing His presence, but He is there nonetheless.

> I wonder what a church would look like that measured its success by the quality of its members' neighborly love.
> —Bob Lupton

> Conflicts seem to dissolve themselves when people live according to 1 Cor. 13. The ultimate prescription for harmonious living is contained in that one chapter.
> —Dr. James Dobson

LOVE

One Sunday afternoon, I felt sad and alone. I knelt before the Lord and cried out, "God, it's sort of like it's just me." In the fog, Jesus whispered to me in His loving way, "I'm here. And I'll always be here, no matter what." I couldn't stop praising Him for His love and presence.

I'm sure you could write ways that God has expressed His love to you. But the bottom line is, He *expresses* His love. His love is not dormant; He actively expresses it day in and day out.

Having looked at some of the ways He expresses His love, we need to see what His love is like because He wants us to express that same type of love toward Him and others. What does God's love look like?

To begin with, His love is perfect. His love is everything it possibly can be. One Sunday morning before coming to church to preach, I knelt by my bed, struggling in spirit. God said to me in His inaudible, yet clear, way, "Charles, you can trust perfect love." I wept with joy. I have clung to that truth ever since. You and I can trust perfect love. And God's love is absolutely perfect.

His perfect love is a gift. We can't work for it. Every time someone gives a gift and the receiver tries to repay the giver, it is no longer a gift. We could never earn His love, and He gives it out of His very nature. God just can't help loving you.

His perfect love that He gives us is everlasting. We need to memorize this verse: "I have loved you with an everlasting love; therefore with loving-kindness I have drawn you" (Jer. 31:3). We can do nothing to make God stop loving us. What good news! God's love never, ever fades.

Furthermore, His perfect, everlasting love that He gives the believer is unconditional. Some people were raised hearing, "I'll love you if . . . ," or "I'll take you back when . . ." There is no if or maybe or fine print or footnotes to God's love. It is totally unconditional. He never says, "I'll take you back *if* . . ."

But it goes farther. God's perfect, everlasting love that He gives us unconditionally is a sacrificial love. That is what the Cross is all about: "God so loved that He gave . . ." God wants us to have this same sacrificial love toward one another. It doesn't make any difference whether people reject us or not, we still express love toward them. Of course, its supernatural source is the Holy Spirit.

And if that is not enough, God's perfect, everlasting, sacrificial, unconditional love that He gives us is immeasurable. The apostle Paul assures us that we are "rooted and grounded in love," and we need to be "able to comprehend with all the saints what is the width and length and depth and height" (Eph. 3:17–18). Paul also tells us that His love "passes knowledge"

> **E**ach time I listen, I'm sending a message: What you say matters; you're important to me. I love you.
> —Christine Suguitan

> **T**wenty-one percent of Americans would ask God if man will ever love his fellow man.
> —100 Questions and Answers

(v. 19). I think Paul is indicating that while we need to try to grasp all the ramifications of such perfect love in every sphere, it is immeasurable; we will never be able to take it all in.

As a grandfather who takes great pleasure in wanting my grandchildren to know how much I love them, I don't think they can ever measure how deeply I love them. I heard a speaker who stated, "I think if our children knew how much we loved them, they couldn't handle it." And yet we express our love in every way possible so they can get a handle on it.

I say this reverently. God has expressed His love in more ways than we could ever count, and yet His love is immeasurable. If we really grasped how much we were loved, it would stagger us. When I realize how much I want my grandchildren to understand my love for them, and then I realize God wants me to understand His love for me even more than that, I am overwhelmed. His love is immeasurable.

Just think of these adjectives describing His love: *perfect, unearned, everlasting, unconditional, sacrificial,* and *immeasurable.* No wonder His heart must be grieved when I don't walk in the sunshine of His love and bask in it.

We are called to love God. Jewish men recited the following verse both morning and evening, "You shall love the LORD your God with all your heart, with all your soul, and with all your strength" (Deut. 6:5). We are to love Him with all of the heart, the seat of the emotions; with all of the soul, the core of personality; with all of our strength, all that is within us; with all of our might—consumed with Him.

How do we work that into our daily lives?

By obedience. Three times in John 14, Jesus reminds us that love equals obedience. In essence He says, "Don't tell Me that you love Me and choose to put up with sin!" My love is to be evident in instantaneous confession when sin is pointed out. That's when He is my center of attention and all my emotional energy moves toward Him.

But there is more. Not only am I to love God, but I am to love myself. "You shall love your neighbor as yourself" (Mark 12:31). Some say, "That sounds haughty and egotistical." The world has corrupted this self-love into the motto, "You gotta look out for number one." The Bible does not teach that. The Bible teaches a healthy love for ourselves because we are His workmanship and worth loving.

Do you know how people can tell whether they love themselves? By the way they treat themselves. If they abuse their bodies with alcohol or tobacco or overeating, they are not loving themselves enough to care for their bodies. Satan will say, "You're not worth loving." But God said, "You are My

Ninety-four percent of teenagers surveyed in a Gallup Poll believed God loves them.
—*100 Questions and Answers*

"Owe no man anything but to love . . ." There is a debt that we are to pay to each other . . . Am I making payments on my debt of love?
—Roger C. Palms

■ Agape *love—sacrificial commitment, dedicated to the well-being of another.* Phileo *love—brotherly affection.* Eros *love—sexual affection.*

workmanship. You are worth My Son's dying for. You are incredibly valuable."

We need to see ourselves as God sees us. Our sense of self-worth can come not from what others think of us but from what God thinks of us. And we are the apple of His eye.

Not only are we called to love God and ourselves, but we are also called to love our neighbors. This is perhaps the hardest of the three commands.

In John 14, 15, 16, and 17, Jesus emphasized that we are to love others. That is how the world is to know we are Christians. True, some people are more lovable than others, but love is *not* an emotion; it *is* a decision. We can choose by our will, with the Holy Spirit indwelling and empowering us, to love. We can ask the most unlovable people, "How can I help you to be all God wants you to be?"

Some people cannot handle love. They are uncomfortable with affection. Sometime they are so scarred emotionally that they are afraid to be loved. They fear you will expect them to love in return and they are incapable of doing that because of damaged emotions. But genuine agape love doesn't expect love in return, so love them anyhow.

Jesus doesn't stop with calling on us to love our neighbors. He calls on us to love our enemies as well. This is a supernatural calling, and we must rely on the Holy Spirit to give us the capacity to love them.

If love is a feeling, we are all in trouble. Our feelings are fickle and they fluctuate. But the decision to do what is the best for others can be steady, no matter what we feel. When the alarm clock goes off on a cold, rainy morning, we get ready for work whether or not we feel like it. By an act of will, we throw back the covers and put our feet on the floor. Oftentimes, loving others demands the same kind of discipline and determination.

A fellow decided to love his wife by taking her shopping. Normally, it was such a stressful time that he found something else to do instead. But knowing how much she enjoyed his company, he went as an act of love. He was determined to put her feelings ahead of his own.

As they approached the women's section of the store, his wife mentioned that she needed a pair of khaki slacks. They all looked the same to him, so he wandered off to a different department. Soon, however, his wife motioned for him to join her. She needed his help in selecting the right pants. Several unpleasant emotions flooded his heart. His head clouded with all kinds of verbal responses. Then he remembered what he was there for—to love his wife. By an act of his will, he went into the women's section. Many pairs of khaki slacks later, his emotions caught up to his will, and he started to enjoy the process. As he recounted the story, it was evident that he made a

We're not projecting love to the world and we're basically losing influence.
—Chuck Colson

The first fruit of the Spirit is love; it is the heart of it all.
—*Decision, Oct. 1995*

There is nothing God loves like He loves you.
—Charles Stanley

giant step forward in learning to love his wife in a practical and, for him, self-sacrificing way.

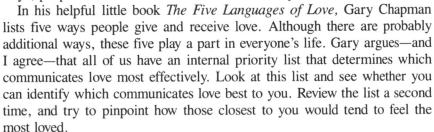

There are many ways to express love to those around you—your neighbors, your family members, and your enemies. Just as love is expressed in different ways, people sense or receive love in different ways as well.

In his helpful little book *The Five Languages of Love,* Gary Chapman lists five ways people give and receive love. Although there are probably additional ways, these five play a part in everyone's life. Gary argues—and I agree—that all of us have an internal priority list that determines which communicates love most effectively. Look at this list and see whether you can identify which communicates love best to you. Review the list a second time, and try to pinpoint how those closest to you would tend to feel the most loved.

1. Physical touch
2. Gift giving
3. Quality time
4. Words of encouragement
5. Acts of service

It behooves you to discover the love language of your children, your spouse, your friends, and your parents and express love to them the way they need to be loved. The tendency, as you might have guessed, is to love others the way you want to be loved, which is the cause of much misunderstanding.

One of the most awesome things I have realized recently about God is that He knows my number one way to feel loved and that is exactly how He deals with me. Is that not just like a loving heavenly Father to do that for His child?

Several years ago I heard a critical statement a man made about me. Because I am human, I didn't feel a great deal of love toward him. Not too long after that, he and I were the only two speakers scheduled at a series of meetings. I preached first, and because I was seated on the first row, I could not get up and leave when he preached. So, I began praying for him. And the strangest thing happened. Tears began streaming down my face because I was loving someone whom I had not even liked several moments earlier.

The only way you can get men to Christ is by love, and you have got to love them into the Kingdom.
—Mel Trotter.

Love

LOVE

■ Agape *love—sacrificial commitment, dedicated to the well-being of another.* Phileo *love—brotherly affection.* Eros *love—sexual affection.*

> **J**esus gave the highest priority to the expression of love for God and for our neighbor, yet we often miss this emphasis in Christian education.
> —Dr. James Dobson

It was totally unexplainable. I walked back to my hotel so I could think about what had happened to me. The speaker was standing inside the hotel lobby. He asked if I'd like to go out to eat, and I immediately said yes. As we sat in the restaurant, he poured out his heart to me, and I realized he was going through a lot of hurt in his life. I listened for a very long time to this precious man and was able to offer some encouragement.

Had the Holy Spirit not flooded my soul with love for him earlier, I would not have gone to eat with him, much less listened to his heart. It was one of the most life-changing events I've experienced. It was absolutely supernatural agape love flooding through my very soul. I had nothing to do with it. I was surprised at the intensity of the love for a man I thought was my enemy.

I have never looked at love the same again.

APPLICATION

After the Resurrection, Peter returned to fishing (John 21). The story of Peter's catching fish after Jesus telling him to cast his net on the other side of the boat is a familiar one.

After breakfast, however, Jesus and Peter talked. Jesus asked Peter three times if he loved Him. Jesus knew the answer but He wanted Peter to realize the answer. Jesus asked the first two times, "Peter, do you *agapao* Me?" That is, "Peter, do you love Me with sacrificial love?" And Peter answered, "Yes, Lord; You know that I *phileo* You." In other words, "Jesus, You know that I love You with brotherly love." The third time Jesus asked, "Peter, do you even *phileo* Me?" Or "Peter, do you even like Me a whole lot?" And Peter was hurt, the Bible says, that Jesus asked him again—and I suspect Peter was stinging that Jesus changed the word, also (John 21:17).

Peter replied, "Lord, You know all things; You know that I *phileo* You." Peter never acknowledged in this passage that he loved Jesus with anything more than a friendship kind of love.

We need only to read the books of 1 and 2 Peter to see that Peter had come a long way after this conversation. He later wrote, "And though you have not seen Him, you love Him" (1 Peter 1:8 NASB). Both epistles are overflowing with love—agape love—for the Lord Jesus Christ.

If Jesus were to meet you and ask you to share a cup of coffee, what would your answer be to the same questions: Do you love Me with sacrificial love? Or do you just like Me a whole lot?

Agape or phileo?

Be honest with your answer.

LOVE

For love to be true, it sometimes has to be velvet and sometimes it has to be steel.

 QUOTES

—Charles Stanley

Life without love is empty and meaningless no matter how gifted we are.

—Charles Stanley

There's nothing you can do to get Him to love you and there's nothing you can do to make Him stop.

—Charles Stanley

PARENTING

■ *The art of raising children.*

SCRIPTURE

PSALM 127:3 NASB

Behold, children are a gift of the LORD; the fruit of the womb is a reward.

COMMENTARY

It is an easy thing for most Christians to understand and quote, "The free gift of God is eternal life" (Rom. 6:23 NASB). We revel in that gift. It is God's greatest gift to us, packaged in His Son. The gift of eternal life was wrapped up in His death and resurrection. None of us who know Him would deny how meaningful the gift is to us.

In the middle of the night as a young parent wearily walks the floor with a red-faced, arched-back, tight-fisted, screaming infant who refuses to settle down, it is almost inconceivable to this dad or mom that the Bible calls this tiny bundle a gift. God calls this a reward? A reward for what, you wonder?

At that exhausting, frustrating moment the parent wonders where Customer Service is so he can complain that the gift didn't come wrapped as expected. A responsibility? No doubt. A gift? He isn't so sure.

Parents remember when they wondered if they'd ever sleep through the night again. They remember the childish spills at meals, especially at restaurants and with company. We remember the earaches. The tantrums. The embarrassing moments.

At such times, it is not so easy to see children as gifts. Inconvenient, yes. Frustrations, yes. Gifts, no.

But God—who calls Himself Father and puts up with us—sees tiny babies, "terrible-twoers," freckle-faced awkward adolescents, stumbling high schoolers, and assertive, yet insecure college students as gifts.

Hannah certainly saw her little boy as a gift. She understood that her long-awaited son was both a gift and a stewardship. We know the story of God's blessing her with a little boy named Samuel. She kept her promise and gave him to the Lord after he was weaned. She took him to the temple and reminded the priest of her vow that this little one would belong in a unique way to the Lord. Hannah knew she was a steward of the marvelous gift named Samuel.

A CLOSER LOOK

In the same way, we need to see ourselves as stewards of our gifts. They are loaned to us for such a short time, but the stewardship is a privilege. Just imagine, you are temporarily in charge of an eternal being!

Never refer to your children as surprises or mistakes. They were in God's mind in eternity past, and He is not the least bit surprised at their appearance into your life. You would do well to memorize these verses. They are powerful in describing each child's uniqueness:

> *For You formed my inward parts;*
> *You covered me in my mother's womb.*
> *I will praise You, for I am fearfully and wonderfully made;*
> *Marvelous are Your works,*
> *And that my soul knows very well.*
> *My frame was not hidden from You,*
> *When I was made in secret,*
> *And skillfully wrought in the lowest parts of the earth.*
> *Your eyes saw my substance, being yet unformed.*
> *And in Your book they all were written,*
> *The days fashioned for me,*
> *When as yet there were none of them (Ps. 139:13–16).*

In these verses there is no hint of a child's being a mistake or surprise. Sometimes the ultimate test of the parents' view of the sovereignty of God is when natural family planning is overruled by God's supernatural family planning.

If we see our children as gifts and see our responsibility as stewards of these wonderful presents, how do we practically go about this?

Let me say this at the very start. I understand all children are different. What gets one child's attention may not necessarily get another's. As James Dobson said, some children come out of the womb shaking their fists. Their agenda is not *whether* they will someday be in charge but *when*. As family lecturer Gary Smalley said, they grow up letting you live in your house. You know kids like that?

Children are unique. Parents complain, "I don't understand why Pete didn't turn out. I raised him exactly the way I raised Rosie and Freddy." That may be part of the problem. The verse, "Train up a child in the way he should go, and when he is old he will not depart from it" (Prov. 22:6), is not the catchall verse we want it to be. It is a precious promise, but we need to cling not to just the last half of the verse. The first part tells us we need to train up a child in the way *he* should go, that is, toward the bent of *his* personality. In the case just mentioned, we need to say gently to the parents, "Pete is Pete. Rosie is Rosie. Freddy is Freddy."

> **I** am persuaded that if mothers and fathers would earnestly seek to know the meaning of full consecration in God's service, they would have clear guidance in the rearing of their children.
> —V. Raymond Edman

PARENTING

We've got to give up cookie-cutter parenting. No more general practitioner approach; we need to specialize. We need to carefully study each child's unique personality from the moment we receive the gift. That will keep us on our toes—and our knees.

God, the giver of good gifts, understands the awesome responsibility and time commitment attached to His gift. And although He does not include a money-back guarantee or a warranty, He does include an Instruction Manual. And the more familiar we are with the Manual, the more effective we will become in our parenting.

APPLICATION

Although children are very different, certain general principles apply to each. Here are several habits every parent should develop and incorporate into parenting skills.

First, *communicate and demonstrate a genuine interest in what goes on in the lives of your children.*

A couple came into my office one afternoon to talk about their daughter. It seemed she had decided to get married against the wishes of her parents. They were concerned and upset.

They had done their best to get their daughter to cancel her plans, even to postpone them, but she was determined to have her way. I agreed to talk to the young woman, and after some persuading, she agreed to talk to me.

Her story was one I have heard many times before. Dad and Mom were always too busy—too busy for the sixth-grade open house, too busy to see her cheer at football games, too busy for her pageants, too busy to meet her friends, too busy to help her choose a major, and on and on it went. But when it was time for her to choose a marriage partner, all of a sudden they had a surge of interest. Suddenly, they wanted to jump into the middle of her life and help her make the "right" decision.

"Well," you may say, "this is the most important decision of her life." That may be true, but when she was thirteen, the most important decision was whether she should have her hair permed or leave it straight. But she was left to face that "crisis" alone. At fifteen, the most important decision of her life was whether she should go to cheerleading camp or church camp. Nobody seemed too concerned about that one, either. Then there was the time she couldn't decide which dress to wear to the prom. Mom looked up from tossing a salad just long enough to tell her that it was her decision. Again, she felt abandoned to do the best she could alone.

Only as genuine Christian holiness and Christlike love are expressed in the life of a parent, can the child have the opportunity to inherit the flame and not the ashes.
—Stephen Green

For years an unspoken message had been coming through loud and clear: "As your parents, we are not really interested in what you do. It is your life. Live it the best you can." So when Mom and Dad stepped in to stop the wedding, their daughter did not see their actions as an expression of love and concern. She saw their actions as interference.

Children spell love *T-I-M-E*. Dad, pitching a ball or fishing with your son is not wasted time. A mother smiled and remembered playing dress-up with her little girl and having tea parties. She said she knew those times paved the way when they went to buy a bathing suit for her daughter at age fifteen. They prayed for something stylish and modest (in other words, a miracle). You know what set the tone of the relationship at fifteen? The mom said, "Playing, making cookies, going to the park and blowing bubbles, reading lots of books, and driving to and from gymnastic classes, talking all the while, paved the way for the teenage years. We were buddies. When the bathing suit came up, we were determined to remain friends. We prayed. God led. And now though she's married, we're still best friends. The foundation was laid way back there tucking in dolls together or sitting in an itchy sandbox together."

I think parents know that a child, or teen, would not walk up to them and say, "Mom, Dad, would you be intimately involved in my life?" If that happened, what would you say? Most likely, you'd say, "Why, of course I will!" To put this principle into practice, you must realize that every time your children ask for advice or share the events of the day they are basically saying, "Will you be involved in my life? Will you be on my team?"

A large part of expressing interest is listening. Learning this lesson challenged me. When my kids accused me of not listening, I always reacted by trying to repeat to them what they had just said to prove that I was listening. Then Andy began playing behavior modification games with me. Every time I would look away he would immediately quit talking. It became rather humorous at times. He would be right in the middle of a highly emotional story and then suddenly stop as I reached for the mail.

Finally, it dawned on me that eye contact reassured him that I was being attentive. The same is true for your children. I began reflecting on how I would feel when I was praying and I thought my heavenly Father was looking away and not being attentive. That would crush me so that eventually, I may not want to tell Him anything. The same is true on a human level.

Another lesson I learned about listening to my children was taught to me by my daughter, Becky. I noticed that every time she talked with me, the rate of her speech and her volume would increase. My response would be, "Slow down, relax." Just like Andy, she had devised a way to keep me

> **A** permissive home is a home where you don't love enough to exercise the authority God gave you.
> —Ben Haden

PARENTING

■ *The art of raising children.*

listening. She said she always felt as if I was going to change the subject, and so she felt pressed to rush through whatever she had to say before the conversation moved in a different direction.

I am grateful for what God has taught me through my children about being a listener. I am grateful that we have a heavenly Father who is vitally interested in what we say. He gives us His full attention, and He doesn't care how long we take to tell Him; He won't change the subject.

Remember, it is not what you think that will have an impact on your kids but what you communicate to them. You communicate your heart and your value system when you spend time with them and listen to what they are saying and feeling.

Second, *love and accept your children unconditionally.* When you think of love, you may think of feeling a certain way. But unconditional love is a habit, not a feeling. It is something you choose to do, not something you wait to feel. Unconditional love means putting others first, in this case, your children.

It is imperative that you accept your children and love them unconditionally. God does that for you, and He wants to do the same for your children through you.

My son is gifted musically. Although I love music, I didn't appreciate the type of music he was interested in when he was a teenager. I wanted him to excel musically but according to my standards. Whenever I criticized his music, however, he understood me to be critical of him. Because children sometimes have a difficult time distinguishing between criticism of them and criticism of their actions or behaviors (as do adults, if we were honest), parents need to be especially careful to make sure the message they convey is an accurate one.

A certain amount of conflict over the music issue carried over into several other areas of our relationship. Looking back now, I can see that much of the conflict was totally unnecessary. The problem was that I was not as tolerant as I should have been, and Andy misunderstood much of what I said about his music. Although in my heart I totally accepted Andy, my comments about his music communicated an entirely different message to him.

Clothing was another area in which I needed to learn how to show unconditional love and acceptance. There was something I would say to Andy that I am ashamed to admit. When he would get all dressed up (to suit my taste), I would pat him on the back and say, "Now, you look like my son." That was my way of saying, "I think you look sharp." But I was communicating conditional acceptance. We have talked about this since he has become an adult, and he admitted that when I said that to him, he wanted to respond, "And whose son do I look like the rest of the time?" What I thought was "dressed up" was a shirt and tie. Andy thought dressed up meant nice jeans.

If your children's behavior brings you personal embarrassment, that is an indication that your personal sense of security is being threatened. You see your children as extensions of yourself, and you want them to reflect perfection. You can forget that.

One way to find out whether or not your children feel unconditional acceptance is to ask them: What do you think it would take for you to make Mom and Dad as proud of you as we could possibly be? Is their answer task oriented? Is it performance oriented? Is it something they must do?

Or is the answer more character oriented? Do they feel they would make you proud by obeying God, regardless of the cost, standing alone for what is right, refusing to compromise at the risk of sacrifice? Their answer will clue you in on the values you are emphasizing—whether you want them to be emphasized or not.

I want to say a word to parents who have the calling of accepting and loving unconditionally children with disabilities. God, who has gifted you with your children, will give you wisdom. Psalm 139 includes children with disabilities. Loving them and accepting them unconditionally are not options for parents. It may be harder, but the rewards will be great. I do not pretend to know what you feel. But *you* know. And more important, *He* knows. All of His children have been disabled one way or the other, and He has accepted us and loved us unconditionally.

Our desire to help our children avoid the mistakes we made hampers our unconditional acceptance. A mother of three preschoolers was asked to list the greatest joys and greatest difficulties in her life with three little ones. One thing she wrote down was particularly insightful: "Seeing them mirror back to me my weaknesses." Probably the child who is the most like us gives us the most difficult time because he or she is our visual aid of things in ourselves that we don't like. It is difficult to be objective in disciplining that child because we tend to be overly strict since we've dealt with this issue over a lifetime, not just in an isolated incident with the child. We need to involve someone else (a friend or spouse) who can help us put things in perspective.

Third, *set limitations*. Since children are unique, the lines might have to be drawn differently for each child. And that is when the accusations come: "Well, Johnny gets to. Why can't I?" That's when you scratch your head and wonder whether you are consistent in your parenting. Just when you think you might be, Susie points a finger that Johnny gets to stay up a half

> **T**he media have gone from "Father knows best" to "Father knows nothing at all."
> —D. James Kennedy

PARENTING

hour later than she does, even though he is younger. Explaining that Johnny gets up when he is called while Susie snoozes away doesn't seem to convince Susie that you are excelling in your consistency.

Nonetheless, God has put limits on His children, and you need to put limits on yours. God's first two children—and every one of them since then—tested the limits, and your children will be no different. But your response must be to hold the line, to follow the original game plan.

Your objective as a parent is to strive to produce responsible adults who are able to function independently of parental authority, yet wholly submitted to God's. Discipline should prepare your children to live outside your home. As someone said, parents are really trying to work themselves out of a job.

Limits need to be clear. Saying, "Be home early," or "Don't waste your money," or "You need to spend more time on your homework," generally doesn't work. Be specific: "Be home by 11:00 P.M."; "Don't spend more than ten dollars"; "Spend an hour each afternoon working on your homework."

When setting the limits, keep in mind the nature of children is to push the limits. Former missionary Elisabeth Elliot tells the story of keeping her grandchildren while her daughter and son-in-law went away for the week. There were quite a few children to look after and one day she had to scold one of them. The little girl looked up and said, "Well, we're all sinners!" Can't you imagine trying to keep a straight face with that response? But the fact is, we are, and her theology was right on target, not to mention convenient.

I can remember taking my son back to the barbershop several times after he had gone alone. Why? Because my general instructions were, "Make sure you get a good haircut." After several incidents, it became obvious that our ideas of a good haircut were altogether different.

Whenever possible, explain the *why* behind the *what*. Tell your children why you have set specific limits. Avoid saying, "Because I said so!" It frustrates you as an adult to hear that response; it frustrates your kids as well. Part of your responsibility as a parent is to help your children internalize certain limits for themselves. There will come a time when you won't be around to set up protective boundaries. If you have not effectively communicated the *why* behind the *what,* it will be easy for your children to leave their standards at home.

Along with loving limitations, there must be clearly defined consequences. "Or else you'll be sorry" isn't enough. Whenever possible, your children should know exactly what to expect when they violate the rules of the house.

Eighteen percent of Americans said they go to church more frequently for their children.

Making the punishment fit the misbehavior takes creativity. For instance, when Andy was in the third grade, he began using a term that my wife decided was unacceptable. She scolded him over and over, but he persisted. Finally, she decided a specific course of action was required. She explained to Andy that the next time he used the offensive word, she was going to wash his mouth out with soap. There was just one problem. She had no idea how you wash someone else's mouth out with anything, much less soap. She prayed that the very thought of such a thing would keep Andy from using the word.

In spite of Annie's prayers, however, Andy soon used the forbidden word. My wife was in the kitchen at the time, and by her own admission, she tried to pretend that she had not heard him correctly. But she knew that to fulfill her responsibility to Andy, she had to punish him for what he said, and she had to do it in the manner she promised.

As she marched him to the bathroom, still unsure of what to do, she spied his toothbrush by the sink. She picked it up, ran it across a bar of soap a couple of times, and then proceeded to brush his teeth with it. It wasn't a pleasant experience for either of them, but it won't be forgotten.

Be sure you are *clear* in your instructions, you are *consistent* in carrying through, and your disciplinary action *corresponds* to the offense.

To take this principle one step farther, work out a system of rewards for your children as well. Just as we avoid behavior that is punished, we repeat behavior that is rewarded.

Extending a teenager's curfew in response to the faithfulness to come home on time is an appropriate reward. As adults, we look forward to bonuses at work, and there is nothing wrong with that. There is no reason that our children can't look forward to bonuses, either. Set limitations, and enforce them with both consequences and rewards.

Fourth, *meet the material needs of your children*. The apostle Paul wrote, "But if anyone does not provide for his own, and especially for those of his household, he has denied the faith and is worse than an unbeliever" (1 Tim. 5:8). These are strong words.

My mom was a widow. She went to work early every morning to provide for me. During the depression, everyone eked by on virtually nothing. Consequently, we did not have much. I had several pairs of overalls, one pair of shoes, a couple of pairs of socks, some underwear, a toothbrush, and a comb. But I never went hungry—even though I do remember wishing we had more to eat. My dear mom, like many of you, did what she could. She worked hard. When I was a little older, I developed a paper route and did my best to help out.

> **C**hristian parents must guard against being so intent on "doing a good job" as parents that their children begin to feel like objects being "worked on," rather than persons with whom to relate in love and enjoyment.

■ *The art of raising children.*

The term *Christian parenting style* means a series of relationships between you and your child that will give you a greater chance of achieving the three primary goals of Christian parenting: (1) knowing your child, (2) helping your child feel right, and (3) leading your child to Christ.
—William Sears, M.D.

I know what it is like to work and work and still not have enough. But the admonition is still there to provide for our families. In providing for our families, we must distinguish between needs and wants.

It is *imperative* that we provide for the *needs* of the family. Needs and wants differ in individual families and take considerable listening to one another and praying together. The promise is there: "And my God shall supply all your need according to His riches in glory by Christ Jesus" (Phil. 4:19). When unemployment is a problem or money is tight, we need to realize God is the ultimate Source. What a time to teach the family to pray!

Praying for direction—and guidance in financial matters—should be a regular event in the Christian home. Let your children see your utter dependence on Him in the area of finances as well as other areas in your life.

My mother once said to me, "I'm sorry I couldn't give you the things other parents gave to their children." And I answered, "Mom, you have nothing to regret. You gave me something that is not for sale in any store, has never been manufactured, and cannot be purchased anywhere. You planted in me a love for God, a desire to be obedient, a desire to be willing to stand, regardless of other people's opinions or attitudes, to do what is right. You taught me to depend upon God for everything. You taught me how to pray. You taught me to trust God as my faithful Father."

She had done all she could for me materially. But as a loving mom with a generous heart, she was sorry she couldn't have done more. I wanted her to know that she passed on to me things that money could not buy.

Fifth, *pass along your faith*. Your primary responsibility as a parent is to pass along your faith and corresponding values to your children. Everything mentioned thus far is part of that.

Our ability to influence our children is tied into their respect for us. It is human nature to resist being influenced by those we don't respect. At the same time, we all find ourselves emulating those whose accomplishments and character we respect. To lead our children toward owning our faith as theirs, we must become leaders worth following. Loving them, accepting them, providing for them, and setting limitations on them are all part of establishing ourselves as respectable leaders.

Our children will never adopt our faith and values because we tell them to. They are even less prone to do so if they are not given ample evidence that what we believe both matters to us and works for us. We must live out our values in such a consistent and sacrificial manner that there is no doubt in their minds that our faith is genuinely a part of our very being.

With that in mind, let's ask the obvious question: How do you hand down your faith and values? You must do two things. First, allow your children to see your faith and values at work for you and your family. Take every opportunity to explain the connection between your decisions and your belief system: "Son, I returned the money because it didn't belong to me and we don't take what doesn't belong to us," or "Sweetie, you will not talk to your mother in that tone of voice. We will respect one another in this house because God has commanded us to be kind to one another."

Explain to your children why you go to church, why you work so hard, why you support the Lord's work financially, and why you treat your spouse with respect. Begin as early as possible helping them see the connection.

The second part of passing down your faith and values is to point out the rewards and consequences connected with what you believe. This doesn't need to be confined to what's taking place in your home. Look for examples—both good and bad—in the homes of others. When things go wrong at home, point out the principle or standard you or your spouse violated. When they come home with a sad story about a friend's family, explain what happened in the context of what you believe. When your family is rewarded for an area of faithfulness, help them see the connection. Point out God's faithfulness whenever possible.

You are shaping your children's worldview—the grid through which they will interpret all the events of life. Take every opportunity to help them develop that framework. This is the essence of passing down your faith.

It makes no difference how many times children attend Sunday school and hear sermons. There is nothing under God's heaven like a mother and a father patterning principles they believe in if they want to hand those principles down to their children. It's more effectively caught than taught.

Moses told the people of God to diligently teach their children "when you sit in your house, when you walk by the way, when you lie down, and when you rise up" (Deut. 6:7). That pretty much covers major portions of life. When they see you tithing, feeding someone who is hungry, gathering up clothes for others, being kind to their friends, driving within the speed limit, or being careful what you watch on television, you can ever so gently let them know a verse that encourages you to do this. Don't preach! Gently share. Boldly live it.

Do you have a faith that is worth handing down? If you hand down your faith the way you are living it now, will your children be the better for having received and accepted your lifestyle?

Sixth, *teach them to be wise.* Soon your children will leave the comfort and security of your home. They will be on their own, making decisions for themselves. In light of this eventuality, they need to understand how to make wise decisions.

> There are three basic building blocks that form the foundation of a successful Christian family: (1) commitment to a God-centered life, (2) a stable and fulfilled Christian marriage, and (3) spiritual leadership.
> —William Sears, M.D.

PARENTING

> **S**pare the rod and spoil the child—that is true. But, beside the rod, keep an apple to give him when he has done well.
> —Martin Luther

The principle of wisdom is in one sense beyond good and evil. That is, it goes beyond what the Scriptures delineate as right and wrong. Wisdom also takes into account people's past experiences, their weaknesses, and their strengths. The commands of Scripture have universal application, but wisdom's prescriptions are more tailor-made, more individualized. What may be wise for one person may be unwise for another.

Learning to live wisely is vital in child rearing because many of the issues facing our children are not clearly addressed in the Bible. The Bible does not explain whether or not dancing is okay; Paul did not include a chapter on rock music; Jesus never discussed dating. I believe such issues must be handled within the context of wisdom.

A high percentage of the "rebellious" children I have counseled came out of homes where the principle of wisdom was ignored, where everything was treated as a moral issue, clearly wrong or clearly right. And there were always "appropriate" verses to support the parents' side of things. Then the parents wondered why their children had no interest in church and spiritual matters. They wondered why their children would not open up and communicate with them. Why should children be associated with an institution that, according to the way their parents present it, has no clue about what they are feeling or thinking? Why should children bother to communicate their feelings to people who treat them as if they cannot think for themselves?

Children who are taught to be wise do not approach the questions of what music to listen to, what movies to watch, and what friends to have from the perspective of what is wrong with these activities. They approach these questions from the perspective of what is the wise thing to do. In light of past experiences, present weaknesses, goals for the future, and God's desires, they consider what is the best thing to do.

We need to play offense before we end up playing catch-up as the world moves in swiftly with its value system. If we only inform and equip and if we only train and teach, we may have protected them, but we haven't prepared them.

It won't take long at all for a university professor to undo everything we've tried to pour into their lives if it was just information we gave them and not help on how to make wise decisions. Make sure the information is there, but make sure you have helped them make tough judgment calls according to what is wise.

Obviously, being effective parents is a time-consuming, difficult, wonderful job. It is surely one of the highest callings in life, and we need God's wisdom in dealing with these gifts from Him. Just when we think we have

> **G**od applies the golden rule to parenting.
> —Buddy Scott

it all figured out, something comes up that we have not a clue how to handle, and again we are pressed to the Lord for wisdom.

See these precious children as gifts, spend time with them, listen to them, love and accept them unconditionally, set limits, provide materially for them, and do everything you can to bring them to Christ, teaching them to live wisely before Him.

Continue to give it all you've got. Pray much. Listen hard. Learn all you can.

God will bless you abundantly as you treasure these gifts in your home: "If any of you lacks wisdom, let him ask of God. . . . Every perfect gift is from above" (James 1:5, 17).

Unwrap your gifts tenderly.

There was once a parent who let his son and daughter play inside a fenced-in yard. They knew the boundaries. And they knew the consequences if they failed to obey and stay within the limits. The father was the best father you could possibly imagine. He loved the two children, and they brought him more joy than anything in his life. But the two children stepped over the boundaries, suffered severe consequences, and broke the father's heart.

The son's name was Adam. The daughter's name was Eve. The Father's name is God.

GROWTH

You've spent time with your kids, you've listened, you've prayed, you've loved and accepted, you've set limitations, you've provided for them, you've handed down your faith, and you've tried to teach as well as model wisdom.

And, because of their will and poor choices, they have broken your heart. Don't beat up on yourself. And don't give up praying.

God the Father was the perfect Parent, but His first two kids didn't turn out to be perfect. He understands.

Children, whether born into the home biologically or ushered into our lives through adoption, are God's greatest gifts to the home, and they need to know it. We need to let our children know how blessed we are that they are ours. We need to reaffirm that they are valuable parts of our lives.

Go into as much detail as you can about the joy of each one's birth. Share with them about the excitement that was yours as you anticipated their arrival. This is especially important if the children are adopted. They need to know how you planned and prayed and longed for them. Tell them as many details as you can. Don't spare the emotions you felt as you relate this to them.

In order to be a good listener, it is also important that we not ridicule what our children say. We may not understand what they are saying, but being critical or ridiculing a child lowers his sense of worth and can cut off meaningful communication.

—Gary Smalley

Your boy wants to know that he is worthy, that he is acceptable, that he measures up in your eyes, and that he means something special to you. It takes so little to confirm him. Tell him that he is the greatest, and back it up with your actions.

—William Beausay II

■ *The process by which God made sinful humankind compatible with Himself.*

RECONCILIATION

SCRIPTURE

COLOSSIANS 1:19–22

For it pleased the Father that in Him all the fullness should dwell, and by Him to reconcile all things to Himself, by Him, whether things on earth or things in heaven, having made peace through the blood of His cross. And you, who once were alienated and enemies in your mind by wicked works, yet now He has reconciled in the body of His flesh through death, to present you holy, and blameless, and above reproach in His sight.

COMMENTARY

To reconcile something is to make it compatible with something else; it is the process of bringing harmony between two or more things. Theologically speaking, reconciliation is the process by which God made sinful humankind compatible with Himself.

In the above passage, Paul used the terms *alienated* and *enemies* to describe our relationship—or lack of relationship—with God. We all suffered from a compatibility problem. In our natural state, we didn't fit with God. He went on to say that our evil behavior set us at odds. It wasn't a matter of our hating God outright. Our acts of sin stemming from our sinful state caused the problem. God is holy. We are sinful. And that makes it impossible for the two to dwell together, thus the need for reconciliation.

Reconciliation is God's work from beginning to end. God engineers the process of reconciliation. But the means or method of reconciliation is Christ's death. His blood brought "peace" between God and humankind (Col. 1:20). Christ's death made friends of enemies. It brought together those who were at one time alienated from one another. His blood removed the barrier brought about by our sinful behavior. Calvary made us compatible with God.

Note that God wasn't changed in the reconciliation process. We were changed. Everything about us that caused us to be alienated from God was altered. Every barrier was removed.

Several years ago, while vacationing in North Carolina, I managed to lock my keys in the trunk of my car. Fortunately, I had an extra ignition key. Unfortunately, it didn't fit the trunk! That afternoon I found a locksmith shop listed in the Yellow Pages. I called and explained my plight. He was sure he could help, so I asked for directions and made my way across town.

When I arrived, he came out to my car with a set of tools and a key that had no teeth cut into it—a blank, as he referred to it. He began by taking my ignition key and holding it up beside the blank. Then he went to work.

> **I** think that if God forgives us we might forgive ourselves. Otherwise it is almost like setting up ourselves as a higher tribunal than Him.
> —C. S. Lewis

Reconciliation **399**

RECONCILIATION

■ *The process by which God made sinful humankind compatible with Himself.*

He cut and chiseled on the blank key until it looked exactly like my ignition key. Next, he put his new creation into the keyhole of my trunk. He pushed it as far as it would go, then pulled it out and whittled on it. He repeated this process several times. Suddenly, it turned, and my trunk opened.

Later, as I thought about what had happened, it occurred to me that the entire process was a picture of reconciliation. The locksmith reconciled the blank key with the trunk lock on my trunk. He altered the blank until it was compatible with the lock.

APPLICATION

God has gone to great lengths to provide the potential for a lasting relationship with us. He initiated and paid for the entire process. Love for us motivated Him to come up with a plan. And that same love moved Him to sacrifice His Son along the way.

The only possible conclusion we can draw is that God intensely desires a relationship with us. It is hard for us to imagine that the God of the universe would care one way or the other. After all, He is so . . . so . . . BIG! He can do anything! Why bother with us?

God answered that question the day He created us. We are made in His image. We are more like God—even in our sinful, alienated state—than any of His other creations. In one sense, when God looks at you, He sees Himself. You are important to God because you are the only part of creation that was made for the expressed purpose of fellowship with Him. To say the least, you are special.

With all that in mind, isn't it sad that we take our freedom to talk with God so casually? Think about it. God has gone to all this trouble and pain to restore us to our intended position of privilege, and oftentimes we ignore Him—that is, until the bottom drops out. Then we come running.

Our heavenly Father paid a high price to provide us with the opportunity to talk to Him, a price that we could never have paid. It is an honor to be given access to the Creator. We should treat our esteemed position more seriously. We should come to Him more often. We should come to Him reverently.

When you sin, you pay Him no tribute by staying away. He has paved the way for you to approach Him immediately after you have sinned. You should take advantage of that. Nothing is gained by running; no one benefits by putting God off. Sure, it is difficult to face Him after you have blown it, but the path is clear. There is no reason to run or fall prey to condemning guilt. He has reconciled you to Himself. Nothing stands between you.

> When we explain as we confess, we are seeking understanding instead of forgiveness. True confession means to admit guilt, not to try to excuse it; it seeks a pardon, not sympathetic understanding.
> —Matt Waymeyer

RECONCILIATION

God fixed the incompatibility problem permanently, eternally. Your good works didn't reconcile you to God. Your good works don't keep you reconciled. And your sin doesn't unreconcile you. So why run? Why ignore Him? God knew you would sin before you sinned. Yet He reconciled you anyway.

The Bible makes it perfectly clear that our acceptance before God is based not on the degree or number of our sins but on the death of His Son. After all, when we become Christians, our past doesn't change. Yet we suddenly become compatible with the holy, righteous God. Sin is not a barrier between the reconciled person and God, for all sin—past, present, and future—has been dealt with.

Take full advantage of the Father's ministry of reconciliation. Don't waste a minute ignoring Him; running from Him; allowing unconfessed sin to keep you from enjoying full fellowship. Face your sin, confess it, and move on. God has done everything He can do to provide you with barrier-free access. When you do, you honor Him.

A CLOSER LOOK

Christ died for everyone, yet not everyone is reconciled to God. Christ's death on the cross paved the way for everyone to be reconciled, but God doesn't force Himself on anyone. It is true that the reconciliation process is God's work from beginning to end, but that process doesn't benefit us until we accept His gift of reconciliation—Jesus Christ.

Reconciliation becomes a reality for us when we accept Christ by faith. Faith, or trust, is the way we acknowledge God's plan of reconciliation and appropriate it as our own.

GROWTH

In 2 Corinthians 5:18–20, Paul states that God has given believers the ministry of reconciliation. In light of what you have learned, how does Paul's admonition affect your responsibility as a believer?

Reconciliation

SEEKING APPROVAL

■ *Desiring favorable opinions of others.*

JOHN 12:42–43 NASB

Nevertheless many even of the rulers believed in Him, but because of the Pharisees they were not confessing Him, lest they should be put out of the synagogue; for they loved the approval of men rather than the approval of God.

The scene takes place in Jerusalem. The Lord Jesus has just come through His triumphal entry into the city, with people waving palm branches. He is making His final appeal to the masses to believe in Him as the Messiah. Trying to make them understand that what He has said and done is from the Father, Jesus urges them to believe the truth.

In John 12:37, we see that although Jesus had performed many miracles right in front of their eyes, some still refused to believe. In verses 39–40, we see that their hearts were hardened. Their continued "will nots" resulted in their final "could nots." God will not harden someone's heart against his will, but He will cooperate with the person who is continually saying, "I will not." God allows him to get to the place that he finally "cannot."

Although some had not believed in Him, others had believed but were secret followers: "The rulers believed in Him, *but* because of the Pharisees they were not confessing Him" (John 12:42 NASB, emphasis added). Do you remember Joseph of Arimathea and Nicodemus? They were secret followers. They formed a secret society of men and women who believed in the Son of God but were not ready to come forward and confess Him as Lord to their friends and neighbors.

Joseph believed but kept his beliefs to himself. Secretly, he went to Pilate to ask for Jesus' body after the Crucifixion. The Bible describes him as "being a disciple of Jesus, but *secretly,* for fear of the Jews" (John 19:38, emphasis added). In the same passage, we read of Nicodemus who had come earlier "by night" (John 3:2; 19:39). The men were like some believers today, confessing Christ in the privacy of their homes but never quite able to do so publicly.

The men remained quiet about their belief for fear of being put out of the synagogue. In their culture, life in the synagogue was very important. Today if a person is put out of one denomination, he or she can join another one. During those days, there was nowhere else to go. If you were put out of the synagogue, it was the Jewish equivalent of being shut out of heaven. In spite of having seen Jesus do miracles, the men were not sure they were willing to pay such a high price for Him. Their story is not so different from our own when we fear the attitude of our friends and keep our faith to ourselves.

SEEKING APPROVAL

What is there inside us that craves the approval of others? How does the approval of others influence our decision-making process? How far are we willing to go to get the approval of other people? Some would answer "too far," as they reap the consequence of doing things that cost them their reputations and, often, their freedom.

The root cause of our wanting approval of others is the fear of rejection and the fear of losing something.

Rejection results in feelings of worthlessness. They are horrible feelings. They are so excruciating, we are willing to do almost anything to avoid them. To some, that means disobeying God and stifling the conscience in order to be accepted—not rejected—by someone else.

We are also fearful of losing something, such as a relationship or a promotion. You and I see this in the business world all the time. It could be about wanting to avoid loss of position, power, and authority or not wanting to lose a lucrative account. Whatever the obvious motivation, the bottom line is the same. We crave the acceptance and approval of others more than we value doing what is right in God's eyes.

People who constantly, and fervently, seek the approval of others live with an identity crisis. They don't know who they are, and they are defined by what others think of them. The sad part is, if your security is built on others, you are fragmented. You might get approval from one person for doing what makes him happy, but the next person you come into contact with will expect something different. You continue the cycle, trying to please everyone, until you reach a point of pleasing no one, especially God. You can't be a whole person and allow others to dictate.

If your approval is built on what others think, your approval rating vacillates. You never know how you stand. How horrible to always be at the mercy of the opinions of others. You need to ask: What is my *identity*? Where do I get my wholeness?

You also may want to ask, How many people's approval is adequate? Do I need the approval of one person, or do I need a multitude? Do I need the people at work to like me, or do I need approval at church and in my neighborhood? How much do I need them to like me? If you're honest, the answer will not settle well because the truth is, most people *never* seem to have enough.

With these questions, you can see that longing for others' acceptance is a snare. Think of all the variables. Different people to please. Different people with different expectations. Different settings with different people with different expectations. Trying to stay on top of all that would wear a person

> **E**very day three thousand American teens reach adulthood as confirmed cigarette smokers. The overriding thing is the image of being cool.

SEEKING APPROVAL ■ *Desiring favorable opinions of others.*

out. But once you cease to perform, you lose. What a horrible way to live! We are a people who tear ourselves into a fractured piece of flesh trying to meet these expectations.

What's the cost of seeking others' endorsement? I think the price we pay not only to gain, but also to retain, the approval of others is a high one. High maintenance is involved. There is a steady dose of polishing people at the right time with the right polish. I don't know anyone who could keep up with that type of pressure for long, but I know a lot of people who keep trying until they break down.

As high as the price is in terms of what we do to our relationships and our health, even higher prices are involved. We pay a dear price when we violate the conscience and the Word of God to attain others' approval. We pay a great price when we keep quiet and deny the truth, knowing that there is wrong going on around us. We pay an exorbitant price when we compromise our convictions. Some church members say "Amen" loud and strong on Sunday, and then go to work, test the emotional and spiritual temperature of the office, and blend right in. It is the same thing the people did when they waved the palm branches before Christ one week and saw Him crucified only days later.

Let me clarify that *wanting* others to like us is natural. There is nothing wrong with that. No one sets out to agitate people just for the sake of agitation. But when we value the approval of others over the approval of God, we get into trouble. None of us wants to be the "odd man out" in the office, but it's a question of who we value more: the relationship with the person on the other side of the office or the God who created us from nothing!

The cost of seeking the approval of our friends or coworkers involves more than we dare to dream. How many people became hooked on alcohol because they didn't want to be the only one at the party not holding a drink? How many teenage girls became involved sexually because they wanted approval? How many teenage guys became involved sexually because they wanted to impress others? How many drug addicts are hooked because they wanted desperately to belong? How many are in gangs because they longed for someone to approve of them? How many are in debt way beyond their ability to pay because they wanted to dress as well as others, live in a house as big as others, and drive something as nice as others? We want others to think we're wonderful, and we're often willing to pay a very high penalty to get approval.

There is a price to pay in compromising our convictions morally as well as monetarily. We can't count as witnesses for the Lord if we are so busy

SEEKING APPROVAL

trying to score points with other people. There is no power in our witness if our eyes are constantly off Jesus and are focused instead on winning friends and influencing people. Powerless, ineffective, guilt-ridden believers have their eyes on their need to win friends, thus assuring the acceptance of those they relate to daily.

If the cause of seeking acceptance is fear of rejection and fear of loss and the cost is paid in terms of compromise, financial stress, guilt, and a myriad of other ways, what is the cure?

To know the cure, you need to ask yourself some questions:

Am I willing to suffer the *consequences* of my actions for the sake of approval? That is the first question.

What will I have when I have the approval of others? If you are honest, you will recognize that you have nothing tangible or permanent.

What will I have to do in order *to retain* approval of others? This is the question that many have asked regarding how far they will go. A person whose eyes are firmly fixed on God's will never have to ask how far because the standard has already been set and is clear.

Am I willing to *continue* what I am about to begin to retain their approval? Once you start giving in to the whims of others, it becomes harder and harder to return to your original standard and easier to stay where you are.

Am I *able* to continue what I am doing to retain their approval? Once you start spending more than you have to get what you think you need to be acceptable, the cost skyrockets. Can you afford to continue?

What have *I lost* when I've lost their approval? Although it is possible you may lose a relationship, could it be much of a relationship to begin with if you had to sacrifice your principles to gain acceptance? I think not.

Will it *profit* me more to gain the approval of others or the approval of God? That should be a no-brainer, yet from the actions of many brothers and sisters in Christ, you would think just the opposite. Let me be loud and clear. I don't care who you think you must have approval from, no one can ever fill up that vacuum in your life like God can. Absolutely no one.

I think if you honestly answer these questions, you will realize that it is a snare to live in the dread of not having the validation of other people. Living for others is selfish. Milking others for their approval is self-seeking. The Bible says to "seek first the kingdom of God and His righteousness, and all these things shall be added to you" (Matt. 6:33).

When we get to heaven, Jesus is not going to ask, "And how well were you liked down there? Did you please everyone?" When we see Him, we are going to be concerned with how much we pleased Him. We will want His "well done."

> **O**nly 16 percent of college students claim to be nondrinkers. College students spend $5.5 billion on alcohol each year, more than they spend on books and other beverages combined.

> **C**omparisons only lead to dead ends.
> —*In Touch*, March 1995

Seeking Approval

405

SEEKING APPROVAL

■ *Desiring favorable opinions of others.*

When a football star runs forty yards at full speed into the end zone for the touchdown, he is cheered. Teammates give him high fives. He dances up and down the turf. He looks into the television camera and holds up his index finger signaling that his team is number one. He may even mouth a "hello" to his proud mom.

Later, with the score tied, the same guy fumbles the ball. The opposing team gets it and scores, winning the game. Our former hero falls from the crowd's grace very, very quickly. The crowd's loud boos confirm it. One minute he can do no wrong. Within a half hour, he can do no right. How fickle the approval of the crowd!

APPLICATION

Seeking the approval of the crowd is just that uncertain. One day, we feel like heroes to everyone. We politely, somewhat modestly, try to stifle the high fives and the dance in the end zone, but we feel pretty special. We're amazed at how many people think we are cool.

Then we fumble.

Most of the time, people around us don't boo loudly. But they leave our playing field quickly, leaving us to stand alone. The crowds we try to please are fickle, too. As long as we need the approval of others, we will be condemned to a life of having to always perform perfectly, and none of us is capable of doing that.

Praise God, we serve One who approves of us unconditionally! We don't have to perform for Him to do so. He confirmed our worth when He sent His Son to die in our place. The Holy Spirit lives within us. Why should we need others to confirm what we already know?

You need to reaffirm who you are—a child of God. Valuable. Accepted. Loved. What more could anyone want? On a scale of one to ten, God thinks you are a ten. Sure, He knows you stumble from time to time. He longs to see you choose what is right and good, but He also stands ready to extend to you the measure of grace that He gives to all His children.

GROWTH

Make a list of people whose approval you value. Is your desire for their approval a balanced one, or are you doing it out of fear of rejection or loss?

Make another list of what you must do to get God's approval. What you will see, as you put these two lists side by side, is that God doesn't expect you to do anything. You are already accepted. Renew your mind to His truth, and you will enjoy the freedom to be who He created you to be, not

SEEKING APPROVAL

what somebody here on earth thinks you ought to be. The difference will change your life.

QUOTE

If a man attracts by his personality, his appeal is along that line; if he is identified with his Lord's personality, then the appeal is along the line of what Jesus Christ can do. The danger is to glory in men; Jesus says we are to lift Him up.

—Oswald Chambers

SEX

■ *The physical union of a man and a woman that results in physical, relational, and spiritual oneness.*

SCRIPTURE

1 CORINTHIANS 6:15–20

Do you not know that your bodies are members of Christ? Shall I then take the members of Christ and make them members of a harlot? Certainly not! Or do you not know that he who is joined to a harlot is one body with her? For "the two," He says, "shall become one flesh." . . . Or do you not know that your body is the temple of the Holy Spirit who is in you, whom you have from God, and you are not your own? For you were bought at a price; therefore glorify God in your body.

COMMENTARY

The apostle Paul's words to the believers in Corinth do not make for easy reading or easy understanding. It is evident from his choice of language that he feels deeply about what he is saying. There was urgency in his pen as he wrote to the wayward band in Corinth. Yet his reasoning doesn't hit home with us the way it probably did with his first-century audience.

This is a culturally oriented passage. Paul was dealing with a specific problem that does not exist in our culture, yet its topic has more relevancy today than ever.

Just outside the town of Corinth stood a pagan temple dedicated to the worship of Aphrodite. The temple housed one thousand prostitute priestesses whose services were part of the worship. Adultery was not immoral to the men of Corinth. On the contrary, it was part of worship; it was good; it was spiritual. In Corinth, men didn't have to sneak around on their wives; they just went to church!

Furthermore, there was no teen culture. Boys and girls married early in those days. There was no dating as we know it. Many of the marriages were arranged by parents. So, by the time boys or girls had reached teen years, they were married. Consequently, the issue of the day was not sex before marriage as much as it was adultery after marriage.

One more bit of information. In the Greek way of thinking, the body and soul were two separate spheres. They saw these two parts as mutually exclusive, having little to do with the other. What you did with your body had nothing to do with your soul as far as they were concerned. So, many of the Christians were prone to worship God with the soul on their day of worship, but the rest of the week they did whatever they wanted with the body—including making an occasional trip to the temple of Aphrodite.

Paul wrote, "The body is not for sexual immorality but for the Lord, and the Lord for the body" (1 Cor. 6:13). Contrary to what many in that culture believed, God does care about the body! He has purchased the body with the blood of His Son and filled it with the Holy Spirit (1 Cor. 6:19–20).

> **T**he sexual impulse is God given, and it must be God guided.
> —James Earl Massey

Our bodies have been purchased and possessed by Another, and He has given strict instructions what to do with them. Part of the instructions are here in this passage. They are specific. And they are given for our protection and pleasure, not for our punishment.

A philosophy about sex that is endorsed every day looks good on the surface. It looks like it's working for a while. The problem is, it isn't.

It appears to work. But it doesn't. Over time, there is a breakdown. There are consequences that surpass the passing pleasure that illicit sex affords.

The Bible is filled with warnings regarding sex outside marriage. And not only warnings, but the reasons behind the warnings as well. Generally speaking, the only thing people know that God said about sex is, "Don't do it." And that's too bad. Because God is not against sex. After all, He created it. God is for sex. After all, everything He created is good. And seeing how He is the Creator, we can safely assume that He knows infinitely more about the subject than anyone else. He knows more than we do.

As the inventor of this marvelous gift, He knows how it works best. He knows how we can receive the maximum joy and benefit from sex. He also know the potential pitfalls.

But we don't like boundaries. So we test the limits; we climb the fences; we charge past the warning signs. And ultimately, we face unnecessary consequences. Our tendency is to ignore Him and make decisions based on our inclinations or what we've heard or experienced. We are prone to adopt the world's philosophy about sex, a philosophy that looks good on paper but in the end collapses. It does not work.

God's very first command to humankind was in regard to sex. And it was *not* "don't do it." It was the very opposite: "Be fruitful and multiply" (Gen. 1:28). God commanded Adam and Eve to get involved physically.

Further evidence of God's positive attitude toward sex is revealed in the Song of Solomon. This book of the Bible is so descriptive that Hebrew boys were not allowed to read it until they reached a certain age.

We need to understand that He is the Creator, and thus He is for sex. He is for great sex. At the same time, He is for us and our well-being. As our heavenly Parent as well as our Creator, He has set up guidelines so that we can enjoy His gift to its fullest. The parameters are for our good, not our misery. He is not out to deny us anything that is good for us. But even good things must be dealt with according to the Manufacturer's Instruction Book.

> **C**heap sex and precious love; you can't have one if you have the other.
> —Jim Conway

SEX

■ *The physical union of a man and a woman that results in physical, relational, and spiritual oneness.*

We know that whenever we ignore guidelines that He has laid down, there will be consequences. But this is especially true in the area of sex. All we need to do is look around at the world we live in and we see the destructive force this good gift can become when removed from its proper context. We know about the consequences of AIDS and sexually transmitted diseases (STDs); we've seen families torn apart by affairs; we cannot escape the staggering statistics of unborn babies aborted in this country every year; we read about people who won't pay child support; we are overwhelmed with stories of incest and rape; prostitution continues to be a threat to young women; pornography is a billion-dollar industry. Sex outside the parameters that God has set forth is destroying families, teenagers, children, churches, and every social institution in this nation. No one can deny that there are devastating consequences to this nation's attitudes about sex. You don't have to be a Christian to see that sex as practiced in our society is having a negative effect.

What are God's parameters? Who is sex for? Well, it is not a gift for "in love" people. God does not permit sex for "ready" people. Being "old enough" isn't the issue. Sex is for married people.

Recent studies show the people who are enjoying sex the most are married people and the people who are having sex the most often are married people. Even our shared experience points to the fact that sex was made for marriage.

God made sex for marriage because sex is not just physical; it is relational. The Bible teaches that when two people have sex, they become united (1 Cor. 6:15–16). The apostle Paul uses the illustration that just as we become united with the Lord Jesus Christ and members of His body, that type of union is also true between sexual partners. That's a potent comparison.

Although oneness is often far from two people's minds when they are in bed together, they are becoming one. Because a couple doesn't know what is happening doesn't mean it isn't happening. The Bible teaches that you become members of each another.

Your body is the vehicle through which you express what's in the soul and spirit. There is no way to communicate with anyone outside your body. You use your five senses to relate. Even in silent prayer you are using your mind. You are not an ethereal being. God has clothed you in flesh so that you can have a vehicle to relate. You talk. You walk. You use your hands to serve. You use your ears to hear others. You use your eyes to see others. Your body houses your soul.

Sex was designed to be the most intimate expression of your soul. You cannot have sex with your body and leave your soul somewhere else. That was the Corinthian mentality.

Culture proclaims that sex is something you do. It is spoken of as an event. But in reality, it is an expression of all that you are. It is relational.

God has designed sex to take place inside a relationship called marriage. Sex is an expression of total abandonment of body, soul, spirit, life, and purpose. It's the ultimate way of saying, "I'm 1,000 percent yours and for you. And you're 1,000 percent mine and for me."

Because this is the zenith of intimacy, when sex is taken out of the context of marriage, there is damage to an individual's ability to be intimate. The more a person abuses this expression of intimacy, the greater the damage.

Thousands of married people go through the motions of sex but experience no intimacy. Their intimacy factor has been damaged through affairs or pornography or other ways.

When Paul said in 1 Corinthians 6:18 that "he who commits sexual immorality sins against his own body," he was essentially saying, "You're just hurting yourself."

When someone has sex but has no intention of giving himself wholly to the other person, he creates an emotional barrier between body and soul. He begins to get detached inwardly. The act of sex is artificially removed from the intent of sex, and consequently, sex is not as fulfilling as it was intended to be. Sometimes, this barrier is created after a breakup. A person gives herself totally to the other person, and then her partner ends the relationship. That explains why a person feels used after a breakup rather than during a relationship.

In either case, this emotional separation of sex from intimacy is a reality. And this reality comes back to haunt after the man or woman decides to marry. Depending on the number of sexual relationships previous to marriage, this wall is difficult to tear down. And suddenly, sex inside the context of marriage is no more fulfilling than it was before. In many cases it is less fulfilling.

Again, the longer one is involved in sex outside marriage, the higher and more impenetrable the wall becomes. And the price he pays relationally increases as well. In this area, as in every other, he reaps what he sows.

It is much easier for a man who has had sex before marriage to have an affair after marriage. Why? Because he is carrying his wall around. He thinks, *Gee, this has nothing to do with my love for my wife. She's great. This is just a physical thing with this other woman.* He has spent years programming his intimacy level with this false message: sex has nothing to do with intimacy.

But it does.

Reasons given for waiting for sex:

1. Want a committed relationship (88%)
2. Worry about STD (85%)
3. Worry about pregnancy (84%)
4. Wait until they're older (84%)
5. Worry about AIDS (83%)

—*Newsweek*, Oct. 17, 1994

SEX

■ *The physical union of a man and a woman that results in physical, relational, and spiritual oneness.*

The emptiness and guilt accompanying sex outside marriage are warning signals. And no matter how much a person brags about what great sex it was, there is something missing. Genuine intimacy.

The apostle Paul warned the Corinthian church that one who commits adultery or fornication is hurting his own body (1 Cor. 6:18). When a person sins sexually, she punishes herself. She alienates herself from intimacy. She sets herself up for a life of isolation.

Another component in all of this is what I call the adventure factor. Men especially are ingrained with a meet, win, conquer mentality. Not a lot of room for relationship.

Then they get married. The intimacy factor has been so damaged in his meeting, winning, and conquering that his marriage lacks any spark. Sex has not been used for intimacy; it was a component of a game. But the game is over. The man thinks, *Gee, there's something wrong with her. I'm not in love anymore.*

Women, on the other hand, quickly learn that sex can be used as a tool. They want a man, and our culture teaches how to get one—sex. So they use sex as a means to an end. They use sex to win and keep the guy they set their sights on. And in the process, they build a wall. Whenever sex is used for anything other than what it was intended for—intimacy and oneness—it loses its ability to accomplish what it was designed for.

In one recent study, 75 percent of high school students said they had already engaged in sex.
—*U.S. News and World Report*, Sept. 26, 1994

When these women get married, they've been through the cycle of trying to rebound unscathed emotionally from a broken sexual liaison so that their wall of detachment is firmly intact. They're hardened. They've learned to keep intimacy at arm's length so long that they become incapable of true intimacy after they're married.

And they lose. They've sinned against their own bodies. They did it to themselves. It's self-abuse.

These women were told to practice safe sex. No one mentioned walls. There is no safe sex outside marriage. You may be able to protect your body, but not your heart.

The sexual revolution has caused a relational famine. We have more sex and less intimacy. We have more sex and fewer lasting relationships than ever before. The world's philosophy doesn't work.

Think about it. Has sex outside marriage made this a better society? Or has sex outside marriage made this a more dangerous society, a more expensive society, a more pain-filled society?

Apparently, sex outside God's boundaries isn't the answer. Apparently, body and soul can't be separated. Apparently, a person becomes one with the sexual partner, whether he wants to or not. Apparently, there are emotional and relational consequences as well as physical ones. And the One who sees His gift of sex and intimacy in total shambles must grieve.

This chapter was not meant to be a how-to on sex. This has been a *why* and *when* chapter. The *why* has been because God gave us the gift to be used in the marital context. He delights in having His children express intimacy. It is a picture of our oneness with Him. It is the height of closeness and joy. It is the feeling of total completeness. It is God given.

The *when* has been the warning that whenever this gift is unwrapped outside God's boundaries, it is disaster. Even when one decides it is only physical, one is deluding herself because body and soul cannot be separated.

God's first command has been tampered with, tinkered with, and trampled on. And it's such a wonderful command. He gave it with such love and delight to His children.

The limits have been tested. The boundaries pushed. And it just hasn't worked. The One who purchased us and indwells us wants us to glorify God in the body (1 Cor. 6:19–20).

Sex can be compared to fire in the fireplace. A fire in the fireplace is lovely. Warm. Comforting. Inviting. Pleasurable. But put that same fire on the sofa or carpet, and it is disastrous. There is nothing inherently wrong with fire, but the location has changed and that has made all the difference.

APPLICATION

If I took the same sharp kitchen knife that I use to cut tomatoes and used it to scrape mud off my shoes, I should not be surprised to find that in time it would no longer do what it was designed to do—cut through tomatoes.

How foolish I would be to get angry at the knife or the manufacturer. I would be the one to blame, not the knife.

The problem is, I used it to do something it was not designed to do. It was designed for one thing—kitchen cutting. I used it for another—shoe scraping. My abuse dulled it.

Sex was designed for one union: marriage. To use it for anything other than what it was designed to do is to abuse it, dull it, ruin it. Sex was originally designed for pure pleasure and oneness. Because we've not used it as the Designer said, we're robbed of intimacy.

Perhaps you have scars of consequences because of sexual sin. The Lord Jesus has scars because of the consequences of your sins, too. There is hope. But you must face reality that the Designer knows best. Look up and thank Him that He can restore you to the intimacy He created you for. Your body and soul cannot be separated. He wants both to belong to Him.

That's the height of intimacy.

SEX

■ *The physical union of a man and a woman that results in physical, relational, and spiritual oneness.*

In fact, it's in marriage, the only coupling in which sex is fully sanctioned by society, where the highest rates of physical satisfaction were reported [88%].

—*Newsweek*, Oct. 17, 1994

Therefore a man shall leave his father and mother and be joined to his wife, and they shall become one flesh.

—Genesis 2:24

SERVICE AND OUTREACH

COMFORT

2 CORINTHIANS 1:3–4

SCRIPTURE

Blessed be the God . . . of all comfort, who comforts us in all our tribulation, that we may be able to comfort those who are in any trouble, with the comfort with which we ourselves are comforted by God.

COMMENTARY

What a marvelous title—God of *all* comfort!

We understand that although suffering is not eradicated, we have Someone who soothes us in the midst of it. Often we cry for even temporary pain relief, but the God of all comfort gives permanent consolation in the midst of excruciating pain. In our text, Paul makes it clear that the comfort from God is not for our benefit only but also for sharing with other hurting people.

When I was a little boy, I sustained my share of scraped knees and stubbed toes. After my mother had evaluated the seriousness of the injury, she would bring out one of two bottles of medicine. One I did not mind. One I hated.

The Mercurochrome was a nice red color. The small bottle was used for scrapes and scratches that weren't deep. I didn't mind it at all, and after the Band-Aid was applied, I ran off to play again.

The other small bottle was a different story. The iodine had an orange-colored tint that even looked like it would sting—which it did. When the cut was deeper, my mother would apply the iodine. No matter how much I begged for the milder red medicine, she knew best. My crying did not acknowledge her wisdom!

After the tiny applicator was rubbed on my wound and I was still loudly protesting, my mother did a wonderful thing. I can still picture it. She would gently blow on the stinging spot. My cries lessened as she soothed my body and, most of all, my heart.

This is perhaps one of the sweetest pictures to me of the God of all comfort. He, by the Holy Spirit, breathes comfort in the scrapes and wounds of life. The deeper the hurt, the more gentle the blowing.

APPLICATION

My mother didn't prevent the hurts, though she tried to warn me to be careful. Hurts are a part of a little boy's life.

Hurts are a part of a big man's life as well.

And the God of all comfort gets out either the gentle medicine or the stronger dose to heal the hurt. But the wonderful part is, He stays to comfort during the pain.

Comfort

COMFORT

■ *To soothe in distress; to bring consolation or hope.*

Comfort is found not in the absence of pain but in the midst of it. So many hurting Christians believe their walk with the Lord is not as it should be because of their intense pain. They don't feel comfortable. Feeling comfortable and being comforted are two different things. The first is a nice feeling but tends to come and go, as feelings do. The second is a fact based on the Comforter, not on circumstances. And He does not come and go: "I will never leave you nor forsake you" (Heb. 13:5).

Those who have experienced hurting or suffering know it gets tiring after a while. The weary saint cries out with Paul to remove the thorn. The Lord Jesus Christ Himself prayed for the cup to be removed. He was so physically and emotionally weary, an angel was sent to strengthen Him (Luke 22:43).

Often, however, the child of God hears nothing from heaven. These are particularly difficult times, especially if the suffering has persisted.

And it is precisely at these times the Comforter is the most precious. The Shepherd in the valley. The Father to His child. The Rock of ages. The Shelter in time of storm.

It is indeed a very natural thing for a parent to mourn a wayward child. It is difficult to feel comforted while the child turns his back on his parents and their God. If they are loving parents, their hearts will break all the years the child drifts. Does that mean they are not comforted? No! Their parental hearts might ache for years until they feel they cannot go on, but their regenerated souls will take great comfort that there is One who loves their child more than they do.

The wife whose husband has abandoned her will grieve and mourn, but does that mean she is not a victorious Christian? No! The victory comes when she goes to her empty bed and realizes there is One who will not abandon her. She hurts, but her soul rests in One who is able to soothe.

The husband who takes fresh flowers to a grave weeps uncontrollably when he remembers his wife's smile the first time he gave her flowers. Are the tears a mark of spiritual immaturity? No! The tears are a mark of a man who dearly loved his wife. His heart breaks, but his soul rests in the Comforter who promises he will see his wife again.

Peace is not the absence of pain. We wouldn't be promised a Comforter— much less need One—if the Christian life was a life of unending bliss.

A woman in our church wrote me a letter describing when she learned this principle. Her deep pain had gone on for years. She continued to serve the Lord with her husband during the long years of distress. One day a particularly overwhelming agony throbbed in the deepest part of her heart.

She was reluctant to tell her husband of her emotional injury, for he was bearing much anguish. Not knowing what had just taken place, her husband

> The typical view of the Christian life is one of deliverance from trouble. Scripture, however, calls us to deliverance *in* trouble.
> —Tim Hansel

> Those who have died in Christ are with Him. This is a fact in which you can find extravagant comfort. The world has no counter offer.
> —*In Touch*, March 1995

COMFORT

greeted her, "Dear, I was just checking the calendar. Don't forget you speak at a women's conference tomorrow." She could contain her emotions no longer. She wept as he held her tightly. She convulsed as she said, "I cannot speak. I have nothing to say. You need to speak in my place."

Her wise husband caressed her until her sobs subsided. He lifted her chin with his hand and said, "I have learned that you can have a pain in your heart and a settled peace in your soul at the same time."

The Comforter used her as she shared that truth the next day with other hurting women. She said, "I surely didn't share out of my fluff but out of a comforted, broken heart."

The Comforter soothes in various ways—through Scripture, through hymns, through other saints (who have probably been hurt), or through myriad tailor-made ways that suit the particular hurts. He is wonderfully creative, perfectly matching the comfort with the sorrow.

We have this assurance: "As one whom his mother comforts, so I will comfort you" (Isa. 66:13). This side of His comfort indicates His tenderness and gentleness, just as my mother cared for my hurts. As a comforting Father, He gives strength to go on in the midst of pain. As the perfect Parent, He has the perfect balance between the two.

The most wonderful thing is, as He is gently blowing on the stinging wound, He is remaining close to His child. One can almost hear Him saying, "Sweet hurting child, you are so special to Me. I hurt with you. I'm staying right here to take good care of you." The slogan of a billboard that was advertising a local hospital sums up the Father's care: "The most critical moments demand exceptional care."

In the year 1874, a passenger steamer, the *Ville de Havre,* was on the way to Europe. There was a family from Chicago on board—Mrs. H. G. Spafford and her four little daughters. The father, a Chicago lawyer, was too busy to go with them at the time, but he intended to follow later.

In midocean a collision took place with a sailing vessel, and nearly all on board were lost. The four children were drowned at sea, but a sailor discovered Mrs. Spafford floating in the water. He rescued her, and she cabled to her husband from shore, "Saved alone." Mr. Spafford started immediately for England to bring his wife back to Chicago. Dr. D. L. Moody left his meetings in Edinburgh and went to Liverpool to try to comfort the bereaved parents, and he was greatly pleased that they were able to say, "It is well; the will of God be done."

From that experience Mr. Spafford wrote the hymn "It Is Well with My Soul" to commemorate his children's tragic deaths. This hymn has been

My prayer for you today is that you will feel the loving arms of God wrapped around you.
—Billy Graham

If I would know the love of my friend, I must see what it can do in the winter.
—George Matheson

The next time you tell someone about Christ, listen carefully, see where the brokenness is and how Christ can put that person's life back together.
—Ravi Zacharias

Comfort

COMFORT

■ *To soothe in distress; to bring consolation or hope.*

Researchers at Southern California College found "that the elderly who actively practice their faith tend to be more optimistic and cope with illness better than their non-religious peers."
—Erling Jorstad

used to comfort others with the comfort he received from the Lord. The first verse says it all:

> *When peace, like a river, attendeth my way,*
> *When sorrows like sea billows roll;*
> *Whatever my lot, Thou hast taught me to say,*
> *It is well, it is well with my soul.*

Peace, such as the writer was describing, is often unexplainable to someone who has not experienced it. In my life, the deeper the sorrow has been, the more indescribable the peace. It may not always be well with my circumstances, my emotions, or my personality, but it is well, it is well with my soul!

GROWTH

Reading biographies of suffering saints often is an encouragement. Read some books about Amy Carmichael or Elisabeth Elliot or Corrie Ten Boom. They suffered greatly but were soothed mightily.

You may want to spend some time with your hymnal singing "Like a River Glorious" or "It Is Well with My Soul." As a hurting child, sing to the God of all comfort, "Jesus Loves Me."

QUOTES

Brokenness attracts brokenness.
—Charles Swindoll

God does not comfort us to make us comfortable, but to make us comforters.

—Dr. J. H. Jowett

EVANGELISM

1 PETER 3:15 NIV

But in your hearts set apart Christ as Lord. Always be prepared to give an answer to everyone who asks you to give the reason for the hope that you have. But do this with gentleness and respect.

COMMENTARY

In his early years, the apostle Peter was an aggressive evangelist. His unbridled zeal for the Savior set him up for embarrassment and even shame before the Cross, yet the same man gave us one of the most succinct statements on the topic of evangelism to be found anywhere in the Scriptures.

I'm sure Peter struggled as we all do with the question of what is our part and what is God's part in evangelism. His tendency at times was to assume both parts! In time, Peter learned that the key is balance. Let's take a closer look at this wonderful verse.

He says to "set apart Christ as Lord." This is a reminder that Christ is your life. He is in control. He is your consuming passion. Since He is in control, you can trust Him to show you how, when, and where to share the gospel. Real evangelism, then, begins with surrender to the lordship of Christ. When Christ is set apart as Lord, He will make your life so appealing to unbelievers that they will ask you about the peace and contentment they observe.

This brings us to the main point of Peter's exhortation: "Always be prepared to give an answer to everyone who asks you to give the reason for the hope that you have."

Preparation takes time. The more prepared we are to present the evidence of God's truth, the better God is able to convict and change lives. Again, this requires some effort on our part. But after all, evangelism is one of the primary reasons God left us here.

In the last part of the verse Peter instructs us to maintain an attitude of gentleness and respect when sharing with others. In other words, "be polite." Communicating the good news of Jesus Christ with a sensitive and tactful spirit keeps us from offending others. The Cross is offensive enough (Gal. 5:11) to the unbeliever without a self-righteous attitude or condemning spirit getting in the way. Attitude and the spirit in which we communicate are as important as the words we say.

APPLICATION

Most believers have a desire to share faith with others. The problem comes in knowing how. The challenge of knowing what, when, and how to speak

EVANGELISM

■ *The process of communicating the message of salvation to unbelievers.*

is usually the major obstacle. The solution, however, is to take the time to get trained. Ignorance is not an acceptable excuse.

Another obstacle to personal evangelism is the time it takes for God to move an unbeliever to saving faith. It is easy to get frustrated when we do not see immediate results. I really struggled with this when I was younger. I wanted to plant the seed, water it, fertilize it, cultivate, and harvest all at once! I would become frustrated when people would not automatically get saved the first time they heard the gospel.

Through the years, I have grown to understand that it's up to God to give "the increase" (1 Cor. 3:6). My part is to faithfully sow His Word and look for those who are ripe for harvest. In our day of instant results it is hard for us to be patient and trust God to work in the hearts of people.

Remember, *evangelism is a process*. You may be doing a better job in evangelism than you realize. God works through your personality and faithfulness to His principles to draw someone into His kingdom. It may be in the form of helping your neighbor with yard work or taking food to a friend after the birth of a child.

Our actions and attitudes build bridges that allow us to share the gospel when the opportunity presents itself. Seeing evangelism as a process takes some pressure off. We shouldn't feel guilty if we don't verbally witness to everyone we meet. But at the same time, we are responsible for building meaningful bridges to the lost. And when the time comes, we are to share verbally what Christ has done in our lives and what He is willing to do in theirs.

The process of evangelism may last months or years. The wonderful experiences of sharing the good news with complete strangers and seeing them converted on the spot are the exceptions, not the rules. And even in these rare cases someone else probably had planted the seed.

It is not unusual to have some bad experiences with personal evangelism. Bad encounters can be so traumatic that they discourage you to the point of giving up. People are easily offended. Oftentimes they feel threatened. Unbelievers may accuse you of excessive piety. Or you may lead someone in a prayer for salvation and see no change in her life. In fact, she may appear to be going backward.

But having a bad experience is no reason to give up. Women who have difficult deliveries or lose a baby through a miscarriage generally don't give up. Often they emerge from the situation more determined than ever to bring another child into this world. Like physical birth, spiritual birth is not without its risks. Seeing a man or woman brought into God's family is no easy undertaking. Some pain and disappointment will be involved.

In upcoming decades, an anticipated 80 million people—new residents and tourists—will flood the U.S. shores. These newcomers will offer immense opportunities for witness and ministry.
—*Missions USA,*
  May–June 1995

EVANGELISM

Jesus said, "A woman, when she is in labor, has sorrow because her hour has come; but as soon as she has given birth to the child, she no longer remembers the anguish, for joy that a human being has been born into the world" (John 16:21). In other words, the reward is worth the pain. The same is true in the evangelism process. There is a price to be paid for being a part of a man's or woman's salvation. But the struggle and disappointments are quickly forgotten when we see those we love birthed into God's family. There is a joy that can't be explained. So don't give up on evangelism. To give up on evangelism is to give up on God. After all, He is the One responsible to save and change lives. He wants us to be a part of the process.

> **W**hen true believers are awed by the greatness of God and by the privilege of becoming His children, then they become sincerely motivated, effective evangelists.
> —Bill Hybels

Brian works for a large corporation. When he started his job, his goal was to reach his work associates for Jesus Christ. He knew he would need to move slowly and wisely. He began by praying for each of them by name. He prayed specifically that God would give him an opportunity to get to know each man. Second, he prayed for an opportunity to share the gospel.

One afternoon, Phil, who works next to Brian, mentioned the need to get to know his neighbors better without becoming a nuisance. Brian told him the Bible talked about becoming a nuisance if we spent too much time with our neighbors. Phil said, "You are kidding!" Brian said, "No," and showed him the verse in Proverbs 25:17. Brian went on to explain the relevant subjects the Bible discussed. He gave Phil some tapes on the family.

Phil listened to the tapes and was hungry for more. He told Brian that was the first time he had ever seen any connection between the Bible and real life. Over a period of six months Phil's appetite for spiritual things increased. Both families spent time together at nonthreatening church-sponsored events. It was becoming clearer and clearer to Phil that becoming a Christian meant a personal relationship with Jesus Christ. Six months after the conversation about neighbors Phil trusted Christ as his Savior. It is exciting to see the grace of God at work in a new believer's life. The evangelism process may be six minutes, six days, six months, six years, or sixty years. We never know how long it will take, but it's worth it.

GROWTH

You can begin the process of personal evangelism right now.

Make a list of the people in your life who are unbelievers. Pray for them at least once a week. As you pray, you will begin to sense a heartfelt burden for the people on your list. When you see them, you will be more conscious of your behavior. You will look for ways to share the gospel. Praying for

EVANGELISM

■ *The process of communicating the message of salvation to unbelievers.*

the lost keeps your perspective in line with God's perspective. It develops sensitivity and compassion for unbelievers.

Make a commitment to spend time studying about evangelism. The life of Jesus is the best place to start. Read the book of John and watch how He related to each individual He came into contact with.

Find an evangelism class that will teach you to share your faith and hold you accountable to do so.

QUOTES

The Evangelistic Harvest is always urgent. The destiny of men and of nations is always being decided. Every generation is strategic. We are not responsible for the past generation, and we cannot bear the full responsibility for the next one; but we do have our generation. God will hold us responsible as to how well we fulfill our responsibilities to this age and take advantage of our opportunities.

—Billy Graham

When the Word produces spiritual birth in the person's heart, we can harvest that crop—a new believer. But we don't just hide that harvest in a barn; we equip and send the new believer to multiply, bearing fruit in others' lives.

—Jim Peterson

GOSPEL

1 CORINTHIANS 15:1–5

Brethren, I declare to you the gospel which I preached to you, which also you received and in which you stand, by which also you are saved, if you hold fast that word which I preached to you—unless you believed in vain. For I delivered to you first of all that which I also received: that Christ died for our sins according to the Scriptures, and that He was buried, and that He rose again the third day according to the Scriptures, and that He was seen by Cephas, then by the twelve.

COMMENTARY

The Greek word for "gospel" is *euangelion*. Originally, it meant "a reward for doing something good." In time it came to mean "good news." The apostle Paul was preaching the good news of the death of Christ for our sins along with His bodily resurrection from the dead. So the gospel is the good news of the death and resurrection of Jesus Christ.

Notice, the gospel includes both His death and His resurrection. If Christ did not rise from the dead, He would be no different from any other religious leader. After all, every other religious leader died for something. But only Jesus validated His claims by coming back to life. Let's examine the gospel with these two events in mind.

The first event of the gospel is Christ's substitutionary death on the cross. Paul says, "Christ died for our sins." That is, He took our punishment for us. Sin created a great chasm between us and God. God came to earth in the person of Jesus Christ to make it possible for us to go to heaven. His very purpose for coming was to save sinners (Luke 19:10). God placed on Him the sin of all humankind (2 Cor. 5:21). Jesus served as the sacrificial Lamb of God: the perfect, sinless Sacrifice to take away the sin of the entire human race. That is what Paul means when he says, "Christ died for our sins." That is the heart and core and pinnacle of the gospel. But the message of the gospel does not end with the Cross.

The second event of the gospel is the resurrection of Jesus Christ. When Christ rose from the dead, it was God's proclamation to all humankind that He accepted Jesus' atoning death on the cross; the Father was satisfied; the barrier of sin had been removed. The Resurrection was proof that God recognized His Son's death as the final payment for the sins of humankind. The Resurrection was a proclamation that Christ had conquered sin, death, and the devil. It guarantees there is life beyond the grave.

Second, the Resurrection serves as further proof of Jesus' identity. He predicted He would come back to life after three days. If there was no

GOSPEL

resurrection, Christ would have been a liar. His resurrection was undeniable evidence of His divine origin.

Jesus Christ rose from the dead to give believers the assurance of forgiveness—a vital part of the gospel of Christ. So the gospel is both Christ's death on the cross and His resurrection from the grave for the sins of humankind.

APPLICATION

There are two ways to apply what I have said about the gospel. The first way is personal appropriation, that is, putting your personal trust in Christ's death on the cross as the payment for your personal sin. It is only when you express personal faith in Christ that His forgiveness is applied to your life. God never forces salvation on anyone. It is a choice you must make.

A second way is sharing the gospel with someone else. An important part of the Christian life is explaining the gospel to others. Although most Christians have confidence in the power of the gospel, many times they lack confidence in their ability to share the gospel. They often fear they will say something inappropriate or be misunderstood. The best way to avoid an awkward situation is to learn to share the gospel in the course of everyday conversation.

One approach is to become familiar with topics that lend themselves to a mention of the gospel. Three topics that fit this description are death, God, and church.

Most people fear death. Current events often involve people in life-threatening situations. These situations lend themselves to discussions about death. It is not unusual in the course of a year to meet people who have lost a friend or relative. In their hearts they are pondering questions about life after death, about God and heaven, about the possibility of an afterlife. Often they are experiencing deep hurt and grief over the loss. Hearing that God loves and cares for them during times of great loss is encouraging. Hearing someone talk with confidence about life after death could be reassuring. So, the reality of death naturally leads into a conversation about the gospel.

The second topic that lends itself to a mention of the gospel is God. Most people believe in a god, although the object of their worship may not be the God of the Bible. There is emphasis today on spiritual belief. I believe this resurgence of interest in the divine is a result of the human hunger for "a god" that can be looked to for inner strength and security. When talk about God occurs, you shouldn't miss the opportunity to point out that the God

> Religions are man's search for God; the Gospel is God's search for man.
> —E. Stanley Jones

of Scripture is personal and desires an intimate relationship with us; He is a God who can be known and experienced through faith in Christ. Discussing the nature and character of God will always bring you back to the gospel.

A third approach is a conversation about church. This is probably the least threatening of the three we have discussed. Unbelievers often caricature the church as irrelevant or an institutional dinosaur on the brink of extinction. At the same time some people have warm feelings about their childhood church experience and turn back to the church when the disappointments of adulthood seem overwhelming.

By explaining how your church experience has helped you handle life's challenges, you are paving the way for a mention of the gospel. People are generally impressed when they hear about people working together to help one another. Many are looking for a place where they can get some help. Take time to share some practical things you have learned at church. Classes you have attended on finance or marriage or child rearing may spark the interest of nonattenders. They may have no idea that a church addresses these topics. Then at the right time, you can share why the ministry of your church is so effective, why your church is interested in the practical needs of men and women.

If your church offers specialty classes that deal with how to manage money or how to have a fulfilling marriage, these are often safe doors through which your unsaved friends can enter the church. Invite them to visit with you. Let them see the good news in action. Provide them with an opportunity to fellowship with men and women who have experienced the good news personally. Continue to discuss these truths and how they have affected you personally.

Two phrases you should become familiar with are these: (1) "since I trusted Christ as my Savior," and (2) "since I put my faith in Christ's death on the cross as payment for my sin." Each contains the core of the gospel. Practice incorporating them into conversation. As you do, you will find that mentioning the gospel comes more naturally.

My son, Andy, and a friend of his frequently eat breakfast at a local restaurant after exercising together. They were discussing the Bible over breakfast when they were abruptly interrupted by a woman at the table across from them. Excitedly, she asked, "Are you talking about the gospel?" "Why, yes," they said, rather surprised by her interruption. She began to pour out her heart over the need she and her husband had for God's direction for their lives. Through tears and a wave of emotion, she told of the lifeless church they were attending and the spiritual hunger they were experiencing.

> The shifting systems of false religion are continually changing their places; but the gospel of Christ is the same forever. While other false lights are extinguished, this true light ever shineth.
> —Theodore Ledyard Cuyler

> The possession of the good news of the gospel involves the obligation to share it.
> —William Barclay

GOSPEL

■ *The good news of the death, burial, and resurrection of Jesus Christ for our sins.*

After asking a couple of probing questions, they discovered that she had believed the gospel as a child but had never been discipled. Consequently, she had never grown much in her faith. She was starving for fellowship and truth. They left her with a map to our church, two gospel-related tapes, but most of all hope. The following Sunday she and her husband were on the front row of our church. After the service they were overwhelmed with gratitude and thanksgiving. They couldn't wait to come back. A major turning point for the couple came over a gospel conversation. There is power in the gospel (Rom. 1:16).

GROWTH

The following list of materials will help you continue to learn more about how to share the gospel with others. The books include *How to Give Away Your Faith* by Paul Little; *Know Why You Believe* by Paul Little; *I'm Glad You Asked* by Ken Boa and Larry Moody; and *More Than a Carpenter* by Josh McDowell.

The periodicals include *Decision* (Billy Graham Association, 1-800-487-0433) and *Christian Research Institute* (CRI Publications, 1-800-443-9797).

QUOTES

The gospel to me is simply irresistible.
—Blaise Pascal

The Gospel is not a secret to be hoarded but a story to be heralded. Too many Christians are stuffing themselves with Gospel blessings, while millions have never had a taste.
—Vance Havner

MISSIONS

MATTHEW 28:19

SCRIPTURE

Go therefore and make disciples of all the nations, baptizing them in the name of the Father and of the Son and of the Holy Spirit.

COMMENTARY

Commonly known as the Great Commission, this Scripture is the cornerstone of the Christian ethic concerning missions. Although the term *mission* or *missions* is never used in the Bible, it is apparent that was Jesus' task assignment to the disciples.

Jesus' ministry on earth was finished, and it was time for Him to ascend to heaven to be with the Father. With His work completed, Jesus took one last opportunity to remind the disciples that their primary job description was to "make disciples" of all nations. It is significant that Jesus emphasized this task. Jesus took this last chance to spell out His assignment to the disciples and left no room for doubt about their primary objective. Simple, no three-point sermon with seven objectives: "Go therefore and make disciples of all the nations, baptizing them in the name of the Father and of the Son and of the Holy Spirit."

This is in no way indicative of Jesus' lack of concern or compassion for people who were hungry or sick. However, He (more than anyone) understood that the first thing the disciples should be concerned with was making disciples or, in our terms, leading people into a growing relationship with Jesus Christ. That was the bottom line, so to speak. Otherwise those left behind might have full stomachs and still spend eternity in hell. It wasn't an either-or situation. Throughout Jesus' ministry, He participated in feeding hungry people and healing sick ones; yet He recognized that a hungry lost person is exactly that, hungry and eternally lost.

Therefore, Jesus gave the disciples their job description, knowing that as they fulfilled this assignment, they would carry on His work. No longer would He be around to preach sermons on the side of a mountain or from a boat anchored near shore. It was up to the disciples to carry on in His absence. The task was clear and probably a little intimidating!

It might have been a little easier had Jesus said, "Make sure that you disciple your neighbors and those who are a part of the local church," but Jesus understood the big picture—that His was a global mission, not merely for the community. The scope of the mission encompassed all nations; thus, it was clear that Jesus was sending the disciples out to disciple the world, not just their neighbors. The reference to all nations had more to do with

While it is projected that by the year 2000 the income of global foreign missions will be $2 billion, the income from the sale of tobacco will be $290 billion.

Missions

MISSIONS

The apostle Paul was one of the first missionaries. He traveled throughout Asia Minor (modern-day Turkey) and Greece, founding churches.
—Mark D. Taylor

peoples, cultures, and languages than countries or political boundaries. The word *nations* is sometimes translated in Scripture as "Gentiles," and it is from this word that we derive our word *ethnic*. A culture is a group of people bound by language, religion, tradition, and worldview. When Jesus spoke to the disciples and issued His last assignment, He used this word to encompass all groups of people, with the mission being to disciple them with the truth of the gospel.

Not only did Jesus recognize the scope of the mission He was sending the disciples out to accomplish, but He understood that it was an emotional time for the disciples. The One whom they had followed, believed in, and observed as Healer and Counselor was leaving them. Having spent the last three years together, Jesus knew it would not be easy for the disciples as they went their separate ways. Therefore, He gave them this assurance: "And lo, I am with you always, even to the end of the age" (Matt. 28:20). He knew it would be a difficult task and that there would be times of discouragement, but He promised to sustain the disciples.

A CLOSER LOOK

Missions was not an afterthought for Jesus as He talked with the disciples on the mountain prior to His ascension. The missions theme that filters through the pages of the Bible is basic to its very existence. If you stop and think about it, there would be no need for the Bible were it not for the fact that God's heart was centered on reconciling us to Him. The Bible became His voice to the lost. Without a missionary heart, perhaps God would not have deemed the Bible necessary or even important. As the inspired Word of God, the Bible has served as the single most significant tool in advancing the gospel to the peoples of the world.

The accounts of those who worked to fulfill this mission are documented throughout its pages. Among them were Paul and Barnabas. Quoting Isaiah, they said, "For so the Lord has commanded us: 'I have set you as a light to the Gentiles'" (Acts 13:47). Many of the Epistles are prayer letters from the missionaries as they went about their task. Whether in jail or in a local church, whether at home or abroad, the biblical missionaries demonstrate their understanding of God's desire to reconcile humankind to Him and their role in His mission.

One of the great changes in the missionary movement today is that non-Western churches (for instance in Korea) are beginning to send out many missionaries.
—Mark D. Taylor

Jesus' words to the disciples that day are vital because they gave the disciples an outline for their continued work, and they do the same for us today. First, Jesus said, "Go." This is where the question of missionary versus witness is addressed. We are to disciple all people, but the admonition to "go therefore and make disciples of all the nations" demonstrates Jesus' desire that we carry the gospel to the world. "Love your neighbor" means that you will witness to that person and share the truth of Jesus Christ. It is a direct response to the leading of Christ when a believer chooses to answer the call and go to another part of the world to disciple people in a different culture. The Great Commission is not difficult to understand; however, what will we do in response? The task is laid out—"make disciples of all the nations, baptizing them." There can be no misunderstanding. Never, *never,* NEVER lose sight of the task at hand.

APPLICATION

As followers of Christ, modern-day disciples, we have His Word as our instruction manual. We have the written Word of God in which Jesus gives us clear and direct instructions and then promises that He will be with us to the very end of the age! We've already received our job assignment. Our responsibility is to complete the task and, in doing so, bring praise, honor, and glory to God.

Not everyone can go abroad. Missionaries are certainly called to foreign countries, but missionaries are working in hospitals and in inner-city projects right here in the United States. The call is to go, whether it be five miles, five hundred miles, or halfway around the world. We are missionaries as we share the truth of Jesus Christ with the lost. Yet God has given a special call to some people to reach those who live outside the comfort zone of their home environment.

For every believer, the task, or mission, is to lead people to the truth of Jesus Christ. In support of those who accept the call to be missionaries, it is the responsibility of every believer to uphold them through prayer, encouragement, and financial support. From prison, Paul spoke to the church at Ephesus about his need for prayer support when he wrote, "Pray also for me, that whenever I open my mouth, words may be given me so that I will fearlessly make known the mystery of the gospel, for which I am an ambassador in chains. Pray that I may declare it fearlessly, as I should" (Eph. 6:19–20 NIV).

The exciting application regarding missions is that ours is not a mission impossible! Jesus gave us a job to do, supplied us with an Instruction Manual on how to do the job, and then gave us His word that He would not desert us in our efforts to do what He commanded. What a wonderful job, to lead the lost to Jesus Christ, the One who destroys Satan's lies with the truth. We have a mission possible. The question for each of us is whether we will

There are now 140,000 Christian missionaries serving around the globe, according to *Operation World*. Evangelical Christianity is the only religion growing because of actual conversions. . . . Reports at a recent missions conference indicate that it is possible that every person on earth may hear the gospel by the year 2000.
—*Wesleyan Advocate,* Oct. 1994

accept the assignment and trust God to prove His faithfulness in empowering us to fulfill what He sent us here to do.

GROWTH

Ask God to give you a heart for missions as you study His Word and seek His will for your life as it relates to the task we are here to do. Whatever His particular will for you, it certainly is that you be involved in completing the task He assigned.

Support missionaries with your prayers, encouragement (letters, birthday gifts, little reminders that you are thinking of them), and financial support. Not everyone can make the trip and perform the duties of an astronaut, but ask any astronaut and he or she will stress the importance of an alert support staff at mission control. Likewise, those who stay behind and daily lift up missionaries in prayer, through personal encouragement, and through financial support, serve as the silent partners in this mission objective. It is a joint effort.

See if your church operates a missionary care center that offers clothes and other necessities to missionaries when they come home. If so, offer your time in organizing donated clothes and household items, helping missionaries as they come through the center and look for the things they need.

Volunteer as a short-term missionary during summer vacation. Not everyone goes to the mission field as a career missionary. There is never a lack of need or opportunity for those who wish to be a part of this vital work. It is a matter of willingness to follow the instructions that Jesus gave the disciples.

QUOTES

For there is no difference between Jew and Gentile—the same Lord is Lord of all and richly blesses all who call on him, for, "Everyone who calls on the name of the Lord will be saved." How, then, can they call on the one they have not believed in? And how can they believe in the one of whom they have not heard? And how can they hear without someone preaching to them? And how can they preach unless they are sent? As it is written, "How beautiful are the feet of those who bring good news!"

—Romans 10:12–15 NIV

Today we are at war and no one seems to know. This very hour our men and women are on the front lines, risking their lives for the most righteous cause. There was no news of it on TV last night. No yellow ribbons hang in remembrance of their plight. Few of us know who their family members are. Even fewer pray for their safety. Rare is the letter that is sent.

—Serving as Senders

Jesus said to them again, "Peace to you! As the Father has sent Me, I also send you."

—John 20:21

The spirit of Christ is the spirit of missions, and the nearer we get to him the more intensely missionary we must become.
—Henry Martyn

NEW AGE MOVEMENT

■ *The infiltration of Eastern religion and occult mysticism into Western civilization.*

SCRIPTURE

GENESIS 3:4–5

The serpent said to the woman, "You will not surely die. For God knows that in the day you eat of it your eyes will be opened, and you will be like God, knowing good and evil."

COMMENTARY

At first glance, it is absurd to think that the best explanation of New Age philosophy can be found in the Bible. Yet Satan first laid out his plan to Eve in the Garden of Eden. As the founding leader of this philosophy, Satan set out his ideas for Eve and for those who would follow as a three-part sermon that went something like this:

First, "you will be like God." The term used for this philosophy is *pantheism,* or the doctrine that identifies God with the entire universe, including every particle, tree, table, animal, and person. God is all and all is God sums it up pretty well.

Second, "you will not die" is the part of the plan that has come to be known as New Age. Reincarnation could best be called the "round and round you go and where you stop nobody knows" way of life. It is the belief in the cyclical evolution of a person's soul that passes from one body to another at death, continuing until the soul reaches a point of perfection.

The third point is extremely cunning, appealing to the intellect, with the promise of a sense of enlightenment that will ultimately lead to truth: "your eyes will be opened, and you will know good and evil." Who wouldn't want to know good from evil? For the New Age thinker, the more you know, the closer you come to truth. But not truth in the Christian sense. For in the New Age movement, truth is fluid. What is true for you may not be true for me.

Although Satan's three-point objective for Eve sounded good, the truth became evident the moment she disobeyed God's commandment. And the truth was not what Eve expected or wanted. Her eyes were opened, and what she discovered should have been a clue to the rest of humanity to come. She wasn't God and she had a clear understanding of how desperately wrong she had been. Prior to her act of disobedience, Eve experienced something we haven't known and will not know until we reach our eternal home in heaven with the Father. She lived in a world free of fear, guilt, rejection, crime, pain, and dishonesty. Yet she did what so many choose to do today;

she listened to Satan's lies. The woman who knew no guilt understood the ravages of disobedience and was never the same again.

What we see happening today in this "New" Age movement has been going on since the Garden of Eden. It is clear from Scripture that this movement should more appropriately be called the Old Age movement because of its inception in the Garden when Satan convinced Eve to move away from *the* truth to what sounded more appealing to her at the moment.

In the December 7, 1987, issue, a writer in *Time* magazine had this to say about this so-called new movement: "So here we are in the New Age, a combination of spirituality and superstition, fad and farce, about which the only thing certain is that it is not new." Even those in the secular media recognized that there was nothing new about this "new" movement. The twentieth-century gurus repackaged their selling points, reintroduced them via marketing, and charged enormous fees at seminars that targeted a new audience. Many have been led to believe, as Eve did, that enlightenment was the path to truth, only to discover that God never abandoned the standard He set from the beginning of creation. Jesus reinforced that by saying, "I am the way, the truth, and the life. No one comes to the Father except through Me" (John 14:6). It wasn't a matter for debate. Jesus doesn't fit the neatly mundane boundaries of New Age philosophers. Contrary to what they think, Jesus wasn't just a good guy. He was Christ, the Savior of humankind. This truth has escaped those who believe in the teachings of New Age.

With so much at stake and so many misconceptions that go with the New Age philosophy, we must never lose our perspective on just who began this whole way of thinking. It was Satan, and anyone who tells you different is telling you a lie. It is essential to the New Age way of life that you believe in the second- and third-chance theory, that proponents devalue the consequence of sin. Many well-meaning people believe that mistakes (*sin* never enters their vocabulary) are not something they need to spend a lot of time worrying about since they'll get another chance to get things right.

As the old hymn says, "My hope is built on Jesus' blood." Anything less is a pitiful failure that will be the eternal nightmare of those who die believing they'll have another chance only to wake up to the error of their belief. As their followers grow in number, the evidence of lives in search of meaning is apparent. It is my obligation (and yours) as a child of God to be a light in this darkened age, to speak the truth in love. The task isn't an easy one because our way is narrow, as Scripture says, but we are given the responsibility of sharing the truth with deceived people.

> When you have taken time to build a relationship with a New Ager, your witness is more likely to be well received. . . . Friendship evangelism has been found to be one of the most effective ways of gaining permanent converts to Jesus Christ.
> —Gordon Lewis

New Age Movement

NEW AGE MOVEMENT

One of the most frustrating things that I encounter when trying to explain or define New Age thinking is that it incorporates so many different avenues of belief. Whatever works for the particular person involved is usually the bottom line. However, those who claim to believe in this philosophy adhere to some basic tenets. One is the belief in reincarnation. In this view, when people die, they do not go to heaven or hell; they just come back to earth and take another shot at life. The quality of the next life depends on the quality of this one. Evil is punished next time around, and good is rewarded as well.

This "system" is based on the law of karma—people get what they deserve. An impersonal force keeps a record of credits and debits, based on behavior, leading to these conclusions:

1. In the end, you win because you get chance after chance.
2. Time is a perpetual merry-go-round.
3. You determine your own destiny.
4. The problem is not sin; it is ignorance.
5. Enlightenment is the path of spiritual progress.

To those who hold firmly to New Age beliefs, God is a force rather than a personal being. Even more basic to New Age beliefs, we are all God. Along with all of nature, we are all one. If that sounds too mysterious, it's only because you have not reached the stage of enlightenment necessary to enter into these truths. Be patient. Next time around, things will become clearer.

The truly dangerous thing is that New Age philosophy is like a sponge. It can absorb all religions, cultures, and governments. There are no real contradictions, only imagined ones. They appear to be contradictions only to unenlightened ones. Jesus is a key figure in much of New Age thought and writing. In their desperate attempt to make Jesus fit into their philosophy, New Agers have found a way to discount what we see as indications of their mistaken ideas. You will never hear New Agers call Jesus a liar or a hoax. Instead, they preach that Jesus was not *the* Christ. Rather, the Christ spirit dwelt in Him and is available to us all. The *Christ spirit* becomes a term for the spirit available to all, the divine energy force of life.

Let's look at the areas that Satan focused on. The last thing that he wanted was for Eve to know the truth, yet he deceived her by playing on her "intellect" with the assurance that she would be "smarter"—even to the point of having something to hold over Adam's head. Recognizing this potential for pride in Eve, Satan pushed the right button, so to speak, and we

The Eastern-influenced views of those following New Age thinking contend that we are our own gods, we dictate what happens in our lives, and we can experience whatever is necessary for ultimate significance.
—George Barna

know what happened. I'm sure that she would have traded her newfound intelligence for her old sense of naivete. She found out, as we know, there is only one God.

Those who believe in this New Age way of thinking say that Jesus is *a* way to God, not *the* way to God. The truth that escapes New Age thinkers is apparent in our belief that God is the Creator of heaven and earth, that Jesus is the Savior of humankind, and that sin results in death without Christ. Because of this "narrow" belief system, many find the New Age movement attractive because it appears to be so fair, so liberating. Good people make progress, bad people suffer, and people get what they deserve. For those who are uncomfortable with the idea of sin and its consequences, the New Age thinker quickly points out the belief in a system that allows a person to go through this life without too much worry because of getting another chance!

The contradiction between what New Agers say and their behavior is obvious and leads those of us who have accepted the truth of Scripture to the conclusion that they speak out of both sides of their mouths! Although they believe that good works lead to a better life next time around, helping someone who is struggling contradicts their belief system since that person is obviously getting what he or she deserves. Can you see their bind? Helping others is a good way to earn points for the next life; yet helping others is not good since that person deserves to struggle. I'm thankful that we don't have to live in that bondage.

The bottom line for those who adhere to the New Age philosophy is the same as it is for every other religion, except Christianity. It boils down to salvation by works. Somewhere a force is keeping score, but we can never be sure what the rules are and where we fit in the sliding scale of good and bad. If we were to accept the teaching that New Agers espouse, we would have to agree that we have no need for a Savior; we just need another chance to get it right. The only problem is, we're not sure what right is!

While it should be obvious to believers how mistaken this New Age philosophy is, it saddens me that a growing segment of society continues to fall for the lies that Satan began teaching in the Garden. Grace plays no part in the New Age thinker's dogma. Everything depends on getting another chance to get it right. But there aren't enough chances, and even if there were, we'd still miss the mark. That's why God knew we needed a Savior, not a guru with nice-sounding words that give us warm, fuzzy feelings. The harsh reality of hell—and our inability to work our way out of our eternal destiny without Christ—is the truth that we must continue to preach to our

> **D**o not assume that just because New Agers use words that sound Christian—such as "Jesus," "Christ," "atonement," "ascension," and so forth—that they are using these words in the same way you are. Ask New Agers to define these words.
> —Ron Rhodes

> **T**he use of fashions in thought is to distract the attention of men from their real dangers.
> —C. S. Lewis

New Age Movement

NEW AGE MOVEMENT

misguided friends. Otherwise, they will discover the truth when this life ends and they arrive at their eternal destination—not the next step up the ladder, but the place in which those without Christ will spend eternity. Hell is not a nice thing to think about. That's why so many have turned to a philosophy that eliminates this obvious mistaken idea that Christians have preached for so long.

As believers, we have the calling to speak the truth at the risk of being labeled narrow-minded and losing friends. That's a risk I'm glad to take.

APPLICATION

Although the contradictions within the New Age philosophy seem obvious, the application is difficult to consider because of the conclusions that we cannot escape. If we take what New Agers say they believe to its logical conclusion, we discover some real problems. If we believe people get what they deserve, we find justification for unkindness, selfishness, and greed. Now wait a minute, you say, isn't that a bit extreme? I don't think so, and I'll explain why.

A look backward at the caste system that once was the ruling way of life in India essentially said that people of good fortune deserved it and people of bad fortune deserved it. Much of that has changed now but is being reinvented in today's New Age philosophies. It says that I am under no obligation to help someone who is in trouble or hurting because they deserve it. The logical extension of this belief is that helping people with bad fortune would slow down their progress and would ultimately cause them more pain. In other words, good becomes evil.

If I had the time and space, I could carry this application out and readily show its impact in every area of life. I could argue that homeless people deserve to be homeless, that hungry people deserve to go to sleep with empty stomachs, that they are just getting what they deserve. And then adding insult to injury, the New Age believer is quick to remind us that what is happening now is only temporary. We must remember they'll have another chance to get it right!

> **"T**hou shalt not interfere with another's reality" might be called the First Commandment of New Age revelation.
> —Elliot Miller

God has not given us the option of a second chance after this life. The cross of Christ is our only hope. When Jesus hung dying on the cross, He didn't correct the thief who believed in Him with his last breath. He didn't say, "Oh, you've got it wrong. This is just the first go-round. Don't worry. You'll get another chance." No, Jesus affirmed for all present that He and the thief would spend eternity in paradise.

NEW AGE MOVEMENT

Genesis 3 contains Satan's version of what has been labeled the New Age movement. But in Revelation 21, we find God's definition of the real new age: "Now I saw a new heaven and a new earth, for the first heaven and the first earth had passed away" (v. 1). Jesus did come back to life but not as someone else. He returned that first Easter morning as the risen Lord and appeared to those who loved Him and were present at His crucifixion. The New Agers are right about us making a round trip—but only once and not as somebody else. When Christ returns, as He promised, we will join Him for the beginning of a new age that is written about in Revelation. It is something that we, as believers, look forward to and something that should cause those who cling to New Age thinking to shudder.

We cannot work our way out of hell. Therefore we do not need a second chance. We need a Savior.

God knew that, and in His all-consuming love, He chose to send that Savior, Jesus Christ, His only Son. We can theorize and dream all we want, but we can never do enough to account for our sins. That's why God showed us such mercy and allowed His Son to die for our sins, not our mistakes. Nothing that we can come up with can outdo Him. My prayer for all of us is that the light will shine through us to a darkened world and that those who falsely believe in their ability to get it right will come to a new and saving understanding of grace. When Jesus said that the truth would set you free, He staked His very life on it.

The application for you, if you believe in Christ as your Savior, is to take every opportunity you are given to tell those who do not know Him as Savior what they are missing and where they will end up without Him. The application, if you are someone who straddles the fence, toying with New Age philosophy, is to find a godly individual who will lead you to the truth. There is no provision made for another chance. Either you accept the grace of God as provided through Jesus' sacrificial death at Calvary, or you will spend your eternity regretting the choice you made. There are few guarantees in life, but this is one of them.

> The study of Kosmin and Lachman, in which 113,000 adults were interviewed, found that less than one-tenth of 1 percent of all adults labeled themselves "New Age."
> —George Barna

OCCULT

■ *The belief in and use of supernatural forces to predict future events or bring about a specific result.*

EPHESIANS 6:12

For we do not wrestle against flesh and blood, but against principalities, against powers, against the rulers of the darkness of this age, against spiritual hosts of wickedness in the heavenly places.

COMMENTARY

If you searched the Bible for the term *occult,* you would come up empty-handed. However, numerous references are made in Scripture to the practice of astrology and to those who act as mediums. These practices, among others, are well within the definition for the occult or occult practices.

With all the references to occult practices in the Bible, in Ephesians Paul defines the true nature of the Christian's struggle. Primarily divided into three sections, Ephesians addresses (1) Christ and the church, (2) the conduct of the believer, and (3) the Christian's warfare, which is the focus of this chapter on the occult. Taking note of Paul's warning, we read in Ephesians 6:10–20, with specific emphasis on 6:12, that the believer's battle is against the forces of darkness. It is spiritual in nature. The very use of words such as *darkness* and *spiritual hosts of wickedness* is inherent to the definition of occult.

Paul's message takes on the tone of a soldier, ready for battle, as he began this part of his letter to the church at Ephesus: "Finally, my brethren, be strong in the Lord and in the power of His might. Put on the whole armor of God, that you may be able to stand against the wiles of the devil" (Eph. 6:10–11). Paul wanted the church to make sure they did not give in to confusion regarding the real source of their struggle. To fight and win, Paul understood the necessity of knowing the enemy and knowing how to wage a successful battle. If Satan can confuse the believers and divert attention from the truth, he can defeat believers in daily trials. There is no escaping the struggle.

Having made it clear that believers are in the middle of spiritual warfare, Paul lays out a plan to defeat Satan's schemes. Being armed with the truth, faith, the helmet of salvation, and the sword of the Spirit (God's Word) is essential to a daily victorious walk. Scripture leaves no doubt that practices such as those I have defined as being occult are spiritual forces of evil, and as such, it is incumbent that believers be equipped to fight a spiritual battle, not "flesh and blood" as our reference verse advises.

The word *occult* may be new to our age, but the practices are documented throughout Scripture. The occult was alive and well in the days of the Bible. The warning of Paul to the church at Ephesus is the same for us today—be alert to the wiles of Satan and be equipped with the armor of God. Although

Some 42 percent of American adults believe they have been in contact with someone who has died. . . . Some 14 percent of Americans endorse the work of spirit mediums or channelers.
—Ron Rhodes

Service and Outreach

we are in a spiritual battle, nowhere does Scripture suggest that we are to live in fear. Alert, yes. Afraid, no. The victory is already ours, though the battle today continues.

As Paul indicated in Ephesians 6:12, believers must understand who we struggle against. Often we blame a person, a circumstance, or an event for our struggles. Paul wants us to be absolutely clear that our battle is not against flesh and blood. We must remember that Satan and his workers do not appear as devilish beings that we fear. Rather, as 2 Corinthians 11:13–15 states, "For such are false apostles, deceitful workers, transforming themselves into apostles of Christ. And no wonder! For Satan himself transforms himself into an angel of light. Therefore it is no great thing if his ministers also transform themselves into ministers of righteousness, whose end will be according to their works."

Some practices of the occult are obvious, and any believer can recognize them as coming from Satan. Satanism is one of the most obvious occult practices. Many of what would be considered the worst occult practices are connected to satanism. They include, but are not limited to, the worship of Satan, black magic, the black mass, sexual and ritual physical abuse, and some areas of the drug culture.

In their book *The Occult,* Josh McDowell and Don Stewart describe the Church of Satan as follows:

> Although the Church of Satan sounds like a contradiction in terms, the emphasis of the organization is on materialism and hedonism. Satan, to followers of this church, is more a symbol than a reality. In this emphasis they depart from other forms of Satanism. They are interested in the carnal and worldly pleasures mankind offers.

In addition to satanism and the Church of Satan, witchcraft is a continuing practice that the believer must be alert to. Again, in the book *The Occult,* the writers give us an idea of the impact of witchcraft on today's world:

> Modern witchcraft bears little resemblance to the witchcraft of the Middle Ages or to witchcraft in still primitive, preliterate societies. Modern witchcraft is a relatively recent development (the last 200 years), embraces hundreds of beliefs and practices and has hundreds of thousands of adherents. The one common theme running through modern witchcraft is the practice of and belief in things forbidden by God in the Bible as occultic.

About 67 percent of American adults claim to have had a psychic experience such as extrasensory perception.
—Ron Rhodes

OCCULT

■ *The belief in and use of supernatural forces to predict future events or bring about a specific result.*

Certainly, the believer would readily recognize the practice of Satan worship and witchcraft as being forbidden by the Bible and occult in nature. Other practices might not be so quickly identified as satanic or occult, however. The practice of astrology, including the use of horoscopes and predicting events by the alignment of planets, is forbidden and rebuked in Deuteronomy 18:10 and Isaiah 47:12–13. Yet many Christians consider it harmless to consult their horoscopes in the daily newspaper. Another practice, divination (fortune-telling) is forbidden in Deuteronomy 18:9–14; Isaiah 44:25; and Jeremiah 27:9. In Ezekiel 13:8, the Lord calls the word of diviners a lie. In Leviticus 20:27, the law of Moses made this practice punishable by death. In Acts 16:16, we find that divination was a lucrative business at Philippi. Other scriptures could be included, but it is abundantly clear that the practice of fortune-telling is occultic in nature and forbidden by Scripture.

The Bible condemns other practices, such as enchantments, sometimes referred to as incantations, spells, or charming. In Deuteronomy 18 and Isaiah 19:3, this practice is condemned. The practice of magic is forbidden by God (Ex. 7:11–12). There is considerable debate about the practice of magic. The term *sleight of hand* or *illusion* has been used to refer to what artists do who commercially perform for paid entertainment. There is a difference between one who practices magic, depending on supernatural forces, and those who perform acts of illusion or sleight of hand, where they admittedly perform acts based on illusion, not supernatural powers.

A friend of mine is a master illusionist. He is great at doing tricks, but he explains to those who see his performance that his tricks are just that—tricks, illusions—and that they have nothing to do with magic or supernatural powers. He leaves no doubt in his performances (a ministry that enables him to talk about the occult) that what he does is sleight of hand, as amazing as it appears to the onlooker.

You have probably enjoyed an illusion or trick performed in a show and never considered it to be anything dangerous. As children, many of us had our "fortunes" told at Halloween parties at school. The use of Ouija boards is thought by some as being a harmless form of entertainment, in no way connected to supernatural powers. But the practice of attempting to contact the dead through the use of a medium is strictly forbidden in the Bible (Deut. 18:10–12; 2 Kings 21:6; Lev. 19:31).

The following is part of the definition of the *Ouija board* found in *The Dictionary of Mysticism*: "An instrument for communication with the spirits of the dead. . . . The common feature of all its varieties is that an object moves under the hand of the medium." If we went no farther, there would

OCCULT

be no question that the use of a Ouija board is condemned by Scripture because it attempts to contact dead spirits through the use of a medium. Harmless play? Again, Satan would have us believe the lie that it is merely a fun game and harmless, but we must be alert to the lie and armed with the truth of Scripture.

The occult has found its way into every imaginable form of the media, portrayed in movies, so-called harmless comic books and games, graphically sung in music. In their book *When the Devil Dares Your Kids,* Bob and Gretchen Passantino make the following comment concerning the emergence of comic books that blatantly include occult practices: "Unfortunately, many of the new comics, some labeled 'for mature readers,' also provide readers with graphic images of infidelity, sexual perversion . . . black magic, destructive occultism . . . sado-masochism and foul language." Certainly, not all comic books, movies, and music contain occult material, but it is vital for Christians to be alert to and aware of how Satan uses the most common devices to spread his lies.

One game that has been the object of considerable debate is Dungeons and Dragons. Some argue with intensity that it is merely a child's game. Josh McDowell and Don Stewart have taken a close look at this game in their book *The Occult,* and they make this observation: "Those who believe it is a harmless game for expanding the imagination have not read the accounts of suicide and crime carried out by its participants." For a more detailed study, these authors note *The Truth About Dungeons and Dragons* by Joan Hake Robie in documenting the occult nature of this game.

It is not necessary to know every device that Satan uses to try to defeat Christians in daily struggles. But understanding his strategy is important, and his strategy is to divert, confuse, and deceive believers. Therefore, being armed with the truth of Scripture and understanding the victory that became ours as we accepted Christ's death as payment for our sins are our only weapons against Satan's devices. He can't win the war, and he can't stand the truth. Satan is a poor loser but a loser nonetheless. The truth of God's Word can't be destroyed, no matter how hard he tries. The devices of Satan are many, but they are worthless when confronted with the truth.

> There is a natural fascination with the supernatural realm. Satan probably capitalized on that by manifesting his overt activity, so as to draw minimal attention to his covert activity—lying, which is where he spends the majority of his effort.
> —John MacArthur, Jr.

 GROWTH

Paul admonished the church at Ephesus to be alert and to continue praying for all the saints. That should be a daily practice as we seek to be aware of Satan's devious ways, grounded in the truth, assured of our standing, and ready for whatever comes. I don't believe that it was Paul's intent to cause

OCCULT ■ *The belief in and use of supernatural forces to predict future events or bring about a specific result.*

the church at Ephesus to live in fear; instead, he wanted them to be sure of the truth and stand firmly on that truth.

Because this topic raises issues that can be dangerous if the believer becomes too engrossed in legitimately seeking to understand and be alert, I agree wholeheartedly with Josh McDowell and Don Stewart when they issue the following warning in their book *The Occult:*

> We realize that by informing people about the world of the occult, we will be exposing certain people to things and practices of which they have previously been ignorant. It is not our desire to stimulate one's curiosity in the realm of the occult to where it becomes an obsession. Seeing that mankind has a certain fascination about evil, it would be wise to take the advice of the apostle Paul, "I want you to be wise in what is good, and innocent in what is evil" (Romans 16:19).

Although it is not necessary or healthy to explore every occult practice, it is incumbent on us to be aware of Satan's strategy and the plan that God has given us to defeat our enemy. As a matter of daily commitment, we who call Jesus Lord must make a practice of putting on the armor that Paul speaks of, of being alert to (but not afraid of) Satan's efforts, and of standing firmly on the truth of Scripture and the authority we have over Satan.

Satan has a plethora of devices to attain his goal of defeating us in everyday struggles. However, Paul reminds us at the end of Ephesians 6 that we must not lose sight of what we are here to do: speak the truth of the gospel. If Satan can divert our attention from our stated purpose, his strategy has worked! Paul urged, "Pray on my behalf, that utterance may be given to me in the opening of my mouth, to make known with boldness the mystery of the gospel" (Eph. 6:19 NASB). Paul warned the church so that they (and us) would not be unaware of the devil's schemes, thus hampering the spread of the gospel.

We are fighting a spiritual battle. The battle is good against evil. God against Satan. Our responsibility is threefold: be alert, be armed to fight, and be ambassadors of the gospel. God has power over Satan and has given us authority over Satan, his devices, and his strategies. Taking Paul's counsel, we must arm ourselves with the truth of God's Word and declare that truth as we wage war against the enemy. If we are to be successful in this spiritual battle (and we certainly can be), we must continually renew our minds to the truth. We may accomplish this by daily study, prayer, and fellowship with other believers in small group study. Otherwise, Satan can bring

The world of the occult is built on one work, experience. It is not built upon Authority, Revealed Authority. We must test all experience by Divine Authority.
—Walter Martin

The Gallup organization found that between 1978 and 1984, belief in astrology among schoolchildren rose from 40 percent to 59 percent.
—Ron Rhodes

Service and Outreach

confusion and doubt into the lives of those who do not take advantage of the support afforded every believer as a part of the family of God.

QUOTES

Now the Spirit expressly says that in latter times some will depart from the faith, giving heed to deceiving spirits and doctrines of demons.

—1 Timothy 4:1

Many of those who had practiced magic brought their books together and burned them in the sight of all.

—Acts 19:19

So Saul died for his unfaithfulness which he had committed against the LORD, because he did not keep the word of the LORD, and also because he consulted a medium for guidance. But he did not inquire of the LORD.

—1 Chronicles 10:13–14

There are so many variables and options to play with that the astrologer is always right. Break a leg when your astrologer told you the signs were good, and he can congratulate you on escaping what might have happened had the signs been bad. Conversely, if you go against the signs and nothing happens, the astrologer can insist that you were subconsciously careful because you were forewarned.

—Time, March 21, 1969

SERVICE

■ *An act of assistance or benefit.*

SCRIPTURE

GALATIANS 5:13–14 NASB

For you were called to freedom, brethren; only do not turn your freedom into an opportunity for the flesh, but through love serve one another. For the whole Law is fulfilled in one word, in the statement, "You shall love your neighbor as yourself."

COMMENTARY

Anyone who has been involved in a church for long knows that there is always a struggle going on somewhere. Where people exist (even in church), there will always be disputes. That has been the case since the days of Paul's ministry. In this letter to the church at Galatia, Paul addressed a problem that existed between two groups within the church.

Some returned to legalism and the "works" theology that was most familiar and most comfortable for them. Others distorted grace and adopted the attitude that they were free from any moral or civil obligation. To reconcile the differences, Paul sought to bring the focus into proper perspective. He encouraged those who regressed to legalism to accept their gift of grace and urged those who used their freedom as moral license to understand that freedom demands responsibility.

In Galatians 5:13, Paul declared that believers are called to freedom and are no longer handcuffed to the standard of acceptance that every other religion in the world had been founded upon, salvation by works. Because of Jesus' death at Calvary, Paul made it clear that we have been set free from condemnation and that our sins are forgiven. However, he exhorted the Galatians not to use their freedom as permission to do as they pleased. Rather, he wrote that the freedom should express itself in the form of service. Two words could have been used for *serve*. The one used is in reference to the service done by a slave and usually refers to the duties of a slave, that is, to fulfill an obligation required by position, not by volunteering. Christians have an obligation to one another that goes beyond volunteering. It is more binding than that. Paul concluded the passage by admonishing the church that there is only way to fulfill the law and that is through love, specifically, through loving one's neighbor as oneself.

Therefore, you are to express your freedom through service and to fulfill the law by loving your neighbor. To serve is to love. Or put another way, if you love, service will be the logical and natural outcome. Service for any other reason is another form of legalism by which you strive for approval or acceptance.

> We worship God through service. The authentic server views each opportunity to lead or serve as an opportunity to worship God.
> —Bill Hybels

SERVICE

Before we consider the right reason for service (love), it is necessary to take a look at the wrong reasons—and there are many. Very often, service is done because there is a need, and on the surface, that appears to be perfectly logical. We automatically think of meeting a need when we think about service. However, that should never be the only criterion for service because tomorrow or next week or next month there will be another need, perhaps of greater importance. Then what will happen? How will priorities be determined? Certainly, it is commendable to want to serve to meet a need, but it should never be the primary reason to serve.

Service is often done by people who are consumed with guilt and feel a need to make up for past wrongs. This is frequently the case when a new Christian hasn't grasped the reality of grace and still feels the need to do something to make up for the past. Others turn their backs on God for a time, and once back into the fellowship, they jump into serving others with great intensity. Service under these conditions is always wrong. It may look as if it's the right thing to do, but it reinforces the notion that they can atone for things that happened in the past. In reality that can't be done. Jesus made up for everything at Calvary.

Sometimes service is done because of tradition or the fact that a person's family has always "been a part of this church." Some families have been a part of a particular church since its organization, and as each generation takes its turn, the hand-me-down theory of service is evident. Grandmother was always involved in something at the church. So was Mother. Now, it's my turn. It's very difficult to criticize someone who wants to serve when there are so many who are indifferent to the responsibility they have as believers; however, service as a result of tradition is misguided.

One of the primary reasons people want to serve is to win God's approval or acceptance. This is a dangerous motivation. Many people serve as a means of seeking God's approval because they spend their entire lives having to perform to get the approval of a parent, spouse, or boss. We can do nothing to increase (or decrease) God's approval and acceptance of us. He can't approve of us more than He already does. He accepts us completely. To enter into service to get God's approval—or for that matter anyone's approval—is to continue to live in bondage to the "works" theology that "if I just do more, I will be accepted more, loved more, or approved of more!" It's a setup for disaster. What happens if that person is forced to give up the service he or she has been performing due to health reasons or time constraints? Fear of loss of approval (love, acceptance) will result. It's a no-win situation.

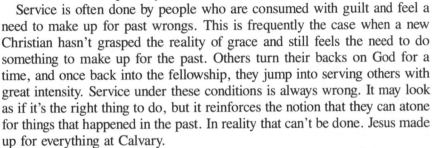

When you're enjoying the fulfillment and fellowship that inevitably accompanies *authentic* [emphasis added] service, ministry is a joy. Instead of exhausting you, it energizes you; instead of burnout, you experience blessing.
—Bill Hybels

SERVICE

■ *An act of assistance or benefit.*

Service under any of these circumstances may result in the gratitude of many, and it may truly benefit those who have been served. However, in some instances, it may result in more problems if the motivation for serving was wrong. Understanding the cause and effect of wrongly motivated acts of service, Paul instructed the Galatians to express their freedom through service and, more specifically, through loving their neighbors.

The result (or outreach) of true freedom is to serve one another and not get caught up in the personal advantages of being a believer while ignoring the community. Because of what Christ did on the cross and the resulting freedom, there is a feeling of gratitude that creates a sense of obligation. That obligation is to love one's neighbor as oneself. When Paul was writing to the Galatians, he left no room for doubt that service must be an expression of love. The way the sentence is structured gives insight into Paul's thinking. He said love, then serve. *Service is the outward expression of the love that motivates every believer who understands that freedom from works does not mean freedom from responsibility.*

APPLICATION

As believers, we are called to express our freedom through loving service. I can hear Paul saying to the church at Galatia and to us today, "This is what I mean:

Come love children by teaching them the Bible.

Come love people who are new to the community.

Come love teenagers, struggling with the relevance of the Bible to their lives.

Come love homeless people.

Come love unwed mothers.

Come love."

Jesus said it this way: "By this all will know that you are My disciples, if you have love for one another" (John 13:35). When service is not others oriented, it becomes self-oriented, and the result is obvious. Suddenly, everything becomes *mine,* and territorialism creeps in. Things like, "This is *my* group, *my* Bible study, *my* church," indicate something far different from others-oriented thinking. When that happens, you can be sure that service is motivated not by a desire to love people through serving them but by a desire to meet one's own needs for attention, fulfillment, or release from the guilt of the past.

On the other hand, when we love someone, it's natural to want to do things for that person. A quick look at an engaged couple is one example of how love motivates. The young bride-to-be just can't do enough for the young man she is about to marry. It's not because she has to or because she needs his attention; she loves him and wants to serve him. Jesus was our best example of love and service. He was always meeting the needs of those He came into contact with. He didn't have to. He did so because of His great love for humankind. He went so far as to die for us. That kind of love is what we've been set free to express, not because we have to but because we want to.

GROWTH

I believe the home is the best place to begin to serve. If you are not sure how to love your family, try serving them. One of the most famous quotes from the era of President John F. Kennedy had to do with service in his statement "Ask not what your country can do for you; ask what you can do for your country." I would paraphrase that for the husbands and wives of this nation: "Ask not what your husband can do for you; ask what you can do for your husband"; "Ask not what your wife can do for you; ask what you can do for your wife."

How many marriages might be saved if this principle were to be lived out? If you will focus on serving the one you married and asking God to open your heart to the connection between love and service, it will become clear that service and love are connected by a single thread, your desire to express your gratitude for the freedom you experience in Christ.

Next, I suggest that you allow God to burden your heart for a particular group or person. If you have no burden, it is entirely possible that you have taken your freedom to an unhealthy extreme and have adopted the attitude that you were saved for your sake alone. If you ask God to open your heart to a place for service, He will.

Opportunities for service abound, and you will be surprised that when you seek God's direction, a place of suitable service will emerge where you can express your love through service.

Finally, make it a part of your daily quiet time to thank God for people who have served you as an expression of their love, and seek Jesus' heart as you pray to adopt His service lifestyle. As you strive to be conformed to His image, ask God to give you a heart for loving service.

> There is not better fuel for service that burns longer and provides more energy than love.
> —Donald Whitney

TESTIMONY

■ *A witness; a statement made to establish a fact.*

SCRIPTURE

JOHN 9:25

He answered and said, "Whether He is a sinner or not I do not know. One thing I know: that though I was blind, now I see."

COMMENTARY

The story given in John 9 is a delightful example of one man's testimony. Unlike blind Bartimaeus, who received his sight immediately (Mark 10:46–52), the young blind man in the text had a different testimony. His story was full of drama and the workings of a "prophet," named Jesus, who spat on the ground, made clay, and put it on the man's blind eyes. The sightless man washed in a pool and "came back seeing" (John 9:6–7). What an incredible testimony this young man had!

Jesus was not a new face in the crowd. That was not His first encounter. John 8 demonstrates that many people were upset with Jesus because He claimed His deity. They had even picked up stones to kill Him. In the very next chapter, He healed this young blind man on the Sabbath, which added to the irritation in the religious community. The Pharisees, who taught that all suffering (including blindness) was due to sin, had their share of questions concerning this miracle. They repeatedly asked, "How?" Yet as they examined and cross-examined the young man, his story never changed.

"I was blind. Now I see."

The religious leaders questioned the young man, argued that no upright person would heal on the Sabbath, and probed for more details. Like many a witness under intense scrutiny and pressure, the young man was challenged as to the accuracy of his story. Trying to answer their continuous questions, the young man finally responded, "He is a prophet" (v. 17). He didn't know much theology, but he knew that what the Man said came true. He had followed Jesus' instructions to wash, and he could see. That didn't satisfy the men who questioned his story.

Because of their discontent with his explanations, they found his parents and interrogated them as well. The parents squirmed, fearing that they would be put out of the synagogue (v. 22), which meant they would lose their jobs and their place of worship and would be disowned by their family. They kept their comments to a minimum, admitting only, "We know that this is our son, and that he was born blind; but by what means he now sees we do not know, or who opened his eyes we do not know. He is of age; ask him. He will speak for himself" (vv. 20–21). They wanted their son to give his own testimony.

> A man who lives right, and is right, has more power in his silence than another has by his words.
> —Phillips Brooks

The son did just that. The religious leaders called him in a second time. He persisted in telling what he knew to be true. Finally, he decided to turn the tables on them and asked, "I told you already, and you did not listen. Why do you want to hear it again? Do you also want to become His disciples?" (v. 27). Apparently, they did not like his leading question. The Bible said they "reviled him" and eventually put him out of the synagogue. The young man, who could now see trees, rocks, grass, and his parents for the first time, was put out of the place of worship because they couldn't accept his miracle.

The account of the man's experience doesn't end there. In verse 35, we read, "Jesus heard that they had cast him out; and when He had found him, He said to him, 'Do you believe in the Son of God?'" Jesus gave him an even greater testimony, because after learning more about the One who had opened his eyes, he said, "'Lord, I believe!' And he worshiped Him" (v. 38). The young man had incredible courage to defy the learned leaders when he knew so little. But he stood firm. Something undeniable had happened to him.

He shared his personal testimony. Simple. Straightforward. Bold. How often do we simply tell that we were once blind to the truth of Christ and now we see? That's really what people want to know. They aren't asking deep theological questions. They just want to know what happened in our lives that makes us different.

Our personal testimony is unique. What we do with our "story" is a responsibility that we must never take lightly. God has entrusted each of us with an opportunity to affect people who watch us daily. Sometimes we never know the influence we have, but people watch us—waiting to see if our words match our actions. You've probably known someone who influenced your life because the testimony spoke so clearly to your heart about your need for a Savior. What would have happened if that person had not taken the responsibility to be a good witness seriously? It's worth a closer look.

> **F**ifty-two percent of Americans reject the idea that sharing religious beliefs with others is a personal responsibility. Sixty-eight percent of born-again believers embrace this!
> —George Barna

A CLOSER LOOK

Your personal testimony is a powerful tool. It is the expression of what God has done and is doing in your life. Some say, "No, you don't understand. My personal testimony isn't dramatic at all. I was saved as a young child. I was never on drugs or anything. I grew up in the church. That's about it." Don't underestimate how powerful that is to a lost person! If you were saved

TESTIMONY

■ *A witness; a statement made to establish a fact.*

> **A** research study at Harvard revealed that there are over seven hundred thousand ways to communicate without words. . . . We don't just speak the message, we are the message.
> —Tim Hansel

at a very young age, there was still a time you passed from death into life—and the world wants to know how to do that.

Not only is your personal testimony a powerful tool, but it will be challenged. Some "religious" people will be uncomfortable around you and will try to catch you off guard. Family members might be embarrassed. Some people will want to debate. When this happens (and it will), you must stand firm. You don't have to get into lengthy discussions. The young man in the Scripture reference didn't have a six-part dissertation. He replied, in layman's terms, "He applied. I washed. I see." The facts were undeniable. *He could see.* And so can you, spiritually, if you have received Christ.

Don't lose heart if people respond negatively to your testimony. You need to be faithful to give out the Word, but the Holy Spirit draws people to life in Christ. If you have been faithful to share your testimony and people respond with a "No, thanks!" remember it is the Spirit's job to convict of sin and save.

They say no because their comfort zone is invaded. All of us know how it feels to be in an environment where we feel out of place. That's what it feels like to lost people surrounded by truth.

They say no because of the fear of what others will say. They want the acceptance of the world more than the acceptance of God. Anytime people make that choice, they are setting themselves up for monumental disappointment; nevertheless, many will avoid responding positively to your testimony because of what other people might think of their decision.

They say no because of unbelief. They don't believe the Bible or God or you. Again, once you have shared the truth with people, the Holy Spirit is the change agent. If they refuse to believe the truth, the consequences will be severe in the end.

They say no because of a rebellious heart. This attitude is dangerous because they can sink deeper into sin and hardness of heart. Scripture is clear that people can rebel for so long that they eventually develop hearts that are unreachable.

You must never allow yourself to think that when people say no, you didn't share your testimony accurately or effectively. Many times you will not see the result of your witness. Often that comes much, much later. Your testimony is a powerful tool that can be challenged, but it has far-reaching consequences. I believe we shortchange ourselves as believers because we don't understand that our testimony is being watched by people that we never have conversation with. If we realized the number of people we affect through our daily activities, we would be astounded.

> **T**here is no set way of doing it, but remember, we are constantly given opportunities to witness.
> —Pat Williams

TESTIMONY

You have no idea who is observing you nearby or from a distance. Sometimes people start out watching with curiosity. They watch to see if your faith really does work. It's a compliment to know that your life has stirred up interest in others. However, three essentials must be operative before you can expect anyone to check out your faith.

First, your *character* needs to be solid. What you are on the inside is so much more important than what you look like on the outside.

Before Philip went to the Ethiopian eunuch, he had already exhibited a godly character. Philip was chosen because of his good reputation (Acts 6). He was humble in that he was willing to serve tables. He was sincere: "And the multitudes with one accord heeded the things spoken by Philip, hearing and seeing the miracles which he did" (Acts 8:6). The people gave him attention because they knew he was sincere. People can generally tell if a person is sincere. I call it feeling static in my spirit when someone doesn't ring true when speaking.

Philip was also obedient. He left an exciting ministry and a tremendous meeting to go to the desert. From my perspective as a preacher, I can only imagine what he was thinking. But he went. Read the description of the meeting: "For unclean spirits, crying with a loud voice, came out of many who were possessed; and many who were paralyzed and lame were healed. And there was great joy in that city" (Acts 8:7–8). All that was going on when an angel of the Lord met Philip and said—with apparently no explanation—"Arise and go toward the south" (Acts 8:26). The Bible adds that it was a desert road.

Can you imagine what it would be like for God to be using you in a great and mighty way and then tell you He needs you in an apparently desertlike experience? Well, Philip's character of obedience matched his humble spirit, and his servant's spirit and he "arose and went" (Act 8:27).

Philip was a man of faith—he went without much instruction. He was zealous in spirit because the Bible says he ran after the chariot that he found in the desert. And he was courageous. Persecution was abounding in the church. Stephen had just been stoned. But Philip ran to give testimony to a man sitting in a chariot.

That's character.

The second essential that must be true before you can expect anyone to be curious about your life is your *conduct,* or what you do. Philip was of a good reputation. He had been watched in the early church, and apparently, his conduct was excellent. He was one of seven men put in charge.

Conduct reveals character. When God said, "Preach to the multitudes, Philip," he preached to the multitudes (Acts 8:6). And when God said,

Fifteen percent of all evangelicals at least once a day share their faith; 22.8 percent at least once a week.

When we commit our lives to Jesus, we receive new life. But it is not life in isolation.
—Ulrich Parzany

Testimony **453**

TESTIMONY

■ *A witness; a statement made to establish a fact.*

"Preach to one, Philip," he ran to catch up with the one. He could have moaned, "Oh, God, come on. I don't want to go to just one. There's a lot going on with the multitudes. Please let me stay with the group." Apparently, no such conversation took place. Philip's conduct matched his character. He did what he was asked, no matter what the task.

What does your conduct say? No, not what do your lips say. What does your conduct say? Words come easily. A godly walk—or conduct—needs to be maintained and carefully watched over. Unbelievers have very high standards for you. They know you shouldn't listen to their jokes. They know you should be a faithful employee. They know your entertainment should be different from theirs.

Your conduct must match your character so that you may be an effective witness for the sake of the kingdom.

A third essential that must be true before you can expect anyone to be curious about your life is your *conversation*. Your conversation will either cloud or confirm your character and your conduct. When Philip ran after the man in the chariot on the desert road, the eunuch was reading out loud, which was customary in those days. Philip's conversation began, "Do you understand what you are reading?" (Acts 8:30). After the Ethiopian eunuch acknowledged he needed someone to help him understand the book of Isaiah, Philip jumped up and sat with him.

Notice that he didn't just jump in and take over before he was invited. He waited until he was invited into the chariot, saw what passage the man was reading, and "Philip opened his mouth, and beginning at this Scripture, preached Jesus to him" (Acts 8:35). Notice, he did not start from Genesis 1. He started where the man was and responded to the man's questions and showed him the Lord Jesus Christ.

That's what a testimony should be. Jesus should be the center of attention, not you.

After Philip's presentation of the gospel, the eunuch got excited and spotted some water in the desert. He immediately wanted to be baptized. Philip went over the gospel once more to make sure the man understood. Philip's conversation made the gospel crystal clear. Your testimony and mine can do the same thing.

It doesn't matter whether your testimony is simple or dramatic. If Jesus is the center of attention, it will sow the seed that the Holy Spirit will nourish into life. Your witness—your testimony—can mean the difference between heaven and hell for others. You don't need to start in Genesis. You need to start where people are and ask God to use your life to make them curious enough to ask what makes such a difference in your life. Then when curiosity

> The very fact that evil can prosper so well in the midst of a nation where 80 percent of the people profess to believe in God and some 20 percent claim Jesus Christ as Lord of their lives is testimony to luke-warmness.
> —Larry Burkett

Service and Outreach

turns to genuine interest, they will ask you to get into their "chariot" and explain the gospel. That's when you must be sure your testimony can withstand cross-examination. If your character, conduct, and conversation line up, the results can be life-changing for those interested in what you have to say.

Whether or not they admit it, most people want to hear about what God has done in your life. If shared wisely and plainly, it can be a magnet that attracts the lost to Christ.

When I became a Christian at the age of twelve, I scooted off the second row in our small church and went forward. As was the custom in our church, they turned me around to face the congregation and said, "Charles, tell these people what you just did."

I had to give a testimony whether I was ready or not! I said, "I don't know all He did. I just know He saved me."

That was my way of saying, "I was blind; now I see."

Simple. Profound.

APPLICATION

Paul told young Timothy to "guard . . . the treasure which has been entrusted to you" (2 Tim. 1:14 NASB). In context, the treasure was his testimony. If you are a Christian, you have a treasure. It's uniquely yours. Better than silver and better than gold. No one else's treasure is quite like yours.

Guard it. It's a sacred trust from One who decided to let you be a bearer of His good news. You need to guard your character, your conduct, and your conversation.

He could have used angels, you know.

But He wants to use you. And will.

What a treasure!

GROWTH

Read Acts 9. How was Paul's testimony one of "I was blind; now I see"? Write out your personal testimony.

QUOTE

Let the redeemed of the LORD say so.
—King David

SPIRITUAL DISCIPLINES

SCRIPTURE

LUKE 9:23–24

Then He said to them all, "If anyone desires to come after Me, let him deny himself, and take up his cross daily, and follow Me. For whoever desires to save his life will lose it, but whoever loses his life for My sake will save it."

COMMENTARY

It was not your ordinary Bible study discussion. It started off innocently enough with a dialogue among Jesus and those present about who they truly believed He was. Peter's quick response "the Christ of God" reflected the mind-set of the group. They had committed their lives to Him, leaving their respective homes and careers to follow Him, to be His disciples. Then Jesus dropped a bombshell on them. There was no easy way to say it. He knew He had to prepare those whom He had called to carry on once He was gone.

He told them He was going to be executed. It is entirely probable that they missed His next statement that He would be raised on the third day. I expect they heard only the part about His death. The One who was supposed to be King was going to die. Things couldn't have been worse. As if that wasn't disconcerting enough, Jesus made it clear that there was a price attached to being a disciple: "If anyone desires to come after Me [follow Me, be My disciple], let him deny himself, and take up his cross daily, and follow Me" (Luke 9:23).

The cross has a different meaning in today's society—a piece of jewelry or a neatly painted picture in a local bookstore. To the disciples, the cross represented torture, physical abuse, and death. They had seen and smelled death firsthand. Jesus' reference to "taking up [the] cross" must have sent waves of fear through the ordinary men whom Jesus had called into extraordinary lives. There probably was a long pause before one of the Twelve was able to speak.

If we could have listened in, the conversation would probably have sounded something like this: "First You asked me to leave my business and my family to follow and learn from You, and now You're telling me that You're going to die and that I have to deny myself and follow in Your steps! Don't You think that's asking a bit much?"

What followed must have sounded like double-talk. "For whoever desires to save his life will lose it, but whoever loses his life for My sake will save it." That had to be even more difficult to understand. How could someone save his life by losing it? The answer to that question would come in time. For it was only as the group of men acted on Christ's call that the true

> **S**alvation and sanctification are the work of God's sovereign grace; our work as His disciples is to disciple lives until they are wholly yielded to God.
> —Oswald Chambers

Disciple

DISCIPLE

■ *A follower and student of Jesus Christ.*

significance of His words became a reality for them. In time, the confusion would disappear, and they would experience the exhilaration of giving their lives totally for the cause of Christ.

A CLOSER LOOK

Jesus stated that we are called beyond simply enjoying the benefits and blessings of salvation; we are to be disciples of Christ. Coming to terms with what a disciple is and what is involved keeps many Christians from pursuing this call. When they start hearing words like *deny* and *sacrifice,* they opt out of the discipling process.

Defining how a disciple must live causes us to hold hands up in protest and say, "Hey, wait a minute! This is starting to sound like a lot more than I bargained for! It's starting to sound like I've got to sacrifice something." And that's exactly what Jesus was saying. Becoming a child of God will cost you nothing because it cost Christ everything. However, becoming a disciple of Jesus Christ could possibly cost a great deal.

The part about denying ourselves and sacrifice bothers Christians today, as it did the disciples that evening. What exactly does that mean? Being a disciple—or follower—of Christ is essentially this: when your desire and God's desire are in conflict, you go with what God wants. When Christ asks for A and you want B, you do A in obedience to Him. Being a follower of Christ is not just believing in something; it's about daily wrestling with this statement: "Here's what I want; here's what God wants. To be a follower of Christ, I have to choose what God wants over what I want."

The idea of having to deny ourselves is one thing, but the notion of losing life if we try to save it and saving it if we "lose it" for Christ is confusing, at best. Jesus' teaching means that when we say no to Him because we're afraid of missing out on life, we will most certainly miss out on life! Jesus knew that life is not found in the things we think it is (job, money, etc.). Life is found in God alone.

Until your purpose lines up with God's purpose, you will never be happy or fulfilled. Christ said that He came that you might have life and have it more abundantly. The only way you can experience abundant life is to surrender your plans to Him.

God's purpose is that we be disciples and then make disciples. By saying no to ourselves, we are allowing God the opportunity to fulfill in us His purpose. It is a choice that every believer must make sooner or later. Everyone who accepts Jesus' death at Calvary as the sufficient payment for sins will go to heaven. Discipleship has nothing to do with whether you will go

> **I**f we were willing to learn the meaning of real discipleship and actually to become disciples, the Church in the West would be transformed, and the resultant impact on society would be staggering.
> —David Watson

to heaven or not. It has everything to do with whether you will find authentic purpose in life.

Jesus declared that we are to "go therefore and make disciples" (Matt. 28:19). However, before we can make disciples, we must be disciples. With this instruction, the next step is to determine what a disciple is and then choose whether we will answer the call. It is possible to be a child of God and never be a disciple of Christ. We can live the Christian life with the assurance of heaven as our ultimate destiny but miss the process of maturing as a disciple.

Nothing worth having is obtained without a price. Being a disciple involves becoming a learner, a student of the Master. That means studying His Word, participating in Bible study, absorbing everything you can through the teaching ministry of your church. It means developing an ongoing relationship with Jesus through prayer and study. A disciple is a learner. You must learn about the One you are to follow and equip yourself for the work He will direct you to do.

A disciple is a follower of Christ. That means you take on His priorities as your own. His agenda becomes your agenda. His mission becomes your mission.

We should be involved in and concerned about many worthy causes, but if all we do is make people more comfortable and feel better about themselves, we miss the heartbeat of discipleship. A disciple of Christ understands that the priority is to impact the outcome of people's journey. That was Christ's mission. This is what He has called us to do as well.

Years ago Dan DeHaan started a Bible study in Atlanta. Over time it grew to more than two thousand people. Dan was a gifted teacher. Later, Dan was killed in a plane crash. To some, it would seem that Dan's ministry came to an abrupt halt. But Dan's influence reaches far beyond his few years as the teacher at a Bible study. Dan was not just a teacher; he was a discipler. He understood what a disciple was, and he committed his time and talents to the task of imparting to others what God had taught him. One of his disciples was my son.

When Andy was about sixteen years old, Dan befriended him. He took him rafting. He invited Andy to his home for one-on-one time. He took him along when he went to speak.

Like many teenagers, Andy went through a stage when it was difficult for him to relate to his mother and me. Dan recognized that Andy needed

> **T**he disciple who abides in Jesus *is* the will of God, and his apparently free choices are God's foreordained decrees. Mysterious? Logically contradictory and absurd? Yes, but a glorious truth to a saint.
> —Oswald Chambers

DISCIPLE

■ *A follower and student of Jesus Christ.*

someone to come alongside him and fill in the gap. He recognized that Andy had potential.

Dan took time to disciple Andy along with about four or five other young men. During their time together, Dan taught Andy how to begin and use a prayer journal. He offered him his own quiet time journal to use as a guide. Dan DeHaan understood that being a disciple meant pouring into the life of Andy and others what had been given to him.

It wasn't that Dan was smarter than anyone else. He wasn't more spiritual, but he understood that God had called him to be a follower of Christ—and then a leader by coming alongside Andy and others who needed his input and insights.

Today when people hear Andy and others from that group who went into ministry, they hear Dan as well. His influence has outlived him. Why? Because of some special talent or gift? No, because he took the time to pour his life into others—as Jesus did. The people who have come to know Christ as a result of Andy's teaching have benefited from the discipleship of Dan DeHaan. The eternal significance of what Dan did will be known only when we get to heaven. This one man, who was just as busy as any of us, opted to follow Christ and make disciples. He discipled my son who learned and followed and now disciples others. That's the way it is supposed to work and will work as we opt to follow Christ.

GROWTH

As Christians, we must first equip ourselves as disciples of Christ and then follow Him obediently. A study of our reference Scripture is just the beginning of learning what Christ expects from us as His present-day disciples. As I've said many times, renewing our minds to what Christ would have us do is essential to a successful Christian life, and success is defined by our obedience to His teachings.

A daily journal, where you keep a personal record of your quiet time, is a learning and growing tool. Use your daily time with God to seek His will for you as a disciple, and then ask Him to give you the courage to follow His leading. Spending time in God's Word daily will be your primary lesson book because it was written to give direction, encouragement, hope, and comfort. It is the disciple's textbook for discipleship. Use it daily to determine what Christ wants you to let Him have so that He can give you the abundant life He said He came to give us.

The use of small groups in discipleship is another way the church has answered the need to make disciples. It is an avenue by which believers can come together to learn and become disciples.

DISCIPLE

Look around at the people God is bringing into your life, perhaps at church but maybe at work or school. Someone needs a discipler—one who will invest time and energy in communicating God's truth to him. Another term for *disciple* might be *mentor* because you become a mentor to those you disciple. Ask God to give you willingness and then opportunity to affect the eternal outcome of someone who needs the truth that you have.

The disciples who were with Jesus were just like you and me—ordinary people who decided to answer the call to make disciples and thereby lived extraordinary lives. That is your call and mine. How God leads you will be different from how He leads me because He has different ways of using the gifts and talents He has given each of us.

Discipleship is an adventure with God. Begin today.

> The secret of a disciple's life is devotion to Jesus Christ, and the characteristic of the life is its unobtrusiveness.
> —Oswald Chambers

QUOTES

It all started by Jesus calling a few men to follow Him. This revealed immediately the direction His evangelistic strategy would take. His concern was not with programs to reach the multitudes, but with men whom the multitudes would follow.

—Robert E. Coleman

When Christ calls a man, He bids him come and die. It may be a death like that of the first disciples who had to leave home and work to follow Him, or it may be a death like Luther's, who had to leave the monastery and go out into the world.

—Dietrich Bonhoeffer

What our Lord said about cross-bearing and obedience is not in fine type. It is in bold print on the face of the contract.

—Vance Havner

Most Christians believe that men are indeed the method of Jesus, but precious few are willing to invest their lives by putting all their eggs in that one basket. Believing this people-oriented philosophy and practicing it are entirely different matters. A large problem in Christendom is that we don't want to take the risk of the time to invest in the lives of people, even though this was a fundamental part of Jesus' ministry. We fear that the basket is really a trap to ensnare us.

—Bill Hull

DISCIPLINE

■ *Training that develops and corrects.*

HEBREWS 12:10 NASB

For they [earthly fathers] disciplined us for a short time as seemed best to them, but He disciplines us for our good, that we may share His holiness.

COMMENTARY

There is a reticence in the church to talk about discipline. All of us understand the value of discipline, but few of us have been the recipient without some resistance. There is always room in our lives to improve, but few of us would readily make the changes necessary were we not prodded into change by some loving parent, teacher, or counselor.

Discipline is a part of life. Not only did our parents have to discipline us, but our teachers did. Later we learned discipline in our workplace. However, the discipline that we receive from a supervisor at work or the teacher in a classroom may not always be as loving as that of our heavenly Father. It would be nice to think that all discipline is handed out justly, but we all know of instances where a person was disciplined unfairly. In a fallen world, inequity abounds. Nevertheless, we must not resist the discipline of our heavenly Father. He disciplines us to conform us to the likeness of His Son. Understanding that, we need to know how to submit to God's discipline.

Discipline is necessary in spite of the hesitancy of some to approach the subject. It was something Jesus considered significant and something worth a closer look.

A CLOSER LOOK

The purpose of godly discipline is positive. The writer of Hebrews tells us it is administered so "we may share His holiness."

Holiness has little to do with a religion or denomination. Holiness is being conformed to the image of Jesus Christ. When our behavior fails to align with our true identity in Christ, God disciplines us for our own good. He is willing to bring into our lives whatever is necessary to accomplish that purpose.

Does that mean we'll be perfect? Of course not. It does mean we'll have a heart bent toward Him—to ultimately be like Him. He brings about correction so that our behavior parallels our identity.

Since God is holy, what method does He use to conform us to that image? The method is discipline through training. Look at this verse: "All discipline for the moment seems not to be joyful, but sorrowful; yet to those who have been trained by it, afterwards it yields the peaceful fruit of righteousness" (Heb. 12:11 NASB).

God is our Father. We are His sons and daughters. It doesn't matter whether we are saved at age five or fifty-five, ten or one hundred, we are always in training. The work of the Holy Spirit is to train us, sift and sand us, chip away at things that are foreign to the family we belong to. As any father who loves his children does, our heavenly Father meets our needs, but He doesn't stop there. He is also our trainer, giving us guidance. When we don't respond to the gentle taps on the shoulder, He will use hardship, failure, and even our sin to bring our behavior in line with our holiness.

God's purpose is our holiness, and His method is training.

Since He is training us for holiness, what should our response be to correction?

We are to take it seriously: "My son, do not regard lightly the discipline of the Lord" (Heb. 12:5 NASB). We need to see it as seriously as God does. We need to see the sin that caused the correction the way God sees the sin. An attitude of indifference or arrogance places us on dangerous spiritual footing.

We are to take our discipline courageously. We are not to faint (Heb. 12:5). We are not to give up and mumble, "Why bother?" We are to endure the chastening and learn from it, much as athletes must persevere through the rigors of training. Do they like the discipline? Do they enjoy getting up at four in the morning to run the laps or swim the length of the pool fifty times? If you asked any of them as they head to the training arena, I doubt any of them would say, "Oh, I absolutely love having to be here eight hours a day, not being with my family, missing out on what other kids are doing." The story is different on the day of their event when they compete and win. The struggle with discipline and training becomes a sweet memory as the medal is placed around the neck. Those who endure, accepting the discipline instead of running from it, benefit in ways they would otherwise miss.

We are to respond to our corrective discipline with the faith that our loving Father is doing what is best. Our tendency is to escape. But when we realize discipline is from the hand of a loving Father, we are able to accept and learn. This has not been an easy lesson for me to learn. I understand how some could say, "How can this be loving? This hurts so bad!" There have been times in my life had I not known God as a loving Father, I would have turned away, unable to accept the discipline. I grew up with an abusive stepfather, so I was able to see the difference. Love is never abusive.

It has been well said that "earthly cares are a heavenly discipline," but they are even something better than discipline; they are God's chariots, sent to take the soul to its high places of triumph.
—Denham Smith

When God does the directing, our life is useful and full of promise, whatever it is doing; and discipline has its perfecting work.
—H. E. Cobb

DISCIPLINE

■ *Training that develops and corrects.*

If you are a parent, think how you discipline your children. You correct them because you see their present and their future. You want them to grow up with mature attitudes and actions. You don't want them to grow up crude and rebellious: "God deals with you as with sons; for what son is there whom his father does not discipline?" (Heb. 12:7 NASB). Children don't believe their parents when they say, "This hurts me more than it hurts you." You have to be a parent to see that is true. I honestly believe our loving Father says, "This hurts Me more than it hurts you." What amazing love!

We need to respond with the belief that it is for our good. "Afterward it yields the peaceable fruit of righteousness" (Heb. 12:11). *Afterward* we see it was worth the pain. God knows we're human and don't relish His chastening hand. It does seem "sorrowful," as Hebrews declares. It *is* sorrowful. But He loves us enough not to leave us where we are. He loves us enough to perfect His holiness in us. We live in an age that tells us parents should let their children do as they please. Many parents believe this lie. No one enjoys the process of discipline, but many men and women have praised their parents who stood firm and meted out the correction. Our heavenly Father understands our resistance but isn't swayed by it. How grateful we should be that He isn't.

We are to respond to our discipline with expectancy, not with shock. We may as well expect it: "God deals with you as with sons" (Heb. 12:7). Children pretty well know when Mom or Dad repeats, "Don't touch the pretty vase," there are consequences when they break it. Cause and effect aren't really all that hard to teach. What God says, He means. And when His children disobey, we should expect consequences of our sin.

We are to respond to our correction with submission: "Furthermore, we had earthly fathers to discipline us, and we respected them; shall we not much rather be subject to the Father of spirits, and live?" (Heb. 12:9 NASB). We need not fight, run, argue, or bargain. We need to yield. You know what I'm talking about. When we think about disciplining our children, it would be a lot easier if they would just submit to a grounding with an "okay, Dad."

Sometimes we're not aware of what He is doing. Perhaps something is going on in your life, and you can't put your finger on it. Or you feel pressure from God in your life, and you're not sure what's going on. Let me offer a suggestion. Why not ask Him, "Father, are You allowing something in my life to get my attention? Are You training me? Is there discipline going on?"

All hardship and difficulty and trials are not necessarily God's hand of discipline for sin. Sometimes He sends things to strengthen our faith and to teach us to endure. John 15:2 tells us that He prunes even the branch that is bringing forth fruit. Don't lose heart.

Just as there are right responses to discipline, there are also wrong ones that demand our attention.

It is wrong to think God is angry. I know that earthly parents sometimes discipline out of anger. That is not correct discipline and teaches the wrong kind of lesson. God is not like that at all. *God is love*. He isn't waiting for us to slip and then knock us down. That's not the biblical view of God. It's the view that Satan wants us to harbor so we will resist the discipline God sends our way.

The wrath and condemnation of God are not for believers anyway: they are for unbelievers. The Lord Jesus took the wrath and condemnation on Himself when He died. He took our judgment. Those who have never received Him are still under wrath and condemnation.

Another wrong response to the chastening of God is to get discouraged and give up. Saying, "Well, I can't please God, so I'm just going to quit trying," is not what God longs for in His children. Some earthly parents may berate their children so much that they break their spirits. This is not discipline; this is child abuse. God's correction is for our welfare. We should never give up; only give in to Christ.

The last wrong response is rationalizing the whole thing away: "Well, these things happen to a lot of people. Even lost people have their share of trouble." They're right in that lost people do have trouble. But there is a major difference between lost and saved people. In the life of the believer, discipline is to prevent future disaster and drifting.

Now that we have seen the right and wrong responses to God's chastening, let me mention something about self-judgment. Paul told the Corinthians to "let a man examine himself" (1 Cor. 11:28). What could that mean?

Self-examination is looking deep inside and being honest about what you see. Self-examination is coming to the same conclusion God does about your sin. Self-examination is confessing—saying the same thing about sin that God says—and repenting, which means turning around. Because sin doesn't fit who you are, if you deal with sin as soon as you identify it in yourself, God won't have to. You need to deal with it immediately. God will give you time to deal with it.

Martin Lloyd Jones, that great English preacher, once said, "Anytime you preach the grace of God according to the Scripture, it will appear to some that it's cheap grace." You may think that my saying that God will give you time to deal with or rid yourself of sin is cheap grace. That is not

> **S**piritual disciplines are those things that—more than likely—most of us would rather not do.
> —Gordon MacDonald

> **N**othing of value is ever acquired without discipline.
> —Gordon MacDonald

> **W**e run without being sent; we speak before God has spoken to us. No wonder we so often fail! Oh, what secret prayer and what heart-searching discipline the heart needs before God can use it!
> —F. Whitfield

DISCIPLINE

what I'm saying at all. I'm saying God detests your sin (not you), and if you won't deal with it, He will.

Although God gives us time to deal with sin, some sins, by their nature, bear consequences—even if we repent immediately. I've had the heart-breaking experience of counseling families torn apart by the unexpected pregnancy of a young daughter. They can either bitterly blame God for their misery or receive His forgiveness and rely fully on His grace to see them through.

Correction is for training in our lives so that we may be conformed to the Lord Jesus Christ. We need to respond seriously and courageously, sensing His love and knowing it's for our best. We need to respond to discipline realizing He said He'd send it, submitting to it, and remembering it is for our good and His glory.

We are not to get angry. We are not to get discouraged and give up. We can see that trials come to the believer and unbeliever for two different reasons: to the Christian for training, and to the non-believer as a warning of future things.

We can examine ourselves and save ourselves heartache if we deal with the sin in confession and repentance. We need to do this immediately.

We need to praise God for loving us through our discipline. Praise God, He trains us in love, not as a duty-bound policeman. We must recognize His wisdom and praise Him for never berating His children. We are blessed by His insistence on disciplining us when we stray. Praise God! He loves us where we are but loves us enough not to leave us there.

> **A**ll discipline is ultimately self-discipline. You have to want to lead a disciplined life.
> —Dr. William Mitchell

APPLICATION

Some children are compliant to the hilt. They eat their vegetables. They don't scream at bedtime. They don't touch the vase. They don't hit the dog. They smile. They do what Mom and Dad ask, without a lot of questions. Other children keep parents humbled.

God has children. Some are more compliant than others, but all need correction. Some respond to a gentle, "Don't do that." Others push the limit before they listen.

Earthly parents get exasperated. They often overcorrect, undercorrect, or abdicate. God never gets exasperated. He has never once been too harsh on one of His children. He has never been too easy. And He won't abdicate His fatherly role. The reason for God's consistent insistence on discipline is simple. He wants all His children to grow up and be like their Elder Brother, the Lord Jesus.

DISCIPLINE

God is the perfect Parent to strong-willed children. We need to thank Him for His constant training. And learn from it.

If you can understand the atonement and realize God punished, judged His Son for your sin and then decide you can go out and live any way you want—you haven't seen discipline yet!

—Charles Stanley

To be very dear to God involves no small degree of chastisement.

—Charles Haddon Spurgeon

Look upon chastening as God's chariots sent to carry your soul into the high places of spiritual achievement.

—Hannah Whitall Smith

FASTING

■ *The biblical discipline of abstaining from food for spiritual purposes.*

MATTHEW 6:17–18

But you, when you fast, anoint your head and wash your face, so that you do not appear to men to be fasting, but to your Father who is in the secret place; and your Father who sees in secret will reward you openly.

COMMENTARY

John Wesley said, "Some have exalted religious fasting beyond all Scripture and reason; and others have utterly disregarded it." It is obvious that there is a great diversity of thought concerning this topic.

We live in a world obsessed with food. It is impossible to drive a city block without passing a local pizza parlor or fast-food restaurant. Some would argue that we have a national addiction to food. There are support groups for people who can't control their eating habits. It is natural to eat. Therefore, the subject of fasting is something that appears unnatural, at least, and strange, at best. For many years Christian authors wrote little on the subject, and only recently has there been a resurgence of interest. However, to understand what fasting is and what it is not, we need to clarify popular misconceptions. Fasting must always be for spiritual purposes, not for public attention, as Jesus indicated in Matthew 6.

The Sermon on the Mount is best known for its "Blessed are . . ." statements, which have inspired many to pattern their lives after Jesus' words to the crowd gathered that day. Because so much attention has been paid to the Beatitudes, we have inadvertently missed what Jesus had to say about certain activities that should be done in privacy, away from neighbors and friends. In Jesus' own way, He admonished the crowd to be careful about what they did in public because of the propensity to do it out of misguided motivation. Jesus talked about three things that we should refrain from doing in public.

First, we should not give for public notoriety (Matt. 6:2). Second, we are admonished to pray in private (Matt. 6:5). Third, we should fast in private (Matt. 6:16). Nothing is intrinsically wrong with doing these things publicly, but I believe Jesus understood the tendency of people to do things for the admiration and respect of their peers rather than for the glory of God. Therefore, to keep their hearts pure, Jesus thought it wise to implement protective measures to help guard them from approaching these things with wrong motives. To be absolutely sure they understood, Jesus emphasized what would happen to those who ignored His teaching. He said the reward would correlate to the motivation. That is, if a person's motivation was to get attention, attention would be the full reward.

It's easy to understand why Jesus would be concerned about the human inclination to get caught up in wrong attitudes about giving. The world has

Fasting is calculated to bring a note of urgency and importance into our praying.
—Arthur Wallis

made the wrong presumption that wealth is a fair measure of a person's value. It makes sense that we would be tempted to fall into that same trap, wanting everyone to know how much we have and are capable of giving. Likewise, public prayer is a prime opportunity for people to come across as pious servants. The Pharisees loved to pray in public so that everyone would know how spiritual they were. Jesus abhorred their hypocrisy and urged the church to be careful not to pattern their prayer life after those hypocrites.

Why would Jesus include fasting in this same list of things to do in private? After all, most people never seriously think about fasting.

I believe Jesus' intent in giving instruction on fasting was the same as it was concerning giving and prayer—to protect people from the tendency toward self-righteousness. There was much confusion about the purpose behind fasting and what it was intended to accomplish. Jesus wanted to be careful that people did not stumble into another exercise in public demonstrations of righteousness.

Before going any farther, we need to look at *what fasting is not intended to do*.

First, fasting is not intended to persuade God to change His mind. Some Christians have the mistaken idea that fasting is a sure way to get God on their team. They learn the hard way that fasting was never intended to be used as a tool to manipulate God. If you regard fasting as a means of motivating God to fix your disasters, you will certainly be disappointed because He never promised to do that.

Second, fasting will not make you more acceptable in God's eyes. It is not another number on the list of things you have to do to be acceptable. Fasting is not commanded in Scripture. There aren't a lot of rules and regulations concerning fasting. The most definitive rule is to do it privately, away from the view of friends and neighbors. It should not be a public exhibition. It is a spiritual exercise, not a public demonstration, and it should be between you and God. There are times when the church or nation should be called to fast, but these times are not as frequent as the times that individuals who seek to glorify God would fast.

Third, biblical fasting is not done to lose weight. That's the way the world would think. Our world has become obsessed with outward appearance. Fitness experts talk to us incessantly through infomercials, filling our minds with the idea that we have to look good to be acceptable. Fasting was never, ever meant to be a diet plan.

God must shake His head in dismay at our misguided thinking. We do not fast to impress God or to convince Him that we are sincere to validate

> **M**en through whom God has worked greatly have emphasized the significance of prayer with fasting.
> —Bill Gothard

> **A**ll of our fasting therefore must be on this basis; we should use it as a spiritual means whereby we are melted into a more complete realization of the purposes of the Lord in our life, church, community, and nation.
> —David Smith

FASTING

■ *The biblical discipline of abstaining from food for spiritual purposes.*

our righteousness. If you are considering a fast or are presently fasting, realize that: (1) it is not a tool to manipulate God to change His mind; (2) it is not a commandment that will make you more acceptable in God's eyes; and (3) it is not a weight-loss gimmick. If you are participating in a fast for any of these three reasons, you are setting yourself up for disappointment.

Now, a closer look at *what fasting is intended for* is the next step in understanding and appropriating the truth of Scripture about this often misunderstood subject.

A CLOSER LOOK

If the purpose we cling to when fasting is not spiritual in nature, focused solely on God, we will never understand or benefit from this discipline. I believe there are specific reasons for fasting that are presented in Scripture.

First, fasting *prepares* us. As we prepare for what God calls us to, fasting puts us in a proper attitude for God to conform us to that purpose and to His image. It is a time when things that seemed vital to our happiness and success lose their allure as we seek Him. We need to take time to separate ourselves from the influence of the world. Fasting provides the opportunity to get away from the negative impact the world has on our decisions and allows us to hear God without outside interference. Fasting prepares us.

Second, it *cleanses*. Fasting is a means of personal cleansing for the physical body, ridding it of impurities. No matter how much we attempt to avoid the impact of living in a fallen world, the influence is obvious. Our souls, like our bodies, need cleansing. Because we are spirit beings, the spirit is accordingly refreshed during times of fasting by the work of the Holy Spirit.

Third, fasting *equips* us for the battle we wage against Satan. A powerful verse deals with fasting and the way it is connected to our victory over the strongholds in our lives. Isaiah made the connection:

> *Is this not the fast that I have chosen:*
> *To loose the bonds of wickedness,*
> *To undo the heavy burdens,*
> *To let the oppressed go free,*
> *And that you break every yoke? (58:6).*

When Satan gains a foothold in our lives, we tend to try everything but fasting. When Satan did his best to tempt Christ, a fasting Messiah triumphed over the evil one.

Few people know that the stupendous achievement of William Carey was fueled by his bedridden sister who prayed for him for over fifty years.
—R. Kent Hughes

FASTING

I'm afraid we busy ourselves with other things because we don't know how to appropriate God's healing power in our lives. Isaiah's words indicate that strongholds can be effectively broken by fasting. Yet we seem hesitant to apply this principle when it comes to the strongholds that put so many of our family in bondage. It's too simple, some would say. Yet, I think we cheat ourselves out of victory by not heeding the truth of Scripture in fasting against strongholds. Fasting breaks strongholds.

We also read about fasting in Scripture where the prophets and teachers were ministering in the early church: "As they ministered to the Lord and fasted, the Holy Spirit said, 'Now separate to Me Barnabas and Saul for the work to which I have called them'" (Acts 13:2). What wonderful direction was given during this time of fasting! It's a lesson to the church today to fast and pray for our children, our young men and women, even before God calls them into a career or ministry. A strong foundation is crucial to ministry, whether done within the walls of a church or outside the church doors in secular society. Fasting obviously was done to benefit the one participating in this exercise.

Scripture gives us striking examples where fasting played a significant role in changing lives and nations. We would be wise to learn the lessons of those who have gone before us.

Fasting is essential in hopeless situations.

Fasting is invaluable in national crisis.

Fasting is invaluable in knowing the will of God.

Hopeless situations respond to fasting. You know the story of Nehemiah, don't you? Judah was in Babylonian captivity, and the city of Jerusalem had been destroyed. The man of God, Nehemiah, was serving as the cupbearer to the king. As a slave in Babylon, he was in a very hopeless situation. The news that Jerusalem's remains were going to be torn down tugged at his heart. On top of that, he saw the sadness of God's people. Nehemiah desperately wanted to help rebuild the walls of Jerusalem so that the people of God would have protection against enemies.

Nehemiah wept and mourned and "was fasting and praying before the God of heaven" (Neh. 1:4). The pagan king had decreed earlier that "this city may not be built until the command is given by me" (Ezra 4:21). You have to understand. The king didn't waffle on decrees. He meant what he said. Nehemiah knew it was time to fast and pray. The king had not seen him sad before, but as Nehemiah took wine to him, he could not hide the grief on his face. Nehemiah took a risk in letting the king see him with a sad face. Kings of that era often had someone decapitated if they didn't like the person's facial expression. The king inquired about his sadness. Nehe-

> **F**asting is to be a voluntary activity and not a forced activity.
> —Bill Gothard

Fasting **473**

FASTING ■ *The biblical discipline of abstaining from food for spiritual purposes.*

miah told him he wanted to go to Jerusalem to rebuild. The Bible records, "So it pleased the king to send me" (Neh. 2:6). That's quite a turn of events! Not only did this man of God get to go, but the king also sent along letters of permission, with officers of the army, horsemen, and written requests for timber to rebuild. Lesson one: fasting is important in hopeless situations.

National interests require extraordinary attention to prayer and fasting. Jehoshaphat understood that. When King Jehoshaphat heard that a great multitude was coming to make war with his people, he called for a national fast. After they fasted and prayed, fighting wasn't necessary because the enemy killed one another! The Bible says, "Then they returned, every man of Judah and Jerusalem, with Jehoshaphat in front of them, to go back to Jerusalem with joy, for the LORD had made them rejoice over their enemies" (2 Chron. 20:27).

Fasting is important in national crisis. Our nation would be wise to heed the lesson of this passage. With the state of the nation in moral disarray, fasting is essential. Lesson two: fasting is crucial during national crisis.

Fasting is important in knowing the will of God. After reading something Jeremiah had written earlier about the desolation of Jerusalem, the prophet Daniel sought to know what would happen to his people. Because he wanted to know the will of God, he said, "Then I set my face toward the Lord God to make request by prayer and supplications, with fasting, sackcloth, and ashes" (Dan. 9:3). We often refer to the messianic prophecy in the book of Daniel, but we seldom realize it was given after the prophet fasted. In this particular story, Daniel fasted, prayed, confessed, and listened, and the angel Gabriel appeared with instructions. Lesson three: fasting is essential to knowing the will of God.

Fasting is one spiritual exercise that the church is not practicing on a regular basis. Remember, though, it is not spiritual arm-twisting. It is directed toward God Himself. We affirm He is more important than our physical desires. It is beneficial to fast in preparation and direction for ministry, for personal cleansing, and for victory over strongholds. It is important to fast during hopeless situations, in national crises, and in discerning the will of God.

Why would something so powerful be practiced so little?

In my ministry at First Baptist in Atlanta, I have felt the need to ask our church family to fast. Although it is not my habit to do this often, there have been times when I believed fasting was the appropriate means of bringing our church into absolute focus on God and His will for our congregation. A few years ago I called for a time of fasting for our church to pray about purchasing

FASTING

new property. A couple just heard part of the sermon and thought I had called for an entire week of fasting. Immediately following the service, they fasted and prayed the whole week.

The next time I saw them, they were obviously anxious to relate what their experience had been during that week of fasting. It was a glorious time for them. God revolutionized their financial situation during that time when they became totally focused on Him. I was a little embarrassed to tell them that I had not meant for them to fast the entire week (since that can be physically dangerous). He used their willingness to seek His will in their lives as a way to teach them lessons they would never have learned otherwise.

APPLICATION

In looking at the biblical instances, we see those who fasted had a very specific thing in mind. We need to know what our objective is.

I do want to caution when fasting, one needs to be aware of physical disabilities that would prohibit it. If, however, there are none, the person who is fasting for a short period of time, or a lengthy period of time, needs to drink a lot of water. Jack Hayford, a pastor on the West Coast, said that when he is hungry during a fast and knows he really needs nourishment, he eats plain bread and drinks a large glass of grape juice. He explained he uses this as a time of worship with the elements. One may fast one meal or two, three, or more. When the time comes to end the fast, it should be done carefully with light food.

There are several things to remember when you are thinking about beginning a fast. How long you fast is between you and God. You can do it as an act of worship. Just don't do it for show.

GROWTH

As a matter of personal study and edification, I suggest you study the kinds of fasts written about in the Bible. Briefly, they are as follows:

The *normal fast* involves abstaining from all food but not from water. Matthew 4:2 explains, "When He had fasted forty days and forty nights, afterward He [Jesus] was hungry." It says nothing about being thirsty. Luke 4:2 says He "ate nothing." Again, it says nothing about being thirsty. Since the body can normally survive no longer than three days without water, we can assume that He drank water during the forty-day fast. The most common Christian fast is to abstain from food but to drink water or, in some cases, fruit juices.

FASTING

■ *The biblical discipline of abstaining from food for spiritual purposes.*

The *partial fast* is a limitation of diet but not total abstinence from food and water. This fast is demonstrated in Daniel 1:12 where we are told that Daniel and some of his friends had only "vegetables to eat and water to drink."

The *absolute fast* means abstaining from both food and water. There are several references in Scripture regarding the absolute fast. We are told that Ezra "ate no bread and drank no water, for he mourned because of the guilt of those from the captivity" (Ezra 10:6). Again, this type of fast is recorded when Esther requested that the Jews fast and pray on her behalf: "Go, gather all the Jews who are present in Shushan, and fast for me; neither eat nor drink for three days, night or day" (Est. 4:16).

The *private fast* is referred to in Matthew 6:16–18. Jesus spoke quite eloquently to the crowd gathered about fasting in a way not to be noticed by others. In direct contrast to the prideful fast exhibited by the Pharisees, Jesus made it clear that He looks deep into the heart of the person observing the fast to motivation. Fasting for public attention or political power was not an acceptable reason to fast.

The *congregational fast* is found in Joel 2:15–16:

> Blow the trumpet in Zion,
> Consecrate a fast,
> Call a sacred assembly;
> Gather the people,
> Sanctify the congregation.

Reference is also made in Acts 13:2 in Luke's words indicating that at least part of the congregation of the church at Antioch were fasting.

The response of King Jehoshaphat to an invasion was to call a *national fast:* "And Jehoshaphat feared, and set himself to seek the LORD, and proclaimed a fast throughout all Judah" (2 Chron. 20:3). Other references are found in Nehemiah 9:1 and Esther 4:16, and the king of Nineveh proclaimed a national fast in response to the preaching of Jonah (Jonah 3:5–8). In the early days of our nation, Congress proclaimed three national fasts. Three presidents (John Adams, James Madison, and Abraham Lincoln) called the nation into fasts, Lincoln doing so three times during the War Between the States.

A study will equip you with knowledge and will give you insight into what role this discipline should or should not play in your life. Not everyone should fast. Anyone with serious health problems should consult a doctor (one who has a relationship with God preferably) before fasting. The more you know about what the Bible has to say about when fasting is appropriate and necessary, the better equipped you will be when God leads you to begin this discipline. Never do so out of pride or in an effort to draw attention to yourself. Scripture says that will be your only reward, shallow as it is.

Whatever you do, do it to the honor and glory of God.

INTERCESSION

■ *To pray on behalf of someone other than yourself.*

SCRIPTURE

1 TIMOTHY 2:1–4 NASB

I urge that entreaties and prayers, petitions and thanksgivings, be made on behalf of all men, for kings and all who are in authority, in order that we may lead a tranquil and quiet life in all godliness and dignity. This is good and acceptable in the sight of God our Savior, who desires all men to be saved and to come to the knowledge of the truth.

COMMENTARY

In Paul's letter to Timothy, he urged—or strongly encouraged—his young friend to intercede for everyone. The emphasis was prayer for others. Paul was asking Timothy to pray not for himself but for those around him. This is the force behind the word *intercession*.

Paul encouraged Timothy to pray for those in authority and included the reason why: "That we may lead a tranquil and quiet life" (1 Tim. 2:2 NASB). The apostle knew that the gospel could be more easily spread in a peaceful environment, in particular, an environment where the governing officials were not hostile toward believers and their practices. Paul believed that intercession was part of the equation that could bring about such an atmosphere.

No doubt Paul also intended for Timothy to pray for the conversion of those in authority. He believed God wanted "all men to be saved" (2:4 NASB). Certainly, he was familiar with what the writer of Proverbs said concerning righteous leadership, "When the righteous are in authority, the people rejoice; but when a wicked man rules, the people groan" (Prov. 29:2).

The apostle Paul believed that through intercession, people could be changed. The term itself, however, implies that intercession does not bring about change. Intercession is the process that links those who need to be changed and the One who can bring about change.

A CLOSER LOOK

The term *intercession* literally means "to come upon," "to meet with," "to come between." When used in the context of prayer—as it is here—it takes on a special meaning. To intercede is to stand between God and someone. It is to represent another person's concern to God. An intercessor is a go-between (Isa. 59:16).

Our prayers are the link between God's inexhaustible resources and people's needs. When we intercede, we stand in the gap between the need and the satisfaction of that need.

INTERCESSION

All of us have had the frustrating experience of praying for others and seeing no results. Often the problem is that we aren't aware of what the Bible teaches about praying for others. According to Scripture, we need to follow some guidelines when we intercede for others.

First, *we are to pray from hearts of love and compassion*. True intercessory prayer is driven by genuine love and concern for the one about whom we are interceding. Prayer motivated by anything else generally doesn't last long. Sometimes we will be the only ones standing in the gap in a situation. When this happens, we must stay involved in the process. So it is equally critical that we are driven with the right motivation, one that will keep us on our knees until the answer comes.

One afternoon a pastor from another city came by seeking advice about a church problem. That evening his church was going to discuss the manner in which deacons were to be selected. Several deacons had threatened to challenge the pastor on the issue before the whole congregation.

He was troubled and fearful. We talked for a while, and I gave him a verse to claim during the business meeting: "I will go in the strength of the Lord GOD; I will make mention of Your righteousness, of Yours only" (Ps. 71:16). Then I told him I would pray. I stood in the gap between the pastor and the victory he needed. I prayed specifically that God would close the mouths of those who would come against my friend as God closed the mouths of the lions that posed a threat to Daniel.

Late that night he called me. He was so excited, I could hardly understand him. He said that it was one of the smoothest business meetings they had ever had.

I was able to identify with the pastor who faced the opposition in his church because I had faced a similar situation when I became the pastor of First Baptist Church of Atlanta. As I prayed, I remembered how I had felt when I faced opposition from deacons. I remembered the feelings of rejection. I remembered the pressure I felt every Sunday as I stood to preach. All of that motivated me to pray earnestly for my friend. Identifying with him allowed me to pray in a way few other people could pray. I felt genuine compassion.

When we are able to identify in some way with the one for whom we are interceding, the passion and intensity of our intercession are heightened. We know how the person feels. It is not unusual for the emotions we felt in the past to resurface. In those situations we are able to pray with genuine compassion—a necessity for real intercessory prayer.

To intercede effectively, we must in some way identify with the needs of others. Spiritually and emotionally, we must feel what they feel. It was

> Seventy-six percent of those surveyed said that God is a heavenly Father who can be reached by prayers.

> If you tell someone you're going to pray for them, pray right that second or you may forget.
> —Frank Sells

INTERCESSION

■ *To pray on behalf of someone other than yourself.*

written of a German pastor, "The sufferings of others became so painful to him that he was pleading for them as if for himself." That is true intercession!

One reason God allows us to suffer is that we can identify with others in our prayers. Until we suffer, we tend to stereotype those who suffer as inferior and weak. We have little patience with them—much less any burden to pray for them.

So if we are going to pray for others, we must ask the Lord to help us see what others see and feel what they feel. When we share in their pain, we will pray with an earnestness we have never known before.

When Jesus looked out over the crowd, He had compassion for them (Matt. 20:34). He felt what they felt. And He knows how we feel in every situation we face. He is our great Intercessor, ever praying for His children, having experienced life on earth. He is not a High Priest who does not know how we feel (Heb. 4:15). The zenith of His identification with us occurred on the cross (Luke 22:44).

Second, *when we intercede for others, we must persevere.* Once we begin interceding for someone, we must not give up. We are to stick with it until either our prayer is answered or the burden is lifted. In this way, intercession can be costly. And often the biggest price is *time.* Time is the most valuable thing we have. There is no way to gain more. To intercede is to invest our most valuable commodity—our time.

Intercession is one link in the chain between a person's need and God's power or intervention. Certainly He can do it without us, but He often chooses to include us in the process. God works through the prayers of His people.

What makes this so difficult is His timing. It may seem that He is never going to act, but His timetable is different from ours. But God is never inactive. He is always at work bringing about His purposes. The problem is our inability to sense what He is up to. For this reason, it is all the more important that we stay on our knees—interceding for those in need.

Third, *when we intercede for others, we must be willing to be part of the answer.* Often God will use the intercessor as part of the answer to the prayer. Nehemiah is a good example. When Nehemiah told the king about his concern, the king sent him back to Jerusalem with enough supplies to be the answer to his own prayer!

When interceding, we must remain open to the possibility of being used by God in a role other than intercessor. If we aren't willing to be used to answer our own prayers, we aren't cooperating fully with God. Someone wrote about the great intercessor Rees Howells, "He was never again to ask

> The real business of your life as a saved soul is intercessory prayer. Wherever God puts you in circumstances, pray immediately, pray that His Atonement may be realized in other lives as it has been in yours.
> —Oswald Chambers

INTERCESSION

God to answer a prayer through others if He could answer it through him. That included his money."

As we pray for others, we must desire their highest good. We must die to all selfish desires concerning them and seek only God's best. We put no conditions on God in our prayers—no matter what the cost to us. For example, if a girl is praying for her boyfriend to be saved, she must be willing to do anything for God to answer her prayer. If she says "I'll do anything but break up with him," God may answer her prayer only on the condition that she is willing to break up.

Carl had been praying for months about his rebellious son. His twenty-two-year-old son had left home and was living with some young men. My friend knew that his son had been involved with drugs before he left home and soon after learned that his son had become a drug dealer. Carl's two main concerns were that God would bring his son home and that his son wouldn't be arrested.

One morning while Carl was praying for his son, God spoke to him. Carl realized that his had been a selfish request. He was well known in his town and would be embarrassed if his son was arrested on drug charges. Carl told the Lord that if the only way to deliver his son from his sin was to allow him to be arrested, he was willing for that to happen, even at the expense of his reputation.

A few days later, Carl received a phone call from the police. His son had been arrested and was charged with possession of illegal drugs. As Carl drove to the police station to pick up his son, he realized that God had been waiting for him to get his attitude right before He could allow his son to come home.

God honored Carl's obedience. He and his son rebuilt their broken relationship, and soon afterward his son left home again, this time to study for the ministry.

When we pray for someone, we must take our hands off the matter completely and let God work any way He desires.

Ask God to show you three people He wants you to pray for—three people who have burdens, heartaches, or specific needs. Tell God you are willing to be part of the answer. Then ask Him to share their burdens with you. Ask God for a genuine spirit of compassion and love for these three. Tell

INTERCESSION

■ *To pray on behalf of someone other than yourself.*

Him you want Him to teach you how to pray and intercede on their behalf. Start with three and add as the Lord leads.

As an intercessor, you must enter into the sufferings and take the place of the one prayed for.

—Rees Howells

The High Priest of old had to enter into the Holy of Holies *alone*, but our High Priest begs for partners to be with Him.

—John Hyde

■ *Quiet contemplation of spiritual truths.*

MEDITATION

JOSHUA 1:8

This Book of the Law shall not depart from your mouth, but you shall meditate in it day and night, that you may observe to do according to all that is written in it. For then you will make your way prosperous, and then you will have good success.

Joshua's mission was that of a military leader. It is significant that his courage and even his hope of victory depended on his obeying the Word of God. God promised success, but there was a condition: meditation and obedience to His Word.

Although most of us are not military leaders, we are certainly in spiritual warfare. Do we need to know God's heart any less than Joshua did? I think not. Do we need encouragement to be prosperous and successful, just as Joshua needed that encouragement? I know so!

Then we need to know Joshua's secret weapon—meditation. When we think about it, it is not a difficult strategy. But when we try to apply it, it seems strangely difficult. Could it be that our enemy wants to see us fail? Definitely.

It is no accident that in the sentence structure of our verse, the word *meditate* precedes the admonition to be obedient. God knows that if His children think, ponder, and ruminate on His promises, obedience is a natural outcome. When we begin to think God's thoughts after Him, a spontaneous overflow of our hearts is to do what He asks.

I am sure leading the children of Israel into Canaan was no easy feat. There were uncertainties, battles, and not a few other trials encountered in the process. Imagine what it meant to Joshua to recall over and over in the heat of the battle this promise: "This Book of the Law shall not depart from your mouth, but you shall meditate in it day and night. . . . For then you will make your way prosperous, and then you will have good success."

God let Joshua know that meditation was his responsibility. God will not force-feed anyone. Joshua had to do what he could in order for God to do what He desired. The promise is a conditional one. God did not say, "*I* will make your way prosperous." He said, "For then *you* will make your way prosperous." I realize we have to be careful here; ultimately, we know that God crowns His children with success. But when God told Joshua to meditate, God expected him to do just that. Joshua was contributing his part in the battle.

MEDITATION

■ *Quiet contemplation of spiritual truths.*

It is foolish for us to think that we can be in daily spiritual warfare and not be armed. We need to do our part while trusting God to do His.

Jeremiah Denton was a prisoner of war in North Vietnam for seven horrendous years. As one of the highest ranking American captives, he was subjected to particularly grueling torture, spending almost his entire incarceration in solitary confinement. In such a barren, brutal situation, it would be hard not to focus on the pain and tedium. Yet Denton not only survived but also came back and was elected a United States senator from Alabama.

How did he survive? He stated on many occasions that an essential survival skill was quoting passages from the Bible. Internalized Scripture became the unseen sword that enabled him to fend off the cruelest weapons of the enemy. By inwardly focusing on the power of God to sustain and strengthen him, he was able to rise above the squalor of his lonely existence.

Joshua, Jeremiah Denton, and the rest of us spiritual warriors must cooperate with God's battle plan. We need to know what our Commander in Chief desires. Let's take a closer look at it.

 A CLOSER LOOK

I received a catalog advertising meditation music. It was not published by a Christian-oriented company and did not claim to have anything biblical in the content. I was interested in how the company recommended the music. The catalog used words like *serenity* and *tranquillity* and admonished the reader to "replace stress and tension as you absorb" the music. The catalog promised that the meditation music would not only "soothe your soul but fill you with the energy that follows blissful complete relaxation." It even told you how long it could take: "286 minutes total."

Just the mention of the word *meditation* conjures up various and sundry images, all somewhat foreign to the Western mind. Many contemporary believers have removed the word from the biblical vocabulary. Its usage has been confined primarily to the practice of Eastern religion and, thus for the Christian, cast into an almost obsolete and forbidden sphere. This abandonment is at our great peril because meditation and its scriptural application are of immense value if we are to listen accurately to God.

Perhaps no other man pursued this godly endeavor more fervently and fruitfully than King David. Many of the psalms are the results of his quietly waiting and reflecting on God. As a "man after God's own heart," David first had to know the mind and heart of God. To a large extent, David accomplished this through the persistent practice of godly meditation. A vivid illustration can be found in 2 Samuel 7. David has reached a place of rest in his reign. His war campaigns are no longer on the drawing board, and he is contemplating building a temple for the Lord. The prophet Nathan gives an encouraging message of God's faithfulness to David and the Lord's plan for constructing the temple. David's response to Nathan's communiqué is found in 2 Samuel 7:18: "Then King David went in and sat before the Lord; and he said: 'Who am I, O Lord God? And what is my house, that You have brought me this far?'" Notice the phrase, David "sat before the Lord." He wasn't sitting in a chair as we would. He was kneeling and sitting back on his heels, listening, and talking to God.

David was meditating.

Meditation was nothing new to David because he had long known what it meant to meditate. We read in the Psalms how often he listened and talked to the Father out in the fields. Even when he was running from Saul and dodging javelins, David took time to meditate on God.

Since meditation is the one activity that should be the daily priority of believers, it is the one discipline Satan will doggedly keep us from observing. When we examine the rewards and the results of meditation, however, we will soon realize it can't be secondary. It has to be primary.

Many believers think that meditation is only for preachers or other spiritual leaders. They do not see its role in a secular world where strife and competition reign. It seems alien to persons who have to get up and hit the expressway in the early morning, be in noisy offices during the day, and then battle the traffic home, where they then must deal with domestic difficulties. Yet in the midst of such constant turmoil believers stand in great need of the quieting effects of meditation so that they may distill God's voice from the roar of everyday living.

> A man of meditation is happy, not for an hour or a day, but quite round the circle of all his years.
> —Isaac Taylor

Personal, private meditation begins when we get alone with the Lord and are quiet before Him. It may be for five minutes, it may be for thirty minutes, it may be for an hour. The important thing is that we get alone with the Lord to find His direction and purpose for our lives. It is an intimate time.

It is no accident that the longest chapter in the Bible, Psalm 119, deals with the Word of God in every single verse. Psalm 119:97–100 lists some of the rewards of meditation, such as wisdom, discernment, keen insight, and heightened obedience. What warrior doesn't need all these things?

Four principles will guide us into meaningful meditation. These principles are liberating truths that cause us to hear the voice of God in a fresh, invigorating manner.

First, reviewing the past is an excellent way to begin our time of meditation because as we do, we will see patterns that God has woven into our lives.

MEDITATION

David remembered his fight with Goliath. He remembered the years spent running from Saul, the battles he had won. Now that he had peace in his life, he had the privilege of savoring God's wonderful works (2 Sam. 7:18). Even in the heat of today's personal battles, we can reflect on His past faithfulness.

One practical way we can reflect on the past is to write in a diary or journal. We tend to forget so easily a victory here or a battle won there. A journal is your private war diary, declaring victories. What a heritage to pass along to your children! Can't you see the delight in the eyes of your children and grandchildren as you point out in your diary, "Look! I was going through a really rough time. It went on a long time and I thought it would never end. But it did end. And His grace was sufficient all along the way. His grace is there for you, too"? I believe most of David's diary is called the book of Psalms.

Second, reviewing the past should be followed by reflecting on God. Listen to what else David said: "And yet this was a small thing in Your sight, O Lord GOD. . . . Now what more can David say to You? For You, Lord GOD, know Your servant. For Your word's sake, and according to Your own heart, You have done all these great things, to make Your servant know them" (2 Sam. 7:19–21).

As we reflect on God, we meditate on His greatness and grace and goodness. Focusing on difficulties intensifies and enlarges the problem. We can moan and groan and tell God how awful everything is, but when we claim His promises and look at His majesty, the problems are put into proper perspective. We are no longer overwhelmed. Long ago I read this encouraging quote: "The future is as bright as the promises of God." It's even more encouraging when we know the promises to claim!

The third principle is remembering God's promises. As David continued to meditate on the Lord, he said, "And now, O Lord GOD, You are God, and Your words are true, and You have promised this goodness to Your servant" (2 Sam. 7:28). David recalled God's promises in establishing his name and family on an everlasting basis. What would happen if we began our personal time with the Lord quoting this verse? God loves to hear His Word spoken to Him. When we tell Him how much we love His promises of peace and provision and protection, this not only gladdens His heart but quiets ours.

Remember when you were little and you asked your parents to take you to the zoo or fishing or somewhere else? More often than not, what was the answer? "We'll see" or "Maybe." Sometimes when they knew the calendar was clear and they knew they could say yes, remember what you said?

> **W**hen we resist these [sensual] impulses by internalizing Scripture . . . we soon build spiritual patterns equal to the sin patterns.
> —Bill Gothard

"Mom, it's almost Saturday. And remember, you *promised*." If your tone was not a sassy one, Mom usually smiled, knowing in your own small way you were holding her to her promise. She was glad you knew she meant what she said. God is delighted when we remember His promises and let Him know we understand He means what He says.

When we meditate on God and remember the promises He has given us in His Word, our faith grows, and our fears dissolve. David understood that. Many times, in the caves hiding from Saul and with from six thousand to twenty thousand men searching for him, David quietly shifted his attention to God. Under the stars or in the darkness of the caves, David focused his attention on God who had equipped him to slay Goliath, who had given him swiftness of body and keenness of mind. He remembered God who had allowed him to avoid Saul's javelin. As he fixed his inner man on God, his fears and frustrations were soothed by the presence of God. We have our own cave and javelin experiences, and we need to remember His wonderful promises in them.

The fourth principle is making requests. On one occasion I was meditating on the Word, and I came to Philippians 4:19: "And my God shall supply all your need according to His riches in glory by Christ Jesus." Suddenly, I stopped. I began to meditate on that verse. Without previous thought on the subject, I prayed for God to provide a large sum of money. I didn't even have a purpose for it. I was burdened to ask for it and to expect it. Several days went by, and my burden grew heavier. All the time I wondered why. Without warning, I had a rather large financial need. Within a matter of hours, God supplied the finances to meet that need. He had burdened me to ask even before I knew I had a need! He had already set in motion to supply a need I didn't know would exist.

If we are to have a profitable time of meditation, we can't rush in, jot down one or two prayer requests, quickly pray, and then go on to dinner. That's not what God wants. He wants us to sit before Him. Meditation isn't a spontaneous occurrence. Certain disciplines must be practical if we are to receive the full benefits of the application. Certain requirements must be heeded if the biblical practice of meditation is to be more than just wishful thinking.

These are the principles that have aided me in personal meditation.

When we think about meditating on the Lord, the first requirement is a season of time. The length of time, whether it's five minutes or an hour, will be determined by our purpose. If we are in deep distress about a subject, the period will usually be lengthened. If we simply want to be quiet, it may

MEDITATION

■ *Quiet contemplation of spiritual truths.*

be a matter of minutes. Psalm 62:5 enjoins us to "wait silently for God alone, for [our] expectation is from Him."

When we tell God we don't have time for Him, we are saying we don't have time for life, for joy, for peace, for direction, for prosperity, because He is the Source of all. The essence of meditation is a period of time set aside to contemplate the Lord, listen to Him, and allow Him to permeate our spirits. When we think about how much time we spend in the world, being in contact with its thinking and value system, we see how desperately we need to be with Him and regain a biblical perspective.

It is amazing what God can do to a troubled heart in a short period of time when the person understands the meaning of meditation. We live in a hurried and rushed world, and it's not going to slow down. So each of us must ask, How am I going to stay in the rush of it all and hear God? I'm convinced that the man who has learned to meditate on the Lord will be able to run on his feet and walk in his spirit. Although he may be hurried by his vocation, that's not the issue. The issue is how fast his spirit is going. To slow it down requires a period to time.

The most important lesson parents can teach their children is the practical importance of prayer and meditation. In doing so, they give their children a lifetime compass. When children learn early to listen to God and obey Him, and when they learn that He is interested in what interests them, they develop a sense of security that no other gift will give them. God is always available, no matter what the circumstances. He will always be there when parents are unavailable.

The only way to teach your children to spend time with the Lord is by example. They need to hear you praying, walk in on you praying, listen to you share how God is speaking to you. They will soon realize that if God hears the prayers of Mom and Dad, He will hear theirs as well. You could not give your children a greater heritage than praying parents.

If we're really going to meditate on the Lord and His Word, stillness is a key: "Be still, and know that I am God" (Ps. 46:10). We'll know God best when we set aside time for Him and learn to be still before Him.

Too often, we're like two-year-old children, sitting, squirming, and wanting God to cram marvelous spiritual insight into our short spiritual attention spans. We like microwave-type devotions. Thirty seconds of spiritual heat and we're pretty warm for the day. Oh, really?

Stillness brings us to the point where we can concentrate. It's difficult to fix our thoughts on God as we barrel down the expressway or stand in the midst of noisy friends. We often miss God's most beautiful intervention in

> **I**n order to meditate, we need to memorize, visualize, and personalize.
> —Bill Gothard

our lives because we are so distracted by other things that we can't see or hear Him. We are not sensitive before Him. We haven't learned to be still in His presence. I shudder to think of how many people "study" their Bibles with a television blaring or utter a brief "Help me through the day, Lord," as they gobble their instant spiritual breakfast heading out the door to work. That is *not* meditation. And a steady diet of that type of praying will lead to spiritual malnutrition.

Mark wrote of Jesus: "Now in the morning, having risen a long while before daylight, He went out and departed to a solitary place; and there He prayed" (Mark 1:35). If the Lord Jesus, who was perfect in His relationship with the Father, felt it necessary to leave the twelve disciples whom He loved the most and seclude Himself before God, shouldn't we make provisions for solitude?

God wants you alone sometimes because He wants your absolute, undivided attention. What a compliment! A King wants to spend time with you? You get to have an audience with royalty? And He listens to you? And though He is King, He allows you to address Him as Father? Why would you want to do that quickly or with a bunch of background noise? Suppose you might miss what He is saying? Surely, you need to be alone with Him.

God doesn't hug two people at a time; He hugs us one at a time. He loves us one at a time, but unless we are willing to get alone with Him, progress in our spiritual journey will be slow. His private workings are often His most precious.

Sometimes, however, when we meditate, we may feel as if nothing is happening outwardly. Just because we can't detect God's functioning overtly doesn't mean that God is not at work.

As you begin to meditate, you may have to labor mentally a bit to focus your attention on God. If that is a problem, you can turn to a psalm and say, "Lord, I have a hard time keeping my mind on the subject at hand. I want to get immersed in this psalm and get my attention on You."

In a few minutes, stop reading and just think about Him. Praise Him for His attributes.

Proverbs 8:34 exclaims, "Blessed is the man who listens to me, watching daily at my gates, waiting at the posts of my doors." Notice the word *daily*. We must take deliberate steps each day to bring our minds, bodies, and lives under control so that we can spend time waiting and listening for God to speak. That may mean going to bed earlier. That may mean turning off the television to do so. A youth worker once wrote, "The key to a successful quiet time is the night before."

> **M**editation is the ultimate activity by which we gain moral freedom.
> —Bill Gothard

MEDITATION

James wrote, "Humble yourselves in the sight of the Lord, and He will lift you up" (James 4:10). If we are rebellious in our hearts and insist on having our own way, we won't meditate. What child wants to sit alone with the parent he is consistently disobeying?

Do you suppose it is possible that you don't spend more time alone with God because you don't want to face the music He keeps sending your way? It is a song that says, "Give up. Surrender. Yield. Let Me love you to the maximum of My potential so that you will reach the maximum of your potential."

The pressures in our lives begin to dissipate when we are secluded, silent, and still before the Lord. God pulls the plug in the pressure tanks of our lives, and our anxieties begin to drain. When we first begin to meditate, our frustration levels are usually at full, but as we focus on Him, the reservoirs of tension empty. Biblical meditation causes something to happen to our spirits, our souls, our emotional beings, and even our human bodies.

We can be tired, weary, and emotionally distraught, but after spending time alone with God, we find that He injects into our bodies energy, power, and strength. God's spiritual dynamics are at work in our inner beings, refreshing and energizing our minds and spirits. There is nothing to match meditation in its impact on our lives and the lives of others.

An unschooled man who knows how to meditate on the Lord has learned far more than the man with the highest education who does not know how to meditate.

I am always moved when I read one special verse in the fourth chapter of Acts. Let me describe the situation leading up to it. Filled with the newly discovered power of the Holy Spirit, Peter and John have been ministering powerfully. Thousands have been saved and great numbers added to the fledgling group of Christians.

Peter and John were arrested by the Sadducees and brought before Annas the high priest, Caiaphas, John, and Alexander, all of high-priestly descent. They placed Peter and John squarely in the center of their contemporaries and asked about the nature of the disciples' work.

Can't you just picture the scene? Peter and John, two large, rough fishermen with a minimum amount of education, stood before a room full of highly educated, influential, skilled, religious rulers.

The outcome of the confrontation is electrifying. Immediately, Peter took the offensive, pushing the Sadducees into the corner. He attacked with power and persuasiveness. His hearers were startled. Luke recorded their

The mightiest works of God are the fruit of silence.
—F. B. Meyer

amazement in Acts 4:13: "Now when they saw the boldness of Peter and John, and perceived that they were uneducated and untrained men, they marveled. And they realized that they had been with Jesus."

It was true then, and it is true today. When we spend time with Him, talking with Him, reading His Word and mulling it over, it shows. The opposite is true as well.

Faced with one of the most difficult decisions of my life, I asked God to speak to my fearful, doubting heart. I was reading chapter 41 in the book of Isaiah, and it was as if God said, "Now, Charles, 'You are My servant, I have chosen you and have not cast you away: fear not, for I am with you; be not dismayed, for I am your God. I will strengthen you, yes, I will help you, I will uphold you with My righteous right hand'" (vv. 9–10). I meditated on that passage day and night for weeks, continually being reminded of His call to fearlessness and His assurance of divine help: "For I, the LORD your God, will hold your right hand, saying to you, 'Fear not, I will help you'" (v. 13).

When the moment of crisis came, I was filled with an awesome sense of peace. That passage had permeated my very being. I felt that I was seeing my situation from God's point of view, relying on His promise and His power. Once again I experienced what Paul meant by the peace that surpasses all understanding.

At another time in my life, the Lord had brought me back to Psalm 81 in my morning meditation for several weeks. Verse 6 kept grabbing my attention: "I removed his shoulder from the burden; his hands were freed from the baskets." I knew God was trying to speak to me through that passage, but I had no idea what He was saying. The more I read and meditated, the more I began to realize that He was preparing me for a change. At the time, I was pastor of a large church in a big city. We had a Christian school, which was growing rapidly, and I was heavily burdened because so much of the responsibility for it rested on me.

After I spent several weeks meditating on that passage and claiming it as a promise of relief, the Lord sent me a staff member who literally removed my shoulder from the burden and freed my hands from the baskets. God is so precise in His instructions!

APPLICATION

When I was a child growing up, my mother would tell me, "Charles, dinner will be ready at 6:00 P.M. Be here." Pretty soon I would get involved in playing and six o'clock came. All of a sudden I would hear a voice crying, "Charles, Charles!" I didn't have to wonder if that was my mother's voice. I knew in a split second whose it was. I had grown up hearing it. A thousand mothers could have called my name, but only *my* mother could have called my name in such a way as to get my attention. When we are saved, it is natural behavior to know our Father when He speaks.

But we must train our ears to listen. And be willing to come and dine when He calls.

PRAYER

LUKE 11:1–4

Now it came to pass, as He was praying in a certain place, when He ceased, that one of His disciples said to Him, "Lord, teach us to pray, as John also taught his disciples." So He said to them, "When you pray, say:

> *Our Father in heaven,*
> *Hallowed be Your name.*
> *Your kingdom come.*
> *Your will be done*
> *On earth as it is in heaven.*
> *Give us day by day our daily bread.*
> *And forgive us our sins,*
> *For we also forgive everyone who is indebted to us.*
> *And do not lead us into temptation."*

Jesus' disciples had undoubtedly logged many hours in prayer by the time this exchange occurred. But after watching Jesus pray, they were keenly aware that something was different about the way He prayed. There was such a stark contrast that asking specific questions in an attempt to fine-tune their skills wasn't adequate. They needed a complete overhaul. So they said to Him, "Teach us to pray." In other words, "Let's start from the very beginning."

Jesus' response is somewhat surprising. The typical response to such a question today is, "It's easy. Prayer is just talking to God." Or you might hear someone say, "You don't learn to pray. You just pray. No one can teach another person to pray. It must come from the heart."

Jesus didn't trivialize their question. He took it seriously. His answer gives us the impression that He was waiting for them to ask. It was a lesson He had been looking forward to teaching for some time. And much to our surprise, He began by giving them the exact words to say, "When you pray, say . . ."

From there He went on to share several principles on prayer. He taught them to persevere (Luke 11:5–8). He explained and illustrated the sincere interest the heavenly Father took in the prayers of His children (Luke 11:11–13). He promised them that their prayers would be heard and answered (Luke 11:9–10).

Prayer is something we learn to do. We are not born knowing how to pray. We are not even born again knowing how to pray. We, like the disciples, must learn to pray.

> **P**rayer is the key of the morning and the bolt of the evening.
> —Matthew Henry

PRAYER

A CLOSER LOOK

One of the first, and yet most difficult, lessons we should learn about prayer regards praying according to God's will. In his first epistle, the apostle John wrote, "Now this is the confidence that we have in Him, that if we ask anything according to His will, He hears us. And if we know that He hears us, whatever we ask, we know that we have the petitions that we have asked of Him" (1 John 5:14–15).

"How can I know that my request is in keeping with the will of God? How will I know that my petition is pleasing to the Father?" These are among the most frequently asked questions regarding prayer.

God makes us a threefold promise in 1 John 5:14–15. First, He promises to listen if we pray according to His will. Second, He promises that we already possess what we have asked for. Third, He promises that we know that we have the petitions we desire. So when we pray according to His will, He hears us, we have what we ask for, and we know that we have what we asked for.

The word *confidence* in verse 14 means "boldness" or "assurance." Among the Greeks, the word was used as a political term and referred to the freedom to speak publicly. So as children of God, we can go to Him openly and boldly make our requests.

We bring God our requests and expect His answer. But there is a little more to it than that. God puts a condition on His promise. This is the condition—that we ask according to His will. We say, "Oh, *that's* the catch." And in one sense, it *is* a catch, but it is built in for our safety.

So how do we know when our request is in keeping with His will? When we are not sure, we should do a couple of things. To begin with, we have the freedom to ask Him what His will is (James 1:5). If we really take John's words seriously, we should probably begin our prayers by asking God how we should pray about any issue. Instead of starting out with a string of requests, we should first seek the mind of God. His will won't run contrary to what He says in His Word. Also, His will is always in keeping with what is wise.

If we still aren't sure after asking, we can ask the Holy Spirit to make intercession for us as we pray (Rom. 8:26). The apostle Paul assures us that when we are stumped—that is, we don't know God's will on a matter—the Holy Spirit will pray through us. And since the Spirit of God knows the mind of God, the Spirit's prayer is always in keeping with the will of the Father.

A barrier to discovering God's will in a matter is our feelings about what should be done. Sometimes we feel so strongly about something, that we can't get past our will to find His! If we feel compelled to pray about a matter, we usually are far from neutral on the subject. We come to God convinced of what He should do.

The average amount of time adults spend in prayer is about five minutes.
—George Barna

PRAYER

Neutrality is essential to finding God's will. That is why Jesus began His model prayer by saying, "Your kingdom come. Your will be done on earth as it is in heaven" (Matt. 6:9–10). As we begin praying, we must be willing for Him to bring us into complete yieldedness. At that point our main concern is that the will of God be done—whatever that is.

Abandonment to God's will removes some of the emotion attached to the request. It clears our hearts and minds and makes it easier for us to hear. Depending on the nature of the request, it may take a long time to come to the point of neutrality. And there are times when the request is so personal or painful that it may be impossible for us to get to that point. At those times the Holy Spirit Himself makes intercession for us.

When our hearts are clean and we have committed ourselves to obey Him, and yet we have not a clue about what to pray, God takes responsibility for showing us. He may use Scripture, or He may use circumstances. If the request isn't in keeping with His will, often He will redirect our attention to other interests.

Remember, prayer is something you learn to do. Like anything else you learn, it takes practice. The more you pray, the easier it will be to discern the voice of God. The easier it will be to know His will. And consequently, your assurance and confidence will grow proportionately.

Another difficult lesson to learn in regard to prayer is to recognize when God has answered the prayer. God answers prayers in one of four ways:

1. Yes.
2. No.
3. Wait.
4. My grace is sufficient.

Or in more personal terms, "Yes, child, you may have it"; "No, child, this is not good for you"; "Wait, child, I have something better"; or "My grace is sufficient for you" (2 Cor. 12:9).

When He answers yes, we are prone to shout, "Praise the Lord!" But when He says no, we have a hard time finding reasons to praise Him. Usually, we don't take "no" for an answer. We keep praying. Or we look for sin in our lives, a reason for His refusal to answer our request. But nowhere in Scripture does it say that God will give us exactly what we ask for every time. He is sovereign. He has the right to say no according to His infinite wisdom.

When my family and I first moved to Atlanta, we couldn't seem to find the right house. It was more than a month before we found a house we felt

More than 200,000 children worldwide ages 8 to 12 participate in the Children's Global Prayer Movement (a prayer workshop for children).

Prayer at the Korean Myong-Song Presbyterian Church begins at 4:00 A.M. and is usually packed with 4,000 believers. With the 5:00 A.M. and 6:00 A.M. services, a total of 12,000 people show up every morning to call upon the Lord.

good about. In the meantime, we had been living with friends. And as you can imagine, we were ready for a place of our own.

We prayed and felt like it was of the Lord, so we applied for a loan. We asked God every day to get the loan approved for us. We really believed He would; we thanked Him in advance.

One week later, the banker told me our loan had been turned down. That was a real shock. To this day, I don't know the reason for the refusal. And we couldn't understand what God was up to. "Why didn't He answer our prayer?" we asked.

God answered that question the next day by sending a tremendous rainstorm. The basement of the house we almost bought was flooded with a foot of water. We had planned to use the basement for a study and for storage. But God was watching out for us even when we misunderstood His will. One week later we found the right house, and we enjoyed living there for eight years.

God says no and wait when it is best for us (Rom. 8:28). Oftentimes it is for our protection. Sometimes God wants to answer our prayer, but the timing is not right. If He says wait, we should wait.

In 1971, our church's television broadcast was taken off the air because of conflict within the church. After the conflict was resolved, we asked the same network if we could be rescheduled at the same broadcast time we had before. The decision makers refused to give us the time. We offered to buy time on the station, but they refused that as well.

We believed God wanted us on television, but for some reason things were not working out. So we prayed that God would once again allow us to begin a television ministry. When we started praying, we thought something would open up soon. But it was a year before anything happened.

One year later two different stations invited us to participate in their weekly programming. One opportunity led to another till today our service is broadcast by In Touch Ministries on satellite throughout the world. God didn't answer our prayer to be put right back on the air for a reason. He waited and provided us with something much better than we asked for.

The Father knows waiting is difficult for His children. But God is more interested in our character than our comfort; His commitment is to our sanctification, not necessarily our satisfaction.

Many young people pray and pray that the Lord will send a marriage partner. As they enter their late twenties, many question God's interest. They say, "What is God waiting for?" He may be waiting till He knows they are ready.

As I reflect on my life, I realize that if God had answered certain prayers according to my timing, I would have missed His best in every single case.

Imagine for a moment a five-year-old who wants a pocketknife and a flashlight. A good father might not mind giving him the flashlight, but the boy needs to grow up a little before he can be trusted with the pocketknife. In the same way, God is waiting for us to grow spiritually in some areas before He can allow us to experience all the spiritual and material blessings He has in store (Eph. 1:3).

God also answers, "My grace is sufficient." There are times when we pray and nothing changes. I know people who have prayed for years for a particular need, and God seems unresponsive. Heaven is silent.

In many cases the problem is not the length or the intensity of our prayers. Neither is it the nature or amount of our faith. Oftentimes God is up to something we don't know about. Something much bigger than we were expecting. Something that requires a different answer from the one we anticipated. But rest assured that if God is not removing your personal "thorn," His grace is sufficient. He will enable you to endure whatever you are facing until He is ready to take the pressure off. Sometimes His silence and seeming lack of response are His way of saying, "My grace is sufficient."

I know a pastor whose son suffered severe brain damage as the result of an accident. Each Wednesday night the father would ask for prayer requests at their church prayer meeting. And every Wednesday night his wife would ask for healing for their brain-damaged son. As time went on, their son's condition worsened. Finally, the mother could no longer bear to publicly ask for prayer. As the pastor's wife, she found it embarrassing to give a weekly report of seemingly unanswered prayer to their flock.

After years of pleading for explanations from God, she finally claimed 2 Corinthians 12:9, "My grace is sufficient." By an act of her will, she decided to trust that God knew what He was doing when there was no logical or rational explanation. Of course, only the God of all grace and comfort can work this in His children.

In difficult or painful situations, it is natural to wonder why God is not intervening in a more tangible way. And contrary to popular Christian opinion, it is fine to ask God why. David did (Ps. 13). Jesus did (Matt. 27:46). Even the apostle Paul asked (2 Cor. 12:7–10). The Father is not offended by your asking. But He is overjoyed when you trust Him when He chooses not to explain. He enjoys the fact that you see Him as a trustworthy Father who will always provide the grace needed to endure whatever He allows to come your way.

> **F**orty-eight percent of Americans spend more time in prayer, meditation, or reading the Bible when they are depressed, and 96 percent of those find that very or somewhat effective.
> —*100 Questions and Answers*

> **I** have lived to thank God that all of my prayers have not been answered.
> —Jean Ingelow

PRAYER

> **P**rayer is the very sword of the Saints.
> —Maurice Goguel

God always answers the prayers of His children. As we learn to pray, we will learn to discern His answers. It may be yes, no, wait, or "My grace is sufficient." But He always answers. As we mature in our faith, and thus our commitment to His will, it will be easier to accept answers that don't align with our expectations. In human terms, it will become easier to take "no" for an answer.

In 1969 while I was preaching a week-long revival in Virginia, I felt God had something specific to say to me. Each night after the service I retired to my room early to pray. One night I pulled out a pad and drew a circle with five lines leading from it. At the end of each line, I wrote one of several things I thought God was saying to me. On the last line I drew a question mark, thinking it was something I had not thought of.

The following night I came back to my room with the same burden. As I prayed and looked over the possibilities, God made it clear that He was going to move me. I asked Him when, and the month of September flashed into my mind. This happened in May of 1969, but I thought that He meant September of 1970. A few months later, however, a pulpit committee from the First Baptist Church of Atlanta came to see me. On September 30, 1969, my family and I moved to Atlanta. God told me ahead of time in order to prepare my heart. He unveiled the hidden when I called on Him to do so.

The sooner you move from your will to His will, the sooner God will show you what you need to know. Remember, God gives us His Word for obedience, not just consideration. He must be assured that you have submitted yourself completely before He unfolds His plan.

Are you facing a decision in your life that is too big for you to handle? Are you going though a difficulty that has left you confused and disheartened? God said, "Call to Me, and I will answer you, and show you great and mighty things, which you do not know" (Jer. 33:3). As you seek God's face and understand who He is and what He is willing and able to do, He will clear away all the mist that surrounds your circumstances. He will show you what to do.

GROWTH

We sing, "Jesus, Jesus, how I trust Him, how I've proved Him o'er and o'er . . . oh, for grace to trust Him more." As we allow God to prove Himself in situation after situation, it becomes easier to trust Him.

One practical way to track the faithfulness of God in your life is to keep a journal of the times you've "proved Him o'er and o'er." These documented reminders will help you trust Him in the future.

Next to the requests in your journal, you could include the answers "yes," "no," "wait," or "His grace is sufficient." As you see specific prayers answered over time, you'll be amazed at the impact it will have on your faith.

 QUOTES

Remember the shortest distance between a problem and the solution is the distance between our knees and the floor.

—Charles Stanley

Prayer is the gymnasium of the soul.

—Samuel Zwamer

Prayer is not conquering God's reluctance, but taking hold of God's willingness.

—Phillips Brooks

Pray for great things, expect great things, work for great things, but above all, pray.

—R. A. Torrey

QUIET TIME

■ *Giving God your undivided attention for a predetermined amount of time for the purpose of talking to and hearing from Him.*

LUKE 5:15–16

The report went around concerning Him all the more; and great multitudes came together to hear, and to be healed by Him of their infirmities. So He Himself often withdrew into the wilderness and prayed.

COMMENTARY

A quiet time, or devotion as some prefer to call it, is personal time alone with God. It is a time set aside to talk to and listen to the Father. It is a time we carve out from our busy schedules to give God our undivided attention. I like to think of it as my personal appointment with the heavenly Father.

Most believers would agree that spending time alone with God is a wonderful habit to develop. You may have even tried it at one time. But if you are like many Christians I know, you do not have a consistent devotional life.

Several reasons may explain the struggle in this area. It could be that you never thought about it. Maybe you were raised in a church where such a thing was never discussed or encouraged. Perhaps your pastor or peers did not emphasize the need for quiet time; for you, the Sunday sermon seemed sufficient. There was not a family devotional time in your home. The idea of spending time alone with God is new for you.

Maybe you have been encouraged to develop this habit, but no one taught you how. You struggled through a couple of devotional times but felt like it was a waste of time. So you quit.

More than likely, however, you are familiar with this concept. You have a general idea of what to do. Your problem, like that of so many believers, is that you don't think it is necessary; you don't believe it is essential.

As busy as Jesus was, as consumed as He was by His mission, as overwhelmed as He must have felt at times, He withdrew often to pray. Even when it meant leaving the physical and spiritual needs of the crowds unmet, He withdrew to lonely places. In those quiet and intimate times, Jesus drew strength for what He knew lay ahead.

Jesus knew that time alone with the heavenly Father was essential. He could not—would not—go without it. By escaping the noise of His day, Jesus established a discipline all believers should follow. After all, if it was necessary for Jesus, it is vital for those who profess to follow Him.

> We need to find a place of quiet for an effective and consistent encounter with God. Our internal space is notably affected by external space.
> —Gordon T. Smith

QUIET TIME

A quiet time is a basic ingredient in a maturing relationship with God. Time alone with God moves our experience as believers out of the realm of religion and into the realm of relationship. It moves us from a religious approach to God to a relational approach.

We all know Christians who go to church every week but show no evidence of faith in their everyday lives. Their approach to God is full of formality. They don't like to talk about it. They say things such as, "I believe one's religious beliefs are a private matter." For them, God is out there somewhere. Insofar as daily activities are concerned, He is irrelevant. What's missing for these folks is the relational side of Christianity. It's not personal.

The tragedy is that they are the losers. God will speak to us through His Word in a real and personal way when we give Him an opportunity to do so. And as is the case in any relationship, communication with God is the key to knowing Him better. Where there is no communication, there is no relationship. Where there is no relationship, there is no trust. And the less you trust someone, the harder it is to follow that person. Fruitful relationships are based on solid, honest two-way communication.

A person with no devotional life generally struggles with faith and obedience. After all, it is difficult to trust someone you don't know, and it is difficult to obey someone you don't trust.

One by-product of a strong devotional life is a heightened sense of accountability to the Father. You will find that it is much more difficult to live with unresolved sin issues when you meet with the Father on a regular basis. A regular devotion time is strong motivation to keep sins confessed and sinful habits in check. It is also a powerful incentive to resolve broken or damaged relationships with others. Holding a grudge against someone else makes it impossible to have genuine intimacy with the Father.

Christ came to create the potential for intimacy between Him and His people. For that potential to become a reality, we must pursue the relationship through regular time alone with the Father. That is why a devotional life is so significant. Without it, the relational side of the Christian faith begins to fade.

No one knew this better than King David. Through the book of Psalms, we are given a behind-the-scenes look at David's devotional life. There he recorded his prayers, his battles with despair, his victories, and his fears. In many ways, the book of Psalms functions as David's quiet time journal.

One cannot help being moved by the personal way in which David communed with God. Being a king, David recognized the importance of treating one's superior with dignity. Furthermore, David lived during the height of

> **S**itting quietly with God is a discipline we need to cultivate. It does not take the place of Bible study, Scripture memory, or prayer. Rather quiet time deepens our walk with the One who seeks our friendship the most.
> —Tim Sanford

Quiet Time

tradition and formality because of the centrality of the law with all its strict regulations. Yet without compromising his respect for the holiness of his King, David moved beyond the formal and addressed his heavenly Monarch as a friend. Intimacy and warmth are evident as he pours out his heart to the heavenly Father. It was not a duty David performed; it was a relationship he was committed to maintaining.

Central to his time alone with God was the Word of God. His ancient Bible ministered to David in a personal way. God's Word functioned as a counselor to him (Ps. 119:24–32). He felt as if God spoke directly to the issues of his life through His Word. And when did that take place? In quiet moments when David broke away from his overwhelming and demanding obligations as king to be alone with his King. In those tranquil moments of solitude, David communed in the most personal way with the Father.

GROWTH

The following are some things I have discovered that have made my devotional life richer.

First, *schedule time with God*. The primary reason people do not have devotions is that they don't plan. Your devotion time is like anything else you intend to do; it must be scheduled, or it doesn't happen.

How many times have you told someone, "Hey, let's get together sometime"? How often do those plans materialize? If you are like me, seldom. If I'm serious about getting together with somebody, I make an appointment; I write it in my planner; I clear my schedule for that period of time.

If you are serious about developing a consistent devotional life, you must schedule your time with God. Life demands it. Specifically, before you go to bed tonight, you need to have already decided when and where you plan to get alone with the Father.

Personally, I find mornings to be the best time to meet with God. I enjoy getting up early and beginning my day listening to and talking with Him. There is something special about focusing on the Father first thing.

Second, *choose a place*. If possible, conduct your quiet time in the same place. In time this spot will take on special significance. It will become your special place. Being there will affect your mood and your ability to concentrate. It will create an air of expectancy in your spirit.

Choose a place off the beaten path of your daily activities. You need a place where there are no distractions. It may be a spare bedroom, your living room, or maybe a conference room at the office. You need a place where the only thing you do there is meet with God.

> **W**hile still in his childhood, John Wesley resolved to dedicate an hour each morning and evening to Bible study and prayer.
> —George Sweeting

I know a man whose special place is under the stairs leading to the basement in his house. A college student pulled his bed away from the wall about eighteen inches and made that his spot. I know several people who have cleared a place in a closet to pray. For me, it is a corner in my study at home. No matter where you live, you can find somewhere to be alone with God.

Third, *use a variety of methods*. One of the most common complaints I hear regarding personal devotions is that after a while they become dry, routine, even boring. God is certainly not boring. And chances are, you are not boring, either. So if spending time with God moves in that direction, the culprit is probably your method. No one method will stay fresh forever. When your devotional life begins to get a little dry, it is time to change your method; modify your routine.

For example, if you have been reading a devotional book, put it down for a while, and journal your thoughts and prayers. If you have been following a reading plan through the Bible, depart from that for a while, and read straight through one book of the Bible. If you have been praying, supplement your prayers by memorizing Scripture. If your devotions have turned into in-depth Bible studies, find a devotional book to lighten things up a while. Remember, this is a relationship. Look for ways to keep it fresh.

> **I** suggest you discipline yourself to spend time daily in a systematic reading of God's Word. Make this "quiet time" a priority that nobody can change.
> —Warren W. Wiersbe

TITHE

■ *One-tenth of our finances that we give back to God for use in His kingdom.*

MALACHI 3:10

66 **B**ring all the tithes into the storehouse,
That there may be food in My house,
And try Me now in this,"
Says the LORD of hosts,
"If I will not open for you the windows of heaven
And pour out for you such blessing
That there will not be room enough to receive it."

COMMENTARY

To tithe is to give 10 percent of our income to God for His work. God provides for His people through His people. All that we have is a gift from God; therefore, a tithe is a mere portion of what He has already given to us.

The message of the prophet Malachi to the Jews in Jerusalem is a reminder of God's love and faithfulness and a rebuke to them for their willful disobedience and contempt for His holy name (1:6). Malachi's words reveal a nation unfaithful and guilty of false worship (1:7–14); they kept God's tithes and offerings for themselves (3:8–12). In so doing, they broke their relationship with God; judgment and punishment resulted.

The good news is that a few were faithful. They loved and honored God, and in turn, He showered His blessings on them (3:16–18). The message of Malachi is more important than ever. If we are obedient to God's Word and cheerfully give the portion He has requested of us, He will bless us and the work of His kingdom. We will continue to enjoy an intimate relationship with Him.

Several years ago, God led us to purchase some property for the church. We knew as a church body that it was what the Lord wanted us to do, so we began to pray that He would provide the funds necessary, above and beyond our tithes. I began to pray about what the Lord would have me give. He began to impress upon me to sell my cameras. Photography is my hobby, and obviously, my cameras are valuable to that pursuit. I was convinced that was what God wanted me to do. As the pastor, I had to set an example, lest I be disobedient as the priests were in Malachi 1. I was also reminded of Jesus' parable of the rich young man. Mark tells us that Jesus said, "Sell whatever you have and give to the poor, and you will have treasure in heaven; and come . . . follow Me" (Mark 10:21). So I sold my cameras and gave the money to the fund. Many of the other members of our congregation gave possessions and treasures. It was a great time in our fellowship for seeking His will in our finances and testing our willingness to obey Him.

American evangelicals have a disposable annual income of about $850 billion. About one-fifth of one percent of that income—$1.5 billion—would support the needed 12,000 church planting teams.

We trusted God to provide, and He did. Several months later I received a call from a woman who asked if I was the Charles Stanley who had owned a particular camera. I said, "Yes," and she said, "I bought this and God told me I needed to give it to you." I was taken aback but realized that because I was willing to part with that camera, God honored my obedience.

APPLICATION

The principle of tithing is relevant for today. However, many make excuses for not returning that portion to God. They fret over the economy and job loss, fear of increased taxes, and generally anticipate the worst. They allow their circumstances to prevent them from giving, and then they wonder why their situation isn't any better. Isn't that just like the unfaithful people in Malachi's day?

> *"Yet from the days of your fathers*
> *You have gone away from My ordinances*
> *And have not kept them.*
> *Return to Me, and I will return to you,"*
> *Says the LORD of hosts.*
> *"But you said, 'In what way shall we return?'*
> *Will a man rob God?*
> *Yet you have robbed Me! But you say,*
> *'In what way have we robbed You?'*
> *In tithes and offerings.*
> *You are cursed with a curse,*
> *For you have robbed Me,*
> *Even this whole nation"* (Mal. 3:7–9).

The percentage of evangelicals claiming to tithe: 44.4 percent.
—Dr. Clyde Narramore

When we give our tithe to God, we provide for His work, prove His faithfulness, and show Him honor in acknowledging Him as the Source of all we possess and as One worthy of our worship. We bring Him the sacrifices of our praise and our possessions. Tithing is another example of God's fairness and equality toward all believers. He requested the same amount (10 percent) and the same portion (the first portion [Prov. 3:9–10]) to be given by all believers.

We are treated equally when we fail to tithe. First, we sin by robbing God of what is rightfully His. Second, we dishonor God when we offer Him only the leftovers (Mal. 1:6–8, 13) and offend the holy name of Jehovah

About 75 percent of Americans are contributing an average of $734 annually to charitable causes, a 20 percent upswing from two years ago.

TITHE

■ *One-tenth of our finances that we give back to God for use in His kingdom.*

God (Mal. 1:12). Finally, we show our arrogance toward God (Mal. 3:15) in believing that it isn't necessary to obey Him.

God's promises await those who are obedient. He challenges us to give Him the privilege to prove Himself. He promised that we would be blessed in return (Prov. 3:9–10; Luke 6:38). He will protect our finances just as He protected the obedient people in the Old Testament from the insects that would devour their crops. Most important, our witness is recognized by others and can be used to attract others to Him through His blessing to us.

A CLOSER LOOK

According to Malachi, the people had been cured of idolatry, but they grew careless and indifferent about many things. The priests became lax and the people neglected the house of God. Many took inferior sacrifices to the temple, and social sin began to abound. Look around. Are we guilty of similar neglect?

Do we view the church as just buildings instead of the house of God where we come to learn about Jesus and see our lives changed? Do we think our hobbies and the economic climate are more important than returning a portion of what God in His graciousness and goodness has given us? We show our ignorance and our arrogance when we fail to acknowledge God's provision for us and His plan to return to Him. We complain about the penalty when Scripture promises God's protection of our resources.

GROWTH

Give God the first portion of your income to show that He has first place in your life and that you know He is the Source of all you have. When you are obedient to Him, you can conquer greed and properly manage God's resources. You have opened your heart to receive His special blessings.

> **G**ive according to your income lest God make your income according to your giving.
> —Peter Marshall

INDEX

INDEX

INDEX

INDEX

ABOUT THE AUTHOR

Charles Stanley is pastor of the 14,000-member First Baptist Church in Atlanta, Georgia. He is the speaker on the internationally popular radio and television program *In Touch*.

Twice elected president of the Southern Baptist Convention, Stanley received his bachelor of arts degree from the University of Richmond, his bachelor of divinity degree from Southwestern Theological Seminary, and his master's and doctor's degrees from Luther Rice Seminary.

Bestsellers from Charles Stanley

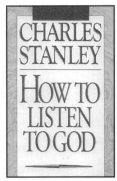

How to Listen to God

This popular book provides direction for Christians who are struggling to hear God's voice and to understand His will for their lives.

0-8407-9041-4 • Hardcover • 160 pages

The Source of My Strength

Sharing some of his personal experiences, this popular author and pastor encourages everyone to face the hurts of the past and receive God's healing and freedom.

0-7852-8273-4 • Hardcover • 256 pages

How to Keep Your Kids on Your Team

Brimming with wisdom and practical advice, this book is a must for all Christian parents who want to ensure that their children grow to be loving and loyal . . . not only to them, but to God and His word.

0-8407-9078-3 • Hardcover • 224 pages

The Wonderful Spirit-Filled Life

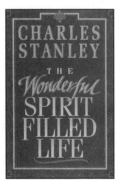

Charles Stanley's bestseller on the power of the Holy Spirit for the journey of faith. In his conversational, illuminating style, Dr. Stanley gives believers the keys to living an abundant life, deepening their personal relationship with Christ, and applying biblical truths.

0-7852-7747-1 • Trade paperback • 256 pages

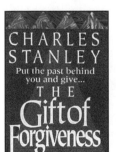

The Gift of Forgiveness

Dr. Stanley shows readers how to give and receive forgiveness in relationships and how to make forgiveness an ongoing, practical experience.

0-8407-9072-4 • Hardcover • 192 pages